中国民政统计年鉴

（中国社会服务统计资料）

CHINA CIVIL AFFAIRS' STATISTICAL YEARBOOK

(Statistics of China Social Services)

2016

中华人民共和国民政部　编

Compiled by Ministry of Civil Affairs of the People's Republic of China

中国统计出版社
China Statistics Press

图书在版编目（CIP）数据

中国民政统计年鉴. 2016 ：汉英对照 / 中华人民共和国民政部编.
-- 北京 ：中国统计出版社, 2016.8（中国社会服务统计资料）
ISBN 978-7-5037-7878-0

I.①中… II.①中… III.①民政事务－统计资料－中国－2016－年鉴－汉、英 IV.①D632-66

中国版本图书馆CIP数据核字(2016)第184276号

中国民政统计年鉴–2016（中国社会服务统计资料）

作　　者/ 中华人民共和国民政部
责任编辑/ 郭　栋　　李　冲
装帧设计/ 李雪燕
出版发行/ 中国统计出版社
通信地址/ 北京市丰台区西三环南路甲6号　　邮政编码/100073
电　　话/ 邮购 (010)63376909　　书店 (010)68783171
网　　址/ http://www.zgtjcbs.com/
印　　刷/ 河北鑫宏源印刷包装有限责任公司
经　　销/ 新华书店
开　　本/ 880×1230mm　　1/16
印　　张/ 46.5
字　　数/ 1450千字
版　　别/ 2016年8月第1版
版　　次/ 2016年8月第1次印刷
定　　价/ 280.00元

本书附同版本CD-ROM一张，光盘内容以书面文字为准。
如有印装错误，本社发行部负责调换。

《中国民政统计年鉴－2016》

（中国社会服务统计资料）

编委会和编辑出版人员

编者说明

《中国民政统计年鉴－2016》(中国社会服务统计资料)是一部全面反映2015年中国社会服务发展的资料性年刊。2015年度社会服务统计资料是根据各省、自治区、直辖市以及计划单列市民政厅（局）报送的社会服务业统计年报及有关部门的报表编制而成。本书内容由六个部分组成：第一部分是专文，2015年社会服务发展统计公报；第二部分是社会服务主要数据图表；第三部分是社会服务综合统计资料；第四部分是社会服务历年统计资料；第五部分是社会服务当年分省统计资料；第六部分是附录，《中国民政统计年鉴－2015》勘误。本书对各级政府有关部门、从事社会服务研究和教学的人员，以及社会各界了解和研究社会服务发展状况、提高政府管理和决策水平，具有重要的参考价值。

书中涉及到的全国性统计数据均不包括香港特别行政区、澳门特别行政区和台湾省；表格中“－”符号表示数据不足本表最小计量单位；“空格”符号表示该项统计数据为零；“#”表示其中主要项。

本书凝聚了全国民政系统广大规划财务部门统计工作者和有关部门统计人员的辛勤汗水和工作成果。本书的编辑出版得到了各级领导和统计战线同仁们的热情支持和帮助。在此，向所有关心和支持该书出版发行的领导和同志表示衷心的谢意。

目　录

第一部分：专文

第二部分：社会服务主要数据图表

综合

社会工作

成员组织和其他社会服务

第三部分：社会服务综合统计资料

综合

社会工作

成员组织和其他社会服务

第四部分：社会服务历年统计资料

综合

社会工作

成员组织和其他社会服务

第五部分：社会服务当年分省统计资料

综合

行政区划和行政机关

社会服务总体情况

社会工作

提供住宿的社会服务活动

为老年人与残疾人提供住宿服务的机构

为智障与精神疾病人提供住宿服务的机构

为儿童提供住宿的社会服务机构

其他提供住宿的社会服务机构

不提供住宿的社会服务活动

为社区居民提供的服务

为老年人提供的服务

为残疾人提供的服务

为儿童提供的服务

为生活困难群众提供的服务

为受灾群众提供的服务

为弱势群体筹集资金的活动

成员组织和其他社会服务

成员组织

其他社会服务

殡葬服务

其他

第六部分：附录

CONTENTS

Part 1: Feature Articles

Part 2: Primary Data Figures of Social Services

I. Synthesis

II. Social Services

III. Member Organizations and Other Social Services

Part Three: Comprehensive statistics of Social Services

I. Synthesis

II. Social Work

III. Member Organizations and Other Social Services

Part Four: Historical Statistics of Social Services

I. Synthesis

II. Social Work

III. Member Organizations and Other Social Services

Part Five: Provincial Statistics of Social Services

I. Synthesis

Administrative Divisions and Administrative Organs

Situation of Social Service Industry

II. Social Work

Social Service Activities with Accommodation

Service Institutions with Accommodation for the Aged and Disabled

Service Institutions with Accommodation for Mental Retardation and Psychopath

Service Institutions with Accommodation for Children

Other Social Service Institutions with Accommodation

Social Service Activities without Accommodation

Social Services for Community Residents

Social Services for the Aged

III. Member Organizations and Other Social Services

Member Organizations

Non-governmental Organizations

Self–governing Organizations

Other Social Services

Marriage Service

Funeral and Interment Service

Other Institutions

Part Six: Appendix

01

专 文

中华人民共和国
2015年社会服务发展统计公报

中华人民共和国民政部

2016年7月4日

2015年，全国民政系统认真贯彻党中央、国务院决策部署，积极顺应人民群众的新期待，深化改革，加强法制，破解难题，扎实推进各项重点工作，民政事业实现了新发展。

一、综合

截至2015年底，全国共有省级行政区划单位34个（其中直辖市4个、省23个、自治区5个、特别行政区2个），地级行政区划单位334个（其中地级市291个、地区10个，自治州30个、盟3个），县级行政区划单位2850个（其中市辖区921个、县级市361个、县1397个、自治县117个、旗49个、自治旗3个、特区1个、林区1个），乡级行政区划单位39789个（其中区公所2个、镇20515个、乡10172个、苏木152个、民族乡990个、民族苏木1个、街道7957个）。

2015年，共联合检查省界14条，完成了总长度约为14468公里的省界联检任务。

图1 乡镇、街道变化情况

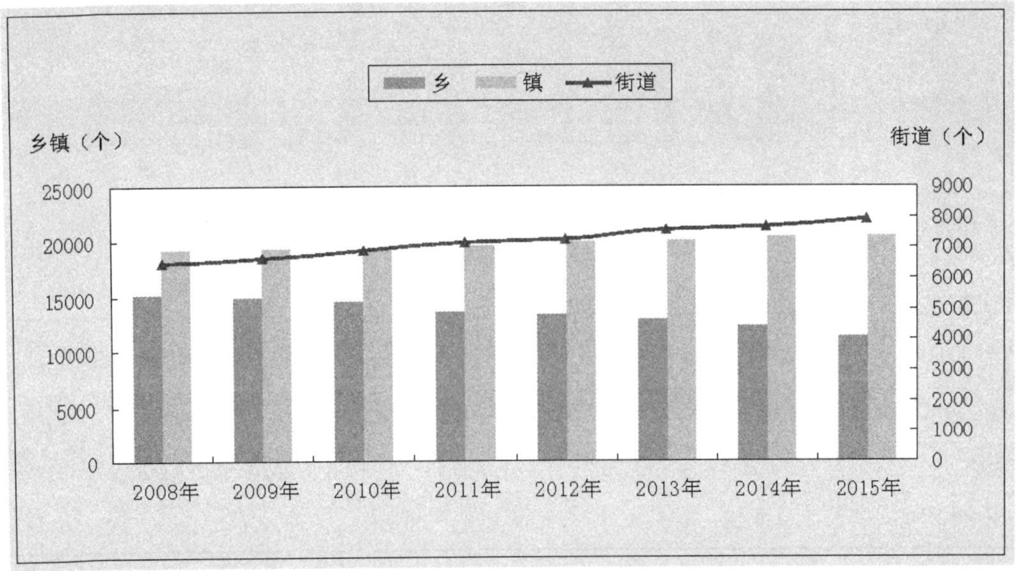

表 1 乡镇、街道变化情况

单位：个

指标	2008年	2009年	2010年	2011年	2012年	2013年	2014年	2015年
乡	15067	14848	14571	13587	13281	12812	12282	11315
镇	19234	19322	19410	19683	19881	20117	20401	20515
街道	6524	6686	6923	7194	7282	7566	7696	7957

截至2015年底，全国共有社会服务机构和设施176.5万个，比上年增长5.8%；职工总数1308.9万人，比上年增长4.6%（全国持证社会工作者共计20.6万人，比上年增长28.8%，其中社会工作师5.2万人，助理工作师15.4万人）；固定资产总价8183.1亿元，比上年增长13.4%；社会服务事业基本建设在建项目建设规模4087.3万平方米，全年实际完成投资总额239.9亿元；全国社会服务事业费支出4926.4亿元，比上年增长11.9%，占国家财政支出比重为3.3%，其中中央财政向各地转移支付社会服务事业费2270.3亿元，比上年增长8.4%，占社会服务事业费比重为46.1%，下降了1.7个百分点。

图2 社会服务基本情况

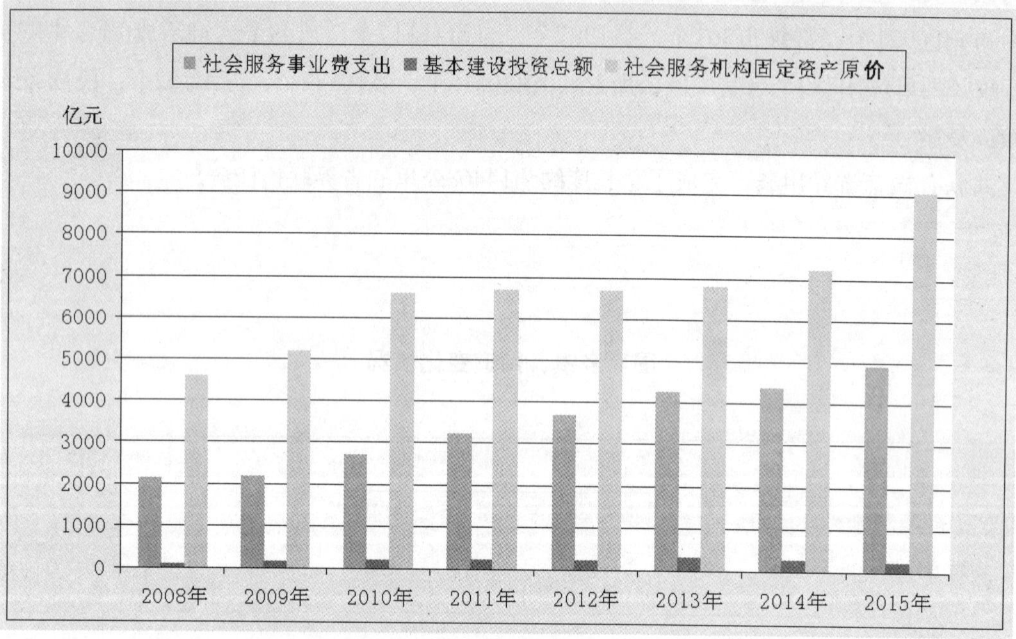

表2 社会服务基本情况

单位：亿元

指标	2008年	2009年	2010年	2011年	2012年	2013年	2014年	2015年
社会服务事业费支出	2146.5	2181.9	2697.5	3229.1	3683.7	4276.5	4404.1	4926.4
基本建设投资总额	66.6	157.0	183.0	218.5	235.0	292.8	282.2	239.9
社会服务机构固定资产原价	4592.8	5198.0	6589.3	6676.7	6675.4	6810.2	7213.0	8183.1

二、社会工作

（一）提供住宿的社会服务

截至2015年底，全国各类办理了注册登记手续的提供住宿的社会服务机构3.1万个，其中登记注册为事业单位的机构1.8万个，比上年增长12.5%，登记注册为民办非企业单位的1.2万个。床位393.2万张。收留抚养236.3万人。

图3 社会服务机构床位

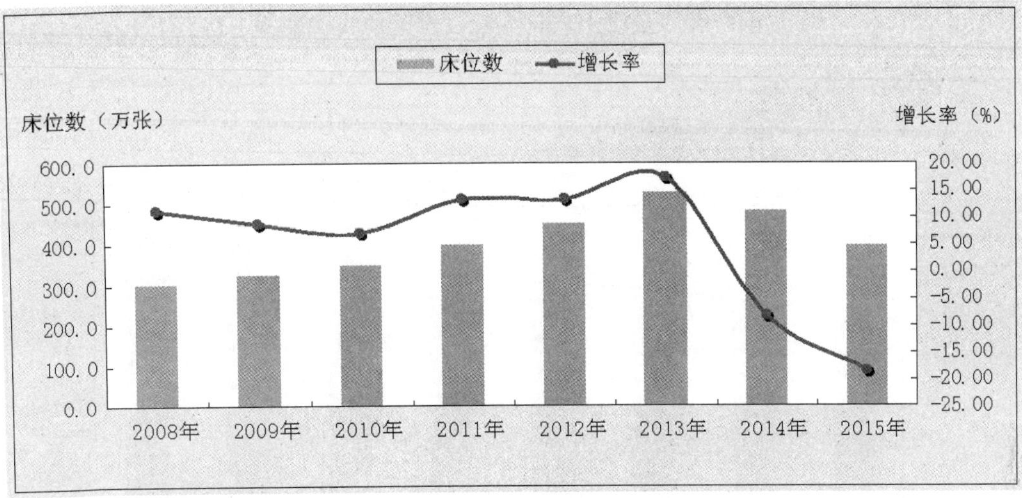

表3 社会服务机构床位

单位：万张、%

指标	2008年	2009年	2010年	2011年	2012年	2013年	2014年	2015年
床位数	300.3	326.5	349.6	396.4	449.3	526.7	482.3	393.2
增长率	11.40	8.72	7.08	13.39	13.35	17.23	−8.43	−18.47

注：自2014年起，调整社会服务机构的统计口径为在工商、编办和民政部门办理了注册登记手续的社会服务单位，原统计口径中未办理注册登记手续的社会服务单位，均已经调整到社会服务设施中。

1.提供住宿的养老服务。全国各类养老服务机构和设施11.6万个，比上年增长23.4%，其中：注册登记的养老服务机构2.8万个，社区养老服务机构和设施2.6万个，互助型养老设施6.2万个；各类养老床位672.7万张，比上年增长16.4%（每千名老年人拥有养老床位30.3张，比上年增长11.4%），其中社区留宿和日间照料床位298.1万张。

2.提供住宿的精神卫生服务。全国民政部门管理的智障与精神疾病服务机构共有242个，床位7.8万张。其中社会福利医院（精神病院）151个，床位数4.9万张，与上年持平，年末收留抚养各类人员4.0万人；复退军人精神病院91个，床位数3.0万张，年末收留抚养各类人员2.4万人。

3.提供住宿的儿童福利和保护服务。全国共有儿童福利和保护服务机构753个，床位10.0万张，年末收留抚养各类人员5.6万人。其中儿童福利机构478个，床位8.9万张；未成年人救助保护中心275个，床位1.1万张，全年共救助流浪乞讨未成年人4.7万人次。

4.其他提供住宿的社会服务。全国共有其他提供住宿的社会服务机构2439个，床位17.1万张。其中各类救助管理机构1766个，床位10.3万张，全年救助生活无着流浪乞讨人员370.5万人次，其中，在站救助318.7万人次，站外救助51.8万人次；安置农场15个；军供站320个。

（二）不提供住宿的社会服务

1.老龄服务。截至2015年底，全国60岁及以上老年人口22200万人，占总人口的16.1%，其中65岁及以上人口14386万人，占总人口的10.5%。全国共有老龄事业单位2280个，老年法律援助中心2.1万个，老年维权协调组织7.1万个，老年学校5.3万个、在校学习人员732.8万人，各类老年活动室37.1万个；享受高龄补贴的老年人2155.1万人，享受护理补贴的老年人26.5万人，享受养老服务补贴的老年人257.9万人。

图4 60岁及以上老年人口占全国总人口比重

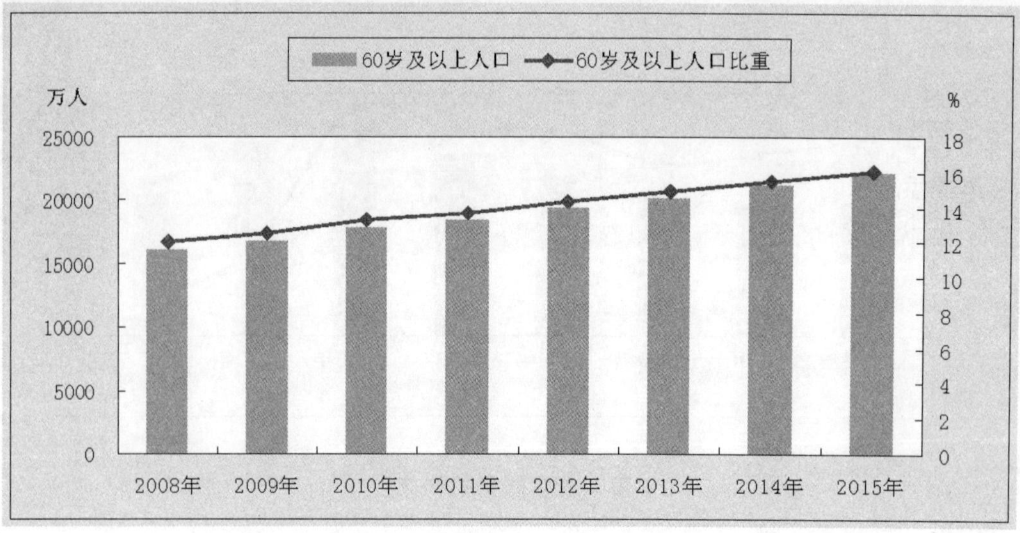

表4 60岁及以上老年人口占全国总人口比重

单位：万人、%

指标	2008年	2009年	2010年	2011年	2012年	2013年	2014年	2015年
60岁及以上人口	15989	16714	17765	18499	19390	20243	21242	22200
60岁及以上人口比重	12.0	12.5	13.26	13.7	14.3	14.9	15.5	16.1

2.儿童福利和收养登记。截至2015年底，全国共有孤儿50.2万人，其中集中供养孤儿9.2万人，社会散居孤儿41.0万人。2015年全国办理家庭收养登记2.2万件，其中：内地居民收养登记1.9万件，港澳台华侨收养179件，外国人收养登记2942件。

表5 家庭收养

单位：件、%

指标	2008年	2009年	2010年	2011年	2012年	2013年	2014年	2015年
家庭收养数	42550	44260	34529	31424	27278	24460	22772	22348
年增长率	−5.8	4.0	−22.0	−9.0	−13.2	−10.3	−6.9	−1.9

图5 家庭收养

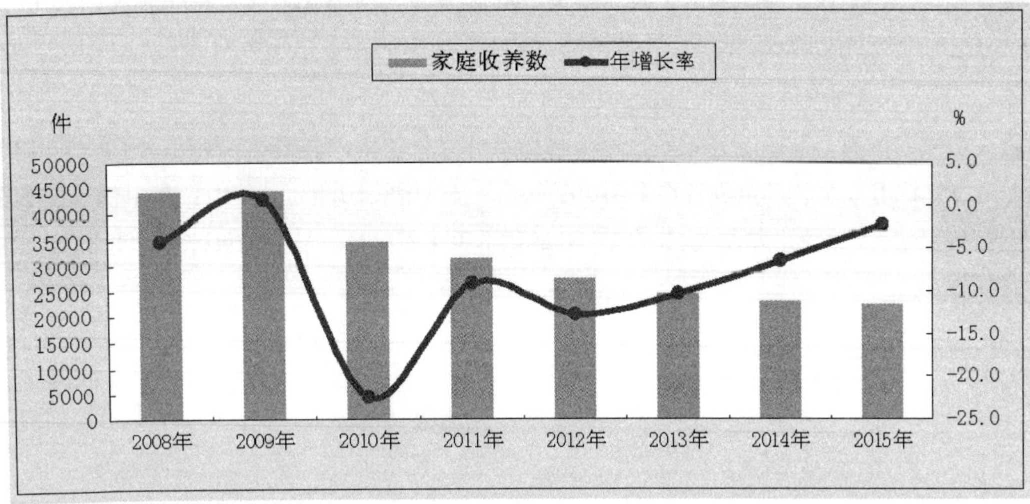

3.为残疾人提供服务的机构。截至2015年底，全国有为残疾人提供服务的机构1.5万个，吸纳残疾职工42.9万人就业，固定资产1778.8亿元，实现利润81.4亿元。

图6 为残疾人提供服务机构中的残疾职工

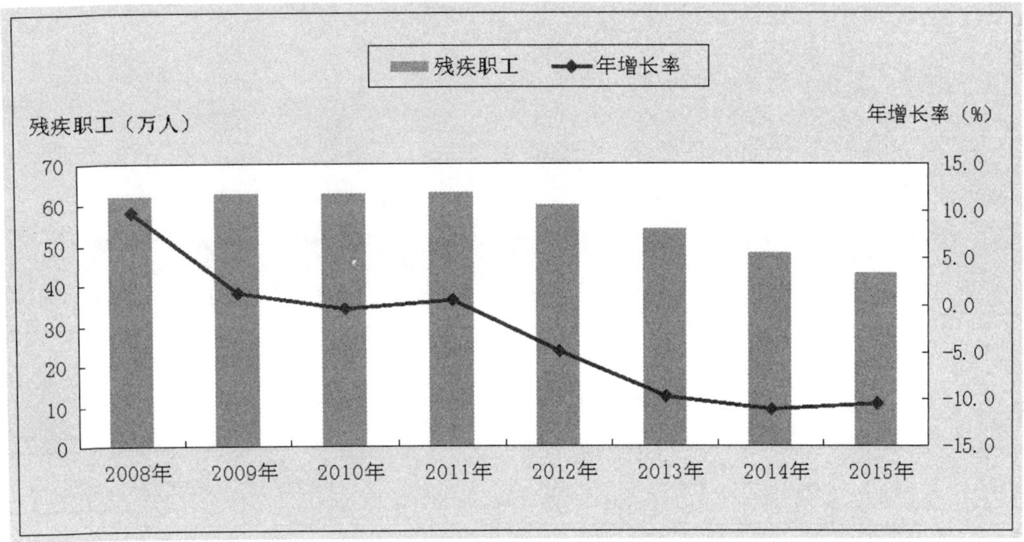

表6 为残疾人提供服务机构中的残疾职工

单位：万人、%

指标	2008年	2009年	2010年	2011年	2012年	2013年	2014年	2015年
福利企业残疾职工	61.9	62.7	62.5	62.8	59.7	53.9	47.9	42.9
年增长率	9.9	1.3	−0.3	0.5	−4.9	−9.7	−11.1	−10.4

4.社会救助

城市低保。截至2015年底，全国有城市低保对象957.4万户、1701.1万人。全年各级财政共支出城市低保资金719.3亿元。2015年全国城市低保平均标准451.1元/人·月，比上年增长9.5%；全国城市低保月人均补助水平316.6元，比上年增长10.9%。

城市“三无”救济。2015年救济城市“三无”人员6.8万人。

农村低保。截至2015年底，全国有农村低保对象2846.2万户、4903.6万人。全年各级财政共支出农村低保资金931.5亿元。2015年全国农村低保平均标准3177.6元/人·年，比上年增长14.4%；全国农村低保年人均补助水平1766.5元，比上年增长13.8%。

农村特困人员救助供养。截至2015年底，全国救助供养农村特困人员516.7万人，比上年下降2.3%。全年各级财政共支出农村特困人员救助供养资金210.0亿元，比上年增长10.6%。其中：集中供养162.3万人，年平均供养标准为6025.7元/人，比上年增长12.2%；分散供养354.4万人，年平均供养标准为4490.1元/人，比上年增长12.1%。

传统救济。2015年传统救济63.8万人。

图7 困难群众基本生活救助情况

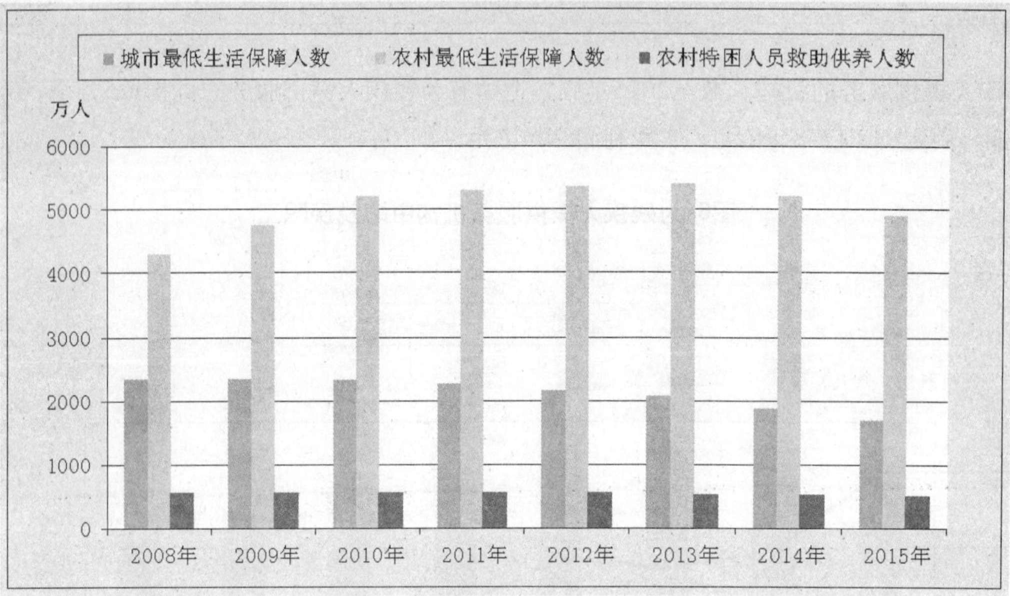

表7 困难群众基本生活救助情况

单位：万人

指标	2008年	2009年	2010年	2011年	2012年	2013年	2014年	2015年
城市最低生活保障人数	2334.8	2345.6	2310.5	2276.8	2143.5	2064.2	1877.0	1701.0
农村最低生活保障人数	4305.5	4760.0	5214.0	5305.7	5344.5	5388.0	5207.2	4903.6
农村特困人员救助供养人数	548.6	553.4	556.3	551.0	545.6	537.2	529.1	516.7

医疗救助。2015年资助参加基本医疗保险6634.7万人，支出资助参加基本医疗保险资金61.7亿元，资助参加基本医疗保险人均补助水平93.0元。2015年直接医疗救助2889.1万人次，其中，住院救助1307.9万人次，门诊救助1581.2万人次；支出资金236.8亿元，其中，住院救助208.7亿元，门诊救助28.0亿元。

2015年全年累计资助优抚对象436.5万人次，优抚医疗补助资金34.6亿元，人均补助水平793元。

临时救助。2015年临时救助655.4万户次，其中，按属地分类救助本地户籍家庭633.5万户次，非本地户籍家庭21.9万户次。

5.防灾减灾。2015年全国各类自然灾害共造成1.9亿人次不同程度受灾，因灾死亡失踪967人，紧急转移安置644.4万人次；农作物受灾面积21769.8千公顷，其中绝收面积2232.7千公顷；倒塌房屋24.8万间，损坏房屋250.5万间；因灾直接经济损失2704.1亿元。国家减灾委、民政部共启动20次国家救灾应急响应，累计救助受灾群众6000余万人次，向受灾省份累计下拨中央自然灾害生活补助资金94.72亿元，紧急调拨4.7万顶救灾帐篷、16.1万床棉被、11万件棉大衣、2.3万个睡袋、5万张折叠床等生活类中央救灾物资，高效有序应对了波及我国西藏日喀则地区的尼泊尔强烈地震、云南沧源地震、新疆皮山地震、台风"苏迪罗"和"彩虹"、南方暴雨洪涝风雹灾害等重特大自然灾害。创建"全国综合减灾示范社区"1390个。

图8 因灾死亡（含失踪）人口

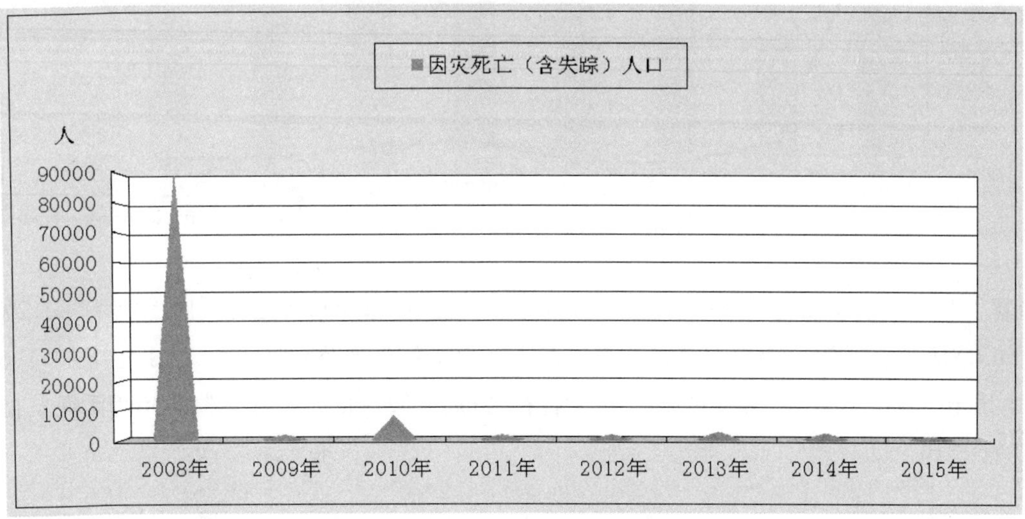

表8 因灾死亡（含失踪）人口

单位：人

指标	2008年	2009年	2010年	2011年	2012年	2013年	2014年	2015年
因灾死亡（含失踪）人口	88928	1528	7844	1126	1530	2284	1818	967

6.慈善事业

慈善捐赠。截至2015年底，全国共建立经常性社会捐助工作站、点和慈善超市3.0万个（其中：慈善超市9654个）。全年共接收社会捐赠款654.5亿元，其中：民政部门直接接收社会各界捐款44.2亿元，各类社会组织接收捐款610.3亿元。全年各地民政部门接收捐赠衣被4537.0万件，捐赠物资价值折合人民币5.2亿元。间接接收其他部门转入的社会捐款4.3亿元，衣被172.5万件，捐赠物资折款6164.4万元。全年有1838.4万人次困难群众受益。全年有934.6万人次在社会服务领域提供了2700.7万小时的志愿服务。

表9 接收社会捐款和衣被

单位：亿元、万件

指标	2008年	2009年	2010年	2011年	2012年	2013年	2014年	2015年
民政部门和社会组织共计接收社会捐赠款	744.5	507.2	596.8	490.1	572.5	566.4	604.4	654.5
民政部门接收社会捐赠衣被	115816.3	12476.6	2750.2	2918.5	12538.2	10405.0	5244.5	4537.0

图9 接收社会捐款和衣被

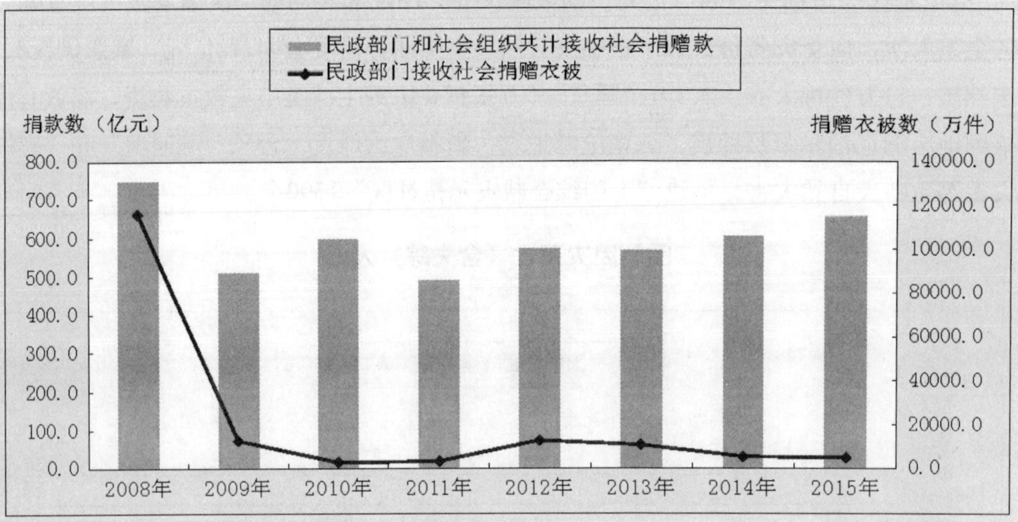

福利彩票。2015年中国福利彩票年销售2015.1亿元，比上年减少44.6亿元，比上年下降2.2%。全年筹集福彩公益金563.8亿元，下降3.7%。全年民政系统共支出彩票公益金288.9亿元，比上年增加57.6亿元，增长24.9%，其中用于抚恤6.9亿元，退役安置0.2亿元，社会福利182.1亿元，社会救助30.0亿元，自然灾害救助1.9亿元，其他43.6亿元。

图10 福利彩票

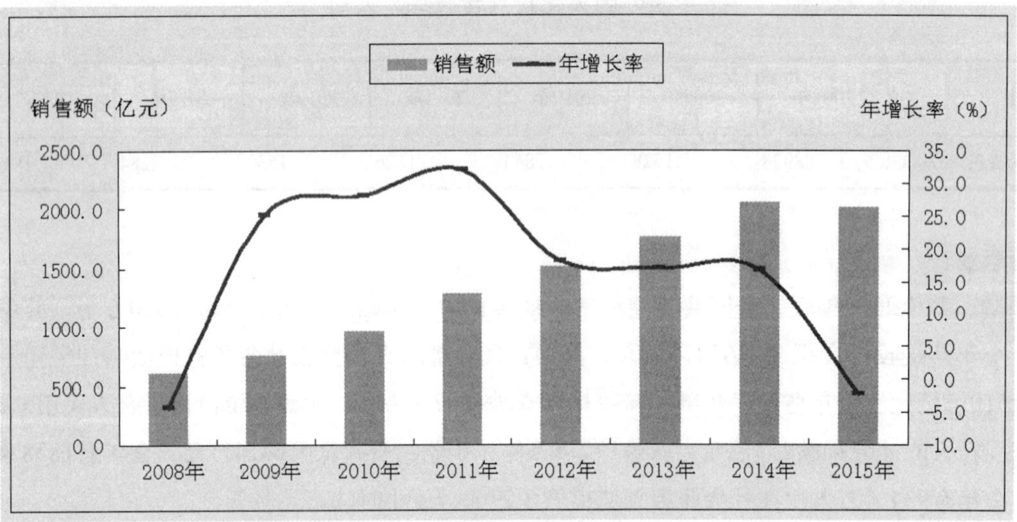

表10 福利彩票

单位：亿元、%

指标	2008年	2009年	2010年	2011年	2012年	2013年	2014年	2015年
销售额	604.0	756.0	968.0	1278.0	1510.3	1765.3	2059.7	2015.1
年增长率	−4.4	25.2	28.0	32.0	18.2	16.9	16.7	−2.2

7.**优抚安置**。截至2015年底，国家抚恤、补助各类重点优抚对象897.0万人。其中：伤残人员73.7万人，

带病回乡退伍军人118.4万人，在乡复员军人79.2万人，60岁以上农村籍退伍军人392.5万人，在乡退伍红军老战士177人，在乡西路军红军老战士64人，红军失散人员3708人；烈士遗属16.1万人，因公牺牲、病故军人遗属10.4万人。

图11 国家抚恤、补助优抚对象

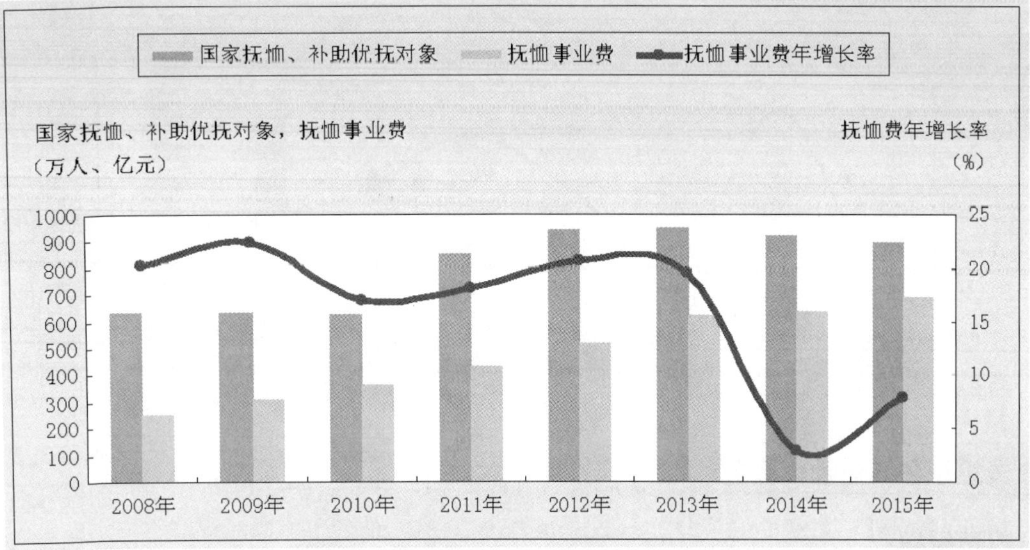

表11 国家抚恤、补助优抚对象

单位：万人、亿元、%

指标	2008年	2009年	2010年	2011年	2012年	2013年	2014年	2015年
国家抚恤、补助优抚对象	633.2	630.7	625.0	852.5	944.4	950.5	917.3	897.0
抚恤事业费	253.6	310.3	362.7	428.3	517.0	618.4	636.6	686.8
抚恤事业费年增长率	20.3	22.4	16.9	18.1	20.7	19.6	2.9	7.9

2015年新增341人享受烈士待遇。截至2015年底，全国共有注册登记的烈士纪念设施管理机构1464个，占地面积4441.7公顷，机构内烈士纪念设施3.5万处；零散烈士纪念设施1.2万处。

2015年共接收军队离退休干部（含退休士官）、无军籍退休退职职工、复员干部1.9万人。军队离退休人员管理中心271个，年末职工0.4万人；军队离退休人员活动中心27个，年末职工0.1万人。

8.社区服务。截至2015年底，全国共有各类社区服务机构和设施36.1万个，覆盖率52.9%，其中，社区服务指导中心863个，社区服务中心2.4万个，比上年增长4.3%，社区服务站12.8万个，比上年增长6.7%，社区养老服务机构和设施2.6万个，比上年增长36.8%，互助型的养老设施6.2万个，比上年增长55%，其他社区服务设施12.0万个，比上年增长12.1%。城镇便民、利民服务网点24.9万个。社区志愿服务组织9.6万个。

表12 社区服务机构和设施

单位：万个、%

指标	2008年	2009年	2010年	2011年	2012年	2013年	2014年	2015年
社区服务机构和设施	14.6	14.6	15.3	16.0	20.0	25.2	31.1	36.1
社区服务中心、站	4.0	6.3	5.7	7.1	10.4	12.8	14.3	15.2
社区服务中心、站增长率	−32.9	58.4	−9.8	23.9	47.8	23.1	11.7	6.2

图12 社区服务机构和设施

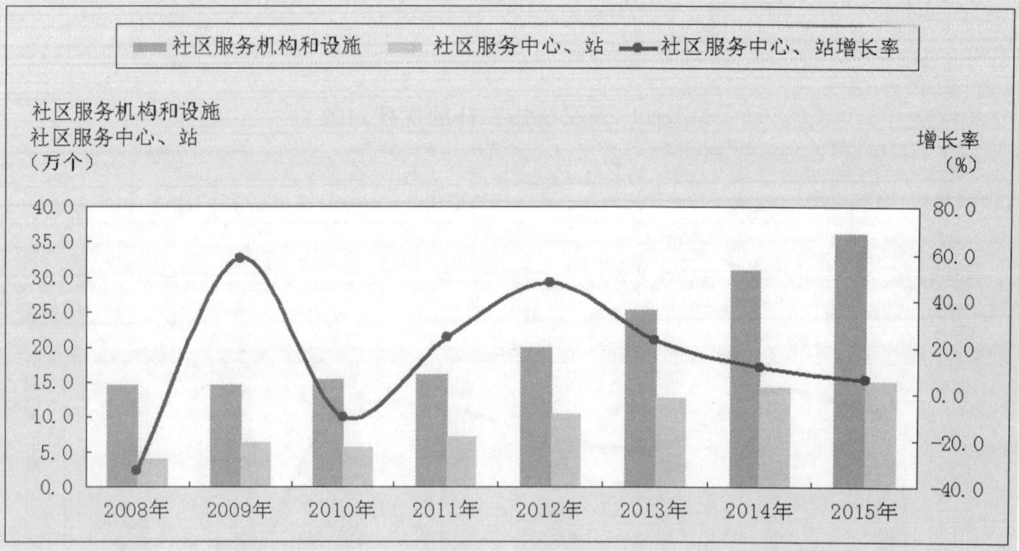

三、成员组织和其他社会服务

（一）成员组织

1.**社会组织**。截至2015年底，全国共有社会组织66.2万个，比上年增长9.2%；吸纳社会各类人员就业734.8万人，比上年增长7.7%；全年累计收入2929.0亿元，支出2383.8亿元，形成固定资产2311.1亿元。接收各类社会捐赠610.3亿元。全年共查处社会组织违法违规案件2951起，其中取缔非法社会组织23起，行政处罚2928起。

全国共有社会团体32.9万个，比上年增长6.1%。其中：工商服务业类3.7万个，科技研究类1.7万个，教育类1.0万个，卫生类1.0万个，社会服务类4.8万个，文化类3.3万个，体育类2.3万个，生态环境类0.7万个，法律类0.3万个，宗教类0.5万个，农业及农村发展类6.2万个，职业及从业组织类2.1万个，其他5.3万个。全年共查处社会团体违法违规案件1681起，其中取缔非法社会团体2起，行政处罚1679起。

全国共有各类基金会4784个，比上年增加667个，增长16.2%，其中：公募基金会1548个，非公募基金会3198个；民政部登记的基金会202个、涉外基金会9个、境外基金会代表机构29个。公募基金会和非公募基金会共接收社会各界捐赠439.3亿元。全年对基金会作出行政处罚16起。

全国共有民办非企业单位32.9万个，比上年增长12.7%。其中：科技服务类1.6万个，生态环境类433个，教育类18.3万个，卫生类2.4万个，社会服务类4.9万个，文化类1.7万个，体育类1.4万个，商务服务类3355个，宗教类114个，国际及其他涉外组织类7个，其他1.9万个。全年共查处民办非企业单位违法违纪案件1254起，其中取缔非法民办非企业单位21起，行政处罚1233起。

表13 社会组织

单位：万个

指标	2008年	2009年	2010年	2011年	2012年	2013年	2014年	2015年
社会团体	23.0	23.9	24.5	25.5	27.1	28.9	31.0	32.9
基金会(个)	1597	1843	2200	2614	3029	3549	4117	4784
民办非企业	18.2	19.0	19.8	20.4	22.5	25.5	29.2	32.9

图13 社会组织

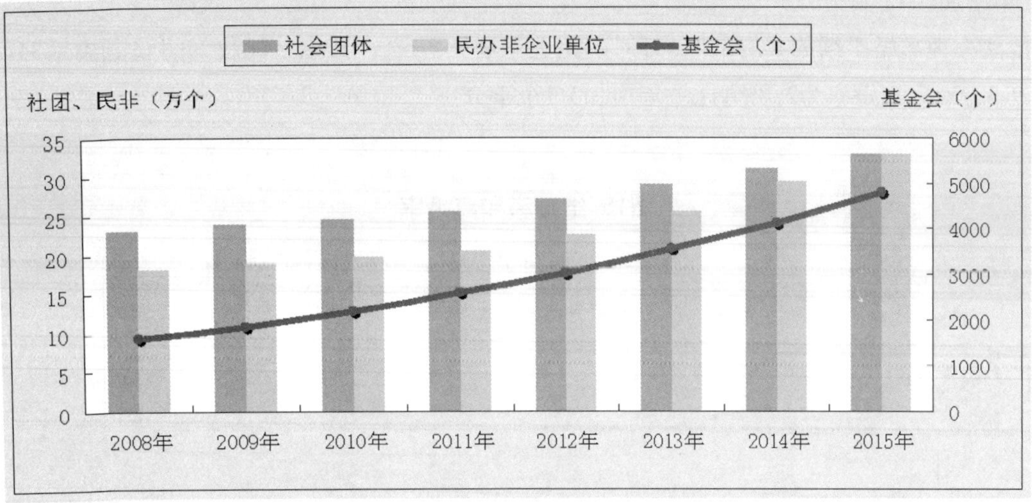

2.自治组织。截至2015年底，基层群众自治组织共计68.1万个，其中：村委会58.1万个，村民小组469.2万个，村委会成员229.7万人；居委会10万个，比上年增长3.1%，居民小组134.7万个，居委会成员51.2万人，比上年增长3.0%。全年共有16.5万个村（居）委会完成选举，参与选举的村（居）民登记数为2.1亿人，参与投票人数为1.6亿人。

图14 自治组织

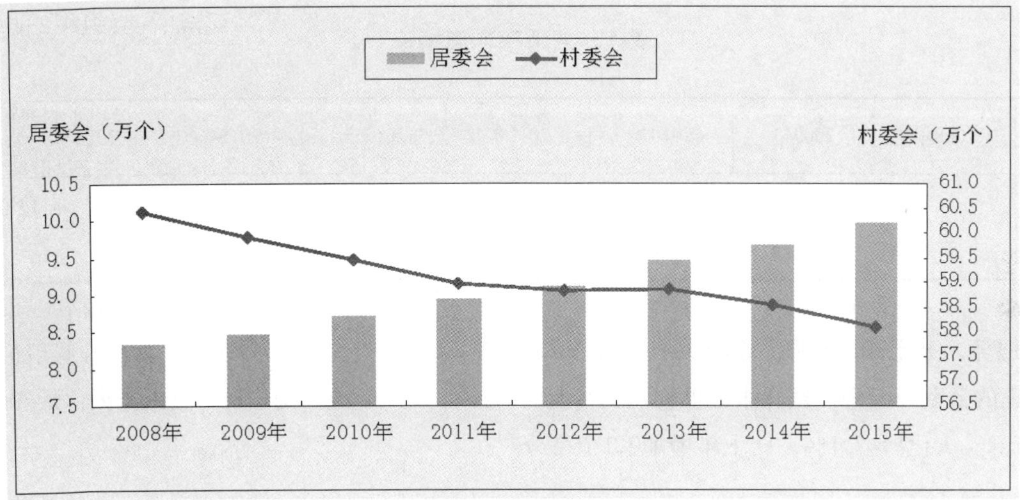

表14 自治组织

单位：万个

指标	2008年	2009年	2010年	2011年	2012年	2013年	2014年	2015年
居委会	8.3	8.5	8.7	8.9	9.1	9.5	9.7	10.0
村委会	60.4	59.9	59.5	59.0	58.8	58.9	58.5	58.1

（二）其他社会服务

1.婚姻登记服务。2015年全国共有事业单位性质的婚姻登记机构2064个，办理婚姻登记事务的处数5714处。各级民政部门和婚姻登记机构共依法办理结婚登记1224.7万对，比上年下降6.3%。其中：涉外及华侨、港澳台居民登记结婚4.1万对。结婚率为9.0‰。2015年25—29岁办理结婚登记占结婚总人口比重最多，占39.4%，比上年增加1.4个百分点。

2015年依法办理离婚手续的共有384.1万对，比上年增长5.6%，其中：民政部门登记离婚314.9万对，法院办理离婚69.3万对。离婚率为2.8‰，比上年增加0.1个千分点。

图15 结婚率和离婚率

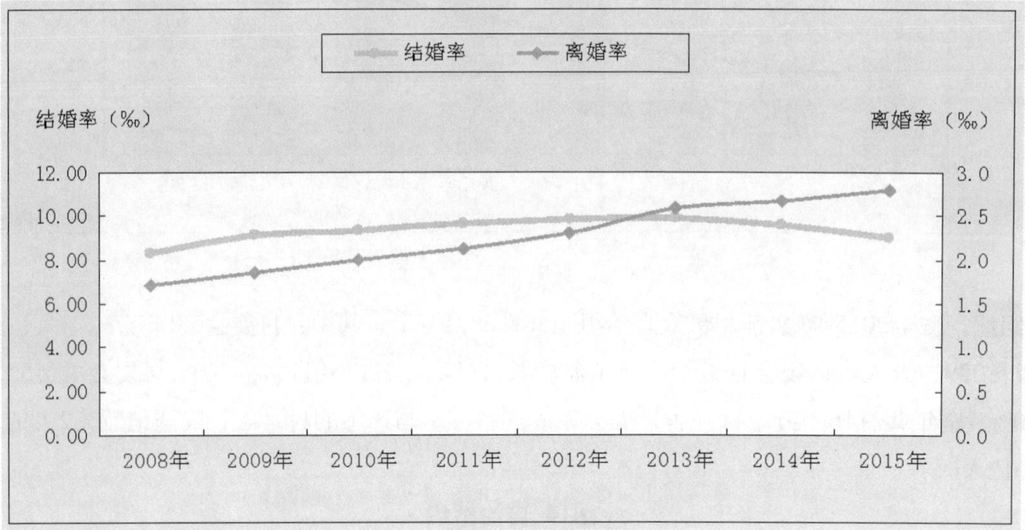

表15 结婚率和离婚率

单位：‰

指标	2008年	2009年	2010年	2011年	2012年	2013年	2014年	2015年
结婚率	8.27	9.10	9.30	9.67	9.80	9.92	9.58	9.00
离婚率	1.71	1.85	2.00	2.13	2.29	2.58	2.67	2.79

2.殡葬服务。截至2015年底，全国共有殡葬服务机构4530个，其中殡仪馆1821个，殡葬管理机构1127个，民政部门管理的公墓1567个。殡葬服务机构职工共有8.4万人，其中殡仪馆职工4.7万人。火化炉6063台，遗体火化459.5万具。火化率47.1%，比上年增加0.1个百分点。

表16 遗体火化情况

单位：万具、%

指标	2008年	2009年	2010年	2011年	2012年	2013年	2014年	2015年
遗体火化数	453.4	454.2	474.1	468.1	477.7	468.9	459.3	459.5
火化率	48.5	48.2	49.0	48.8	49.5	48.2	47.0	47.1

图16 遗体火化情况

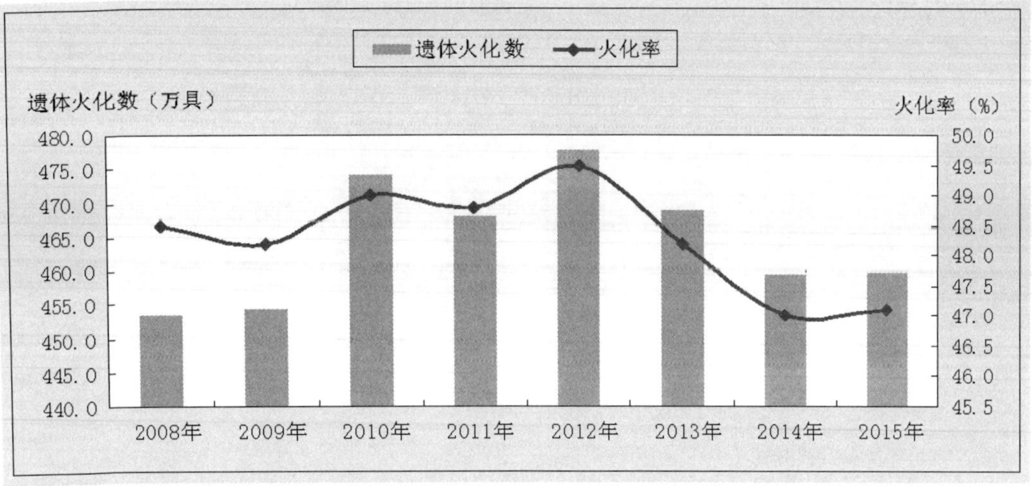

注释：

1．图1和表1中“乡”包含“民族乡、苏木和民族苏木”。

2．财政部、民政部下拨中央资金不包含中央级救灾物资采购经费和部分拨付新疆生产建设兵团资金等。

3．社会组织捐赠数使用的是2015年年检（内容是2014年的情况报告）数据。

4．离婚登记服务中法院判决、调解离婚数据来源于最高人民法院。

5．本资料中的民政对象人数和机构数均为当年实际发生数和注册登记的法定机构数，与当年批准数、计划数和预算数不可比。

6．本资料部分数据因四舍五入原因，存在分项数据与合计数据不等情况，由此产生的误差，均未作机械调整。

7．各项统计数据均未包括香港特别行政区、澳门特别行政区和台湾省。

Statistical Report of the People's Republic of China on the Development of Social Services in 2015

Ministry of Civil Affairs of
the People's Republic of China
July 4th, 2016

In 2015, the system of national civil affairs earnestly implemented decisions and arrangements of the Party Central Committee and the State Council, actively conformed to new expectations of people, intensified reforms, tightened up the legal system, solved difficult problems, worked to secure solid progress in all important work and made new development of civil affairs.

I. Synthesis

By the end of 2015, there were altogether 34 administrative areas at the provincial level in China (4 municipalities directly under the central government, 23 provinces, 5 autonomous regions and 2 special administrative regions), 334 administrative areas at the prefecture level (291 cities at the prefecture level, 10 prefectures, 30 autonomous prefectures and 3 leagues), 2,850 administrative areas at the county level (921 districts under the jurisdiction of cities, 361 cities at the county level, 1,397 counties, 117 autonomous counties, 49 banners, 3 autonomous banners, 1 special zone and 1 forestry district), 39,789 administrative areas at the township level (2 district public offices, 20,515 towns, 10,172 townships, 152 sumus, 990 ethnic townships, 1 ethnic sumu, 7,957 street communities).

In 2015, the joint inspections covered 14 provincial boundaries (14,468 kilometers).

Figure 1: Changes in Townships, Towns and Street Communities

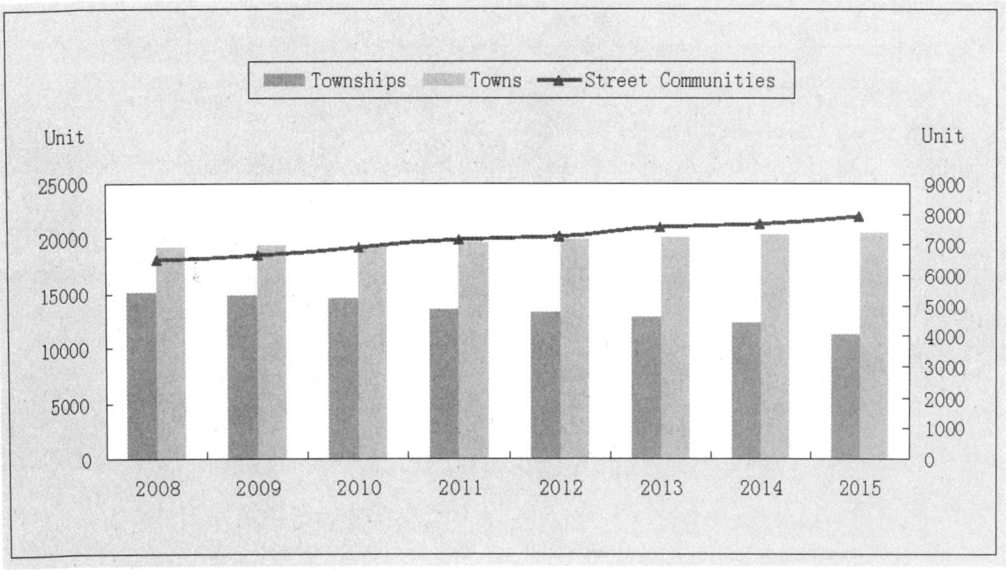

Table 1: Changes in Townships, Towns and Street Communities

Indicators	2008	2009	2010	2011	2012	2013	2014	2015
Townships (Unit)	15067	14848	14571	13587	13281	12812	12282	11315
Towns (Unit)	19234	19322	19410	19683	19881	20117	20401	20515
Street Communities (Unit)	6524	6686	6923	7194	7282	7566	7696	7957

By the end of 2015, there were 1.765 million organizations and facilities on social services, a rise of by 5.8 percent over the previous year. The total number of staff was 13.089 million, a rise of by 4.6 percent over the previous year (The total number of national certified social workers was 206,000, a rise of by 28.8 percent over the previous year, 52,000 of them were social workers and 154,000 of them were assistant social workers). The total fixed assets stood at 818.31 billion yuan, which rose 13.4 percent over the previous year. The area of construction projects for social services was 40,873,000 square meters and the total investment reached 23.99 billion yuan. By the end of 2015, the total expenditure on social service industry reached 492.64 billion yuan, a rise of 11.9 percent over the previous year. The proportion of total expenditure on social service industry in the share of national financial expenditure was 3.3 percent. Thereinto, the transferred payment of the central government to social service industry amounted to 227.03 billion yuan, a rise of 8.4 percent over the previous year. It took up 46.1 percent of the total social service expenditure, decreased 1.7 percent over the previous year.

Figure 2: Basic Situation of Social Service Industry

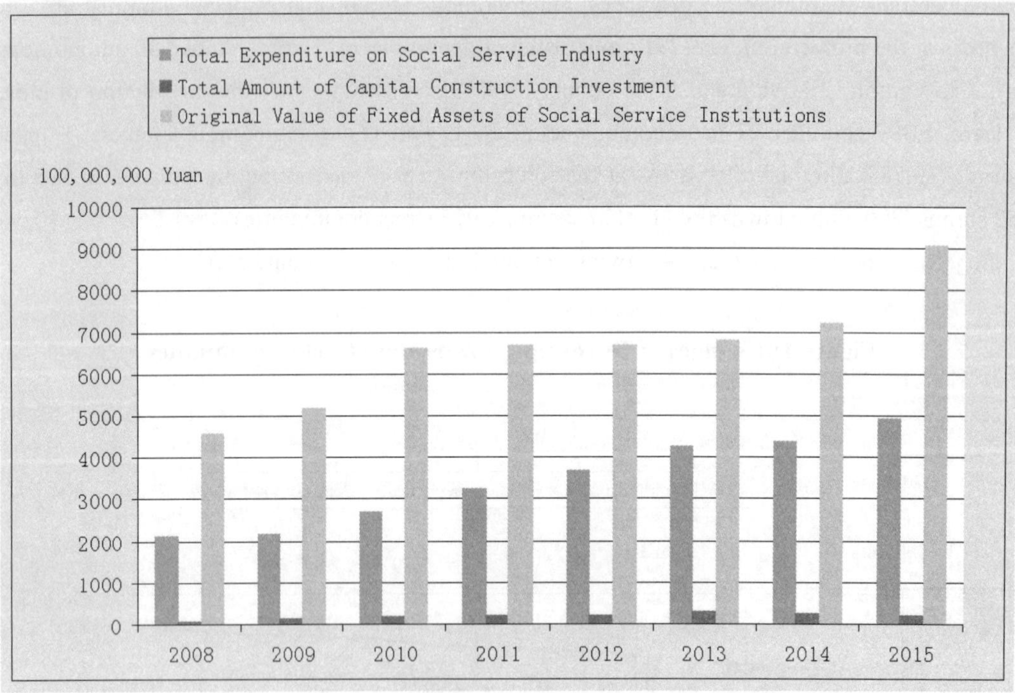

Table 2: Basic Situation of Social Service Industry

Indicators	2008	2009	2010	2011	2012	2013	2014	2015
Total Expenditure on Social Service Industry (100,000,000 Yuan)	2146.5	2181.9	2697.5	3229.1	3683.7	4276.5	4404.1	4926.4
Total Amount of Capital Construction Investment (100,000,000 Yuan)	66.6	157.0	183.0	218.5	235.0	292.8	282.2	239.9
Original Value of Fixed Assets of Social Service Institutions (100,000,000 Yuan)	4592.8	5198.0	6589.3	6676.7	6675.4	6810.2	7213.0	8183.1

II. Social Services

A. Social Services with Accommodation

By the end of 2015, there were 31 thousand social service institutions with accommodation which were registered. Thereinto, 18 thousand of them were public institutions, a rise of 12.5 percent over that of the previous year, and 12 thousand of them were non-governmental and non-commercial enterprises.They offered 3.932 million beds and the number of adoptees reached 2.363 million.

Figure 3: Beds in Social Service Institutions

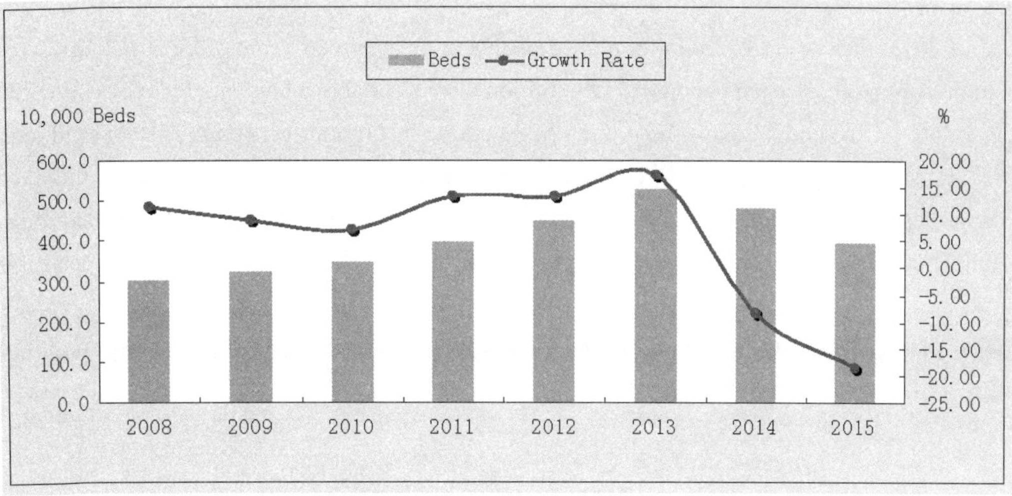

Table 3: Beds in Social Service Institutions

Indicators	2008	2009	2010	2011	2012	2013	2014	2015
Bed (10,000 Beds)	300.3	326.5	349.6	396.4	449.3	526.7	482.3	393.2
Growth Rate (%)	11.40	8.72	7.08	13.39	13.35	17.23	−8.43	−18.47

Note : From 2014, organizations on social services were those which were registered in bureau of industry and commerce, state commission office of public sectors reform and civil affairs departments. Facilities on social services were those which were not registered.

1. Social Services with Accommodation for the Aged

The number of welfare institutions and facilities for the aged was 116,000, a rise of 23.4 percent over the previous year. Thereinto, there were 28,000 welfare institutions which were registered, 26,000 community welfare institutions and facilities, 62,000 mutual aid facilities. The number of all kinds of beds for aged people was 6.727 million, a rise of 16.4 percent over the previous year (the average number of beds per thousand seniors was 30.3, a rise of 11.4 percent in comparison with last year).Thereinto, 2,981 thousand were used for community accommodation and daytime care.

2. Service Agencies with Accommodation for Psychiatric Disorders

There were 242 service agencies for mental retardations and psychiatric disorders under the management of the civil affairs departments with 78 thousand beds. Thereinto, there were 151 social welfare homes (mental hospitals) with 49 thousand beds, basically the same as that in the previous year. By the end of 2015, 40 thousand people were adopted. There were 91 mental hospitals with 30 thousand beds for ex-servicemen and 24 thousand people were adopted by the end of the year.

3. Welfare and Protection Institutions with Accommodation and for the Children

By the end of the year, there were 753 welfare and protection institutions with 100 thousand beds for children, and 56 thousand children were adopted. Thereinto, there were 478 welfare institutions for children. They offered 89 thousand beds. There were 275 children relief and protection centers with 11 thousand beds. They received 47 thousand minor vagabonds (person-times) in the whole year.

4. Other Social Service Institutions with Accommodation Service

There were 2,439 other social service institutions with 171 thousand beds. Thereinto, there were 1,766 relief and management institutions with 103 thousand beds. In the whole year, they received 3.705 million street people (person-times) who had no means of support. Thereinto, 3.187 million of those got in-shelter reliefs and 518 thousand got out-shelter reliefs. There were 15 arrangement farms. There were 320 military depots for military supplies.

B. Social Services without Accommodation

1. Aging Service

By the end of 2015, there were 222.0 million aged people at or above 60 years old, consisting of 16.1 percent of the total population. Among those aged people, 143.86 million were at or above 65 years old, consisting of 10.5 percent of the total population. By the end of 2015, there were 2,280 public institutions on aging, 21 thousand legal aid centers for the aged, 71 thousand rights safeguarding institutions for the aged, 53 thousand schools for the aged with 7.328 million students in these schools and 371 thousand activity rooms for the aged. There were 21.551million aged people who received elderly subsidy, 265 thousand received nursing care subsidy, 2.579 million received aged service subsidy.

Figure 4: Percentage of Aged Population 60 Years Old or above in the Total National Population

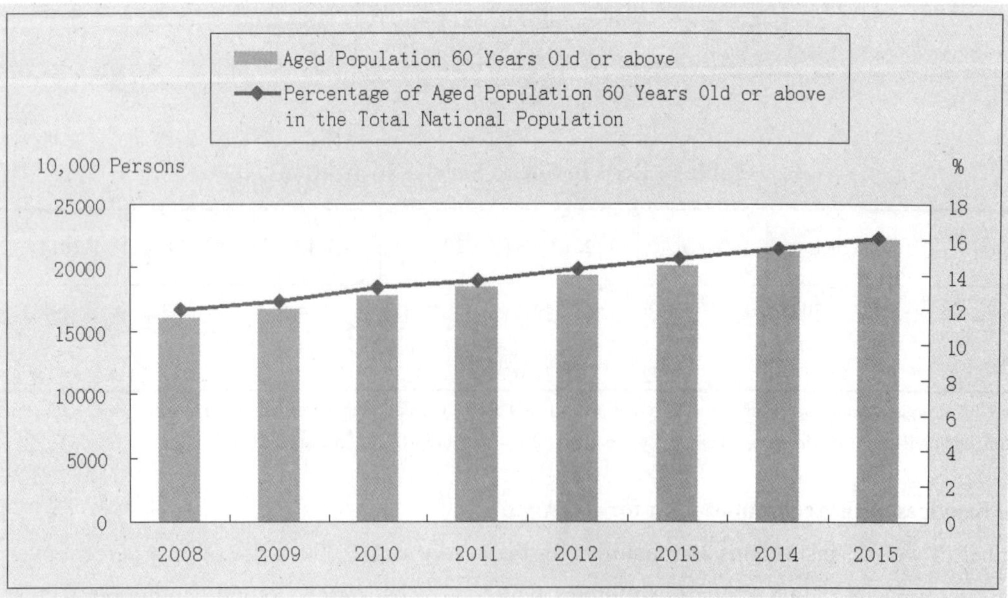

Table 4: Percentage of Aged Population 60 Years Old or above in the Total National Population

Indicators	2008	2009	2010	2011	2012	2013	2014	2015
Aged Population 60 Years Old or above (10,000 Persons)	15989	16714	17765	18499	19390	20243	21242	22200
Percentage of Aged Population 60 Years Old or above in the Total National Population (%)	12.0	12.5	13.26	13.7	14.3	14.9	15.5	16.1

2. Children Welfare and Adoption

By the end of 2015, there were 502 thousand orphans in China, of which 92 thousand orphans were collectively adopted, 410 thousand orphans scattered. In 2015, registered family adoptions totaled 22,000 cases. Thereinto, 19,000 cases were completed by mainland citizens, 179 cases were completed by overseas Chinese and residents in Hong Kong, Macao and Taiwan, 2,942 cases were completed by foreigners.

Figure 5: Children Adopted by Families

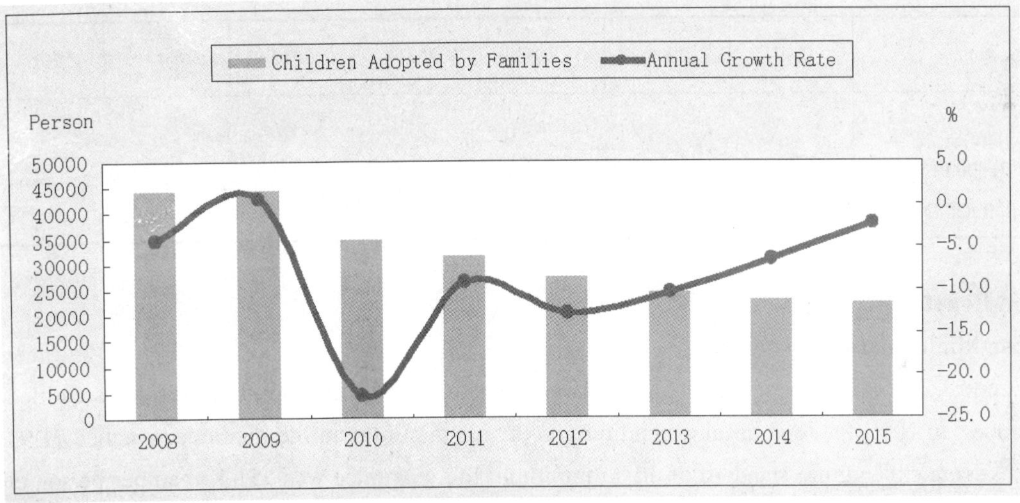

Table 5: Children Adopted by Families

Indicators	2008	2009	2010	2011	2012	2013	2014	2015
Children Adopted by Families (Person)	42550	44260	34529	31424	27278	24460	22772	22348
Annual Growth Rate (%)	−5.8	4.0	−22.0	−9.0	−13.2	−10.3	−6.9	−1.9

3. Agencies Providing Services for Disabled

By the end of 2015, there were 15,000 social welfare agencies providing services for disabled across the country. These agencies employed 429 thousand disabled people. The fixed assets valued 177.88 billion yuan and the profits reached 8.14 billion yuan.

Figure 6: Disabled Employees in Social Welfare Enterprises

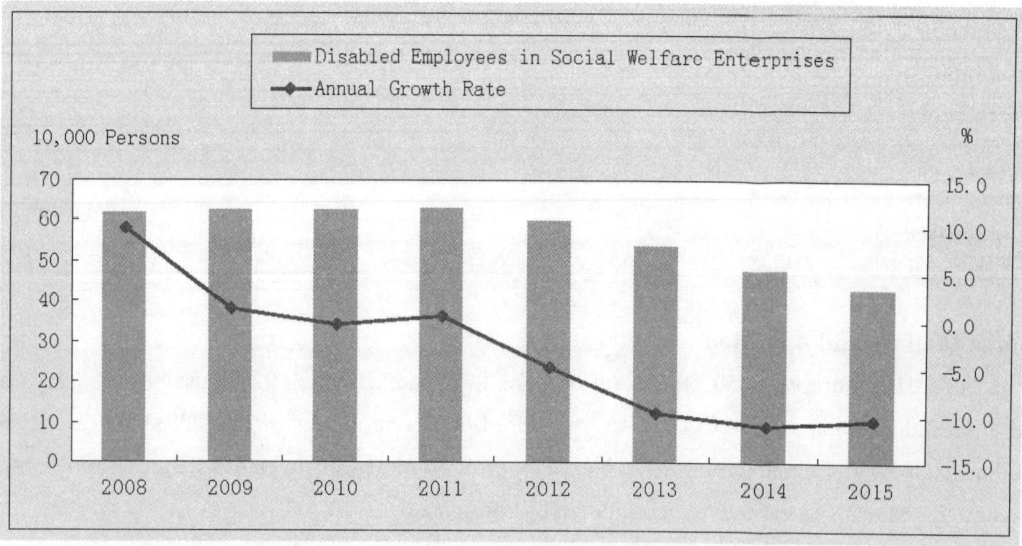

Table 6 Disabled Employees in Social Welfare Enterprises

Indicators	2008	2009	2010	2011	2012	2013	2014	2015
Disabled Employees in Social Welfare Enterprises(10,000 Persons)	61.9	62.7	62.5	62.8	59.7	53.9	47.9	42.9
Annual Growth Rate(%)	9.9	1.3	−0.3	0.5	−4.9	−9.7	−11.1	−10.4

4. Social Relief

- Urban Minimum Life Guarantee

By the end of 2015, there were 9.574 million households or 17.011 million urban residents entitled to minimum living allowances. In 2015, the total fiscal expenditure on the urban minimum life guarantee reached 71.93 billion yuan. In 2015, the average expenditure standard of urban minimum life guarantee was 451.1 yuan per person every month, a rise of 9.5 percent over the previous year. The per capita urban minimum life guarantee was 316.6 yuan every month, a rise of 10.9 percent over the previous year.

- Relief of the Urban Three-Without People

In 2015, 68 thousand urban Three-Without people had been relieved.

- Rural Minimum Life Guarantee

By the end of 2015, there were 28.462 million households, 49.036 million people who were covered by the rural minimum life guarantee system. A total of 93.15 billion yuan was distributed by governments at all levels in the whole year. In 2015, the average expenditure standard of rural minimum life guarantee of the country was 3,177.6 yuan per person per year, a rise of 14.4 percent. The per capita rural minimum life guarantee was 1,766.5 yuan every year, a rise of 13.8 percent over the previous year.

- Five Guarantees in Rural Areas

By the end of 2015, there were 5.167 million people who had received relief allowances from the five guarantees system in rural areas across the country, decreased 2.3 percent over the previous year. A total of 21.0 billion yuan for rural five guarantees was distributed by government at all levels in the whole year. It was an increase of 10.6 percent over the previous year. There were 1.623 million people who were cared collectively, with an average expenditure standard of 6025.7 yuan per person per year, a rise of 12.2 percent in comparison with last year. There were 3.544 million people who were cared separately, with an average expenditure standard of 4,490.1 yuan per person every year, a rise of 12.1 percent in comparison with last year.

● Traditional Rural Relief

In 2015, there were 638 thousand residents who received the traditional rural relief.

Figure 7: Situation of Basic Relief for People in Difficulties

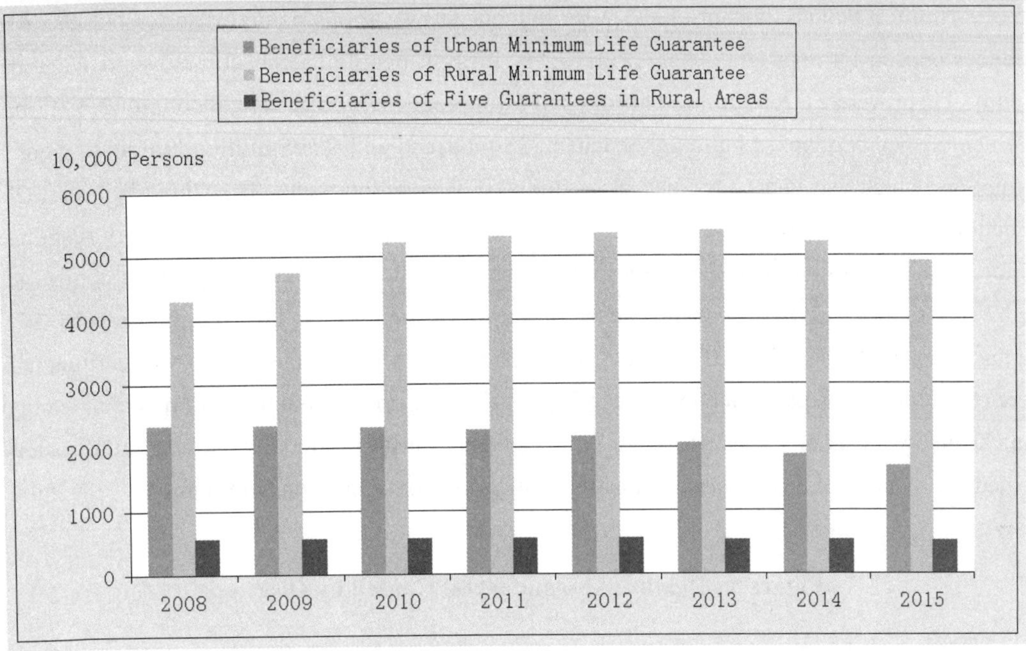

Table 7: Situation of Basic Relief for People in Difficulties

Indicators	2008	2009	2010	2011	2012	2013	2014	2015
Beneficiaries of Urban Minimum Life Guarantee (10,000 Persons)	2334.8	2345.6	2310.5	2276.8	2143.5	2064.2	1877.0	1701.0
Beneficiaries of Rural Minimum Life Guarantee (10,000 Persons)	4305.5	4760.0	5214.0	5305.7	5344.5	5388.0	5207.2	4903.6
Beneficiaries of Five Guarantees in Rural Areas (10,000 Persons)	548.6	553.4	556.3	551.0	545.6	537.2	529.1	516.7

● Medical Aid

In 2015, 66.347 million people received subsidized aid for medical insurance. The fund for subsidized aid for medical insurance was 6.17 billion yuan and the average expenditure was 93 yuan per person. There were 28.891 million people (person-times) that received direct medical aid. Thereinto, 13.079 million of them were aided as inpatients and 15.812 million were aided as outpatients. The total expenditure on medical aid was 23.68 billion yuan. It includes the fund for medical aid as inpatients of 20.87 billion yuan, the fund for medical aid as outpatients of 2.8 billion yuan.

In 2015, the number of people who were covered by state pension and preferential treatment program reached 4.365

million (person-times). The financial expenditure on medical subsidy totaled 3.46 billion yuan. The average expenditure was 793 yuan per person.

- The Provisional Relief

In 2015, there were 6.554 million households (times) that received provisional relief. According to the classification of the household registration, 6.335 million households (times) belonged to local permanent residence and 219 thousand households (times) belonged to non-local permanent residence.

5. Disaster Prevention and Relief

In 2015, 190 million people (person-times) were influenced by various natural disasters. There were 967 deaths and abscondences caused by disasters. There were 6.444 million people (person-times) who were transferred and resettled urgently. There were 21.7698 million hectares of farm crops hit by disasters, thereinto, 2.2327 million hectares of crops were demolished. Collapsed buildings reached 248 thousand and 2.505 million buildings were damaged. The direct economic loss which was caused by disasters stood at 270.41 billion yuan. The China National Commission for Disaster Reduction and the Ministry of Civil Affairs totally started disaster assistance emergency response for 20 times and helped more than 60 million people (person-times). They allocated 9.472 billion yuan as central natural disaster relief funds, 47 thousand tents, 161 thousand pieces of cotton-padded quilts, 110 thousand pieces of cotton-padded clothes, 23 thousand sleeping bags and 50 thousand folding beds. They did efficiently in some serious natural disasters, such as, severe earthquake in Nepal which influenced Xigazê (Xizang) in our country, earthquake in Cangyuan (Yunnan) and in Pishan (Xinjiang), typhoon "Soudelor" and "Mujigae" and rainstorm, flood, wind and hail disasters of the south. And they created 1,390 national comprehensive disaster mitigation demonstration community.

Figure 8 : Deaths (Abscondences) Caused by Disasters

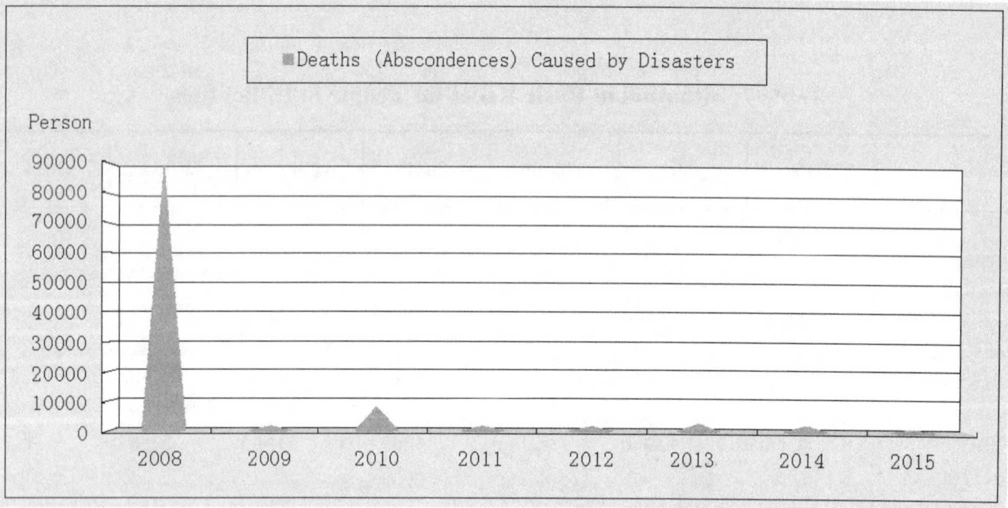

Table 8 : Deaths (Abscondences) Caused by Disasters

Indicators	2008	2009	2010	2011	2012	2013	2014	2015
Deaths (Abscondences) Caused by Disasters (Person)	88928	1528	7844	1126	1530	2284	1818	967

6. Social Charity

- Charitable Donations

By the end of 2015, there were 30 thousand regular workstations of social donations and charity supermarkets

(9,654 of which were charity supermarkets). The total social donations reached 65.45 billion yuan. Of this total, the civil affairs departments received direct donations of 4.42 billion yuan and social organizations received donations of 61.03 billion yuan. In 2015, the donated quilts and clothes reached 45.37 million pieces, valued at 520 million yuan. The indirect social donations which were transferred from other departments were 430 million yuan, and there were also 1.725 million pieces of indirect-donated quilts and clothes. The donated materials were worth 61.644 million yuan. Over 18.384 million people (person-times) in difficulties benefited from the charitable donations. There were 9.346 million volunteers (person-times) who provided 27.007 million hours of social services in 2015.

Figure 9: Social Donations and Donated Quilts and Clothes

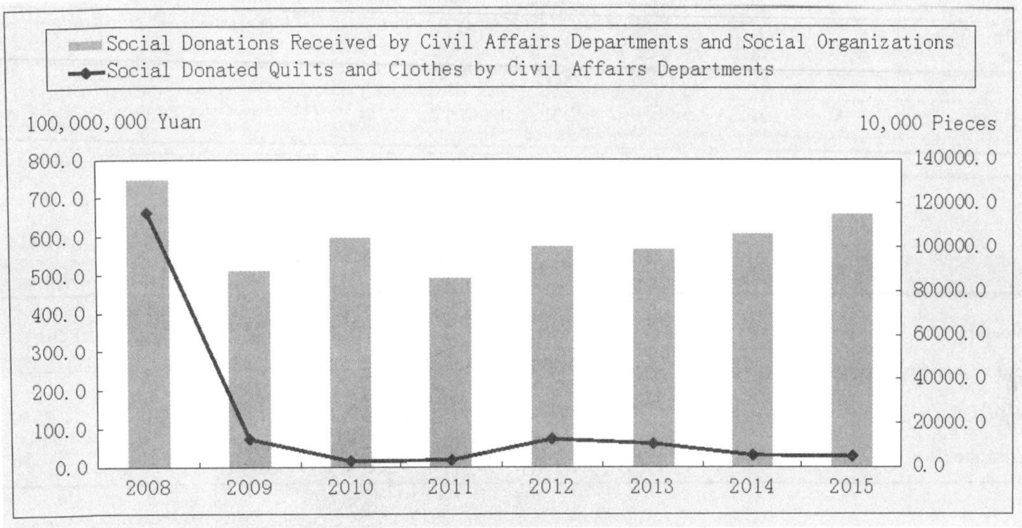

Table 9: Social Donations and Donated Quilts and Clothes

Indicators	2008	2009	2010	2011	2012	2013	2014	2015
Social Donations Received by Civil Affairs Departments and Social Organizations (100,000,000 Yuan)	744.5	507.2	596.8	490.1	572.5	566.4	604.4	654.5
Social Donated Quilts and Clothes by Civil Affairs Departments (10,000 Pieces)	115816.3	12476.6	2750.2	2918.5	12538.2	10405.0	5244.5	4537.0

- Welfare Lottery

In 2015, the sales of welfare lottery reached 201.51 billion yuan, a decrease of 4.46 billion yuan (2.2 percent) over the previous year. The public lottery funds reached 56.38 billion yuan, a decline of 3.7 percent in comparison with last year. The expenditure of public lottery funds by the civil affairs departments totaled 28.89 billion yuan, an increase of 5.76 billion yuan over the previous year, with an increase of 24.9 percent. It included 690 million yuan on state pension, 20 million yuan on the placement of retired servicemen, 18.21 billion yuan on social welfare, 3 billion yuan on social relief, 190 million yuan on disaster relief and 4.36 billion yuan on other expenses.

Figure 10: Welfare Lottery

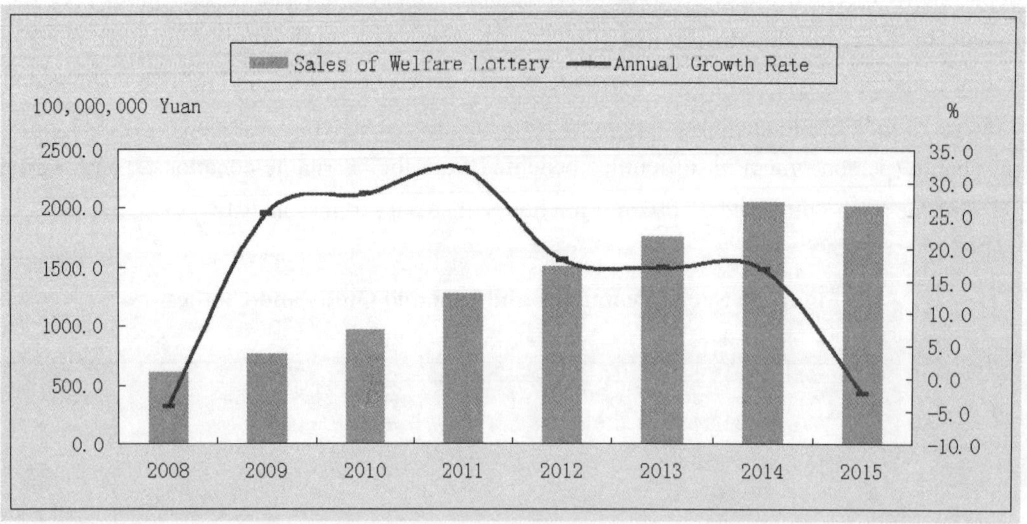

Table 10: Welfare Lottery

Indicators	2008	2009	2010	2011	2012	2013	2014	2015
Sales of Welfare Lottery (100,000,000 Yuan)	604.0	756.0	968.0	1278.0	1510.3	1765.3	2059.7	2015.1
Annual Growth Rate (%)	−4.4	25.2	28.0	32.0	18.2	16.9	16.7	−2.2

7. Preferential Treatment and Placement

By the end of 2015, there were 8.97 million people who were covered by state pension and preferential treatment program. Of this total, there were 737 thousand wounded servicemen, 1.184 million ailing ex-servicemen, 0.792 million rural retired servicemen, 3.925 million ex-servicemen above 60 years old with rural registration households, 177 veterans of the Red Army in rural areas, 64 veterans of the West-Road Red Army in the rural areas, 3,708 veterans who lost touch with the Red Army, 161 thousand family members of martyrs, 104 thousand family members of servicemen who died on duty or of illness.

Table 11: Beneficiaries of State Pension and Preferential Treatment

Indicators	2008	2009	2010	2011	2012	2013	2014	2015
Beneficiaries of State Pension and Preferential Treatment (10,000 Persons)	633.2	630.7	625.0	852.5	944.4	950.5	917.3	897.0
Operating Expense on State Pension (100,000,000 Yuan)	253.6	310.3	362.7	428.3	517.0	618.4	636.6	686.8
Annual Growth Rate of Operating Expense on State Pension (%)	20.3	22.4	16.9	18.1	20.7	19.6	2.9	7.9

Figure 11: Beneficiaries of State Pension and Preferential Treatment

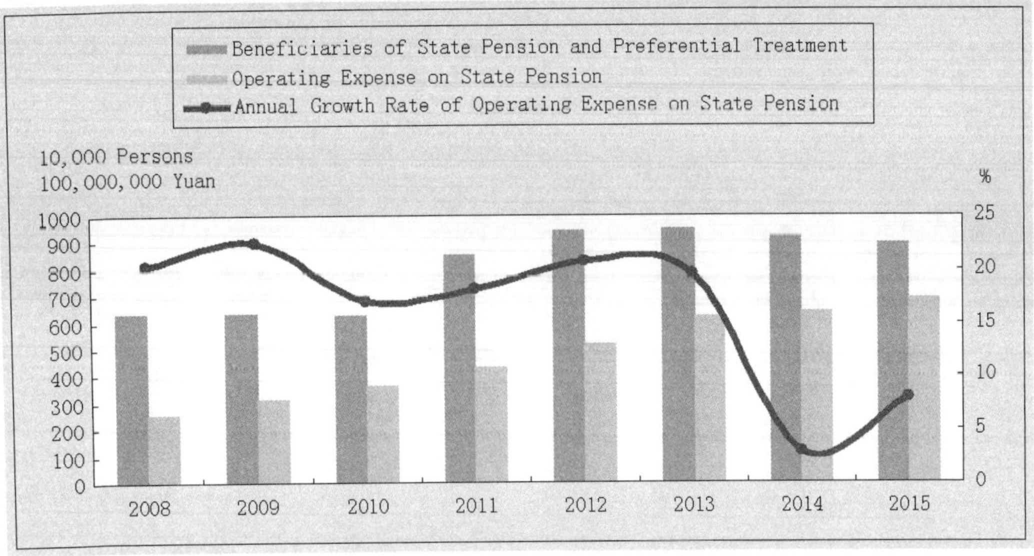

In 2015, the government applied special treatment to the newly increased 341 martyrs. By the end of 2015, there were 1,464 registered management organizations of martyrs' monuments, taking up the space of 4,441.7 hectares. There were 35,000 martyrs' monuments which were within management organizations and there were 12,000 scattered monuments.

In 2015, there were 19,000 retired military cadres (including demobilized sergeants), retirees military employees who had no military registration and demobilized officers. There were 271management centers for the emeritus and retired personnel who were from troops and 4,000 employees worked in these management centers. There were 27 activity centers granted for the emeritus and retired personnel who were from troops and one thousand employees worked in these places.

8. Community Services

By the end of 2015, there were 361 thousand community service institutions, and the coverage rate of community service institutions was 52.9 percent. Among these institutions, 863 were community service instruction centers and 24,000 were community service centers, an increase of 4.3 percent over the previous year. There were 128 thousand community service stations with an increase of 6.7 percent over the previous year. There were 26 thousand community welfare institutions and facilities for the aged with an increase of 36.8 percent over the previous year. There were 62,000 mutual aid facilities with an increase of 55 percent over the previous year, 120 thousand other community service institutions with an increase of 12.1 percent over the previous year. There were 249 thousand convenience stations and 96 thousand community organizations of volunteers in urban areas.

Table 12: Community Service Institutions and Facilities

Indicators	2008	2009	2010	2011	2012	2013	2014	2015
Community Service Institutions and Facilities (10,000 Units)	14.6	14.6	15.3	16.0	20.0	25.2	31.1	36.1
Community Service Centers and Stations (10,000 Units)	4.0	6.3	5.7	7.1	10.4	12.8	14.3	15.2
The growth rate of Community Service Stations (%)	−32.9	58.4	−9.8	23.9	47.8	23.1	11.7	6.2

Figure 12: Community Service Institutions and Facilities

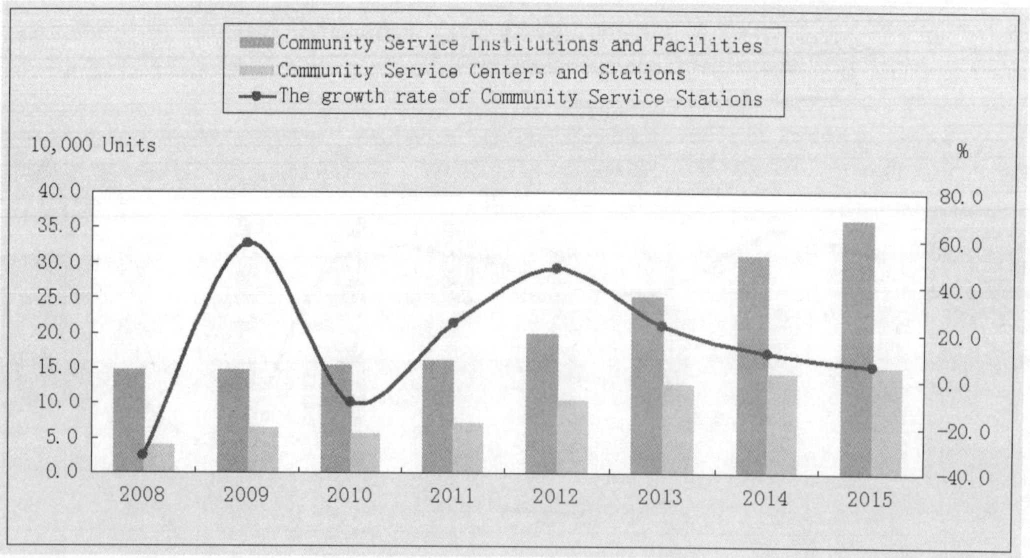

III. Member Organizations and Other Social Services

A. Member Organizations

1. Non-Government Organizations (NGOs)

By the end of 2015, there were altogether 662 thousand NGOs, an increase of 9.2 percent over that of the previous year. There were 7.348 million employees, an increase of 7.7 percent over the previous year. The total annual income was 292.9 billion yuan, and the total expenditure was 238.38 billion yuan, the total value of fixed assets was 231.11 billion yuan. The NGOs received donations of 61.03 billion yuan. There were 2,951 law-breaking cases which concerned NGOs and were investigated and penalized. As a result, 23 illegal NGOs were banned and 2,928 administrative punishments took place.

There were 329 thousand social organizations, a growth of 6.1 percent over the previous year. Among these social organizations, 37,000 were engaged in industry and commercial services, 17,000 in science and technology services, 10,000 in education, 10,000 in health, 48,000 in social services, 33,000 in culture, 23,000 in sports, 7,000 in eco-environment, 3,000 in legal services, 5,000 in religion, 62,000 in agricultural and rural development, 21,000 in profession and 53,000 in other fields. In 2015, there were 1,681 law-breaking cases which concerned social organizations and were investigated and penalized. Thereinto, 2 illegal social organizations were banned and 1,679 administrative punishments took place.

In 2015, there were 4,784 foundations across the country, an increase of 667, rose by 16.2 percent over that of the previous year. Of this total, there were 1,548 public-raising foundations, 3,198 nonpublic raising foundations. There were 202 foundations registered in the Ministry of Civil Affairs, 9 foundations concerning foreign affairs, 29 representative offices of overseas foundations. The publicraising foundations and non-public-raising foundations totally received donations of 43.93 billion yuan. In 2015, 16 administrative punishments took place.

There were altogether 329 thousand non-governmental and non-commercial enterprises, a rise of 12.7 percent over the previous year. Among these enterprises, there were 16,000 engaged in science and technology services, 433 in ecological environment, 183,000 in education, 24,000 in health, 49,000 in social services, 17,000 in culture, 14,000 in sports, 3,355 in commercial services, 144 in religion, 7 in international and other overseas affairs and 19,000 in other fields. In 2015, there were 1,254 lawbreaking and discipline violation cases which concerned non-governmental and non-commercial enterprises and were investigated and penalized. Thereinto, 21 illegal non-governmental and non-commercial enterprises were banned, and 1,233 administrative punishments took place.

Figure 13: Non-Governmental Organizations

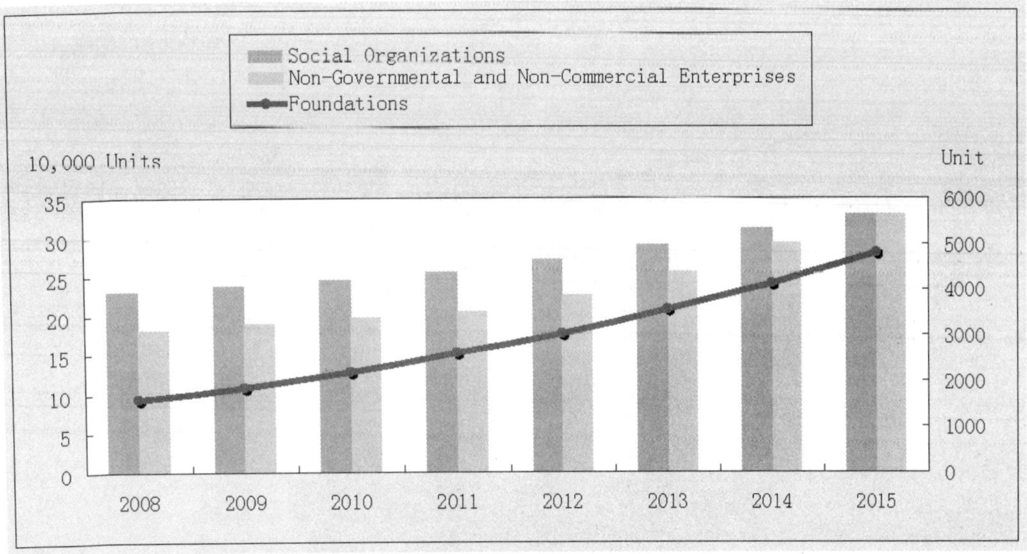

Table 13: Non-Governmental Organizations

Indicators	2008	2009	2010	2011	2012	2013	2014	2015
Social Organizations (10,000 Units)	23.0	23.9	24.5	25.5	27.1	28.9	31.0	32.9
Foundations(Unit)	1597	1843	2200	2614	3029	3549	4117	4784
Non- Governmental and Non-Commercial Enterprises (10,000 Units)	18.2	19.0	19.8	20.4	22.5	25.5	29.2	32.9

2. Self-Governing Organizations

By the end of 2015, self-governing organizations at the grass-roots totaled 681 thousand. Of this total, there were 581 thousand village committees. The number of village groups was 4.692 million. There were 2.297 million members in the village committees. There were 100,000 community neighborhood committees, a rise of 3.1 percent over that of the previous year. There were 1.347 million neighborhood groups. There were 512 thousand members of neighborhood committees, a rise of 3.0 percent over that in the previous year. In 2015, elections in 165 thousand neighborhood committees and village committees were completed. The registered number of residents and villagers who participated in the elections was 210 million. The number of voters was 160 million.

Table 14: Self-Governing Organizations

Indicators	2008	2009	2010	2011	2012	2013	2014	2015
Community Neighborhood Committees (10,000 Units)	8.3	8.5	8.7	8.9	9.1	9.5	9.7	10.0
Village Committees (10,000 Units)	60.4	59.9	59.5	59.0	58.8	58.9	58.5	58.1

Figure14: Self-Governing Organizations

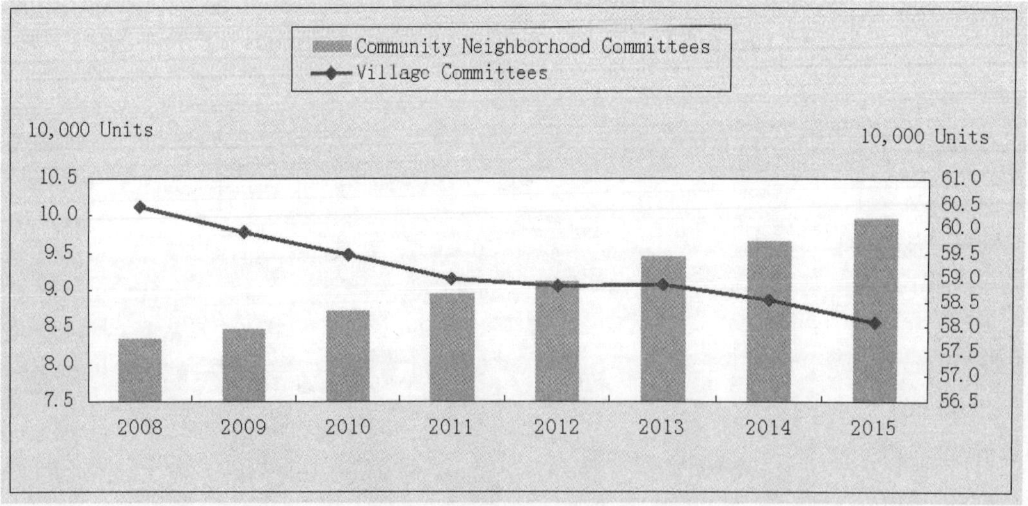

B. Other Social Services

1. Marriage Service

In 2015, there were 2,064 service institutions of marriage registration (qualified as public institutions) and 5,714 service offices of marriage registration in China. The number of people that registered their marriage through civil affairs departments or marriage registration institutions reached 12.247 million couples, a decline of 6.3 percent. Of this total, there were 41 thousand couples concerning foreigners, overseas Chinese and residents of Hong Kong, Macau and Taiwan. The crude nuptiality was 9.0 per thousand. The proportion of people ranged from 25 to 29 years old accounted for 39.4 percent of all registered for marriage, taking the lead among other age groups and it increased by 1.4 percent over that of the previous year.

In 2015, there were 3.841 million couples handling divorce, which was an increase of 5.6 percent over the previous year. Of this total, 3.149 million couples were registered through the civil affairs departments and those who divorced through courts were 693 thousand couples. The crude divorce rate was 2.8 per thousand, which was an increase of 0.1 per thousand over that in 2014.

Figure 15: Crude Nuptiality and Divorce Rate

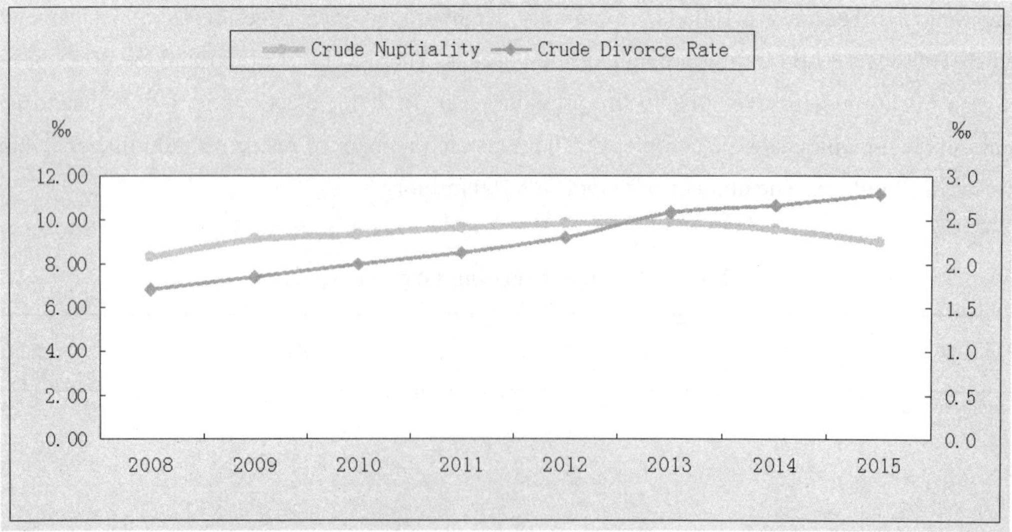

Table 15: Crude Nuptiality and Divorce Rate

Indicators	2008	2009	2010	2011	2012	2013	2014	2015
Crude Nuptiality (‰)	8.27	9.10	9.30	9.67	9.80	9.92	9.58	9.00
Crude Divorce Rate (‰)	1.71	1.85	2.00	2.13	2.29	2.58	2.67	2.79

2. Funeral and Interment

By the end of 2015, there were 4,530 funeral and interment service institutions. Of this total, there were 1,821 funeral parlors, 1,127 funeral management organizations. There were 1,567 public cemeteries under the management of the civil affairs departments. There were 84 thousand employees in the funeral and interment service institutions. Among these institutions, 47 thousand people worked for funeral parlors. There were 6,063 cremators, which cremated 4.595 million remains. The cremation rate stood at 47.1 percent, 0.1 percent over that of the previous year.

Figure 16: Cremation of Funeral Service

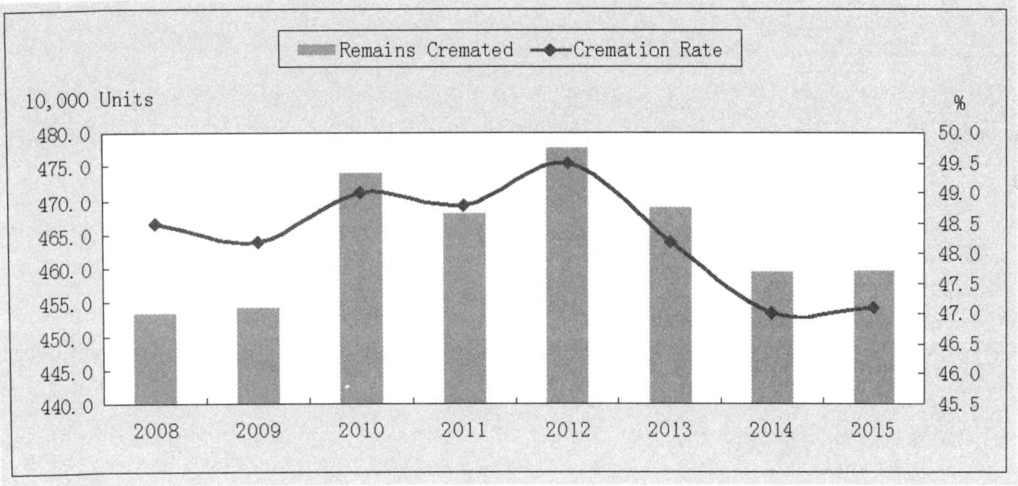

Table 16: Cremation of Funeral Service

Indicators	2008	2009	2010	2011	2012	2013	2014	2015
Remains Cremated (10,000 Units)	453.4	454.2	474.1	468.1	477.7	468.9	459.3	459.5
Cremation Rate(%)	48.5	48.2	49.0	48.8	49.5	48.2	47.0	47.1

Notes:

[1] Townships in figure 1 and table 1 include ethnic townships, sumus and ethnic sumus.

[2] The relief funds allocated by the Ministry of Finance and the Ministry of Civil Affairs do not include the purchasing funds for central relief material and the relief funds that the central government allocated to Xinjiang Production and Construction Corps.

[3]Non-Government Organizations' donations data of the annual inspection in 2015(with the report of the year 2014) was used.

[4] The statistics of judicial decisions and mediate divorces recorded in the divorce registration service comes from the supreme peoples' court.

[5] In this report, the numbers of people were the actual amount and the numbers of institutions were the numbers of authorized ones. These numbers should not be compared with approved numbers and predicted numbers.

[6] The itemized figures may not match the totalized ones in this report, this is because some of the statistics in the report were rounded off and no mechanical adjustments have been made for mending the error.

[7] Statistics of Hong Kong, Macau and Taiwan province were not included into the report.

02

社会服务
主要数据图表

图1-1　市、区、县

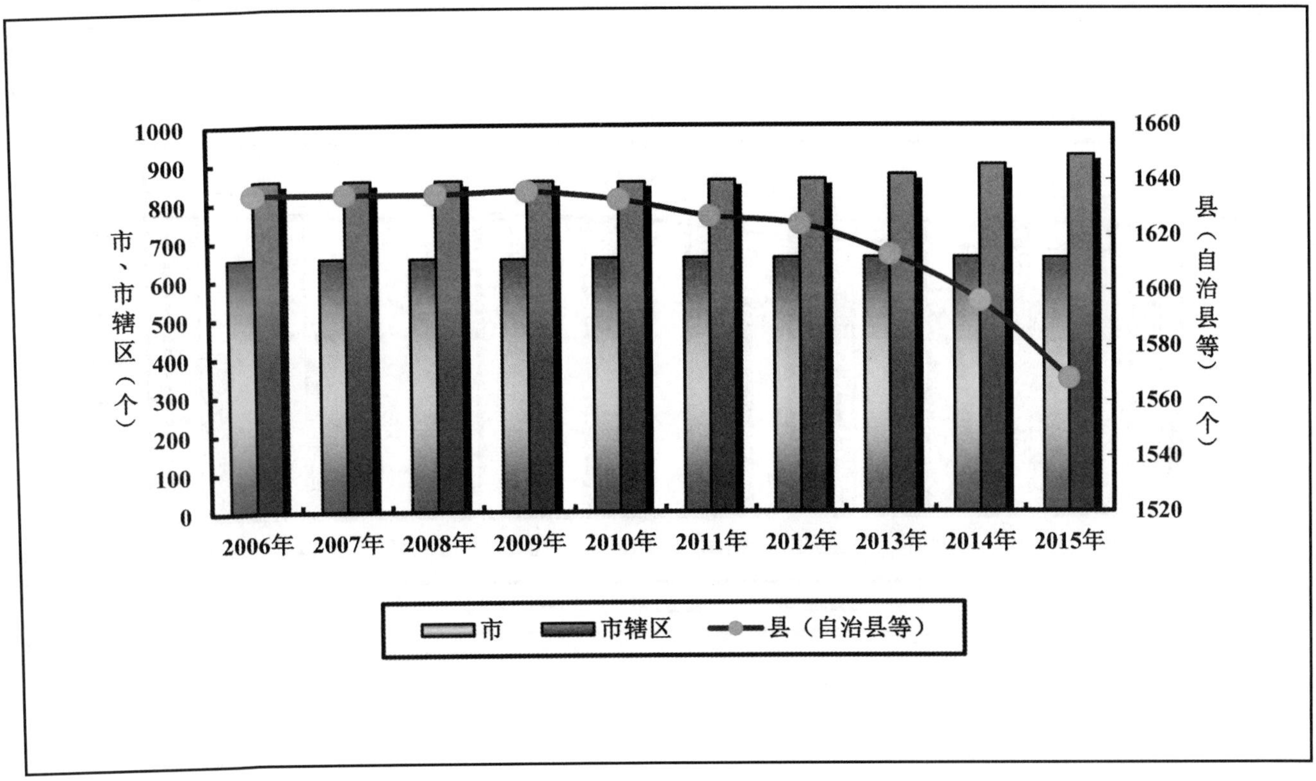

单位：个

指　标	2006年	2007年	2008年	2009年	2010年	2011年	2012年	2013年	2014年	2015年
市	656	655	655	654	657	657	657	658	658	656
市辖区	856	856	856	855	853	857	860	872	897	921
县（自治县等）	1635	1635	1635	1636	1633	1627	1624	1613	1596	1568

注：市含直辖市、地级市及县级市。

图1-2　乡镇与街道

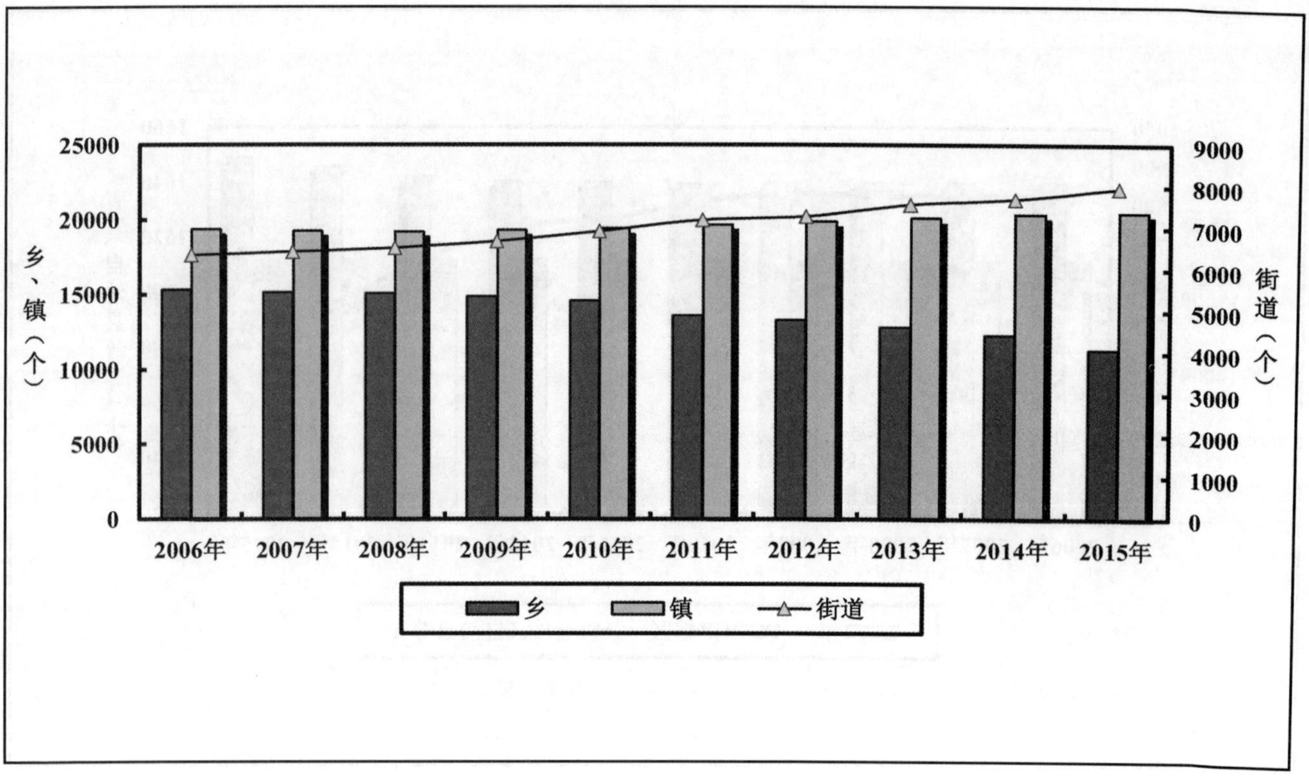

单位：个

指　标	2006年	2007年	2008年	2009年	2010年	2011年	2012年	2013年	2014年	2015年
乡	15306	15120	15067	14848	14571	13587	13281	12812	12282	11315
镇	19369	19249	19234	19322	19410	19683	19881	20117	20401	20515
街道	6355	6434	6524	6686	6923	7194	7282	7566	7696	7957

图1-3　60岁及以上老年人口占全国总人口比重

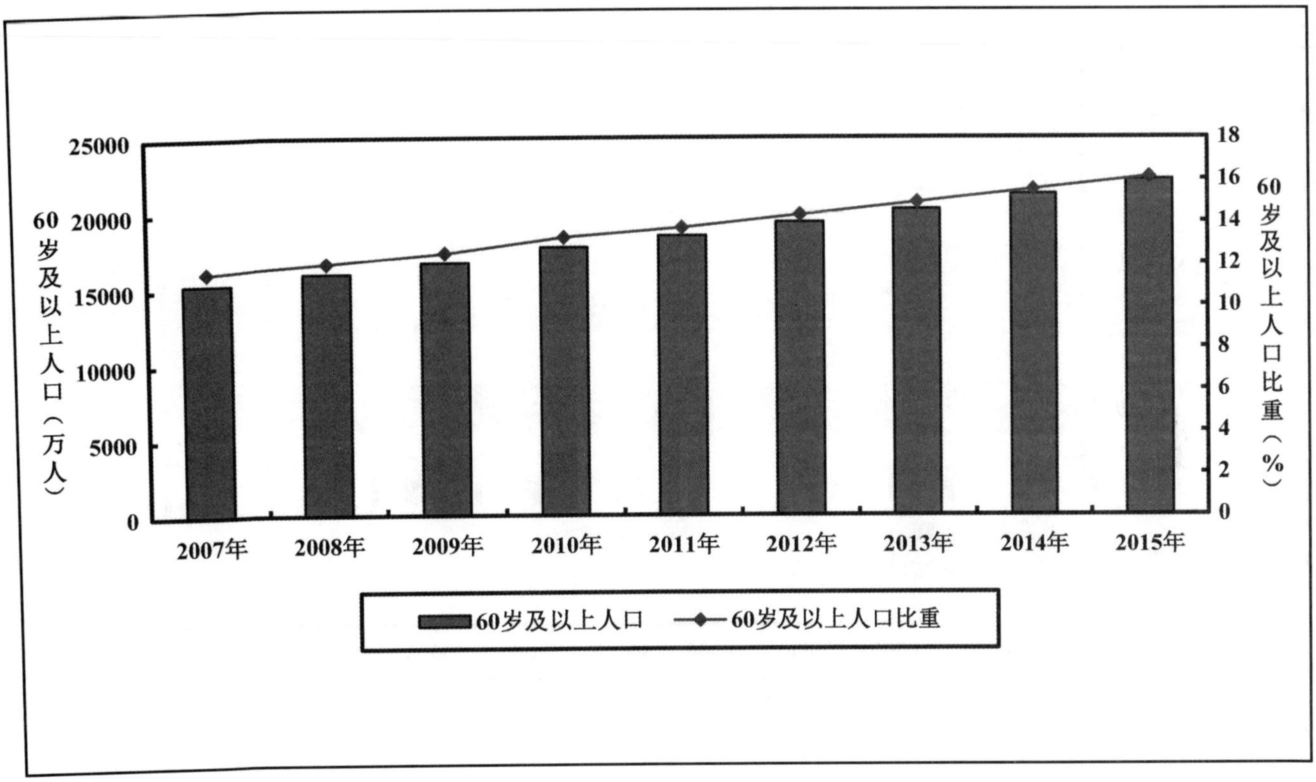

单位：万人、%

指　标	2007年	2008年	2009年	2010年	2011年	2012年	2013年	2014年	2015年
60岁及以上人口	15340	15989	16714	17765	18499	19390	20243	21242	22200
60岁及以上人口比重	11.60	12.00	12.50	13.26	13.70	14.30	14.90	15.50	16.10

注：本表数据来源于国家统计局。

图1-4　人口年龄结构

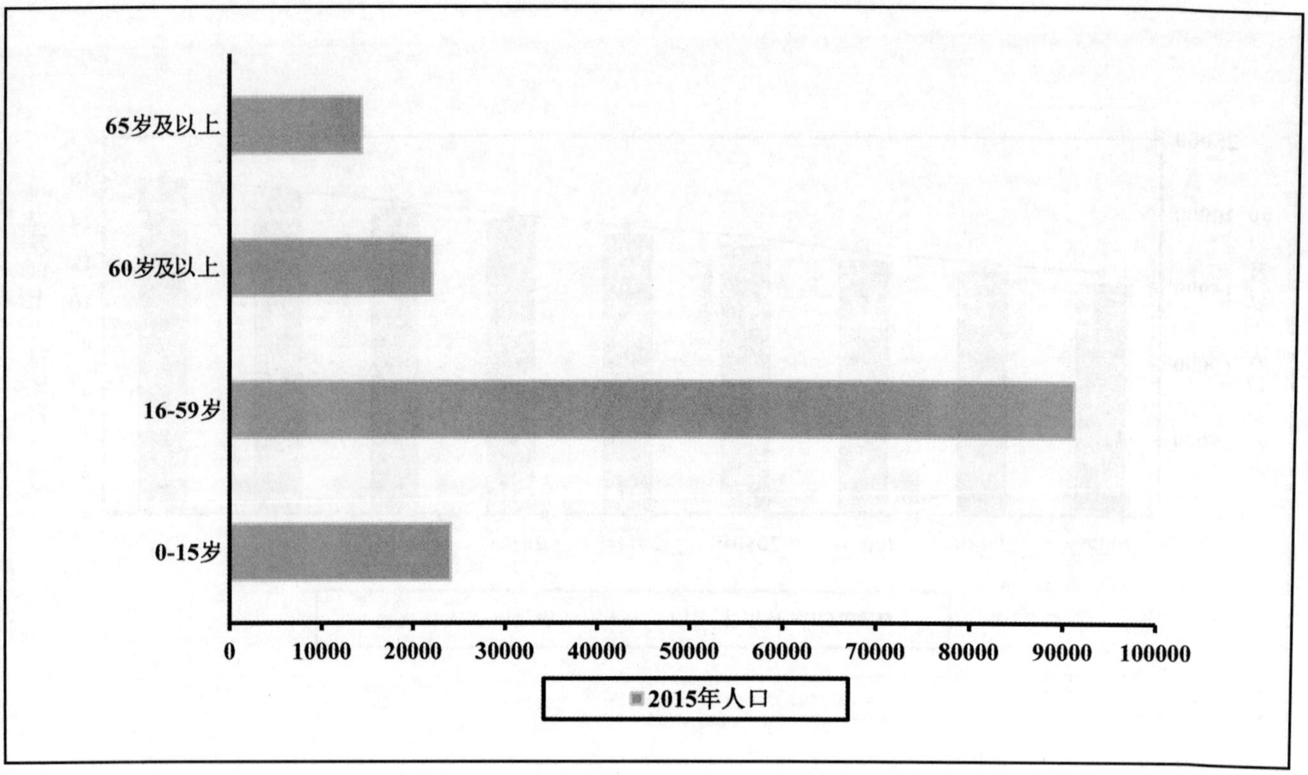

单位：万人、%

指　标	0−15岁	16−59岁	60岁及以上	65岁及以上
2015年人口	24166	91096	22200	14386
不同年龄段人口比重	17.6	66.3	16.1	10.5
比2014年增减百分点	0.1	-0.7	0.6	0.4

注：本表数据来源于国家统计局。

图1-5　社会服务机构和设施职工

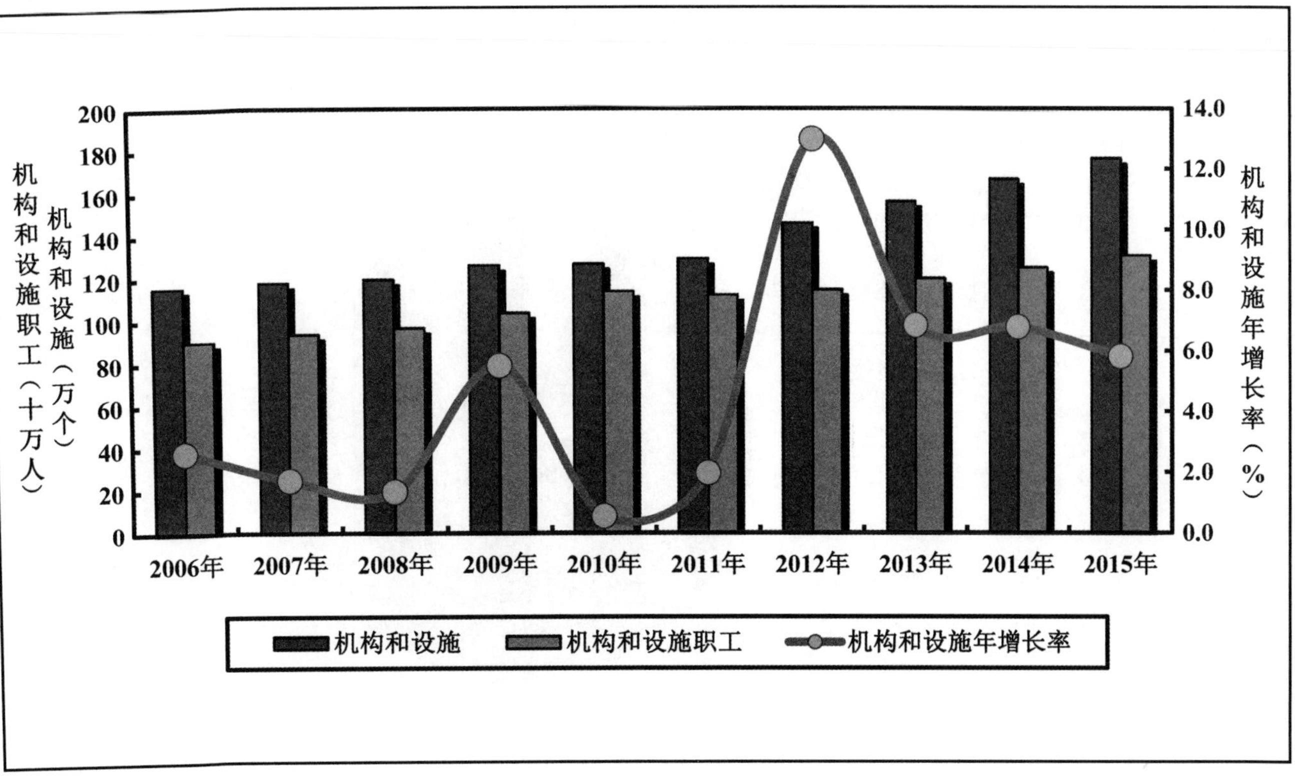

单位：万个、%、十万人

指　标	2006年	2007年	2008年	2009年	2010年	2011年	2012年	2013年	2014年	2015年
机构和设施	116.0	118.0	119.6	126.2	126.9	129.4	146.2	156.2	166.8	176.5
机构和设施职工	90.4	93.8	96.7	103.8	113.8	112.1	114.7	119.8	125.1	130.9
机构和设施年增长率	2.7	1.7	1.4	5.5	0.6	2.0	13.0	6.8	6.8	5.8

图1-6 社会服务对象占全国总人口比重

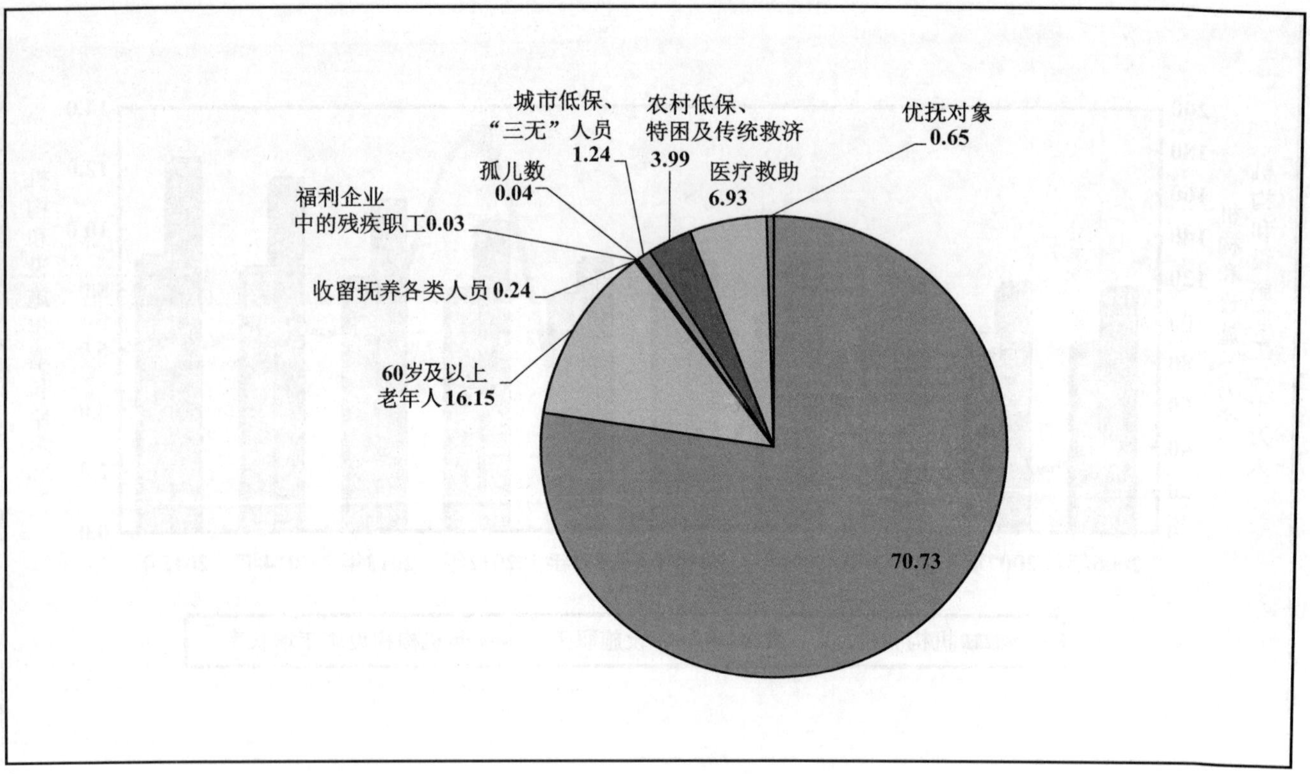

单位：万人、%

指　标	2015年	比　重
全国总人口	137462.0	100.0
社会服务对象	40236.7	29.27
# 60岁及以上老年人	22200.0	16.15
收留抚养各类人员	330.8	0.24
福利企业中的残疾职工	42.9	0.03
孤儿数	50.2	0.04
城市低保、“三无”人员	1707.9	1.24
农村低保、特困及传统救济	5484.1	3.99
医疗救助	9523.8	6.93
优抚对象	897.0	0.65

注：医疗救助为人次数。

图1-7　社会服务机构和设施固定资产原价

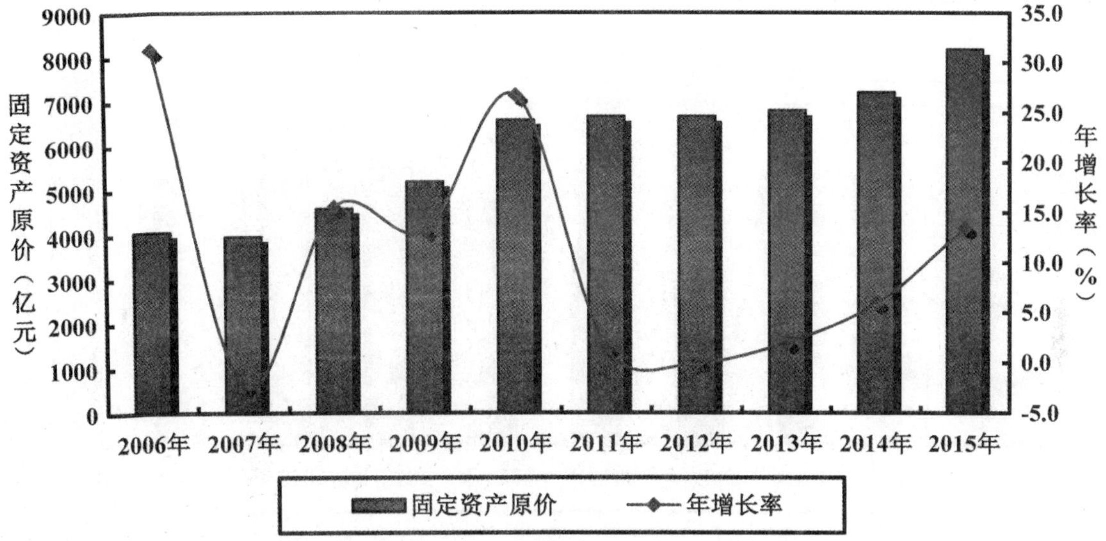

单位：亿元、%

指　标	2006年	2007年	2008年	2009年	2010年	2011年	2012年	2013年	2014年	2015年
固定资产原价	4066.7	3973.0	4592.8	5198.0	6589.3	6676.7	6675.4	6810.2	7213.0	8183.1
年增长率	31.3	-2.3	15.6	13.2	26.8	1.3	-	2.0	5.9	13.4

图1-8 社会服务事业费

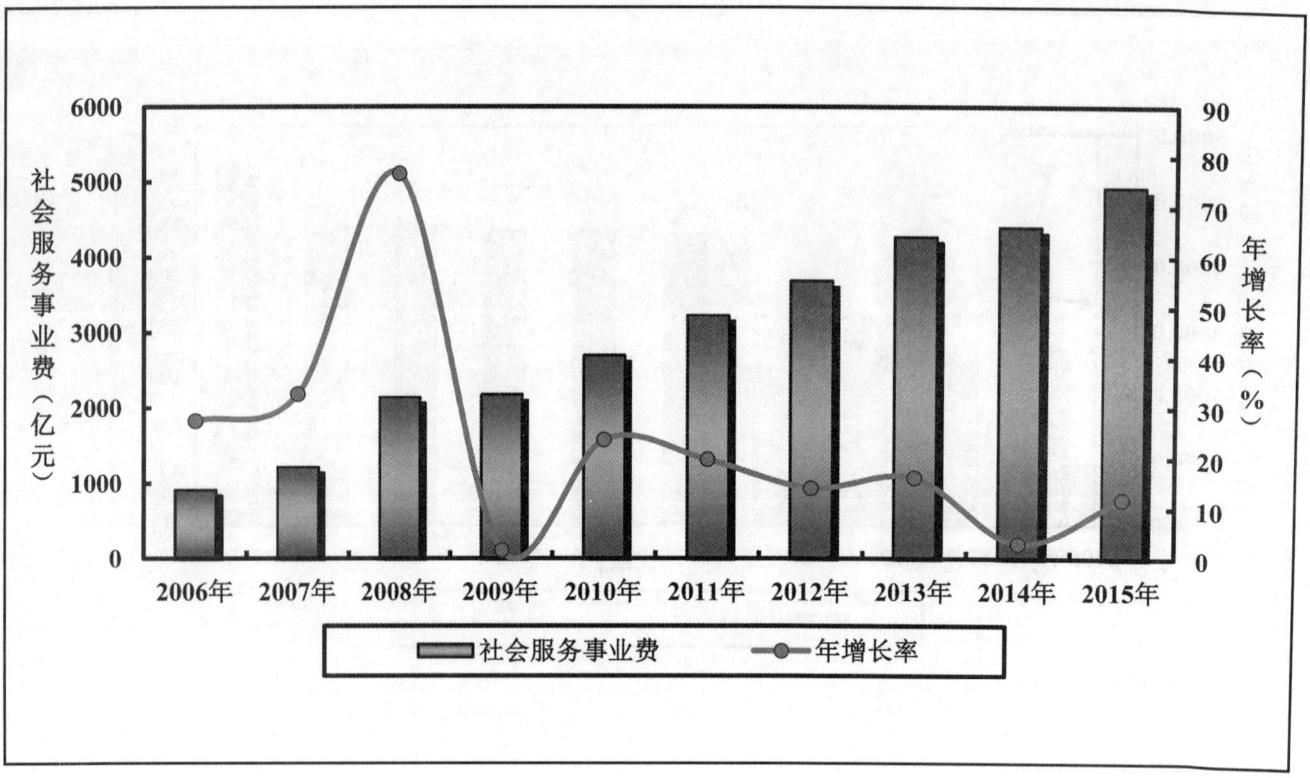

单位：亿元、%

指　标	2006年	2007年	2008年	2009年	2010年	2011年	2012年	2013年	2014年	2015年
社会服务事业费	915.4	1215.5	2146.5	2181.9	2697.5	3229.1	3683.7	4276.5	4404.1	4926.4
年增长率	27.4	32.8	76.6	1.6	23.6	19.7	14.1	16.1	3.0	11.9

图1—9 社会服务事业费支出占国家财政支出的比重

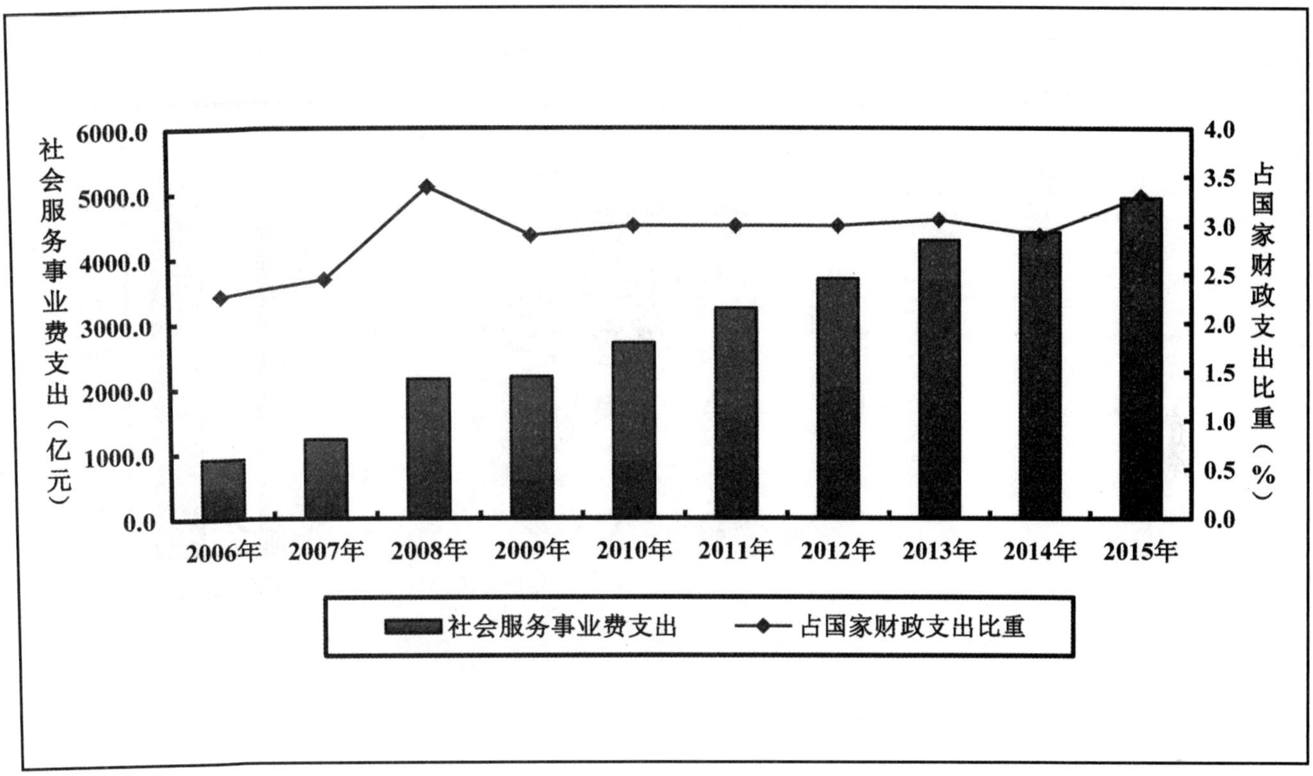

单位：亿元、%

指　标	2006年	2007年	2008年	2009年	2010年	2011年	2012年	2013年	2014年	2015年
社会服务事业费支出	915.4	1215.5	2146.5	2181.9	2697.5	3229.1	3683.7	4276.5	4404.1	4926.4
占国家财政支出比重	2.3	2.5	3.4	2.9	3.0	3.0	3.0	3.1	2.9	3.3

图1-10　按用项分社会服务事业费

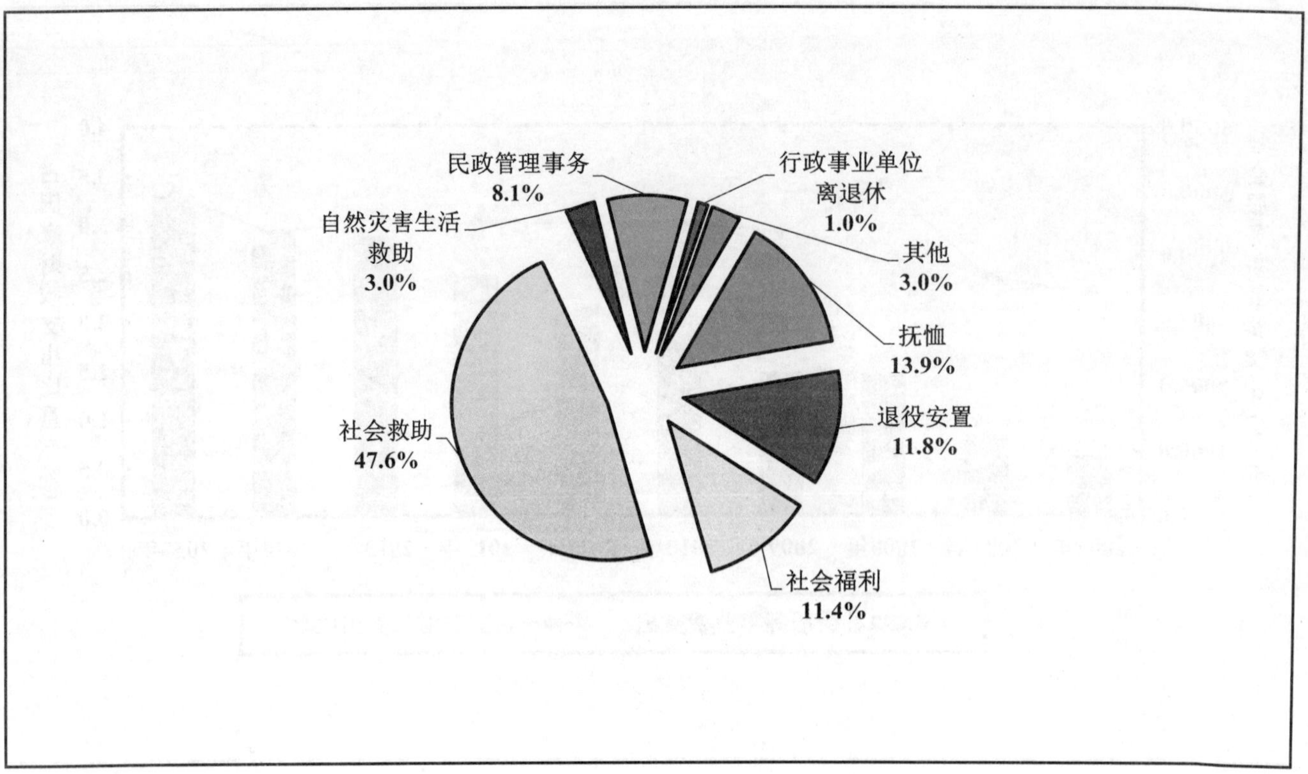

单位：亿元、%

指　标	社会服务事业费	抚恤	退役安置	社会福利	社会救助	自然灾害生活救助	民政管理事务	行政事业单位离退休	其他
金　额	4926.4	686.8	582.7	562.8	2347.4	148.5	399.6	50.1	148.5
比　重	100.0	13.9	11.8	11.4	47.6	3.0	8.1	1.0	3.0

图1-11　中央转移支付社会服务事业费

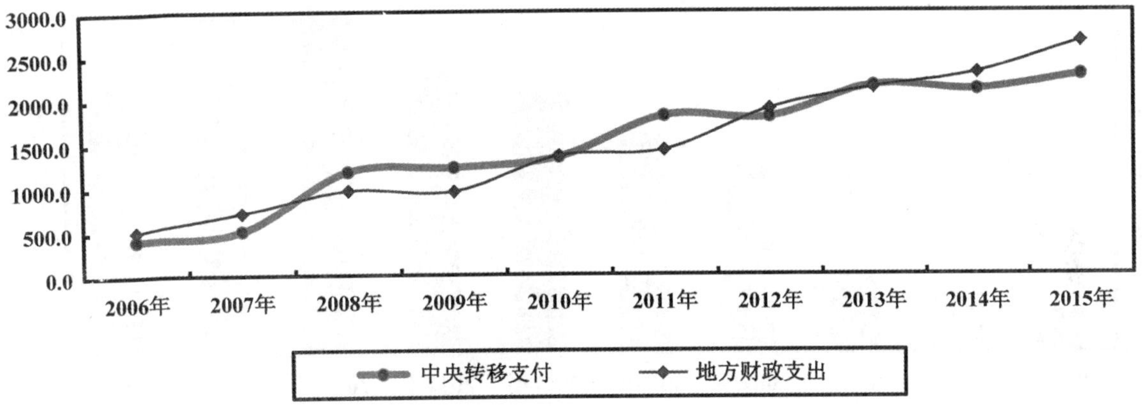

单位：亿元、%

指　标	2006年	2007年	2008年	2009年	2010年	2011年	2012年	2013年	2014年	2015年
社会服务事业费支出	915.4	1215.5	2146.5	2181.9	2697.5	3229.1	3683.7	4276.5	4404.1	4926.4
中央转移支付	404.0	504.4	1181.1	1227.0	1342.4	1808.0	1794.6	2149.7	2105.0	2270.3
地方财政支出	511.4	711.1	965.4	954.9	1355.1	1421.1	1889.1	2126.8	2299.1	2656.1
中央转移支付比重	44.1	42.6	55.0	56.2	49.8	56.0	48.7	50.3	47.8	46.1

图1-12　社会服务基本建设投资

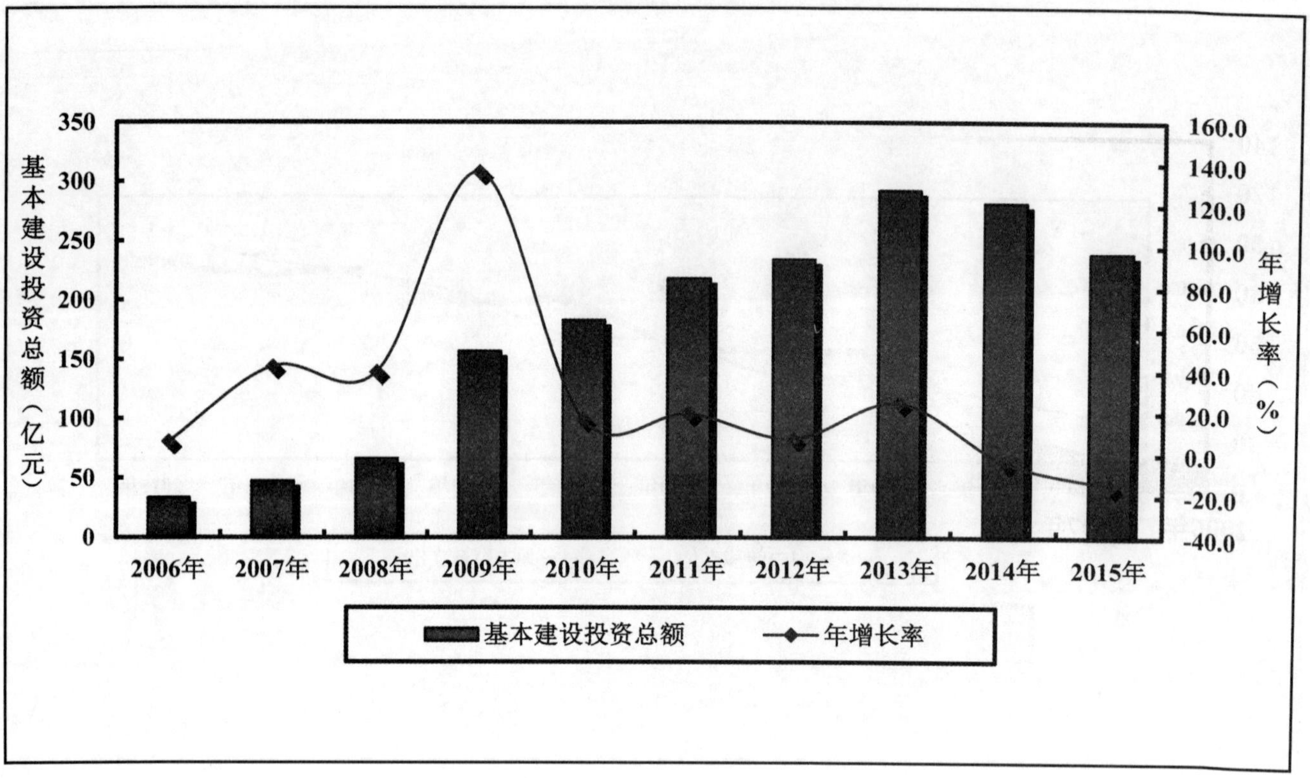

单位：亿元、%

指　标	2006年	2007年	2008年	2009年	2010年	2011年	2012年	2013年	2014年	2015年
基本建设投资总额	33.5	47.7	66.6	157	183	218.5	234.7	292.8	282.2	239.9
年增长率	6.0	42.4	39.6	135.7	16.6	19.4	7.4	24.8	-3.6	-15.0

图1-13　基本建设预算内支出和中央转移支付情况

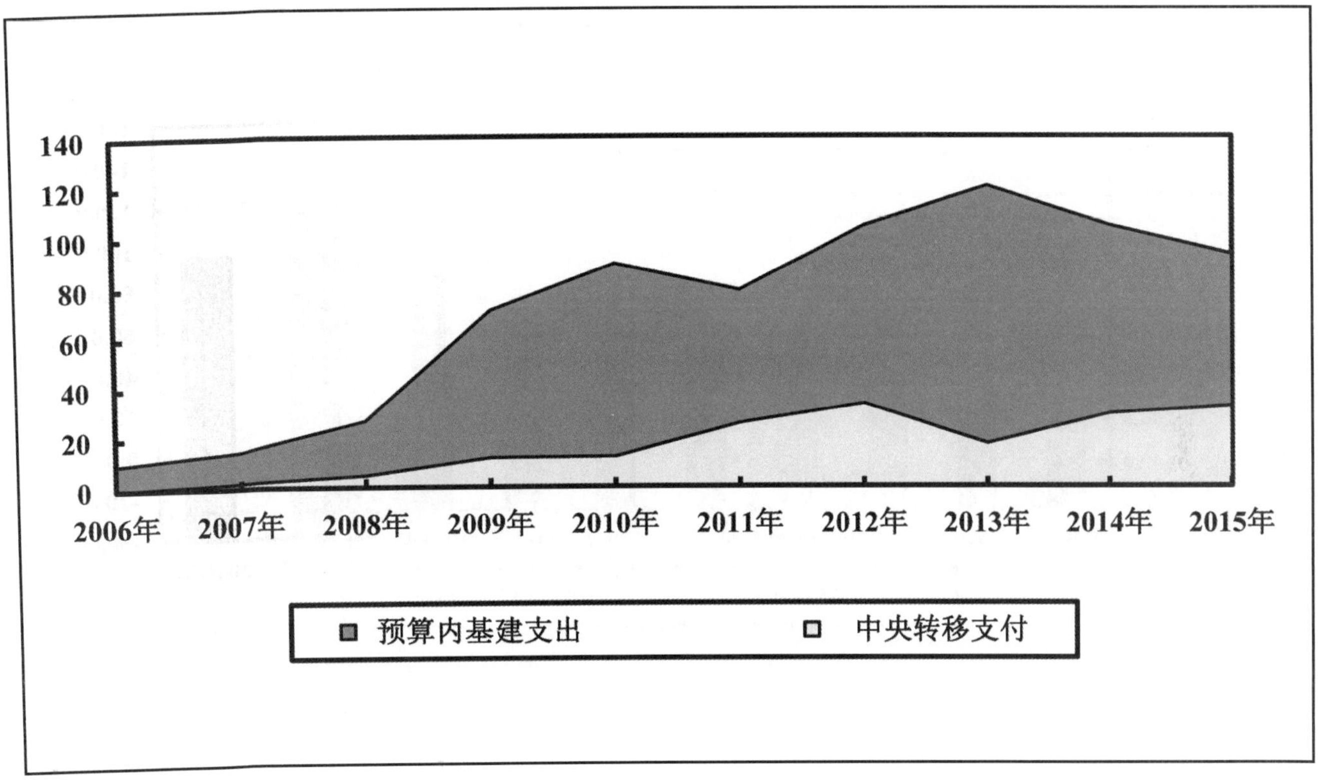

单位：亿元、%

指　标	2006年	2007年	2008年	2009年	2010年	2011年	2012年	2013年	2014年	2015年
社会服务事业费支出	915.4	1215.5	2146.5	2181.9	2697.5	3229.1	3683.7	4276.5	4404.1	4926.4
预算内基建支出	9.9	14.5	26.6	70.6	89.1	78.5	104.2	120.1	104.3	92.8
中央转移支付		2.0	4.7	11.7	12.0	25.3	33.0	17.0	29.0	32.0

图2-1 社会服务床位数

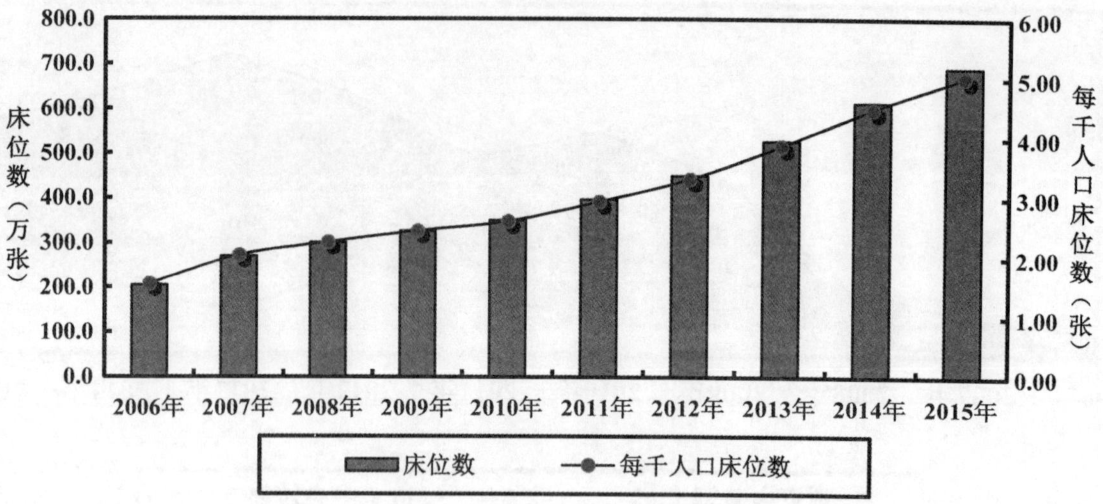

单位：万张、张

指　标	2006年	2007年	2008年	2009年	2010年	2011年	2012年	2013年	2014年	2015年
床位数	204.5	269.6	300.3	326.5	349.6	396.4	449.3	526.7	613.5	732.9
每千人口床位数	1.56	2.04	2.26	2.45	2.61	2.94	3.32	3.87	4.49	5.33

图2-2　养老服务床位数

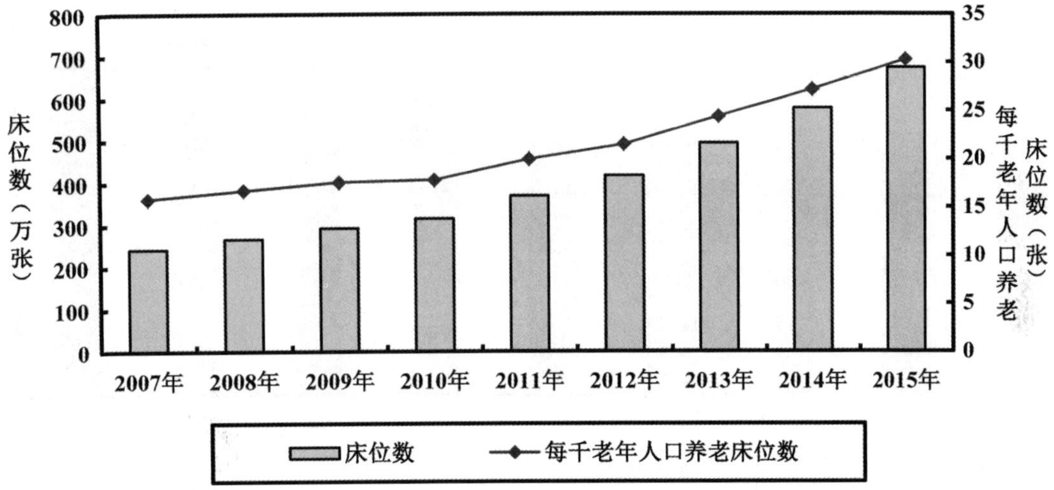

单位：万张、%、张

指　标	2007年	2008年	2009年	2010年	2011年	2012年	2013年	2014年	2015年
床位数	242.9	267.4	293.5	316.1	369.2	416.5	493.7	577.7	672.7
增长率	35.2	10.1	9.8	7.7	16.8	12.8	18.5	17.0	16.4
每千老年人口养老床位数	15.83	16.72	17.56	17.79	19.96	21.48	24.39	27.20	30.30

图2-3　智障和精神疾病服务床位数

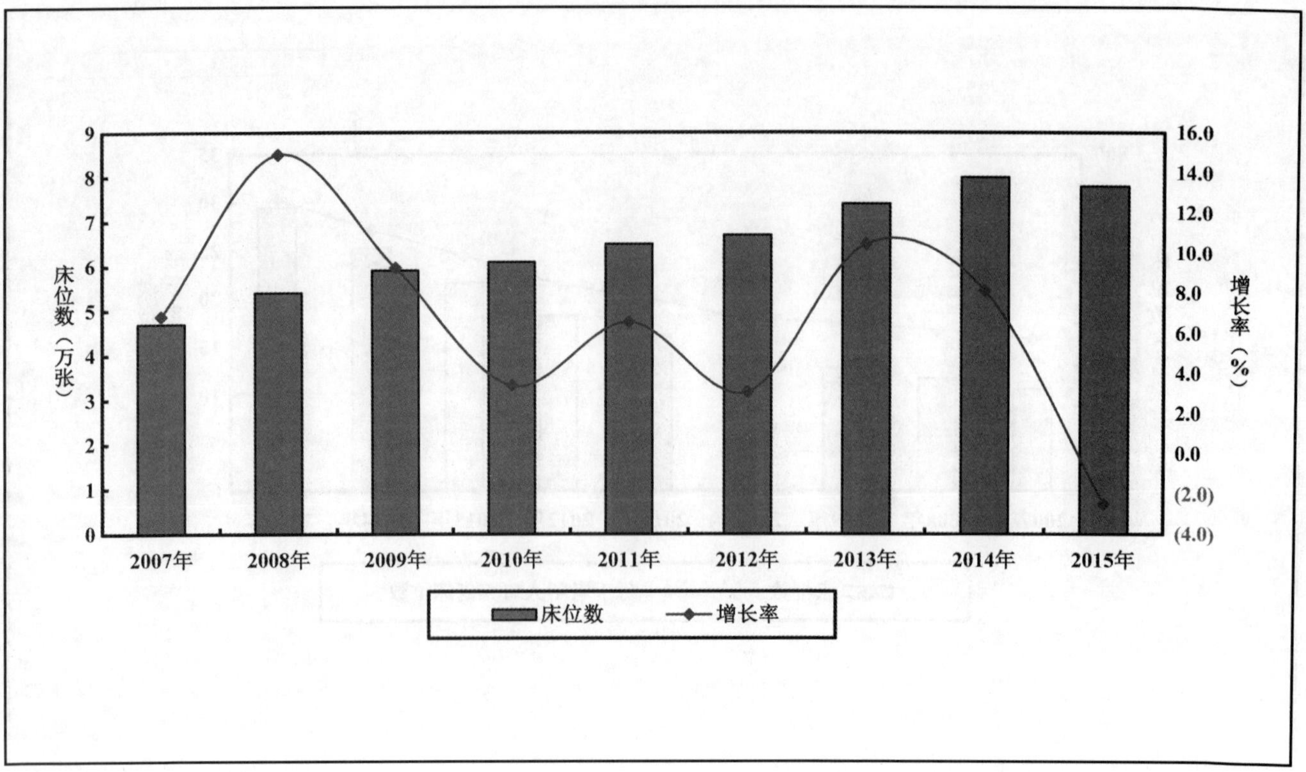

单位：万张、%

指　标	2007年	2008年	2009年	2010年	2011年	2012年	2013年	2014年	2015年
床位数	4.7	5.4	5.9	6.1	6.5	6.7	7.4	8.0	7.9
增长率	6.8	14.9	9.3	3.4	6.6	3.1	10.4	8.1	−1.3

图2-4　儿童服务床位数

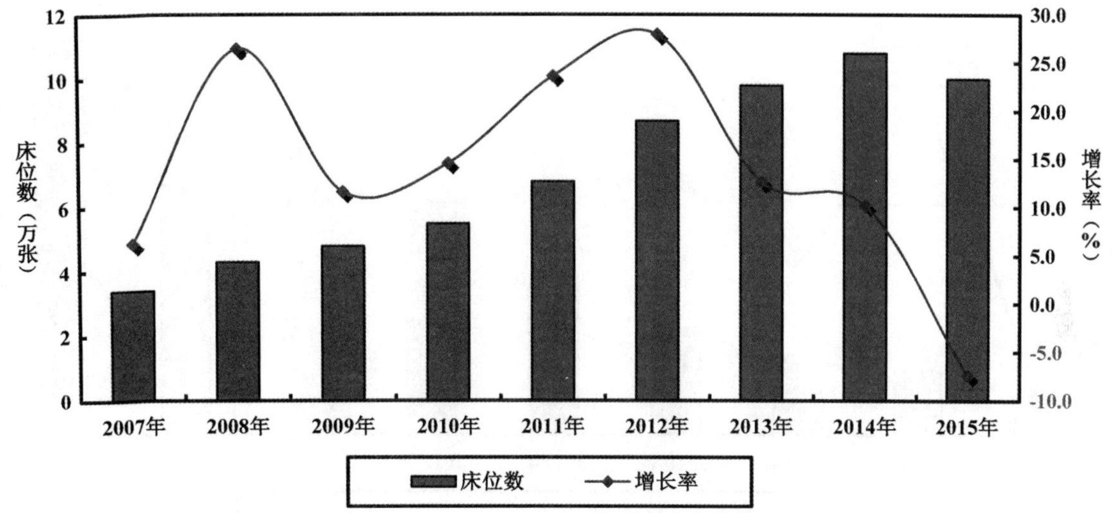

单位：万张、%

指　标	2007年	2008年	2009年	2010年	2011年	2012年	2013年	2014年	2015年
床位数	3.4	4.3	4.8	5.5	6.8	8.7	9.8	10.8	10.0
增长率	6.2	26.5	11.6	14.6	23.6	27.9	12.6	10.2	−7.4

图2-5 老年福利

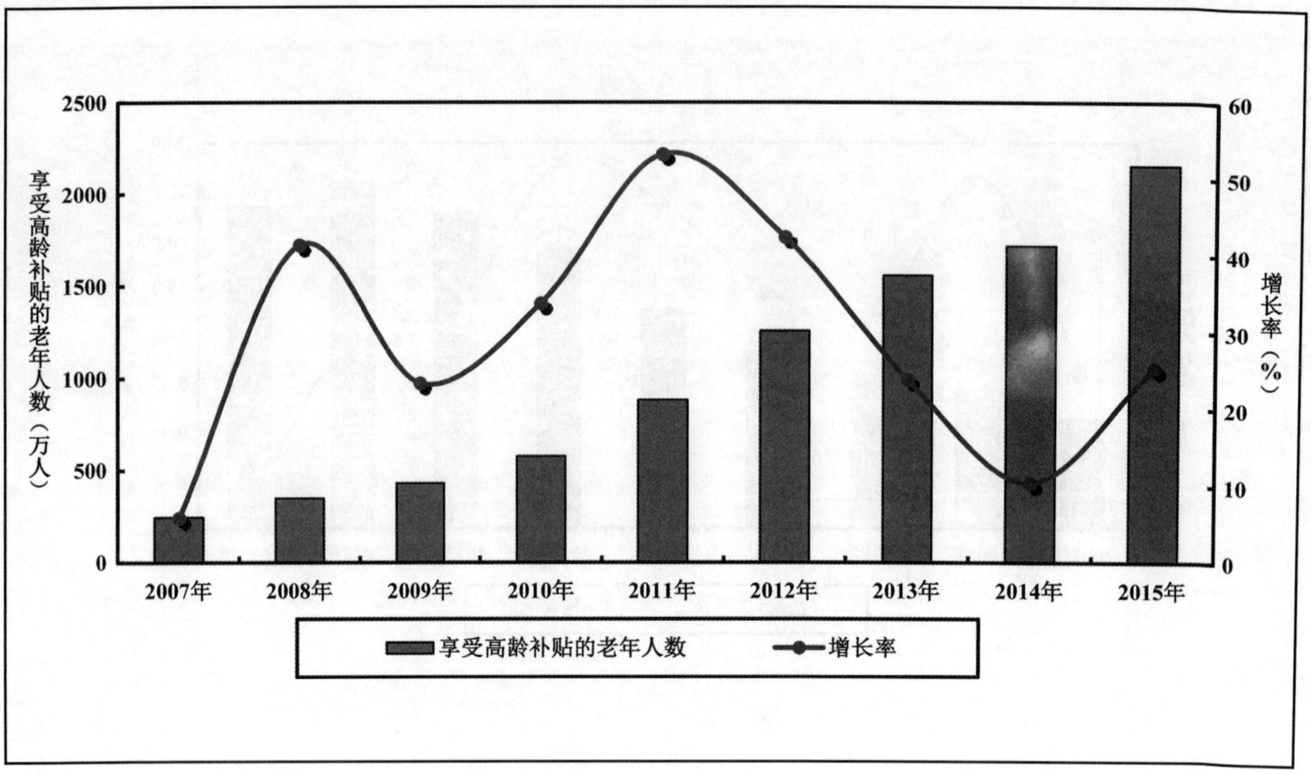

单位：万人、%

指　标	2007年	2008年	2009年	2010年	2011年	2012年	2013年	2014年	2015年
享受高龄补贴的老年人数	247.1	349.3	430.9	576.4	883.1	1257.7	1557.9	1719.6	2155.1
增长率	5.8	41.4	23.4	33.8	53.2	42.4	23.9	10.4	25.3

图2–6　家庭收养

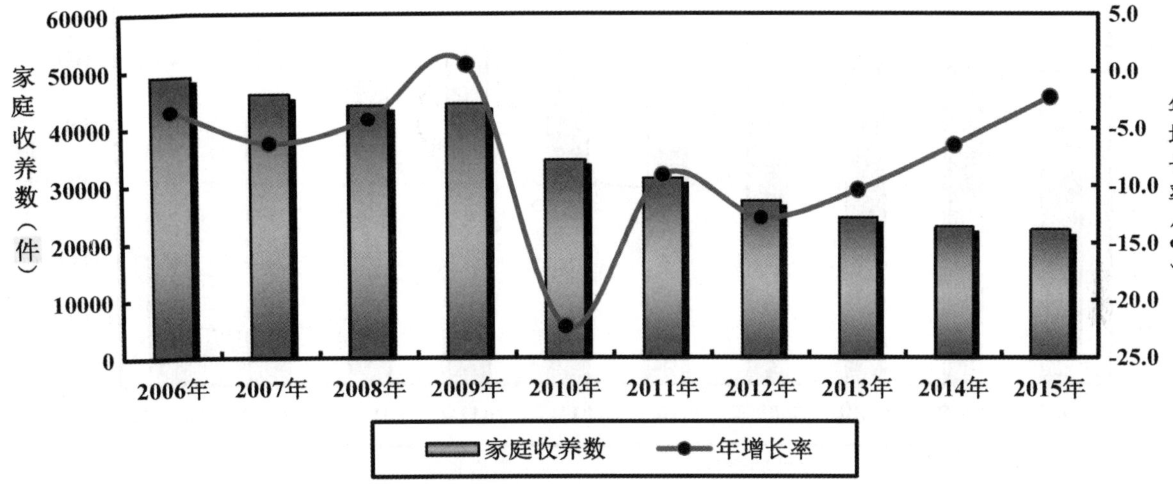

单位：件、%

指　标	2006年	2007年	2008年	2009年	2010年	2011年	2012年	2013年	2014年	2015年
家庭收养数	48178	45192	42550	44260	34529	31424	27278	24460	22772	22348
年增长率	-2.7	-6.2	-5.8	4.0	-22.0	-9.0	-13.2	-10.3	-6.9	-1.9

图2-7 为残疾人提供服务机构中的残疾职工

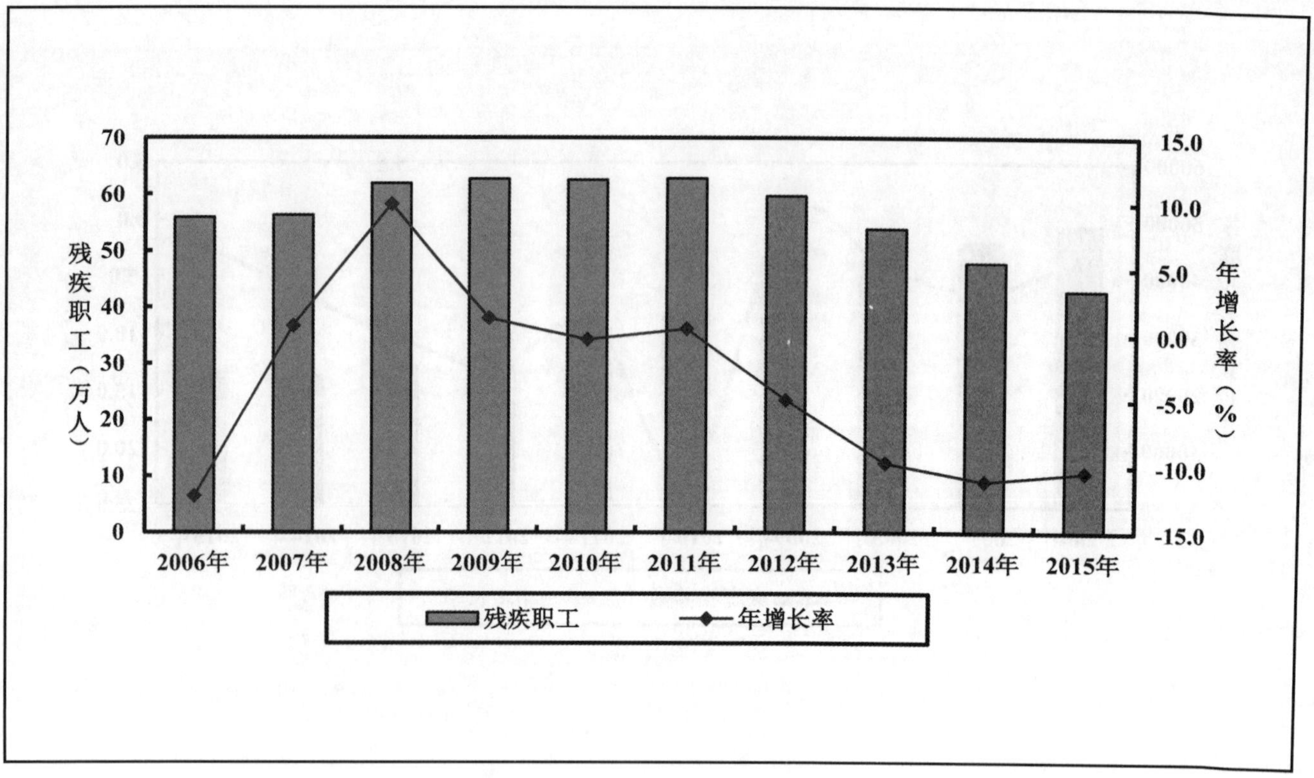

单位：万人、%

指　标	2006年	2007年	2008年	2009年	2010年	2011年	2012年	2013年	2014年	2015年
残疾职工	55.9	56.3	61.9	62.7	62.5	62.8	59.7	53.9	47.9	42.9
年增长率	-12.2	0.7	9.9	1.3	-0.3	0.5	-4.9	-9.7	-11.1	-10.4

图2-8　城市最低生活保障

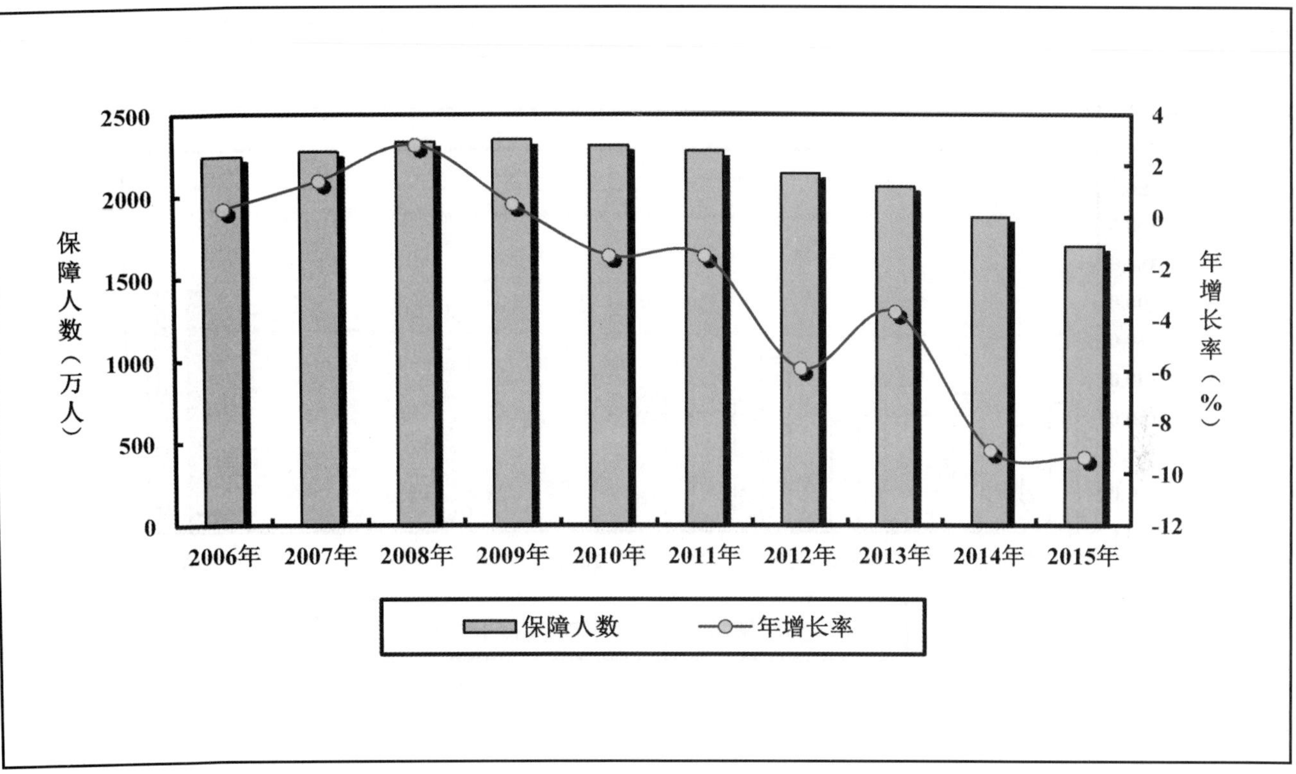

单位：万人、%

指　标	2006年	2007年	2008年	2009年	2010年	2011年	2012年	2013年	2014年	2015年
保障人数	2240.1	2272.1	2334.8	2345.6	2310.5	2276.8	2143.5	2064.2	1877.0	1701.1
年增长率	0.3	1.4	2.8	0.5	-1.5	-1.5	-5.9	-3.7	-9.1	-9.4

图2-9　城市低保平均标准与平均支出水平

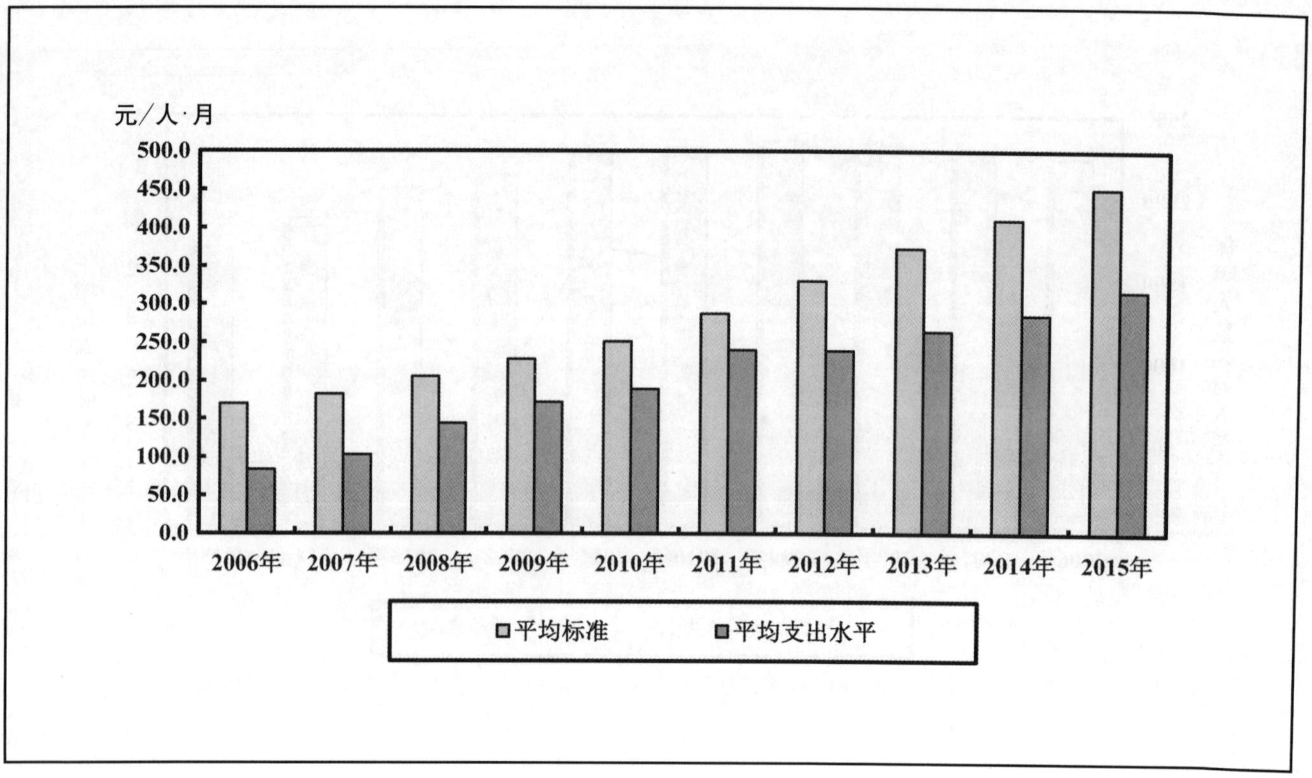

单位：元/人·月

指　标	2006年	2007年	2008年	2009年	2010年	2011年	2012年	2013年	2014年	2015年
平均标准	169.6	182.4	205.3	227.8	251.2	287.6	330.1	373.3	410.5	451.1
平均支出水平	83.6	102.7	143.7	172.0	189.0	240.3	239.1	264.2	285.6	316.6

图2-10　分省城市低保平均标准与支出水平

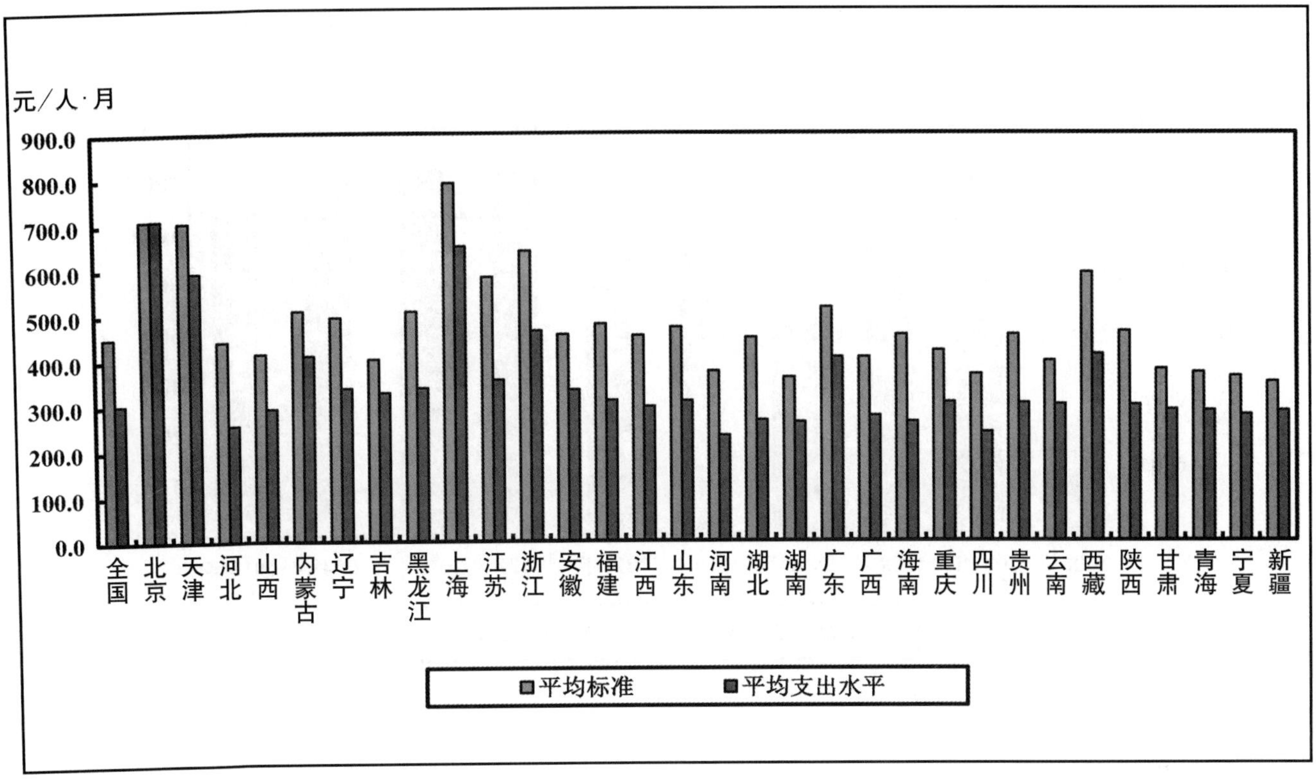

单位：元/人·月

地　区	平均标准	平均支出水平	地　区	平均标准	平均支出水平	地　区	平均标准	平均支出水平	地　区	平均标准	平均支出水平
全　国	**451.1**	**316.6**	黑龙江	506.4	338.4	河　南	374.1	231.9	贵　州	453.4	302.9
北　京	710.0	710.3	上　海	790.0	650.9	湖　北	447.1	265.2	云　南	395.9	300.6
天　津	705.0	593.4	江　苏	581.7	355.7	湖　南	359.8	260.7	西　藏	591.3	410.5
河　北	441.4	255.7	浙　江	640.5	463.5	广　东	513.8	404.2	陕　西	460.7	299.1
山　西	413.2	291.7	安　徽	455.0	333.6	广　西	404.4	274.4	甘　肃	378.1	288.2
内蒙古	508.0	409.1	福　建	478.1	310.0	海　南	466.8	261.7	青　海	370.4	286.3
辽　宁	493.5	337.5	江　西	452.0	296.2	重　庆	419.1	305.2	宁　夏	361.8	277.3
吉　林	401.6	328.3	山　东	470.1	308.6	四　川	367.0	238.3	新　疆	349.2	285.9

图2-11　农村最低生活保障

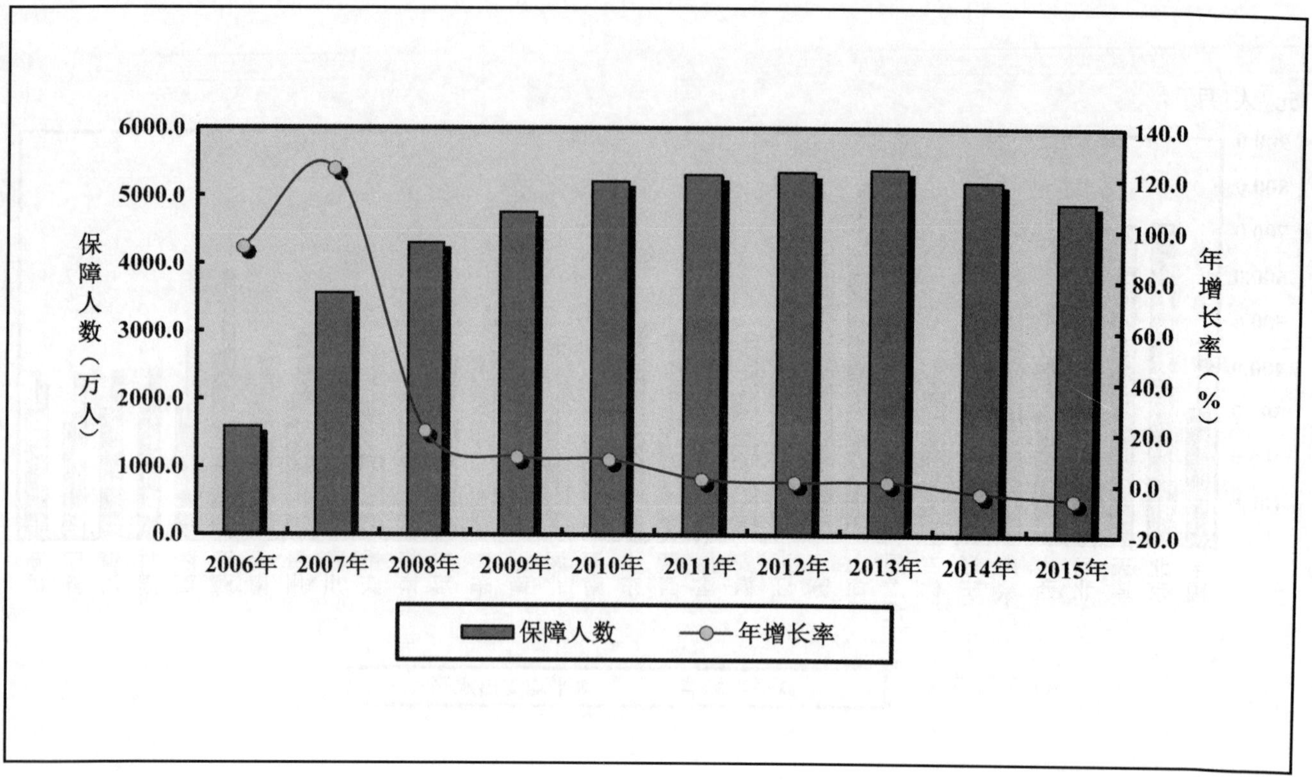

单位：万人、%

指　标	2006年	2007年	2008年	2009年	2010年	2011年	2012年	2013年	2014年	2015年
保障人数	1593.1	3566.3	4305.5	4760.0	5214.0	5305.7	5344.5	5388.0	5207.2	4903.6
年增长率	93.1	123.9	20.7	10.6	9.5	1.8	0.7	0.8	-3.4	-5.8

图2-12　农村低保平均标准与平均支出水平

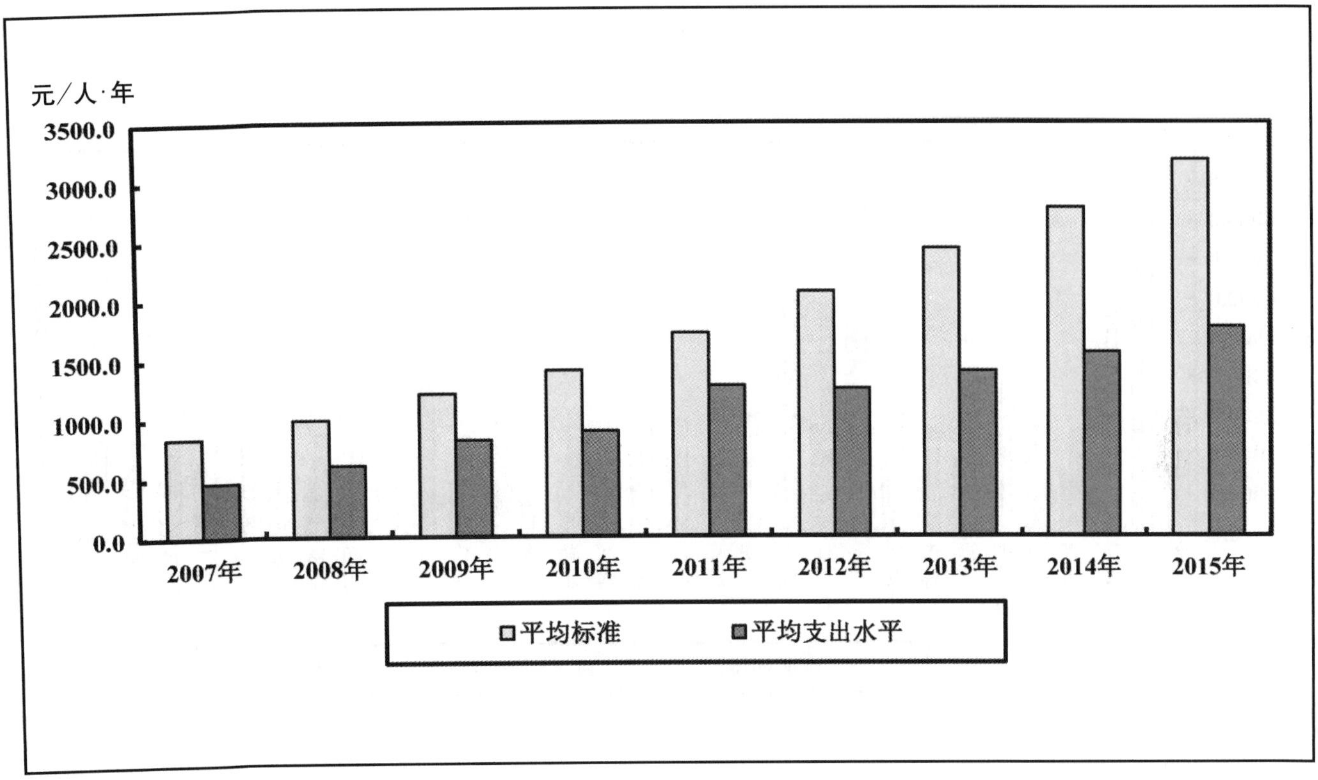

单位：元/人·年

指　标	2007年	2008年	2009年	2010年	2011年	2012年	2013年	2014年	2015年
平均标准	840.0	987.6	1209.6	1404.0	1718.4	2067.8	2433.9	2776.6	3177.6
平均支出水平	465.6	604.8	816.0	888.0	1273.2	1247.9	1393.5	1552.3	1766.5

图2-13　分省农村低保平均标准与支出水平

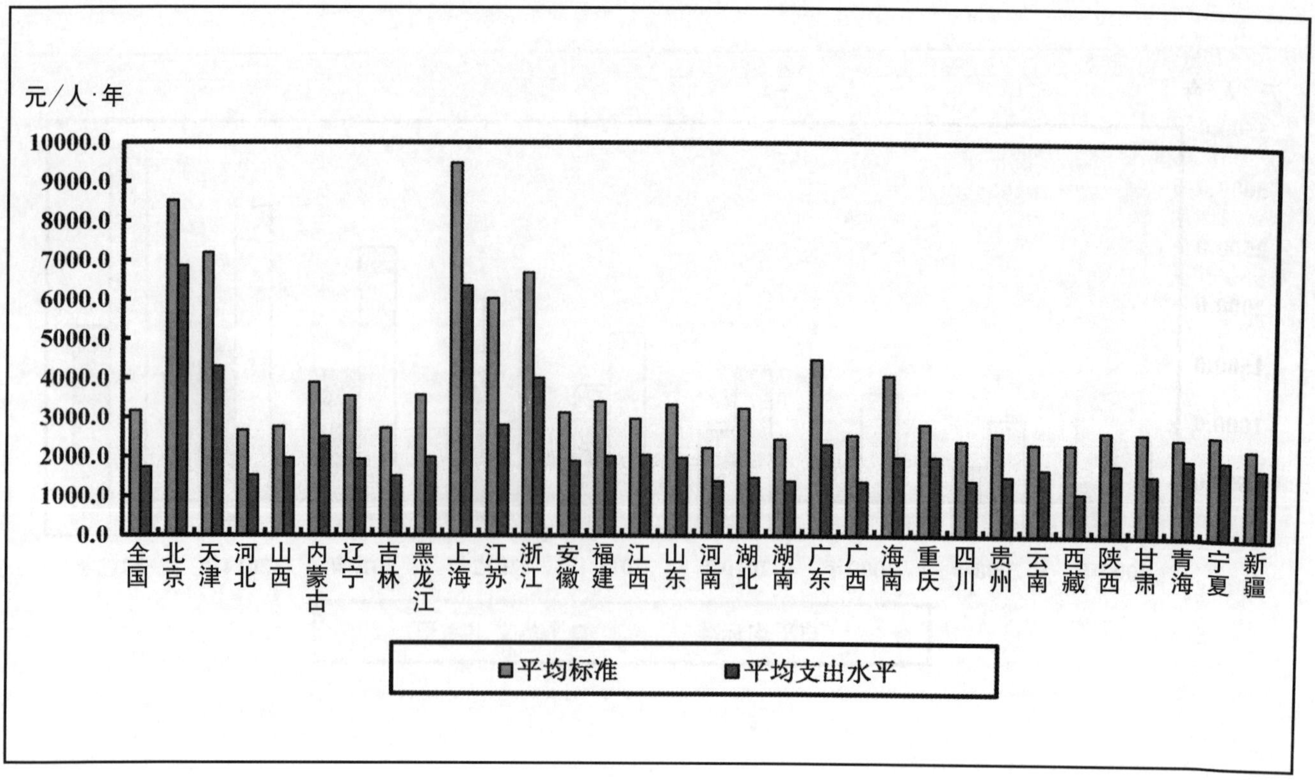

单位：元/人·年

地　区	平均标准	平均支出水平	地　区	平均标准	平均支出水平	地　区	平均标准	平均支出水平	地　区	平均标准	平均支出水平
全　国	**3177.6**	**1766.5**	黑龙江	3573.9	1989.7	河　南	2232.3	1390.3	贵　州	2620.0	1521.0
北　京	8520.0	6862.7	上　海	9480.0	6342.6	湖　北	3235.2	1476.2	云　南	2341.9	1697.2
天　津	7194.0	4301.4	江　苏	6029.8	2804.6	湖　南	2446.4	1387.9	西　藏	2337.5	1100.8
河　北	2670.7	1524.2	浙　江	6683.9	4007.5	广　东	4489.9	2324.0	陕　西	2654.2	1823.3
山　西	2757.8	1959.8	安　徽	3121.1	1887.1	广　西	2556.1	1376.3	甘　肃	2617.7	1564.1
内蒙古	3891.2	2506.1	福　建	3405.9	2017.3	海　南	4168.4	2006.2	青　海	2494.2	1968.1
辽　宁	3548.5	1930.2	江　西	2965.7	2050.9	重　庆	2841.0	2009.5	宁　夏	2606.1	1974.1
吉　林	2721.2	1510.3	山　东	3340.0	1975.4	四　川	2409.1	1405.4	新　疆	2287.4	1793.3

图2-14　农村特困人员救助供养

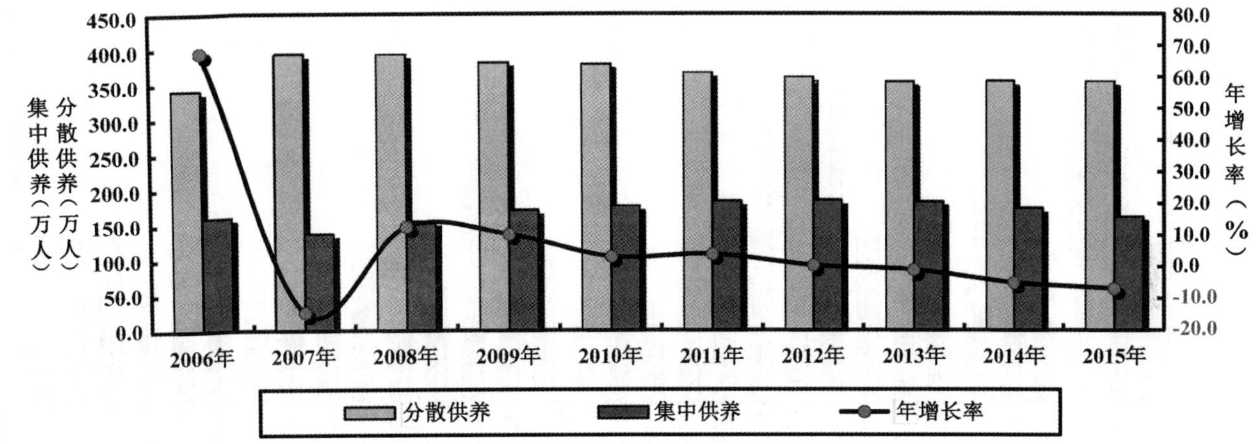

单位：万人、%

指　标	2006年	2007年	2008年	2009年	2010年	2011年	2012年	2013年	2014年	2015年
救助供养合计	503.3	531.3	548.6	553.4	556.3	551.0	545.6	537.3	529.1	516.7
分散供养	342.2	393.3	393.0	381.6	378.9	366.5	360.3	353.8	354.8	354.4
集中供养	161.1	138.0	155.6	171.8	177.4	184.5	185.3	183.5	174.3	162.3
年增长率	67.8	-14.3	12.8	10.4	3.3	4.0	0.4	-1.0	-5.0	-6.9

图2-15　分省农村特困集中供养平均标准与支出水平

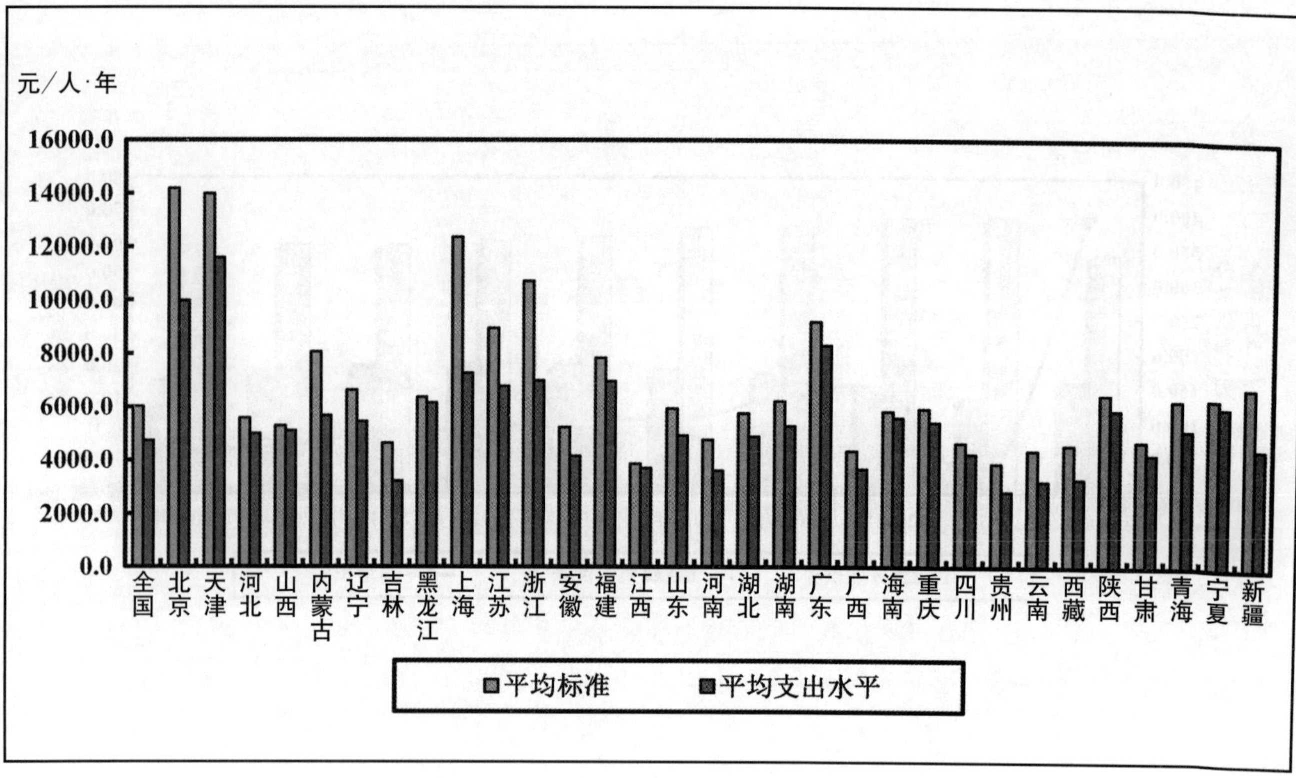

单位：元/人·年

地　区	平均标准	平均支出水平	地　区	平均标准	平均支出水平	地　区	平均标准	平均支出水平	地　区	平均标准	平均支出水平
全　国	**6025.7**	**4790.4**	黑龙江	6371.7	6160.2	河　南	4770.4	3616.9	贵　州	3889.0	2848.8
北　京	14183.2	9974.3	上　海	12360.0	7269.6	湖　北	5760.1	4885.3	云　南	4383.2	3232.6
天　津	13989.9	11587.1	江　苏	8949.0	6779.9	湖　南	6215.1	5282.6	西　藏	4586.3	3327.0
河　北	5578.9	4989.2	浙　江	10702.7	6994.4	广　东	9193.1	8310.2	陕　西	6468.4	5896.1
山　西	5280.8	5100.2	安　徽	5225.5	4155.6	广　西	4362.9	3685.1	甘　肃	4732.0	4239.5
内蒙古	8063.7	5664.4	福　建	7840.7	6968.2	海　南	5886.3	5599.6	青　海	6254.9	5155.2
辽　宁	6626.1	5443.9	江　西	3872.0	3711.2	重　庆	5934.7	5429.3	宁　夏	6344.7	6047.2
吉　林	4634.6	3219.8	山　东	5931.5	4921.7	四　川	4659.3	4250.5	新　疆	6797.9	4521.4

图2-16　分省农村特困分散供养平均标准与支出水平

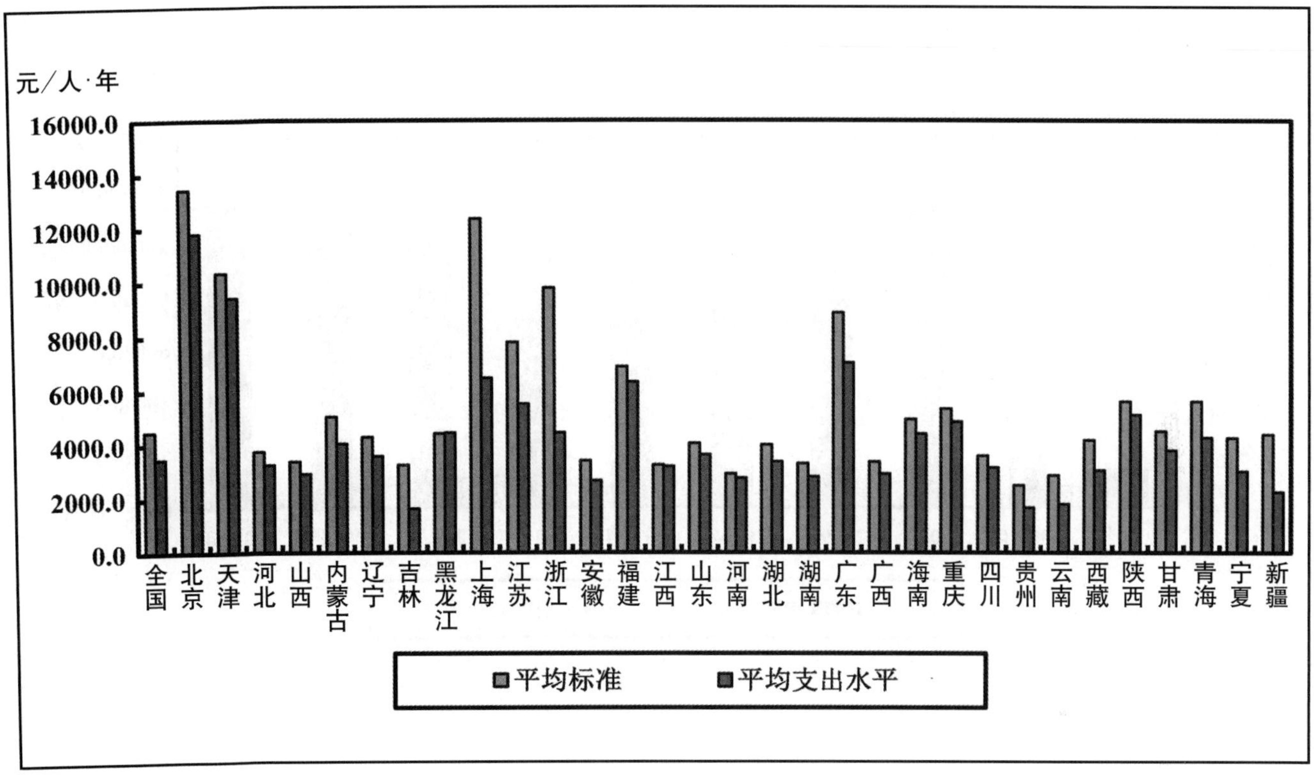

单位：元/人·年

地　区	平均标准	平均支出水平	地　区	平均标准	平均支出水平	地　区	平均标准	平均支出水平	地　区	平均标准	平均支出水平
全　国	**4490.1**	**3674.3**	黑龙江	4409.2	4440.7	河　南	2909.2	2756.4	贵　州	2501.7	1674.1
北　京	13452.6	11818.4	上　海	12360.0	6462.5	湖　北	3988.6	3358.8	云　南	2864.9	1796.0
天　津	10360.4	9435.5	江　苏	7785.5	5515.2	湖　南	3288.4	2807.8	西　藏	4163.5	3041.3
河　北	3736.4	3242.3	浙　江	9798.5	4439.0	广　东	8871.0	7030.9	陕　西	5601.9	5095.1
山　西	3378.0	2913.6	安　徽	3393.6	2663.8	广　西	3354.7	2914.2	甘　肃	4486.8	3786.0
内蒙古	5030.4	4030.8	福　建	6882.8	6316.9	海　南	4970.5	4389.5	青　海	5602.6	4248.2
辽　宁	4283.2	3566.0	江　西	3246.3	3189.2	重　庆	5324.0	4844.4	宁　夏	4242.5	3002.0
吉　林	3238.8	1627.2	山　东	4041.8	3627.0	四　川	3588.3	3149.4	新　疆	4375.4	2248.4

图2-17　社会捐赠

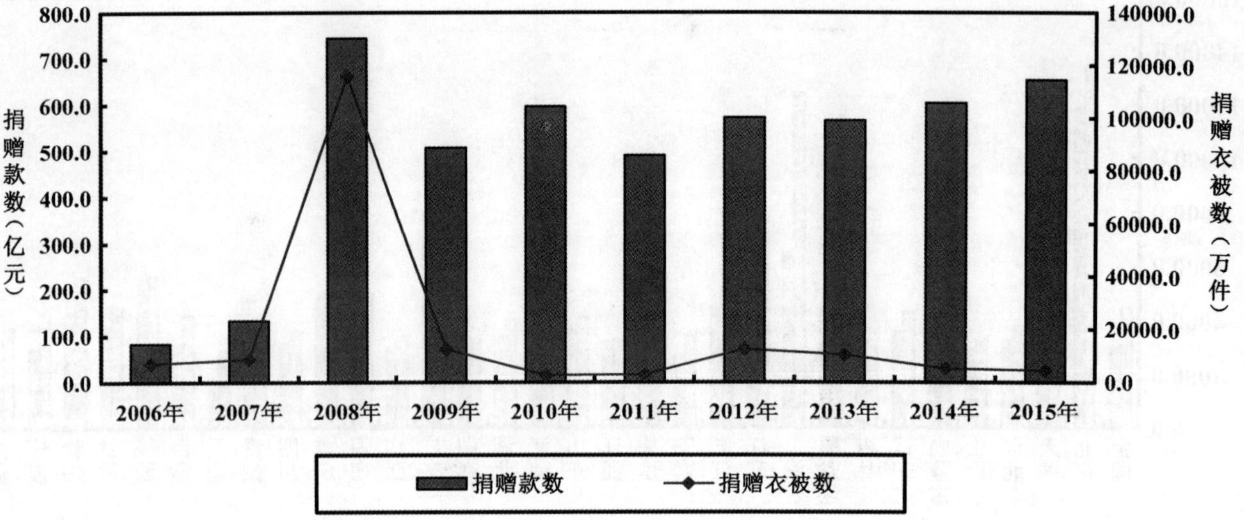

单位：亿元、万件

指　标	2006年	2007年	2008年	2009年	2010年	2011年	2012年	2013年	2014年	2015年
捐赠款数	83.1	132.8	744.5	507.2	596.8	490.1	572.5	566.4	604.4	654.5
捐赠衣被	7123.6	8756.8	115816.3	12476.6	2750.2	2918.5	12538.2	10405.0	5244.5	4537.0

注：捐赠款为民政部门和社会组织接收的合计数。

图2-18　福利彩票

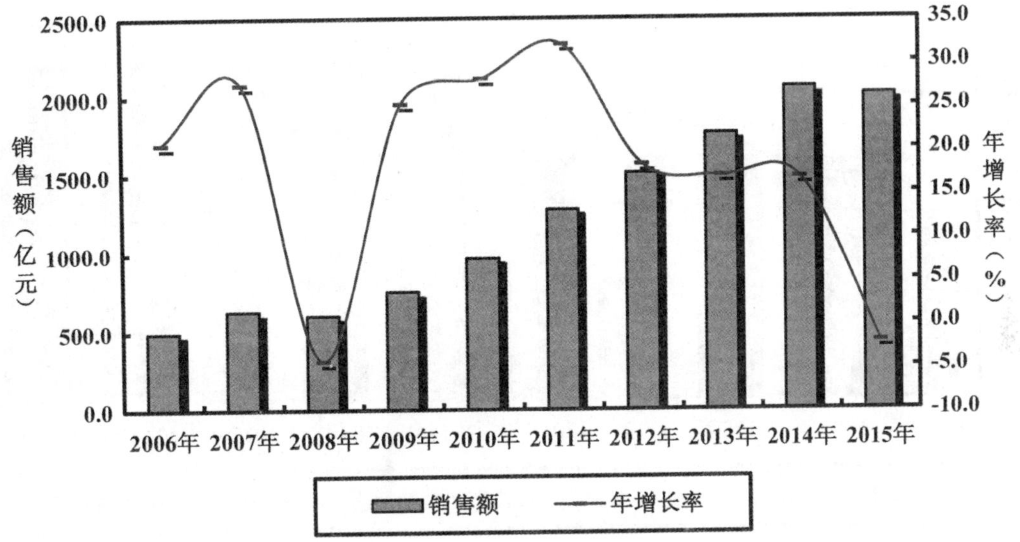

单位：亿元、%

指　标	2006年	2007年	2008年	2009年	2010年	2011年	2012年	2013年	2014年	2015年
销售额	495.7	631.6	604.0	756.0	968.0	1278.0	1510.3	1765.3	2059.7	2015.1
年增长率	20.5	27.4	(4.4)	25.2	28.0	32.0	18.2	16.9	16.7	−2.2

图2-19 国家抚恤、补助优抚对象

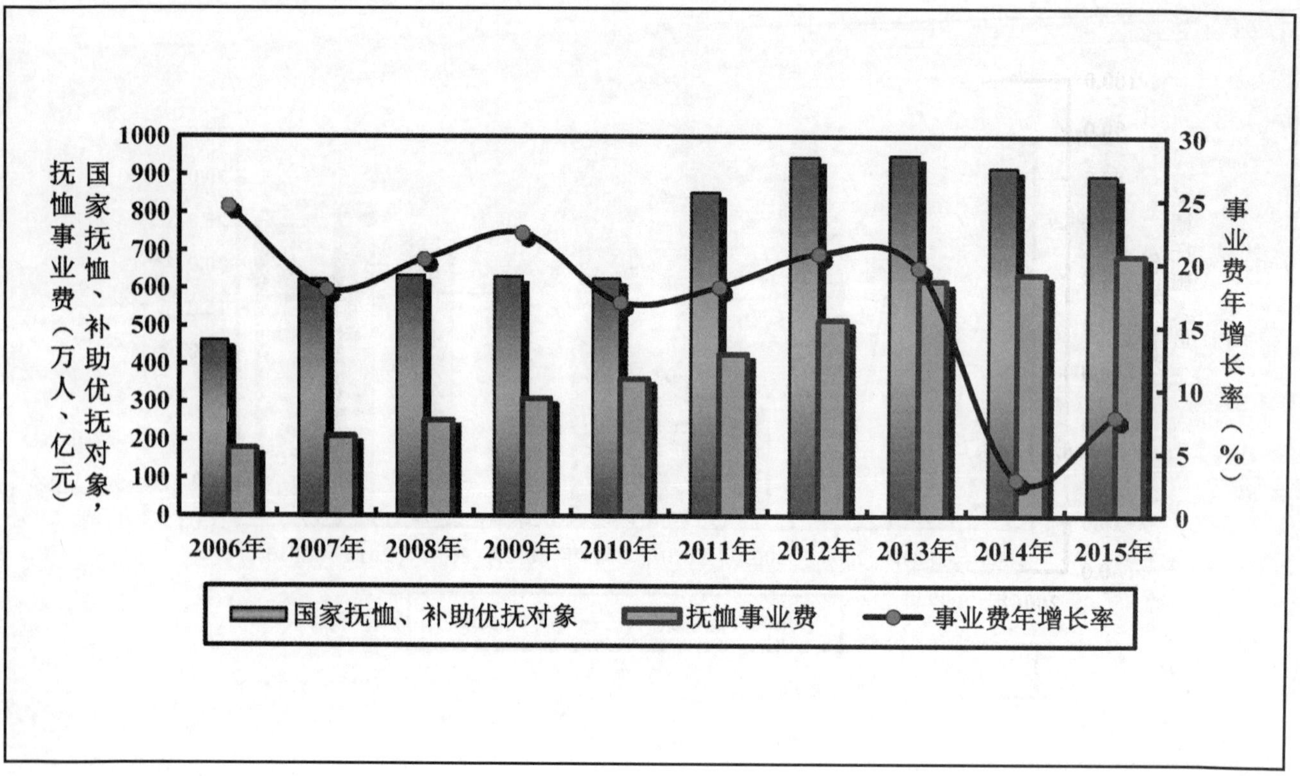

单位：万人、亿元、%

指　标	2006年	2007年	2008年	2009年	2010年	2011年	2012年	2013年	2014年	2015年
国家抚恤、补助优抚对象	462.6	622.4	633.2	630.7	625	852.5	944.4	950.5	917.3	897.0
抚恤事业费	178.8	210.8	253.6	310.3	362.7	428.3	517	618.4	636.6	686.8
事业费年增长率	24.5	17.9	20.3	22.4	16.9	18.1	20.7	19.6	2.9	7.9

图2-20　优抚对象分类

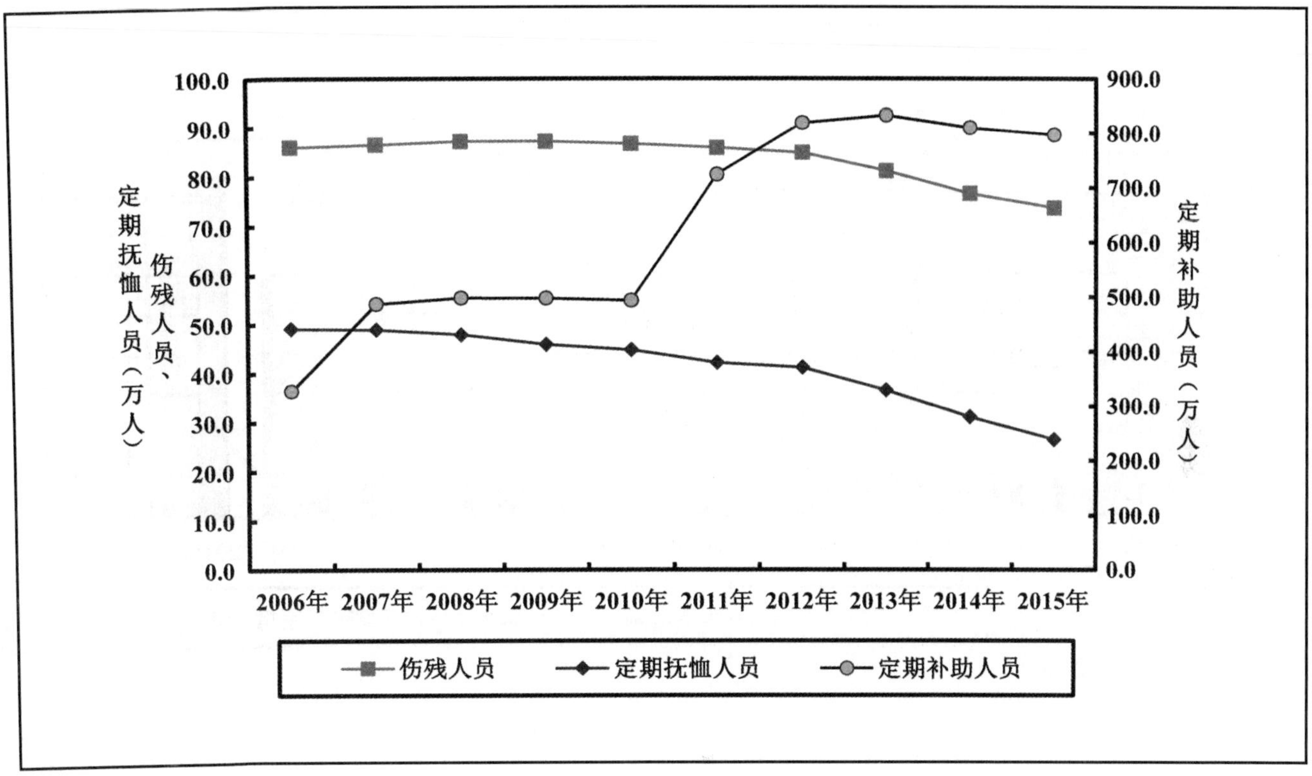

单位：万人

指　标	2006年	2007年	2008年	2009年	2010年	2011年	2012年	2013年	2014年	2015年
伤残人员	86.0	86.5	87.2	87.2	86.7	85.9	84.9	81.2	76.6	73.7
定期抚恤人员	49.1	48.9	47.9	45.9	44.8	42.2	41.2	36.6	31.1	26.5
定期补助人员	327.4	487.1	498.2	497.7	493.5	724.4	818.4	832.6	809.6	796.8

图2-21 接收安置军休干部、军休职工

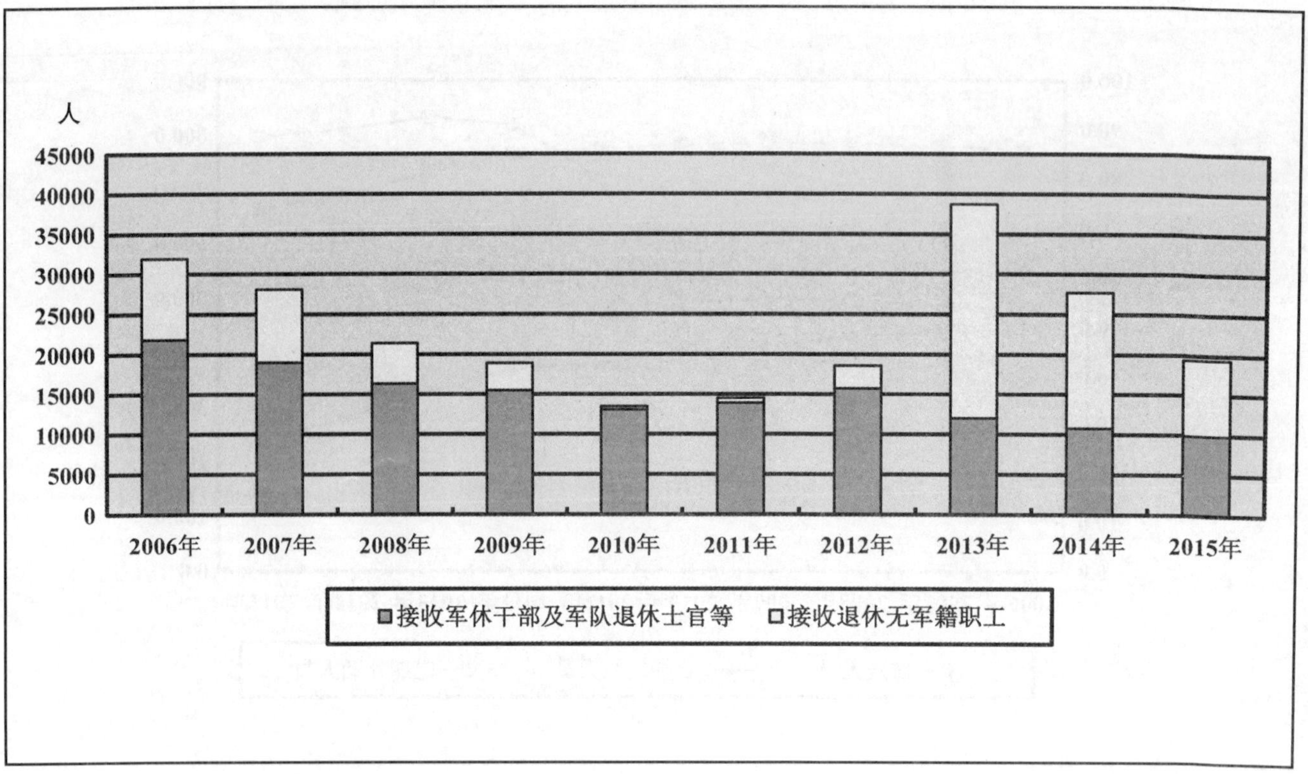

单位：人

指 标	2006年	2007年	2008年	2009年	2010年	2011年	2012年	2013年	2014年	2015年
接收军休干部及军队退休士官等	21832	18997	16331	15492	13070	13901	15723	11997	10791	9921
接收退休无军籍职工	10136	9061	5047	3412	381	629	2847	26709	16908	9508

图2-22 烈士纪念建筑物管理机构和藏品量

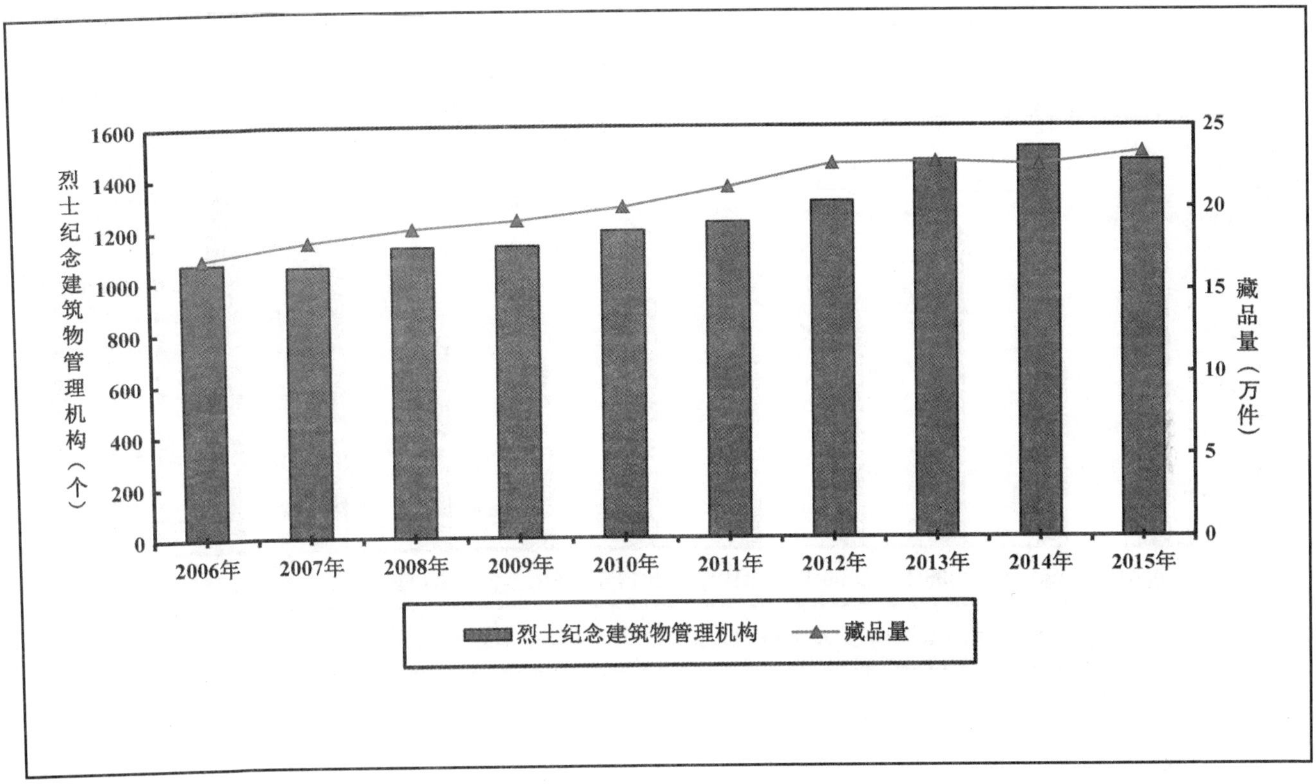

单位：个、万件

指　标	2006年	2007年	2008年	2009年	2010年	2011年	2012年	2013年	2014年	2015年
烈士纪念建筑物管理机构	1072	1056	1133	1137	1195	1227	1306	1463	1516	1464
藏品量	17.0	18.0	18.8	19.3	20.1	21.3	22.7	22.8	22.6	23.4

图2-23　烈士褒扬和零散烈士纪念设施

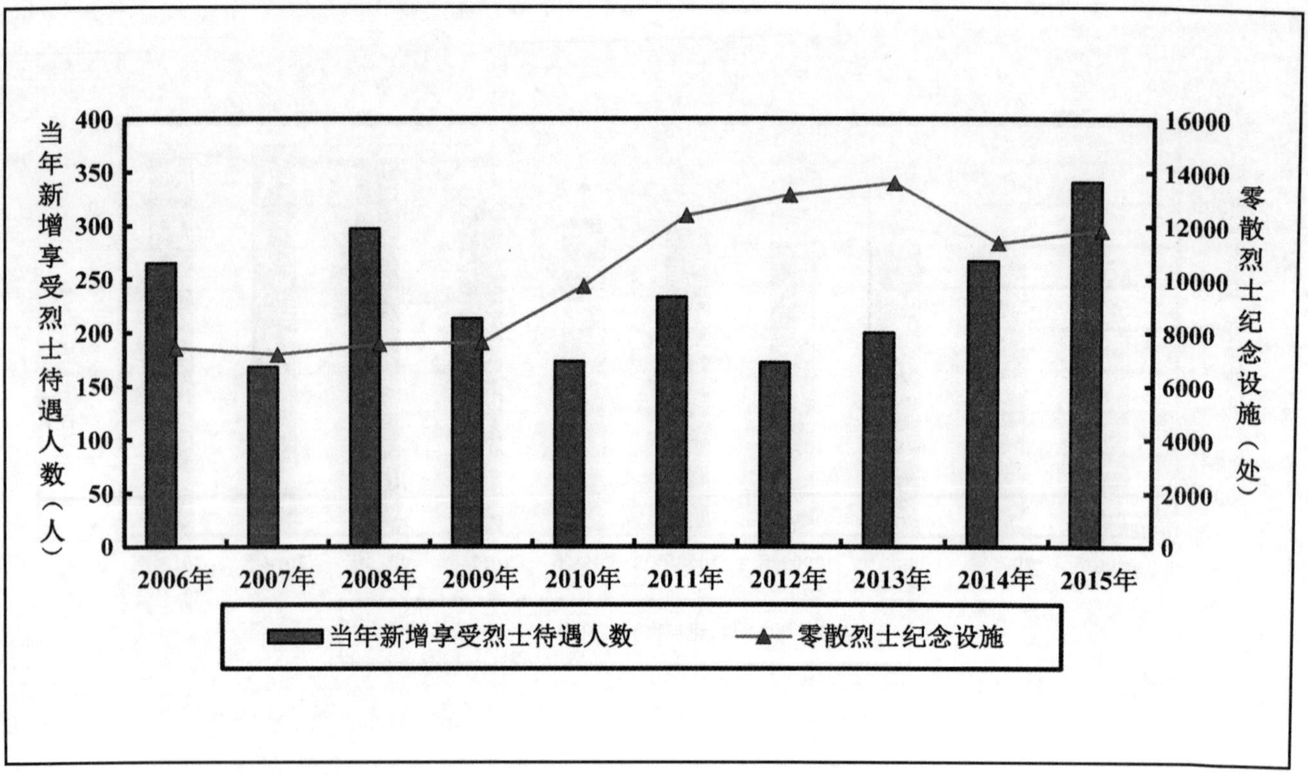

单位：人、处

指　标	2006年	2007年	2008年	2009年	2010年	2011年	2012年	2013年	2014年	2015年
当年新增享受烈士待遇人数	265	168	297	213	173	233	172	200	267	341
零散烈士纪念设施	7414	7186	7569	7622	9729	12378	13151	13601	11365	11838

图2-24　因灾死亡失踪人口

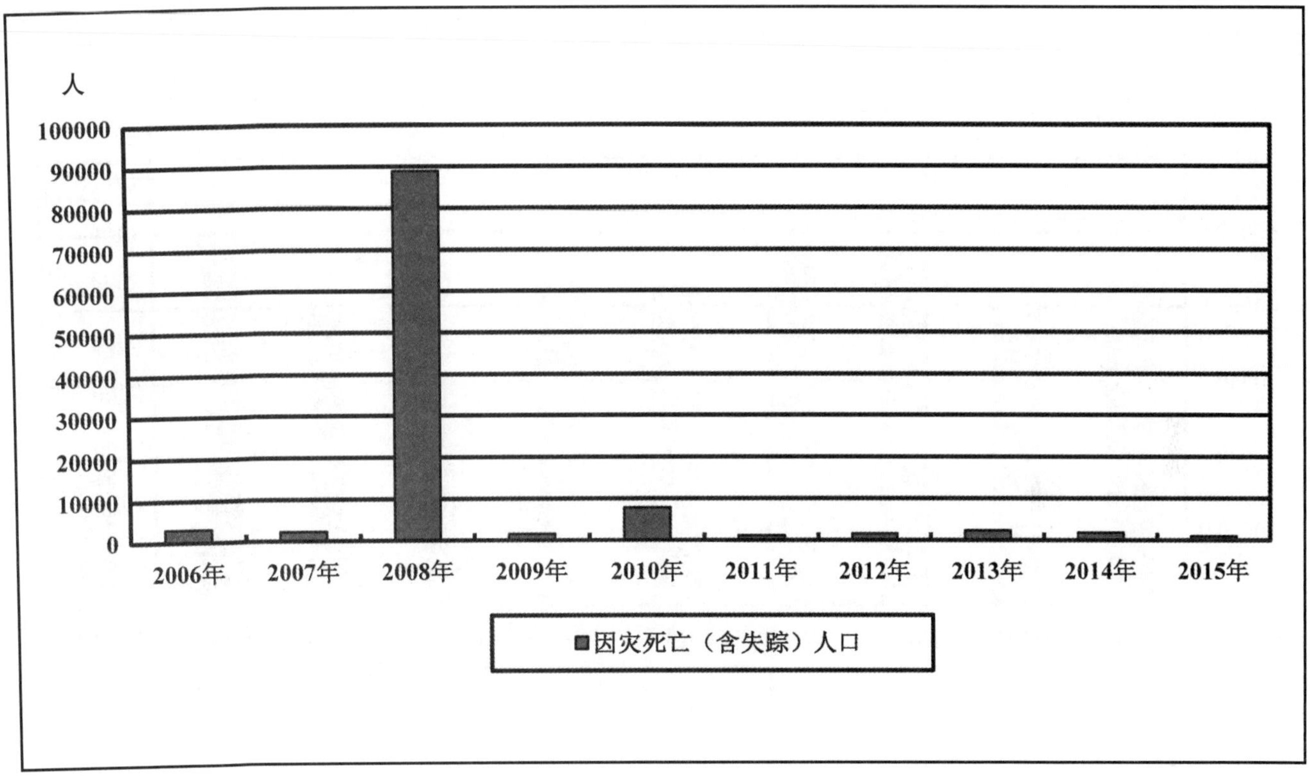

单位：人

指　标	2006年	2007年	2008年	2009年	2010年	2011年	2012年	2013年	2014年	2015年
因灾死亡(含失踪)人口	3186	2325	88928	1528	7844	1126	1530	2284	1818	967

图2-25　受灾人口

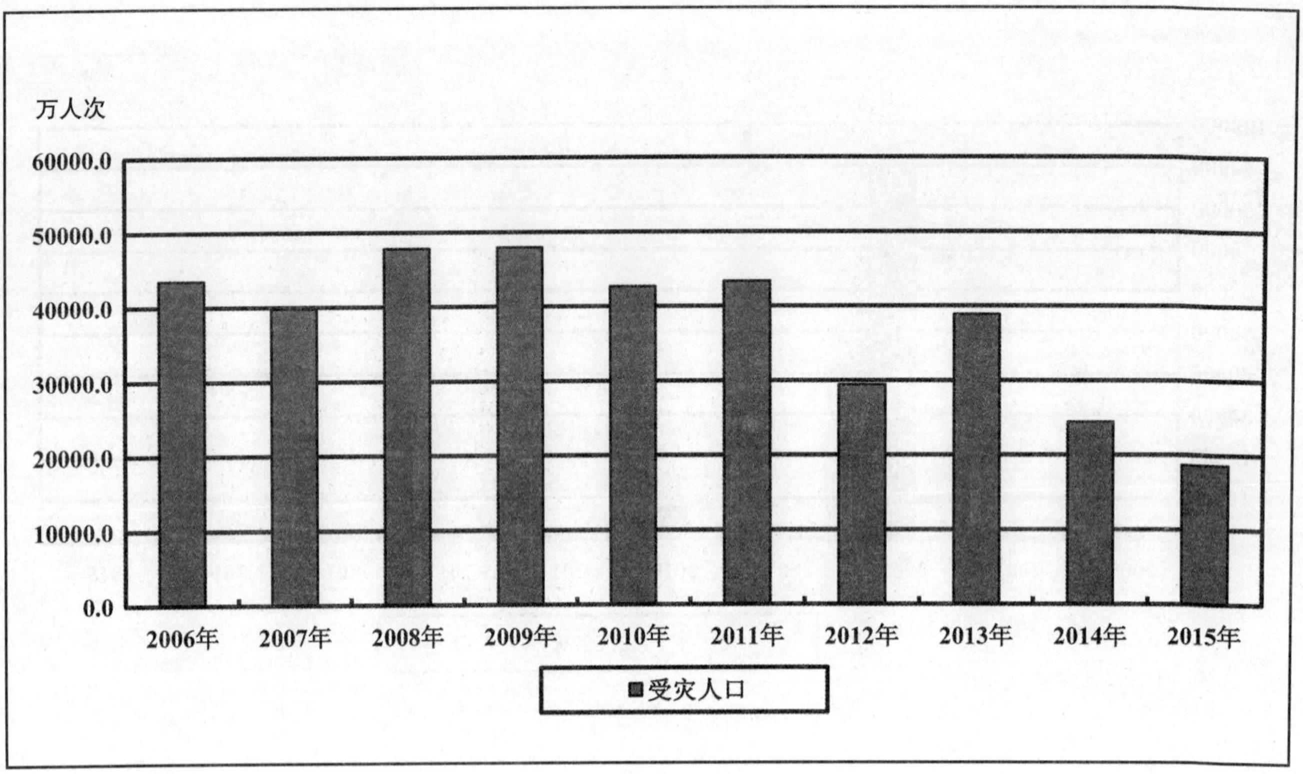

单位：万人次

指　标	2006年	2007年	2008年	2009年	2010年	2011年	2012年	2013年	2014年	2015年
受灾人口	43453.3	39777.9	47795.0	47933.5	42610.2	43290.0	29421.7	38818.7	24353.7	18620.3

图2-26　社区服务机构和设施

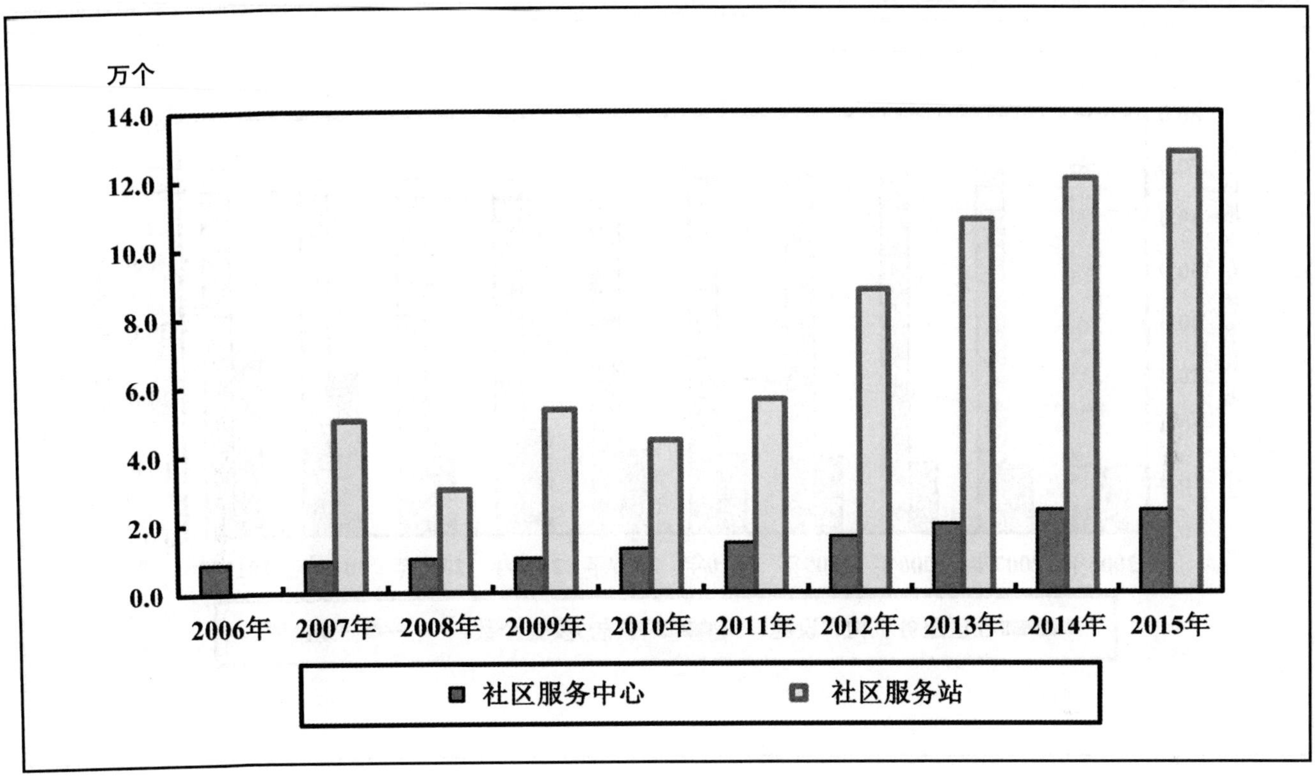

单位：万个

指　标	2006年	2007年	2008年	2009年	2010年	2011年	2012年	2013年	2014年	2015年
社区服务机构和设施	12.5	12.9	14.6	14.6	15.3	16.0	20.0	25.2	31.1	36.1
#社区服务中心	0.9	0.9	1.0	1.0	1.3	1.4	1.6	2.0	2.4	3.3
社区服务站		5.0	3.0	5.3	4.4	5.6	8.8	10.8	12.0	12.8

注：2014年以后社区服务中心中含社区服务指导中心。

图2-27 社区服务机构和设施覆盖率

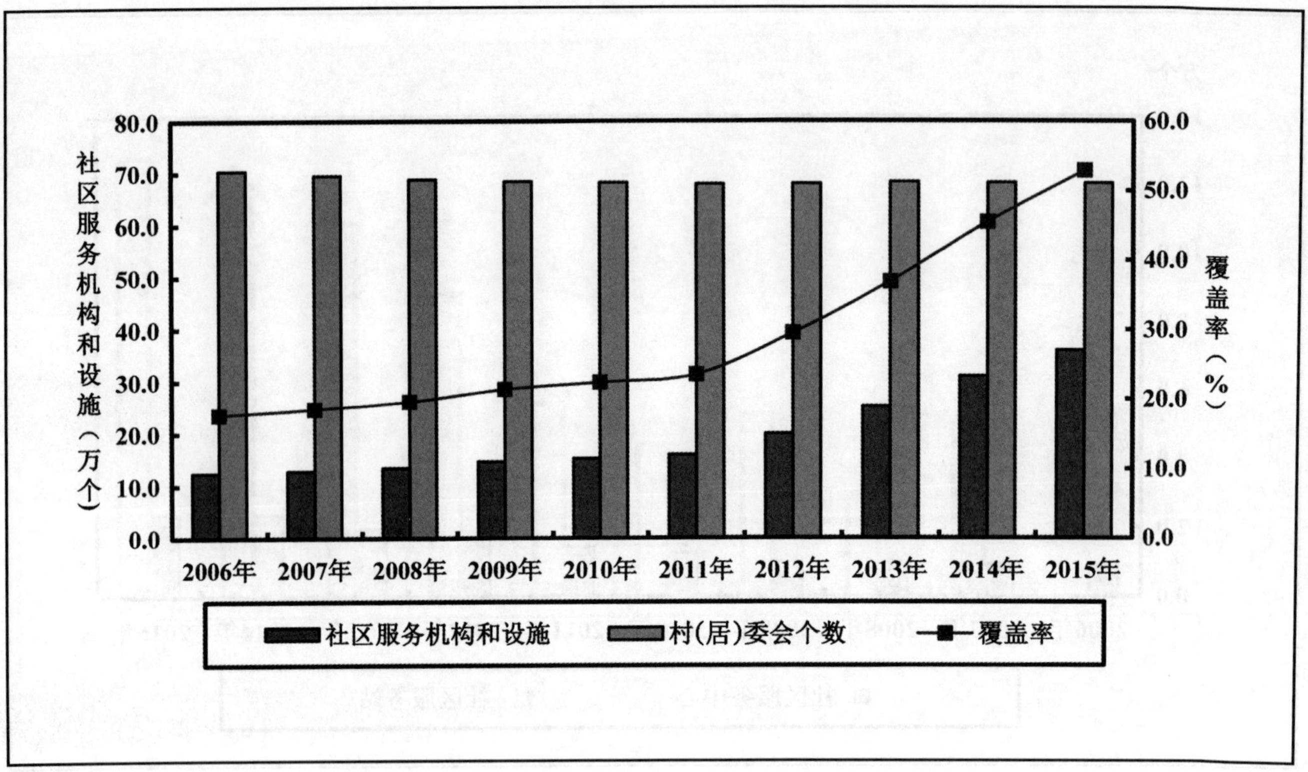

单位：万个、%

指　标	2006年	2007年	2008年	2009年	2010年	2011年	2012年	2013年	2014年	2015年
社区服务机构和设施	12.5	12.9	13.5	14.7	15.3	16.0	20.0	25.2	31.1	36.1
村(居)委会个数	70.4	69.5	68.8	68.4	68.2	67.9	68.0	68.3	68.2	68.1
覆盖率	17.7	18.6	19.6	21.4	22.4	23.6	29.5	36.9	45.5	52.9

图3-1　社会组织

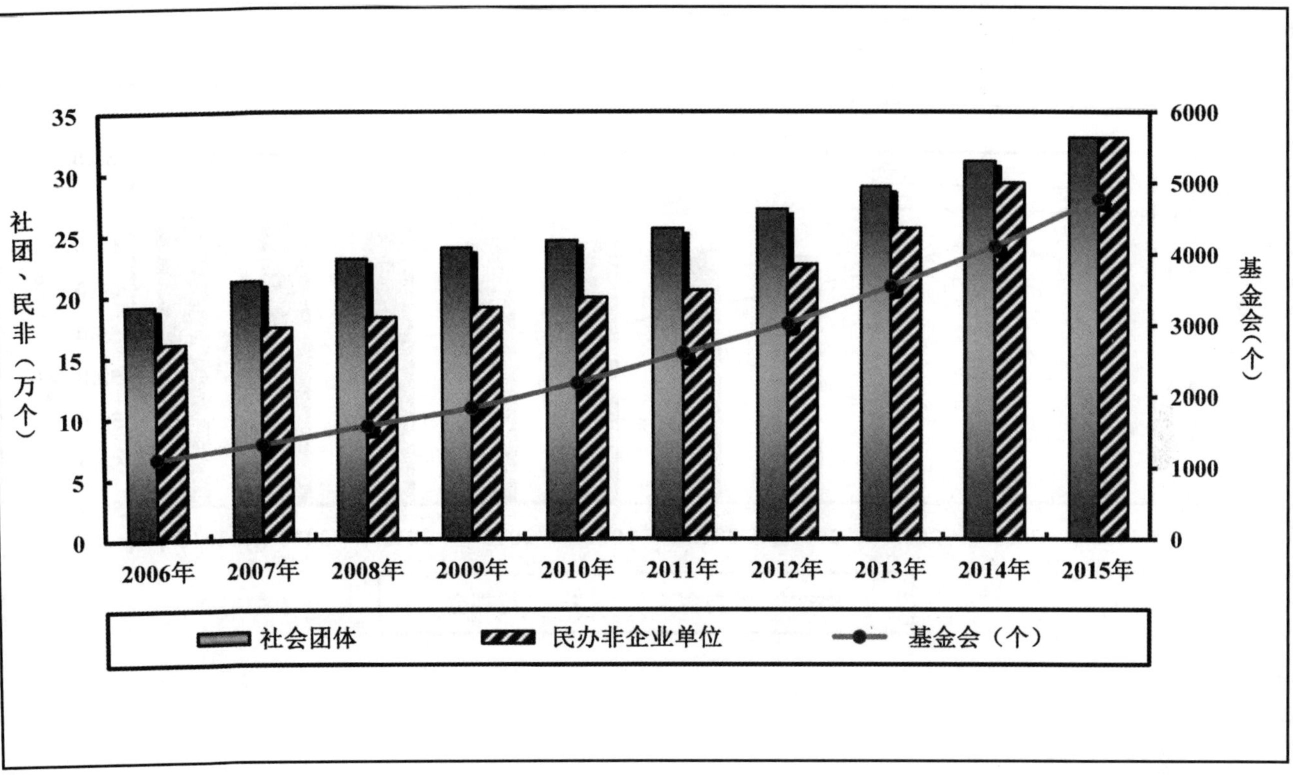

单位：万个

指　标	2006年	2007年	2008年	2009年	2010年	2011年	2012年	2013年	2014年	2015年
社会组织	35.4	38.7	41.4	43.1	44.6	46.2	49.9	54.7	60.6	66.2
社会团体	19.2	21.2	23.0	23.9	24.5	25.5	27.1	28.9	31.0	32.9
基金会(个)	1144	1340	1597	1843	2200	2614	3029	3549	4117	4784
民办非企业单位	16.1	17.4	18.2	19.0	19.8	20.4	22.5	25.5	29.2	32.9

图3-2　自治组织

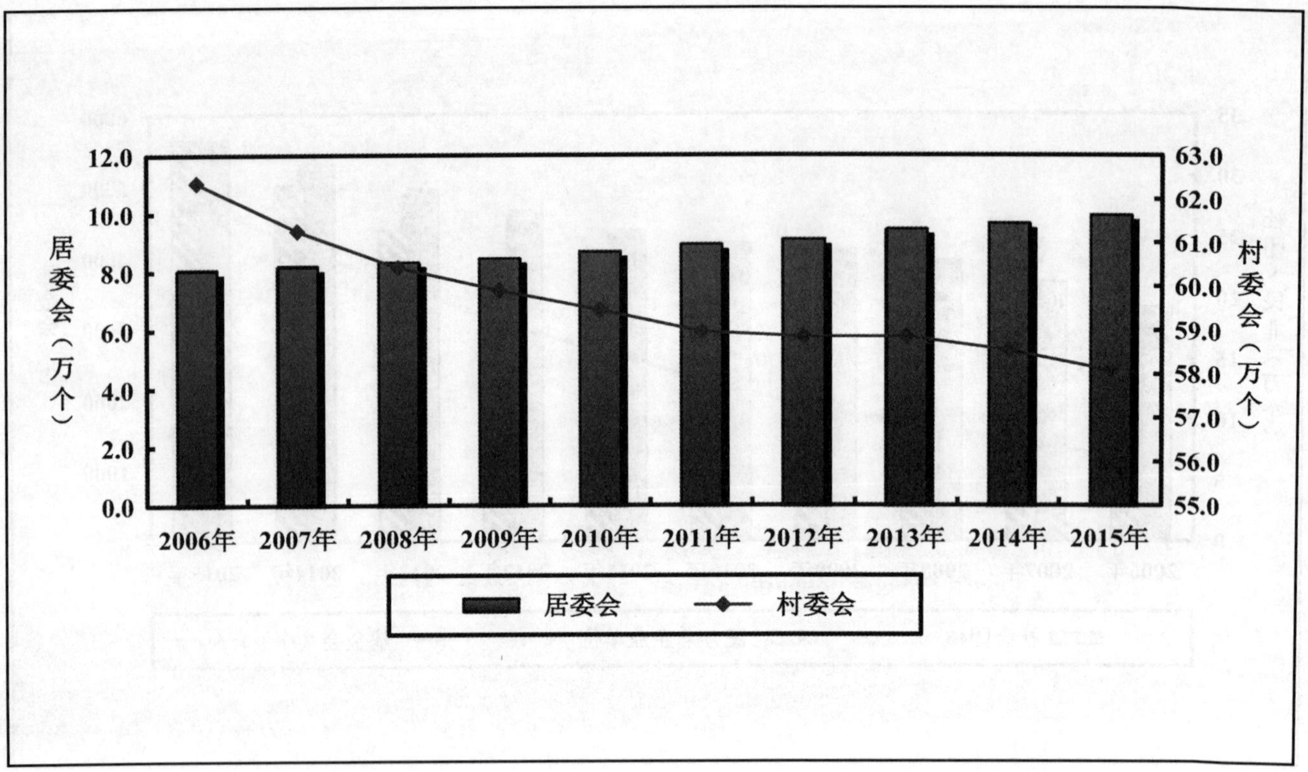

单位：万个

指　标	2006年	2007年	2008年	2009年	2010年	2011年	2012年	2013年	2014年	2015年
自治组织	70.4	69.5	68.8	68.4	68.2	67.9	68.0	68.3	68.2	68.1
居委会	8.1	8.2	8.3	8.5	8.7	8.9	9.1	9.5	9.7	10.0
村委会	62.4	61.3	60.4	59.9	59.5	59.0	58.8	58.9	58.5	58.1

图3-3 结婚登记

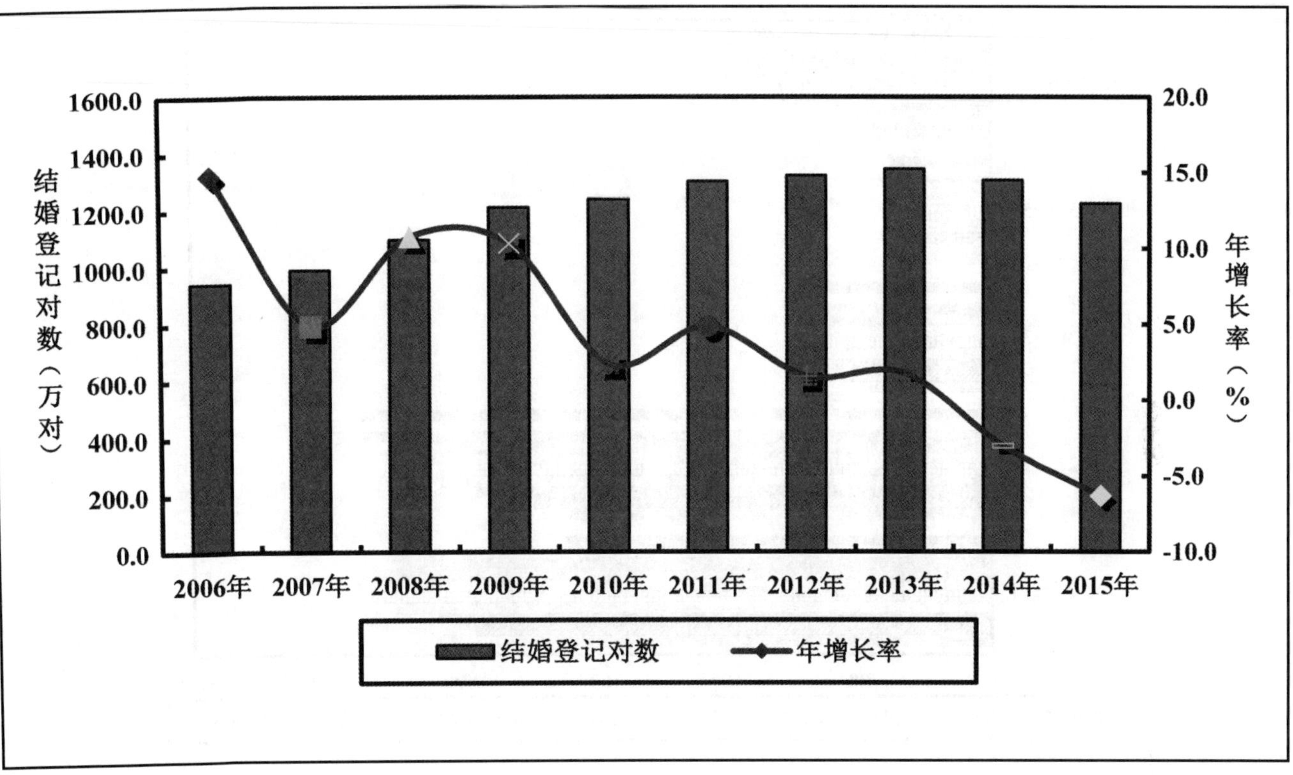

单位：万对、%

指　标	2006年	2007年	2008年	2009年	2010年	2011年	2012年	2013年	2014年	2015年
结婚登记对数	945.0	991.4	1098.3	1212.2	1241.0	1302.4	1323.6	1346.9	1306.7	1224.7
年增长率	14.8	4.9	10.8	10.4	2.4	4.9	1.6	1.8	-3.0	-6.3

图3-4　分年龄组结婚登记

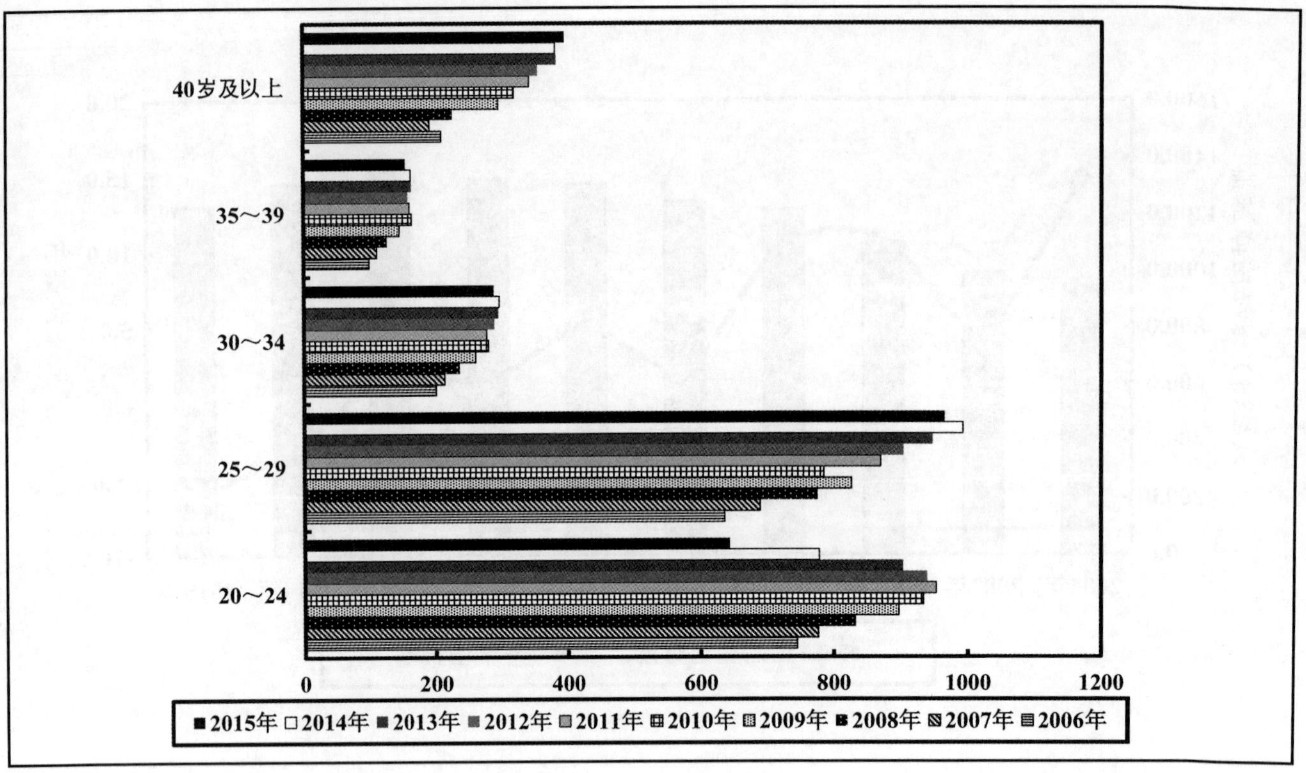

单位：万人

年　份	20～24岁	25～29岁	30～34岁	35～39岁	40岁及以上
2006	744.8	636.3	200.8	99.0	209.1
2007	776.7	689.5	214.0	110.9	191.6
2008	832.3	775.7	236.1	126.5	226.2
2009	896.7	826.4	260.3	145.4	295.5
2010	933.4	784.6	279.9	164.5	319.6
2011	953.0	870.2	277.6	161.5	342.4
2012	939.6	904.1	289.0	158.9	355.6
2013	903.4	947.5	295.1	164.3	383.5
2014	778.2	993.1	296.5	163.5	382.2
2015	643.9	965.7	288.1	155.3	396.4

图3-5 结婚率和离婚率

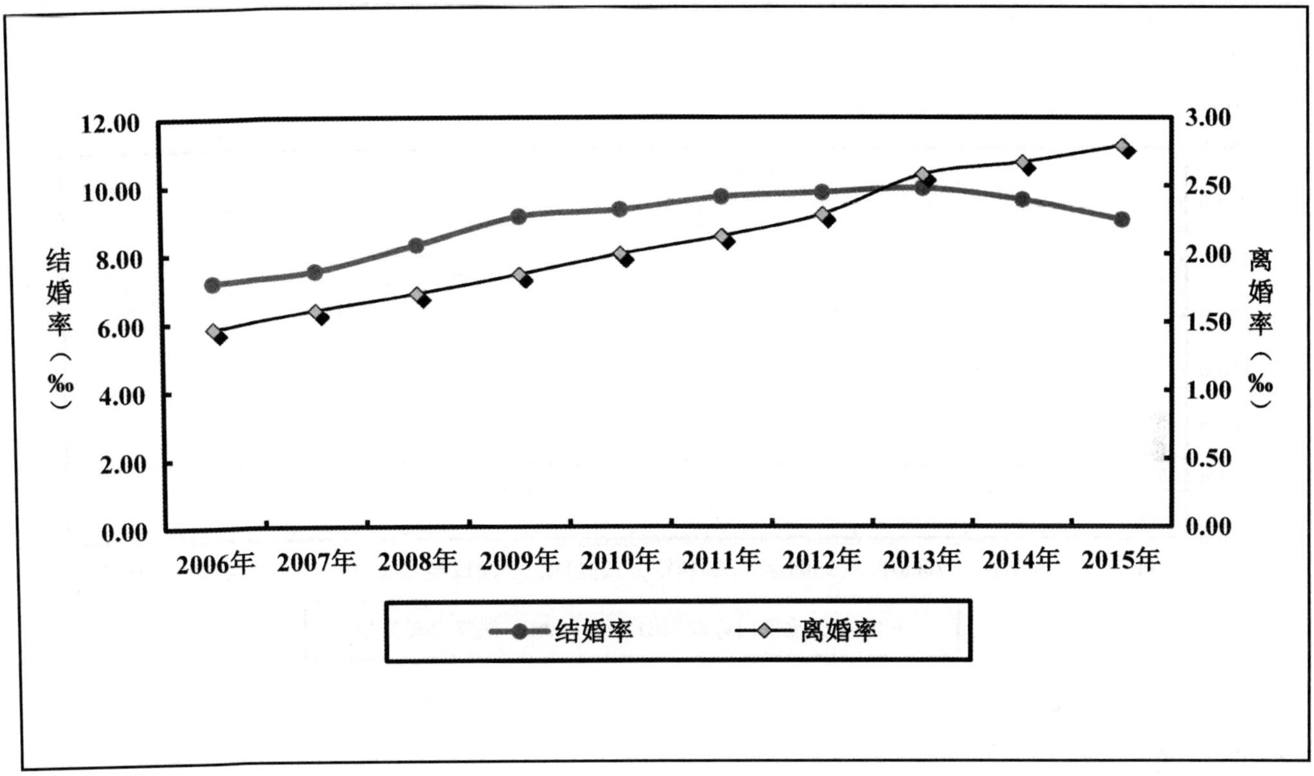

单位：‰

指　标	2006年	2007年	2008年	2009年	2010年	2011年	2012年	2013年	2014年	2015年
结婚率	7.19	7.50	8.27	9.10	9.30	9.67	9.80	9.92	9.58	9.00
离婚率	1.46	1.59	1.71	1.85	2.00	2.13	2.29	2.58	2.67	2.79

注：结（离）婚率计算方法：结（离）婚对数除以当期人口平均数。

图3-6　民政部门和法院办理离婚

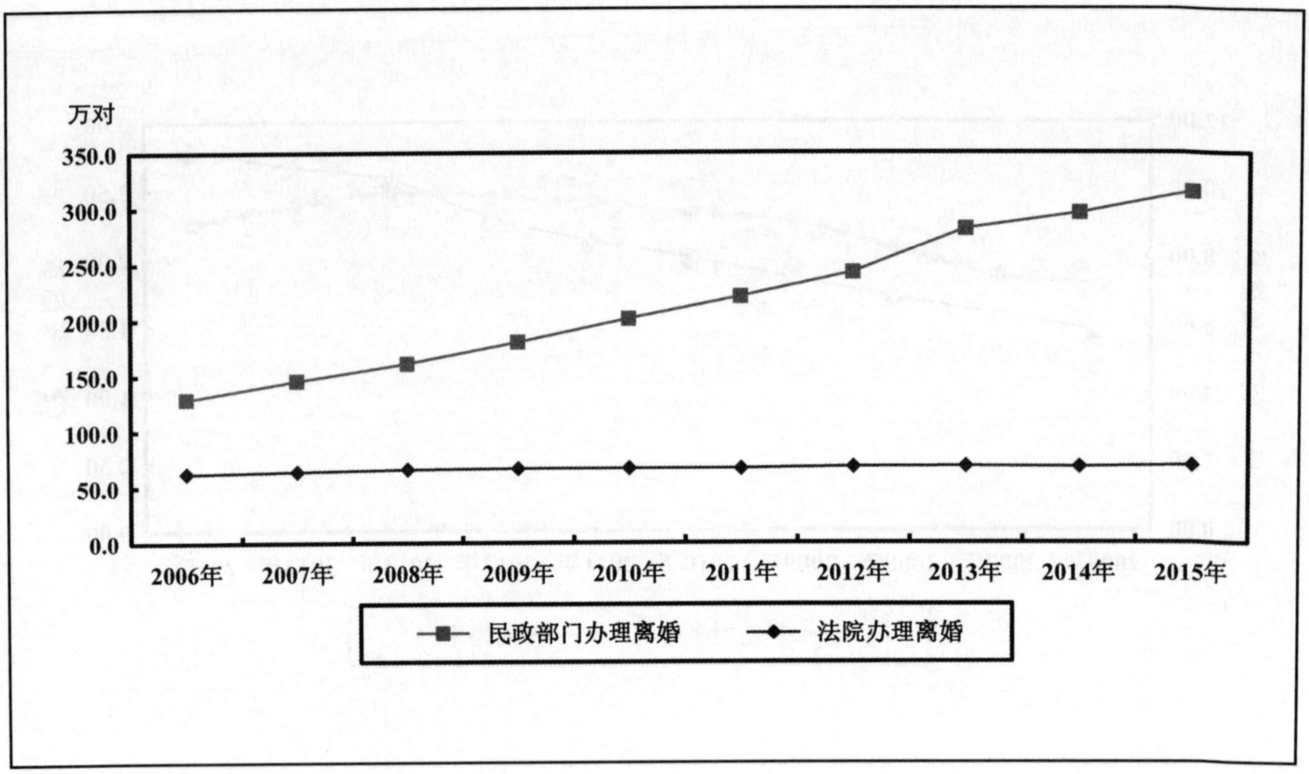

单位：万对

指　标	2006年	2007年	2008年	2009年	2010年	2011年	2012年	2013年	2014年	2015年
离婚对数	191.3	209.8	226.9	246.8	267.8	287.4	310.4	350.0	363.6	384.1
民政部门办理离婚	129.1	145.7	161.0	180.2	201.0	220.7	242.3	281.5	295.7	314.9
法院办理离婚	62.2	64.1	65.9	66.6	66.8	66.7	68.1	68.5	67.9	69.3

图3-7　遗体火化

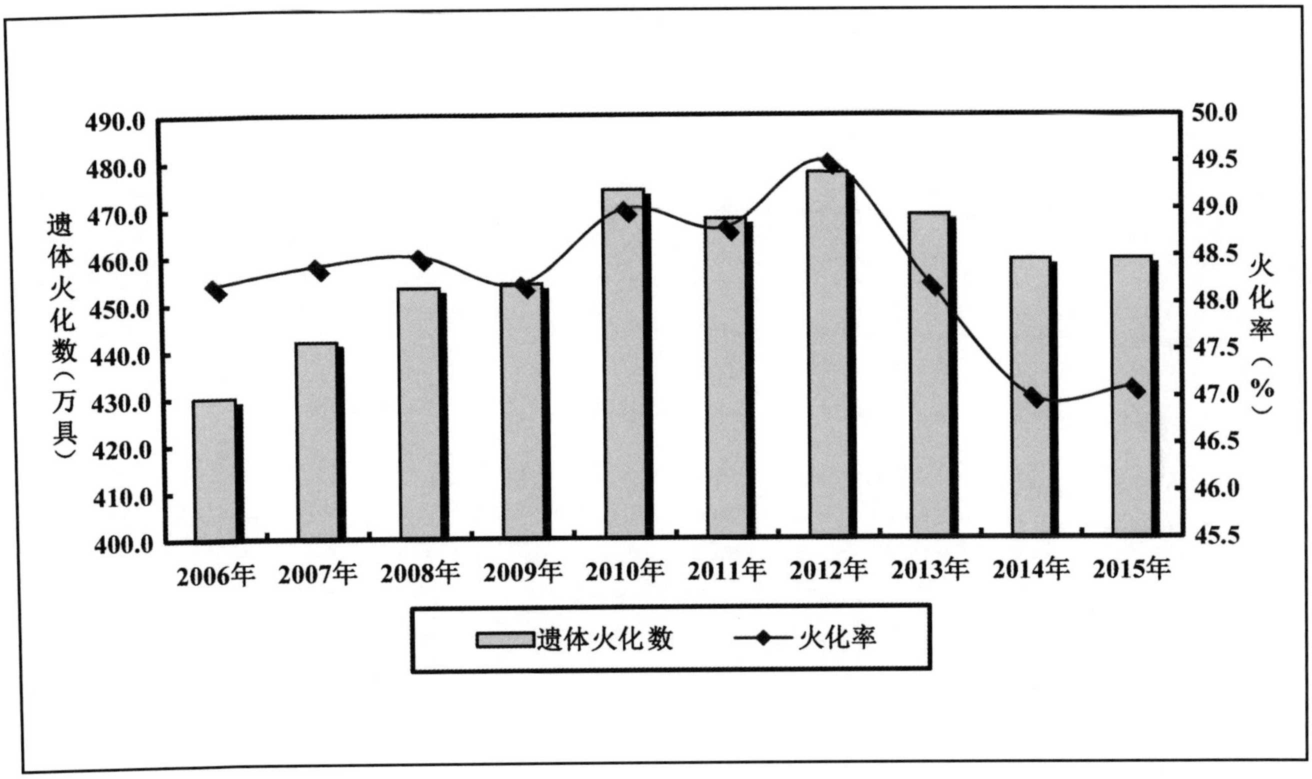

单位：万具、%

指　标	2006年	2007年	2008年	2009年	2010年	2011年	2012年	2013年	2014年	2015年
遗体火化数	430.2	442.1	453.4	454.2	474.1	468.1	477.7	468.9	459.3	459.5
火化率	48.2	48.4	48.5	48.2	49.0	48.8	49.5	48.2	47.0	47.1

03

社会服务综合统计资料

A-1-1 “七五”—“十二五”时期社会服务发展速度

单位：%

指　标	“七五”时期平均增长速度	“八五”时期平均增长速度	“九五”时期平均增长速度	“十五”时期平均每年增长速度	“十一五”时期平均增长速度	“十二五”时期平均增长速度
一、综合						
行政区划						
镇	5.7	7.7	3.0	-0.8	-0.1	1.1
乡	-11.6	-7.8	-4.7	-7.2	-1.8	-4.9
60岁及以上老年人口					4.3	4.6
事业费支出	11.9	14.8	17.3	25.6	30.3	12.8
固定资产原价	20.8	22.5	53.1	9.9	16.3	4.4
二、社会工作						
社会服务床位	9.7	4.6	3.0	7.7	13.8	14.6
# 养老床位				5.0	15.3	16.3
智障和精神疾病床位				10.0	8.8	6.7
儿童床位				11.7	11.5	21.2
家庭收养				-2.0	-7.5	-8.9
福利企业	23.0	7.6	-7.6	-5.2	-6.6	-7.4
福利彩票		54.5	14.6	29.4	18.7	15.8
城市最低生活保障				40.9	0.7	-5.9
优抚对象	8.5	1.1	-0.3	0.8	6.3	7.5
社区服务中心			8.0	5.6	8.2	13.7
三、成员组织和其他社会服务						
社会组织		75.5	-3.2	15.8	6.9	8.2
社会团体				5.6	7.5	6.1
基金会					17.7	16.8
民办非企业单位				45.5	6.1	10.7
自治组织						
村民委员会	1.1	-6.9	-4.7	-3.0	-1.1	-0.5
社区居委会	4.1	2.5	-0.6	-5.9	1.7	2.8
婚姻						
办理结婚登记	2.7	-0.4	-0.2	-0.6	8.6	-0.3
办理离婚登记	11.7	5.7	2.8	8.0	8.5	7.5
殡葬						
遗体火化数	5.3	5.5	7.3	3.8	1	-0.6

A-1-2 社会服务发展主要指标预期值

指　标	单　位	2016年预期值	2020年预期值	2030年预期值
一、综合				
行政区划				
镇	万个	2.1	2.2	2.5
乡	万个	1.2	0.9	0.6
人口	万人	137408.9	140808.9	147863.4
60岁及以上老年人口	万人	22243.9	27453.5	42425.8
事业费支出	亿元	5814.4	12532.9	58229.3
固定资产原价	亿元	7401.2	7354.9	8209.4
二、社会工作				
社会服务床位	万张	710.8	1192.4	4661.2
# 养老床位	万张	655.5	1148.3	5198.4
智障和精神疾病床位	万张	8.6	12.2	25.1
儿童床位	万张	12.6	18.9	48.5
家庭收养	万件	1.9	1.0	0.3
福利企业	万个	1.4	1.1	0.6
福利彩票	亿元	2414.9	7172.8	53149.2
城市最低生活保障	万人	1760.0	1586.8	1089.8
优抚对象	万人	940.0	1290.7	1998.1
社区服务中心	万个	2.8	5.7	25.2
三、成员组织和其他社会服务				
社会组织	万个	66.3	88.1	173.9
社会团体	万个	33.1	42.5	73.7
基金会	万个	4.8	1.1	5.3
民办非企业单位	万个	32.9	46.0	106.9
自治组织				
村民委员会	万个	58.3	57.5	55.6
社区居委会	万个	10.0	11.7	15.6
婚姻				
办理结婚登记	万对	1308.1	1630.5	2142.2
办理离婚登记	万对	393.4	653.6	1595.4
殡葬				
遗体火化数	万具	456.4	618.4	918.4

注：发展速度为“十二五”时期平均增长速度，其中床位数、优抚对象和遗体火化数用的是1978年至2014年的平均速度。

A-1-3 2011-2015年社会服务发展主要指标数据

指 标	单 位	2011年	2012年	2013年	2014年	2015年
一、综合						
乡镇级行政区划						
镇	个	19683	19881	20117	20401	20515
乡	个	13587	13281	12812	12282	11315
# 民族乡	个	1086	1064	1035	1020	991
街道办事处	个	7194	7282	7566	7696	7957
区公所	个	2	2	2	2	2
社会服务基本情况						
机构和设施	万个	129.4	136.7	156.2	166.8	176.5
职工人数	万人	1120.8	1144.7	1197.6	1251.0	1308.9
固定资产原价	亿元	6676.7	6675.4	6810.2	7213.0	8183.1
基本建设投资	亿元	218.5	234.7	292.8	282.2	239.9
# 预算内投资	亿元	78.5	104.2	120.1	104.3	92.8
公益金投资	亿元	53.4	51.1	64.7	57.5	61.7
预算内基本建设投资占事业费比重	%	2.4	2.8	2.8	2.4	1.9
公益金基本建设投资占公益金支出的比重	%	41.8	32.1	33.1	24.9	21.4
事业费	亿元	3229.1	3683.7	4276.5	4404.1	4926.4
# 抚恤	亿元	428.3	517.0	618.4	636.6	686.8
退役安置	亿元	302.3	372.1	435.3	456.8	582.7
社会福利	亿元	232.2	319.5	397.6	480.9	562.8
社会救助	亿元	1766.3	1866.1	2172.4	2197.5	2347.4
自然灾害生活救助	亿元	128.7	163.4	178.7	124.4	148.5
民政管理事务	亿元	220.7	248.4	296.7	308.3	399.6
离退休人员经费	亿元	35.3	39.0	43.6	44.2	50.1
其他	亿元	115.3	158.3	133.9	155.3	148.5
# 公益金支出	亿元	127.9	159.0	195.5	231.3	288.9
中央转移支付的事业费占全国总事业费比重	%	56.0	48.7	50.3	47.8	46.1
全国总事业费占财政支出的比重	%	3.0	3.0	3.1	2.9	3.3
二、社会工作						
提供住宿的社会服务						
机构数	万个	4.6	4.8	4.6	3.7	3.1
机构和设施各类床位数	万张	396.4	449.4	526.7	613.5	732.9
# 养老机构和设施床位数	万张	369.2	416.5	493.7	577.8	672.7
机构和设施收养人数	万人	293.4	309.5	322.5	336.8	330.8
每千人口社会服务床位数	张	2.9	3.3	3.9	4.5	5.3
每千老年人口养老床位数	张	20.0	21.5	24.4	27.2	30.3
不提供住宿的社会服务						
机构和设施数	万个	10.0	13.3	27.7	33.4	38.2
老龄人口						
60岁及以上老年人口	万人	18499	19390	20243	21242	22200
占全国总人口	%	13.7	14.3	14.9	15.5	16.1

A-1-3续表1

指　标	单　位	2011年	2012年	2013年	2014年	2015年
儿童						
孤儿数	万人	49.1	57.0	54.9	52.5	50.2
家庭收养	万人	3.1	2.7	2.4	2.3	2.2
流浪儿童救助	万人次	17.9	15.2	18.4	17.0	16.7
残疾人						
为残疾人提供服务的机构数	万个	2.2	2.0	1.8	1.6	1.5
残疾职工数	万人	62.8	59.7	53.9	47.9	42.9
社会救助						
最低生活保障						
城市最低生活保障人数	万人	2276.8	2143.5	2064.2	1877.0	1701.1
城市最低生活保障户数	万户	1145.7	1114.9	1097.2	1026.1	957.4
城市最低生活保障平均标准	元/人·月	287.6	330.1	373.3	410.5	451.1
城市最低生活保障平均支出水平	元/人·月	240.3	239.1	264.2	285.6	316.6
农村最低生活保障人数	万人	5305.7	5344.5	5388.0	5207.2	4903.6
农村最低生活保障户数	万户	2672.8	2814.9	2931.1	2943.6	2846.2
农村最低生活保障平均标准	元/人·年	1718.4	2067.8	2433.9	2776.6	3177.6
农村最低生活保障平均支出水平	元/人·年	1273.2	1247.9	1393.5	1552.3	1766.5
农村特困人员救助供养	万人	551.0	545.6	537.3	529.1	516.7
集中供养人数	万人	184.5	185.3	183.5	174.3	162.3
集中供养平均标准	元/人·年	3399.7	4060.9	4685.0	5371.3	6025.7
集中供养平均支出水平	元/人·年	3081.9	3496.6	4078.3	4676.1	4790.4
分散供养人数	万人	366.5	360.3	353.8	354.8	354.4
分散供养平均标准	元/人·年	2470.5	3008.0	3498.5	4005.9	4490.1
分散供养平均支出水平	元/人·年	1774.9	2237.3	2724.3	3228.9	3674.3
医疗救助						
直接医疗救助	万人次	2144.0	2173.7	2126.4	2395.3	2889.1
资助参加医疗保险	万人	6375.1	5877.5	6358.8	6723.7	6634.7
生活无着人员救助						
生活无着人员救助	万人次	241.0	276.6	348.5	351.7	375.2
为弱势群体筹集资金的活动						
民政部门接收赠款数	亿元	96.6	101.7	107.6	79.6	44.2
民政部门接收捐赠衣被数	亿件	0.3	1.3	1.0	0.5	0.5
民政部门接收捐赠其他物资价值	亿元	4.8	6.3	8.7	8.0	5.2
受益人次数	万人次	1459.7	1325.0	1246.0	1694.9	1838.4
社会捐赠接收站、点数	万个	3.4	3.1	3.1	3.2	3.0
销售福利彩票	亿元	1278.0	1510.3	1765.3	2059.7	2015.1
筹集社会福利基金	亿元	382.0	449.4	510.7	585.7	563.8

A-1-3续表2

指　标	单　位	2011年	2012年	2013年	2014年	2015年
优抚安置						
国家抚恤、补助各类优抚对象	万人	852.5	944.4	950.5	917.3	897.0
接收军队离退休人员人数	万人	1.5	1.9	3.9	2.8	1.9
社区服务						
社区服务机构和设施	万个	16.0	20.0	25.2	31.1	36.1
# 社区服务中心	个	14391	16306	19904	24006	24138
社区服务站	个	56156	87931	108377	120188	128083
社区服务机构和设施覆盖率	%	23.6	29.5	36.9	45.5	52.9
便民、利民网点	万个	45.3	39.7	35.9	30.9	24.9
自然灾害情况						
受灾人口	万人次	43290.0	29421.7	38818.7	24353.7	18620.3
因灾死亡（含失踪）人口	人	1126	1530	2284	1818	967
直接经济损失	亿元	3096.4	4185.5	5808.4	3373.8	2704.1
三、成员组织和其他社会服务						
社会组织	万个	46.2	49.9	54.7	60.6	66.2
社会团体	万个	25.5	27.1	28.9	31.0	32.9
基金会	个	2614	3029	3549	4117	4784
民办非企业单位	万个	20.4	22.5	25.5	29.2	32.9
社会组织接收捐款数	亿元	393.5	470.8	458.8	524.8	610.3
自治组织	万个	67.9	67.9	68.3	68.2	68.1
村委会	万个	59.0	58.8	58.9	58.5	58.1
居委会	万个	8.9	9.1	9.5	9.7	10.0
婚姻服务						
结婚登记	万对	1302.4	1323.6	1346.9	1306.7	1224.7
# 涉外及华侨、港澳台	万对	4.9	5.3	5.5	4.7	4.1
结婚率	‰	9.7	9.8	9.9	9.6	9.0
离婚登记	万对	287.4	310.4	350.0	363.7	384.1
离婚率	‰	2.1	2.3	2.6	2.7	2.8
殡葬服务						
遗体火化数	万具	468.1	477.7	468.9	459.3	459.5
火化率	%	48.8	49.5	48.2	47.0	47.1

A-1-4 社会服务发展主要数据与上年比较

指　标	单　位	2015年	2014年	比上年增长(%)
一、综合				
行政区划				
镇	个	20515	20401	0.6
乡	个	11315	12282	-7.9
# 民族乡	个	991	1020	-2.8
街道办事处	个	7957	7696	3.4
区公所	个	2	2	
老龄人口				
60岁及以上老年人口	万人	22200	21242	4.5
占全国总人口	%	16.1	15.5	0.6(百分点)
65岁及以上老年人口	万人	14386	13755	4.6
占全国总人口	%	10.5	10.1	0.4(百分点)
资产				
社会服务事业费总支出	亿元	4926.4	4404.1	11.9
# 抚恤	亿元	686.8	636.6	7.9
退役安置	亿元	582.7	456.8	27.6
社会福利	亿元	562.8	481.0	17.0
社会救助	亿元	2347.4	2197.5	6.8
自然灾害生活救助	亿元	148.5	124.4	19.4
民政管理事务	亿元	399.6	330.5	20.9
行政事业单位离退休	亿元	50.1	44.2	13.3
其他	亿元	148.5	133.1	11.6
基本建设支出	亿元	239.9	282.2	-15.0
固定资产原价	亿元	8183.1	7213.0	13.4
二、社会工作				
提供住宿的社会服务机构				
单位数	万个	3.1	3.7	-16.2
床位数	万张	393.2	397.0	-1.0
收养人数	万人	236.3	255.4	-9.3
每千人口社会服务床位数	张	5.3	4.5	17.8

A-1-4续表1

指　标	单　位	2015年	2014年	比上年增长(%)
社会救助				
城市				
城市最低生活保障人数	万人	1701.1	1877.0	-9.4
城市最低生活保障户数	万户	957.4	1026.1	-6.7
城市最低生活保障平均标准	元/人·月	451.1	410.5	9.9
城市最低生活保障平均支出水平	元/人·月	316.6	285.6	10.9
农村				
农村最低生活保障人数	万人	4903.6	5207.2	-5.8
农村最低生活保障户数	万户	2846.2	2943.6	-3.3
农村最低生活保障平均标准	元/人·年	3177.6	2776.6	14.4
农村最低生活保障平均支出水平	元/人·年	1766.5	1552.3	13.8
农村特困供养				
农村特困人员供养总人数	万人	516.7	529.1	-2.3
集中供养人数	万人	162.3	174.3	-6.9
集中供养平均标准	元/人·年	6025.7	5371.3	12.2
集中供养平均支出水平	元/人·年	4790.7	4676.1	2.5
分散供养人数	万人	354.4	354.8	-0.1
分散供养平均标准	元/人·年	4490.1	4005.9	12.1
分散供养平均支出水平	元/人·年	3674.3	3228.9	13.8
医疗救助				
直接医疗救助	万人次	2889.1	2395.3	20.6
资助参加医疗保险	万人	6634.7	6723.7	-1.3
儿童收养				
家庭收养	万人	2.2	2.3	-4.3
为残疾人提供服务的机构				
为残疾人提供服务的机构数	万个	1.5	1.6	-6.3
残疾职工人数	万人	42.9	47.9	-10.4
福利彩票				
销售福利彩票	亿元	2015.1	2059.7	-2.2
筹集社会公益金	亿元	563.8	585.7	-3.7
优抚安置				
国家抚恤、补助各类优抚对象	万人	897.0	917.3	-2.2
接收军队离退休人员人数	万人	1.9	2.8	-32.1

A-1-4续表2

指　标	单　位	2015年	2014年	比上年增长(%)
社会捐赠				
社会捐赠款数	亿元	44.2	79.6	-44.5
捐赠衣被总数	亿件	0.5	0.5	
捐赠其他物资价值	亿元	5.2	8.0	-35.0
受益人次数	万人次	1838.4	1694.9	8.5
社会捐赠接收站、点数	万个	3.0	3.2	-6.3
社区服务机构和设施				
社区服务机构和设施总数	个	360956	310652	16.2
社区服务指导中心	个	863	918	-6.0
社区服务中心	个	24138	23088	4.5
社区服务站	个	128083	120188	6.6
社区养老机构和设施	个	26067	18927	37.7
社区互助型养老设施	个	62027	40357	53.7
其他	个	119778	107174	11.8
社区服务机构和设施覆盖率	%	52.9	45.5	7.4(百分点)
便民利民网点	个	24.9	30.9	-19.4
三、成员组织和其他社会服务				
社会组织				
社会组织总数	万个	66.2	60.6	9.2
社会团体	万个	32.9	31.0	6.1
基金会	个	4784	4116	16.2
民办非企业	万个	32.9	29.2	10.1
自治组织				
村委会	万个	58.1	58.5	-0.7
居委会	万个	10.0	9.7	3.1
婚姻				
结婚登记	万对	1224.7	1306.7	-6.3
# 涉外及华侨、港澳台	万对	4.1	4.7	-12.8
结婚率	‰	9.0	9.6	-0.6(千分点)
离婚登记	万对	384.1	363.7	5.6
离婚率	‰	2.8	2.7	0.1 (千分点)
殡葬				
遗体火化数	万具	459.5	459.3	
火化率	%	47.1	47.0	0.1(百分点)

A-1-5 行政区划与上年比较

单位：个

指 标	2015年	2014年	比上年增长(%)
地级行政区划合计	**334**	**333**	**0.3**
# 地级市	291	288	1.0
地区	10	12	-16.7
自治州	30	30	
盟	3	3	
县级行政区划合计	**2850**	**2854**	**-0.1**
# 市辖区	921	897	2.7
县级市	361	361	
县	1397	1425	-2.0
自治县	117	117	
旗	49	49	
自治旗	3	3	
特区	1	1	
林区	1	1	
乡镇、街道级行政区划合计	**39789**	**40381**	**-1.5**
# 镇	20515	20401	0.6
乡	11315	12282	-7.9
苏木	152	151	0.7
民族乡	990	1020	-2.9
民族苏木	1	1	
街道办事处	7957	7696	3.4
区公所	2	2	

A-1-6 社会服务机构和设施与上年比较

单位：个

指　标	2015年	2014年	比上年增长(%)
社会服务	**1765004**	**1668143**	**5.8**
一、社会工作	**413372**	**370893**	**11.5**
提供住宿的社会服务机构	**31187**	**36810**	**-15.3**
老年人与残疾人服务机构	**27752**	**33043**	**-16.0**
城市养老服务机构	7656	7642	0.2
农村养老服务机构	15587	20261	-23.1
社会福利院	1717	1864	-7.9
光荣院	1106	1411	-21.6
荣誉军人康复医院	46	44	4.5
复员军人疗养院	36	38	-5.3
军休所	1604	1783	-10.0
智障与精神疾病服务机构	**242**	**254**	**-4.7**
社会福利医院	151	156	-3.2
复退军人精神病院	91	98	-7.1
儿童收养救助服务机构	**753**	**890**	**-15.4**
儿童福利机构	478	545	-12.3
未成年人救助保护中心	275	345	-20.3
其他提供住宿的服务机构	**2440**	**2623**	**-7.0**
生活无着人员救助管理站	1766	1949	-9.4
安置农场	15	13	15.4
军供站	320	327	-2.1
其他提供住宿的机构	339	334	1.5

A-1-6续表

单位：个

指　标	2015年	2014年	比上年增长(%)
不提供住宿的社会服务机构	**382185**	**334083**	**14.4**
老龄机构	2280	2558	-10.9
为残疾人提供服务的机构	14585	16389	-11.0
救助低保服务机构	965	992	-2.7
救灾储备机构	776	868	-10.6
福利彩票发行机构	861	893	-3.6
军队离退休人员管理中心	271	185	46.5
军队离退休人员活动中心	27	30	-10.0
烈士纪念建筑物管理机构	1464	1516	-3.4
社区服务机构和设施	360956	310652	16.2
二、成员组织和其他社会服务	**1349554**	**1294987**	**4.2**
成员组织	**1342960**	**1288192**	**4.3**
社会组织	**662425**	**606048**	**9.3**
社会团体	328500	309736	6.1
基金会	4784	4117	16.2
民办非企业	329141	292195	12.6
自治组织	**680535**	**682144**	**-0.2**
居委会	99679	96693	3.1
村委会	580856	585451	-0.8
其他社会服务	**6594**	**6795**	**-3.0**
婚姻服务机构	**2064**	**2236**	**6.9**
殡葬服务机构	**4530**	**4559**	**-0.6**
殡仪馆	1821	1801	1.1
公墓	1567	1598	-1.9
骨灰堂	15	19	-21.1
殡葬管理单位	1127	1141	-1.2
三、其他事业单位	**2078**	**2263**	**-8.2**
行政机关	**3482**	**3491**	**-0.3**

A－1－7 社会服务机构和设施职工与上年比较

单位：万人

指　标	2015年	2014年	比上年增长(%)
社会服务	**1308.9**	**1251.1**	**4.6**
一、社会工作	**281.9**	**277.3**	**1.7**
提供住宿的社会服务机构	**38.4**	**40.4**	**-5.0**
老年人与残疾人服务机构	**31.8**	**33.4**	**-4.8**
城市养老服务机构	13.2	12.2	8.2
农村养老服务机构	10.9	13.0	-16.2
社会福利院	4.3	4.5	-4.4
光荣院	0.9	1.2	-25.0
荣誉军人康复医院	0.6	0.5	20.0
复员军人疗养院	0.3	0.3	-
军休所	1.6	1.7	-5.9
智障与精神疾病服务机构	**2.5**	**2.6**	**-3.8**
社会福利医院	1.4	1.4	-
复退军人精神病院	1.1	1.2	-8.3
儿童收养救助服务机构	**1.4**	**1.5**	**-6.7**
儿童福利机构	1.2	1.3	-7.7
未成年人救助保护中心	0.2	0.2	-
其他提供住宿的服务机构	**2.7**	**2.9**	**-6.9**
生活无着人员救助管理站	1.7	1.8	-5.6
安置农场	-	-	-
军供站	0.5	0.5	-
其他提供住宿的机构	0.5	0.6	-16.7

A–1–7续表

单位：万人

指　标	2015年	2014年	比上年增长(%)
不提供住宿的社会服务机构	**243.5**	**236.8**	**2.8**
老龄机构	0.9	1.0	-10.0
为残疾人提供服务的机构	111.3	125.4	-11.2
救助低保服务机构	0.8	0.7	14.3
救灾储备单位	0.2	0.2	-
福利彩票发行机构	1.2	1.1	9.1
军队离退休人员管理中心	0.4	0.2	100.0
军队离退休人员活动中心	0.1	0.1	-
烈士纪念建筑物管理机构	1.0	1.0	-
社区服务机构和设施	127.6	107.1	19.2
二、成员组织和其他社会服务	**1025.2**	**971.8**	**5.5**
成员组织	**1015.7**	**962.5**	**5.5**
社会组织	**734.8**	**682.3**	**7.7**
社会团体	390.2	373.6	4.4
基金会	2.5	2.0	25.1
民办非企业	342.1	306.6	11.6
自治组织	**280.9**	**280.2**	**0.3**
居委会	51.2	49.7	3.1
村委会	229.7	230.5	-0.3
其他社会服务	**9.5**	**9.3**	**2.2**
婚姻服务机构	**1.0**	**1.0**	**3.7**
殡葬服务机构	**8.5**	**8.3**	**2.4**
殡仪馆	4.7	4.6	1.6
公墓	2.7	2.7	1.0
骨灰堂	0.1	-	-
殡葬管理单位	1.0	1.0	-2.4
三、其他事业单位	**1.8**	**2.0**	**-10.0**
行政机关	**9.5**	**9.5**	**0.1**

A-1-8 社会服务机构和设施中社会工作师人员情况

单位：人

指 标	社会工作师			助理社会工作师		
	2015年	2014年	比上年增长(%)	2015年	2014年	比上年增长(%)
社会服务	**44480**	**25782**	**72.5**	**52104**	**50770**	**2.6**
一、社会工作	**12931**	**10252**	**26.1**	**19588**	**18295**	**7.1**
提供住宿的社会服务机构	**4461**	**3795**	**17.5**	**4624**	**4070**	**13.6**
老年人与残疾人服务机构	**3009**	**2567**	**17.2**	**3363**	**2839**	**18.5**
城市养老服务机构	905	650	39.2	1345	926	45.2
农村养老服务机构	396	407	-2.7	401	397	1.0
社会福利院	1020	867	17.6	1108	968	14.5
光荣院	135	149	-9.4	118	164	-28.0
荣誉军人康复医院	65	69	-5.8	40	47	-14.9
复员军人疗养院	69	42	64.3	30	13	130.8
军休所	419	383	9.4	321	324	-0.9
智障与精神疾病服务机构	**246**	**218**	**12.8**	**238**	**265**	**-10.2**
社会福利医院	139	117	18.8	123	124	-0.8
复退军人精神病院	107	101	5.9	115	141	-18.4
儿童收养救助服务机构	**543**	**466**	**16.5**	**398**	**394**	**1.0**
儿童福利机构	492	421	16.9	344	334	3.0
未成年人救助保护中心	51	45	13.3	54	60	-10.0
其他提供住宿的服务机构	**663**	**544**	**21.9**	**625**	**572**	**9.3**
生活无着人员救助管理站	535	464	15.3	490	455	7.7
安置农场	39			27	6	350.0
军供站	51	46	10.9	54	56	-3.6
其他提供住宿的机构	38	34	11.8	54	55	-1.8

A–1–8续表

单位：人

指　标	社会工作师			助理社会工作师		
	2015年	2014年	比上年增长(%)	2015年	2014年	比上年增长(%)
不提供住宿的社会服务机构	**8470**	**6457**	**31.2**	**14964**	**14255**	**5.0**
老龄机构	141	140	0.7	102	92	10.9
救助低保服务机构	155	136	14.0	140	112	25.0
救灾储备单位	40	38	5.3	40	29	37.9
福利彩票发行机构	125	104	20.2	184	152	21.1
军队离退休人员管理中心	110	72	52.8	84	45	86.7
军队离退休人员活动中心	4	4		4	6	-33.3
烈士纪念建筑物管理机构	183	172	6.4	115	117	-1.7
社区服务机构和设施	7712	4946	55.9	14295	11802	21.1
二、成员组织和其他社会服务	**31141**	**14442**	**115.6**	**32232**	**32184**	**-2.5**
成员组织	**30385**	**14442**	**110.4**	**31381**	**31381**	
社会组织	**24206**	**9324**	**159.6**	**16651**	**16651**	
社会团体	12050	3537	240.7	8298	7360	12.7
基金会	233	76	206.6	343	90	281.1
民办非企业	11923	5711	108.8	12868	9201	39.9
自治组织	**6179**	**5118**	**20.7**	**16833**	**14730**	**14.3**
居委会	557	4602	-87.9	1700	13151	-87.1
村委会	5622	516	989.5	15133	1579	858.4
其他社会服务	**756**	**681**	**11.0**	**851**	**803**	**6.0**
婚姻服务机构	**205**	**200**	**2.5**	**194**	**173**	**12.1**
殡葬服务机构	**551**	**481**	**14.6**	**657**	**630**	**4.3**
殡仪馆	278	239	16.3	404	367	10.1
公墓	137	107	28.0	166	161	3.1
殡葬管理单位	136	135	0.7	87	102	-14.7
三、其他事业单位	**408**	**407**	**0.2**	**284**	**291**	**-2.4**
行政机关	**1787**	**1475**	**21.2**	**1630**	**1404**	**16.1**

A-1-9 性别统计情况

指　标	职工总数（人）		女性占比（%）	比上年增长（百分点）
		#女性		
社会服务	**13089248**	**4128377**	**31.5**	**0.8**
一、社会工作	**2820819**	**1070394**	**37.9**	**0.5**
提供住宿的社会服务机构	**385951**	**216236**	**56.0**	**1.3**
老年人与残疾人服务机构	**318240**	**180915**	**56.8**	**1.5**
城市养老服务机构	132296	83927	63.4	0.9
农村养老服务机构	109350	54078	49.5	0.7
社会福利院	43411	26903	62.0	0.6
光荣院	9407	4478	47.6	0.5
荣誉军人康复医院	5566	3045	54.7	-0.2
复员军人疗养院	2639	1481	56.1	1.0
军休所	15571	7003	45.0	1.0
智障与精神疾病服务机构	**25736**	**15278**	**59.4**	**1.5**
社会福利医院	14393	8357	58.1	1.4
复退军人精神病院	11343	6921	61.0	1.6
儿童收养救助服务机构	**13789**	**8903**	**64.6**	**0.2**
儿童福利机构	12038	8235	68.4	
未成年人救助保护中心	1751	668	38.1	-1.4
其他提供住宿的服务机构	**28186**	**1140**	**39.5**	
生活无着人员救助管理站	17419	5939	34.1	0.6
安置农场	590	181	30.7	1.2
军供站	5201	2023	38.9	-0.1
其他提供住宿的机构	4976	2997	60.2	-2.6

A-1-9续表

指　标	职工总数（人）	#女性	女性占比（%）	比上年增长（百分点）
不提供住宿的社会服务机构	**2434868**	**854158**	**35.1**	**0.6**
老龄机构	9316	4082	43.8	-0.1
为残疾人提供服务的机构	1113183	367219	33.0	0.8
救助低保服务机构	7651	3428	44.8	0.6
救灾储备单位	2288	724	31.6	0.9
福利彩票发行机构	11972	5114	42.7	1.6
军队离退休人员管理中心	3696	1650	44.6	-1.9
军队离退休人员活动中心	584	238	40.8	1.7
烈士纪念建筑物管理机构	10050	3948	39.3	-0.2
社区服务机构和设施	1276128	467755	36.7	-0.3
二、成员组织和其他社会服务	**10251373**	**3050199**	**29.8**	**0.9**
成员组织	**10157149**	**3019335**	**29.7**	**0.9**
社会组织	**7347892**	**2241648**	**30.5**	**1.1**
社会团体	3901849	912812	23.4	1.6
基金会	25028	7251	29.0	2.4
民办非企业	3421015	1321585	38.6	0.1
自治组织	**2809257**	**777687**	**27.7**	**0.3**
居委会	512196	251946	49.2	0.8
村委会	2297061	525741	22.9	0.1
其他社会服务	**94224**	**30864**	**32.8**	**0.6**
婚姻服务机构	**10373**	**6734**	**64.9**	**-0.7**
殡葬服务机构	**83851**	**24130**	**28.8**	**1.0**
殡仪馆	46725	12108	25.9	0.5
公墓	27277	9412	34.5	1.7
骨灰堂	90	18		
殡葬管理单位	9759	2592	26.6	1.2
三、其他事业单位	**17056**	**7784**	**45.6**	**1.3**
行政机关	**95141**	**31254**	**32.9**	**0.8**

A-1-10 社会服务机构固定资产原价与上年比较

单位：亿元

指　标	2015年	2014年	比上年增长(%)
社会服务	**8183.1**	**7213.0**	**13.4**
一、社会工作	**2892.1**	**3273.0**	**-11.6**
提供住宿的社会服务机构	**868.2**	**859.2**	**1.0**
老年人与残疾人服务机构	**726.0**	**719.0**	**1.0**
城市养老服务机构	260.6	233.7	11.5
农村养老服务机构	243.9	269.8	-9.6
社会福利院	131.3	123.7	6.1
光荣院	18.3	25.1	-27.1
荣誉军人康复医院	23.2	21.4	8.4
复员军人疗养院	11.9	8.7	36.8
军休所	36.8	36.6	0.5
智障与精神疾病服务机构	**49.1**	**46.9**	**4.7**
社会福利医院	26.9	24.9	8.0
复退军人精神病院	22.2	22.0	0.9
儿童收养救助服务机构	**37.6**	**38.2**	**-1.6**
儿童福利机构	35.5	34.1	4.1
未成年人救助保护中心	2.1	4.1	-48.8
其他提供住宿的服务机构	**55.5**	**55.4**	**0.2**
生活无着人员救助管理站	31.6	33.7	-6.2
安置农场	0.7	0.3	133.3
军供站	15.8	13.8	14.5
其他提供住宿的机构	7.4	7.5	-1.3

A-1-10续表

单位：亿元

指　标	2015年	2014年	比上年增长(%)
不提供住宿的社会服务机构	**2023.9**	**2413.8**	**-16.2**
老龄机构	8.3	7.9	5.1
为残疾人提供服务的机构	1778.8	1789.5	-0.6
救助低保服务机构	1.6	1.5	6.7
救灾储备单位	11.8	12.0	-1.7
福利彩票发行机构	76.0	69.7	9.0
军队离退休人员管理中心	17.2	14.2	21.1
军队离退休人员活动中心	7.2	7.0	2.9
烈士纪念建筑物管理机构	52.6	51.2	2.7
社区服务机构和设施	70.4	460.8	-84.7
二、成员组织和其他社会服务	**5242.4**	**3893.1**	**34.7**
成员组织	**4950.4**	**3609.3**	**37.2**
社会组织	**2311.1**	**1560.6**	**48.1**
社会团体	379.6	337.7	12.4
基金会	35.8	24.5	46.1
民办非企业	1895.7	1198.4	58.2
自治组织	**2639.3**	**2048.6**	**28.8**
居委会	485.5	372.2	30.4
村委会	2153.8	1676.4	28.5
其他社会服务	**292.0**	**283.8**	**2.9**
婚姻服务机构	**8.0**	**9.4**	**-14.9**
殡葬服务机构	**284.0**	**270.5**	**5.0**
殡仪馆	174.8	166.1	5.2
公墓	87.4	82.3	6.2
骨灰堂	0.7		6900.0
殡葬管理单位	21.1	22.1	-4.5
三、其他事业单位	**48.5**	**46.8**	**3.6**
行政机关	**251.5**	**168.3**	**49.4**

A-1-11 基本建设投资与上年比较

单位：亿元、万平方米

指 标	2015年	2014年	比上年增长(%)
计划总投资	**882.9**	**915.2**	**-3.5**
本年计划投资	**217.2**	**266.0**	**-18.4**
#提供住宿的社会服务机构	128.9	147.4	-12.6
老年人与残疾人服务机构	107.4	128.5	-16.4
智障与精神疾病服务机构	9.7	6.2	56.7
儿童收养救助服务机构	8.4	8.1	3.2
其他提供住宿的服务机构	3.4	4.6	-26.2
不提供住宿的社会服务机构	32.5	36.1	-9.9
其他	55.7	35.3	57.8
开工累计完成投资	**450.2**	**501.3**	**-10.2**
本年实际完成投资	**239.9**	**282.2**	**-15.0**
#提供住宿的社会服务机构	147.4	156	-5.5
老年人与残疾人服务机构	123.8	134.2	-7.7
智障与精神疾病服务机构	9.5	6.5	45.4
儿童收养救助服务机构	10.4	10.4	0.4
其他提供住宿的服务机构	3.6	4.9	-25.9
不提供住宿的社会服务机构	36.9	41.5	-11.0
其他	55.6	84.7	-34.4
国家预算内投资	92.8	104.3	-11.0
国内贷款	4.7	3.5	34.8
利用外资	0.8	1.7	-53.5
福利彩票公益金	61.7	57.5	7.2
其他	79.9	115.3	-30.7
本年完工项目规模	**1048.4**		

A-1-12 社会服务事业费与上年比较

单位：亿元

指　标	2015年	2014年	比上年增长(%)
社会服务事业费合计	**4926.4**	**4404.0**	**11.9**
占国家财政支出比重（%）	3.3	2.9	0.4(百分点)
# 中央转移支付的事业费	2270.3	2105.0	7.9
占社会服务事业费的比重（%）	46.1	47.8	-1.7
# 国家预算内基本建设投资	92.8	104.3	-11.0
# 公益金支出	288.9	231.3	24.9
按支出性质分			
抚恤	686.8	636.6	7.9
退役安置	582.7	456.8	27.6
社会福利	562.8	480.9	17.0
社会救助	2347.4	2197.5	6.8
# 最低生活保障	1650.8	1592.0	3.7
临时救助	106.2	57.6	84.4
特困人员供养	214.9	189.8	13.2
其他社会救助	71.8	74.2	-3.2
医疗救助	303.7	284.0	6.9
自然灾害生活救助	148.5	124.4	19.4
民政管理事务	399.6	330.5	20.9
行政事业单位离退休	50.1	44.2	13.3
其他	148.5	133.1	11.6

A-1-13 中央财政转移支付的社会服务事业费与上年比较

单位：亿元

指　标	2015年	2014年	比上年增长(%)
中央财政转移支付的社会服务事业费合计	**2270.3**	**2105.0**	**7.8**
# 抚恤	350.0	338.0	3.6
退役安置	352.9	288.8	22.2
社会福利	73.0	63.4	15.1
社会救助	1391.6	1318.3	5.6
# 最低生活保障	1166.7	1101.3	5.9
临时救助	41.0	32.0	28.1
医疗救助	163.9	165.0	-0.7
生活无着人员救助	20.0	20.0	0.0
自然灾害生活救助	94.6	96.3	-1.8
民政管理事务	8.1	0.2	3950.0
# 预算内基本建设投资	32.0	29.0	10.3
# 养老服务	28.0	24.4	14.8
社区服务	2.0	2.0	2.0
儿童福利	2.0	2.0	0.0
# 公益金支出	52.4	40.6	29.1

A-1-14 按支出形式分类的社会服务事业费支出情况

单位：亿元

指 标	2015年	2014年	占全部（%）	比上年增长额	比上年增长（%）
总计	**4926.4**	**4404.1**	**100.0**	**522.3**	**11.86**
直接发放	**3918.8**	**3542.4**	**79.6**	**376.3**	**10.62**
按标准发放和报销	2959.7	2674.0	60.1	285.7	10.68
发放数	2904.0	2619.1	59.0	284.9	10.88
定期发放	2874.2	2590.8	58.3	283.4	10.94
军队干部离休金	41.5	30.4	0.8	11.1	36.59
军队干部退休金	214.0	167.2	4.3	46.7	27.96
军队无军籍退休金	58.9	42.4	1.2	16.5	39.01
地方干部、人员退休金、退职金	12.2	12.3	0.3	-0.1	-0.6
离休、退休、退职金小计	326.6	252.2	6.6	74.3	29.47
烈属和牺牲病故定期抚恤金	34.9	34.8	0.7	0.0	0.13
伤残抚恤金	123.0	106.7	2.5	16.3	15.28
在乡退伍红军老战士生活费	0.1	0.2	0.0	-0.1	-41.21
红军失散人员补助费	0.7	1.7	0.0	-1.1	-60.78
复员退伍军人定期定量补助费	162.0	156.5	3.3	5.5	3.53
“参战”退伍军人补助费	64.8	57.2	1.3	7.6	13.3
“涉核”退伍军人补助费	10.2	9.0	0.2	1.2	13.04
抚恤、补助费小计	395.6	366.1	8.0	29.5	8.07
军队离休干部遗属、退休人员遗属定期定量补助费	2.7	1.6	0.1	1.0	62.49
农村特困供养救济费	209.9	189.8	4.3	20.1	10.59
农村最低生活保障金	893.5	818.2	18.1	75.2	9.2
城市最低生活保障金	719.3	721.7	14.6	-2.5	-0.34
传统救济	71.8	30.5	1.5	41.3	135.26
定期定量救济费小计	1897.2	1762.0	38.5	135.2	7.67
分散安置伤残军人护理费	3.2	2.8	0.1	0.4	15.22
军队离休、退休人员护理费	4.1	3.6	0.1	0.5	12.94
儿童福利支出	54.8	52.4	1.1	2.4	4.56
老年人福利	192.7	151.7	3.9	41.1	27.08
非定期发放	29.8	28.3	0.6	1.5	5.19
烈士和牺牲病故人员一次性抚恤金	25.8	22.6	0.5	3.2	14.08
企事业退休人员一次性抚恤金	0.7	0.8	0.0	0.0	-3.75
离休、退休干部死亡丧葬补助费	3.3	5.0	0.1	-1.7	-33.93
城市最低生活保障对象临时补助	39.5	49.7	0.8	-10.2	-20.49
农村最低生活保障对象临时补助	38.1	52.0	0.8	-14.0	-26.87
报销数	55.7	54.9	1.1	0.8	1.5
伤残补助费	7.0	7.1	0.1	-0.1	-0.99
离休、退休干部其他费用	48.7	47.8	1.0	0.9	1.87

A-1-14续表

单位：亿元

指　标	2015年	2014年	占全部(%)	比上年增减额	比上年增长(%)
临时性发放	959.0	868.4	19.5	90.6	10.44
烈军属复员退伍军人临时补助费	253.7	236.4	5.2	17.3	7.32
退伍军人建房补助费	2.1	2.0	0.0	0.1	3
义务兵优待金	128.4	113.1	2.6	15.3	13.54
退役士兵自谋职业金	95.7	88.2	1.9	7.5	8.55
城镇退役士兵生活补助	17.6	14.4	0.4	3.3	22.64
优抚对象临时补助费小计	497.6	454.1	10.1	43.5	9.58
灾民生活救济费	92.1	72.7	1.9	19.4	26.67
医疗救助	303.7	284.0	6.2	19.7	6.93
其他对象临时救助	65.7	57.6	1.3	8.1	14.04
单位拨款	**352.2**	**296.1**	**7.2**	**56.0**	**18.93**
民政部门举办事业单位经费	287.9	240.2	5.8	47.7	19.85
优抚事业单位	47.5	48.2	1.0	-0.7	-1.35
荣誉军人康复医院	8.0	7.3	0.2	0.7	9.19
复员军人疗养院	3.6	4.2	0.1	-0.6	-13.94
复员退伍军人精神病院	10.4	10.1	0.2	0.3	2.98
光荣院	8.6	8.7	0.2	-0.1	-1.63
烈士纪念建筑物管理机构	9.2	9.4	0.2	-0.2	-1.89
其他优抚事业单位	7.7	8.4	0.2	-0.7	-8.51
社会福利事业单位	106.4	99.9	2.2	6.6	6.56
社会福利院	56.0	51.8	1.1	4.1	7.93
儿童福利院	15.7	15.4	0.3	0.3	2.18
精神病人福利院	18.1	16.3	0.4	1.8	11.05
流浪乞讨人员救助站	16.7	16.3	0.3	0.3	1.9
军队离退休干部管理机构	66.5	30.7	1.4	35.8	116.41
殡葬事业单位	67.5	61.4	1.4	6.0	9.8
火葬场	29.0	25.3	0.6	3.6	14.32
其他殡葬事业单位	38.5	36.1	0.8	2.4	6.63
集体办事业单位补贴	45.5	37.7	0.9	7.8	20.66
优抚事业单位	0.1	0.3	0.0	-0.1	-48.41
社会福利事业单位	45.4	37.5	0.9	7.9	21.13
生产单位拨款	3.6	1.9	0.1	1.7	93.77
假肢厂、站	1.0	1.0	0.0	0.0	4.84
安置农场	2.6	0.9	0.1	1.7	189.36
灾民紧急抢救、转移、安置费	8.5	8.2	0.2	0.2	2.7
救灾储备	6.7	8.1	0.1	-1.4	-17.24
其他支出	**655.5**	**565.6**	**13.3**	**89.9**	**15.9**

A-1-15 按支出性质分类的社会服务事业费支出情况

单位：亿元

指 标	2015年	2014年	占全部(%)	比上年增长额	比上年增长(%)
总计	**4926.4**	**4404.1**	**100.0**	**522.3**	**11.9**
优待抚恤支出合计	**686.8**	**636.6**	**13.9**	**50.2**	**7.9**
死亡抚恤	65.3	61.8	1.3	3.5	5.6
伤残抚恤	130.0	113.8	2.6	16.2	14.3
在乡复员、退伍军人生活补助	237.7	224.6	4.8	13.2	5.9
优抚事业单位	63.0	69.1	1.3	-6.1	-8.9
义务兵优待金	128.4	113.1	2.6	15.3	13.5
其他优抚支出	62.3	54.2	1.3	8.1	15.1
退役安置	**582.7**	**456.8**	**11.8**	**125.9**	**27.6**
退伍军人安置	131.0	117.2	2.7	13.8	11.8
军队移交政府的离退休人员安置	363.1	287.8	7.4	75.3	26.2
军队移交政府离退休干部管理机构	66.5	30.7	1.4	35.8	116.4
其他退役安置支出	22.2	21.1	0.5	1.0	5.0
社会福利	**562.8**	**480.9**	**11.4**	**81.8**	**17.0**
儿童福利	54.8	52.4	1.1	2.4	4.6
老年人福利	192.7	151.7	3.9	41.1	27.1
假肢矫形	2.5	2.1	0.1	0.4	18.8
殡葬	67.5	61.4	1.4	6.0	9.8
社会福利事业单位	137.8	121.9	2.8	15.9	13.0
其他社会福利支出	107.5	91.4	2.2	16.1	17.6
社会救助	**2347.4**	**2197.5**	**47.7**	**149.8**	**6.8**
最低生活保障	1650.8	1592.0	33.5	58.8	3.7
城市最低生活保障	719.3	721.7	14.6	-2.5	-0.3
农村最低生活保障	931.5	870.3	18.9	61.3	7.0

A−1−15续表

单位：亿元

指　标	2015年	2014年	占全部(%)	比上年增减额	比上年增长(%)
其他社会救助	71.8	321.5	1.5	-249.7	-77.7
医疗救助	303.7	284.0	6.2	19.7	6.9
民政部门资助参合	36.8	32.3	0.8	4.5	13.8
民政部门资助参保	17.7	16.2	0.4	1.6	9.8
直接医疗救助	214.6	204.1	4.4	10.4	5.1
优抚对象医疗补助	34.6	31.4	0.7	3.2	10.2
自然灾害生活救助	**148.5**	**124.4**	**3.0**	**24.1**	**19.4**
生活救济费	92.1	72.7	1.9	19.4	26.7
紧急抢救、安置、转移灾民支出	8.5	8.2	0.2	0.2	2.7
救灾储备	6.7	8.1	0.1	-1.4	-17.2
自然灾害灾后重建补助	30.4	25.2	0.6	5.1	20.4
其他救助	10.9	10.2	0.2	0.7	7.2
民政管理事务	**399.6**	**330.5**	**8.1**	**69.1**	**20.9**
行政运行	94.8	76.8	1.9	17.9	23.3
一般行政管理事务	19.1	14.6	0.4	4.6	31.4
机关服务	2.3	2.3	0.1	0.0	1.2
拥军优属	22.6	21.3	0.5	1.3	6.3
老龄事务	33.5	28.8	0.7	4.8	16.6
民间组织管理	7.8	7.3	0.2	0.6	8.0
行政区划和地名管理	12.1	5.0	0.3	7.0	140.2
基层政权和社区建设	105.9	89.6	2.2	16.3	18.2
部队供应	5.0	5.8	0.1	-0.8	-13.2
其他民政管理事务支出	96.5	79.2	2.0	17.3	21.9
行政事业单位离退休	**50.1**	**44.2**	**1.0**	**5.9**	**13.3**
地方离退休人员经费	13.5	13.6	0.3	-0.1	-0.7
行政单位离退休	20.1	16.8	0.4	3.3	20.0
事业单位离退休	13.5	12.3	0.3	1.2	9.5
离退休人员管理机构	0.4	0.2	0.0	0.2	75.5
其他行政事业单位离退休支出	2.7	1.4	0.1	1.3	93.5
其他	**148.5**	**133.1**	**3.0**	**15.5**	**11.6**

A-2-1 社会工作类机构财务状况

单位：万元

指　标	2015年	2014年	比上年增长(%)
执行企业会计制度单位情况			
固定资产原价	18045518.1	18272589.6	-1.24
本年折旧	1723915.5	1918752.3	-10.15
营业收入	43959557.0	47465545.4	-7.39
营业成本	20234453.5	20169413.8	0.32
营业税金及附加	640889.6	830669.3	-22.85
销售费用	1746581.9	1899756.3	-8.06
管理费用	2090815.4	2344568.5	-10.82
# 税金	250320.4	257835.7	-2.91
差旅费	83073.9	90625.2	-8.33
财务费用	1555403.3	1558746.9	-0.21
# 利息支出	1190935.8	1183391.4	0.64
公允价值变动收益	4261.2	13881.9	-69.30
投资收益	56915.5	29325.9	94.08
营业利润	1211099.0	1270512.4	-4.68
营业外收入	298479.5	261314.5	14.22
# 政府补助	91860.8	53777.7	70.82
应付职工薪酬	3253550.4	3386388.0	-3.92

A-2-1续表

单位：万元

指　标	2015年	2014年	比上年增长(%)
执行行政事业单位会计制度情况			
固定资产原价	8376074.4	10530176.0	-20.46
上年结转和结余	937524.3	829170.0	13.07
本年收入合计	8051375.2	8311246.1	-3.13
#事业收入	3205999.7	3332713.6	-3.80
经营收入	135331.5	204722.3	-33.90
本年支出合计	7452602.4	8152083.5	-8.58
#工资福利支出	1392427.5	1732467.0	-19.63
商品和服务支出	1447749.9	1626295.0	-10.98
#取暖费	45050.7	57652.2	-21.86
差旅费	19219.2	24381.5	-21.17
因公出国（境）费用	837.2	740.5	13.06
劳务费	112327.7	112498.1	-0.15
工会经费	8952.3	8213.1	9.00
福利费	20271.4	27581.5	-26.50
对个人和家庭的补助	2726659.6	2630196.4	3.67
#抚恤金	29890.4	28193.6	6.02
生活补助	406016.2	397172.1	2.23
救济费	138773.2	130495.9	6.34
助学金	1560.5	2635.0	-40.78
奖励金	11236.0	6374.0	76.28
生产补贴	537.0	692.7	-22.48
经营支出	66925.7	63868.9	4.79
销售税金	4792.4	9640.3	-50.29
执行民间非营利组织单位会计制度情况			
固定资产原价	2500456.1	3927116.6	-36.33
上年结余	87222.8	74842.0	16.54
本年收入合计	1130226.3	1399974.9	-19.27
# 捐赠收入	42860.9	109196.5	-60.75
会费收入	51509.5	107999.0	-52.31
本年费用合计	965823.9	1315556.6	-26.58
# 业务活动成本	512054.1	777037.6	-34.10
# 人员费用	206067.1	396229.1	-47.99
日常费用	101833.4	149793.8	-32.02
固定资产折旧	57570.8	100590.9	-42.77
税费	3650.7	2708.1	34.81
管理费用	345206.3	399369.6	-13.56
# 人员费用	150299.1	175921.6	-14.56
日常费用	61732.5	88394.4	-30.16
固定资产折旧	30675.8	43420.7	-29.35
税费	13057.6	24826.3	-47.40
净资产变动额	31737.2	63155.7	-49.75

A-2-2 提供住宿的社会服务机构和社区养老情况与上年比较

指 标	机构与设施数（个）			职工人数（万人）		
	2015年	2014年	比上年增长(%)	2015年	2014年	比上年增长(%)
机构和设施合计	**392143**	**96094**	**308.1**	**166.0**	**54.7**	**203.4**
机构合计	**31187**	**36810**	**-15.3**	**38.4**	**40.4**	**-5.0**
养老机构和设施	**388708**	**92327**	**321.0**	**159.4**	**47.7**	**234.1**
机构类	**27752**	**33043**	**-16.0**	**31.8**	**33.4**	**-4.8**
城市养老服务机构	7656	7642	0.2	13.2	12.2	8.4
农村养老服务机构	15587	20261	-23.1	10.9	13.0	-15.9
社会福利院	1717	1864	-7.9	4.3	4.5	-4.4
光荣院	1106	1411	-21.6	0.9	1.2	-21.6
荣誉军人康复医院	46	44	4.5	0.6	0.5	11.3
复员军人疗养院	36	38	-5.3	0.3	0.3	-12.0
军休所	1604	1783	-10.0	1.6	1.7	-8.4
社区机构和设施类	**360956**	**310652**	**16.2**	**127.6**	**107.1**	**19.1**
社区养老机构和设施	26067	18927	37.7	12.2	7.0	74.3
社区互助型养老设施	62027	40357	53.7	12.4	7.3	69.9
其他社区机构和设施	272862	251368	8.6	103.0	92.8	11.0
智障与精神疾病服务机构	**242**	**254**	**-4.7**	**2.5**	**2.6**	**-3.8**
社会福利医院	151	156	-3.2	1.4	1.4	-
复退军人精神病院	91	98	-7.1	1.1	1.2	-8.3
儿童收养救助服务机构	**753**	**890**	**-15.4**	**1.4**	**1.5**	**-6.7**
儿童福利院	478	545	-12.3	1.2	1.3	-7.7
流浪儿童救助保护中心	275	345	-20.3	0.2	0.2	-
其他提供住宿的服务机构	**2440**	**2623**	**-7.0**	**2.7**	**2.9**	**-6.9**
生活无着人员救助管理站	1766	1949	-9.4	1.7	1.8	-5.6
军供站	320	327	-2.1	0.5	0.5	-
安置农场	15	13	15.4	-	-	-
其他	339	334	1.5	0.5	0.6	-16.7

A-2-2续表

指　标	床位数（万张）			收留抚养救助人数（万人）			年末床位利用率（%）
	2015年	2014年	比上年增长（%）	2015年	2014年	比上年增长（%）	
机构和设施（含在建）合计	**732.9**	**651.4**	**12.5**	**330.8**	**337.8**	**-2.1**	
机构合计	**393.1**	**426.0**	**-7.7**	**236.3**	**271.5**	**-13.0**	
养老机构和设施	**672.7**	**593.8**	**13.3**	**295.7**	**307.9**	**-4.0**	
机构类	**358.2**	**390.3**	**-8.2**	**219.4**	**255.9**	**-14.3**	**61.3**
城市养老服务机构	116.4	108.5	7.3	59.6	57.7	3.3	51.2
农村养老服务机构	177.1	219.6	-19.3	115.2	155.7	-26.0	65.0
社会福利院	37.7	37.0	2.0	21.1	21.7	-2.8	55.9
光荣院	7.6	9.4	-18.8	4.3	5.4	-19.6	56.8
荣誉军人康复医院	1.0	0.9	11.7	0.6	0.6	-3.9	57.4
复员军人疗养院	0.7	0.7	-4.8	0.4	0.5	-26.0	55.5
军休所（万户）	17.6	14.2	23.9	18.2	14.3	27.4	103.5
社区机构和设施类	**298.1**	**187.5**	**59.0**	**94.5**	**66.3**	**42.5**	**31.7**
社区养老机构和设施	134.2	71.1	88.7	55.7	35.4	57.3	41.5
社区互助型养老设施	70.7	50.1	41.1	21.1	18.5	14.1	29.8
其他社区机构和设施	93.2	66.3	40.6	17.7	12.4	42.7	19.0
智障与精神疾病服务机构	**7.9**	**8.0**	**-1.3**	**6.4**	**6.5**	**-1.5**	**81.0**
社会福利医院	4.9	4.9	-	4.0	4.0	-	81.6
复退军人精神病院	3.0	3.1	-3.2	2.4	2.5	-4.0	80.0
儿童收养救助服务机构	**10.0**	**10.8**	**-7.4**	**5.6**	**5.9**	**-5.1**	**56.0**
儿童福利院	8.9	9.6	-7.3	5.5	5.7	-3.5	61.8
流浪儿童救助保护中心	1.1	1.2	-8.3	0.1	0.2	-50.0	9.1
其他提供住宿的服务机构	**17.0**	**16.9**	**0.6**	**4.9**	**3.2**	**53.1**	**28.8**
生活无着人员救助管理站	10.3	9.9	4.0	3.4	1.5	126.7	33.0
军供站	3.8	3.7	2.7	-	-	-	-
安置农场	-	-	-	-	-	-	-
其他	2.9	3.3	-12.1	1.5	1.7	-11.8	51.7
在建机构和设施	**41.7**	**37.9**	**10.0**				
在建养老机构和设施	34.0	30.2	12.6				
其他在建机构和设施	7.7	7.7	-				

A-2-3 家庭收养与上年比较

单位：人、件、%

指　标	2015年	2014年	比上年增长(%)
孤儿数	**502105**	**525179**	**-4.39**
集中供养孤儿	91712	93522	-1.94
社会散居孤儿	410393	431657	-4.93
家庭收养服务			
收养登记合计(件)	22348	22772	-1.86
中国公民收养登记	19406	19885	-2.41
# 香港居民	105	120	-12.50
澳门居民	3	12	-75.00
台湾居民	42	39	7.69
华侨	29	20	45.00
外国人收养登记	2942	2887	1.91
被收养人合计（人）	22363	22876	-2.24
# 女性	14751	16158	-8.71
残疾儿童	3290	2637	24.76
社会福利机构抚养的儿童	10704	10336	3.56
# 被外国人收养	2804	2608	7.52
社会孤儿	5645	6802	-17.01
# 被外国人收养	113	184	-38.59
近亲属抚养人数	1143	1375	-16.87
# 被外国人收养	7	184	-38.59
生父母有特殊困难无力抚养人数	539	527	2.28
# 被外国人收养	9	29	-68.97
其他	4332	3836	12.93

A-2-4 社会救助与上年比较

指　标	2015年	2014年	比上年增长(%)
社会救助总人数	**17746.4**	**17816.8**	**-0.40**
城市最低生活保障人数（万人）	1701.1	1877.0	-9.4
# 女性	727.1	792.4	-8.2
残疾人	165.7	161.1	2.9
三无对象	43.8	50.0	-12.3
# 老年人	293.5	315.8	-7.1
在职人员	31.1	37.5	-17.1
灵活就业	377.3	425.8	-11.4
登记失业	264.1	312.5	-15.5
未登记失业	394.0	398.7	-1.2
在校生	235.9	266.0	-11.3
其他未成年人	105.1	120.7	-12.9
城市最低生活保障家庭数（万户）	957.4	1026.1	-6.7
城市最低生活保障费（亿元）	719.3	721.7	-0.3
城市最低生活保障平均标准（元/人·月）	451.1	410.5	9.9
城市最低生活保障平均支出水平（元/人·月）	316.6	285.6	10.9
农村最低生活保障人数（万人）	4903.6	5207.2	-5.83
农村最低生活保障家庭数（万户）	2846.2	2943.6	-3.31
农村最低生活保障费（亿元）	931.5	870.3	7.04
农村最低生活保障平均标准（元/人·年）	3177.6	2776.6	14.44
农村最低生活保障平均支出水平（元/人·年）	1766.5	1552.3	13.8

注：社会救助总人数是救助人数和人次数的合计。

A-2-4续表

指　标	2015年	2014年	比上年增长(%)
特困人员救助供养			
农村特困人员救助供养总人数	516.8	529.1	-2.32
集中供养人数（万人）	162.3	174.3	-6.85
集中供养费（亿元）	82.9	79.8	3.89
集中供养平均标准(元/人·年)	6025.7	5371.3	12.18
集中供养平均支出水平(元/人·年)	4790.4	4676.1	2.45
分散供养人数（万人）	354.4	354.8	-0.10
分散供养费（亿元）	127.1	110.1	15.45
分散供养平均标准(元/人·年)	4490.1	4005.9	12.09
分散供养平均支出水平(元/人·年)	3674.3	3228.9	13.79
城市“三无”救助人数（万人）	**6.8**	**7.6**	**-10.1**
传统救济人数（万人）	**63.8**	**74.5**	**-14.44**
临时救助(万人次)	**655.4**	**650.7**	**0.72**
医疗救助			
直接救助人次数(万人次)	2889.1	2395.3	20.62
资助参加基本医疗保险人数（万人）	6634.7	6723.7	-1.32
生活无着人员救助（万人次）	**375.2**	**351.7**	**6.68**

A-2-5 分省城市最低生活保障平均标准与上年比较

单位：元/人·月

地 区	2015年	2014年	比上年增长(%)
全 国	**451.1**	**410.5**	**9.9**
北 京	710.0	650.0	9.2
天 津	705.0	640.0	10.2
河 北	441.4	431.9	2.2
山 西	413.2	383.7	7.7
内蒙古	508.0	481.4	5.5
辽 宁	493.5	452.8	9.0
吉 林	401.6	371.1	8.2
黑龙江	506.4	446.8	13.3
上 海	790.0	710.0	11.3
江 苏	581.7	536.1	8.5
浙 江	640.5	573.3	11.7
安 徽	455.0	421.5	7.9
福 建	478.1	404.4	18.2
江 西	452.0	418.3	8.1
山 东	470.1	451.9	4.0
河 南	374.1	328.8	13.8
湖 北	447.1	411.0	8.8
湖 南	359.8	352.8	2.0
广 东	513.8	454.5	13.1
广 西	404.4	340.1	18.9
海 南	453.5	379.6	19.5
重 庆	419.1	369.0	13.6
四 川	367.0	336.2	9.2
贵 州	453.4	395.0	14.8
云 南	395.9	359.6	10.1
西 藏	591.3	533.9	10.8
陕 西	460.7	388.5	18.6
甘 肃	378.1	328.3	15.2
青 海	370.4	351.0	5.5
宁 夏	361.8	304.8	18.7
新 疆	349.2	329.2	6.1

A-2-6 分省城市最低生活保障支出水平与上年比较

单位：元/人·月

地 区	2015年	2014年	比上年增长(%)
全 国	**316.6**	**269.1**	**17.7**
北 京	710.3	820.7	-13.4
天 津	593.4	626.3	-5.2
河 北	255.7	268.4	-4.7
山 西	291.7	219.8	32.7
内蒙古	409.1	335.1	22.1
辽 宁	337.5	275.7	22.4
吉 林	328.3	158.1	107.7
黑龙江	338.4	343.9	-1.6
上 海	650.9	425.1	53.1
江 苏	355.7	500.7	-29.0
浙 江	463.5	353.3	31.2
安 徽	333.6	201.3	65.7
福 建	310.0	451.6	-31.3
江 西	296.2	280.3	5.7
山 东	308.6	292.3	5.6
河 南	231.9	208.1	11.4
湖 北	265.2	221.1	19.9
湖 南	260.7	214.1	21.8
广 东	404.2	566.1	-28.6
广 西	274.4	220.6	24.4
海 南	261.7	383.6	-31.8
重 庆	305.2	368.8	-17.2
四 川	238.3	279.0	-14.6
贵 州	302.9	102.8	194.5
云 南	300.6	119.7	151.0
西 藏	410.5	229.5	78.8
陕 西	299.1	407.8	-26.7
甘 肃	288.2	260.3	10.7
青 海	286.3	314.1	-8.8
宁 夏	277.3	253.1	9.6
新 疆	285.9	205.1	39.4

A-2-7 社会捐赠与上年比较

指　标	2015年	2014年	比上年增长(%)
社会捐赠合计（万元）	**6597061.4**	**6124155.3**	**7.7**
直接接收捐赠情况			
捐赠款数额（万元）	442029.5	795542.9	-44.4
捐赠衣被合计（万件）	4537.0	5244.5	-13.5
捐赠其他物资价值（万元）	52408.2	80053.2	-34.5
间接接收捐赠情况			
捐赠款数额（万元）	42562.3	21519.1	97.8
捐赠衣被合计（万件）	172.5	105.6	63.4
捐赠其他物资价值（万元）	6164.4	39011.6	-84.2
受益人次数（万人次）	1838.4	1695.0	8.5
社会捐赠接收工作站、点数（个）	30362	32061	-5.3
# 社会捐赠接收工作站数（个）	12810	14126	-9.3
慈善超市数（个）	9654	10174	-5.1
各类社会组织接收捐赠（万元）	**6102623.7**	**5248559.2**	**16.3**

注：由于社会组织年检工作滞后于年报汇总工作，社会组织捐赠数据为2014年数据。

A-2-8 自然灾害与上年比较

指　标	2015年	2014年	比上年增长(%)
农作物受灾情况总计(千公顷)			
受灾	21769.8	24890.7	-12.5
绝收	2232.7	3090.3	-27.8
旱灾			
受灾	10609.7	12271.7	-13.5
绝收	1046.1	1484.7	-29.5
洪涝(含山体滑坡和泥石流)			
受灾	5620.2	4738.9	18.6
绝收	659.5	628.2	5.0
风雹			
受灾	2918.0	3225.4	-9.5
绝收	309.1	457.7	-32.5
台风			
受灾	1721.1	2483.1	-30.7
绝收	181.5	348.7	-47.9
地震			
受灾	0.5	36.4	-98.6
绝收		2.8	-100.0
雪灾、低温冷冻			
受灾	900.3	2132.5	-57.8
绝收	36.5	168.2	-78.3
人口受灾情况			
受灾（万人次）	18620.3	24353.7	-23.5
死亡人口（含失踪）（人）	967.0	1818	-46.8
紧急转移人口（万人次）	644.4	601.7	7.1
损失情况			
倒塌房屋（万间）	24.8	45.0	-44.9
损坏房屋（万间）	49.2	354.2	-86.1
直接经济损失（亿元）	2704.1	3373.8	-19.9

A-2-9 国家优抚、安置对象与上年比较

单位：人

指　标	2015年	2014年	比上年增长(%)
优抚对象人数	**8970288**	**9173281**	**-2.2**
抚恤	1001843	1077331	-7.0
烈士家属抚恤	160948	197955	-18.7
因公牺牲抚恤	43711	48179	-9.3
病故军人家属抚恤	60316	65076	-7.3
伤残人员抚恤	736868	766121	-3.8
补助	7968445	8095950	-1.6
在乡红军老战士	177	341	-48.1
在乡西路军红军老战士	64	87	-26.4
红军失散人员	3708	11269	-67.1
在乡复员军人	792440	993204	-20.2
带病回乡退伍军人	1183750	1242020	-4.7
60岁以上农村籍退伍军人	3924604	3748039	
参战退役人员	1409601	1448018	-2.7
参试退役人员	184840	188072	-1.7
部分60周岁以上烈士(含错杀被平反)人员子女	241257	229308	
其他补助人数	228004	235592	-3.2
本年接收离退休人员和安置复原干部数	**22311**	**30237**	**-26.2**
军队干部（含地方）	9511	10288	-7.6
军队退休士官	410	503	-18.5
军队无军籍职工	9508	16908	-43.8
复员干部	2882	2538	13.6
本年新增享受烈士待遇人数	**341**	**267**	**27.7**
零散烈士纪念设施	**11838**	**11365**	**4.2**
优待			
优待优抚对象（万户）	317.0	335.5	-5.5
# 军属（万户）	85.8	88.3	-2.8
优待金（亿元）	193.0	151.0	27.8
# 军属（亿元）	76.6	69.3	10.6

A-2-10 社区服务与上年比较

单位：个、张、%

指　标	2015年	2014年	比上年增长(%)
社区服务机构和设施总数	**360956**	**310592**	**16.1**
社区服务指导中心	863	918	-6.0
社区服务中心	24138	23088	4.5
社区服务站	128083	120188	6.6
社区养老机构和设施	26067	18927	37.7
社区互助型养老设施	62027	40357	53.7
其他机构和设施	119778	107114	11.8
社区服务机构和设施覆盖率	**52.9**	**45.5**	**16.3**
便民利民网点数（万个）	**24.9**	**30.9**	**-19.4**
社区养老床位数	**2981379**	**1875053**	**59.0**
日间照料床位	1212564	759655	59.6
留宿照料床位	1768815	1115398	58.6
社区服务志愿者组织数（万个）	**9.6**	**10.9**	**-11.9**

A-3-1 社会组织财务状况

单位：万元

指　标	2015年	2014年	比上年增长(%)
执行行政事业单位会计制度情况			
固定资产原价	276899.1	259575.3	6.7
上年结转和结余	23062.1	21959.1	5.0
本年收入合计	515717.5	378379.6	36.3
# 事业收入	34263.6	33507.6	2.3
经营收入	23759.7	27056.1	-12.2
本年支出合计	228967.1	89551.3	155.7
# 工资福利支出	34607.8	37714.3	-8.2
商品和服务支出	144077.9	19563.9	636.4
# 取暖费	252.7	253.3	-0.2
差旅费	638.7	834.1	-23.4
因公出国（境）费用	0.0	0.0	0.0
劳务费	79762.7	692.1	11424.7
工会经费	44045.4	399.4	10927.9
福利费	517.3	778.1	-33.5
对个人和家庭的补助	6332.4	5507.5	15.0
# 抚恤金	0.0	11.0	-100.0
生活补助	213.7	245.2	-12.8
救济费	14.5	14.6	-0.7
助学金	72.2	163.4	-55.8
奖励金	226.0	230.0	-1.7
生产补贴	286.8	273.3	4.9
经营支出	257.7	176.4	46.1
收支结余	1985.3	1492.5	33.0
销售税金	421.50	1040.3	-59.5

A−3−1续表

单位：万元

指　标	2015年	2014年	比上年增长(%)
执行民间非营利组织单位会计制度情况			
固定资产原价	22833898.0	15346719.3	48.8
上年结余	11070290.0	7923623.1	39.7
本年收入合计	28774009.2	20059288.4	43.4
# 捐赠收入	6102623.7	5248559.2	16.3
会费收入	2420408.6	1819941.6	33.0
本年费用合计	23608642.7	19070964.1	23.8
# 业务活动成本	11099752.6	12052804.3	-7.9
# 人员费用	3942515.4	3287752.4	19.9
日常费用	2033252.6	1708722.5	19.0
固定资产折旧	912313.7	844283.2	8.1
税费	165658.6	162669.6	1.8
管理费用	5181971.0	4216776.2	22.9
# 人员费用	1865588.3	1613243.2	15.6
日常费用	670059.8	609987.1	9.8
固定资产折旧	301515.2	308016.6	-2.1
税费	85545.4	87400.1	-2.1
净资产变动额	8552726.4	9806108.6	-12.8

A-3-2 社会组织分类情况与上年比较

单位：个

指　标	2015年	2014年	比上年增长(%)
社会组织合计	**662425**	**606048**	**9.3**
社会团体	**328500**	**309736**	**6.1**
按活动区域分			
中央级	1974	1941	1.7
省级	29233	27973	4.5
地级	80220	76211	5.3
县级	217073	203611	6.6
基金会	**4784**	**4117**	**16.2**
按性质分类			
公募性	1548	1470	5.3
非公募性	3198	2610	22.5
涉外基金会	9	9	
境外代表机构	29	28	3.6
民办非企业	**329141**	**292195**	**12.6**
按性质分类			
法人	260479	228366	14.1
合伙	8791	7033	25.0
个体	59871	56796	5.4

A-3-3 自治组织财务状况

单位：万元

指　标	2015年	2014年	比上年增长(%)
执行企业会计制度单位情况			
固定资产原价	2727337.9	2863527.7	-4.8
本年折旧	148945.1	154016.3	-3.3
营业收入	1580476.7	1362536.0	16.0
营业成本	1108891.8	1057966.8	4.8
营业税金及附加	21022.0	20949.6	0.3
销售费用	29720.1	39664.3	-25.1
管理费用	265244.6	262901.7	0.9
# 税金	4821.0	4113.0	17.2
差旅费	305.4	566.7	-46.1
财务费用	-13441.4	-8149.7	64.9
# 利息支出	-24942.3	-21569.3	15.6
公允价值变动收益	-1020.7	30.1	-3491.0
投资收益	64131.6	41995.8	52.7
营业利润	62691.9	24846.5	152.3
营业外收入	168935.6	141390.6	19.5
#政府补助	61798.3	48597.7	27.2
应付职工薪酬	95143.3	99631.6	-4.5

A−3−3续表

单位：万元

指　标	2015年	2014年	比上年增长(%)
执行行政事业单位会计制度情况			
固定资产原价	21189913.5	15128537.8	40.1
上年结转和结余	1365844.5	878930.5	55.4
本年收入合计	7817047.8	8366917.6	-6.6
#事业收入	2174753.8	2100182.4	3.6
经营收入	665861.9	633541.5	5.1
本年支出合计	6997608.0	11373307.6	-38.5
#工资福利支出	2009732.5	1936016.0	3.8
商品和服务支出	1810948.1	1860147.8	-2.6
#取暖费	52962.9	75776.8	-30.1
差旅费	66494.3	65561.3	1.4
因公出国（境）费用	1147.1	1102.1	4.1
劳务费	169461.7	167477.6	1.2
工会经费	15370.4	14159.3	8.6
福利费	154715.4	152721.0	1.3
对个人和家庭的补助	306354.5	308360.0	-0.7
#抚恤金	3661.0	3489.9	4.9
生活补助	89784.9	85213.6	5.4
救济费	6988.6	5162.0	35.4
助学金	8384.0	8173.2	2.6
奖励金	5940.4	6149.4	-3.4
生产补贴	8966.8	9790.9	-8.4
经营支出	51954.6	49546.2	4.9
收支结余	81111.5	30651.1	
销售税金	9922.7	13423.3	-26.1
执行民间非营利组织单位会计制度情况			
固定资产原价	2476078.9	2494387.5	-0.7
上年结余	97398.4	90812.2	7.3
本年收入合计	891636.6	2246029.9	-60.3
# 捐赠收入	24917.2	27275.8	-8.6
会费收入	96592.1	95641.6	1.0
本年费用合计	804695.1	833931.8	-3.5
# 业务活动成本	453388.1	461111.6	-1.7
# 人员费用	143659.8	143556.9	0.1
日常费用	79205.2	87746.0	-9.7
固定资产折旧	78485.3	79719.1	-1.5
税费	8987.0	8888.2	1.1
管理费用	225951.1	216370.0	4.4
# 人员费用	83409.4	86798.0	-3.9
日常费用	44670.9	46458.5	-3.8
固定资产折旧	20543.1	19475.2	5.5
税费	5719.9	5709.0	0.2
净资产变动额	89227.2	86599.9	3.0

A-3-4 自治组织主要指标与上年比较

单位：个、人

指 标	2015年	2014年	比上年增长(%)
城市			
社区居委会	99679	96693	3.1
居民小组	1347274	1357913	-0.8
居民委员会成员人数	512196	497038	3.0
# 女性	251946	240739	4.7
居委会选举情况			
当年进行选举的居委会数	29970	27337	9.6
当年参选人口数	62635078	60995065	2.7
# 登记选民数	52699497	54530894	-3.4
参选人数	40804184	42225351	-3.4
农村			
村民委员会	580856	585451	-0.8
村民小组	4691632	4704267	-0.3
村民委员会成员人数	2297061	2305024	-0.3
# 女性	525741	526409	-0.1
村委会选举情况			
当年进行选举的村委会数	134675	302832	-55.5
当年参选村人口数	149455947	368872058	-59.5
# 登记选民数	134197410	343801097	-61.0
参选人数	118633157	301390325	-60.6

A-3-5 其他社会服务机构财务状况

单位：万元

指　标	2015年	2014年	比上年增长(%)
执行企业会计制度单位情况			
固定资产原价	970507.7	922067.8	5.3
本年折旧	81492.1	80285.4	1.5
营业收入	1074715.6	909193.5	18.2
营业成本	242462.5	364205.6	-33.4
营业税金及附加	12084.7	10265.4	17.7
销售费用	90090.1	74504.2	20.9
管理费用	179853.9	158282.6	13.6
# 税金	4683.3	5032.9	-6.9
差旅费	1659.6	2335.3	-28.9
财务费用	6562.6	6675.4	-1.7
# 利息支出	796.1	2044.0	-61.1
公允价值变动收益			
投资收益	2919.0	418.0	598.3
营业利润	218696.8	171638.9	27.4
应付职工薪酬	94422.6	69787.5	35.3

A-3-5续表

单位：万元

指　标	2015年	2014年	比上年增长(%)
执行行政事业单位会计制度情况			
固定资产原价	1884846.3	1858650.8	1.4
上年结转和结余	88285.3	109889.2	-19.7
本年收入合计	1378451.0	1462109.8	-5.7
#事业收入	697503.5	702973.6	-0.8
经营收入	286039.9	262144.2	9.1
本年支出合计	1322894.3	1367846.6	-3.3
#工资福利支出	360530.6	331822.0	8.7
商品和服务支出	512347.7	515119.2	-0.5
#取暖费	6736.0	6955.2	-3.2
差旅费	4336.9	4548.5	-4.7
因公出国（境）费用	47.7	59.2	-19.4
劳务费	39521.2	38679.6	2.2
工会经费	2638.0	2226.7	18.5
福利费	7131.4	7453.4	-4.3
对个人和家庭的补助	65120.1	63470.1	2.6
#抚恤金	889.2	1408.2	-36.9
生活补助	4434.0	3429.2	29.3
救济费	433.3	593.0	-26.9
助学金	90.1	134.1	-32.8
奖励金	1733.5	1360.8	27.4
生产补贴	411.1	1386.3	-70.3
经营支出	152914.6	131134.0	16.6
销售税金	4190.0	3790.3	10.5
执行民间非营利组织单位会计制度情况			
固定资产原价	64594.5	57747.2	11.9
上年结余	6341.5	2992.7	111.9
本年收入合计	16510.0	13247.5	24.6
# 捐赠收入	400.8	611.7	-34.5
会费收入	553.0	1184.6	-53.3
本年费用合计	11523.0	10394.6	10.9
# 业务活动成本	6778.6	7104.3	-4.6
# 人员费用	2142.6	1930.0	11.0
日常费用	2465.2	1784.0	38.2
固定资产折旧	1063.3	1640.4	-35.2
税费	219.5	159.0	38.1
管理费用	3250.2	2895.9	12.2
# 人员费用	1208.4	912.5	32.4
日常费用	715.4	1091.6	-34.5
固定资产折旧	367.3	213.3	72.2
税费	27.8	25.0	11.2
净资产变动额	882.2	1080.6	-18.4

A-3-6 其他社会服务主要指标与上年比较

指　标	2015年	2014年	比上年增长(%)
婚姻服务			
事业单位性质的婚姻登记机构（个）	2064	2236	-7.7
办理婚姻登记业务的处数（处）	5714	6797	-15.9
结婚登记（对）	12247056	13067426	-6.3
内地居民登记结婚对数（对）	12205888	13020405	-6.3
初婚人数（人）	21089700	22868064	-7.8
再婚人数（人）	3404412	3266788	4.2
#女性	1772263	1686629	5.1
恢复结婚（对）	398527	348285	14.4
涉外及华侨、港澳台居民登记结婚（对）	41168	47021	-12.4
结婚率（‰）	9.0	9.6	-0.6 (千分点)
离婚登记（对）	3841407	3636754	5.6
民政部门办理离婚对数（对）	3148779	2957295	6.5
内地居民办理离婚	3142542	2950581	6.5
华侨、港澳台居民登记离婚	6237	6714	-7.1
各级法院办理离婚件数（件）	692628	679459	1.9
离婚率（‰）	2.8	2.7	0.1 (千分点)
殡葬服务			
殡仪服务机构（个）	4530	4559	-0.6
火化炉数(台)	6063	5908	2.6
全年遗体火化数（具）	4595065	4593037	-
火化率(%)	47.1	47.0	0.1 (百分点)
穴位数（个）	15811006	14318347	10.4
安葬数（具）	10379760	8963554	15.8

04

社会服务历年统计资料

B-1-1 县及以上行政区划

单位：个

年份	省级	地级（不含地级市）	县级（不含县级市、市辖区）	市			市辖区	县级合计
					地级	县级		
1978	30	212	2153	193	98	92	408	2653
1979	30	211	2153	216	104	109	428	2690
1980	30	211	2151	223	107	113	511	2775
1981	30	208	2144	233	108	122	514	2780
1982	30	210	2140	245	112	130	527	2797
1983	30	178	2091	289	144	142	552	2785
1984	30	175	2069	300	147	150	595	2814
1985	30	165	2046	324	162	159	621	2826
1986	30	159	2017	353	166	184	629	2830
1987	30	156	1986	381	170	208	632	2826
1988	31	151	1936	434	183	248	647	2831
1989	31	151	1919	450	185	262	648	2829
1990	31	151	1903	467	185	279	651	2833
1991	31	151	1894	479	187	289	650	2833
1992	31	148	1848	517	191	323	662	2833
1993	31	139	1795	570	196	371	669	2835
1994	31	127	1735	622	206	413	697	2845
1995	31	124	1716	640	210	427	706	2849
1996	31	117	1696	666	218	445	717	2858
1997	33	110	1693	668	222	442	727	2862
1998	33	104	1689	668	227	437	737	2863
1999	34	95	1682	667	236	427	749	2858
2000	34	74	1674	663	259	400	787	2861
2001	34	67	1660	662	265	393	808	2861
2002	34	57	1649	660	275	381	830	2860
2003	34	51	1642	660	282	374	845	2861
2004	34	50	1636	661	283	374	852	2862
2005	34	50	1636	661	283	374	852	2862
2006	34	50	1635	656	283	369	856	2860
2007	34	50	1635	655	283	368	856	2859
2008	34	50	1635	655	283	368	856	2859
2009	34	50	1636	654	283	367	855	2858
2010	34	50	1633	657	283	370	853	2856
2011	34	48	1627	657	284	369	857	2853
2012	34	48	1624	657	285	368	860	2852
2013	34	47	1613	658	286	368	872	2853
2014	34	45	1596	649	288	361	897	2854
2015	34	43	1568	652	291	361	921	2850

B-1-2 乡镇级行政区划

单位：个

年 份	乡镇级					
		镇数	乡数	#民族乡	街道办事处	区公所
1978	6195	2173				4022
1979	10424	2361			4444	3619
1980						
1981	11434	2678			4965	3791
1982						
1983	49695	2968	35514		5304	5909
1984	106439	7186	85290		5844	8119
1985	104900	9140	82450	3144	5402	7908
1986	83954	10718	61353	2936	5718	6165
1987	81025	11103	58739	3020	5680	5503
1988	65345	11481	45195	1571	5099	3570
1989	65419	11873	44624	1755	5420	3502
1990	65188	12084	44397	1980	5269	3438
1991	63391	12455	42654	1403	5186	3096
1992	54830	14539	33827	1348	5233	1231
1993	54863	15805	32445	1351	5470	1143
1994	54605	16702	31463	1322	5372	1068
1995	53360	17532	29502	1330	5596	730
1996	51336	18171	27056	1383	5565	544
1997	50967	18925	25966	1545	5678	398
1998	50999	19216	25712	1517	5732	339
1999	50750	19756	24745	1222	5904	345
2000	51024	20312	24555	1356	5902	255
2001	46369	20358	20012	1165	5972	27
2002	44822	20600	18640	1162	5516	66
2003	44067	20226	18064	1149	5751	26
2004	43275	19892	17534	1127	5829	20
2005	41636	19522	15951	1093	6152	11
2006	41040	19369	15306	1089	6355	10
2007	40813	19249	15120	1094	6434	10
2008	40828	19234	15067	1097	6524	3
2009	40858	19322	14848	1098	6686	2
2010	40906	19410	14571	1096	6923	2
2011	40466	19683	13587	1086	7194	2
2012	40446	19881	13281	1064	7282	2
2013	40497	20117	12812	1035	7566	2
2014	40381	20401	12282	1020	7696	2
2015	39789	20515	11315	991	7957	2

B–1–3 全国人口情况

单位：万人、%

年份	总人口			农村贫困人口	65岁及以上老年人口	65岁及以上人口比重	60岁及以上老年人口	60岁及以上人口比重	出生人口	死亡人口	当年净增人口
		城镇	乡村								
1978	96259	17245	79014	25000							
1979	97542	18495	79047								1283
1980	98705	19140	79565								1163
1981	100072	20171	79901								1367
1982	101654	21480	80174		4991	4.9					1469
1983	103008	22274	80734								954
1984	104357	24017	80340	12800							
1985	105851	25094	80757	12500							1164
1986	107507	26366	81141	13100							1476
1987	109300	27674	81626	12200	5968	5.4					1500
1988	111026	28661	82365	9600							1541
1989	112704	29540	83164	10200							1577
1990	114333	30195	84138	8500	6368	5.6			2391	762	1629
1991	115823	31203	84260						2258	768	1490
1992	117171	32175	84996	8000					2119	771	1348
1993	118517	33173	85344						2126	780	1346
1994	119850	34169	85681	7000					2104	771	1333
1995	121121	35174	85947	6540	7510	6.2			2063	792	1271
1996	122389	37304	85085		7833	6.4			2067	799	1268
1997	123626	39449	84177	4962	8085	6.5			2038	801	1237
1998	124761	41608	83153	4210	8359	6.7			1942	807	1135
1999	125786	43748	82038	3412	8679	6.9			1834	809	1025
2000	126743	45906	80837	3209	8821	7.0			1771	814	957
2001	127627	48064	79563	2927	9062	7.1			1702	818	884
2002	128453	50212	78241	2820	9377	7.3			1647	821	826
2003	129227	52376	76851	2900	9692	7.5			1599	825	774
2004	129988	54283	75705	2610	9857	7.6			1593	832	761
2005	130756	56212	74544	2365	10055	7.7	14408	11.03	1617	849	768
2006	131448	57706	73742	2148	10419	7.9	14901	11.3	1584	892	692
2007	132129	59379	72750	4320	10636	8.1	15340	11.6	1594	913	681
2008	132802	60667	72135	4007	10956	8.3	15989	12	1608	935	673
2009	133450	62186	71288	3597	11309	8.5	16714	12.5	1615	943	672
2010	134091	66558	67415	2688	11883.2	8.9	17764.9	13.26	1596	953	642
2011	134735	69079	65656	12238	12288	9.1	18499	13.7	1604	960	644
2012	135404	71182	64222	9899	12714	9.4	19390	14.3	1635	966	669
2013	136072	73111	62961	8249	13161	9.7	20243	14.9	1640	972	668
2014	136782	74916	61866	7017	13755	10.1	21242	15.5	1687	977	710
2015	137462	77116	60346	5575	14386	10.5	22200	16.1	1655	975	680

注：本表资料来源于国家统计局。

B-1-4 社会服务机构和设施（按登记类型分类）

单位：万个

年 份	合 计	事业单位（含设施）	福利企业	社会组织	自治组织	行政机关
1978	1.1	1.1	0.1			
1979	1.3	1.2	0.1			
1980	1.4	1.3	0.1			
1981	1.5	1.3	0.2			
1982	1.7	1.6	0.2			
1983	40.2	1.9	0.6		37.7	
1984	103.6	2.6	0.7		100.3	
1985	107.7	3.3	1.5		103.0	
1986	101.2	3.9	2.0		95.3	
1987	100.1	4.2	2.8		93.2	
1988	106.7	4.3	4.0	0.4	97.8	
1989	111.8	4.4	4.2	0.5	102.8	
1990	119.8	4.5	4.2	1.1	110.0	
1991	129.2	4.7	4.4	8.3	111.9	
1992	136.1	4.8	5.0	15.5	110.8	
1993	139.7	5.3	5.7	16.8	112.0	
1994	140.3	5.2	6.0	17.4	111.7	
1995	133.7	5.2	6.0	18.1	104.4	
1996	133.9	5.3	5.9	18.5	104.2	
1997	131.4	5.3	5.6	18.1	102.4	
1998	122.2	5.4	5.1	16.6	95.2	
1999	115.7	5.4	4.5	14.3	91.6	
2000	109.5	6.1	4.1	15.3	84.0	
2001	109.8	5.7	3.8	21.1	79.2	0.6
2002	110.5	5.8	3.6	24.5	76.7	0.5
2003	109.9	5.8	3.4	26.7	74.0	0.4
2004	111.1	6.7	3.2	28.9	72.2	0.4
2005	112.6	6.6	3.1	32.0	70.9	0.4
2006	115.7	6.7	3.0	35.4	70.5	0.4
2007	117.7	7.0	2.5	38.7	69.5	0.3
2008	119.2	6.6	2.4	41.4	68.8	0.4
2009	125.9	12.1	2.3	43.1	68.4	0.3
2010	126.6	11.6	2.2	44.6	68.2	0.3
2011	129.4	13.1	2.2	46.2	67.9	0.3
2012	146.2	26.3	2	49.9	68	0.3
2013	156.2	31.4	1.8	54.7	68.3	0.3
2014	166.5	36.0	1.7	60.6	68.2	0.3
2015	176.5	40.7	1.5	66.2	68.1	0.3

B-1-5 社会服务机构和设施（按行业分类分）

单位：万个

年份	合计							行政机关
		社会工作	成员组织	社会组织	自治组织	其他社会服务	其他事业单位	
1978	1.1	0.8				0.3		
1979	1.3	1.0				0.3		
1980	1.4	1.1				0.3		
1981	1.5	1.2				0.3		
1982	1.7	1.4				0.3		
1983	40.2	2.2	37.7		37.7	0.3		
1984	103.6	3.0	100.3		100.3	0.3		
1985	107.7	4.5	103.0		103.0	0.3		
1986	101.2	5.6	95.3		95.3	0.3		
1987	100.1	6.6	93.2		93.2	0.3		
1988	106.7	8.1	98.3	0.4	97.8	0.3		
1989	111.8	8.3	103.3	0.5	102.8	0.3		
1990	119.8	8.4	111.1	1.1	110.0	0.3		
1991	129.2	8.7	120.2	8.3	111.9	0.3		
1992	136.1	9.5	126.3	15.5	110.8	0.3		
1993	139.7	10.7	128.7	16.8	112.0	0.3		
1994	140.3	10.9	129.1	17.4	111.7	0.3		
1995	133.6	10.9	122.4	18.1	104.4	0.3		
1996	133.9	10.9	122.7	18.5	104.2	0.3		
1997	131.4	10.6	120.5	18.1	102.4	0.3		
1998	122.2	10.2	111.8	16.6	95.2	0.3		
1999	115.7	9.5	105.9	14.3	91.6	0.3		
2000	109.5	9.8	99.3	15.3	84.0	0.3		
2001	109.8	9.2	100.3	21.1	79.2	0.3		0.6
2002	110.5	9.1	101.2	24.5	76.7	0.3		0.5
2003	109.9	8.9	100.7	26.7	74.0	0.3		0.4
2004	111.1	9.6	101.1	28.9	72.2	0.3		0.4
2005	112.6	9.5	102.9	32.0	70.9	0.3		0.4
2006	115.7	9.2	105.9	35.4	70.5	0.5		0.4
2007	117.7	9.0	108.2	38.7	69.5	0.5		0.3
2008	119.2	8.4	110.2	41.4	68.8	0.6		0.4
2009	125.9	13.8	111.5	43.1	68.4	0.6		0.3
2010	126.6	13.2	112.8	44.6	68.2	0.6		0.3
2011	129.4	14.6	114.1	46.2	67.9	0.7		0.3
2012	146.2	27.5	117.9	49.9	68	0.6	0.2	0.3
2013	156.1	32.3	123.0	54.7	68.3	0.6	0.2	0.3
2014	166.8	37.1	128.8	60.6	68.2	0.7	0.2	0.3
2015	176.5	41.3	134.3	66.2	68.1	0.7	0.2	0.3

注：2012年开始社会工作中包含其他社区服务设施。

B-1-6 社会服务机构和设施职工

单位：万人

年 份	合 计	社会工作	成员组织			其他社会服务	其他事业单位	行政机关	乡、镇民政助理员
				社会组织	自治组织				
1978	19.7	19.7							
1979	21.9	21.9							
1980	25.3	25.3							
1981	27.8	27.8							
1982	29.1	29.1							
1983	41.5	41.5							
1984	48.0	48.0							
1985	497.9	83.4	414.5		414.5				
1986	506.2	104.1	402.1		402.1				
1987	529.1	132.2	396.9		396.9				
1988	569.6	166.9	402.7		402.7				
1989	587.5	171.5	416.0		416.0				
1990	631.8	179.3	452.5		452.5				
1991	661.2	192.7	468.5		468.5				
1992	691.3	213.9	477.4		477.4				
1993	733.9	230.0	503.9		503.9				
1994	749.6	243.1	506.5		506.5				
1995	694.2	245.7	448.5		448.5				
1996	676.0	229.2	446.8		446.8				
1997	666.8	238.2	428.6		428.6			14.3	
1998	634.4	225.0	409.4		409.4			14.8	
1999	615.1	213.7	401.4		401.4			14.8	5.9
2000	566.8	203.4	363.4		363.4			13.5	5.7
2001	565.2	202.4	362.8		362.8			12.1	4.6
2002	526.2	192.4	333.8		333.8			11.2	4.1
2003	551.8	193.0	358.8		358.8			10.8	3.7
2004	532.4	197.8	334.6		334.6			11.3	3.9
2005	500.6	189.5	311.1		311.1			8.4	5.5
2006	895.5	183.0	712.5	425.2	287.3			8.3	4.6
2007	930.0	190.4	739.6	456.9	282.7			8.4	4.7
2008	958.7	206.9	751.8	475.8	276.0			8.7	4.5
2009	1029.3	207.5	821.8	544.7	277.1			8.8	4.7
2010	1129.5	234.0	895.5	618.2	277.3			8.9	5.0
2011	1120.8	235.7	876.6	599.3	277.3	8.5		9.0	4.9
2012	1144.7	241.4	892.5	613.3	279.2	8.6	2.2	9.3	5.2
2013	1197.6	269.2	917.3	636.6	280.7	9.1	2.0	9.4	5.2
2014	1250.9	277.3	962.5	682.3	280.2	9.3	1.9	9.5	5.4
2015	1308.9	281.9	1015.7	734.8	280.9	9.5	1.8	9.5	5.3

注：合计数不含乡镇助理员。

B-1-7 社会工作师

单位：人

年　份	报考人数	考试通过人数	社会服务行业在业人数	行政机关	社会工作	成员组织	其他社会服务	其他事业单位
2008	77698	4192	3144	286	1496	1191	171	
2009	46015	4227	7360	758	3809	2544	249	
2010	25547	2664	9901	922	5176	3473	330	
2011	25500	2338	11604	854	5165	5247	338	
2012	34245	6104	18215	1114	6276	10056	443	326
2013	48287	11658	23197	1280	8014	12994	560	349
2014	62881	7427	27257	1475	10252	14442	681	407
2015	79535	13155	45248	1787	11912	30385	756	408

B-1-8 助理社会工作师

单位：人

年　份	报考人数	考试通过人数	社会服务行业在业人数	行政机关	社会工作	成员组织	其他社会服务	其他事业单位
2008	60139	20648	17574	609	4727	11840	398	
2009	38204	6611	24095	798	5530	17388	379	
2010	46047	5428	24700	969	6724	16517	490	
2011	54515	8068	29626	963	10686	17419	558	
2012	92621	23846	37599	1163	11998	23513	645	280
2013	121937	27300	44565	1264	15471	26871	694	265
2014	144813	28431	52174	1404	18295	31381	803	291
2015	196965	34274	60379	1630	19272	38342	851	284

B-1-9 社会服务职业技能人员情况

单位：人

年 份	合格总人数	养老护理员	假肢类技能人员	孤残儿童护理员	灾害信息员	殡葬类技能人员
2007	114		21			93
2008	1027		139			888
2009	3575	24	302	23	1397	1829
2010	16809	171	252	196	14554	1636
2011	33240	1538	164	1270	27842	2426
2012	34931	4220	219	2590	25608	2294
2013	17612	4072	193	2216	8989	2142
2014	13246	5934	338	2093	2765	2116
2015	12871	8127	268	1570	791	2115

说明：1.以上数据为民政部职业技能鉴定指导中心及分布在全国31个省、自治区、直辖市76个鉴定站鉴定人数和竞赛晋级人数（不含地方自行组织的鉴定人数）。

2.假肢师（初中高技师高级技师5个级别）、矫形器师（初中高技师高级技师5个级别）。

3.殡仪服务员（初中高技师4个级别）、遗体接运工（初中高3个级别）、遗体防腐师（初中高技师高级技师5个级别）、遗体整容师（初中高技师高级技师5个级别）、遗体火化师（初中高技师高级技师5个级别）、墓地管理员（初中高技师4个级别）。

B-1-10 医疗救助

单位:万人次、万人

年 份	民政部门资助参加城市医疗保险人数	民政部门资助参加农村合作医疗人数	民政部门直接医疗救助人次数	住院救助	门诊救助
2004		552.6	121.1		
2005		654.9	199.6		
2006		1317.1	201.3		
2007		2517.3	819.1		
2008	642.6	3432.4	1203.1		
2009	1095.9	4059.1	1140.4		
2010	1461.2	4615.4	1479.3		
2011	1549.8	4825.3	2144		
2012	1387.1	4490.4	2173.7	1141.4	1032.3
2013	1490.1	4868.7	2126.4	1074.0	1052.4
2014	1702	5021.7	2395.3	1106.6	1288.7

年 份	资助基本医疗保障人数	民政部门认定并实施	民政部门认定、有关方面实施	直接医疗救助	门诊救助	住院救助	民政部门认定并实施	民政部门认定、有关方面实施
2015	6634.7	6213	421.7	2889.1	1581.2	1307.9	2515.9	373.2

B-1-11 历年性别情况统计（1996-2015）

单位：万人

年份	城市最低生活保障人数	女	农村最低生活保障人数	女	农村特困人员集中救助供养人数	女	农村特困人员分散救助供养人数	女	本年在站救助人次数	女	年末残疾职工人数	女
1996	84.9											
1997	87.9											
1998	184.1											
1999	256.9										79.0	19.2
2000	402.6										72.9	26.8
2001	1170.7		304.6								69.9	25.2
2002	2064.7		407.8								68.3	25.1
2003	2246.8		367.1						634528		67.9	24.0
2004	2205.0		488.0						820254		66.2	23.0
2005	2234.2	592.4	825.0	235.1					1196305	209632	63.7	21.8
2006	2240.1	787.5	1593.1	455.1					1295506	221164	55.9	18.3
2007	2272.1	922.5	3566.3	1169.2	138.0	38.3	393.3	99.2	1544492	281987	56.3	16.9
2008	2334.8	947.7	4305.5	1337.0	155.6	36.4	393.0	91.1	1573484	269609	61.9	19.3
2009	2345.6	961.4	4760.0	1502.4	171.8	38.0	381.6	85.9	1680532	281387	62.7	19.8
2010	2310.5	943.4	5214.0	1673.4	177.4	36.9	378.9	83.8	1719008	314866	62.5	19.6
2011	2276.8	920.2	5305.7	1700.6	184.5	37.7	366.5	77.9	2409701	373103	62.8	19.7
2012	2143.5	889.9	5344.5	1814.5	185.3	36.1	360.3	73.3	2765761	383262	59.7	18.4
2013	2064.2	867.0	5388.0	1866.5	183.5	34.1	353.8	67.9	3479536	609333	53.9	16.6
2014	1877.0	792.4	5207.2	1826.4	174.3	30.6	354.8	63.5	2953359	568551	47.9	15.0
2015	1701.1	727.1	4903.6	1795.0	162.3	27.8	354.4	59.4	3233912	608786	42.9	13.5

B-1-11续表

单位：万人

年份	社团负责人数	女	基金会负责人数（人）	女	民办非企业单位负责人数	女	居委会主任数	女	村委会主任数	女
1996										
1997										
1998										
1999	47.6	6.0			0.9	0.2				
2000	45.4	6.1			3.2	0.7				
2001	43.3	5.7			10.1	3.6				
2002	45.5	6.1			14.4	5.1				
2003	51.8	6.2			16.6	5.8				
2004	56.0	6.6			19.1	6.5				
2005	64.0	6.9	2940	450	23.1	7.0				
2006	36.4	7.0	3014	738	20.9	6.5				
2007	39.2	7.9	3113	925	25.9	7.4	8.2	3.7	61.1	9.1
2008	49.5	10.2	3231	600	30.6	8.9	7.8	3.4	57.6	5.9
2009	49.4	9.4	3856	637	31.1	9.6	7.8	3.4	56.3	6.2
2010	56.9	9.1	4797	1019	35.7	10.1	8.1	3.5	56.3	5.9
2011	59.4	8.2	6257	1388	33.6	11.0	8.0	3.5	54.5	6.1
2012	61.6	9.1	6896	1167	35.9	11.9	9.1	3.8	58.7	6.9
2013	61.0	10.0	7331	1429	37.7	12.6	9.4	3.9	58.7	7.0
2014	63.9	10.7	8952	1687	41.3	13.9	9.6	3.9	58.4	7.2
2015	66.3	12.2	12491	2852	48.4	16.0	9.9	4.1	57.9	6.7

B-1-12 社会服务机构固定资产原价

单位：亿元

年 份	合计							行政机关
		社会工作	成员组织	社会组织	自治组织	其他社会服务	其他事业单位	
1978								
1979								
1980								
1981								
1982								
1983	13.0	13.0						
1984	14.9	14.9						
1985	20.1	20.1						
1986	24.2	24.2						
1987	28.7	28.7						
1988	40.8	40.8						
1989	44.1	44.1						
1990	51.7	51.7						
1991	63.6	63.6						
1992	75.6	75.6						
1993	100.3	100.3						
1994	119.0	119.0						
1995	142.6	142.6						
1996	168.1	168.1						
1997	211.5	211.5						
1998	962.4	962.4						
1999	1017.3	1017.3						
2000	1199.3	1199.3						
2001	1317.0	1317.0						
2002	1394.9	1394.9						
2003	1644.3	1644.3						
2004	1755.6	1755.6						62.8
2005	3032.9	1858.0	1174.9		1174.9			64.9
2006	3972.4	2103.0	1869.4	423.0	1446.4			94.3
2007	3840.2	1934.3	1905.9	682.0	1223.9			132.8
2008	4459.9	2186.8	2273.1	805.8	1467.3			132.9
2009	5078.8	2326.4	2752.4	1030	1722.4			119.2
2010	6467.5	2671.9	3795.6	1864.1	1931.5			121.8
2011	6705.6	2790.4	3684.2	1885.0	1799.2	231		284.2
2012	6675.4	2898.9	3477.7	1425.4	2052.3	251.8	47	344.1
2013	6810.2	3030.7	3465.7	1496.6	1969.1	267	46.8	185.4
2014	7212.9	3273.0	3609.3	1560.6	2048.64	283.8	46.8	169.3
2015	8183.1	2892.2	4950.4	2311.1	2639.3	292	48.5	251.5

B-1-13 历年财政支出和社会服务事业费支出情况

单位：亿元

年　份	国家财政支出	社会服务事业费支出	占财政支出%	年　份	国家财政支出	社会服务事业费支出	占财政支出%
1950	68.04	1.32	1.94	1981	1138.41	19.23	1.69
1951	122.32	1.37	1.12	1982	1229.98	19.19	1.56
1952	175.78	2.83	1.61	1983	1409.52	21.61	1.53
1953	220.50	3.55	1.61	1984	1701.02	24.24	1.43
1954	280.93	6.04	2.15	1985	2004.25	29.58	1.48
1955	474.29	4.98	1.05	**“七五”时期**	**12865.67**	**208.49**	**1.62**
“一五”时期	**1367.89**	**25.99**	**1.90**	1986	2204.91	34.41	1.56
1956	536.79	5.69	1.06	1987	2262.18	35.93	1.59
1957	303.43	5.31	1.75	1988	2491.21	39.56	1.59
1958	408.75	3.27	0.80	1989	2823.78	46.65	1.65
1959	553.09	4.48	0.81	1990	3083.59	51.94	1.68
1960	652.25	7.24	1.11	**“八五”时期**	**24387.46**	**386.59**	**1.59**
“二五”时期	**3760.99**	**53.03**	**1.41**	1991	3386.62	62.54	1.85
1961	367.66	9.89	2.69	1992	3742.20	63.71	1.70
1962	305.33	7.45	2.44	1993	4642.30	69.87	1.51
1963	339.15	8.75	2.58	1994	5792.62	87.02	1.50
1964	398.77	16.15	4.05	1995	6823.72	103.45	1.52
1965	467.10	10.79	2.31	**“九五”时期**	**57043.46**	**840.90**	**1.47**
“三五”时期	**2523.24**	**35.83**	**1.42**	1996	7937.55	121.15	1.53
1966	540.49	8.81	1.63	1997	9233.56	133.52	1.45
1967	441.40	8.21	1.86	1998	10798.18	161.84	1.50
1968	359.62	5.61	1.56	1999	13187.67	194.70	1.48
1969	525.20	6.67	1.27	2000	15886.50	229.69	1.45
1970	646.53	6.53	1.01	**“十五”时期**	**127800.69**	**2471.74**	**1.93**
“四五”时期	**3924.37**	**46.70**	**1.19**	2001	18902.58	284.75	1.51
1971	734.41	6.83	0.93	2002	22053.15	392.27	1.78
1972	768.87	8.15	1.06	2003	24649.95	498.92	2.02
1973	810.57	9.97	1.23	2004	28486.89	577.39	2.03
1974	792.98	9.04	1.14	2005	33708.12	718.41	2.13
1975	820.00	12.71	1.55	**“十一五”时期**	**317654.99**	**9156.70**	**2.88**
“五五”时期	**5198.77**	**84.22**	**1.62**	2006	40213.16	915.35	2.28
1976	804.48	16.17	2.01	2007	49565.40	1215.49	2.45
1977	842.27	18.53	2.20	2008	62427.03	2146.45	3.44
1978	1122.09	13.71	1.22	2009	75874.00	2181.90	2.88
1979	1281.79	18.33	1.43	2010	89575.40	2697.51	3.01
1980	1228.83	17.48	1.42	**“十二五”时期**	**676383.92**	**20529.88**	**3.04**
“六五”时期	**7483.18**	**113.85**	**1.52**	2011	108929.67	3229.14	2.96
				2012	125712.25	3683.74	2.93
				2013	139744.00	4276.50	3.06
				2014	151662.00	4414.10	2.91
				2015	150336.00	4926.40	3.28

B-1-14 按用项分社会服务事业费

单位：亿元

年份	社会服务事业费	抚恤费	离休费	社会福利及其他社会救济费	最低生活保障事业费	自然灾害救济费	退休费	其他社会服务事业费
1978	13.7	2.8		4.4		4.2	2.3	
1979	18.4	3.5		5.2		6.8	2.9	
1980	17.5	4.4		5.2		4.5	3.4	
“六五”时期	**114.2**	**27.3**	**0.9**	**32.1**		**35.2**	**16.8**	**1.7**
1981	19.2	4.4		5.1		6.3	3.4	
1982	19.6	4.8		5.1		6.0	3.5	
1983	21.6	5.3		6.5		6.4	3.4	
1984	24.2	6.1	0.2	8.0		6.9	3.0	
1985	29.6	6.7	0.7	7.4		9.6	3.5	1.7
“七五”时期	**208.4**	**59.2**	**11.4**	**46.7**		**56.4**	**22.0**	**12.8**
1986	34.4	8.4	1.2	8.3		10.7	3.8	1.9
1987	35.9	9.6	1.8	8.6		9.9	4.1	2
1988	39.6	11	2.3	9		10.4	4.3	2.5
1989	46.6	14	2.9	10		12.3	4.6	2.9
1990	51.9	16.2	3.2	10.8		13.1	5.2	3.5
“八五”时期	**386.6**	**107.8**	**23.2**	**75.6**		**94.1**	**45.5**	**40.5**
1991	62.5	16.8	3.6	11.7		20.9	5.4	4.2
1992	63.7	18	4.2	12.4		17.1	6.6	5.4
1993	69.9	20.1	3.6	14.5		14.9	8.3	8.4
1994	87	24.4	5.5	17.3		17.7	12.1	10.1
1995	103.5	28.5	6.3	19.7		23.5	13.1	12.4

年份	社会服务事业费	抚恤费	军队离退休、退职费	社会福利及其他社会救济费	最低生活保障事业费	自然灾害救济费	地方离、退休人员费	其他社会服务事业费
“九五”时期	**840.9**	**220.6**	**76.9**	**201.8**	**48.7**	**171.5**	**58.0**	**112.2**
1996	121.2	31.9	6.2	22.8	3	30.8	13.9	15.5
1997	133.5	36.1	12.4	27.1	2.9	28.7	10.3	19
1998	161.8	39.4	15.2	34	7.1	41.2	10.9	21.3
1999	194.7	49.7	18.4	52.5	13.8	35.6	11.2	27.2
2000	229.7	63.5	24.7	65.4	21.9	35.2	11.7	29.2

年份	社会服务事业费	抚恤	退役安置	社会福利	社会救助	城市低保及其他城市社会救济	农村低保及其他农村社会救济	医疗救助	自然灾害生活救助	离退休人员经费	其他
“十五”时期	**2471.8**	**479.8**	**302.7**	**444.7**		**668**	**127.6**	**11**	**247.6**	**66.9**	**273.7**
2001	284.8	69.5	31.2	90.6		41.6			41	13	39.5
2002	392.3	74.7	49.5	167.5		108.7			40	13.2	47.3
2003	498.9	87.9	59	78.9	153.1	153.1			52.9	13.1	54
2004	577.4	104.1	74.1	52.1	223.6	172.7	47.7	3.2	51.1	13.9	58.5
2005	718.4	143.6	88.9	55.6	279.6	191.9	79.9	7.8	62.6	13.7	74.4
“十一五”时期	**9156.8**	**1316.2**	**956**	**490**	**3673.6**	**1941.7**	**1710.7**	**436.1**	**1205**	**125.7**	**975.4**
2006	915.4	178.8	115.7	65.3	372	224.2	126.6	21.2	79	14	90.6
2007	1215.5	210.8	165	87.6	509.7	277.4	189.8	42.5	79.8	24.8	137.8
2008	2146.5	253.6	180.6	103.1	806.7	393.4	326.8	86.5	609.8	26.5	166.2
2009	2181.9	310.3	225.7	124.1	1098.1	482.1	487.9	128.1	199.2	30	194.5
2010	2697.5	362.7	269	109.9	1302	564.6	579.6	157.8	237.2	30.4	386.3

年份	社会服务事业费	抚恤	退役安置	社会福利	社会救助	城乡低保	其他社会救助	医疗救助	自然灾害生活救助	民政管理事务	行政事业单位离退休	其他
“十二五”时期	**20520**	**2887.1**	**2149.2**	**1993.1**	**10349.7**	**7586.3**	**1471.4**	**1292**	**743.7**	**1496.1**	**212.2**	**688.9**
2011	3229.2	428.3	302.3	232.2	1766.3	1327.6	222.4	216.3	128.7	220.8	35.3	115.3
2012	3683.8	517	372.1	319.5	1866.1	1392.3	243.2	230.6	163.4	248.5	39	158.2
2013	4276.5	618.4	435.3	397.6	2172.4	1623.6	291.4	257.4	178.7	296.7	43.6	133.8
2014	4404.1	636.6	456.8	481	2197.5	1592.0	321.5	284.0	124.4	330.5	44.2	133.1
2015	4926.4	686.8	582.7	562.8	2347.4	1650.8	392.9	303.7	148.5	399.6	50.1	148.5

B-1-15 中央转移支付社会服务事业费

单位：万元

年 份	合 计	中央级社会服务事业费	中央专项转移支付	抚恤、退休、救济费	救 灾	社会福利救济事业费	其 他
1978	11	11					
1979	44	44					
1980	103	103					
“六五”时期	**335594**	**1108**	**334486**	**63306**	**270745**	**220**	**215**
1981	138	138					
1982	74120	78	74042	14247	59795		
1983	74368	163	74205	14205	60000		
1984	78872	286	78586	18586	60000		

年 份	合 计	中央级社会服务事业费	中央专项转移支付	抚 恤	安 置	救 灾	社会福利救济事业费	其 他
1985	108096	443	107653	9698	6570	90950	220	215
“七五”时期	**778310**	**9267**	**769043**	**148718**	**105230**	**512500**		
1986	132802	2526	130276	16396	9285	102000		
1987	133877	2742	131135	21726	19409	90000		
1988	158355	1297	157058	24110	21948	111000		
1989	174374	1185	173189	43206	26483	103500		
1990	178902	1517	177385	43280	28105	106000		
“八五”时期	**1488090**	**15897**	**1472193**	**328272**	**315101**	**828820**		
1991	309432	1792	307640	49010	34210	224420		
1992	209360	3217	206143	52156	40587	113400		
1993	238083	3108	234975	60494	53481	121000		
1994	353831	4077	349754	79084	90670	180000		
1995	377384	3703	373681	87528	96153	190000		
“九五”时期	**2943934**	**104302**	**2839632**	**749824**	**773058**	**1122750**	**190000**	**4000**
1996	426354	6371	419983	102394	102589	215000		
1997	455309	5954	449355	110430	114925	220000		4000
1998	568049	50783	517266	120000	149516	247750		

年 份	合 计（亿元）	中央级社会服务事业费（亿元）	中央专项转移支付（亿元）	抚恤（亿元）	安置（亿元）	救灾（亿元）	低保（亿元）	临时救助（亿元）	医疗救助（亿元）	福利（亿元）	其他（亿元）
1999	62.8	1.2	61.6	18.0	17.6	22.0	4.0				
2000	86.6	2.9	83.7	23.7	23.0	22.0	15.0				
“十五”时期	**1004.3**	**11.9**	**992.4**	**212.1**	**217.3**	**170.1**	**373.1**		**12.0**		**7.9**
2001	109.6	1.4	108.2	26.3	28.7	30.2	23.0				
2002	140.2	1.8	138.4	31.6	37.0	24.3	45.5				
2003	213.6	1.8	211.8	37.1	39.2	40.5	92.0		3.0		0.1
2004	227.7	3.9	223.8	40.7	47.4	32.0	100.6		3.0		0.1
2005	313.2	2.9	310.3	76.4	65.0	43.1	112.0		6.0		7.7
“十一五”时期	**4761.3**	**89.3**	**4658.9**	**767.6**	**699.9**	**856.1**	**1941.6**		**319.6**		**74.2**
2006	406.8	2.8	404.0	111.7	73.9	49.4	136.0		14.3		18.7
2007	523.1	5.6	504.4	110.9	117.4	49.9	189.9		36.3		0.1
2008	1207.7	26.6	1181.1	142.1	142.9	478.4	363.1		54.5		0.1
2009	1232.5	5.5	1227.0	187.3	160.2	174.7	620		84.5		0.3
2010	1391.2	48.8	1342.4	215.6	205.5	103.7	632.6		130		55
“十二五”时期	**10189.2**	**61.5**	**10127.7**	**1668.5**	**1390.9**	**489.5**	**5312.0**	**73.0**	**785.6**	**258.0**	**150.2**
2011	1817.4	9.4	1808.0	277.4	206.4	84	1004.7		150	25.2	60.3
2012	1804.6	10	1794.6	333.3	265.4	112.7	870.5		150	42	20.7
2013	2163.5	13.7	2149.8	369.8	277.4	101.9	1168.8		156.7	54.4	20.8
2014	2117.8	12.8	2105.0	338	288.8	96.3	1101.3	32	165	63.4	20.2
2015	2285.9	15.6	2270.3	350	352.9	94.6	1166.7	41	163.9	73	28.2

B-1-16 彩票公益金支出

单位：亿元

年 份	合计	抚恤	退役安置	社会福利	低保及其他社会救济	医疗救助	自然灾害生活救助	其他
2001								
2002								
2003								
2004								
2005								
“十一五”时期	**485.3**	**17.6**	**6**	**204.9**	**26.2**	**48.8**		**175.6**
2006	52.6	2.6	1	24.1	3.3			21.6
2007	77.6	3	0.9	35.5	4.3			33.9
2008	119.2	3.7	1.3	44.9	7.2	17.5		38.5
2009	113.4	3.4	1.2	49.3	5.9	15.5		38
2010	122.5	4.9	1.6	51.1	5.5	15.8		43.6
“十二五”时期	**1002.6**	**30.5**	**2.6**	**596.4**	**42.7**	**90.4**	**8.8**	**206.7**
2011	127.9	4.8	0.4	61.4	7.4	16.3	0.8	36.6
2012	159.0	5.4	0.5	92.2	7.3	16.8	1.3	35.6
2013	195.5	7.5	0.6	117.1	8.7	17.5	2.6	41.5
2014	231.3	5.9	0.9	143.6	10.0	19.1	2.2	49.4
2015	288.9	6.9	0.2	182.1	9.3	20.7	1.9	43.6

B-1-17 中央彩票公益金使用情况

单位：亿元

年 份	合 计	中央级	转移支付					
				养老	残疾人	儿童	社会公益	医疗救助
“十五”时期	**14.91**		**14.91**	**0.70**		**2.06**	**0.15**	**12.0**
2001								
2002								
2003	3.00		3.00					3.0
2004	5.91		5.91	0.70		2.06	0.15	3.0
2005	6.00		6.00					6.0
“十一五”时期	**112.29**	**2.47**	**109.82**	**21.64**		**16.37**	**1.81**	**70.0**
2006	14.03	0.10	13.93	1.59		3.24	0.10	9.0
2007	16.98	0.88	16.10	1.53		1.24	0.33	13.0
2008	28.14	0.10	28.04	4.79		6.67	0.58	16.0
2009	26.61	0.09	26.52	7.79		2.05	0.68	16.0
2010	26.53	1.30	25.23	5.94		3.17	0.12	16.0
“十二五”时期	**220.81**	**8.20**	**212.61**	**75.83**	**25.34**	**22.88**	**8.56**	**80.0**
2011	30.03	1.30	28.73	7.86		3.48	1.39	16.0
2012	35.98	2.30	33.68	10.67	0.99	4.35	1.67	16.0
2013	48.71	1.80	46.91	22.16	1.98	5.08	1.69	16.0
2014	35.95	1.10	34.85	10.20	2.97	3.97	1.71	16.0
2015	70.14	1.70	68.44	24.94	19.40	6.00	2.10	16.0

B-1-18 社会服务事业基本建设投资（按投资来源分）

单位：亿元、万平方米

年 份	计划总投资	本年完成投资	国家投资	国内贷款	自 筹	福利彩票公益金	其 他	本年完工项目个数
1988								
1989	5.8	2.0	0.7	0.1	0.8		0.2	
1990	6.9	2.4	0.8	0.1	1.0		0.3	
“八五”时期	**63.4**	**27.6**	**10.3**	**1.2**	**13.4**		**2.8**	
1991	7.0	3.0	1.0	0.1	1.5		0.3	
1992	7.3	3.2	1.0	0.1	1.9		0.4	
1993	12.8	5.6	1.4	0.2	3.4		0.7	
1994	15.5	6.2	2.3	0.5	2.9		0.6	
1995	20.9	9.6	4.6	0.3	3.8		0.9	
“九五”时期	**237.9**	**89.8**	**21.3**	**5.9**	**54.3**	**6.8**	**8.3**	**2793**
1996	29.8	10.1	2.1	0.4	6.4		1.1	
1997	35.7	13.8	2.7	0.8	8.6		1.6	
1998	41.0	16.6	2.8	0.8	11.1		1.9	
1999	63.2	24.7	6.0	2.3	14.6	3.5	1.8	1456
2000	68.2	24.7	7.7	1.6	13.6	3.3	1.9	1337
“十五”时期	**376.9**	**151.7**	**47.9**	**8.8**	**78.4**	**21.0**	**16.6**	**22117**
2001	77.5	30.8	10.4	2.2	15.1	3.6	3.1	1360
2002	88.7	30.1	9.5	1.4	15.9	3.3	3.3	3659
2003	87.3	30.0	9.9	1.7	15.1	3.5	3.3	3867
2004	89.7	29.2	8.9	2.4	14.4	4.7	3.5	8982
2005	33.8	31.6	9.1	1.0	17.9	5.8	3.5	4249
“十一五”时期	**485.6**	**487.8**	**210.7**	**12.4**	**148.8**	**96.8**	**82.3**	**62453**
2006	34.8	33.5	9.9	0.9	19.9	8.4	2.5	3626
2007	47.6	47.7	14.5	3.0	26.9	13.0	2.9	2446
2008	63.5	66.6	26.6	1.9	34.6	16.5	3.2	3906
2009	166.5	157.0	70.6	3.7	67.4	26.6	15.3	6457

年 份	本年计划总投资	本年完成投资	国家投资	国内贷款	利用外资	福利彩票公益金	其 他	本年完工项目规模
2010	173.2	183.0	89.1	2.9	0.2	32.3	58.5	46018
“十二五”时期	**1234.7**	**1268.1**	**499.9**	**19.6**	**5.8**	**288.3**	**454.5**	**38309.3**
2011	217.3	218.5	78.5	6.2	0.5	53.4	79.9	4533
2012	222.3	234.7	104.2	3.8	1.1	51	74.6	6095
2013	311.9	292.8	120.1	1.4	1.7	64.7	104.8	15328
2014	266	282.2	104.3	3.5	1.7	57.5	115.3	11355
2015	217.2	239.9	92.8	4.7	0.8	61.7	79.9	1048.4

注：2015年后，本年完工项目个数指标更改为本年完工项目规模，单位为万平方米。

B-1-19 国家对社会服务事业基本建设投资(按项目分)

单位：亿元

年 份	国家预算内基本建设投资	优抚安置单位	社区服务设施	收养性福利机构	殡仪	救助	其他
1989	0.7						0.7
1990	0.8			0.2	0.1		0.5
“八五” 时期	**10.3**	**4.2**		**1.4**	**1.1**	**0.2**	**3.4**
1991	1.0	0.1		0.2	0.1		0.6
1992	1.0			0.2			0.8
1993	1.4			0.2	0.4		0.8
1994	2.3	1.2		0.3	0.3		0.5
1995	4.6	2.9		0.5	0.3	0.2	0.7
“九五” 时期	**21.3**	**2.0**	**1.6**	**6.6**	**6.5**		**4.6**
1996	2.1	0.1		0.5	0.5		1.0
1997	2.7			0.7	1.1		0.9
1998	2.8	0.2		1.8	0.8		
1999	6.0	0.9	0.6	1.5	1.7		1.3
2000	7.7	0.8	1.0	2.1	2.4		1.4
“十五” 时期	**47.9**	**5.0**	**9.4**	**14.3**	**9.2**		**10.0**
2001	10.4	0.7	1.5	3.1	2.1		3.0
2002	9.5	0.7	2.1	2.8	1.9		2.0
2003	9.9	1.2	2.4	3.3	1.5		1.5
2004	9.0	1.1	2.3	2.5	1.1		2.0
2005	9.1	1.3	1.1	2.6	2.6		1.5
“十一五” 时期	**210.8**	**27.8**	**31.5**	**85.2**	**19.2**	**8.1**	**39.0**
2006	9.9	1.8	0.8	3.9	1.4	0.3	1.6
2007	14.5	2.5	0.9	6.5	2.4	0.4	1.8
2008	26.6	8.2	1.9	8.5	3.7	1.1	3.2
2009	70.6	7.4	14.0	30.1	5.7	2.5	11.0
2010	89.2	7.9	13.9	36.2	6.0	3.8	21.4
“十二五” 时期	**499.9**	**20.8**	**29.4**	**277.3**	**12.9**	**63.5**	**95.9**
2011	78.5	9.5	11.1	31.1	5.8	3.8	17.2
2012	104.2	11.3	18.3	45.1	7.1	6.1	16.2

年 份	国家预算内基本建设投资	提供住宿的社会工作机构	为老年人与残疾人提供服务的机构	为智障与精神病提供服务的机构	为儿童提供收养救助服务的机构	不提供住宿的社会工作机构	其他
2013	120.1	76.2	66.5	3.2	4.6	22.2	21.7
2014	104.3	66.4	58.1	2.7	4.5	16.2	21.7
2015	92.8	58.5	51.6	2.2	4.0	15.2	19.1

B-1-20 中央预算内

年份	项目合计（个）	投资合计	本级情况				养老	
			本级项目数	本级投资	地方项目小计	补助地方投资小计	项目数	资金额
1989								
1990		0.1		0.1				
“八五”时期		**0.2**		**0.2**				
1991		0.2		0.2				
1992								
1993								
1994								
1995								
“九五”时期								
1996								
1997								
1998								
1999								
2000								
“十五”时期	**24**	**0.8**	**24**	**0.8**				
2001	3	0.3	3	0.3				
2002	10	0.2	10	0.2				
2003	6	0.1	6	0.1				
2004	3	0.1	3	0.1				
2005	2	0.1	2	0.1				
“十一五”时期	**2088**	**35.9**	**18**	**5.5**	**2070**	**30.4**	**189**	**5.0**
2006	2	0.2	2	0.2				
2007	218	2.8	5	0.8	213	2.0		
2008	575	6.8	3	2.1	572	4.7		
2009	774	13.0	4	1.3	770	11.7	63	2.0
2010	519	13.1	4	1.1	515	12.0	126	3
“十二五”时期	**1860**	**135.2**	**4**	**0.7**	**1856**	**134.5**	**1364**	**107.4**
2011	433	26.0	4	0.7	429	25.3	338	9
2012	692	33.0			692	33.0	669	31
2013	735	17.0			735	17.0	357	15

年　份	建设规模	投资合计	本级情况				养老		精神
			建设规模	本级投资	建设规模	补助地方投资小计	建设规模	资金额	建设规模
2014	383.28	29.0			383.28	29.0	330	24.39	
2015	342.89	30.2			342.89	30.2	302	28	

基本建设投资情况

单位：亿元、个、万平方米

地方情况									
精神卫生		儿童		流浪		社区		烈建	
项目数	资金额	项目数	资金额	项目数	资金额	项目数	资金额	项目数	资金额
26	**4.4**	**134**	**5.0**	**254**	**5.0**	**1334**	**6.0**	**133**	**5.0**
		15	0.5	28	0.8	170	0.7		
		32	1.3	65	1.4	475	2.0		
		33	1.3	78	1.4	463	2.0	133	5.0
26	4.37	54	1.9	83	1.4	226	1.3		
91	**16.3**		**4.0**		**0.7**	**401**	**6.2**		
91	16.3								
						23	2		
						378	2		

地方情况								
卫生	儿童		社会事务		社区		烈建	
资金额	建设规模	资金额	建设规模	资金额	建设规模	资金额	建设规模	资金额
	22.33	2	5.37	0.65	25.58	1.96		
	17.51	2			23.51	0.2		

B-2-1 提供住宿的社会服务机构

单位：个

年 份	单位数	老年及残疾人	智障和精神疾病	儿童	其他	#救助管理站	#安置农场	#军供站
1978	8571	8365	139	67				
1979	8988	8801	135	52				
1980	9669	9460	150	59				
1981	10031	9813	155	63				
1982	12275	12046	165	64				
1983	15807	15582	165	60				
1984	22796	22566	167	63				
1985	29100	28852	161	59	28			
1986	35008	34750	166	58	34			
1987	37372	37109	170	60	33			
1988	39030	38767	173	62	28			
1989	39743	39472	180	64	27			
1990	40583	40340	181	62				
1991	42264	42013	188	63				
1992	43319	43063	189	67				
1993	43681	43375	190	67	49			
1994	43240	42911	188	73	68			
1995	43074	42735	190	77	72			
1996	42829	42518	155	84	72			
1997	42385	42027	192	91	75			
1998	42131	41755	195	105	76			
1999	40430	40030	191	110	99			
2000	40491	39321	201	126	843			
2001	38785	38106	200	160	319			
2002	38200	37591	200	178	231			
2003	37294	36224	205	192	1587			
2004	38593	37880	211	208	1320			
2005	42487	40641	226	224	1396			
2006	43187	40964	219	249	1755			
2007	44958	42713	234	269	1742			
2008	41099	38674	244	290	1891			
2009	43944	39671	266	419	3588			
2010	44482	39904	251	480	3847			
2011	45973	42828	251	638	2256	1547		327
2012	48078	44304	257	724	2793	1770	27	328
2013	45977	42475	261	803	2438	1891	26	325
2014	36810	33044	254	890	2622	1949	13	327
2015	31187	27752	242	753	2440	1766	15	320

B-2-2 提供住宿的社会服务机构床位

单位：万张

年 份	床位数合计	老年及残疾人床位	智障和精神疾病床位	儿童床位	其他床位	#救助管理站	#军供站	每千人口拥有社会服务床位数	每千老年人口拥有养老床位数
1978	16.3	15.7	0.6					0.17	
1979	22.6	20.1	2.1	0.4				0.23	
1980	24.2	21.3	2.4	0.5				0.25	
1981	25.3	22.2	2.5	0.6				0.25	
1982	28.2	24.8	2.8	0.6				0.28	
1983	32.4	29.0	2.8	0.6				0.31	
1984	42.5	39.0	2.9	0.6				0.41	
1985	49.1	45.7	2.9	0.5	0.2			0.46	
1986	58.7	55.0	3.1	0.6	0.3			0.55	
1987	64.9	61.0	3.3	0.6	0.3			0.59	
1988	69.5	65.5	3.4	0.6	0.2			0.63	
1989	73.8	69.5	3.6	0.7	0.2			0.65	
1990	78.0	73.5	3.7	0.8				0.68	
1991	82.8	78.3	3.8	0.7				0.71	
1992	89.8	85.2	3.8	0.8				0.77	
1993	92.7	87.8	4.0	0.9	0.4			0.78	
1994	95.5	90.6	4.0	0.9	0.5			0.80	
1995	97.6	92.5	4.0	1.1	0.6			0.81	
1996	100.8	95.6	4.0	1.2	0.6			0.82	
1997	103.1	97.8	4.0	1.3	0.6			0.83	
1998	105.8	100.2	4.1	1.5	0.6			0.85	
1999	108.9	102.4	4.1	1.6	0.8			0.87	
2000	113.0	104.5	4.1	1.8	2.6			0.89	
2001	140.7	114.6	4.2	2.3	19.6			1.10	
2002	141.5	114.9	4.3	2.5	19.8			1.10	
2003	142.9	120.6	4.5	2.7	15.1			1.11	
2004	157.2	139.5	4.5	3.0	10.2			1.21	
2005	180.7	158.1	4.4	3.2	15.0			1.38	10.97
2006	204.5	179.6	4.4	3.2	17.3			1.56	12.05
2007	269.6	242.9	4.7	3.4	18.6			2.04	15.83
2008	300.3	267.4	5.4	4.3	23.2			2.26	16.72
2009	326.5	293.5	5.9	4.8	22.3			2.45	17.56
2010	349.6	316.1	6.1	5.5	21.9			2.61	17.79
2011	396.4	369.2	6.5	6.8	13.9	7.1	3.8	2.94	19.96
2012	449.3	416.5	6.7	8.7	17.4	9.0	3.8	3.32	21.48
2013	462.4	429.5	7.4	9.8	15.7	9.7	3.7	3.87	24.39
2014	426.0	390.2	8.0	10.8	17.0	9.9	3.7	4.49	27.20
2015	393.2	358.2	7.9	10.0	17.1	10.3	3.8	5.30	30.30

B-2-3 提供住宿的社会服务机构收养人员情况

单位：万人

年 份	总人数	老年及残疾人	智障和精神疾病人	儿童	其他
1978	16.3	14.0	1.9	0.4	
1979	18.6	16.3	1.9	0.4	
1980	19.1	16.7	2.0	0.4	
1981	19.7	17.0	2.2	0.5	
1982	22.5	19.7	2.3	0.5	
1983	25.9	23.0	2.4	0.5	
1984	34.1	31.0	2.6	0.5	
1985	40.8	37.5	2.6	0.5	0.2
1986	47.4	43.9	2.8	0.5	0.2
1987	51.8	48.2	2.9	0.5	0.2
1988	54.8	51.1	3.0	0.6	0.1
1989	56.9	53.0	3.1	0.6	0.2
1990	59.9	56.1	3.2	0.6	
1991	64.6	60.8	3.2	0.6	
1992	69.6	65.6	3.3	0.7	
1993	72.4	68.0	3.4	0.7	0.3
1994	73.6	69.2	3.3	0.8	0.3
1995	74.7	70.1	3.2	1.0	0.4
1996	76.9	72.3	3.1	1.1	0.4
1997	78.5	73.7	3.2	1.2	0.4
1998	80.0	74.9	3.2	1.4	0.5
1999	82.7	77.6	3.2	1.4	0.5
2000	85.4	78.6	3.2	1.8	1.8
2001	88.5	82.0	3.3	2.1	1.1
2002	91.6	85.0	3.4	2.2	1.0
2003	96.5	89.1	3.5	2.5	1.4
2004	110.9	103.9	3.6	2.8	0.6
2005	123.6	116.2	3.7	2.9	0.8
2006	147.0	138.5	3.8	3.2	1.5
2007	200.0	191.3	4.1	3.0	1.6
2008	240.0	211.5	4.5	3.4	20.6
2009	256.0	227.5	5.0	3.7	19.8
2010	278.2	247.0	5.3	4.2	21.7
2011	293.4	279.7	5.5	4.6	3.6
2012	309.5	293.6	5.8	5.4	4.7
2013	322.5	307.4	6.0	5.6	3.5
2014	337.0	320.4	6.5	5.9	4.2
2015	236.3	219.4	6.4	5.6	4.9

B-2-4 按城乡分类的提供住宿的社会服务机构情况

年份	单位数（个）	城市	农村	床位数（万张）	城市	农村	收养人数（万人）	城市	农村
1978	8571	728	7843	16.3	0.1	16.2	16.3	5.7	10.6
1979	8988	1518	7470	22.6	6.4	16.2	18.6	8	10.6
1980	9669	1407	8262	24.2	7.1	17.1	19.1	7.9	11.2
1981	10031	1487	8544	25.3	7.4	17.9	19.7	8.2	11.5
1982	12275	1689	10586	28.2	7.6	20.6	22.5	8.7	13.8
1983	15807	1760	14047	32.4	7.7	24.7	25.9	9	16.9
1984	22796	1925	20871	42.5	8.5	34	34.1	10	24.1
1985	29100	5478	23622	49.1	18.2	30.9	40.8	14.6	26.2
1986	35008	8330	26678	58.7	23.6	35.1	47.4	18.9	28.5
1987	37372	9358	28014	64.9	25.8	39.1	51.8	20.5	31.3
1988	39030	10498	28532	69.5	28.4	41.1	54.8	22.3	32.5
1989	39743	10118	29625	73.8	28.7	45.1	56.9	22.3	34.6
1990	40583	12697	27886	78	34.5	43.5	59.9	26.8	33.1
1991	42264	13197	29067	82.8	36.7	46.1	64.6	28.5	36.1
1992	43319	16847	26472	89.8	44.6	45.2	69.6	34.5	35.1
1993	43681	17400	26281	92.7	47	45.7	72.4	37.2	35.2
1994	43240	18035	25205	95.5	50	45.5	73.6	39.1	34.5

年份	单位数（个）	国有社会福利院	社会办敬老院	床位数（万张）	国有社会福利院	社会办敬老院	收养人数（万人）	国有社会福利院	社会办敬老院
1995	43074	11184	31890	97.6	18.6	79	74.7	14.4	60.3
1996	42829	11216	31613	100.8	19.2	81.6	76.9	14.8	62.1
1997	42385	10417	31968	103.1	19.9	83.2	78.5	15.4	63.1
1998	42131	9895	32236	105.8	21	84.8	80	16.1	63.9
1999	40430	3086	37344	108.9	23.6	85.3	82.7	17.9	64.8

年份	单位数（个）	城市	农村	床位数（万张）	城市	农村	收养人数（万人）	城市	农村
2000	40491	14915	25576	113	57.4	55.6	85.4	42.6	42.8
2001	38785	12135	26650	140.7	72.3	68.4	88.5	39.6	48.9
2002	38200	12503	25697	141.5	75.3	66.2	91.6	42.2	49.4
2003	37294	12951	24343	142.9	75.3	67.6	96.5	46.1	50.4
2004	38593	12151	26442	157.2	79.7	77.5	110.9	51.5	59.4
2005	42487	12806	29681	180.7	91.2	89.5	123.6	55.7	67.9
2006	43187	11814	31373	204.5	90.9	113.6	147.0	55.0	92.0
2007	44958	10274	34684	269.6	89.8	179.8	200.0	43.9	149.3
2008	41099	10731	30368	300.3	107.2	193.1	240.0	79.5	160.5
2009	43944	12658	31286	326.5	117.7	208.8	256.0	83.0	173.0
2010	44482	13010	31472	349.6	124.7	224.9	278.2	95.7	182.5
2011	45973	13833	32140	396.4	154.5	241.9	293.4	100.9	192.5
2012	48078	15291	32787	449.3	188.3	261	309.5	109.5	200.0
2013	45977	15730	30247	462.4	189.6	272.8	322.5	121.3	201.2
2014	36810	16549	20261	426.0	206.4	219.6	334.0	127.6	155.7
2015	31187	15600	15587	393.2	216.1	177.1	236.3	121.1	115.2

B-2-5 老年福利与福利企业

单位：万人

年 份	老年福利			福利企业		
	享受高龄补贴的老年人数	享受护理补贴的老年人数	享受养老服务补贴的老年人数	单位数（个）	残疾职工人数（万人）	利润额（亿元）
1978				920	3.5	0.8
1979				1106	4.8	0.8
1980				1309	5.5	0.9
1981				1574	6.1	0.7
1982				1704	6.4	0.8
1983				5930	9.6	0.9
1984				6710	11.6	1.3
1985				14872	23.2	5.1
1986				19865	31.4	4.2
1987				27793	43.3	8.8
1988				40496	55.9	16.5
1989				41565	60.5	16.1
1990				41827	63.8	17.8
1991				43805	70.1	21.3
1992				49836	77.8	32.6
1993				56881	84.5	44.7
1994				60233	90.9	44.1
1995				60237	93.9	49.1
1996				59397	93.6	45.1
1997				55509	91.0	66.3
1998				50514	85.6	63.9
1999				44628	79.0	76.7
2000				40670	72.5	99.0
2001				37980	69.9	119.5
2002				35758	68.3	148.3
2003				33976	67.9	189.9
2004				32410	66.2	219
2005				31211	63.7	225.2
2006	233.5			30199	55.9	237.8
2007	247.1			24974	56.3	169.3
2008	349.3			23780	61.9	119.2
2009	430.9			22783	62.7	125.4
2010	576.4			22226	62.5	150.8
2011	883.1			21507	62.8	140.1
2012	1257.7			20205	59.7	118.4
2013	1557.9	11.7	101.9	18227	53.9	106.9
2014	1719.6	20	154.7	16389	47.9	95.2
2015	2155.1	26.5	257.9	14585	42.9	81.4

B-2-6 孤儿和收养

单位：件、人

年份	孤儿数	收养登记总数	中国公民收养登记	外国公民收养登记	被收养人合计	福利机构抚养的儿童	被中国公民收养	被外国人收养
1996		18896	14804	4092	20389	2201		
1997		21548	17193	4355	21548	975		
1998		26498	20611	5887	26498	677		
1999		38074	31916	6158	38019	1670	31882	6137
2000		55802	49037	6765	56191	1847	49500	6691
2001		44706	36089	8617	45844	1908	37200	8644
2002		45336	35372	9964	47860	2404	37642	10218
2003		54159	44884	9275	54159	3427	44884	9275
2004		52603	40084	12519	55572	3189	44708	10864
2005		49506	35470	14036	50921	3564	38057	12864
2006		48178	38393	9785	49148	2867	39424	9724
2007		45192	36893	8299	46047	1146	37790	8257
2008	67921	42550	37009	5541	44115	1846	38617	5498
2009	127599	44260	39801	4459	44359	1605	39964	4395
2010	252110	34529	29618	4911	34473	1878	29978	4495
2011	509695	31424	27579	3845	31329	1679	28117	3212
2012	570075	27278	23157	4121	27310	1760	23189	4121
2013	548845	24460	21230	3230	24491	9657	21261	3230
2014	525179	22772	19885	2887	22876	10336	20055	2821
2015	502105	22348	19406	2942	22363	10704	19430	2933

注：福利机构抚养的儿童2012年以前是孤儿，2013年以后含弃婴。

B-2-7 城市社会救济和城市最低生活保障

单位：万人

年份	城市传统救济总人数	城市传统定救人数	城市精简退职老职工人数		
				享受40%人数	定量救济人数
1978					
1979	33.6	23.7	*9.9*		
1980	32.9	22.9	*10*		
1981	31.5	21.5	*10*		
1982	34.7	21.4	*13.3*		
1983	47.1	22.6	*24.5*		
1984	*207.4*	*160.6*	*46.8*	*25.3*	
1985	30.0	18.2	11.8	6.4	5.4
1986	49.0	35.6	13.4	7.1	6.3
1987	29.8	16.2	13.6	7.2	6.4
1988	32.9	17.6	15.3	7.7	7.6
1989	30.5	16.2	14.3	7.1	7.2
1990	41.8	16.4	25.4	16.4	9.0
1991	33.7	16.1	17.6	8.5	9.0
1992	39.5	19.2	20.3	9.7	10.6
1993	24.6	13.8	10.8	5	5.8
1994	23.0	12.4	10.6	4.9	5.7
1995	109.0	55.2	53.8	23.9	29.9
1996	120.1	66.5	53.6	23.6	30.0

年份	城市最低生活保障人数	在职人员	下岗人员	退休人员	失业人员	"三无"人员	其他人员
1996	84.9						
1997	87.9						
1998	184.1						
1999	256.9						
2000	402.6						
2001	1170.7						
2002	2064.7	186.8	554.5	90.8	358.3	91.9	783.1
2003	2246.8	179.3	518.4	90.7	409	99.9	949.3
2004	2205	141	468.9	73.1	423.1	95.4	1003.5
2005	2234.2	114.1	430.7	61.3	410.1	95.8	1122.1
2006	2240.1	97.6	350	53.2	420.8	93.1	1225.3

年份	城市最低生活保障人数	残疾人	三无人员	老年人	成年人				未成年人	
					在职人员	灵活就业	登记失业	未登记失业	在校生	其他
2007	2272.1	161.0	125.8	298.4	93.9	343.8	627.2	364.3	321.6	223
2008	2334.8	169.1	106.9	316.7	82.2	381.7	564.3	402.2	358.1	229.6
2009	2345.6	181.0	94.1	333.5	79.0	432.2	510.2	410.9	369.1	210.7
2010	2310.5	180.7	89.3	338.6	68.2	432.4	492.8	420.0	357.3	201.2
2011	2276.8	184.1	80.3	346.9	61.5	429.7	472.5	426.7	348.5	191
2012	2143.5	174.5	64.9	339.3	49.6	459.3	400.4	422.1	318.3	154.5
2013	2064.2	169.2	58	330.3	45.1	462.1	365.5	416.8	303.2	141.3
2014	1877.0	161.1	50	315.8	37.5	425.8	312.5	398.7	266	120.7
2015	1701.1	165.7	43.8	293.5	31.1	377.3	264.1	394	235.9	105.1

注：1984年的精简退职老职工人数含农村的数据。

B-2-8 农村社会救济和农村最低生活保障

单位：万人、万户

年　份	农村社会救济总人数	农村定期定量救济人数	农村精简退职老职工人数	享受40%人数	定量救济人数
1978					
1979	6847.6	*6837.7*	*9.9*		
1980	4651.8	*4641.8*	*10*		
1981	4265.1	*4255.1*	*10*		
1982	4270.7	*4257.4*	*13.3*		
1983	3526.7	*3502.2*	*24.5*		
1984	3842.7	*3795.9*	*46.8*	*25.3*	
1985	116.7	75.1	41.6	18.1	23.5
1986	103	63.1	39.9	18.1	21.7
1987	92.2	53.2	39	17.7	21.3
1988	93	54.1	38.9	17.6	21.4
1989	75.7	35.0	40.7	18.3	22.3
1990	100.2	46.7	53.5	23.6	29.9
1991	97	43.8	53.2	23.5	29.8
1992	97.5	45.6	51.9	23.3	28.6
1993	80.1	36.3	43.8	19.5	24.3
1994	82.1	38.5	43.6	19.2	24.3
1995	98.3	55.2	43.1	19	24.1
1996	109.2	66.5	42.7	18.6	24.1
1997	104.5	51.4	53.1	23.2	29.8
1998	120.5	65.6	54.9	24.9	30
1999	107.1	55.6	51.5	22.5	28.7
2000	112.2	62.5	49.7	22.1	27.6
2001	130.5	80.7	49.8	21.3	27.8
2002	138.7	*90*	48.7	20.9	27.8

年　份	农村困难群众救助总人数	农村最低生活保障人数	农村特困户救助人数	农村困难群众救助总户数	农村最低生活保障户数	困难户	其　他	农村特困户救助户数	困难户	其　他	农村特困供养户数	农村传统救济人数
2001	385.3	304.6	80.7									
2002	497.8	407.8	*90.0*	156.7	156.7							
2003	1160.5	367.1	793.4	632.8	146.5	114.5	32	282.1	192.7	89.3	204.2	
2004	1402.1	488	914.1	780.8	197.9	165.2	33.6	317.1	260.4	56.6	265.8	
2005	1891.8	825	1066.8	1061	356.5	298.8	57.7	354.8	290.4	64.4	349.7	
2006	2987.8	1593.1	775.8	1606.3	777.2			325.8			503.3	115.6

年　份	农村救助总人数	农村最低生活保障人数	农村特困人员集中供养人数	农村特困分散供养	传统救济人数
2007	4172.6	3566.3	138.0	393.3	75.0
2008	4926.3	4305.5	155.6	393.0	72.2
2009	5375.6	4760.0	171.8	381.6	62.2
2010	5829.8	5214.0	177.4	378.9	59.5
2011	5925.4	5305.7	184.5	366.5	68.7
2012	5969.7	5344.5	185.3	360.3	79.6
2013	5998.3	5388.0	183.5	353.8	73.0
2014	5810.8	5207.2	174.3	354.8	74.5
2015	5484.1	4903.6	162.3	354.4	63.8

注：1984年以前含应保未保的农村救济人数。

B-2-9 最低生活保障和社会救济平均标准

年　份	城市最低生活保障平均标准（元/人·月）	农村最低生活保障平均标准（元/人·年）	农村特困集中供养平均标准（元/人·年）	农村特困分散供养平均标准（元/人·年）
1999	149.0			
2000	157.0			
2001	147.0			
2002	148.0			
2003	149.0			
2004	152.0			
2005	156.0			
2006	169.6	850.8	1608.2	1224.5
2007	182.4	840.0	1953.0	1432.0
2008	205.3	987.6	2176.1	1624.4
2009	227.8	1210.1	2587.5	1842.7
2010	251.2	1404.0	2951.4	2102.1
2011	287.6	1718.4	3399.7	2470.5
2012	330.1	2067.8	4060.9	3008.0
2013	373.3	2433.9	4685.0	3498.5
2014	410.5	2776.6	5371.3	4005.9
2015	451.1	3177.6	6025.7	4490.1

B-2-10 最低生活保障和社会救济平均支出水平

年　份	城市最低生活保障平均支出水平（元/人·月）	农村最低生活保障平均支出水平（元/人·年）	农村特困集中供养平均支出水平（元/人·年）	农村特困分散供养平均支出水平（元/人·年）
1999	44.8			
2000	45.3			
2001	29.6			
2002	43.9			
2003	58.0			
2004	65.0			
2005	72.3			
2006	83.6	414.0		
2007	102.7	465.6		
2008	143.7	604.8	2055.7	1121.0
2009	172.0	816.0	2316.0	1284.0
2010	189.0	888.0	2460.0	1416.0
2011	240.3	1273.2	3081.9	1774.9
2012	239.1	1247.9	3496.6	2237.3
2013	264.2	1393.5	4078.3	2724.3
2014	285.6	1552.3	4676.1	3228.9
2015	316.6	1766.5	4790.4	3674.3

B-2-11 社会捐赠

单位：亿元、亿件

年份	社会捐赠款物合计	社会捐赠款	民政部门	各类社会组织	社会捐赠其他物资折款	接收社会捐赠衣被数量
1997	14.0	4.2			9.9	0.9
1998	113.2	50.2	50.2		63.0	2.9
1999	17.8	6.9	5.0	2.0	10.8	0.6
2000	16.3	9.3	5.4	3.9	7.0	0.8
2001	20.0	11.7	7.6	4.1	8.3	1.3
2002	20.8	19.0	11.1	7.9	1.8	2.3
2003	43.4	41.0	29.2	11.9	2.4	2.0
2004	35.1	34.0	17.1	16.9	1.2	0.9
2005	61.9	60.3	31.3	29.0	1.6	1.0
2006	89.5	83.1	43.0	40.1	6.4	0.7
2007	148.3	132.8	50.9	81.9	15.6	0.9
2008	764.1	744.5	479.3	265.2	19.6	11.6
2009	485.9	483.7	66.5	417.2	2.2	1.2
2010	601.7	596.8	179.8	417.0	4.9	0.3
2011	494.9	490.1	96.6	393.5	4.8	0.3
2012	578.8	572.5	101.7	470.8	6.3	1.3
2013	575.1	566.4	107.6	458.8	8.7	1
2014	612.4	604.4	79.6	524.9	8.0	0.5
2015	659.7	654.5	44.2	610.3	5.2	0.5

B-2-12 城市生活无着人员救助

年 份	救助站（个）	未成年人救助保护中心（个）	生活无着人员救助（人次）	# 未成年人救助	救助类单位床位数（张）	# 未成年人救助保护中心床位
1978	783					
1979	845					
1980	665					
1981	598					
1982	610					
1983	615					
1984	628					
1985	636					
1986	647					
1987	639					
1988	644					
1989	669					
1990	666					
1991	691					
1992	692					
1993	719					
1994	712					
1995	722					
1996	720					
1997	728					
1998	742					
1999	800					
2000	857					
2001	838					
2002	861					
2003	864		634528	60257		
2004	977		820254	104455	47086	
2005	1079	40	1196305	120487	45603	1849
2006	1189	50	1295506	129337	45661	1133
2007	1261	90	1544492	159989	46800	3621
2008	1334	88	1573484	155794	50642	3543
2009	1372	116	1680532	167283	51049	3670
2010	1448	145	1719008	146329	55562	5221
2011	1547	241	2409701	178705	71109	8165
2012	1770	261	2765761	152070	99901	10038
2013	1891	274	3484727	183802	108360	11499
2014	1949	345	3474544	128033	110806	11584
2015	1766	275	3752106	166723	113402	10682

B-2-13 中国福利彩票销售

年 份	福利彩票发行单位（个）	福利彩票销售额（亿元）	提取公益金（亿元）	公益金支出（亿元）
1978				
1979				
1980				
"六五"时期				
1981				
1982				
1983				
1984				
1985				
"七五"时期		**14.2**	**4.6**	
1986				
1987		0.2	0.1	
1988		3.8	1.2	
1989		3.8	1.3	
1990		6.5	2.0	
"八五"时期		**115.2**	**34.3**	
1991		7.7	2.5	
1992		13.8	4.1	
1993		18.4	5.5	
1994		18.0	5.3	
1995		57.3	16.9	
"九五"时期		**358.7**	**103.5**	**72.7**
1996		64.8	19.1	
1997		36.4	10.1	
1998		63.2	19.6	14.1
1999	1169	104.4	30.5	19.9
2000	1253	89.9	24.2	38.7
"十五"时期		**1145.2**	**377.1**	**161.9**
2001	1185	139.6	41.9	19.7
2002	1121	168.0	52.3	25.5
2003	1145	200.1	67.2	30.6
2004	1128	226.4	79.4	33.8
2005	1113	411.2	136.3	52.3
"十一五"时期		**3455.3**	**1127.4**	**484.0**
2006	989	495.7	168.8	52.6
2007	985	631.6	211.0	77.6
2008	999	604.0	205.4	119.2
2009	988	756.0	243.4	113.4
2010	993	968.0	298.8	121.2
"十二五"时期		**8628.7**	**2491.6**	**1002.6**
2011	974	1278.0	382.0	127.9
2012	955	1510.3	449.4	159
2013	940	1765.3	510.7	195.5
2014	893	2060.0	585.7	231.3
2015	861	2015.1	563.8	288.9

B-2-14 定期抚恤优抚对象

单位：人

年份	抚恤补助总人数（万人）	定期抚恤人数	烈属	牺牲、病故军人家属	伤残人员（万人）
1978	205.9				73.4
1979	173.6				75.6
1980	222.4				78.6
1981	233.6				79.6
1982	240.8	590104	541516	48588	81.6
1983	251.2	577791	526826	50965	83.0
1984	267.3	585403	536523	48880	84.4
1985	283.3	518566	440000	78566	85.3
1986	339.8	533245	446209	87036	86.5
1987	366.3	548063	453480	94583	88.0
1988	378.5	537472	429271	108201	88.7
1989	411.7	525134	422656	102478	89.1
1990	425.7	516638	407276	109362	87.4
1991	434.8	614945	504462	110483	87.5
1992	433.7	602163	492457	109706	87.6
1993	441.2	495994	383924	112070	88.3
1994	442.0	487256	372850	114406	88.5
1995	448.8	486250	370685	115565	88.8
1996	447.0	484270	366216	118054	89.3
1997	448.3	480464	362086	118378	89.5
1998	447.0	473901	357492	116409	89.2
1999	445.1	458079	336587	121492	88.7
2000	442.4	448276	325116	123160	88.1

年份	抚恤补助总人数（万人）	定期抚恤人数	烈属	牺牲军人家属	病故军人家属	伤残人员（万人）
2001	450.7	480852	348521	60081	72250	85.5
2002	459.0	480466	341109	63953	75404	85.8
2003	464.9	488820	345141	65303	78376	86.0
2004	462.0	485733	339817	65695	80221	85.6
2005	460.3	492517	349253	63603	79661	84.5
2006	462.6	491320	346089	64248	80983	86.0
2007	622.4	488675	342101	64478	82096	86.5
2008	633.2	478880	332390	65001	81489	87.2
2009	630.7	458578	317675	62304	78599	87.2
2010	625.0	447824	307587	62338	77899	86.7
2011	852.5	422439	286449	60534	75456	85.9
2012	944.4	411711	277712	59478	74521	84.9
2013	950.5	366400	240375	55734	70291	81.2
2014	917.3	311210	197955	48179	65076	76.6
2015	897.0	264975	160948	43711	60316	73.7

B-2-15 定期补助优抚对象

单位：人

年份	定期补助总人数	红军老战士合计	在乡红军老战士	西路军	红军失散人员	在乡复员军人	带病回乡退伍军人	60岁及以上农村籍退伍军人	其他
1978	9251	9251	9251						
1979	7872	7872	7872						
1980	6922	6922	6922						
1981	6567	6567	6567						
1982	1002181	6383	6383			859055	136743		
1983	1104586	6142	6142			952993	145451		
1984	1243633	6159	6159			1081350	156124		
1985	1461180	6329	6329			1185502	183129		86220
1986	1999872	6315	6315			1673990	210445		109122
1987	2230873	7466	7466			1833402	241290		148715
1988	2360462	7415	7415			1950641	247009		155397
1989	2715258	6628	6628			2272639	283075		152916
1990	2866579	7514	7514			2373873	305045		180147
1991	2939074	7015	7015			2419453	346021		166585
1992	2975175	6599	6599			2402869	373989		191718
1993	2947209	113728	5531	2997	105200	2424984	408497		
1994	2963965	112054	5058	2430	104566	2424435	427476		
1995	2987751	108484	4659	2318	101507	2423191	456076		
1996	3018047	115317	4480	2303	108534	2421517	481213		
1997	3037367	122115	4195	2214	115706	2396017	519235		
1998	3033826	118245	3996	2157	112092	2367266	548315		
1999	3056727	111096	3687	2106	105303	2363466	582165		
2000	3057257	105632	3326	1997	100309	2320739	630886		
2001	3170877	98345	3325	1889	93131	2246954	782802		42776
2002	3251971	94848	3136	1691	90021	2274657	882090		376
2003	3300232	90767	2893	1610	86264	2262264	919349		27852
2004	3277914	87521	2701	1454	83366	2214467	950428		25498
2005	3265797	79639	2681	1370	75588	2145421	977424		63313
2006	3274059	71707	2417	1220	68070	2064713	1072684		64955
2007	4870800	66220	2049	966	63205	1988977	1134414		1681189
2008	4981893	49198	1622	440	47136	1920235	1193622		1818838
2009	4976839	42945	1351	322	41272	1809019	1219752		1905123
2010	4935399	38630	1226	273	37131	1703396	1265664		1927709
2011	7243706	30309	911	190	29208	1587006	1321786	2373772	1930833
2012	8183693	26882	757	164	25961	1474790	1324325	3210986	2146710
2013	8326336	19740	647	117	18976	1260945	1306479	3566766	2172406
2014	8095950	11697	341	87	11269	993204	1242020	3748039	2100990
2015	7968445	3949	177	64	3708	792440	1183750	3924604	2063702

B-2-16 接收军队离退休、退职人员

单位：人

年 份	合 计	军队离退休干部	地方(含军队职工)人员
1978			
1979			
1980			
1981			
1982	21993	801	21192
1983	20038	1507	18531

年 份	合 计	军队离退休干部	#离 休	地方人员	军队职工
1984	9916	1873	117	6228	1815
1985	12429	6137	3327	4472	1820
1986	29260	21564	15598	4236	3460
1987	14146	10035	6224	1719	2392
1988	6050	4242	2329	1287	521
1989	4858	3441	1530	994	423
1990	6214	4988	2573	1008	218
1991	6558	5568	2703	806	184
1992	4420	3551	1516	693	176
1993	5578	916	283	543	4318
1994	5773	1016	447	566	4190
1995	3531	1056	323	476	1999
1996	9346	3210	371	282	5854
1997	6311	3246	401	230	2835
1998	8156	5868	785	691	1597

年 份	合 计	军队离退休干部	地方离退休干部	军队无军籍职工
1999	12380	9464	305	2611
2000	15238	10197	219	4822
2001	13738	6236	373	7129

年 份	合 计	军队离退休干部(含地方)	#离 休	军队退休士官	军队无军籍职工
2002	14428	3640		161	10627
2003	11057	5055	143	140	6312
2004	10794	8884	200	90	1820

年 份	合 计	军队离退休干部	#离 休	地方离退休干部	#离 休	军队退休士官	军队无军籍职工
2005	18512	17280	223	136	14	192	904
2006	31968	20794	259	673	85	365	10136
2007	28058	18534	258	303	23	160	9061
2008	21378	15829	78	205	15	297	5047
2009	18904	13836	143	348	5	1308	3412
2010	13451	11775	148	183	4	1112	381
2011	14530	12355	140	141	8	1405	629
2012	18570	14341	416	335	45	1047	2847
2013	38762	10927	108	500	29	570	26709
2014	27699	10067	246	221	9	503	16908
2015	19429	9102	600	409	81	410	9508

B-2-17 烈士褒扬和优待

年 份	烈士纪念建筑物管理机构（个）	本年新增享受烈士待遇的人数（人）	零散烈士纪念设施（个）	优待优抚对象户数（户）	#优待军属户数	优待总金额（万元）	#固定优待军属总额
1978			5347				
1979			3779			20393	
1980			2825			31459	
1981			2915			47255	
1982	965	8601	3592	4730756		58750	
1983	928	11024	3826	4387292		59588	
1984	786	8478	3953	4102419		62263	
1985	579	5887	3716	3567165	2884906	71655	577018
1986	582	11758	3871	3355694	2710272	75243	62205
1987	587	10644	4121	3223550	2562036	80915	66321
1988	632	9035	4236	3225253	2477699	87160	71735
1989	637	3960	4466	3086285	2423418	92169	77764
1990	632	3067	6065	2941486	2522476	99535	86739
1991	630	1556	6474	2967881	2540714	106354	93069
1992	684	1338	6957	2967002	2535037	116573	102008
1993	696	1467	6956	3009163	2470099	131555	113330
1994	718	1215	7279	3027420	2462671	155627	133070
1995	715	1277	7067	3051322	2476261	194379	166414
1996	740	1187	7020	3040439	2449077	251798	217527
1997	737	888	7048	3334000	2427586	321741	261865
1998	752	749	7322	3250395	2415838	356413	292305
1999	774	616	7252	3818210	2380675	402998	305386
2000	795	468	7427	3855797	2282584	469054	363675
2001	845	460	7802	3973085	2086464	385859	275456
2002	873	403	8051	4130817	1929011	374819	251854
2003	918	461	7781	3962425	1672205	391581	239410
2004	938	316	7425	3632630	1430630	418499	267458
2005	989	314	7483	3393218	1224036	379631	213968
2006	1072	265	7414	3220933	1183674	421010	224354
2007	1056	168	7186	3277318	1145223	454090	233479
2008	1133	297	7569	3301682	1108878	666011	267750
2009	1137	213	7622	3280522	1190816	751065	297448
2010	1195	173	9729	3308766	1169833	671536	340382
2011	1227	233	12378	3330859	1050918	968175	555402
2012	1306	172	13151	3471611	1008477	1121135	520520
2013	1463	200	13601	3402629	958255	1351368	646023
2014	1516	267	11365	3354536	883066	1510252	693201
2015	1464	341	11838	3170333	858330	1929548	766241

注：2011年由于部分省份指标理解错误，数据有调整。

B-2-18 自然灾害情况

年 份	受灾人口 （万人次）	因灾死亡人口 （含失踪） （人）	紧急转移人口 （万人）	直接经济 损失 （亿元）	倒塌房屋 （万间）	农作物受灾面积 （万公顷）
1978		4965			73.1	4844
1979		6962			152.1	3937
1980		6821			137.3	5003
1981	26710.0	7422			261.5	3979
1982	22900.7	7935			320.3	3313
1983	22439.0	10952		260.9	345.4	3471
1984	20894.0	6927			274.7	3189
1985	26446.0	4394	290.5	410.4	224.9	4437
1986	29928.0	5410	345.8		209.7	4714
1987	23512.0	5495	348.0	326.3	180.0	4207
1988	36169.0	7306	582.9		258.0	5087
1989	34569.0	5952	365.3	525.0	194.1	4699
1990	29348.0	7338	579.2	616.0	247.4	3847
1991	41941.0	7315	1308.5	1215.1	581.5	5547
1992	37174.0	5741	303.6	853.9	196.6	5133
1993	37541.0	6125	307.7	933.2	271.6	4867
1994	43799.0	8549	1054.0	1876.0	512.1	5504
1995	24215.0	5561	1064.0	1863.0	439.3	4587
1996	32305.0	7273	1216.0	2882.0	809.0	5975
1997	47886.0	3212	511.3	1975.0	288.0	5343
1998	35216.0	5511	2082.4	3007.4	821.4	2229
1999	35319.0	2966	664.8	1962.4	174.5	4998
2000	45652.3	3014	467.1	2045.3	147.3	5469
2001	37255.9	2583	211.1	1942.0	92.2	5215
2002	37841.8	2840	471.8	1717.4	175.7	4711.9
2003	49745.9	2259	707.3	1884.2	343.0	5438.6
2004	33920.6	2250	563.2	1602.3	155.0	3710.6
2005	40653.7	2475	1570.3	2042.1	226.4	3881.8
2006	43453.3	3186	1384.5	2528.1	193.3	4109.1
2007	39777.9	2325	1499.1	2363.0	146.7	4899.3
2008	47795.0	88928	2682.2	11752.4	1097.7	3999.0
2009	47933.5	1528	709.9	2523.7	83.8	4721.4
2010	42610.2	7844	1858.4	5339.9	273.3	3742.6
2011	43290.0	1126	939.4	3096.4	93.5	3247.1
2012	29421.7	1530	1109.6	4185.5	90.6	2496.2
2013	38818.7	2284	1215.0	5808.4	87.5	3135
2014	24353.7	1818	601.7	3373.8	45.0	2489.1
2015	18620.3	967	644.4	2704.1	24.8	2177

B-2-19 社区服务机构和设施

单位：个

年份	城乡各类社区服务机构和设施合计	社区服务中心	其他社区服务机构	便民利民网点
1987				
1988	69699		69699	
1989	71357		71357	
1990	84757		84757	
1991	89918		89918	
1992	112171		112171	
1993	92946	3711	89235	169503
1994	98679	4034	94645	204229
1995	115175	4380	110795	234024
1996	132309	5055	127254	259201
1997	138366	5113	133253	307226
1998	154196	6154	148042	345075
1999	164962	7623	157339	405740
2000	187888	6444	181444	451567
2001	201758	6179	195579	539544
2002	206743	7898	198845	622986
2003	203945	7520	196425	668418
2004	205926	7804	198122	703760
2005	203275	8479	194796	664764
2006	160007	8565	151442	457896

年份	城乡各类社区服务机构和设施合计	社区指导中心	社区服务中心	社区服务站	其他社区服务机构	便民利民网点
2007	134852		9319	50116	75417	892656
2008	146322		9873	30021	106428	748684
2009	146341		10003	53170	83168	692625
2010	152941		12720	44237	95984	539136
2011	160352		14391	56156	89805	452868
2012	200162	809	15497	87931	95925	397222
2013	251939	890	19014	108377	123658	358518

年份	城乡各类社区服务机构和设施合计	#社区指导中心	#社区服务中心	#社区服务站	#社区养老机构和设施	#互助型养老设施
2014	310652	918	23088	120188	18927	40357
2015	360956	863	24138	128083	26067	62027

B-3-1 社会组织

单位：个

年　份	社会组织合计	社会团体	基金会	民办非企业
1978				
1979				
1980				
1981				
1982				
1983				
1984				
1985				
1986				
1987				
1988	4446	4446		
1989	4544	4544		
1990	10855	10855		
1991	82814	82814		
1992	154502	154502		
1993	167506	167506		
1994	174060	174060		
1995	180583	180583		
1996	184821	184821		
1997	181318	181318		
1998	165600	165600		
1999	142665	136764		5901
2000	153322	130668		22654
2001	210939	128805		82134
2002	244509	133297		111212
2003	266612	141167	954	124491
2004	289432	153359	892	135181
2005	319762	171150	975	147637
2006	354393	191946	1144	161303
2007	386916	211661	1340	173915
2008	413660	229681	1597	182382
2009	431069	238747	1843	190479
2010	445631	245256	2200	198175
2011	461971	254969	2614	204388
2012	499268	271131	3029	225108
2013	547245	289026	3549	254670
2014	606048	309736	4117	292195
2015	662425	328500	4784	329141

注：2001年以前的基金会含在社会团体内。

B-3-2 自治组织

年份	自治组织合计（万个）	居民委员会（个）	居民小组（万个）	居民委员会成员（万人）	村民委员会（万个）	村民小组（万个）	村民委员会成员（万人）
1978							
1979		46810					
1980							
1981		57169					
1982							
1983	37.7	65519			31.2		
1984	100.3	75609			92.7		
1985	103.0	80943		34.9	94.9		379.6
1986	95.3	86824		36.2	86.6		365.9
1987	93.2	86799		37.0	84.5		359.9
1988	97.8	95684		36.1	88.3		366.6
1989	102.8	93691		36.6	93.4		379.4
1990	110.0	98814		43.1	100.1		409.4
1991	111.9	100347		44.1	101.9		424.4
1992	110.8	104136		46.5	100.4		430.9
1993	112.0	107173		47.9	101.3		456.0
1994	111.7	110112		48.0	100.7		458.5
1995	104.4	111860		48.0	93.2		400.5
1996	104.2	113690		49.3	92.8		397.5
1997	102.4	117915	108.3	49.8	90.6	535.8	378.8
1998	95.2	119042	117.2	50.8	83.3	537.1	358.6
1999	91.6	114815	124.7	50.1	80.1	555.7	351.3
2000	84.0	108424	127.2	48.4	73.2	553.4	315.0
2001	79.2	91893	125.9	46.4	70.0	541.9	316.4
2002	76.7	86087	124.4	39.6	68.1	528.6	294.2
2003	74.1	77431	122.2	39.7	66.3	519.2	319.1
2004	72.2	77884	129.6	42.5	64.4	507.9	292.1
2005	70.9	79947	123.3	45.4	62.9	490.5	265.7
2006	70.4	80717	123.5	44.3	62.4	453.3	243.0
2007	69.5	82006	122.3	41.6	61.3	466.9	241.1
2008	68.8	83413	128.7	42.2	60.4	480.9	233.9
2009	68.4	84689	129.5	43.1	59.9	480.5	234.0
2010	68.2	87057	130.7	43.9	59.5	479.1	233.4
2011	67.9	89480	134.0	45.4	59.0	476.4	231.9
2012	68.0	91153	133.5	46.9	58.8	469.4	232.3
2013	68.3	94620	135.7	48.4	58.9	466.4	232.3
2014	68.2	96693	135.8	49.7	58.5	470.4	230.5
2015	68.1	96679	134.7	51.2	58.1	469.2	229.7

B-3-3 结婚

年　份	结婚登记总数（万对）	内地居民登记结婚数（万对）	涉外华侨港澳台登记结婚数（万对）	结婚登记人数（万人）
1978	597.8	597.8		
1979	637.1	636.3	0.8	
1980	720.9	719.8	1.1	
1981	1041.7	1040.3	1.4	
1982	836.9	835.5	1.4	
1983	765.4	764.2	1.3	
1984	784.8	783.4	1.4	
1985	831.3	829.1	2.2	
1986	884.0	882.3	1.7	
1987	926.7	924.7	2.0	
1988	899.2	897.2	2.0	
1989	937.2	935.2	2.0	
1990	951.1	948.7	2.4	
1991	953.6	951.0	2.6	
1992	957.5	954.5	3.0	
1993	915.4	912.2	3.3	
1994	932.4	929.0	3.4	
1995	934.1	929.7	4.4	
1996	938.7	934.0	4.7	1877.4
1997	914.1	909.1	5.1	1828.3
1998	891.7	886.7	5.0	1783.4
1999	885.3	879.9	5.4	1770.6
2000	848.5	842.0	6.5	1697.0
2001	805.0	797.1	7.9	1610.0
2002	786	778.8	7.3	1572.0
2003	811.4	803.5	7.8	1622.8
2004	867.2	860.8	6.4	1734.4
2005	823.1	816.6	6.4	1646.2
2006	945	938.2	6.8	1890.0
2007	991.4	986.3	5.1	1982.8
2008	1098.3	1093.2	5.1	2196.6
2009	1212.4	1207.5	4.9	2424.8
2010	1241	1236.1	4.9	2482.0
2011	1302.4	1297.5	4.9	2604.8
2012	1323.6	1318.3	5.3	2647.2
2013	1346.9	1341.4	5.5	2693.8
2014	1306.7	1302.0	4.7	2613.5
2015	1224.7	1220.6	4.1	2449.4

结婚率计算方法：

$$结婚率=\frac{登记结婚人数}{（当年期初人口数+当年期末人口数）/2}\times 1000‰$$

登记

初婚人数（万人）	再婚人数（万人）	#女（万人）	#恢复结婚（对）	结婚率（‰）
				6.2
				6.7
				7.3
				10.4
				8.3
				7.5
				7.5
				7.9
				8.2
				8.6
				8.3
				8.4
				8.2
				8.3
				8.3
				7.8
				7.8
				7.7
1781.7	86.2	41.1	48044	7.7
1726.0	92.2	46.3	62752	7.4
1675.4	97.9	49.8	69160	7.2
1659.4	100.5	50.0	57815	7.1
1581.4	102.6	50.8	56324	6.7
1481.7	112.5	58.0	63442	6.3
1440.3	117.2	60.2	68081	6.1
1483.9	123.3	60.7	68204	6.3
1569.6	152.0	77.1	84799	6.7
1483.0	163.1	74.3	115003	6.3
1705.6	184.4	86.7	107113	7.2
1779.7	203.1	97.3	138967	7.5
1972.5	224.1	108.0	162244	8.3
2168.8	256.0	124.7	181162	9.1
2200.9	281.1	138.8	190356	9.3
2309.9	294.9	146.5	209781	9.7
2361.2	286.0	145.8	229607	9.8
2386.0	307.9	156.5	298766	9.9
2286.8	326.7	168.7	348285	9.6
2109.0	340.4	177.2	398527	9.0

B-3-4 离婚登记

年 份	离婚总数（万对）	民政部门登记离婚数（万对）			法院部门办理离婚数（万件）	离婚率（‰）
			内地居民登记离婚数（万对）	涉外华侨港澳台登记离婚数（对）		
1978	28.5	17.0	17		11.5	0.18
1979	31.9	19.3	19.3	82	12.6	0.33
1980	34.1	18.0	18	330	16.1	0.35
1981	38.9	18.7	18.7	46	20.2	0.39
1982	42.8	21.1	21.1	116	21.7	0.42
1983	41.8	19.7	19.7	126	22.1	0.42
1984	45.4	19.9	19.9	110	25.5	0.40
1985	45.8	19.6	19.6	108	26.2	0.44
1986	50.6	21.4	21.4	205	29.2	0.47
1987	58.1	23.6	23.6	220	34.5	0.55
1988	65.5	26.4	26.4	310	39.1	0.60
1989	75.3	28.8	28.7	518	46.5	0.68
1990	80.0	30.1	30	602	49.9	0.69
1991	83.1	30.1	30	588	53	0.72
1992	85.0	31.6	31.5	833	53.4	0.74
1993	91.0	33.6	33.5	968	57.4	0.77
1994	98.2	35.5	35.4	737	62.7	0.82
1995	105.6	36.8	36.7	813	68.8	0.88
1996	113.4	39.4	39.3	1175	74	0.93
1997	119.9	44.0	43.9	1385	75.9	0.97
1998	119.2	46.6	46.5	948	72.6	0.96
1999	120.2	47.8	47.7	975	72.4	0.96
2000	121.3	48.9	48.8	1075	72.4	0.96
2001	125.0	52.8	52.5	2856	72.2	0.98
2002	117.7	57.3	56.8	5221	60.4	0.90
2003	133.0	69	68.7	3333	64	1.05
2004	166.5	104.6	104.0	5830	61.9	1.28
2005	178.5	118.4	117.5	8267	60.1	1.37
2006	191.3	129.1	128.3	8414	62.2	1.46
2007	209.8	145.7	144.8	8852	64.1	1.59
2008	226.9	161.0	160.0	9470	65.9	1.71
2009	246.8	180.2	179.6	5608	66.6	1.85
2010	267.8	201.0	200.4	5783	66.8	2.00
2011	287.4	220.7	220.2	5761	66.7	2.13
2012	310.4	242.3	241.7	6161	68.1	2.29
2013	350.0	281.5	280.9	6538	68.5	2.58
2014	363.9	295.7	295.1	6714	67.9	2.67
2015	384.3	314.9	314.3	6237	69.3	2.79

离婚率计算方法：

$$离婚率=\frac{离婚人数}{（当年期初人口数+当年期末人口数）/2}\times 1000‰$$

B-3-5 殡葬服务

年 份	殡仪馆（个）	公墓（个）	骨灰堂	殡葬管理机构（个）	火化炉数（台）	遗体火化数（万具）	火化率（%）
1978					1712	117.5	
1979					2300	102.1	
1980					2510	98.7	
1981					2586	85.4	
1982					2622	96.2	
1983					2622	108.0	
1984					2686	128.2	
1985	9	24		122	2729	155.2	
1986	5	25		143	2745	155.5	26.2
1987	6	29		195	2752	162.0	27.0
1988	14	37		219	2729	180.9	29.5
1989	17	50		217	2768	182.3	30.1
1990	1260	73		211	2795	201.3	31.5
1991	1283	84		234	2714	215.6	34.0
1992	1288	88		228	2852	242.6	31.2
1993	1264	136		296	2891	247.6	31.6
1994	1272	163		284	2882	257.1	33.4
1995	1281	209		302	2927	262.7	33.2
1996	1283	256		313	3005	282.7	35.2
1997	1289	359		340	2959	295.0	36.8
1998	1310	425		374	3157	319.7	39.6
1999	1318	624		402	*3340*	336.4	41.5
2000	1363	692		466	*3565*	373.7	46.0
2001	1415	757		540	4299	386.7	47.3
2002	1486	854		542	3945	415.2	50.6
2003	1515	855		599	4159	434.9	52.7
2004	1549	937		633	4792	436.9	52.5
2005	1594	1009		681	5037	450.2	53.0
2006	1635	1109		805	5649	430.2	48.2
2007	1708	1162		799	4838	442.1	48.4
2008	1692	1209		853	4789	453.4	48.5
2009	1729	1266		901	5123	454.2	48.2
2010	1724	1308		919	5229	474.1	49.0
2011	1745	1406		952	5209	468.1	48.8
2012	1782	1597		978	5539	477.7	49.5
2013	1784	1506	29	1063	5743	468.9	48.2
2014	1801	1598	19	1141	5908	459.3	47.0
2015	1821	1567	15	1127	6063	459.5	47.1

注：斜体下划线数据经过修正。1989年以前部分数据统计不完全。

05

社会服务当年分省统计资料

C-1-1 省级行政区划

地 区	面积（万平方千米）	省级合计（个）	直辖市	省	自治区	特别行政区
全 国	**960**	**34**	**4**	**23**	**5**	**2**
北 京	1.68	1	1			
天 津	1.1	1	1			
河 北	19	1		1		
山 西	15	1		1		
内蒙古	110	1			1	
辽 宁	15	1		1		
吉 林	18	1		1		
黑龙江	46	1		1		
上 海	0.58	1	1			
江 苏	10	1		1		
浙 江	10	1		1		
安 徽	13	1		1		
福 建	12	1		1		
江 西	16	1		1		
山 东	15	1		1		
河 南	16	1		1		
湖 北	18	1		1		
湖 南	21	1		1		
广 东	18	1		1		
广 西	23	1			1	
海 南	3.4	1		1		
重 庆	8.23	1	1			
四 川	48	1		1		
贵 州	17	1		1		
云 南	38	1		1		
西 藏	120	1			1	
陕 西	19	1		1		
甘 肃	39	1		1		
青 海	72	1		1		
宁 夏	6.6	1			1	
新 疆	160	1			1	
香 港		1				1
澳 门		1				1
台 湾		1		1		

C-1-2 地级与县级行政区划

单位:个

地 区	地级合计	地级市	地区	自治州	盟	县级合计	市辖区	县级市	县	自治县	旗	自治旗	特区	林区
全 国	**334**	**291**	**10**	**30**	**3**	**2850**	**921**	**361**	**1397**	**117**	**49**	**3**	**1**	**1**
北 京						16	16							
天 津						16	15		1					
河 北	11	11				170	42	20	102	6				
山 西	11	11				119	23	11	85					
内蒙古	12	9			3	102	22	11	17		49	3		
辽 宁	14	14				100	57	16	19	8				
吉 林	9	8		1		60	21	20	16	3				
黑龙江	13	12	1			128	65	18	44	1				
上 海						16	15		1					
江 苏	13	13				97	55	21	21					
浙 江	11	11				90	36	20	33	1				
安 徽	16	16				105	44	6	55					
福 建	9	9				85	28	13	44					
江 西	11	11				100	22	10	68					
山 东	17	17				137	51	28	58					
河 南	17	17				158	51	21	86					
湖 北	13	12		1		103	39	24	37	2				1
湖 南	14	13		1		122	35	16	64	7				
广 东	21	21				119	62	20	34	3				
广 西	14	14				110	37	8	53	12				
海 南	4	4				23	8	5	4	6				
重 庆						38	23		11	4				
四 川	21	18		3		183	50	16	113	4				
贵 州	9	6		3		88	14	7	55	11			1	
云 南	16	8		8		129	14	14	72	29				
西 藏	7	4	3			74	5		69					
陕 西	10	10				107	27	3	77					
甘 肃	14	12		2		86	17	4	58	7				
青 海	8	2		6		43	6	3	27	7				
宁 夏	5	5				22	9	2	11					
新 疆	14	3	6	5		104	12	24	62	6				

C-1-3 乡镇级行政区划

单位:个

地区	乡镇级合计	镇	乡	#民族乡	街道办事处	区公所
全 国	**39789**	**20515**	**11315**	**991**	**7957**	**2**
北 京	331	143	38	5	150	
天 津	244	121	6	1	117	
河 北	2251	1067	890	50	293	1
山 西	1398	564	632		202	
内蒙古	1010	496	275	18	239	
辽 宁	1532	648	213	56	671	
吉 林	901	429	182	28	290	
黑龙江	1234	512	374	52	348	
上 海	213	107	2		104	
江 苏	1281	767	72	1	442	
浙 江	1350	641	265	14	444	
安 徽	1494	946	303	9	245	
福 建	1105	633	294	19	178	
江 西	1552	820	582	8	150	
山 东	1826	1115	75		636	
河 南	2433	1105	703	12	625	
湖 北	1233	761	168	10	304	
湖 南	1911	1119	417	83	375	
广 东	1584	1128	11	7	445	
广 西	1251	773	350	59	128	
海 南	218	175	21		22	
重 庆	1025	617	195	14	213	
四 川	4635	2032	2271	98	332	
贵 州	1370	796	401	194	173	
云 南	1389	681	545	140	163	
西 藏	694	140	544	9	10	
陕 西	1291	989	23		279	
甘 肃	1351	628	600	34	123	
青 海	399	140	225	28	34	
宁 夏	236	102	90		44	
新 疆	1047	320	548	42	178	1

C-1-4 民政部门

地 区	单位数	年末职工人数		受教育程度		职业资
			女性	大学专科人数	大学本科及以上人数	助理社会工作师人数
全 国	**3482**	**95141**	**31254**	**36651**	**41243**	**1630**
中央级	1	372	112	8	364	
北 京	18	1150	473	175	914	63
天 津	18	604	167	161	379	
河 北	195	6238	2337	2273	2063	110
山 西	131	2587	803	1107	1027	24
内蒙古	117	3217	1083	1390	1414	7
辽 宁	119	2981	924	1067	1681	19
吉 林	70	1344	314	380	630	6
黑龙江	151	2550	933	1063	1206	58
上 海	18	685	276	138	534	64
江 苏	121	3491	954	994	2147	213
浙 江	102	2516	693	906	1351	24
安 徽	122	2765	784	1067	1266	101
福 建	97	1719	366	653	722	16
江 西	117	3167	945	1103	1086	33
山 东	180	6427	2038	2386	3125	128
河 南	182	8147	2957	3547	2665	112
湖 北	119	4172	1315	1836	1603	27
湖 南	145	6474	2239	2380	2426	93
广 东	142	4006	1246	1476	1949	109
广 西	127	2309	744	914	1076	10
海 南	22	624	194	286	226	21
重 庆	41	1184	367	389	731	6
四 川	209	5488	1868	2284	2247	78
贵 州	100	3221	1023	1444	1319	14
云 南	148	4461	1469	1810	1776	25
西 藏	83	1166	505	515	449	2
陕 西	118	3721	1071	1541	1371	20
甘 肃	101	3158	936	1181	1221	108
青 海	55	881	317	334	366	37
宁 夏	28	796	283	265	467	82
新 疆	285	3520	1518	1578	1442	20

行政机构

单位：个、人、人次、时

格水平	年龄结构				志愿服务	
社会工作师人数	35岁及以下人数	36岁至45岁人数	46岁至55岁人数	56岁及以上人数	志愿者服务人次数	志愿服务时间
1787	**24480**	**34737**	**28794**	**7130**	**282542**	**599080.4**
	133	126	69	44		
25	307	369	396	78	5	15.0
	126	171	239	68	550	1120.0
94	1830	2266	1793	349	1134	5154.0
20	675	923	838	151	206	465.0
13	848	1154	984	231	5760	14901.0
28	636	934	1096	315	753	1508.0
25	161	627	458	98		
35	616	965	846	123	9065	18218.0
91	150	204	222	109	924	2265.0
247	559	1204	1330	398	35085	67483.4
52	442	748	995	331	74586	90651.0
102	509	1094	905	257	31564	83262.0
55	283	558	694	184	70308	178997.0
30	625	1223	1019	300	2833	8673.0
174	2095	2347	1666	319		
154	2810	2951	1865	521	40	150.0
45	821	1447	1355	549	287	931.0
78	2031	2420	1570	453	8736	29591.0
126	914	1416	1342	334	8218	27004.0
23	297	789	987	236	14	112.0
5	124	221	211	68		
23	224	357	484	119	1917	5809.0
68	1316	2156	1662	354	24281	45914.0
9	814	1311	919	177	634	2749.0
35	914	1695	1552	300	588	852.0
4	591	403	151	21	172	370.0
57	1105	1307	1049	260	2495	7995.0
75	1077	1140	784	157	576	1707.0
18	218	388	231	44	396	936.0
65	208	299	238	51	48	98.0
11	1021	1524	844	131	1367	2150.0

C-1-4续表

地 区	职工按行政级别分				乡、镇、街道民政助理员
	中央级	省级	地级	县级	
全 国	**372**	**3884**	**13916**	**76969**	**53345**
中央级	372				
北 京		231		919	710
天 津		131		473	359
河 北		114	659	5465	3326
山 西		91	390	2106	1448
内蒙古		82	469	2666	1628
辽 宁		88	747	2146	1080
吉 林		119	291	934	279
黑龙江		28	622	1900	269
上 海		175		510	411
江 苏		166	675	2650	1681
浙 江		111	411	1994	1649
安 徽		115	528	2122	1942
福 建		120	307	1292	1533
江 西		80	381	2706	1045
山 东		131	834	5462	5005
河 南		141	793	7213	2305
湖 北		101	598	3473	1372
湖 南		170	734	5570	5225
广 东		149	976	2881	712
广 西		111	431	1767	2811
海 南		76	100	448	324
重 庆		193		991	2972
四 川		128	746	4614	4522
贵 州		109	401	2711	2675
云 南		142	650	3669	1951
西 藏		178	290	698	81
陕 西		142	496	3083	3541
甘 肃			677	2481	1386
青 海		105	173	603	426
宁 夏		145	142	509	183
新 疆		212	395	2913	494

单位：人、万元

执行行政事业单位会计制度财务指标				
固定资产原价	上年结转和结余	本年收入合计	本年支出合计	收支结余
2515454.7	**722478.8**	**8254501.0**	**8106588.4**	**511214.0**
84149.2	33413.1	150890.8	153813.0	30490.8
39888.4	62785.4	550361.0	538915.3	69036.0
14838.9	7050.9	199837.9	178049.9	1094.0
59904.1	12596.3	426796.4	416388.3	15729.7
53319.5	17911.7	145252.6	146917.1	6362.8
55042.9	15771.0	102862.4	94343.6	14147.8
62105.8	18315.1	143653.9	156729.9	13846.1
30608.0	1859.8	69679.9	50964.4	3982.9
26293.3	859.9	109299.5	108541.0	210.5
35935.4	49619.3	421947.8	421709.3	20921.3
76480.1	17350.0	427391.9	418538.2	13957.6
63857.0	37306.1	799053.8	800698.8	14493.6
67955.4	9153.8	281107.2	276194.3	5433.8
37873.9	48397.7	333203.1	332826.5	29614.5
37288.6	13331.8	74489.4	75950.8	10935.1
90506.8	12706.8	307598.1	311101.5	
40675.8	27305.8	211204.5	196000.0	9694.5
100871.0	5064.7	139341.1	139903.1	3809.1
63781.4	3915.3	429153.5	414387.5	1107.0
135966.5	25852.4	682198.4	692397.0	12008.0
82013.3	44010.2	391398.8	397807.4	27773.2
13024.7	30797.5	138114.1	125402.7	25960.9
41588.2	4554.3	143022.1	133376.0	11188.7
78590.6	19079.3	319652.3	309852.7	17990.4
47736.3	41612.5	158301.9	169731.5	17682.3
107030.3	95886.8	409574.7	372046.9	47860.0
35111.8	2081.5	18921.2	40585.4	
47791.6	3550.2	206932.6	186800.0	23490.4
11824.5	13776.2	44756.8	40077.9	17799.2
26030.7	2988.7	105915.9	117093.8	5617.0
22912.0	21918.2	112634.5	96070.3	20045.6
824458.7	21656.5	199952.9	193374.3	18931.2

C-1-5 社会服务

地区	机构和设施数	按登记类型分				按行业	
		工商登记	编制登记	民政登记	设施	社会工作	成员组织
全 国	**1765004**	**15753**	**30958**	**710315**	**1007978**	**413367**	**1342960**
中央级	2346		30	2316		2	2316
北 京	29558	543	809	10697	17509	12792	16632
天 津	13171	224	146	5430	7371	2621	10488
河 北	111406	535	933	20157	89781	38912	72237
山 西	47856	345	841	13260	33410	4713	42928
内蒙古	31553	162	657	13583	17151	4691	26681
辽 宁	47067	1652	912	22401	22102	10102	36394
吉 林	25089	331	1240	10828	12690	3048	21802
黑龙江	31179	284	670	14840	15385	4469	26503
上 海	26629	834	296	16664	8835	7381	19102
江 苏	146415	2594	1769	102412	39640	44123	101880
浙 江	110232	1800	1277	46573	60582	33706	76078
安 徽	52552	367	677	25816	25692	9699	42617
福 建	47457	295	630	24174	22358	6470	40723
江 西	42013	287	2384	16107	23235	5603	35789
山 东	155339	1187	1289	45878	106985	31146	123855
河 南	88940	708	1399	30863	55970	7552	80974
湖 北	72188	519	2092	28345	41232	14829	57008
湖 南	87960	431	2286	28091	57152	14219	73320
广 东	139869	224	1897	55001	82747	59183	80199
广 西	52701	135	751	22430	29385	14057	38393
海 南	10612	22	68	5523	4999	2107	8429
重 庆	35488	664	705	15759	18360	8856	26443
四 川	116689	747	3023	41591	71328	22907	93200
贵 州	52511	88	1161	10790	40472	22812	29231
云 南	39483	252	628	21411	17192	3872	35387
西 藏	6606	7	100	999	5500	545	6037
陕 西	52959	205	814	20396	31544	7794	44956
甘 肃	45304	77	440	18911	25876	8951	36096
青 海	9635	32	64	3654	5885	1341	8252
宁 夏	8961	61	142	5174	3584	1249	7611
新 疆	25236	141	828	10241	14026	3615	21399

总表

单位:个、人

分类分		年末职工人数		按登记类型分			
其他社会服务	其他事业单位		女性	工商登记	编制登记	民政登记	设施
6594	**2078**	**13088674**	**4128057**	**1138391**	**361895**	**7698359**	**3890029**
	28	35513	15715		1449	34064	
64	70	243073	109576	24433	14251	134872	69517
42	20	99098	44219	16478	3363	46215	33042
221	36	686173	235898	29090	16035	379822	261226
138	77	311533	92963	28328	8808	153597	120800
161	20	184972	62982	11717	7693	97419	68143
459	112	424725	149026	82204	14935	216702	110884
211	24	149562	41259	16513	14627	75928	42494
175	32	250867	92434	10520	12362	158041	69944
92	54	333070	108163	63428	8508	219876	41258
341	71	1144679	360507	230055	23371	689123	202130
293	155	781023	256214	172892	14432	400454	193245
209	27	405470	119104	17423	9731	265687	112629
202	62	390600	96221	16041	6253	278954	89352
201	420	329388	97478	24144	14063	205419	85762
282	56	921605	268248	88599	19525	382076	431405
296	118	571164	167310	54770	19975	256715	239704
270	81	545680	183137	31955	22923	330426	160376
324	97	510418	169015	26564	20372	261061	202421
447	40	954130	373368	16012	26349	629673	282096
175	76	477195	109761	8229	10058	358403	100505
63	13	81015	25352	1870	1050	54094	24001
168	21	311723	124623	58539	6758	167325	79101
444	137	899592	283353	52448	22840	558743	265561
378	90	378527	95781	4045	10876	183731	179875
201	23	562305	189744	23408	5949	450138	82810
24		40972	12074	205	528	14685	25554
168	41	424247	107489	11996	10071	282944	119236
225	32	290865	53115	3347	5122	194018	88378
37	5	51523	13083	1869	996	25854	22804
88	13	77483	17594	4076	1904	55360	16143
195	27	220484	53251	7193	6718	136940	69633

C-1-5续表1

地 区	受教育程度		职业资格水平	
	大学专科人数	大学本科及以上人数	助理社会工作师人数	社会工作师人数
全 国	**2210770**	**1325663**	**59043**	**45248**
中央级	560	25828	443	6585
北 京	54100	73410	6083	3596
天 津	22780	26500	1959	554
河 北	67126	37794	2347	2578
山 西	56040	24168	355	316
内蒙古	43679	17589	860	490
辽 宁	81784	61704	1736	940
吉 林	22299	8125	1112	2051
黑龙江	43344	17041	689	677
上 海	82169	30170	2385	4580
江 苏	215053	127322	7962	2830
浙 江	139857	75562	3229	2239
安 徽	82724	44988	3834	1255
福 建	36708	29090	1393	924
江 西	37601	12210	881	326
山 东	213550	123929	1861	1058
河 南	94025	44846	1000	653
湖 北	102594	37972	2410	1275
湖 南	99352	55131	1366	816
广 东	214096	136445	7728	4633
广 西	53405	32698	900	938
海 南	9776	6990	105	71
重 庆	61120	51209	3122	2553
四 川	134520	78453	2268	1160
贵 州	62505	48966	213	158
云 南	52295	32271	744	275
西 藏	1538	1030	3	1
陕 西	45281	21321	390	286
甘 肃	29113	14876	1131	1093
青 海	5380	1727	96	73
宁 夏	9330	5748	72	48
新 疆	37066	20550	366	216

单位：个、人、人次、时

年龄结构				志愿服务	
35岁及以下人数	36岁至45岁人数	46岁至55岁人数	56岁及以上人数	志愿者服务人次数	志愿服务时间
3986785	**5088111**	**2885508**	**1127910**	**9345968**	**27006683.3**
9691	13521	7788	4513		
74151	85777	63792	19353	4327575	14635738.0
28611	30906	26564	13017	78626	154647.0
171876	321623	148152	44522	71015	307874.0
91214	113008	75582	31729	12292	28592.4
57078	69503	42371	15979	30385	70587.0
120447	162040	91507	50715	43527	66954.0
31369	93111	17676	7406	23368	46668.0
85342	97546	52969	15010	29782	88424.0
101178	110265	85273	36354	76134	222626.5
319623	435365	285650	104041	732384	1637152.5
230599	294554	178909	76961	614719	1129823.0
115763	161631	97598	30478	199780	466069.0
97333	134742	99181	59343	132244	364601.0
107176	145427	59155	17630	8255	25565.7
284070	379895	200048	57592	1066435	2476391.6
201021	217394	109156	43593	10115	34386.0
176910	196946	133977	37847	92314	266483.0
166449	210985	102955	29964	216608	693645.0
405555	309252	175782	63541	108459	491075.9
115470	171656	123221	66848	10795	37855.0
24651	35890	15912	4562	12473	21937.0
108220	112375	67637	23491	600603	1500060.9
304352	340038	166571	88631	187714	577435.5
108630	154875	83711	31311	575506	1374083.1
166022	200286	115539	80458	9401	44507.0
10481	14331	10902	5258	146	232.0
111755	148834	128513	35145	24940	78089.2
73073	136932	64694	16145	12529	56722.0
12872	25584	9995	2871	8971	13792.0
13556	50157	10438	3317	2595	6393.0
62247	113662	34290	10285	26278	88273.0

C-1-5续表2

地 区	执行企业会计制度单位财务指标					执行行政
	固定资产原价	营业收入	费用合计	营业利润	固定资产原价	上年结转和结余
全 国	**21766960.0**	**46638545.2**	**5961948.3**	**1493758.1**	**32189161.3**	**2511356.7**
中央级	6287.7	15684.1	6677.7	962.0	135719.8	32054.4
北 京	2977497.1	2196429.8	391498.4	122813.2	949533.9	348605.4
天 津	233461.7	599320.9	84713.6	6064.2	315803.0	36261.7
河 北	485731.8	982363.8	102338.2	3332.3	2864934.7	61050.2
山 西	247679.5	227630.3	35532.3	-5266.9	815537.2	34908.7
内蒙古	79246.6	95136.2	17368.4	5000.1	318037.4	25879.4
辽 宁	1428126.5	1644140.9	207187.7	35085.4	571399.7	40304.6
吉 林	147376.9	248872.9	28143.5	-95.7	343601.7	8648.4
黑龙江	713660.6	162865.1	41461.3	3085.4	707263.2	55995.8
上 海	1698597.8	3221958.6	277986.9	244667.6	1308537.1	130273.8
江 苏	3416446.8	11107965.1	1196200.5	245451.3	6781831.8	806253.1
浙 江	5066194.3	14330230.5	2154556.5	538857.7	4009601.6	139642.7
安 徽	178204.1	921221.4	71497.3	21150.8	764751.3	36631.2
福 建	194403.7	277516.8	58292.2	1563.2	262075.0	32629.2
江 西	120883.0	2011932.4	21308.4	4478.2	449594.1	49794.9
山 东	1099329.5	1754375.0	339584.1	134195.1	2062036.7	10211.6
河 南	362320.0	510088.7	92347.7	21813.6	579095.0	21011.8
湖 北	317539.3	468629.0	95107.1	4825.6	1454829.5	11554.4
湖 南	309410.7	643072.0	60996.2	6318.0	830306.9	11797.5
广 东	306907.3	317140.0	47224.6	14034.2	2613774.8	164015.5
广 西	99580.1	353399.6	23082.4	-545.3	401041.7	45294.3
海 南	21413.9	36785.3	8969.1	-1207.7	64531.5	17225.6
重 庆	700405.5	1864753.4	224202.0	35901.0	363158.9	39298.6
四 川	554777.5	1313392.6	126977.3	8431.2	947980.4	88718.5
贵 州	95426.4	61114.6	21961.5	6030.0	229064.8	35708.5
云 南	423608.4	744014.8	136960.6	11022.8	629883.1	116058.7
西 藏	13687.7	498.0	399.0	139.0	87343.0	22672.0
陕 西	164931.2	330822.6	50315.2	20882.9	562700.3	23688.2
甘 肃	33290.1	15817.1	3226.8	1155.8	290281.6	7698.4
青 海	9119.7	15711.5	3666.0	195.6	40480.9	9652.2
宁 夏	95302.8	68462.5	7323.7	-1928.3	120107.3	10874.3
新 疆	166111.8	97199.7	24842.1	5345.8	314323.4	36943.1

单位：万元

事业单位会计制度财务指标			执行民间非营利组织单位会计制度财务指标			
本年收入合计	本年支出合计	收支结余	固定资产原价	上年结余	本年收入合计	本年费用合计
18182455.0	**16436562.7**	**813765.7**	**27875027.5**	**11261252.7**	**30812382.1**	**25390684.7**
197014.7	159098.6	47462.9	953052.1		5569041.1	4424685.2
1516713.1	1234950.4	63550.7	1342128.0	1736427.5	1847659.3	1256250.4
295981.6	290958.8	20018.7	451537.2	19100.2	222618.3	294520.0
763481.0	736670.0	33565.7	1816422.8	643881.3	5574274.4	1924562.5
343711.2	349549.2	23128.1	377652.2	12804.4	192740.3	175128.2
212705.9	221993.6	27953.4	131182.4	2253.9	87482.0	86973.9
813903.0	631272.5	18844.2	1268036.7	882777.9	424186.3	439860.2
172809.3	164650.3	2643.4	10761.9	342.2	97493.6	22892.3
473150.9	204070.2	2639.3	215949.1	7015.8	122049.5	202881.3
845644.8	761147.4	39407.6	489314.3	2545989.0	3003609.0	2612021.5
1744975.8	1586301.0	72255.9	2860827.7	2068816.2	3100628.9	2836057.2
1663693.1	1431675.7	51661.3	2647666.7	1037307.2	1756405.8	1530872.7
366294.0	354602.3	5463.1	1289860.6	302463.0	615871.0	598414.3
338291.2	329032.0	18591.6	435752.7	153129.4	258460.1	274020.6
220756.4	186169.5	46107.0	353116.0	7875.1	275768.9	948455.2
1935960.5	1940164.3	121.5	1087306.2	6631.5	1160998.1	1150237.8
425870.9	409402.4	8700.0	794680.2	55431.2	719467.1	460718.3
684554.7	655627.0	15955.7	614862.3	4995.9	581991.1	545142.7
628644.8	622880.3	17093.0	560183.9	72682.8	393011.7	346931.5
1567969.7	1321445.5	67565.3	6330391.2	327664.6	1989515.7	2210366.9
316699.1	267053.9	16880.3	200008.1	74362.4	107898.8	97097.8
77832.6	73195.2	12319.5	75296.2	1606.9	336721.0	100679.8
314635.1	276690.7	75435.6	764797.2	195423.7	640542.4	543928.7
627105.0	635474.4	25142.4	923287.4	669864.0	961039.2	1359382.1
440628.3	454252.3	10199.8	341127.8	46092.4	157917.1	144843.4
267747.4	257893.1	12720.9	586458.2	257130.6	288679.5	329199.3
13265.4	28096.1	8038.4	5444.7	13863.7	3404.8	2956.7
433432.7	408422.9	17647.8	581560.8	5131.5	122735.5	210357.8
153689.6	147475.8	14422.1	133965.8	3861.9	54796.3	55698.7
30337.4	25555.2	2050.2	59293.2	969.2	30028.1	35013.3
52989.9	55688.2	12466.9	65864.2	27557.5	40091.8	92986.2
241965.9	215103.9	23713.4	107239.7	77799.8	75255.4	77548.2

C-1-6 社会服务发展

地区	社会服务综合指数(%)	每万人口社会服务机构和设施数(个/万人)	每万人口社会服务职工人数(人/万人)	每百万人口社工助工师(人/百万人)	每千人口固定资产原价(万元/千人)
全国	**100.0**	**12.8**	**95.2**	**76.8**	**59.5**
北京	248.9	13.6	112.0	445.8	242.7
天津	127.2	8.5	64.1	162.4	64.7
河北	94.1	15.0	92.4	66.3	69.6
山西	61.6	13.1	85.0	18.3	39.3
内蒙古	95.8	12.6	73.7	53.8	21.0
辽宁	104.5	10.7	96.9	61.1	74.6
吉林	80.8	9.1	54.5	114.9	18.2
黑龙江	85.2	8.2	65.8	35.8	42.9
上海	173.3	11.0	137.9	288.4	144.8
江苏	174.9	18.4	143.5	135.3	163.7
浙江	167.1	19.9	141.0	98.7	211.7
安徽	100.2	8.6	66.0	82.8	36.3
福建	99.8	12.4	101.7	60.4	23.2
江西	64.7	9.2	72.1	26.4	20.2
山东	96.0	15.8	93.6	29.6	43.1
河南	65.0	9.4	60.2	17.4	18.3
湖北	104.4	12.3	93.2	63.0	40.8
湖南	82.0	13.0	75.2	32.2	25.1
广东	132.5	12.9	87.9	113.9	85.3
广西	84.8	11.0	99.5	38.3	14.6
海南	82.3	11.6	88.9	19.3	17.7
重庆	122.1	11.8	103.3	188.1	60.6
四川	89.6	14.2	109.7	41.8	29.6
贵州	89.8	14.9	107.2	10.5	18.9
云南	81.7	8.3	118.6	21.5	34.6
西藏	37.7	20.4	126.5	1.2	32.9
陕西	85.6	14.0	111.8	17.8	34.5
甘肃	81.3	17.4	111.9	85.5	17.6
青海	45.3	16.4	87.6	28.7	18.5
宁夏	75.5	13.0	112.6	17.4	40.9
新疆	67.4	10.7	93.4	24.7	24.9

综合指数

社会服务事业费占财政支出的比重(‰)	每千人口社会服务事业费(万元/千人)	每百万人口乡镇街道数(个/百万人)	万人口社会服务床位(张/万人)	千老年人口养老床位(张/千人)	每十万人口孤儿数(人/十万人)	每百万人口家庭收养数(件/百万人)
32.8	**35.8**	**28.9**	**53.3**	**30.3**	**36.5**	**16.3**
38.7	102.3	15.2	71.4	29.0	9.9	8.0
23.8	49.7	15.8	44.4	23.7	5.6	5.6
32.1	24.3	30.3	70.3	40.9	21.6	5.1
35.1	32.8	38.2	26.9	16.3	37.0	7.0
33.2	56.2	40.2	90.9	56.7	22.0	7.3
34.2	42.1	35.0	51.0	21.1	17.6	5.0
32.9	38.4	32.7	30.0	14.3	18.9	1.2
37.4	39.5	32.4	53.0	27.0	19.6	1.2
15.6	40.0	8.8	56.9	27.2	8.1	8.2
26.9	32.7	16.1	82.9	41.0	22.2	29.2
21.2	30.2	24.4	90.1	51.7	8.7	61.2
34.6	29.5	24.3	62.5	36.1	43.9	14.3
19.4	23.5	28.8	37.9	24.9	15.7	32.9
35.6	34.4	34.0	46.3	30.9	50.7	9.1
30.3	29.2	18.5	71.5	37.1	17.8	24.5
33.7	24.2	25.7	40.6	24.2	45.6	7.7
37.0	38.8	21.1	57.4	30.1	40.5	12.8
40.2	34.0	28.2	36.2	19.2	64.3	16.0
15.9	23.9	14.6	25.1	19.9	35.8	13.4
36.7	31.1	26.1	40.6	25.8	49.2	33.1
23.9	32.6	23.9	24.1	17.6	18.0	12.3
30.2	38.0	34.0	70.0	33.2	36.7	7.1
42.0	38.4	56.5	65.8	30.7	36.2	12.3
37.4	41.7	38.8	57.4	35.3	59.6	8.0
49.0	48.7	29.3	29.5	19.9	50.2	33.0
12.7	54.0	214.2	96.6	61.9	179.0	146.6
42.2	48.7	34.0	41.9	23.6	33.0	9.9
46.2	52.6	52.0	52.5	33.8	79.3	3.7
30.5	78.7	67.9	42.0	31.6	276.7	7.1
36.0	59.6	34.3	38.6	30.4	100.1	6.8
34.0	54.8	44.4	34.3	24.8	97.6	10.7

C-1-6续表

地 区	每万人口流浪救助人次数（人次/万人）	每十万人口福利企业残疾职工人数（人/十万人）	城市低保平均标准（十元/人·月）	农村低保平均标准（十元/人·月）	农村特困集中供养平均标准（十元/人·月）	农村特困分散供养平均标准（十元/人·月）	每万人口优抚对象人数（人/万人）
全 国	**27.3**	**3.1**	**45.1**	**26.5**	**50.2**	**37.4**	**65.3**
北 京	245.8	4.4	71.0	71.0	118.2	112.1	20.4
天 津	30.2	4.0	70.5	60.0	116.6	86.3	29.8
河 北	10.9	1.6	44.1	22.3	46.5	31.1	76.4
山 西	26.4	3.6	41.3	23.0	44.0	28.1	49.1
内蒙古	19.5	1.8	50.8	32.4	67.2	41.9	19.5
辽 宁	14.2	8.3	49.3	29.6	55.2	35.7	50.7
吉 林	13.0	2.5	40.2	22.7	38.6	27.0	44.5
黑龙江	8.7	1.4	50.6	29.8	53.1	36.7	31.2
上 海	11.5	8.1	79.0	79.0	103.0	103.0	16.5
江 苏	14.5	9.8	58.2	50.2	74.6	64.9	60.4
浙 江	11.4	10.9	64.0	55.7	89.2	81.7	54.0
安 徽	23.8	1.1	45.5	26.0	43.5	28.3	74.9
福 建	24.1	1.9	47.8	28.4	65.3	57.4	49.1
江 西	21.2	2.1	45.2	24.7	32.3	27.1	64.7
山 东	11.4	3.3	47.0	27.8	49.4	33.7	91.2
河 南	18.2	2.4	37.4	18.6	39.8	24.2	79.0
湖 北	63.6	2.1	44.7	27.0	48.0	33.2	80.9
湖 南	84.7	1.9	36.0	20.4	51.8	27.4	128.0
广 东	20.1	0.5	51.4	37.4	76.6	73.9	39.5
广 西	27.4	0.6	40.4	21.3	36.4	28.0	60.9
海 南	56.2	1.1	45.3	34.0	48.7	41.1	29.3
重 庆	18.8	7.0	41.9	23.7	49.5	44.4	87.7
四 川	31.2	2.5	36.7	20.1	38.8	29.9	102.6
贵 州	22.9	0.2	45.3	21.8	32.4	20.8	63.0
云 南	11.5	2.0	39.6	19.5	36.5	23.9	74.5
西 藏	37.4	0.3	59.1	19.5	38.2	34.7	14.4
陕 西	22.4	1.0	46.1	22.1	53.9	46.7	65.8
甘 肃	14.0	0.4	37.8	21.8	39.4	37.4	46.8
青 海	36.4	1.5	37.0	20.8	52.1	46.7	25.5
宁 夏	20.4	2.2	36.2	21.7	52.9	35.4	17.9
新 疆	9.8	1.4	34.9	19.1	56.6	36.5	14.6

每千人口福利彩票销售（万元/千人）	社区服务设施覆盖率(%)	城市社区服务中心（站）覆盖率(%)	每十万人口社会组织（个/十万人）	每十万人口村居委会个数（个/十万人）	每万人口结婚对数（对/万人）	每万人口离婚对数（对/万人）	火化率(%)
14.7	**53.0**	**82.0**	**48.2**	**49.5**	**89.1**	**27.9**	**47.0**
23.2	166.8	98.7	44.8	31.8	76.5	37.9	85.1
24.5	38.7	80.4	33.2	34.6	65.4	33.6	78.1
10.3	70.1	58.5	26.0	71.3	82.1	26.8	44.1
11.6	10.6	57.6	34.1	83.0	94.6	19.7	10.6
21.3	27.9	70.5	52.8	53.5	86.8	36.6	50.8
25.0	42.5	95.9	47.2	35.9	72.3	34.8	95.9
12.7	15.7	61.6	38.5	40.7	85.2	46.3	65.0
13.1	24.0	47.5	35.6	33.9	83.5	49.8	69.6
17.8	102.1	67.7	55.3	23.8	58.7	27.6	100.0
18.1	181.4	129.3	100.8	26.9	98.6	28.7	89.6
26.5	94.0	81.6	79.0	58.3	70.9	25.2	100.0
10.7	44.3	83.0	40.1	29.3	120.3	29.5	73.1
13.3	33.5	94.4	62.4	43.7	91.0	23.3	83.8
7.1	16.3	37.2	33.6	44.7	67.1	20.8	23.5
14.7	34.4	84.6	44.1	81.7	71.2	24.5	89.3
6.6	10.4	29.4	31.1	54.3	115.4	26.6	23.9
16.0	41.4	94.4	47.2	50.2	97.9	28.5	64.4
11.5	25.2	60.9	40.9	67.2	80.0	26.7	17.5
18.9	217.6	134.0	49.7	24.2	77.5	17.8	96.1
10.6	80.8	30.7	46.3	33.8	87.8	21.8	26.6
19.1	64.1	84.0	58.8	33.7	91.2	16.6	5.5
15.1	66.9	77.8	50.9	36.7	97.0	45.5	36.1
10.2	35.3	90.1	48.8	64.8	90.4	34.9	36.3
7.1	115.6	137.5	29.8	53.0	139.5	30.7	31.9
13.7	21.0	52.4	44.6	30.1	96.6	23.0	22.1
32.9	6.0	62.0	17.7	168.7	47.7	7.3	4.6
21.8	26.5	86.5	51.9	66.6	93.9	25.7	22.8
17.4	47.1	118.4	72.0	66.8	84.7	17.8	11.6
19.9	24.5	92.0	61.8	78.6	86.8	21.7	18.5
22.3	36.5	112.7	70.6	40.0	88.5	26.4	11.5
16.9	22.4	69.8	40.5	50.1	117.2	43.1	26.8

C-1-7 社会工作师、助理

地 区	社会工作师和助理社会工作师累计合格人数	社会工作师		
		累计合格人数	当年考试通过人数	当年报考人数
全 国	**206183**	**51722**	**13155**	**79535**
北 京	20723	5063	894	4538
天 津	4754	1002	344	1751
河 北	3652	1326	270	1587
山 西	2149	873	190	1554
内蒙古	1178	403	141	1727
辽 宁	6993	1953	429	3010
吉 林	4185	885	248	2599
黑龙江	3457	904	214	1527
上 海	9412	2881	530	4239
江 苏	27830	6385	1781	7875
浙 江	16134	5132	1264	6343
安 徽	5606	1427	486	2457
福 建	6523	1867	579	3064
江 西	2488	611	107	604
山 东	9078	3219	936	5388
河 南	4454	1337	257	1615
湖 北	5450	1021	299	1919
湖 南	4471	1165	253	2136
广 东	43100	8678	2185	13879
广 西	2674	585	110	836
海 南	299	71	22	155
重 庆	3594	1511	460	2929
四 川	6931	141	33	495
贵 州	818	435	124	1368
云 南	1851	5	1	12
西 藏	17	979	325	1836
陕 西	5068	891	438	1546
甘 肃	980	233	66	632
青 海	290	59	4	138
宁 夏	443	149	28	369
新 疆	1581	531	137	1407

社工师人员情况

单位:人

	助理社会工作师			
当年实考人数	累计合格人数	当年考试通过人数	当年报考人数	当年实考人数
59851	**154461**	**34274**	**196965**	**155337**
3782	15660	1865	10821	8918
1562	3752	1040	5388	4720
1270	2326	432	1824	1524
1160	1276	337	1605	1326
1201	775	243	2179	1476
2477	5040	1171	8555	6941
1977	3300	870	7983	6645
1176	2553	464	2972	2405
2782	6531	1494	8905	6273
6245	21445	4894	23449	19104
4586	11002	2116	9063	6910
1765	4179	891	4850	3610
2348	4656	1015	5594	4266
490	1877	296	1537	1254
3318	5859	1194	5769	3912
1293	3117	478	2037	1714
1533	4429	1011	6555	5332
1419	3306	828	5350	3967
10645	34422	7749	49220	38410
638	2089	380	2338	2010
124	228	70	922	784
2257	5420	1503	9053	7284
304	677	158	1364	987
921	1416	475	3699	2762
9	12	6	135	99
1423	2615	801	5189	4304
1308	4177	1964	4776	3994
414	747	172	906	608
93	231	18	524	364
293	294	93	994	864
1038	1050	246	3409	2570

C-1-8 社会服务职业

地 区	累计鉴定合格人数	2015年鉴定合格人数	养老护理员		假肢类技能人员	
			累计鉴定合格人数	2015年鉴定合格人数	累计鉴定合格人数	2015年鉴定合格人数
全 国	**133425**	**12871**	**24086**	**8127**	**1896**	**268**
中央级	7725	1615	2940	708	595	134
北 京	12657	196	238		58	
天 津	731	115	144		2	
河 北	1084	412	634	274	10	
山 西	2804	398	988	336		
内蒙古	2284	303	379	230	21	
辽 宁	2682		346		128	
吉 林	3026	120	187	100	5	
黑龙江	3254	9	463	9	4	
上 海	2705	16	8		170	16
江 苏	3332	256	98	57	198	37
浙 江	31572	98	53	31	80	19
安 徽	2267		182		24	
福 建	2443	930	951	389	8	4
江 西	2594	118	69		24	
山 东	5804	672	1090	435	87	25
河 南	6136	1488	3077	1272	63	
湖 北	2591	10	360		23	10
湖 南	5081	406	124		27	1
广 东	8087	1975	4661	1648	138	3
广 西	2525	544	1260	378	112	4
海 南	311	68	189	52		
重 庆	4166	349	17	10	39	
四 川	5506	1784	3668	1657	1	
贵 州	2524	97	294	14	8	
云 南	2845	172	147		23	
西 藏	193	89	128	57		
陕 西	671	94	73			
甘 肃	1045	44	201		34	15
青 海	323	56	254	56		
宁 夏	3500	293	503	260		
新 疆	957	176	360	154	14	

说明：1.以上数据为民政部职业技能鉴定指导中心及分布在全国31个省、自治区、直辖市76个鉴定站鉴定人数和竞赛晋级人数（不含地方自行组织的鉴定人数）。

2.殡葬类职业包括：殡仪服务员（初中高技师4个级别）、遗体接运工（初中高3个级别）、遗体防腐师（初中高技师高级技师5个级别）、遗体整容师（初中高技师高级技师5个级别）、遗体火化师（初中高技师高级技师5个级别）、墓地管理员（初中高技师4个级别）。

3.假肢类职业包括：假肢师（初中高技师高级技师5个级别）、矫形器师（初中高技师高级技师5个级别）。

技能人员情况

单位：人

孤残儿童护理员		灾害信息员		殡葬类技能人员	
累计鉴定合格人数	2015年鉴定合格人数	累计鉴定合格人数	2015年鉴定合格人数	累计鉴定合格人数	2015年鉴定合格人数
9958	**1570**	**81946**	**791**	**15539**	**2115**
1110	405	1005	23	2075	345
204	20	10651		1506	176
109		246		230	115
302	138	11		127	
323	62	1493			
370		1145	73	369	
219		1573		416	
168	20	2666			
214		2440		133	
96		2420		11	
499		1869		668	162
363		30671		405	48
176		1498		387	
88	42	1396	495		
409	96	1840		252	22
454		3052		1121	212
783	216	2041		172	
302		1691		215	
346	55	2157		2427	350
708	133	1238		1342	191
337	70	177		639	92
84	16	30		8	
174	31	3058	200	878	108
383	105	1245		209	22
299	42	1603		320	41
296		1517		862	172
49	32			16	
591	94	7			
128		479		203	29
64		5			
128	25	2611		258	8
182		111		290	22

C-1-9 分省社会服务

地 区	1952年	1953年	1954年	1955年	1956年	1957年
全 国	**28265**	**35484**	**60390**	**49842**	**56906**	**53119**
中央级	6	443	20619	8736	270	85
北 京	198	237	276	247	584	302
天 津	208	315	131	157	217	240
河 北	2849	4558	4764	4526	9681	6640
山 西	1253	1398	1531	1373	2096	1953
内蒙古	912	370	306	364	625	417
辽 宁	611	1434	1392	1298	1638	1339
吉 林	346	595	880	856	1331	1610
黑龙江	640	831	912	952	1442	1336
上 海	550	306	411	729	1121	1073
江 苏	1980	1993	2051	3003	4052	5051
浙 江	398	426	505	757	1430	988
安 徽	2051	4061	3382	3453	4748	4306
福 建	828	732	789	933	1473	866
江 西	1519	1040	1368	2253	1889	1802
山 东	2624	3993	5082	3975	3664	5261
河 南	1440	2745	2307	2494	4360	5539
湖 北	2719	1058	2765	2664	1306	1505
湖 南	1255	1089	3381	2205	2259	2177
广 东	1762	1454	1270	1407	2725	2729
广 西	516	645	735	700	1414	1589
海 南						
重 庆						
四 川	1583	2035	2052	2646	3570	2606
贵 州	368	686	633	567	618	494
云 南	630	695	875	740	908	599
西 藏			43	207	91	
陕 西	519	1023	984	1135	1794	1250
甘 肃	390	1074	675	1171	1083	871
青 海	52	134	140	154	281	237
宁 夏						
新 疆	58	114	131	140	236	254

事业费历年支出情况

单位：万元

1958年	1959年	1960年	1961年	1962年	1963年
32693	**44786**	**72444**	**98912**	**74475**	**87533**
82	192	262	39		
376	751	824	658	542	638
194					
2494	4148	5070	10807	5780	15681
2279	1656	2659	2896	2556	2640
505	873	525	785	1468	1124
1098	1249	4475	4392	3933	3467
1126	764	1055	1271	1660	2138
948	782	991	1485	2151	2362
464	475	471	422	539	874
2617	2956	4843	4107	4873	7282
672	874	857	1414	1597	1166
1642	3169	3161	4704	3530	5431
823	4141	2823	2798	1493	1687
1717	1691	2179	3224	3168	2273
3795	4494	8141	11332	6963	7201
2990	2672	10271	11417	8107	10099
1210	2466	4428	4569	3767	3468
1344	967	1690	4299	2697	2834
1223	2982	4608	3475	2830	3146
582	903	997	2687	1505	2125
1982	2583	6315	9758	5918	4227
331	613	750	2390	1429	1792
514	675	880	1692	773	1250
2	1	25	48	117	
588	1109	1113	1530	1422	1640
539	681	1778	4522	2464	2988
164	447	576	1028	1005	
92	239	428	303	365	
300	233	249	860	1823	

C-1-9续表1

地 区	1964年	1965年	1966年	1967年	1968年	1969年
全 国	**161510**	**107869**	**88112**	**81887**	**56154**	**66683**
中央级	31	2325	454	534	308	11
北 京	816	1047	914	939	868	820
天 津				473	439	572
河 北	31433	18545	12395	6983	4443	5333
山 西	2361	2899	4447	2692	2478	2579
内蒙古	1360	1440	2182	2401	1194	842
辽 宁	3382	2942	2572	2781	2473	3542
吉 林	2235	1798	1704	1745	1579	1890
黑龙江	2796	2611	2548	2169	1775	2355
上 海	1074	1220	1472	1654	1410	1359
江 苏	11070	5506	7298	5400	3756	3839
浙 江	1152	1351	1142	1366	1486	1481
安 徽	10567	3347	4119	6861	4025	4246
福 建	1394	1463	1673	1738	1727	1922
江 西	3081	1989	2145	2318	1637	1924
山 东	11079	15807	9458	9844	5878	7622
河 南	48554	17841	9303	8611	4105	6983
湖 北	3319	2790	2579	3177	2651	3509
湖 南	4522	2482	2141	2562	1848	2019
广 东	3056	2664	2454	2644	2046	2639
广 西	4006	1983	1997	2541	1641	1607
海 南						
重 庆						
四 川	4495	5179	4774	4067	3374	3439
贵 州	1808	1726	1730	1926	1224	1314
云 南	1494	1596	1772	1412	807	1018
西 藏	133	192	374			96
陕 西	1918	3137	3623	1874	1477	1733
甘 肃	2310	1611	1161	1963	671	989
青 海	465	695	409	185	190	246
宁 夏	378	284	272	287	200	238
新 疆	1212	1399	1000	740	444	516

单位：万元

1970年	1971年	1972年	1973年	1974年	1975年
65349	**68269**	**81549**	**99675**	**90406**	**127082**
		8	10		
895	974	1192	1506	1284	1461
405	407	546	762	937	881
2054	3591	5482	8727	5925	5960
4777	4563	4025	4696	3587	3420
891	649	1020	1914	1575	1559
2867	3922	4574	5590	3902	18731
1837	1968	1753	2174	2500	2448
2247	2317	2768	3701	3884	3701
1442	1554	1676	1885	2088	2263
4191	4969	7368	6988	7258	8001
1496	1517	2399	2103	1973	1984
5547	3365	4639	4625	3981	5828
1463	1481	1721	2142	2150	1991
2047	2357	2357	4039	3220	2964
6442	9034	8801	8110	8601	10417
4947	4699	4799	5474	4190	24152
4197	3116	3462	4747	3487	4471
1668	1602	2272	3321	2580	2942
2734	2410	2800	4041	5051	3836
1555	1827	1713	1597	1669	1653
3678	4518	5615	6780	5936	6061
1646	1535	2116	3574	1955	2352
2460	1454	1746	1509	2245	2242
100	104	173	228	195	206
1778	2099	2415	3435	2986	2579
952	968	2206	3421	4183	2603
207	291	366	311	342	521
242	354	810	1369	1813	600
584	651	727	896	909	1255

C-1-9续表2

地 区	1976年	1977年	1978年	1979年	1980年	1981年
全 国	**161690**	**185288**	**137135**	**183279**	**174769**	**192267**
中央级			11	44	103	138
北 京	1742	3068	1990	2238	2802	3167
天 津	933	13670	1061	1482	1474	1670
河 北	7041	36568	11605	9140	11165	13597
山 西	4111	4813	5437	8154	6749	7893
内蒙古	2502	1873	2040	5922	5714	6218
辽 宁	14705	7427	6103	5607	6671	8073
吉 林	2834	3677	3869	3477	4482	4970
黑龙江	4176	5463	5545	5149	5370	6562
上 海	2469	2581	2777	3290	3375	3381
江 苏	7719	8031	9208	10019	11269	12914
浙 江	2424	2641	2853	3475	3703	3897
安 徽	15690	6300	6756	13263	9385	9550
福 建	2432	2826	2730	3272	3625	4268
江 西	3606	3981	3953	8610	6289	5309
山 东	9746	10599	12292	15169	16327	14126
河 南	40056	21437	14140	19495	12007	10921
湖 北	5463	5160	6149	9597	9265	12458
湖 南	3442	3550	4380	6747	7026	8924
广 东	4884	5546	5435	8146	8337	7767
广 西	1963	2355	2073	4019	3213	3674
海 南						
重 庆						
四 川	9037	12602	8511	12722	12063	15429
贵 州	2748	3296	2740	4767	4123	4718
云 南	3428	3783	2948	3478	4172	4599
西 藏	289	270	379	1366	1704	1208
陕 西	3174	4575	4834	5780	5390	8198
甘 肃	2240	5485	4030	5204	4801	4338
青 海	407	514	696	853	862	915
宁 夏	1150	1780	1090	1040	1385	1118
新 疆	1279	1417	1500	1754	1918	2267

单位：万元

1982年	1983年	1984年	1985年	1986年	1987年
191874	**216116**	**242371**	**295841**	**344064**	**359278**
78	163	286	443	2526	2742
3416	4063	4904	5719	7287	8906
1669	2194	3101	3583	4113	4531
10179	9692	12427	16654	16581	20578
7854	7015	7924	10683	10193	11833
5135	7379	7909	9030	11684	10867
10591	11727	11741	18341	22112	18104
4951	6300	5952	8391	13570	14016
8005	9546	8782	10119	13791	13686
3215	3170	3540	4467	5503	5603
11991	14750	16403	16254	20586	21208
4070	4808	6480	8174	10211	12353
7521	12093	14059	14340	13524	12942
4773	5506	5601	8298	7657	9238
6183	7093	8360	8364	9768	11546
18998	17811	17413	22757	22496	29017
12862	15216	13710	18456	20939	2260
7956	10798	10760	11860	14581	14846
7546	10428	10373	12357	15013	15167
9550	9035	12337	14516	15526	17076
3897	4779	6382	9438	9634	9054
14542	13943	17823	20667	24973	25524
4354	5211	5833	9182	8657	9092
4231	5251	7025	10137	13752	12712
1151	1357	1821	1391	1789	1828
6271	5820	6313	7545	8586	9299
5778	4902	8983	6541	7655	7238
1068	1270	1674	1918	2134	1837
1819	2329	1497	1826	1990	1780
2220	2467	2958	4395	4768	4896

C-1-9续表3

地 区	1988年	1989年	1990年	1991年	1992年	1993年
全 国	**395646**	**466492**	**519383**	**625359**	**637097**	**698708**
中央级	1297	1185	1517	1792	3217	3108
北 京	11355	12805	14738	16249	19073	26105
天 津	5209	5861	6585	7176	8173	9218
河 北	24272	26484	32162	30785	33344	38161
山 西	13977	15845	15976	17378	19264	19515
内蒙古	11254	10975	13510	13449	14250	15314
辽 宁	19595	22233	26318	26380	29561	32903
吉 林	10692	11439	14155	14619	16553	18461
黑龙江	14205	15127	15982	18411	19734	19377
上 海	3965	4741	5364	6270	7742	10368
江 苏	23816	27647	33150	50604	48290	47590
浙 江	16113	18710	21111	22094	22124	26924
安 徽	14854	16444	19755	80611	39002	26982
福 建	10332	11213	13935	15070	18423	20141
江 西	13240	15076	15791	16915	21249	21410
山 东	31890	39382	44965	46744	52525	62616
河 南	21784	26566	24275	27675	31304	34498
湖 北	17804	20704	21092	23318	23677	28918
湖 南	19110	22384	24981	23436	24712	29096
广 东	16675	20206	21863	25022	29602	43983
广 西	9757	11955	11313	12728	14317	16760
海 南	2338	3659	3366	3843	4270	4630
重 庆						
四 川	28123	32186	36228	39004	42563	49037
贵 州	9408	11568	12079	11043	11761	15154
云 南	14934	31640	33901	38725	41026	30502
西 藏	1795	2116	2909	3499	2647	2598
陕 西	10602	12277	13688	13412	16805	20107
甘 肃	8346	7681	8813	9124	11256	12186
青 海	1750	1802	2086	2036	2387	2965
宁 夏	2609	1805	2000	2206	2456	2464
新 疆	4549	4776	5775	5741	5790	7617

单位：万元

1994年	1995年	1996年	1997年	1998年	1999年
870194	**1034502**	**1211500**	**1335202**	**1618445**	**1946843**
4077	3703	6371	5954	50783	11856
36146	44073	54012	61184	74406	97748
11970	15023	17254	19738	20952	20611
48303	58804	74364	71151	79064	88202
22995	31008	37882	37150	39519	45466
18378	20470	26012	26773	35484	35659
44239	60067	59580	65370	74946	85394
24648	30876	31416	33928	52337	53311
26195	28798	30459	33020	55977	60566
15557	19773	23984	30860	37336	54151
59349	69907	80163	93383	108862	121349
40044	43610	50852	60657	65733	88269
26883	37348	43979	50559	56473	72895
25502	31904	34498	46134	49421	50996
23815	30354	33883	35962	47177	45334
71995	76826	88009	101613	112960	131746
44163	52458	59353	64155	68311	80338
39148	40291	50385	58511	85285	75622
35093	42680	53778	48234	54533	73272
53653	64806	75354	88748	96993	112133
30480	28730	36280	28944	30995	31950
6163	7210	8828	8274	9472	10818
			25048	35054	51123
59629	70257	77059	63016	72283	89492
15641	20528	26419	27866	27126	30834
31529	36916	46048	52043	53384	63169
5304	4466	5228	6987	11749	6824
20404	26336	32108	31702	25791	43230
13897	17748	21484	20366	20554	26371
3454	4342	6473	8088	8669	23784
3244	3458	4279	4397	5442	8651
8297	11732	15706	25387	22690	55676

C-1-9续表4

地 区	2000年	2001年	2002年	2003年	2004年	2005年	2006年
全 国	**2296954**	**2847548**	**3922695**	**4989171.81**	**5773906.5**	**7184146**	**9153527**
中央级	29338	13965	18467	18027.2	39289.8	37423	27907
北 京	150746	196540	233429	303795.3	327957	370918	450229
天 津	30547	41580	58202	62682.2	71091.4	92462	121917
河 北	113381	125698	153525	185640.8	216769.6	283480	356510
山 西	56815	71776	105897	124002.5	147569.6	192257	236469
内蒙古	44674	55328	70606	99367.7	126236.7	141727	187147
辽 宁	131675	180547	227704	279736.9	304551.2	368476	437608
吉 林	51153	76026	118392	166702.2	182133.4	218688	284676
黑龙江	61753	80658	177852	167487.2	193823.3	222865	376619
上 海	87021	121538	167719	222539.6	228764.3	282196	316864
江 苏	159691	170800	205763	256062.56	309196	419996	502744
浙 江	97755	124023	159432	189645.4	294720.4	354320	415110
安 徽	72568	89476	138918	208605.9	195411.9	250782	312519
福 建	67797	68897	85353	94060.8	139539.3	157015	226313
江 西	49521	57966	92013	149217.2	176371.5	225667	340990
山 东	159315	180470	233918	283989.3	311522.3	408419	526836
河 南	102698	117574	159157	221712.8	251438.9	337872	425038
湖 北	113381	122382	167653	229233.85	270653.4	345556	440298
湖 南	80343	104818	158443	210815.4	252891.5	326694	422998
广 东	144461	198362	278022	341821	386221.4	483430	635940
广 西	35135	49819	82929	109901	113722.5	156841	175928
海 南	13568	15372	18032	24304.1	27949.8	38103	49003
重 庆	55934	70571	117114	125112.4	145713	174682	216847
四 川	105249	139493	194774	244374.4	302566.3	376043	500440
贵 州	36085	51264	67973	82093.5	102696.6	151257	181266
云 南	78944	98782	115945	150814	183854.7	202346	228950
西 藏	9920	14979	15358	17912.7	23199.7	22574	30224
陕 西	54365	72136	103474	147038.8	149120.1	186935	244342
甘 肃	35251	42851	58315	75346	91876.1	111530	149598
青 海	16159	19790	24812	36616	39139.1	47402	51844
宁 夏	13775	21289	28724	30448.1	34071.3	35346	57593
新 疆	56940	52768	104762	130065	133844.4	160847	222762

单位：万元

2007年	2008年	2009年	2010年	2011年	2012年	2013年	2014年	2015年
12154874	**21464484**	**21819430.2**	**26975149**	**32291356.0**	**36837379.4**	**42765370.8**	**44041244.2**	**49264448.4**
32841	263213	55240.2	488035.9	93505.4	100110.8	137419.9	128646.0	155949.2
575756	575302	745435.4	982144.3	1031493.0	1260515.9	1555734.8	1600353.6	2220633.5
149046	196893	244982.6	313824.7	375011.5	444250.9	552118.0	591814.0	769084.9
488387	678036	843485.2	969269.1	1244217.3	1438698.1	1672465.7	1653297.9	1805161.2
339210	457567	562518.4	634004.6	876097.5	936468.5	1130400.3	1144649.5	1201392.7
283105	420111	575897.9	768526.2	968084.5	1127395.6	1236610.0	1409253.2	1410121.9
575209	724799	887386.5	1066504.6	1347428.2	1567755.2	1672890.8	1694087.8	1844543.3
341920	470519	642777.6	750632.3	801698.3	765275.0	986245.5	942015.8	1057440.4
478896	643011	800947.6	854398.8	1050480.9	1152380.1	1589618.1	1373441.2	1504605.0
406118	515828	557187.9	572521.7	662862.5	727872.8	832211.6	857287.8	966471.0
632560	811832	996449.2	1265312.3	1711513.8	1970955.5	2335259.9	2460508.3	2605552.1
508925	610800	704117.9	884859.5	1061597.3	1253870.2	1428845.7	1502557.1	1674651.1
490974	659432	804010.6	971558.4	1263090.4	1421837.3	1601142.2	1699609.2	1812233.9
247500	282403	322487.9	422187.8	503195.6	614533.8	729824.6	775607.4	903162.9
434664	596019	693704.1	847650.9	986614.7	1075144.7	1224409.1	1472214.2	1571857.7
715079	885720	1122739	1437374.8	1691804.7	2183629.3	2502270.9	2706751.9	2871388.9
598726	785189	1035342.8	1230796.6	1586875.1	1740800.2	2097496.0	2054924.0	2292633.2
514067	748412	897367.7	1082788.8	1408483.1	1531263.7	1849392.5	1852790.6	2269799.1
521304	771404	997685.9	1165255.4	1545645.5	2003252.4	1996276.3	2085354.4	2305544.2
720130	834465	1021108.9	1154286.9	1480652.6	1668953.2	1981669.0	2237116.3	2595187.3
247212	410162	492763.3	731162.4	971372.9	1173997.1	1292515.6	1391271.4	1492923.0
65929	96527	142315.6	190264.1	223849.3	240254.6	254400.4	287775.5	296623.7
307697	435014	514479.6	674873.3	783120.4	907587.4	999446.7	1027739.5	1146517.8
734868	4848630	2289514.1	2408738.2	2168767.6	2375722.4	2880631.2	2917857.6	3152459.5
264299	443051	560108.4	728242.8	1116447.6	1248670.9	1341494.8	1391678.3	1472311.4
420914	687354	930167.6	1224026.2	1432131.1	1730472.3	1845730.7	1979476.0	2310934.8
38363	69982	82169.4	85017.8	130279.7	155073.7	156074.8	136789.5	175034.3
365358	849627	867024.3	1139380.6	1356364.3	1424205.1	1838401.7	1679000.3	1847868.8
226791	1063855	577204.8	740624.8	1000902.5	1051754.7	1299304.5	1214834.5	1367615.6
81455	123508	189659.7	330701.5	359785.5	341516.9	377594.3	381598.0	462567.9
79705	110375	143479.2	161335.6	195226.4	220055.6	266258.2	264662.5	409809.1
267867	395446	519670.9	698848.1	862756.8	983105.5	1101217.0	1126280.9	1292369.0

C-1-10 社会服务事业费

地 区	预算指标		
	2015年	2014年	增长(%)
全 国	**49587430.1**	**45130767.70**	**9.9**
中央级	162275.6	160968.30	0.8
北 京	1933909.2	1584025.20	22.1
天 津	841748.4	613841.00	37.1
河 北	1821618.6	1732833.60	5.1
山 西	1249590.2	1207672.50	3.5
内蒙古	1427487.8	1416401.60	0.8
辽 宁	1809406.2	1684919.20	7.4
吉 林	1129292.7	1055354.40	7.0
黑龙江	1519390.0	1404905.70	8.1
上 海	1171982.6	994656.30	17.8
江 苏	2582318.3	2463224.80	4.8
浙 江	1664446.4	1514614.10	9.9
安 徽	1802709.5	1659327.30	8.6
福 建	901048.7	812657.20	10.9
江 西	1570132.1	1459303.50	7.6
山 东	2824994.4	2702182.50	4.5
河 南	2240757.3	2137429.40	4.8
湖 北	2352767.5	2051670.00	14.7
湖 南	2327130.3	2121593.70	9.7
广 东	2557435.2	2230664.50	14.6
广 西	1485762.4	1381693.70	7.5
海 南	347546.4	361912.90	-4.0
重 庆	1406014.3	1072614.30	31.1
四 川	3181029.2	2969415.30	7.1
贵 州	1567198.2	1516174.50	3.4
云 南	2285288.3	1957799.10	16.7
西 藏	274419.5	210770.90	30.2
陕 西	1862287.4	1769283.10	5.3
甘 肃	1376628.3	1221824.80	12.7
青 海	481697.7	357353.50	34.8
宁 夏	431753.8	272324.50	58.5
新 疆	1159639.2	1031356.30	12.4

预算指标地方安排情况

单位：万元

地方预算安排预算指标		
2015年	2014年	增长(%)
26900610.7	**24023782.4**	**12.0**
1185583.2	976640.2	21.4
674581.4	472402.0	42.8
891142.6	835564.6	6.7
614571.2	590413.5	4.1
813863.8	841676.6	-3.3
870363.2	830428.2	4.8
454564.7	419342.4	8.4
646421.0	572905.7	12.8
1019670.6	871216.3	17.0
2034444.3	1988514.8	2.3
1409046.4	1313343.1	7.3
918448.5	839501.3	9.4
612647.7	580091.2	5.6
785887.1	695115.5	13.1
1685703.4	1714136.5	-1.7
880466.3	854706.4	3.0
1190181.5	956153.0	24.5
1007903.3	900103.7	12.0
2072325.2	1786459.5	16.0
710860.4	652565.7	8.9
192194.4	204446.9	-6.0
831771.3	521997.3	59.3
1426587.2	1332462.3	7.1
493271.2	426446.5	15.7
1089918.3	881657.1	23.6
119918.5	85571.9	40.1
932475.4	861078.1	8.3
446512.3	387905.8	15.1
222736.7	134415.5	65.7
246736.8	100366.5	145.8
419812.8	396154.3	6.0

C-1-11 中央专项

地 区	合计	抚恤合计	财社[2015]84号	财社[2015]68号	
			追减抚恤	抚恤补助资金（优抚对象）	老党员生活补贴
全 国	**22702834**	**3499497**	**-318**	**1078011**	**2511**
北 京	748326	25810		10753	40
天 津	167167	19548		7487	17
河 北	933954	187538		36018	738
山 西	635019	89802		18669	115
内蒙古	613624	36203		5785	26
辽 宁	939043	77263		13827	26
吉 林	674811	68728		25238	-25
黑龙江	872969	59153		6418	21
上 海	153042	15462		6446	1
江 苏	547874	161439		48440	456
浙 江	257386	74028		29814	65
安 徽	884261	156954		44921	19
福 建	288401	55749		17166	3
江 西	784245	123872		25909	3
山 东	1139291	398419		118002	740
河 南	1360291	256553		83412	152
湖 北	1162586	197107		53639	32
湖 南	1319227	341156		139483	2
广 东	485110	110614		40786	5
广 西	774902	91978		29877	0
海 南	155352	14302		3013	10
重 庆	574243	118588		43201	0
四 川	1754442	357486		128668	6
贵 州	1073647	93488		23922	-1
云 南	1195370	147486		53299	7
西 藏	154501	5881		2093	0
陕 西	943750	118734		25083	44
甘 肃	890116	46513		17494	0
青 海	258819	10215		3889	0
宁 夏	185017	7245		2180	1
新 疆	739827	31652		13079	8
兵 团	36221	531	-318		

拨款对账单

单位：万元

财社[2015]69号	财社[2015]70号	财社[2015]116号	财社[2015]162号	财社[2015]220号	
优抚事业单位补助资金	兵团优抚事业单位抚恤资金	烈士褒扬	一次性生活补助金	抚恤提标(优抚对象抚恤补助金)	抚恤提标(老党员生活补助)
72140	**650**	**12137**	**30**	**189388**	**588**
300		147		1139	6
810		640		830	3
2230		316		10184	167
2970		309		4696	43
1790		254		1602	7
1705		0		3698	8
3390		301		3388	5
2415		81		3092	8
		478		685	0
1540		382		8401	68
1870		521		3990	12
3175		382		7845	5
2390		162		3210	1
2970		155		7633	0
5350		595		20687	191
4250		389		13809	39
4210		647		10984	3
4920		786		19354	1
2460		81		5910	1
2140		228		5768	0
320		316		795	2
1600		155		6278	1
4965		602		19753	2
2790		763		5408	0
2210		578		8772	1
400		220		255	0
3960		832		6539	11
1170		316		2501	2
610		74		467	0
830		0		336	0
2400		1427		1379	1
	650		30		

C-1-11续表1

地 区	财社[2015]221号	财社[2014]128号	财社[2014]129号	财社[2015]14号	财社[2015]221号
	抚恤提标	提前下达2015年优抚对象补助资金(第一批)	提前下达2015年优抚对象补助资金(第二批)老党员	墓地维修和烈属接待	墓地维修和烈属接待
全 国	**169**	**2098171**	**14702**	**500**	**500**
北 京		12498	127		
天 津		9514	78		
河 北		130210	4197		
山 西		60199	1125		
内蒙古		25536	190		
辽 宁		57319	253		
吉 林		35785	180		
黑龙江		46379	232		
上 海		7597	2		
江 苏		96286	1481		
浙 江		36964	269		
安 徽		98726	151		
福 建		32740	17		
江 西		86575	8		
山 东		241200	4832		
河 南		152165	968		
湖 北		126444	57		
湖 南		174706	33		
广 东		60787	19		
广 西		53363	6	500	
海 南		9184	37		
重 庆		67275	21		
四 川		203001	43		
贵 州		60495	8		
云 南		81642	28		500
西 藏		2913			
陕 西		81465	277		
甘 肃		24933	47		
青 海		5143	2		
宁 夏		3863	4		
新 疆		13264	10		
兵 团	169				

单位：万元

财社[2015]254号 国家级抗战纪念设施遗址修缮保护	财社[2015]161号 抗战胜利70周年为部分老战士发放一次性补助	优抚医疗合计	财社[2015]71号 优抚对象医疗补助资金	财社[2015]72号 兵团对象优抚医疗补助	财社[2014]134号 提前下达2015年优抚对象医疗补助资金预算指标
8000	**22318**	**237244**	**71078**	**148**	**166018**
270	530	1928	553		1375
	169	3116	1019		2097
750	2728	11105	2617		8488
250	1426	5689	1429		4260
750	263	3392	1158		2234
150	277	5882	1850		4032
150	316	5398	1591		3807
200	307	5200	1366		3834
	253	1221	270		951
1080	3305	11421	3519		7902
130	393	5860	1992		3868
500	1230	11305	3306		7999
	60	5067	1596		3471
450	169	8055	2316		5739
2150	4672	23336	6902		16434
	1369	15497	4484		11013
220	871	13216	3772		9444
450	1421	19239	5979		13260
	565	10046	3141		6905
	96	6149	1987		4162
250	375	2064	637		1427
	57	8561	2705		5856
	446	19700	6034		13666
	103	6857	2006		4851
250	199	9725	3127		6598
		1074	366		708
	523	8198	2492		5706
	50	3049	977		2072
	30	1918	696		1222
	31	1364	443		921
	84	2464	748		1716
		148		148	

C-1-11续表2

地区	安置合计	财社[2015]62号			财社[2015]63号
		退役安置补助资金(第一批，退役士兵职业教育和技能培训)	退役安置补助资金(第一批，退役士兵待分配期间管理教育补助)	退役安置补助资金(第一批,一级至四级分散供养残疾退役士兵购建房补助)	退役安置补助资金(第二批，军休人员)
全国	**3529327**	**70832**	**575**	**1900**	**1393345**
北京	695601	121	9	20	276038
天津	85137	174	4		33669
河北	191686	3315	49	120	75183
山西	62486	1352	17	60	23340
内蒙古	40256	1031	17	30	15501
辽宁	337511	3201	24	120	134010
吉林	72387	1330	9	30	28680
黑龙江	59618	2410	6	70	23019
上海	114244	323	4	10	45483
江苏	190976	5041	21	90	77317
浙江	71176	1970	21	60	28980
安徽	51783	3899	17	70	19087
福建	56710	1277	10	30	21871
江西	31865	2845	26	40	12026
山东	285803	5757	50	190	112624
河南	109656	6481	41	170	41328
湖北	130819	4817	20	110	50200
湖南	82031	4954	55	140	32403
广东	144340	2513	13	80	55383
广西	33881	2138	11	10	12739
海南	18738	429	3		7719
重庆	58631	1468	7	80	23308
四川	153033	5222	40	100	62422
贵州	21528	1893	15	70	8460
云南	95359	1741	25	60	36869
西藏	14763	265	1		6169
陕西	156633	1789	36	90	62926
甘肃	62007	1792	17	40	24722
青海	17527	295	2		7303
宁夏	10718	576	2		4260
新疆	72179	413	3	10	30306
兵团	245				

单位：万元

财社[2015]64号 退役安置补助资金（第三批，离退休人员服务管理）	财社[2015]65号 退役安置补助资金（退役士兵职业教育和技能培训）	财社[2015]66号 退役安置补助资金（第四批，军休干部管理机构用房）	财社[2015]67号 退役安置补助资金（军休干部住房保障）	财社[2014]130号 提前下达军休管理机构补助资金（第一批）	财社[2014]131号 提前下达军休管理机构补助资金（第二批）
46382	**245**	**123531**	**457**	**1816827**	**75233**
9125		58939	685	336350	14314
1014		2249	2107	44281	1639
2747		2993	-6	102794	4491
758		960	-501	35126	1374
674		655	21	21143	1184
4302		6887	-38	181955	7050
1058		983	-24	38539	1782
939		915	98	30577	1584
1541		6653	-61	57828	2463
2458		2966	356	98522	4205
968		1806	82	35704	1585
759		891	454	25352	1254
801		1744	8	29693	1276
398		459	-30	15419	682
3610		5657	180	152521	5214
1504		2898	83	54702	2449
1578		2866	-1832	70424	2636
1109		1280	40	40234	1816
1721		5363	-318	76756	2829
512		1022	78	16512	859
303		1090	-7	8752	449
727		1475	-285	30738	1113
2005		3868	-12	76331	3057
331		176	-561	10576	568
1271		1561	19	51519	2294
-2		187	0	7776	367
2085		3356	71	83171	3109
804		1453	14	31658	1507
226		267	0	9055	379
129		285	-102	5277	291
927		1627	-62	37542	1413
	245				

C-1-11续表3

地 区	福利(孤儿救助)合计	财社[2015]61号 本次下达孤儿基本生活保障资金	财社[2014]132号 预拨2015孤儿基本生活保障资金	城乡低保、临时救助合计	财社[2015]94号 低保补助资金	临时救助资金
全 国	**205920**	**54848**	**151072**	**12076843**	**3991633**	**191020**
北 京	539	144	395	5332		1650
天 津	213	72	141	48604	14280	1854
河 北	5679	1828	3851	426658	137451	6583
山 西	5519	1436	4083	373694	120367	5936
内蒙古	3330	1007	2323	423179	136911	5708
辽 宁	1870	567	1303	445000	144332	5387
吉 林	1998	529	1469	433419	140489	5659
黑龙江	2844	806	2038	628444	204145	8208
上 海	493	133	360	13200		7425
江 苏	4432	1165	3267	121615	36718	6715
浙 江	1241	362	879	58026	15756	5804
安 徽	9876	3028	6848	526657	170373	7374
福 建	1562	445	1117	109119	38642	4216
江 西	10755	4756	5999	462145	156956	8924
山 东	4239	1257	2982	345089	128207	8897
河 南	16776	4609	12167	822099	268433	7383
湖 北	10078	2460	7618	662725	215705	7724
湖 南	15912	2636	13276	678839	220725	8063
广 东	10064	2629	7435	144746	44796	6575
广 西	11377	3816	7561	509910	164982	6986
海 南	775	192	583	85644	29789	4464
重 庆	5968	1414	4554	301051	96201	6551
四 川	14671	4467	10204	956268	312456	9305
贵 州	10485	2544	7941	786604	268152	5788
云 南	11633	-109	11742	765816	273884	6814
西 藏	2820	821	1999	64250	20200	2893
陕 西	6252	1717	4535	531540	172236	8087
甘 肃	10378	2868	7510	629366	209405	7186
青 海	7856	2360	5496	152143	55059	5083
宁 夏	3398	1023	2375	112095	34094	3571
新 疆	12887	3866	9021	453566	160889	4207
兵 团						

单位：万元

财社[2014]140号		城乡医疗救助合计	财社[2015]88号 城乡医疗救助补助资金		
2015年救助补助资金预算指标下达(低保补助资金)	2015年救助补助资金预算指标下达(临时救助补助资金)		本次下达小计	一般公共预算资金	彩票公益金
7675808	**218382**	**1402053**	**284204**	**124204**	**160000**
	3682	2183	441	193	248
28559	3911	3247	659	288	371
274900	7724	45875	9621	4386	5235
240735	6656	38418	7787	3403	4384
273820	6740	44644	9397	4302	5095
288665	6616	29494	5741	2375	3366
280977	6294	55290	10762	4452	6310
408290	7801	70880	14938	6849	8089
	5775	2099	426	186	240
70610	7572	14751	2990	1307	1683
30301	6165	7163	1452	635	817
340745	8165	62663	13206	6055	7151
60109	6152	11639	2359	1031	1328
288911	7354	70290	14863	6842	8021
199434	8551	30783	6240	2727	3513
536867	9416	81342	17035	7752	9283
431408	7888	61976	12997	5924	7073
441451	8600	88393	17206	7119	10087
86148	7227	14564	2952	1290	1662
329965	7977	56068	11858	5460	6398
46339	5052	17280	3503	1531	1972
192401	5898	39471	8321	3817	4504
624914	9593	127928	24901	10302	14599
504574	8090	73703	14347	5936	8411
476635	8483	82020	15965	6605	9360
34744	6413	16651	3491	1591	1900
344471	6746	67220	13085	5414	7671
404537	8238	78560	15292	6327	8965
85646	6355	28434	5974	2729	3245
68187	6243	21228	4303	1880	2423
281465	7005	57796	12092	5496	6596

C-1-11续表4

地 区	财社[2014]127号 提前下达城乡医疗救助补助资金预算指标 公共财政预算资金	流浪乞讨救助合计	财社[2015]59号 流浪乞讨本次下达	财社[2014]146号 提前下达2015年流浪乞讨救助补助预算指标
全 国	**1117849**	**199983**	**60031**	**139952**
北 京	1742	8911		8911
天 津	2588	1194		1194
河 北	36254	5558		5558
山 西	30631	6000	3029	2971
内蒙古	35247	3800	1838	1962
辽 宁	23753	4375	333	4042
吉 林	44528	3756	1559	2197
黑龙江	55942	3357	1395	1962
上 海	1673	2152	394	1758
江 苏	11761	9606	3410	6196
浙 江	5711	5288	1406	3882
安 徽	49457	10406	3269	7137
福 建	9280	4249	1310	2939
江 西	55427	6271	1301	4970
山 东	24543	8241	3249	4992
河 南	64307	10207	2333	7874
湖 北	48979	17000	5800	11200
湖 南	71187	18712	6195	12517
广 东	11612	13310	5382	7928
广 西	44210	9000	5412	3588
海 南	13777	1908	508	1400
重 庆	31150	3451	453	2998
四 川	103027	17949	4066	13883
贵 州	59356	5384	1033	4351
云 南	66055	3477	1189	2288
西 藏	13160	603		603
陕 西	54135	6844	2354	4490
甘 肃	63268	2878	815	2063
青 海	22460	1975	660	1315
宁 夏	16925	1000	455	545
新 疆	45704	3121	883	2238
兵 团				

单位：万元

救灾合计	财社[2015]3号 冬春补助	财社[2015]4号 救灾	财社[2015]12号 救灾	财社[2015]31号 救灾储备物资管理费	财社[2015]32号 救灾
946119	**140000**	**2000**	**9000**	**7149**	**15000**
157	100			57	
336				336	
32632	6580				
35576	5000				
41283	5800				
23027	4480			442	
17629	5360				
23367	5400			639	
7811	1360				
20241	660				
29551	3720			253	
28144	880			144	
47831	6920				
14563	2560				
18977	4940			675	
46607	7180			471	
45591	7040			453	
20190	1680				
37232	4760			186	
5653	2600				
17841	5400				
72344	10140			630	
54790	9160				
57452	8320		9000	386	
36072	3260			102	15000
33739	6100			861	
40805	8700			361	
22029	3420			551	
17435	3300				
74828	5180			602	
22386		2000			

C-1-11续表5

地 区	财社[2015]56号	财社[2015]57号	财社[2015]97号	财社[2015]98号
	救灾	救灾	救灾	救灾
全 国	**8600**	**5400**	**10000**	**8000**
北 京				
天 津				
河 北				
山 西				
内蒙古				
辽 宁				
吉 林				
黑龙江				
上 海				
江 苏				
浙 江				
安 徽				
福 建		5400		
江 西	8600			
山 东				
河 南				
湖 北			10000	
湖 南				8000
广 东				
广 西				
海 南				
重 庆				
四 川				
贵 州				
云 南				
西 藏				
陕 西				
甘 肃				
青 海				
宁 夏				
新 疆				
兵 团				

单位：万元

财社[2015]99号	财社[2015]104号	财社[2015]132号	财社[2015]133号	财社[2015]148号	财社[2015]149号
救灾	救灾(捐赠资金)	救灾	救灾	救灾	救灾
8000	**1281**	**10000**	**12000**	**31000**	**9000**
	600	10000			
8000					
	681				
			12000	31000	
					9000

C-1-11续表6

地区	财社[2015]150号	财社[2015]151号	财社[2015]153号	财社[2015]154号
	救灾	救灾	收回救灾应急车辆结余资金	收回救灾应急车辆结余资金
全　国	**10000**	**2000**	**-4347**	**-64**
北　京				
天　津				
河　北			-276	
山　西			-241	
内蒙古			-237	
辽　宁				
吉　林			-77	
黑龙江			-181	
上　海				
江　苏				
浙　江	10000	2000		
安　徽			-194	
福　建				
江　西			-246	
山　东				
河　南			-190	
湖　北			-146	
湖　南			-207	
广　东				
广　西			-224	
海　南			-25	
重　庆			-69	
四　川			-375	
贵　州			-280	
云　南			-345	
西　藏				
陕　西			-267	
甘　肃			-246	
青　海			-142	
宁　夏			-25	
新　疆			-354	
兵　团				-64

单位：万元

财社[2015]157号	财社[2015]158号	财社[2015]170号	财社[2015]171号	财社[2015]172号	财社[2015]245号
救灾	救灾	救灾	救灾	救灾	救灾
7000	**5500**	**10000**	**5600**	**3000**	**10000**

5600

7000

5500 10000

10000

3000

C-1-11续表7

地　区	财社[2015]246号	财社[2015]247号	财社[2015]248号	财社[2015]270号
	救灾	救灾	救灾	冬春
全　国	**7000**	**6000**	**7000**	**589550**
北　京				
天　津				
河　北				26328
山　西			7000	23817
内蒙古		6000		29720
辽　宁				18105
吉　林				12346
黑龙江				17509
上　海				
江　苏				6451
浙　江				1981
安　徽				18772
福　建				6220
江　西				32557
山　东				12003
河　南				13552
湖　北				29102
湖　南				30305
广　东				8510
广　西	7000			25510
海　南				3078
重　庆				12510
四　川				51349
贵　州				37910
云　南				39410
西　藏				17710
陕　西				27045
甘　肃				31990
青　海				18200
宁　夏				11160
新　疆				26400
兵　团				

单位：万元

财社[2015]271号	彩票公益金合计	财社[2015]73号			
冬春		老年人福利	残疾人福利	儿童福利	社会公益
11450	**524474**	**138605**	**39550**	**59610**	**20930**
	7077	1883	450	3080	500
	5004	2267	500	950	129
	23444	6210	1300	1170	968
	14859	3378	1050	1720	627
	14010	4189	1000	2740	903
	12481	3665	1200	1460	720
	14377	3152	2000	1380	535
	16820	3599	1500	1570	637
	3441	1952	750	630	109
	24005	6481	2300	2110	950
	12668	4333	1050	1420	583
	22584	6809	1150	1720	792
	14212	2494	1550	1500	439
	20340	5401	900	1160	765
	26494	6719	2050	2260	950
	25628	7411	1800	4070	888
	20521	5417	2100	2110	916
	25888	7253	2100	2250	900
	15241	4650	2250	2160	704
	15763	5591	1500	2300	799
	7934	2032	300	940	363
	19113	4795	1050	1480	851
	30278	9212	3300	2000	1272
	17251	4311	1300	1730	709
	18443	4727	1200	2320	800
	8818	2613	300	3970	363
	11484	4319	950	1780	688
	12939	3986	850	1770	525
	13730	3506	500	1640	593
	8930	2667	500	1050	390
	27786	3583	800	3170	562
11450	12911				

C-1-11续表8

地区	财社[2015]74号			
	老年人福利	残疾人福利	儿童福利	社会公益
全 国	**2000**	**450**	**390**	**70**
北 京				
天 津				
河 北				
山 西				
内蒙古				
辽 宁				
吉 林				
黑龙江				
上 海				
江 苏				
浙 江				
安 徽				
福 建				
江 西				
山 东				
河 南				
湖 北				
湖 南				
广 东				
广 西				
海 南				
重 庆				
四 川				
贵 州				
云 南				
西 藏				
陕 西				
甘 肃				
青 海				
宁 夏				
新 疆				
兵 团	2000	450	390	70

单位：万元

财综[2015]33号	财综[2015]31号	财综[2015]89号	财综[2015]21号	财社[2015]29号
农村幸福院	精神病福利院	精神病福利院	新疆福利设施	地名普查
100169	**50000**	**104000**	**8700**	**81374**
1164				788
1158				768
5796	2000	6000		3779
3084	2000	3000		2976
2178		3000		3527
2436	3000			2140
2310	2000	3000		1829
2514		7000		3286
				730
4164		8000		1818
3282	2000			1695
4113	3000	5000		2482
2229		6000		1950
3114	3000	6000		2821
7515		7000		2324
6459	3000	2000		3556
3978	2000	4000		2537
5385	2000	6000		3466
3477	2000			1995
3573	2000			3544
1299	3000			1054
2937	3000	5000		1568
7494	2000	5000		4785
3201	3000	3000		3557
3396	3000	3000		3959
1572				3569
3747				3106
2808		3000		3621
1491	3000	3000		2992
1323		3000		1604
1971	2000	7000	8700	3548
1001	3000	6000		

C-1-12 收入支出情况

单位：万元

地 区	收入合计	上年结余	本年收入合计	本年实际支出	收支结余	用事业基金弥补收支差额	结余分配	年末净结余
全 国	**54279261.7**	**2822577.4**	**51456684.3**	**50701961.5**	**3577300.2**	**46287.5**	**113891.2**	**3509696.5**
中央级	246115.0	60508.5	185606.5	176949.9	69165.1	29.4	2018.3	67176.2
北 京	2924880.2	308814.4	2616065.8	2478268.5	446611.7	2001.8	7425.4	441188.1
天 津	973985.2	84533.8	889451.4	807986.6	165998.6	2833.1	7054.1	161777.6
河 北	1931901.3	84797.1	1847104.2	1805816.0	126085.3	212.5	136.9	126160.9
山 西	1378286.6	128911.0	1249375.6	1222092.1	156194.5	115.0	877.3	155432.2
内蒙古	1513674.1	72144.3	1441529.8	1416974.9	96699.2	574.9	1185.7	96088.4
辽 宁	1903734.6	62339.4	1841395.2	1873846.6	29888.0	6.9	444.3	29450.6
吉 林	1068284.2	1647.9	1066636.3	1058852.4	9431.8	1.4	255.9	9177.3
黑龙江	1525814.3	19026.3	1506788.0	1504875.5	20938.8		58.3	20880.5
上 海	1255595.8	181116.7	1074479.1	1029644.6	225951.2	152.7	4955.8	221148.1
江 苏	2729820.3	35750.2	2694070.1	2672006.2	57814.1	177.4	14610.2	43381.3
浙 江	1871333.0	92115.1	1779217.9	1763203.7	108129.3	433.6	11721.1	96841.8
安 徽	1821262.7	8719.9	1812542.8	1812451.4	8811.3	102.0	586.9	8326.4
福 建	1035129.7	80077.2	955052.5	923547.4	111582.3	159.6	3835.7	107906.2
江 西	1574104.3	468.2	1573636.1	1572906.4	1197.9			1197.9
山 东	2991115.2	19792.1	2971323.1	2984512.4	6602.8	6929.0		13531.8
河 南	2401372.9	66773.5	2334599.4	2333937.8	67435.1	91.2	2151.4	65374.9
湖 北	2339985.5	23152.9	2316832.6	2292777.2	47208.3	3934.7	5900.9	45242.1
湖 南	2449575.8	27736.0	2421839.8	2406458.2	43117.6	5898.8	7492.4	41524.0
广 东	2831863.2	86579.0	2745284.2	2732078.0	99785.2	90.3	5549.6	94325.9
广 西	1743655.3	209969.7	1533685.6	1516478.0	227177.3		5982.6	221194.7
海 南	418133.6	95378.8	322754.8	299338.5	118795.1	184.2	16.7	118962.6
重 庆	1256373.8	58542.6	1197831.2	1149163.2	107210.6	162.3	2715.7	104657.2
四 川	3445929.2	185590.0	3260339.2	3230090.9	215838.3	2009.3	2718.2	215129.4
贵 州	1957236.7	367804.9	1589431.8	1483062.6	474174.1	453.9	1679.2	472948.8
云 南	2519237.8	177629.6	2341608.2	2341099.1	178138.7	19413.1	19427.6	178124.2
西 藏	402508.1	69094.5	333413.6	390225.4	12282.7	269.7	142.2	12410.2
陕 西	1982311.0	56864.8	1925446.2	1876627.3	105683.7		2472.9	103210.8
甘 肃	1439870.4	45059.4	1394811.0	1367615.6	72254.8	50.7		72305.5
青 海	482444.6	9518.6	472926.0	476272.6	6172.0		2290.9	3881.1
宁 夏	510540.2	63787.6	446752.6	410430.0	100110.2		185.0	99925.2
新 疆	1353187.1	38333.4	1314853.7	1292372.5	60814.6			60814.6

C-1-13 行政事业性收费收入情况

单位：万元

地区	行政事业性收费	婚姻登记收费	收养登记收费	殡葬收费
全国	**304586.3**	**8555.4**	**668.6**	**295362.3**
中央级				
北京	17264.5	7.2	4.4	17252.9
天津	11396.9	110.2		11286.7
河北	11093.5	36.2	256.0	10801.3
山西	15606.5	298.2	7.9	15300.4
内蒙古	11248.9	141.5	1.0	11106.4
辽宁	11379.6	128.0	63.9	11187.7
吉林	2907.5	97.0		2810.5
黑龙江	15294.2	103.4	0.4	15190.4
上海				
江苏	27364.5	25.0	13.1	27326.4
浙江	9264.8	124.5	27.4	9112.9
安徽	17377.6	274.9	12.2	17090.5
福建	16226.7	268.5	22.7	15935.5
江西	3.1		3.1	
山东	17020.0	445.9	36.3	16537.8
河南	3933.2	756.6		3176.6
湖北	14380.2	294.9	6.0	14079.3
湖南	1236.5	193.2	14.1	1029.2
广东	30739.5	588.1	20.3	30131.1
广西	15647.2	600.2	23.5	15023.5
海南	1.3	1.3		
重庆	850.7	844.8	5.9	
四川	34306.8	1656.2	18.3	32632.3
贵州	492.2	482.6	4.6	5.0
云南	2785.6	225.3	32.6	2527.7
西藏	70.6		70.6	
陕西	8752.3	94.2	0.4	8657.7
甘肃	6412.7	234.2	1.6	6176.9
青海	59.2	58.7	0.5	
宁夏	90.0	35.8	0.1	54.1
新疆	1380.0	428.8	21.7	929.5

C-1-14 财政性资金

地区	上年结余合计	抚恤	退役安置	社会福利
全国	**2489371.8**	**285555.8**	**273468.7**	**483531.0**
中央级	47352.9	8460.7		20700.7
北京	178282.5	7143.8	90098.0	35544.9
天津	78358.8	3016.8	6149.0	10512.5
河北	84787.0	13040.8	19502.4	15440.2
山西	124959.8	23645.7	7090.3	24422.6
内蒙古	71843.0	6936.4	6149.2	11863.5
辽宁	59649.5	1981.7	6837.5	3444.9
吉林	1647.9			
黑龙江	19026.3	963.3	366.7	1220.6
上海	135209.3	14491.7	15117.7	23614.1
江苏	30461.9	1607.3	3168.9	6850.5
浙江	82780.1	15403.6	5637.3	28209.5
安徽	8719.9	230.0	849.0	1982.3
福建	76247.7	10993.6	13290.5	14953.1
江西	468.2	18.2		74.2
山东	14784.8	2481.7	1842.2	5569.5
河南	66012.2	3720.2	3938.9	9140.1
湖北	22164.3	22.3	7834.4	9159.7
湖南	7850.5	1642.0	339.7	63.9
广东	71455.7	8927.0	12435.3	14747.6
广西	195338.3	40604.5	8614.1	44909.3
海南	92887.4	9216.2	8884.5	14891.4
重庆	57715.2	5472.2	450.5	29425.2
四川	174281.4	10286.2	7805.4	50269.1
贵州	357797.7	45801.2	13416.0	64429.4
云南	169096.5	27528.1	20157.7	15104.7
西藏	69094.5	7567.9	112.6	1708.1
陕西	51008.1	2206.7	1691.9	5169.7
甘肃	42330.2	1613.0	2771.2	3972.0
青海	9518.6	1162.9	1544.4	2651.6
宁夏	49908.2	1792.0	1252.3	3195.5
新疆	38333.4	7578.1	6121.1	10290.6

收、支、余情况

单位：万元

社会救助	自然灾害生活救助	民政管理事务	行政事业单位离退休	其他款项用于民政支出
790874.9	**165503.9**	**213704.2**	**9631.7**	**232449.0**
	5558.0	7365.0	835.5	4433.0
17636.5	734.9	6718.9	519.1	19885.6
20901.2	4365.1	16626.5	353.9	16354.5
22349.2	4212.0	8367.5	1023.1	655.5
60095.5	4759.6	3834.8	23.0	1088.3
17920.7	2828.9	7827.5	25.8	17302.4
18406.6	2846.8	6987.3	320.6	11414.4
932.6	164.0	0.3		551.0
15302.8	250.4	370.6		143.3
46195.3	800.0	28534.3	148.6	6307.6
949.5	54.0	2254.3		15576.5
16904.7	3454.7	9254.2	1416.6	2475.9
4737.8	506.0			414.8
13976.8	2138.8	13527.4	1443.7	4093.8
375.8				
469.4	20.0	4401.9		
43449.0	485.0	750.8		4340.2
1548.5	206.9	2511.6		443.9
5248.9	244.6	281.5		29.9
22205.2	1222.4	6666.9	2384.3	2511.4
58606.1	13608.6	12572.1	91.4	12877.3
25992.2	4227.9	12058.5	50.7	16550.9
10194.9	5302.8	3178.3	82.4	3608.9
54772.9	22640.6	3924.5	151.3	24349.6
181088.2	29887.7	11197.4	118.6	11859.2
45286.3	19097.7	16309.5	485.2	24268.5
15392.1	20918.0	9582.8		12828.8
23141.6	314.5	1853.3	1.7	821.4
17335.9	5120.7	5285.5	93.6	6138.3
1446.6	1754.3	938.7		1.6
20028.0	7344.8	5992.5	40.5	9751.1
7984.1	434.2	4529.8	22.1	1371.4

C-1-14续表1

地 区	本年收入合计	抚恤	退役安置	社会福利
全 国	**49544853.1**	**6811900.3**	**5896714.3**	**5804544.4**
中央级	162275.6	3669.8		11125.0
北 京	2314427.2	139731.0	1309746.8	241305.5
天 津	793982.5	71985.9	97475.0	116615.8
河 北	1839299.3	380281.4	333829.4	201473.0
山 西	1225046.0	217909.0	96924.7	106983.3
内蒙古	1414346.2	101718.3	92279.2	168939.5
辽 宁	1797022.8	182480.3	402612.4	150591.3
吉 林	1063740.7	128279.5	84873.5	67888.5
黑龙江	1473016.7	95452.9	85459.3	87149.1
上 海	1019670.6	102088.7	226948.3	184509.4
江 苏	2553719.7	452667.8	356675.5	463705.0
浙 江	1678035.0	254877.4	147320.4	401101.4
安 徽	1809990.5	288799.3	170582.0	183618.4
福 建	930103.8	144582.2	100679.7	148921.6
江 西	1570193.1	217364.5	58226.5	149654.1
山 东	2859518.1	778619.0	445389.5	370869.5
河 南	2293035.6	440177.3	189356.8	179446.5
湖 北	2252129.8	345917.1	192320.4	210537.9
湖 南	2309551.4	459324.2	118477.3	235375.0
广 东	2605109.7	372734.2	305058.4	422646.9
广 西	1496299.9	173631.3	61078.9	185940.9
海 南	308070.2	25306.1	28922.3	51888.9
重 庆	1146918.4	179641.8	103446.4	145831.3
四 川	3162217.0	508754.9	261086.9	400706.2
贵 州	1575455.7	143521.1	41888.9	144191.4
云 南	2282939.2	198801.3	118377.2	126671.8
西 藏	157929.0	6590.3	14377.8	21397.8
陕 西	1880314.7	242116.3	213299.9	229532.0
甘 肃	1384803.4	64560.4	90200.0	126716.5
青 海	463090.5	17080.5	29217.2	55557.9
宁 夏	407756.3	12505.8	19982.8	21859.3
新 疆	1314844.5	60730.7	100600.9	191793.7

单位：万元

社会救助	自然灾害生活救助	民政管理事务	行政事业单位离退休	其他款项用于民政支出
23596742.1	**1517524.2**	**3834405.3**	**493556.0**	**1589466.5**
	13500.0	74954.4	5481.2	53545.2
191931.2	2441.7	186627.7	61434.1	181209.2
239001.2	1201.8	180515.7	3289.7	83897.4
738932.6	44539.5	100812.0	28569.2	10862.2
658800.3	42880.1	77022.9	10962.8	13562.9
850458.3	50307.1	71731.8	18209.4	60702.6
709493.7	45425.1	183291.5	26023.0	97105.5
649167.6	23725.0	69402.4	9626.4	30777.8
1100213.3	30603.8	60206.4	11056.0	2875.9
343607.1	1032.0	142895.5	6071.0	12518.6
855899.6	26327.0	234244.8	27212.7	136987.3
516900.2	41249.9	236524.3	23906.6	56154.8
986207.5	38571.2	79596.7	16388.1	46227.3
350204.5	38357.4	87059.7	22265.6	38033.1
1008559.1	59368.2	57723.3	11393.3	7904.1
998078.2	24677.1	184470.8	15396.2	42017.8
1240655.1	32507.6	117357.9	21621.1	71913.3
1185136.5	98098.9	158317.9	19620.5	42180.6
1264886.1	56570.0	135072.8	8266.2	31579.8
974611.5	52609.2	283663.7	41617.2	152168.6
831452.7	61958.8	125778.4	16849.6	39609.3
136301.1	17367.3	34055.4	5293.3	8935.8
543151.6	41766.0	103985.4	11845.9	17250.0
1588856.1	106886.7	233684.1	25166.8	37075.3
1031255.5	88431.9	114551.0	1389.3	10226.6
1359122.7	194433.1	153361.6	15927.0	116244.5
76032.2	17821.8	11552.4	965.8	9190.9
949189.4	67400.9	149740.3	10336.9	18699.0
986795.5	56760.8	33186.9	5415.6	21167.7
265043.7	17101.8	30349.7	2138.7	46601.0
201913.0	24447.6	34253.8	3568.8	89225.2
764885.0	99154.9	88414.1	6248.0	3017.2

C-1-14续表2

地 区	本年支出合计	抚恤	退役安置	社会福利
全 国	**49264448.4**	**6867691.8**	**5827136.8**	**5627554.5**
中央级	155949.2	11419.2		21450.1
北 京	2220633.5	126294.0	1235641.4	241851.5
天 津	769084.9	71566.9	102680.7	78008.5
河 北	1805161.2	380933.5	329381.3	190435.1
山 西	1201392.7	222109.8	93926.9	104541.5
内蒙古	1410121.9	103076.8	89989.3	162693.5
辽 宁	1844543.3	182468.9	400605.1	137367.6
吉 林	1057440.4	128565.2	82877.2	60846.7
黑龙江	1504605.0	95953.7	84143.7	87461.9
上 海	966471.0	105035.5	199101.4	167725.3
江 苏	2605552.1	463109.4	392274.2	465334.7
浙 江	1674651.1	265897.5	145389.1	394537.7
安 徽	1812233.9	295774.9	165427.2	183619.2
福 建	903162.9	147650.7	98942.8	125550.9
江 西	1571857.7	218302.0	56819.3	147661.2
山 东	2871388.9	780175.1	446392.2	376390.5
河 南	2292633.2	444599.3	189087.8	192465.7
湖 北	2269799.1	351444.8	205800.5	214501.5
湖 南	2305544.2	456639.8	119179.0	237938.7
广 东	2595187.3	358106.5	299817.6	408948.2
广 西	1492923.0	176871.1	59681.9	173703.1
海 南	296623.7	25861.5	27568.4	44953.9
重 庆	1146517.8	181717.1	100960.9	153573.8
四 川	3152459.5	523803.0	259246.9	373325.7
贵 州	1472311.4	146077.1	39860.0	143976.5
云 南	2310934.8	202119.7	131775.7	131427.7
西 藏	175034.3	6661.3	17273.1	21439.0
陕 西	1847868.8	240597.0	211916.5	227329.9
甘 肃	1367615.6	62917.2	87530.7	98806.2
青 海	462567.9	17756.1	29705.5	60401.2
宁 夏	409809.1	13963.5	22491.4	23133.8
新 疆	1292369.0	60223.7	101649.1	176153.7

单位：万元

社会救助	自然灾害生活救助	民政管理事务	行政事业单位离退休	其他款项用于民政支出
23473778.5	**1485214.2**	**3996486.2**	**501099.2**	**1485487.2**
	19058.0	72069.8	6302.9	25649.2
189310.7	4340.6	185927.9	60898.0	176369.4
240289.3	1468.8	186918.0	3781.8	84370.9
729992.8	37977.2	100835.0	27572.6	8033.7
641175.8	41607.6	75285.6	10972.8	11772.7
843269.6	45546.5	94107.4	18345.6	53093.2
747086.5	45235.2	241886.4	26200.8	63692.8
651948.7	23891.1	79903.8	9658.9	19748.8
1134486.3	30622.2	58034.4	11056.0	2846.8
337321.5	832.0	143389.5	6080.9	6984.9
861363.4	24695.6	239760.2	27394.5	131620.1
512651.1	37955.5	236926.2	24347.0	56947.0
987511.6	38823.3	79831.2	16394.4	44852.1
348290.4	35496.1	85759.9	22707.3	38764.8
1010696.5	60781.4	57822.0	11702.8	8072.5
998124.5	24697.1	188195.5	15396.2	42017.8
1238963.2	31893.0	117263.5	22003.4	56357.3
1179690.4	98076.3	174746.7	19768.3	25770.6
1262120.1	56585.6	137167.1	8227.1	27686.8
968438.8	51051.2	301490.5	41977.2	165357.3
843360.0	54284.8	125808.1	17240.5	41973.5
125418.3	17857.7	37205.9	5243.0	12515.0
518833.2	37817.3	123741.6	12364.6	17509.3
1594515.8	104505.1	226877.8	29264.9	40920.3
942113.8	80434.3	107073.6	1430.7	11345.4
1361550.6	196844.1	157863.8	16204.8	113148.4
87390.9	19555.0	12753.6	1141.9	8819.5
925296.0	65003.2	150896.4	10016.7	16813.1
981764.8	58828.5	40942.7	5608.3	31217.2
252857.6	18329.5	31345.5	2175.9	49996.6
202582.2	22038.7	34448.1	3401.6	87749.8
755364.1	99081.7	90208.5	6217.8	3470.4

C-1-14续表3

地 区	年末结余合计	抚恤	退役安置	社会福利
全 国	**3080464.0**	**279722.2**	**423630.7**	**609904.4**
中央级	53679.3	711.3		10375.6
北 京	272076.2	20207.5	164575.3	35551.0
天 津	151484.5	5961.9	14119.5	54728.7
河 北	125230.6	14231.3	28240.5	26962.4
山 西	148535.3	19444.9	9912.9	26942.8
内蒙古	95672.9	8586.6	9105.5	16559.7
辽 宁	27128.8	951.0	10551.2	972.2
吉 林	9177.3			
黑龙江	20776.5	984.7	1123.6	2115.2
上 海	181440.2	11964.9	44922.0	35997.6
江 苏	26938.2	1448.1	2408.5	7682.4
浙 江	86863.2	15060.7	6756.7	24757.9
安 徽	8326.4	544.6	308.2	2493.3
福 建	99554.2	11189.2	14200.8	31705.0
江 西	1166.2	1054.7		
山 东	9842.9	4238.7	839.5	48.5
河 南	63878.3	3155.3	3788.4	7799.9
湖 北	43832.5	56.0	20297.6	11371.0
湖 南	10858.4	2123.0	1578.8	231.4
广 东	71181.2	8863.7	9017.0	15196.8
广 西	203175.2	33520.9	9383.5	49896.9
海 南	113541.6	8432.7	12473.1	16953.1
重 庆	101018.9	4595.2	3310.3	39672.2
四 川	204346.7	9750.9	9726.2	58711.1
贵 州	460942.0	43245.2	15444.9	64644.3
云 南	172590.3	32287.9	14163.4	16206.2
西 藏	11497.6	207.3	44.8	504.1
陕 西	83344.8	3766.4	3075.3	8517.4
甘 肃	70265.5	3278.8	8174.4	15492.5
青 海	3881.1	631.8		684.8
宁 夏	87402.6	1327.0	931.2	3870.2
新 疆	60814.6	7900.0	5157.6	23260.2

单位：万元

社会救助	自然灾害生活救助	民政管理事务	行政事业单位离退休	其他款项用于民政支出
981303.4	**187415.1**	**254366.2**	**4688.0**	**276296.4**
		10249.6	13.7	32329.1
19592.0	40.0	7478.8	556.8	24074.8
30479.0	4098.0	27294.1	231.8	13961.4
31842.7	11251.7	9120.8	93.4	248.7
77720.0	6032.1	5574.6	13.0	2895.0
26030.6	5560.9	22948.2	26.9	5823.1
1203.7	3188.8	4092.5	306.9	5862.5
715.6	60.0	38.8		
13074.3	47.2	2610.0		408.6
50359.5	1000.0	29448.7	237.4	7510.1
2494.2	2131.2	4611.4	4.6	6157.7
19799.5	6645.8	11277.8	983.8	1580.9
3890.3	409.3	166.3		203.8
16121.8	5540.0	14840.7	870.9	2859.3
111.5				
423.1		4293.1		
45345.3	97.2	773.8		2906.4
7679.2	230.0	2331.9		1110.8
6452.4	1.6	441.3		29.9
23505.0	2395.1	5641.9	596.5	5429.8
48284.1	20422.6	11995.9	61.7	16999.3
40489.3	3572.8	11625.0	110.8	17353.8
36772.0	6786.5	6445.2		3445.2
59205.1	26597.5	7352.8	110.6	31205.2
270229.9	37885.3	18674.8	77.2	10740.4
41691.5	19174.7	18080.5	372.6	30410.8
767.3	8491.4	1339.1		
43953.7	2539.2	2456.2	1.3	610.0
19545.4	4391.8	3675.9	27.3	14991.3
2564.5				
23907.1	8081.4	4052.5	6.3	36158.4
17053.8	743.0	5434.0	1.2	990.1

C-1-15 预算指标

地 区	本年预算指标合计	上年结转预算指标	本级财政安排预算指标	本年上级下达预算指标	本年下达所属地方预算指标	本年抚恤预算指标
全 国	**52556311.9**	**3188309.6**	**49920922.7**	**74502411.0**	**75055331.4**	**6966932.2**
中央级	162275.6		22847187.0		22684911.4	3669.8
北 京	2318537.1	384627.9	1185583.2	2022372.1	1274046.1	140691.7
天 津	807531.7	12980.4	674581.4	329898.1	209928.2	75355.4
河 北	1984618.0	136706.7	907219.5	3274209.2	2333517.4	392688.7
山 西	1349188.4	99597.5	614571.2	2318834.2	1683814.5	228123.3
内蒙古	1527734.2	102345.8	817139.9	2424657.4	1816408.9	106795.4
辽 宁	1885281.0	60068.7	874726.9	2809910.8	1859425.4	183872.8
吉 林	1076593.1	18645.8	454564.7	1418025.6	814643.0	128416.7
黑龙江	1500278.1	46596.7	652930.5	3283048.7	2482297.8	95836.8
上 海	1043609.6	45141.8	1019670.6	152312.0	173514.8	102088.7
江 苏	2759469.8	175212.8	2070653.2	2221438.0	1707834.2	462729.5
浙 江	1759169.6	95016.6	1409046.4	753139.8	498033.2	264317.7
安 徽	1837896.4	28022.2	925613.0	1978649.4	1094388.2	292186.9
福 建	1007573.7	98302.6	620870.1	1111841.9	823440.9	150490.9
江 西	1603732.2	28540.0	790947.2	2799463.2	2015218.2	217642.9
山 东	2896611.8	71617.3	1685703.4	4099427.7	2960136.6	778872.6
河 南	2360437.4	97761.8	920897.4	4542735.1	3200956.9	441348.0
湖 北	2581549.7	236260.0	1190181.5	3027544.6	1872436.4	346801.1
湖 南	2358857.2	43323.4	1008709.6	4602536.0	3295711.8	460664.4
广 东	2686159.4	104083.8	2096889.7	2902516.8	2417330.9	380045.6
广 西	1691419.1	204928.9	711588.2	2228677.3	1453775.3	196666.0
海 南	403513.0	76040.8	197271.9	329427.3	199227.0	29544.4
重 庆	1538880.4	146465.6	831771.3	1633406.0	1072762.5	180507.5
四 川	3278259.8	91368.7	1432449.3	5938691.9	4184250.1	515944.6
贵 州	1795954.2	228756.0	493271.2	3645716.8	2571789.8	153674.3
云 南	2313331.8	20371.5	1097590.3	4687755.2	3492385.2	202713.0
西 藏	204081.5	25866.7	119918.5	214723.4	156427.1	11777.9
陕 西	2077206.3	296849.6	932475.4	3589977.5	2742096.2	266874.6
甘 肃	1426121.7	48178.3	447827.1	2110108.7	1179992.4	65072.6
青 海	464049.9	24357.0	222523.5	944790.6	727621.2	17080.5
宁 夏	457659.7	27966.7	246736.8	539536.8	356580.6	13197.3
新 疆	1398730.5	112308.0	419812.8	2567038.9	1700429.2	61240.6

收入情况

单位：万元

上年结转预算指标	本级财政安排预算指标	本年上级下达预算指标	本年下达所属地方预算指标	本年退役安置预算指标	上年结转预算指标	本级财政安排预算指标
219828.9	**6775245.4**	**10858648.2**	**10886790.3**	**6101538.3**	**650395.9**	**5772454.4**
	3503955.2		3500285.4			3529620.0
15918.2	99763.4	60311.9	35301.8	1309746.8	341727.8	272418.2
699.3	57603.9	37908.0	20855.8	103128.2	5240.0	25881.4
22465.2	189167.9	660274.0	479218.4	347358.7	13617.0	120831.1
21693.0	116628.3	290757.5	200955.5	99976.6	5452.6	32038.0
2217.5	67163.0	129200.0	91785.1	96412.1	8302.0	57739.9
5148.4	105940.6	239995.1	167211.3	415795.9	8922.0	95660.9
506.0	60626.2	163285.5	96001.0	84901.3	5.0	54455.7
1286.3	38056.5	201700.7	145206.7	85887.4	1509.9	27640.1
	102088.7	15462.0	15462.0	244249.3	41447.4	226948.3
12703.9	286095.4	583978.2	420048.0	373963.1	17775.0	188193.0
12170.9	176307.6	173443.4	97604.2	149902.1	4822.4	74044.8
3063.6	124169.0	331675.3	166721.0	172586.2	2067.1	119190.6
7630.5	87111.4	208435.7	152686.7	111466.1	13150.4	41605.7
	93770.9	417562.3	293690.3	58226.5		26331.3
2781.0	375672.7	1296596.8	896177.9	450072.6	16702.2	147567.4
883.7	183396.8	830758.9	573691.4	191025.6	2988.0	79081.7
853.1	149924.5	460364.9	264341.4	193262.2	3002.2	59537.0
1530.8	117665.0	1069872.4	728403.8	118769.3	292.0	43407.6
9500.2	259786.4	484875.4	374116.4	341463.8	45888.5	151234.4
32461.0	70917.0	256437.2	163149.2	67011.2	8854.6	24275.6
4095.7	13760.5	26507.5	14819.3	38294.7	5666.7	19084.0
961.9	60957.6	262392.9	143804.9	104876.1	1242.9	45002.2
4265.9	155858.4	1130786.2	774965.9	273611.8	9817.0	110607.1
11972.4	48213.9	300185.0	206697.0	43441.6	1675.8	19676.8
2333.7	52893.3	480548.3	333062.3	119904.0	1789.5	22755.5
1090.6	3568.2	9799.4	2680.3	26815.9	9.4	9621.8
40462.6	123222.0	463838.0	360648.0	231980.2	81384.5	63770.5
542.1	18017.5	97318.5	50805.5	96109.5	5604.9	28497.6
	6562.4	38260.2	27742.1	29217.2	549.0	18868.1
179.7	5653.1	15355.1	7990.6	21481.4	888.7	9529.3
411.7	20728.1	120761.9	80661.1	100600.9	1.4	27338.8

C-1-15续表1

地 区	本年上级下达预算指标	本年下达所属地方预算指标	本年社会福利预算指标	上年结转预算指标	本级财政安排预算指标	本年上级下达预算指标
全 国	**8651875.1**	**8973187.1**	**6304741.8**	**614373.2**	**5749637.9**	**4352891.4**
中央级		3529620.0	11125.0		700517.0	
北 京	1788990.3	1093389.5	242461.9	14379.6	155281.9	89500.8
天 津	170123.5	98116.7	118451.5	5108.9	109918.1	11179.0
河 北	547451.1	334540.5	238356.3	35092.2	175448.2	183204.5
山 西	157709.2	95223.2	122584.1	13960.3	88245.8	97289.7
内蒙古	92993.9	62623.7	199178.1	26234.7	123810.5	190066.4
辽 宁	746460.8	435247.8	152153.5	2854.4	118305.1	66610.3
吉 林	109247.0	78806.4	67907.8	4651.0	63638.7	49866.1
黑龙江	127781.1	71043.7	87510.1	11364.5	69193.5	71773.5
上 海	114305.0	138451.4	191147.4	3197.0	184509.4	3934.0
江 苏	559442.4	391447.3	479398.4	23180.8	450115.7	217120.5
浙 江	147900.0	76865.1	436642.9	45083.7	392356.6	106268.0
安 徽	118135.5	66807.0	191716.4	3998.0	173544.2	91893.8
福 建	138824.9	82114.9	181694.2	57514.3	108785.9	75312.6
江 西	87449.3	55554.1	149746.4	860.0	117791.3	160100.7
山 东	749716.6	463913.6	374166.4	23775.3	325660.9	265069.0
河 南	282666.9	173711.0	183533.8	14537.4	174473.1	199088.2
湖 北	295748.1	165025.1	213205.9	13222.3	175460.6	116054.1
湖 南	223995.4	148925.7	247690.4	8255.8	238065.7	377147.4
广 东	444235.1	299894.2	431997.0	19337.1	387354.9	288038.4
广 西	80885.2	47004.2	264431.4	61378.1	188485.9	171379.4
海 南	30147.5	16603.5	65532.9	8166.5	51241.2	25235.6
重 庆	121579.2	62948.2	157155.5	15344.0	130773.5	71577.9
四 川	463331.8	310144.1	443357.4	27371.9	374506.4	427332.3
贵 州	65597.3	43508.3	178069.0	43961.3	106371.7	157329.6
云 南	271900.3	176541.3	129416.1	2398.4	100337.7	140024.0
西 藏	20193.9	3009.2	24709.6	1163.2	37169.9	19681.8
陕 西	368154.3	281329.1	250604.1	27638.8	192719.7	222475.2
甘 肃	123891.0	61884.0	141352.8	4297.3	73738.5	160482.4
青 海	54453.5	44653.4	55593.6	8088.0	52463.9	84780.2
宁 夏	25764.0	14700.6	26853.7	783.6	11130.1	19465.0
新 疆	122801.0	49540.3	246998.2	87174.8	98222.3	193611.0

单位：万元

本年下达所属地方预算指标	本年社会救助预算指标	上年结转预算指标	本级财政安排预算指标	本年上级下达预算指标	本年下达所属地方预算指标
4412160.7	**25211287.8**	**1090964.3**	**24200132.3**	**45723383.0**	**45803191.8**
689392.0			13897358.0		13897358.0
16700.4	193749.0	6555.1	165125.9	34733.6	12665.6
7754.5	240724.2	607.4	195550.9	105445.6	60879.7
155388.6	802627.7	44553.2	275630.1	1747931.2	1265486.8
76911.7	734912.6	38879.6	272232.0	1628667.5	1204866.5
140933.5	873965.2	16128.6	379801.7	1775793.8	1297758.9
35616.3	774065.7	37032.2	231870.6	1539681.1	1034518.2
50248.0	661188.8	12526.4	165247.1	1041057.9	557642.6
64821.4	1108684.2	8843.8	444018.1	2778683.4	2122861.1
493.0	343607.1	497.4	343607.1	18672.0	19169.4
211018.6	1010440.0	112148.0	747320.2	736229.1	585257.3
107065.4	535418.5	19262.6	436159.2	260172.3	180175.6
77719.6	996800.9	14595.2	370700.6	1326577.5	715072.4
59918.6	361062.2	10980.5	220758.6	529677.0	400353.9
129005.6	1009170.5		462409.8	1982344.6	1435583.9
240338.8	1013374.1	11675.9	593726.3	1692331.9	1284360.0
204564.9	1271961.4	39711.0	313182.2	3072141.6	2153073.4
91531.1	1494339.7	181458.0	557662.9	1949191.6	1193972.8
375778.5	1268181.6	2522.0	453514.9	2699863.7	1887719.0
262733.4	997954.2	23283.6	792150.3	1479965.7	1297445.4
156812.0	872449.3	52179.6	236267.1	1539574.1	955571.5
19110.4	172941.3	23380.9	64637.7	226539.8	141617.1
60539.9	902016.9	101369.1	447798.8	1107868.3	755019.3
385853.2	1619594.9	33667.5	463036.4	3596185.9	2473294.9
129593.6	1175801.5	146850.1	156403.4	2843695.2	1971147.2
113344.0	1372568.5	7742.0	503788.5	3201927.8	2340889.8
33305.3	93602.1	22219.2	41394.8	118153.7	88165.6
192229.6	1059936.4	96883.1	364793.4	2232349.4	1634089.5
97165.4	1006195.7	15794.8	276547.7	1633048.8	919195.6
89738.5	265967.4	15.0	78353.8	650478.1	462879.5
4525.0	211518.4	8519.9	70955.2	322797.2	190753.9
132009.9	766467.8	1082.6	178129.0	1851603.6	1264347.4

C-1-15续表2

地 区	本年城市最低生活保障预算指标	上年结转预算指标	本级财政安排预算指标	本年上级下达预算指标	本年下达所属地方预算指标	本年农村最低生活保障预算指标	上年结转预算指标
全 国	**8630278.6**	**405140.1**	**10416584.7**	**19774375.1**	**21965821.3**	**9484744.1**	**463953.0**
中央级			7632684.5		7632684.5		
北 京	71259.1		71259.1			32545.2	
天 津	115495.6		84234.4	84678.0	53416.8	50642.0	593.3
河 北	498134.8	29094.5	163693.6	1330850.2	1025503.5	81735.8	3415.5
山 西	404674.6	20956.3	22396.3	849776.4	488454.4	161658.4	7420.9
内蒙古	356622.0	9891.7	127143.1	837134.8	617547.6	311008.9	1116.9
辽 宁	424332.5	25270.7	62736.5	874325.4	538000.1	186574.3	4229.2
吉 林	380365.4	7345.4	91860.1	745852.9	464693.0	156985.9	3554.0
黑龙江	567908.9	2972.8	228956.3	1698705.4	1362725.6	270186.9	461.1
上 海	141296.0		141296.0			17317.2	
江 苏	136358.5	836.3	131449.8	105754.2	101681.8	504373.1	108402.6
浙 江	54639.4	2115.1	45866.2	20475.3	13817.2	230769.0	11115.0
安 徽	294204.6	6508.9	93835.1	809578.8	615718.2	385827.9	4641.8
福 建	55033.1	1783.1	25187.7	89754.3	61692.0	153665.3	375.0
江 西	375443.4		95518.6	944769.9	664845.1	322462.6	
山 东	179815.5	3823.8	126026.4	326437.9	276472.6	518515.4	4749.0
河 南	353263.7	30535.4	64713.9	1486883.1	1228868.7	588868.8	6449.7
湖 北	566842.9	102409.3	117628.6	821191.9	474386.9	499800.5	49283.0
湖 南	469348.1	2323.5	168203.0	1536372.6	1237551.0	426831.6	
广 东	161708.7	3374.5	157368.1	176540.1	175574.0	407594.8	12768.3
广 西	147227.9	19747.4	10761.2	664396.2	547676.9	455188.5	12352.1
海 南	71088.4	10147.8	24647.6	101986.0	65693.0	28528.3	5173.0
重 庆	391687.2	53458.0	132846.2	544263.5	338880.5	231280.2	39449.2
四 川	644531.4	12029.5	64255.0	1685459.6	1117212.7	471830.3	13225.1
贵 州	212002.4	13374.1	39780.8	513266.6	354419.1	795159.9	116670.6
云 南	402815.6	1529.2	186023.8	973702.3	758439.7	749929.6	3045.2
西 藏	26878.4	129.5	12447.7	36331.6	22030.4	36421.2	8619.1
陕 西	302760.6	31540.0	76270.7	630922.2	435972.3	445607.6	40182.3
甘 肃	262504.5	12519.5	65803.0	403152.6	218970.6	553346.7	840.0
青 海	134728.1		31421.5	331864.7	228558.1	57730.1	
宁 夏	67853.9	973.0	43137.9	60410.0	36667.0	97491.9	5653.1
新 疆	359453.4	450.8	77132.0	1089538.6	807668.0	254866.2	168.0

单位：万元

本级财政安排预算指标	本年上级下达预算指标	本年下达所属地方预算指标	本年其他社会救济预算指标	上年结转预算指标	本级财政安排预算指标	本年上级下达预算指标	本年下达所属地方预算指标
7111060.2	**17111153.5**	**15201422.6**	**3957837.9**	**108884.7**	**3628255.0**	**3403711.2**	**3183013.0**
4130564.5		4130564.5			503844.0		503844.0
32545.2			66354.9	5689.1	40780.8	28589.2	8704.2
49048.7	1000.0		32087.9	14.1	26132.1	13404.6	7462.9
11757.7	108332.0	41769.4	121220.8	6832.1	60813.7	116854.0	63279.0
154457.5	490539.4	490759.4	85175.1	3106.7	63476.4	120229.4	101637.4
118692.5	664463.7	473264.2	123704.3	2843.3	100994.3	106566.7	86700.0
71263.2	505510.5	394428.6	100388.0	2925.6	69112.9	55272.1	26922.6
18924.8	134507.1		44346.9	16.0	34077.2	37195.7	26942.0
39718.9	519907.7	289900.8	123798.4	1103.8	104960.9	218043.4	200309.7
17317.2			157027.7	497.4	157027.7	15352.0	15849.4
279753.6	428615.8	312398.9	231406.4	1512.9	226426.6	82787.7	79320.8
180227.0	126725.6	87298.6	142037.1	3197.9	119555.7	53075.9	33792.4
69352.2	320011.0	8177.1	190797.4	2699.7	156276.6	35886.5	4065.4
84547.1	269715.5	200972.3	88580.4	2854.2	67683.5	88626.5	70583.8
156573.2	499552.2	333662.8	133274.0		111092.8	241563.7	219382.5
247712.2	1012498.2	746444.0	166977.2	1629.4	127492.4	118434.5	80579.1
31849.3	1088555.6	537985.8	203753.0	2274.7	176761.0	197741.7	173024.4
284493.7	701727.1	535703.3	270761.5	12172.2	99008.6	250108.4	90527.7
65418.6	613690.3	252277.3	221709.1	198.5	176887.1	218595.2	173971.7
263882.5	743848.4	612904.4	243819.4	3012.1	214661.2	262370.4	236224.3
64462.9	573286.6	194913.1	182641.6	12175.0	143773.8	139468.4	112775.6
24473.4	44196.9	45315.0	47210.4	3029.9	11766.1	43379.5	10965.1
108612.0	273957.5	190738.5	168501.0	5474.0	146977.0	151015.8	134965.8
83851.0	1251717.6	876963.4	270741.5	5493.0	232465.6	152742.5	119959.6
64610.8	1996956.7	1383078.2	65957.9	7793.8	38902.1	82540.5	63278.5
156344.2	1821067.2	1230527.0	88020.7	1830.8	117970.3	89999.3	121779.7
20949.2	56424.2	49571.3	3943.4	4879.3	2873.4	2040.8	5850.1
81103.7	1062906.0	738584.4	171131.0	12639.6	153181.2	241575.2	236265.0
122746.7	968015.4	538255.4	96523.6	1521.4	76700.0	98072.2	79770.0
20254.7	163821.2	126345.8	32202.2	15.0	15722.6	47792.2	31327.6
21811.7	190254.0	120226.9	22427.0	1189.5	4423.3	27738.2	10924.0
33740.3	479350.1	258392.2	61318.1	263.7	46434.1	66649.0	52028.7

C-1-15续表3

地　区	本年医疗救助预算指标	上年结转预算指标	本级财政安排预算指标	本年上级下达预算指标	本年下达所属地方预算指标
全　国	**3138427.2**	**112986.5**	**3044232.4**	**5434143.2**	**5452934.9**
中央级			1630265.0		1630265.0
北　京	23589.8	866.0	20540.8	6144.4	3961.4
天　津	42498.7		36135.7	6363.0	
河　北	101536.3	5211.1	39365.1	191895.0	134934.9
山　西	83404.5	7395.7	31901.8	168122.3	124015.3
内蒙古	82630.0	2276.7	32971.8	167628.6	120247.1
辽　宁	62770.9	4606.7	28758.0	104573.1	75166.9
吉　林	79490.6	1611.0	20385.0	123502.2	66007.6
黑龙江	146790.0	4306.1	70382.0	342026.9	269925.0
上　海	27966.2		27966.2	3320.0	3320.0
江　苏	138302.0	1396.2	109690.2	119071.4	91855.8
浙　江	107973.0	2834.6	90510.3	59895.5	45267.4
安　徽	125971.0	744.8	51236.7	161101.2	87111.7
福　建	63783.4	5968.2	43340.3	81580.7	67105.8
江　西	177990.5		99225.2	296458.8	217693.5
山　东	148066.0	1473.7	92495.3	234961.3	180864.3
河　南	126075.9	451.2	39858.0	298961.2	213194.5
湖　北	156934.8	17593.5	56532.0	176164.2	93354.9
湖　南	150292.8		43006.2	331205.6	223919.0
广　东	184831.3	4128.7	156238.5	297206.8	272742.7
广　西	87391.3	7905.1	17269.2	162422.9	100205.9
海　南	26114.2	5030.2	3750.6	36977.4	19644.0
重　庆	110548.5	2987.9	59363.6	138631.5	90434.5
四　川	232491.7	2919.9	82464.8	506266.2	359159.2
贵　州	102681.3	9011.6	13109.7	250931.4	170371.4
云　南	131802.6	1336.8	43450.2	317159.0	230143.4
西　藏	26359.1	8591.3	5124.5	23357.1	10713.8
陕　西	140437.2	12521.2	54237.8	296946.0	223267.8
甘　肃	93820.9	913.9	11298.0	163808.6	82199.6
青　海	41307.0		10955.0	107000.0	76648.0
宁　夏	23745.6	704.3	1582.3	44395.0	22936.0
新　疆	90830.1	200.1	20822.6	216065.9	146258.5

单位：万元

本年自然灾害生活救助预算指标	上年结转预算指标	本级财政安排预算指标	本年上级下达预算指标	本年下达所属地方预算指标
1852156.8	**412119.0**	**1438708.6**	**3103690.8**	**3102361.6**
13500.0		935732.0		922232.0
2441.7	1220.0	1064.7	657.0	500.0
1201.8		865.8	336.0	
59289.4	17221.3	9320.1	107539.6	74791.6
60545.0	16477.0	8492.0	120749.5	85173.5
76047.2	17358.9	15320.1	139497.1	96128.9
50414.8	2681.6	6929.8	77216.8	36413.4
24358.9	957.4	10684.6	31755.9	19039.0
48175.8	23016.8	2882.1	77680.1	55403.2
1032.0		1032.0		
27482.7	6044.5	13993.2	42314.0	34869.0
47908.2	5410.1	20690.1	45869.0	24061.0
39994.5	1786.2	8657.2	62004.2	32453.1
51532.1	4285.7	19082.4	92478.5	64314.5
91925.2	27680.0	16414.3	138306.2	90475.3
27313.9	6020.0	6730.9	51727.5	37164.5
47529.3	22355.9	7992.4	71754.0	54573.0
103109.8	29956.3	26831.5	142447.3	96125.3
87028.0	30319.0	11112.5	139684.5	94088.0
54370.8	1735.9	32444.9	110557.4	90367.4
89021.3	30179.0	21025.3	130536.1	92719.1
37724.7	24283.5	2713.1	16227.0	5498.9
57433.3	25756.4	13775.9	50305.2	32404.2
119231.9	13353.5	33535.2	242958.4	170615.2
109762.0	20668.3	34023.7	204694.0	149624.0
199947.5	3297.3	139198.2	389400.9	331948.9
24349.3	1154.6	1324.6	41467.1	19597.0
74486.1	28624.1	15442.3	161014.3	130594.6
57045.8	6740.0	9500.7	87212.0	46406.9
17101.8	15680.0	1324.8	32715.0	32618.0
25258.3	4546.8	3199.5	35872.0	18360.0
125593.7	23308.9	7372.7	258714.2	163802.1

C-1-15续表4

地 区	本年民政管理事务预算指标					本年行政事业单位离退休预算指标	
		上年结转预算指标	本级财政安排预算指标	本年上级下达预算指标	本年下达所属地方预算指标		上年结转预算指标
全 国	**3920457.7**	**73617.9**	**3786530.1**	**1083076.5**	**1022766.8**	**494146.9**	**523.3**
中央级	74954.4		158992.4		84038.0	5481.2	
北 京	186627.7		185414.3	1213.4		61434.1	
天 津	181386.1	525.0	198007.0	1536.0	18681.9	3289.7	
河 北	104565.8	3457.8	97533.0	27666.5	24091.5	28569.2	
山 西	78079.4	2681.3	72422.1	23218.1	20242.1	10962.8	
内蒙古	77368.6	4208.2	65003.6	37249.1	29092.3	18209.4	
辽 宁	185370.4	2089.9	146121.7	94141.4	56982.6	26027.5	0.4
吉 林	69415.4		66803.0	15518.4	12906.0	9626.4	
黑龙江	60251.9	575.4	57208.3	25429.9	22961.7	11056.0	
上 海	142895.5		142895.5			6071.0	
江 苏	235285.3	1106.3	233477.1	46190.6	45488.7	27212.7	100.0
浙 江	242866.1	7758.8	228455.7	16402.1	9750.5	23928.5	10.3
安 徽	79684.0	1392.4	78262.6	8973.8	8944.8	16388.1	30.8
福 建	88634.1	1481.8	84384.3	33165.7	30397.7	22552.0	251.7
江 西	57723.3		54902.3	13730.0	10909.0	11393.3	
山 东	184624.6	186.0	179074.5	39872.4	34508.3	15396.2	
河 南	117592.3	87.5	105502.5	32461.8	20459.5	21621.1	
湖 北	165371.2	5804.7	159709.6	45702.2	45845.3	19620.6	111.6
湖 南	136677.5	403.8	114462.5	78299.1	56487.9	8266.2	
广 东	284440.1	3508.6	278869.1	55794.0	53731.6	41617.2	
广 西	136474.6	8956.9	123177.4	41412.3	37072.0	16854.9	14.8
海 南	39871.9	4792.9	33486.4	1952.6	360.0	5478.4	0.5
重 庆	105581.6	1265.6	102959.5	16482.5	15126.0	11870.5	
四 川	243106.9	1249.8	236861.2	70774.3	65778.4	25197.2	3.2
贵 州	121634.6	1067.0	117010.6	72333.8	68776.8	1421.9	
云 南	154890.9	1365.1	146170.8	93703.6	86348.6	15927.0	
西 藏	12474.7	46.4	16721.9	5299.1	9592.7	965.8	
陕 西	161823.2	17686.2	141264.9	117201.5	114329.4	10336.9	
甘 肃	33374.9	53.7	29700.2	8142.0	4521.0	5415.6	
青 海	30349.7		24783.6	23301.8	17735.7	2138.7	
宁 夏	38646.9	1866.2	26870.7	17910.0	8000.0	3568.8	
新 疆	88414.1	0.6	80021.8	17998.5	9606.8	6248.0	

单位：万元

本级财政安排预算指标	本年上级下达预算指标	本年下达所属地方预算指标	本年其他款项用于民政支出预算指标	上年结转预算指标	本级财政安排预算指标	本年上级下达预算指标	本年下达所属地方预算指标
488802.0	**5678.0**	**856.4**	**1705050.4**	**126487.1**	**1709412.0**	**723168.0**	**854016.7**
5481.2			53545.2		115531.2		61986.0
61434.1			181384.2	4827.2	245080.7	46965.1	115488.8
3659.6		369.9	83994.8	799.8	83094.7	3370.0	3269.7
28452.7	116.5		11162.2	300.0	10836.4	25.8	
10962.8			14004.6	453.7	13550.2	442.7	442.0
18209.4			79758.2	27895.9	90091.7	59857.1	98086.5
21872.8	4154.3		97580.4	1339.8	148025.4	41651.0	93435.8
9458.4	168.0		30777.8		23651.0	7126.8	
11056.0			2875.9		2875.9		
6071.0			12518.6		12518.6	-61.0	-61.0
26679.0	615.7	182.0	142958.1	2154.3	124779.6	35547.5	19523.3
23918.2	11.0	11.0	58185.6	497.8	57114.2	3074.0	2500.4
16357.3			48539.4	1088.9	34731.5	39389.3	26670.3
22300.3			40142.1	3007.7	36841.5	33947.5	33654.6
11393.3			7904.1		7934.0	-29.9	
15396.2			52791.4	10476.9	41874.5	4113.5	3673.5
21621.1			85825.9	17198.3	35647.6	53863.7	20883.7
19475.0	34.0		45839.2	1851.8	41580.4	18002.4	15595.4
8139.9	178.6	52.3	31579.8		22341.5	13494.9	4256.6
41617.2			154270.7	829.9	153432.5	39050.8	39042.5
16840.1			48510.4	10904.9	30599.8	8453.0	1447.3
5371.2	106.7		14124.7	5654.1	6977.8	2710.6	1217.8
11870.5			19439.0	525.7	18633.3	3200.0	2920.0
25174.0	20.0		38215.1	1639.9	32870.6	7303.0	3598.4
1421.9			12149.3	2561.1	10149.2	1881.9	2442.9
15927.0	29.2	29.2	117964.8	1445.5	116519.3	110221.1	110221.1
965.8	77.0	77.0	9386.2	183.3	9151.5	51.4	
10304.9	167.0	135.0	21164.8	4170.3	20957.7	24777.8	28741.0
5415.6			21554.8	15145.5	6409.3	14.0	14.0
2138.7			46601.0	25.0	38028.2	60801.8	52254.0
3568.8			117134.9	11181.8	115830.1	102373.5	112250.5
6248.0			3167.2	328.0	1752.1	1548.7	461.6

C-1-15续表5

地 区	本年预算指标结余	抚恤	退役安置	社会福利
全 国	**3011458.8**	**155031.9**	**204824.0**	**500197.4**
中央级				
北 京	4109.9	960.7		1156.4
天 津	13549.2	3369.5	5653.2	1835.7
河 北	145318.7	12407.3	13529.3	36883.3
山 西	124142.4	10214.3	3051.9	15600.8
内蒙古	113388.0	5077.1	4132.9	30238.6
辽 宁	88258.2	1392.5	13183.5	1562.2
吉 林	12852.4	137.2	27.8	19.3
黑龙江	27261.4	383.9	428.1	361.0
上 海	23939.0		17301.0	6638.0
江 苏	205750.1	10061.7	17287.6	15693.4
浙 江	81134.6	9440.3	2581.7	35541.5
安 徽	27905.9	3387.6	2004.2	8098.0
福 建	77469.9	5908.7	10786.4	32772.6
江 西	33539.1	278.4		92.3
山 东	37093.7	253.6	4683.1	3296.9
河 南	67401.8	1170.7	1668.8	4087.3
湖 北	329419.9	884.0	941.8	2668.0
湖 南	49305.8	1340.2	292.0	12315.4
广 东	81049.7	7311.4	36405.4	9350.1
广 西	195119.2	23034.7	5932.3	78490.5
海 南	95442.8	4238.3	9372.4	13644.0
重 庆	391962.0	865.7	1429.7	11324.2
四 川	116042.8	7189.7	12524.9	42651.2
贵 州	220498.5	10153.2	1552.7	33877.6
云 南	30392.6	3911.7	1526.8	2744.3
西 藏	46152.5	5187.6	12438.1	3311.8
陕 西	196891.6	24758.3	18680.3	21072.1
甘 肃	41318.3	512.2	5909.5	14636.3
青 海	959.4			35.7
宁 夏	49903.4	691.5	1498.6	4994.4
新 疆	83886.0	509.9		55204.5

单位：万元

社会救助	自然灾害生活救助	民政管理事务	行政事业单位离退休	其他款项用于民政支出
1614545.7	**334632.6**	**86052.4**	**590.9**	**115583.9**
1817.8				175.0
1723.0		870.4		97.4
63695.1	14749.9	3753.8		300.0
76112.3	17664.9	1056.5		441.7
23506.9	25740.1	5636.8		19055.6
64572.0	4989.7	2078.9	4.5	474.9
12021.2	633.9	13.0		
8470.9	17572.0	45.5		
154540.4	1155.7	1040.5		5970.8
18518.3	6658.3	6341.8	21.9	2030.8
10593.4	1423.3	87.3		2312.1
10857.7	13174.7	1574.4	286.4	2109.0
611.4	32557.0			
15295.9	2636.8	153.8		10773.6
31306.3	15021.7	234.4		13912.6
309203.2	5010.9	7053.3	0.1	3658.6
3295.5	30458.0	1604.7		
23342.7	1761.6	776.4		2102.1
40996.6	27062.5	10696.2	5.3	8901.1
36640.2	20357.4	5816.5	185.1	5188.9
358865.3	15667.3	1596.2	24.6	2189.0
30738.8	12345.2	9422.8	30.4	1139.8
144546.0	21330.1	7083.6	32.6	1922.7
13445.8	5514.4	1529.3		1720.3
17569.9	6527.5	922.3		195.3
110747.0	7085.2	12082.9		2465.8
19400.2	285.0	188.0		387.1
923.7				
9605.4	810.7	4393.1		27909.7
1582.8	26438.8			150.0

C−1−16 当年预算

地区	全国预算安排合计	中央安排合计	全省安排合计				抚恤	
				省级	市级	县级及以下		中央安排
全国	**49587430.1**	**22686819.4**	**26900610.7**	**9129187.8**	**4189150.8**	**13582272.1**	**6741735.3**	**3500285.4**
中央级								
北京	1933909.2	748326.0	1185583.2	490358.4		695224.8	124773.4	25010.0
天津	841748.4	167167.0	674581.4	146328.8		528252.6	77151.9	19548.0
河北	1821618.6	930476.0	891142.6	346253.4	162399.5	382489.7	367718.4	184060.0
山西	1249590.2	635019.0	614571.2	216318.6	172339.0	225913.6	206430.3	89802.0
内蒙古	1427487.8	613624.0	813863.8	278164.6	174630.3	361068.9	103087.3	36203.0
辽宁	1809406.2	939043.0	870363.2	179003.0	258089.2	433271.0	181998.4	76836.0
吉林	1129292.7	674728.0	454564.7	161414.6	115101.8	178048.3	128754.2	68128.0
黑龙江	1519390.0	872969.0	646421.0	405571.5	46003.5	194846.0	96929.6	59153.0
上海	1171982.6	152312.0	1019670.6	110679.8		908990.8	117550.7	15462.0
江苏	2582318.3	547874.0	2034444.3	427354.3	314501.3	1292588.7	444908.6	161439.0
浙江	1664446.4	255400.0	1409046.4	223475.9	172520.6	1013049.9	250335.6	74028.0
安徽	1802709.5	884261.0	918448.5	163849.3	141696.4	612902.8	288085.6	164954.0
福建	901048.7	288401.0	612647.7	153310.6	130549.1	328788.0	142207.7	55749.0
江西	1570132.1	784245.0	785887.1	290306.3	37962.1	457618.7	215704.3	123872.0
山东	2824994.4	1139291.0	1685703.4	374250.3	378904.7	932548.4	774091.7	398419.0
河南	2240757.3	1360291.0	880466.3	314296.1	143205.9	422964.3	428578.9	256553.0
湖北	2352767.5	1162586.0	1190181.5	491453.5	204514.9	494213.1	347031.5	197107.0
湖南	2327130.3	1319227.0	1007903.3	429926.0	120206.0	457771.3	456723.6	339285.0
广东	2557435.2	485110.0	2072325.2	718280.4	492862.5	861182.3	367387.8	110614.0
广西	1485762.4	774902.0	710860.4	299958.6	148481.4	262420.4	162765.1	91978.0
海南	347546.4	155352.0	192194.4	61381.0	33644.6	97168.8	28062.5	14302.0
重庆	1406014.3	574243.0	831771.3	549857.7		281913.6	179545.6	118588.0
四川	3181029.2	1754442.0	1426587.2	352478.9	247224.5	826883.8	512763.2	357486.0
贵州	1567198.2	1073927.0	493271.2	165656.1	94675.3	232939.8	141701.9	93488.0
云南	2285288.3	1195370.0	1089918.3	527482.9	207274.9	355160.5	199348.5	147486.0
西藏	274419.5	154501.0	119918.5	54422.7	20443.6	45052.2	10523.2	6955.0
陕西	1862287.4	929812.0	932475.4	432048.5	230968.0	269458.9	241378.0	118156.0
甘肃	1376628.3	930116.0	446512.3	287992.6	57200.1	101319.6	64142.8	46513.0
青海	481697.7	258961.0	222736.7	143291.4	4682.0	74763.3	16777.4	10215.0
宁夏	431753.8	185017.0	246736.8	180325.4	20603.0	45808.4	12898.1	7245.0
新疆	1159639.2	739826.4	419812.8	153696.6	58466.6	207649.6	52379.5	31651.4

安排情况

单位：万元

全省安排	省　级	市　级	县级及以下	退役安置	中央安排	全省安排	省　级
3241449.9	**787029.9**	**314457.1**	**2139962.9**	**5750115.2**	**3529620.0**	**2220495.2**	**611286.8**
99763.4	4340.2		95423.2	968019.2	695601.0	272418.2	209969.5
57603.9	5367.7		52236.2	111018.4	85137.0	25881.4	142.9
183658.4	81093.3	20702.0	81863.1	309994.6	191686.0	118308.6	51261.9
116628.3	13923.4	20248.5	82456.4	94524.0	62486.0	32038.0	11156.4
66884.3	10168.6	4743.5	51972.2	97724.2	40256.0	57468.2	14477.8
105162.4	13844.8	14909.8	76407.8	432046.2	337511.0	94535.2	9472.0
60626.2	32810.5	653.4	27162.3	127282.7	72827.0	54455.7	8547.4
37776.6	22308.9	710.6	14757.1	86761.3	59618.0	27143.3	2895.3
102088.7	7128.3		94960.4	341253.3	114305.0	226948.3	8065.7
283469.6	58581.3	19145.5	205742.8	373578.9	190976.0	182602.9	34844.0
176307.6	16897.4	8217.7	151192.5	145138.8	71094.0	74044.8	1863.9
123131.6	785.6	10083.4	112262.6	169027.8	51329.0	117698.8	11873.9
86458.7	18834.1	8619.2	59005.4	97574.6	56710.0	40864.6	3254.2
91832.3	32333.0	838.9	58660.4	58189.8	31865.0	26324.8	8095.1
375672.7	61936.5	54612.9	259123.3	433370.4	285803.0	147567.4	29308.0
172025.9	34169.1	15951.4	121905.4	186268.6	109656.0	76612.6	15058.4
149924.5	44027.0	15809.1	90088.4	190356.0	130819.0	59537.0	15105.7
117438.6	42046.9	13717.8	61673.9	125396.1	82031.0	43365.1	15579.8
256773.8	75458.7	42317.9	138997.2	288609.1	144340.0	144269.1	25126.4
70787.1	35485.2	9095.5	26206.4	58115.4	33881.0	24234.4	8904.1
13760.5	1260.1	2352.5	10147.9	37525.5	18738.0	18787.5	3008.5
60957.6	26344.3		34613.3	103633.2	58631.0	45002.2	4486.4
155277.2	35731.7	9452.6	110092.9	263384.9	153045.0	110339.9	20713.0
48213.9	10336.4	8953.3	28924.2	41765.8	22089.0	19676.8	3550.0
51862.5	19657.3	3712.7	28492.5	118094.1	95359.0	22735.1	5798.4
3568.2	468.1	1356.5	1743.6	24384.8	14763.0	9621.8	556.6
123222.0	62964.8	22338.6	37918.6	220403.5	156633.0	63770.5	42718.3
17629.8	5146.6	3216.0	9267.2	90504.6	62007.0	28497.6	18182.7
6562.4	3707.3	70.0	2785.1	36404.3	17527.0	18877.3	17752.0
5653.1	745.6	1133.0	3774.5	20247.3	10718.0	9529.3	4148.3
20728.1	9127.2	1494.8	10106.1	99517.8	72179.0	27338.8	5370.2

C-1-16续表1

地 区	市级	县级及以下	社会福利	中央安排	全省安排	省级	市级	县级及以下
全 国	**342264.0**	**1266944.4**	**5714550.9**	**691300.0**	**5023250.9**	**1765257.3**	**1319211.5**	**1938782.1**
中央级								
北 京		62448.7	162897.9	7616.0	155281.9	65040.6		90241.3
天 津		25738.5	115135.1	5217.0	109918.1	69362.6		40555.5
河 北	32418.0	34628.7	201873.5	29123.0	172750.5	50726.5	48180.2	73843.8
山 西	7406.2	13475.4	108623.8	20378.0	88245.8	23345.0	48720.1	16180.7
内蒙古	4776.3	38214.1	132290.7	8508.0	123782.7	40331.6	33737.2	49713.9
辽 宁	32063.9	52999.3	119797.5	1870.0	117927.5	6790.4	77083.1	34054.0
吉 林	37758.8	8149.5	80013.7	16375.0	63638.7	29968.4	20318.2	13352.1
黑龙江	6080.2	18167.8	88347.6	19664.0	68683.6	46660.5	8711.0	13312.1
上 海		218882.6	188443.4	3934.0	184509.4	41108.1		143401.3
江 苏	23382.1	124376.8	470955.7	28437.0	442518.7	98992.5	113532.6	229993.6
浙 江	8737.7	63443.2	406265.6	13909.0	392356.6	95377.4	61750.1	235229.1
安 徽	22142.1	83682.8	186966.0	13989.0	172977.0	50892.0	51718.9	70366.1
福 建	9981.4	27629.0	124208.8	15774.0	108434.8	20615.9	40737.7	47081.2
江 西	801.3	17428.4	148663.8	31095.0	117568.8	70639.5	10115.8	36813.5
山 东	24526.9	93732.5	356393.9	30733.0	325660.9	72111.6	116559.8	136989.5
河 南	26976.5	34577.7	212691.7	42404.0	170287.7	88102.4	40712.1	41473.2
湖 北	10579.8	33851.5	195981.6	20521.0	175460.6	33788.6	61523.9	80148.1
湖 南	9289.9	18495.4	279801.7	41800.0	238001.7	173603.7	31901.5	32496.5
广 东	19107.6	100035.1	407192.5	25305.0	381887.5	82664.7	162224.1	136998.7
广 西	7887.8	7442.5	215604.0	27140.0	188464.0	102660.1	54324.9	31479.0
海 南	11591.6	4187.4	56949.9	8709.0	48240.9	12118.6	10764.7	25357.6
重 庆		40515.8	155003.5	24230.0	130773.5	70773.2		60000.3
四 川	6907.8	82719.1	418939.0	44949.0	373990.0	148196.3	115166.1	110627.6
贵 州	4375.5	11751.3	134107.7	27736.0	106371.7	44270.1	29184.4	32917.2
云 南	4975.6	11961.1	126569.9	26680.0	99889.9	22346.7	36797.1	40746.1
西 藏	8787.8	277.4	49410.9	12241.0	37169.9	29493.0	4774.8	2902.1
陕 西	12521.7	8530.5	206708.7	13989.0	192719.7	62383.8	75084.0	55251.9
甘 肃	3490.1	6824.8	137045.5	63317.0	73728.5	41035.3	23706.6	8986.6
青 海	0.8	1124.5	74243.9	21586.0	52657.9	35816.1	2125.0	14716.8
宁 夏	2187.1	3193.9	14528.1	3398.0	11130.1	5679.7	1125.2	4325.2
新 疆	3509.5	18459.1	138895.3	40673.0	98222.3	30362.4	38632.4	29227.5

单位：万元

社会救助	中央安排合计	全省安排合计	省级	市级	县级及以下	城市最低生活保障	中央安排	全省安排
24138760.2	**13897358.0**	**10241402.2**	**4368065.5**	**892690.3**	**4980646.4**	**10399146.1**	**7632684.5**	**2766461.6**
181551.9	16426.0	165125.9	9221.3		155904.6	71259.1		71259.1
251711.9	56161.0	195550.9	37927.1		157623.8	127073.4	42839.0	84234.4
762570.6	489196.0	273374.6	139360.4	30079.2	103935.0	589981.2	426658.0	163323.2
696033.0	423801.0	272232.0	152124.3	58931.5	61176.2	383498.3	361102.0	22396.3
852849.3	475015.0	377834.3	131771.9	87892.9	158169.5	358928.3	232032.0	126896.3
706092.1	474494.0	231598.1	71416.0	42628.3	117553.8	287736.5	225000.0	62736.5
663110.1	497863.0	165247.1	59760.0	23609.2	81877.9	513326.1	421466.0	91860.1
1148516.5	707881.0	440635.5	295896.1	23275.5	121463.9	840002.8	612435.0	227567.8
362279.1	18672.0	343607.1	14251.3		329355.8	141296.0		141296.0
895165.7	157393.0	737772.7	204100.0	44742.2	488930.5	127183.5		127183.5
512496.2	76337.0	436159.2	89580.5	27875.2	318703.5	52489.2	6623.0	45866.2
979702.3	611031.0	368671.3	66174.8	25288.2	277208.3	630510.3	537063.0	93447.3
346852.9	130074.0	216778.9	61163.7	24924.8	130690.4	53093.7	28000.0	25093.7
1006824.3	546761.0	460063.3	163049.4	15680.4	281333.5	330778.6	236310.0	94468.6
1001175.3	407449.0	593726.3	192620.0	103434.3	297672.0	229553.4	103527.0	126026.4
1225180.6	929145.0	296035.6	139886.5	20637.3	135511.8	885361.5	822099.0	63262.5
1322657.9	764995.0	557662.9	323161.0	41752.7	192749.2	473540.6	355912.0	117628.6
1258589.9	805183.0	453406.9	164181.1	28138.5	261087.3	830369.0	662176.0	168193.0
965699.6	182666.0	783033.6	461123.4	53819.1	268091.1	154554.5		154554.5
816896.6	581127.0	235769.6	120096.5	7855.3	107817.8	505651.8	494947.0	10704.8
171533.7	106896.0	64637.7	35660.0	3316.5	25661.2	70986.6	46339.0	24647.6
800332.8	352534.0	447798.8	404337.3		43461.5	338229.2	205383.0	132846.2
1582067.1	1121845.0	460222.1	101998.3	41569.4	316654.4	520762.2	457252.0	63510.2
1028951.4	872548.0	156403.4	54712.0	23744.4	77947.0	198628.3	158847.5	39780.8
1359635.3	861038.0	498597.3	277890.6	74308.6	146398.1	455660.7	273884.0	181776.7
122295.8	80901.0	41394.8	1206.0	1260.9	38927.9	35540.7	23093.0	12447.7
963762.4	598969.0	364793.4	196793.1	72137.9	95862.4	266079.7	189809.0	76270.7
989683.9	713853.0	275830.9	210369.9	12524.6	52936.4	249673.5	184182.0	65491.5
262823.8	184470.0	78353.8	46678.0	517.2	31158.6	125599.5	94178.0	31421.5
206642.2	135687.0	70955.2	50387.5	134.5	20433.2	43137.9		43137.9
695076.0	516947.0	178129.0	91167.5	2611.7	84349.8	508660.0	431528.0	77132.0

C-1-16续表2

地 区	省级	市级	县级及以下	农村最低生活保障	中央安排	全省安排	省级	市级
全 国	**1317728.5**	**266748.5**	**1181984.6**	**7098410.5**	**4130564.5**	**2967846.0**	**1424980.4**	**259439.7**
中央级								
北 京			71259.1	32545.2		32545.2		
天 津			84234.4	49048.7		49048.7		
河 北	128000.0	14419.7	20903.5	11707.5		11707.5		2718.2
山 西		10319.6	12076.7	154457.5		154457.5	109109.0	28472.2
内蒙古	73069.9	23293.8	30532.6	296064.1	178699.0	117365.1	28355.0	43207.2
辽 宁	15000.0	3815.8	43920.7	291263.2	220000.0	71263.2	48016.0	7243.0
吉 林	43227.0	12137.1	36496.0	18924.8		18924.8		3891.7
黑龙江	161806.0	16166.7	49595.1	39080.7		39080.7		2622.8
上 海	4639.7		136656.3	17317.2		17317.2		
江 苏	47619.0	13473.6	66090.9	386802.2	107328.0	279474.2	105381.0	2923.6
浙 江	5622.1	3698.6	36545.5	219661.0	39434.0	180227.0	44525.6	1649.1
安 徽	56500.0	5236.2	31711.1	69352.2		69352.2		6760.7
福 建	966.2	3748.8	20378.7	153642.1	70751.0	82891.1	26415.5	8823.1
江 西	500.0	4949.2	89019.4	365380.2	209557.0	155823.2	54042.0	2680.3
山 东	44496.0	24475.6	57054.8	489274.2	241562.0	247712.2	103823.0	43782.5
河 南	53093.0	1924.3	8245.2	27622.8		27622.8		6677.0
湖 北	29414.0	26880.3	61334.3	575694.7	291201.0	284493.7	244066.0	165.8
湖 南	100085.0	17671.8	50436.2	65388.6		65388.6		1016.1
广 东	83548.0	12624.7	58381.8	392339.3	130944.0	261395.3	168431.0	14202.5
广 西		1155.6	9549.2	64162.9		64162.9	50500.0	576.4
海 南	19354.0	196.0	5097.6	54262.4	29789.0	24473.4	15526.0	545.0
重 庆	133497.5		-651.3	191831.0	83219.0	108612.0	107519.5	
四 川	22967.0	5400.5	35142.7	563621.4	480118.0	83503.4	24033.0	16488.7
贵 州	15000.0	7635.1	17145.7	678489.3	613878.5	64610.8	22500.0	9844.2
云 南	110567.7	25704.9	45504.1	632507.2	476635.0	155872.2	86665.7	27654.4
西 藏	206.0	798.0	11443.7	62106.2	41157.0	20949.2		
陕 西	26791.5	24022.6	25456.6	408001.7	326898.0	81103.7	31345.5	25709.6
甘 肃	34788.6	7000.0	23702.9	552421.5	429760.0	122661.5	108495.4	1357.2
青 海	20209.3		11212.2	66781.7	46527.0	20254.7	16431.7	428.4
宁 夏	36667.0		6470.9	124092.7	102281.0	21811.7	13266.5	
新 疆	50094.0		27038.0	44566.3	10826.0	33740.3	16533.0	

单位：万元

县级及以下	其他社会救助	中央安排	全省安排	省级	市级	县级及以下	医疗救助	中央安排
1283425.9	**3605599.8**	**503844.0**	**3101755.8**	**1048712.2**	**235532.8**	**1817510.8**	**3035603.8**	**1630265.0**
32545.2	55023.8	14243.0	40780.8	7442.9		33337.9	22723.8	2183.0
49048.7	33091.1	6959.0	26132.1	1870.2		24261.9	42498.7	6363.0
8989.3	65102.3	5558.0	59544.3	560.0	9770.2	49214.1	95779.6	56980.0
16876.3	82068.4	18592.0	63476.4	29193.3	11551.4	22731.7	76008.8	44107.0
45802.9	116919.1	16248.0	100671.1	22639.0	11971.0	66061.1	80937.8	48036.0
16004.2	68943.8		68943.8	3400.0	17566.7	47977.1	58148.6	29494.0
15033.1	49786.2	15709.0	34077.2	11233.0	2280.6	20563.6	81073.0	60688.0
36457.9	123328.5	19366.0	103962.5	78717.6	3286.4	21958.5	146104.5	76080.0
17317.2	172379.7	15352.0	157027.7	9509.6		147518.1	31286.2	3320.0
171169.6	245984.9	23893.0	222091.9	28100.0	20211.4	173780.5	135195.1	26172.0
134052.3	136812.7	17257.0	119555.7	12468.4	15192.4	91894.9	103533.3	13023.0
62591.5	155501.1		155501.1		11466.2	144034.9	124338.7	73968.0
47652.5	80284.2	14617.0	65667.2	18503.0	8253.5	38910.7	59832.9	16706.0
99100.9	133395.3	22549.0	110846.3	78498.4	6082.1	26265.8	177270.2	78345.0
100106.7	135733.4	8241.0	127492.4	11550.0	21877.5	94064.9	146614.3	54119.0
20945.8	177563.2	10207.0	167356.2	72410.5	9740.7	85205.0	134633.1	96839.0
40261.9	141698.6	42690.0	99008.6	38796.0	10899.8	49312.8	131724.0	75192.0
64372.5	212234.1	35375.0	176859.1	56654.1	5539.5	114665.5	150598.2	107632.0
78761.8	240693.0	27112.0	213581.0	98532.6	20268.7	94779.7	178112.8	24610.0
13086.5	167595.7	23963.0	143632.7	58796.4	4766.5	80069.8	79486.2	62217.0
8402.4	23190.1	11424.0	11766.1	480.0	1760.5	9525.6	23094.6	19344.0
1092.5	162877.0	15900.0	146977.0	120613.5		26363.5	107395.6	48032.0
42981.7	268007.4	36847.0	231160.4	25578.3	10123.0	195459.1	229676.1	147628.0
32266.6	58164.1	19262.0	38902.1	12212.0	4756.7	21933.4	93669.7	80560.0
41552.1	136501.6	18774.0	117727.6	67381.8	4421.7	45924.1	134965.8	91745.0
20949.2	2873.4		2873.4	1000.0	254.9	1618.5	21775.5	16651.0
24048.6	160025.2	6844.0	153181.2	103916.1	17726.2	31538.9	129655.8	75418.0
12808.9	94681.9	18302.0	76379.9	61468.0	3822.7	11089.2	92907.0	81609.0
3394.6	29135.6	13413.0	15722.6	2037.0	88.8	13596.8	41307.0	30352.0
8545.2	15237.3	10814.0	4423.3	110.0	122.0	4191.3	24174.3	22592.0
17207.3	60767.1	14333.0	46434.1	15040.5	1731.7	29661.9	81082.6	60260.0

C-1-16续表3

地 区	全省安排	省级	市级	县级及以下	自然灾害生活救助	中央安排	全省安排	省级
全 国	**1405338.8**	**576644.4**	**130969.3**	**697725.1**	**1423766.4**	**922232.0**	**501534.4**	**300862.8**
中央级								
北 京	20540.8	1778.4		18762.4	1221.7	157.0	1064.7	500.0
天 津	36135.7	36056.9		78.8	1201.8	336.0	865.8	800.0
河 北	38799.6	10800.4	3171.1	24828.1	41917.1	32632.0	9285.1	3600.0
山 西	31901.8	13822.0	8588.3	9491.5	44068.0	35576.0	8492.0	4299.1
内蒙古	32901.8	7708.0	9420.9	15772.9	56503.1	41283.0	15220.1	4955.1
辽 宁	28654.6	5000.0	14002.8	9651.8	29856.8	23027.0	6829.8	495.0
吉 林	20385.0	5300.0	5299.8	9785.2	28390.6	17706.0	10684.6	3425.2
黑龙江	70024.5	55372.5	1199.6	13452.4	26182.8	23367.0	2815.8	2266.4
上 海	27966.2	102.0		27864.2	1032.0		1032.0	1032.0
江 苏	109023.1	23000.0	8133.6	77889.5	21624.7	7811.0	13813.7	6145.0
浙 江	90510.3	26964.4	7335.1	56210.8	38931.1	18241.0	20690.1	780.0
安 徽	50370.7	9674.8	1825.1	38870.8	38197.2	29551.0	8646.2	3170.8
福 建	43126.9	15279.0	4099.4	23748.5	46939.2	28144.0	18795.2	12450.0
江 西	98925.2	30009.0	1968.8	66947.4	64105.3	47831.0	16274.3	3330.0
山 东	92495.3	32751.0	13298.7	46445.6	21293.9	14563.0	6730.9	1500.0
河 南	37794.1	14383.0	2295.3	21115.8	26697.9	18977.0	7720.9	4195.0
湖 北	56532.0	10885.0	3806.8	41840.2	73438.5	46607.0	26831.5	21550.0
湖 南	42966.2	7442.0	3911.1	31613.1	56703.5	45591.0	11112.5	6200.0
广 东	153502.8	110611.8	6723.2	36167.8	52634.9	20190.0	32444.9	26304.5
广 西	17269.2	10800.1	1356.8	5112.3	58257.3	37232.0	21025.3	16676.7
海 南	3750.6	300.0	815.0	2635.6	8366.1	5653.0	2713.1	100.0
重 庆	59363.6	42706.8		16656.8	31616.9	17841.0	13775.9	11449.4
四 川	82048.1	29420.0	9557.2	43070.9	105857.4	72344.0	33513.4	15614.0
贵 州	13109.7	5000.0	1508.4	6601.3	89093.7	55070.0	34023.7	21067.0
云 南	43220.8	13275.4	16527.6	13417.8	196610.6	57452.0	139158.6	103311.5
西 藏	5124.5	208.0		4916.5	37396.6	36072.0	1324.6	651.6
陕 西	54237.8	34740.0	4679.5	14818.3	49181.3	33739.0	15442.3	10987.6
甘 肃	11298.0	5617.9	344.7	5335.4	50105.4	40805.0	9300.4	5892.9
青 海	10955.0	8000.0		2955.0	23505.8	22171.0	1334.8	
宁 夏	1582.3	344.0	12.5	1225.8	20634.5	17435.0	3199.5	2677.4
新 疆	20822.6	9500.0	880.0	10442.6	82200.7	74828.0	7372.7	5436.6

单位：万元

市级	县级及以下	民政管理事务	中央安排	全省安排	省级	市级	县级及以下
64846.9	**135824.7**	**3687339.8**	**84038.0**	**3603301.8**	**580160.9**	**789231.1**	**2233909.8**
	564.7	186202.3	788.0	185414.3	49985.0		135429.3
	65.8	198775.0	768.0	198007.0	17026.5		180980.5
2930.2	2754.9	99339.1	3779.0	95560.1	12658.0	18656.3	64245.8
1924.3	2268.6	75398.1	2976.0	72422.1	4676.7	27698.0	40047.4
6771.6	3493.4	68090.8	3527.0	64563.8	13841.6	13763.4	36958.8
816.4	5518.4	146617.5	2140.0	144477.5	4799.6	54414.1	85263.8
39.0	7220.4	68632.0	1829.0	66803.0	16565.0	18656.6	31581.4
50.0	499.4	59743.5	3286.0	56457.5	27485.9	5743.4	23228.2
		142895.5		142895.5	37400.5		105495.0
556.4	7112.3	227731.3	1818.0	225913.3	21692.3	55128.1	149092.9
9198.1	10712.0	230150.7	1695.0	228455.7	14068.3	41818.0	172569.4
430.3	5045.1	77013.7		77013.7	11205.4	20023.1	45785.2
3597.3	2747.9	84200.7	1950.0	82250.7	24354.6	21591.2	36304.9
1873.3	11071.0	57442.3	2821.0	54621.3	9117.0	6022.9	39481.4
2645.4	2585.5	181398.5	2324.0	179074.5	9045.2	61540.9	108488.4
1019.4	2506.5	105194.9	3556.0	101638.9	5776.8	30062.6	65799.5
721.8	4559.7	159709.6		159709.6	30796.9	55861.0	73051.7
1078.3	3834.2	117574.1	3466.0	114108.1	17298.7	30093.6	66715.8
1647.1	4493.3	280864.1	1995.0	278869.1	21400.9	100761.1	156707.1
2107.5	2241.1	126684.1	3544.0	123140.1	14019.3	42301.4	66819.4
203.9	2409.2	31783.4		31783.4	5714.8	3554.1	22514.5
	2326.5	105378.5	2419.0	102959.5	25271.3		77688.2
4717.1	13182.3	240048.9	4785.0	235263.9	30225.6	49247.8	155790.5
3245.1	9711.6	120567.6	3557.0	117010.6	31551.8	22523.9	62934.9
16508.3	19338.8	152880.5	7355.0	145525.5	36825.9	37914.5	70785.1
143.5	529.5	20290.9	3569.0	16721.9	13096.0	3359.9	266.0
1577.3	2877.4	149590.9	8326.0	141264.9	37944.2	42038.2	61282.5
780.3	2627.2	33321.2	3621.0	29700.2	6130.1	9083.1	14487.0
140.0	1194.8	27775.6	2992.0	24783.6	11071.6	1048.7	12663.3
125.0	397.1	28474.7	1604.0	26870.7	9123.8	5704.0	12042.9
	1936.1	83569.8	3548.0	80021.8	9991.6	10621.2	59409.0

C-1-16续表4

地　区	行政事业单位离退休	全省安排	省级	市级	县级及以下
全　国	**479321.6**	**479321.6**	**70779.5**	**105109.9**	**303432.2**
中央级					
北　京	61434.1	61434.1	2764.5		58669.6
天　津	3659.6	3659.6			3659.6
河　北	27477.9	27477.9	5765.2	7153.9	14558.8
山　西	10962.8	10962.8	2421.4	3265.5	5275.9
内蒙古	18030.4	18030.4	1028.7	5844.3	11157.4
辽　宁	21807.3	21807.3	2766.9	7717.8	11322.6
吉　林	9458.4	9458.4	806.3	3630.3	5021.8
黑龙江	10954.3	10954.3	8058.4	1094.6	1801.3
上　海	6071.0	6071.0	1404.3		4666.7
江　苏	25771.4	25771.4	1179.7	3901.7	20690.0
浙　江	23918.2	23918.2	1090.9	7410.8	15416.5
安　徽	16224.3	16224.3	2278.6	4033.5	9912.2
福　建	22223.3	22223.3	1238.1	5039.7	15945.5
江　西	11268.3	11268.3	2153.9	1972.7	7141.7
山　东	15396.2	15396.2	5147.0	3896.8	6352.4
河　南	20629.4	20629.4	3393.5	6728.4	10507.5
湖　北	19475.0	19475.0	4440.7	3606.5	11427.8
湖　南	8128.9	8128.9	101.0	1429.1	6598.8
广　东	41614.7	41614.7	5398.4	17721.8	18494.5
广　西	16840.1	16840.1	905.3	3744.6	12190.2
海　南	5293.5	5293.5	2897.0	628.9	1767.6
重　庆	11870.5	11870.5	3479.3		8391.2
四　川	25118.2	25118.2		7675.7	17442.5
贵　州	1421.9	1421.9			1421.9
云　南	15630.1	15630.1	2037.4	2163.2	11429.5
西　藏	965.8	965.8	677.1	287.7	1.0
陕　西	10304.9	10304.9	3507.1	2230.4	4567.4
甘　肃	5415.6	5415.6	1039.4	1775.0	2601.2
青　海	2138.7	2138.7	1176.4	346.2	616.1
宁　夏	3568.8	3568.8	1381.9	794.7	1392.2
新　疆	6248.0	6248.0	2241.1	1016.1	2990.8

单位：万元

其他款项用于民政支出	中央安排	全省安排		
			省级	市级	县级及以下
1651840.7	**61986.0**	**1589854.7**	**645745.1**	**361340.0**	**582769.6**
247808.7	2728.0	245080.7	148537.3		96543.4
83094.7		83094.7	15702.0		67392.7
10727.4		10727.4	1788.1	2279.7	6659.6
13550.2		13550.2	4372.3	4144.9	5033.0
98912.0	8832.0	90080.0	61589.3	17101.1	11389.6
171190.4	23165.0	148025.4	69418.3	28455.8	50151.3
23651.0		23651.0	9531.8	10436.3	3682.9
1954.4		1954.4		338.2	1616.2
12457.6	-61.0	12518.6	289.6		12229.0
122582.0		122582.0	1819.5	54112.7	66649.8
57210.2	96.0	57114.2	3817.5	7513.0	45783.7
47492.6	13407.0	34085.6	17468.2	7976.9	8640.5
36841.5		36841.5	11400.0	16057.8	9383.7
7934.0		7934.0	1588.4	656.8	5688.8
41874.5		41874.5	2582.0	11687.7	27604.8
35515.3		35515.3	23714.4	1118.2	10682.7
44117.4	2537.0	41580.4	18583.6	14660.1	8336.7
24212.5	1871.0	22341.5	10914.8	4557.3	6869.4
153432.5		153432.5	20803.4	95263.8	37365.3
30599.8		30599.8	1211.4	21164.4	8224.0
8031.8	1054.0	6977.8	622.0	1232.4	5123.4
18633.3		18633.3	3716.5		14916.8
32850.5	-12.0	32862.5		12488.0	20374.5
9588.2	-561.0	10149.2	168.8	2648.7	7331.7
116519.3		116519.3	59615.1	30894.9	26009.3
9151.5		9151.5	8274.3	472.5	404.7
20957.7		20957.7	14749.6	3039.9	3168.2
6409.3		6409.3	195.7	2624.4	3589.2
38028.2		38028.2	27090.0	434.1	10504.1
124760.1	8930.0	115830.1	106181.2	9399.5	249.4
1752.1		1752.1		580.9	1171.2

C-1-17 预算资金

地 区	预算内经费实际支出	抚恤	死亡抚恤	一次性抚恤金	定期抚恤金	其他	伤残抚恤
全 国	**49264448.4**	**6867691.8**	**652844.0**	**257811.2**	**348695.4**	**46337.4**	**1300263.3**
中央级	155949.2	11419.2					
北 京	2220633.5	126294.0	42996.7	38805.5	4064.1	127.1	18418.1
天 津	769084.9	71566.9	7313.1	4762.9	1887.0	663.2	14184.5
河 北	1805161.2	380933.5	27833.1	12146.1	14874.4	812.6	69599.2
山 西	1201392.7	222109.8	15229.0	5463.2	8684.6	1081.2	35748.7
内蒙古	1410121.9	103076.8	6322.4	3416.9	2453.4	452.1	17220.9
辽 宁	1844543.3	182468.9	22681.4	13334.2	7938.1	1409.1	44301.7
吉 林	1057440.4	128565.2	11230.3	3975.4	6386.4	868.5	33991.2
黑龙江	1504605.0	95953.7	9522.3	2443.0	6730.6	348.7	22965.0
上 海	966471.0	105035.5	16613.2	8923.6	6111.2	1578.4	17744.6
江 苏	2605552.1	463109.4	47109.0	16813.4	24422.3	5873.3	96943.9
浙 江	1674651.1	265897.5	20619.6	8548.6	10797.4	1273.6	43462.3
安 徽	1812233.9	295774.9	16762.2	4713.0	10955.4	1093.8	55296.4
福 建	903162.9	147650.7	17349.2	4527.9	12224.6	596.7	20279.0
江 西	1571857.7	218302.0	36221.5	4572.1	24451.4	7198.0	34558.2
山 东	2871388.9	780175.1	57810.1	19737.2	35153.9	2919.0	226614.7
河 南	2292633.2	444599.3	30345.5	11279.4	17462.1	1604.0	95442.7
湖 北	2269799.1	351444.8	44438.2	9132.4	34872.0	433.8	50225.0
湖 南	2305544.2	456639.8	48666.6	12894.3	28820.1	6952.2	88447.6
广 东	2595187.3	358106.5	25388.9	12462.2	12027.6	899.1	43313.5
广 西	1492923.0	176871.1	8311.9	2340.1	5662.0	309.8	16915.5
海 南	296623.7	25861.5	4414.8	1263.7	2749.7	401.4	3496.5
重 庆	1146517.8	181717.1	14623.0	4596.7	6696.1	3330.2	34471.7
四 川	3152459.5	523803.0	44148.9	12626.1	30204.3	1318.5	92715.3
贵 州	1472311.4	146077.1	9185.6	4544.6	3921.9	719.1	21155.7
云 南	2310934.8	202119.7	17547.9	8922.8	8137.4	487.7	31016.9
西 藏	175034.3	6661.3	3152.4	657.0	2378.0	117.4	1545.1
陕 西	1847868.8	240597.0	22480.2	10585.3	10778.7	1116.2	33960.6
甘 肃	1367615.6	62917.2	9880.6	5945.9	2881.4	1053.3	16152.3
青 海	462567.9	17756.1	3259.5	1949.7	930.3	379.5	3676.5
宁 夏	409809.1	13963.5	2667.2	1533.2	552.4	581.6	2958.2
新 疆	1292369.0	60223.7	8719.7	4894.8	3486.6	338.3	13441.8

总体支出情况

单位：万元

伤残抚恤金	在乡伤残抚恤金	在职保健金	伤残补助费	分散安置残疾军人护理费	在乡复员、退伍军人生活补助	在乡复退军人定期定量补助费	在乡红军老战士定期定量补助费	红军失散人员定期定量补助费
1230013.8	**930669.9**	**299343.9**	**70249.5**	**32068.9**	**2377296.4**	**1619858.5**	**965.2**	**6842.5**
17195.5	9054.0	8141.5	1222.6	441.5	11591.9	8002.5	5.6	
13610.8	6735.5	6875.3	573.7	391.8	24790.7	17628.3		
65637.5	65120.8	516.7	3961.7	809.9	116682.7	83758.7		
34709.3	20799.0	13910.3	1039.4	830.5	45665.1	37845.7	25.0	1.7
16155.3	8265.6	7889.7	1065.6	140.8	18014.2	17081.3	16.3	1.9
42710.4	32698.8	10011.6	1591.3	471.7	46314.3	41477.1	10.0	
32815.3	25257.9	7557.4	1175.9	832.5	28107.5	25344.4		1.9
21454.1	15853.6	5600.5	1510.9	232.7	35611.8	33099.0	25.3	21.6
16618.9		16618.9	1125.7	369.5	12500.3	9228.4		
88133.8	66936.0	21197.8	8810.1	3707.1	121595.0	100046.1		1.9
40790.3	26662.6	14127.7	2672.0	726.4	77568.9	60866.8		92.6
53384.1	41071.6	12312.5	1912.3	1112.3	124307.4	102304.1		339.2
19274.6	16473.9	2800.7	1004.4	190.2	48461.3	27131.8		337.0
32357.0	30049.3	2307.7	2201.2	1199.8	91627.1	62452.4	28.4	2009.4
213310.3	154502.0	58808.3	13304.4	9976.2	193453.4	153005.4		
91654.5	66906.1	24748.4	3788.2	1891.5	161389.2	108527.9	12.7	420.1
47430.3	40982.1	6448.2	2794.7	1128.4	133847.6	97485.1	8.2	649.8
83512.8	69654.0	13858.8	4934.8	1620.0	209232.1	132448.1	8.4	1636.9
40587.7	32462.2	8125.5	2725.8	643.8	154299.5	56044.6		67.9
16067.6	13755.2	2312.4	847.9	381.2	80651.5	34267.8		378.8
3433.7	3324.2	109.5	62.8	21.1	7009.8	4321.0		16.4
32203.5	23301.1	8902.4	2268.2	1643.8	90946.9	64347.0		
88576.9	73218.0	15358.9	4138.4	1790.5	265032.5	192687.4	180.8	590.4
19916.4	15270.2	4646.2	1239.3	371.6	71419.2	35464.3	4.2	11.5
30278.9	22130.8	8148.1	738.0	152.5	75632.1	31756.4		5.8
1537.1	828.8	708.3	8.0		816.6	486.6	326.7	3.3
32759.2	26810.8	5948.4	1201.4	499.8	85697.6	54993.7	219.5	246.8
15169.5	10784.2	4385.3	982.8	341.0	22613.9	11278.7	68.0	3.9
3168.3	2570.0	598.3	508.2	2.8	3590.6	2426.3		
2904.3	2816.9	87.4	53.9	21.5	3127.5	2458.0	4.3	1.8
12655.9	6374.7	6281.2	785.9	126.5	15698.2	11593.6	21.8	1.9

C-1-17续表1

地 区	"参战"退伍军人生活补助	"涉核"退伍军人生活补助	优抚事业单位	烈士纪念建筑物管理维修经费
全 国	**648069.2**	**101561.0**	**629802.8**	**245546.5**
中央级			11419.2	11419.2
北 京	2729.0	854.8	5246.8	1242.1
天 津	7100.2	62.2	10532.7	3464.8
河 北	22943.0	9981.0	66768.3	21464.5
山 西	4482.7	3310.0	42214.9	17753.6
内蒙古	820.2	94.5	13046.4	4955.6
辽 宁	2722.2	2105.0	13535.8	3585.7
吉 林	2090.3	670.9	11209.2	2937.3
黑龙江	2308.1	157.8	8111.4	2446.7
上 海	2709.1	562.8	11481.6	7850.3
江 苏	18074.9	3472.1	39586.0	17720.1
浙 江	15068.8	1540.7	23281.5	9152.7
安 徽	15760.8	5903.3	19189.2	13428.5
福 建	20783.9	208.6	15633.9	4230.5
江 西	25121.8	2015.1	15233.1	6276.5
山 东	33096.0	7352.0	81358.0	32451.9
河 南	41062.2	11366.3	22782.6	9771.0
湖 北	31327.2	4377.3	30331.9	5903.5
湖 南	67409.3	7729.4	32517.8	10063.6
广 东	92675.5	5511.5	32039.8	11844.2
广 西	43857.2	2147.7	23496.9	7983.5
海 南	2623.6	48.8	3902.0	2112.0
重 庆	22723.3	3876.6	7292.5	2401.5
四 川	61317.3	10256.6	33810.8	12383.6
贵 州	35831.6	107.6	7988.2	4313.0
云 南	43784.5	85.4	8946.4	3185.8
西 藏			570.6	380.6
陕 西	19763.0	10474.6	22087.7	6213.7
甘 肃	7627.9	3635.4	3455.6	2157.9
青 海	596.7	567.6	836.9	551.0
宁 夏	494.1	169.3	1499.8	775.5
新 疆	1164.8	2916.1	10395.3	5126.1

单位：万元

烈士纪念建筑物管理单位经费	荣誉军人康复医院经费	在院人员生活费	复员军人疗养院经费	在院人员生活费
92402.0	**80045.1**	**6320.6**	**36404.5**	**4310.9**
11419.2				
461.1				
2745.8			503.1	29.7
4307.2	522.4		5285.9	187.6
4589.6	2847.4	280.4	3743.5	658.9
3373.3	2066.0		15.0	
1818.2	1517.1			
1526.4	4806.3			
594.0	2620.7	58.3		
6308.2	1141.2	31.6		
8620.6	3868.0		2022.5	298.5
2641.3	6388.1			
2382.1	518.6			
1450.0	190.6	178.0		
1884.2	3389.8	108.3	95.8	10.0
7814.4	14462.9	180.0	15536.0	871.1
4948.4	5187.4	381.8	1305.9	188.7
2801.1	3425.8	600.0	30.0	
2678.6	990.2		50.0	
4166.3	3017.3	301.0	4031.6	550.0
1099.0	2022.6		833.4	
384.7				
655.7	2199.5	271.0		
3109.7	9086.1	674.2	176.9	38.2
1521.6	1685.5	162.5		
1684.3	2158.2			
64.6				
2201.7	4434.0	3033.5	2774.9	1478.2
1675.8	344.5			
258.0				
175.3	502.1			
3041.6	652.8	60.0		

C-1-17续表2

地 区	复退军人精神病院经费	在院人员生活费	光荣院经费	在院人员生活费
全 国	**103703.9**	**8699.0**	**85741.0**	**20308.6**
中央级				
北 京			3483.2	538.3
天 津	2230.2	117.2	3078.3	309.9
河 北	2838.9		12307.1	2248.6
山 西	5952.6	465.2	7483.5	1879.8
内蒙古	1440.6	134.6	3188.1	780.7
辽 宁	2374.5	95.6	5151.3	1163.3
吉 林	347.0	265.0	1409.8	392.6
黑龙江	1755.6	234.2	864.7	416.1
上 海	110.0	110.0		
江 苏	8174.5		1180.1	265.1
浙 江	6355.7		782.1	215.7
安 徽	10.0		3234.2	901.7
福 建	7227.5	769.6	1508.2	426.5
江 西	5.5	3.5	4764.2	1819.9
山 东	14751.5	1413.7	2591.2	803.7
河 南	3079.3	435.0	2091.4	588.8
湖 北	14108.5	1163.2	5272.9	1750.0
湖 南	4290.9	370.0	10828.9	2565.0
广 东	8526.9	926.0	2415.1	718.2
广 西	8041.6	161.7	1700.7	246.3
海 南			351.7	139.9
重 庆			2348.3	333.0
四 川	6615.6	353.2	3181.2	839.7
贵 州			1029.8	281.8
云 南	167.9		8.0	5.0
西 藏				
陕 西	4865.0	1681.3	2338.7	500.3
甘 肃	407.1		17.5	2.5
青 海				
宁 夏			12.2	6.2
新 疆	27.0		3118.6	170.0

单位：万元

其他优抚事业单位经费	集体办优抚事业单位补助费	义务兵优待金	城市义务兵优待金	农村义务兵优待金	其他优抚支出
77035.8	**1326.0**	**1284461.2**	**635013.8**	**649447.4**	**623024.1**
521.5		21360.5	16750.9	4609.6	26680.0
1256.3		9707.9	5165.4	4542.5	5038.0
24303.8	45.7	88900.1	38814.2	50085.9	11150.1
4414.3	20.0	71909.2	43491.9	28417.3	11342.9
1381.1		38574.1	24176.7	14397.4	9898.8
907.2		44174.4	24198.9	19975.5	11461.3
1693.8	15.0	36504.9	20967.1	15537.8	7522.1
423.7		13318.5	9206.4	4112.1	6424.7
2380.1		38315.1	32657.5	5657.6	8380.7
6159.2	461.6	87582.8	50345.9	37236.9	70292.7
602.9		75498.8	30135.3	45363.5	25466.4
1996.7	1.2	58462.6	23004.1	35458.5	21757.1
2458.1	19.0	32487.0	11965.4	20521.6	13440.3
636.3	65.0	27292.3	13534.9	13757.4	13369.8
1564.5		130913.2	45977.0	84936.2	90025.7
1347.6		110513.7	54012.4	56501.3	24125.6
1591.2		74562.5	35888.2	38674.3	18039.6
5799.2	495.0	53181.3	31562.9	21618.4	24594.4
2080.6	124.1	51110.2	21986.8	29123.4	51954.6
2915.1		24454.5	8175.8	16278.7	23040.8
1428.7	9.6	1321.9	806.8	515.1	5716.5
343.2		20342.5	9402.0	10940.5	14040.5
2347.4	20.0	65328.8	27030.4	38298.4	22766.7
959.9		19214.4	10264.7	8949.7	17114.0
3390.7	35.8	11918.0	4378.0	7540.0	57058.4
190.0		479.3	153.5	325.8	97.3
1447.4	14.0	58555.8	29794.8	28761.0	17815.1
528.6		5345.2	1732.4	3612.8	5469.6
285.9		3002.1	1994.4	1007.7	3390.5
210.0		3092.1	1763.1	1329.0	618.7
1470.8		7037.5	5676.0	1361.5	4931.2

C-1-17续表3

地 区	退役安置	退伍军人安置	一次性建房补助费	退役士兵自谋职业金	城镇退役士兵生活补助	军队移交政府的离退休人员安置	军队离休干部离休金	军队退休干部退休金
全 国	**5827136.8**	**1309983.0**	**20540.0**	**957289.7**	**176312.0**	**3630802.5**	**415174.2**	**2139522.7**
中央级								
北 京	1235641.4	34039.2	16.5	33819.6	88.5	778188.5	22940.1	479739.0
天 津	102680.7	18942.2		16042.0	90.4	75783.5	5925.6	49991.9
河 北	329381.3	87183.9	171.7	48266.0	20227.2	209724.4	23933.6	136084.8
山 西	93926.9	19634.8	94.0	7931.4	8375.0	60213.5	6740.4	34796.2
内蒙古	89989.3	40659.7	37.3	24128.5	12152.8	40270.6	3894.8	28414.5
辽 宁	400605.1	50439.8	557.9	36456.0	7559.9	315252.8	129969.9	125873.1
吉 林	82877.2	14608.0	341.0	8260.0	3869.7	59053.7	7062.1	38172.9
黑龙江	84143.7	24965.0	409.3	14515.9	6176.3	53916.1	17135.6	25633.6
上 海	199101.4	40246.9	72.4	33080.2	4214.7	135890.2	5902.9	75056.5
江 苏	392274.2	126992.8	629.0	113410.1	5549.8	225672.1	16449.7	142560.7
浙 江	145389.1	51992.7	139.8	40529.3	6984.1	74748.8	8345.9	33669.5
安 徽	165427.2	94451.7	531.2	81049.2	7951.4	57027.3	8416.5	32314.6
福 建	98942.8	33602.0	1500.0	27212.3	2254.1	53414.6	7197.7	37839.9
江 西	56819.3	25434.1	83.5	16307.3	5036.5	27083.5	6375.1	9809.7
山 东	446392.2	117451.1	6328.0	78218.6	13846.6	284468.8	39222.2	173710.0
河 南	189087.8	59491.8	954.3	33748.2	16772.5	110150.8	12496.9	73261.9
湖 北	205800.5	42129.9	430.0	29671.1	6688.1	146791.4	14996.6	79962.6
湖 南	119179.0	30511.1	656.4	15100.7	9219.4	71062.2	7375.9	42713.7
广 东	299817.6	116532.6	1435.3	95636.2	6255.8	147376.5	13890.6	92415.3
广 西	59681.9	17685.4	927.8	11984.7	2234.5	34378.6	2259.3	20483.3
海 南	27568.4	6469.5		4807.1	847.7	18141.5	558.0	13147.2
重 庆	100960.9	34628.9	208.2	30797.9	1153.5	59113.4	3442.9	38659.9
四 川	259246.9	91014.1	1407.2	73868.0	4514.6	147731.5	14199.6	99385.3
贵 州	39860.0	14927.3	272.4	11691.9	1912.4	21570.1	2413.0	12211.1
云 南	131775.7	24671.1	1261.5	15913.3	3814.4	95353.3	7740.0	48732.1
西 藏	17273.1	7899.4		1225.5	224.6	8946.8	678.6	4803.7
陕 西	211916.5	30652.6	1560.4	15856.3	10924.7	159513.1	15965.0	104466.8
甘 肃	87530.7	21384.6	76.0	12786.6	5295.5	56121.0	4114.8	32492.3
青 海	29705.5	5623.9	50.8	3343.0	879.4	22549.5	935.6	3474.8
宁 夏	22491.4	7863.5	363.1	5568.9	528.3	4179.2	1199.5	1115.8
新 疆	101649.1	17853.4	25.0	16063.9	669.6	77115.2	3395.8	48530.0

单位：万元

军队无军籍职工退休金	军队离退休人员其他费用	死亡丧葬费	护理费	遗属生活困难补助费		其他费用	军队移交政府离退休干部管理机构	其他退役安置支出
					定期定量补助费			
589023.3	**487082.3**	**32797.2**	**41159.2**	**26658.8**	**10858.4**	**386467.1**	**664657.9**	**221693.4**
128736.1	146773.3	2878.7	9290.8	395.2	114.5	134208.6	398632.0	24781.7
8239.0	11627.0	600.7	1231.2	295.0	159.3	9500.1	6749.8	1205.2
26700.1	23005.9	2366.5	2116.5	4171.1	1387.4	14351.8	29052.6	3420.4
12020.1	6656.8	568.0	1409.6	1440.6	512.3	3238.6	5410.8	8667.8
4964.0	2997.3	439.8	14.8	693.4	350.5	1849.3	4655.4	4403.6
39835.4	19574.4	2694.9	1248.0	1430.6	1049.4	14200.9	21974.0	12938.5
12791.3	1027.4	280.2	66.6	156.4	34.7	524.2	6239.3	2976.2
9429.9	1717.0	261.0	300.2	280.0	67.6	875.8	4049.4	1213.2
23473.1	31457.7	1025.7	1549.4	113.4	100.5	28769.2	18039.2	4925.1
42275.5	24386.2	3830.8	2317.2	1350.3	675.4	16887.9	22420.5	17188.8
13985.2	18748.2	462.4	1452.7	436.2	230.9	16396.9	10366.0	8281.6
6067.3	10228.9	1158.1	1059.5	1224.4	420.0	6786.9	7050.5	6897.7
4335.9	4041.1	814.6	339.5	303.8	174.2	2583.2	9197.4	2728.8
4767.1	6131.6	192.9	177.9	171.9	69.5	5588.9	2167.8	2133.9
33781.6	37755.0	5209.2	7210.5	3138.0	1878.9	22197.3	20107.1	24365.2
14230.3	10161.7	1380.1	1605.2	1583.2	530.4	5593.2	7839.9	11605.3
28329.4	23502.8	1107.2	2446.1	1397.1	216.8	18552.4	11519.4	5359.8
15577.4	5395.2	800.4	967.4	1148.5	263.0	2478.9	10353.9	7251.8
28810.1	12260.5	883.4	536.1	346.1	192.0	10494.9	11012.5	24896.0
7205.1	4430.9	412.6	521.2	330.4	226.7	3166.7	4859.3	2758.6
2700.6	1735.7	15.3	29.2	102.0	47.1	1589.2	2096.0	861.4
9837.8	7172.8	525.4	254.6	478.7	81.0	5914.1	5597.0	1621.6
22761.6	11385.0	1862.5	913.3	1229.3	503.5	7379.9	13457.2	7044.1
3544.8	3401.2	137.1	306.1	168.0	55.1	2790.0	1584.0	1778.6
11388.8	27492.4	389.7	509.1	1304.0	205.1	25289.6	7128.3	4623.0
3464.5							259.5	167.4
26184.4	12896.9	1317.0	2021.3	1744.9	774.5	7813.7	10328.4	11422.4
14469.6	5044.3	451.5	1200.9	570.1	310.7	2821.8	3839.1	6186.0
9577.3	8561.8	75.8		123.4	0.8	8362.6	968.0	564.1
1683.3	180.6	71.2	18.5	49.7	5.1	41.2	2499.2	7949.5
17856.7	7332.7	584.5	45.8	483.1	221.5	6219.3	5204.4	1476.1

C-1-17续表4

地区	社会福利	儿童福利	老年人福利	假肢矫形
全 国	**5627554.5**	**548361.9**	**1927421.1**	**24712.1**
中央级	21450.1			
北 京	241851.5	22075.8	132646.3	905.2
天 津	78008.5	2052.8	26287.1	1637.4
河 北	190435.1	14936.1	78834.8	358.0
山 西	104541.5	11655.7	27940.4	828.7
内蒙古	162693.5	7653.1	70262.7	
辽 宁	137367.6	14190.9	34084.2	2.2
吉 林	60846.7	3939.4	12287.6	67.9
黑龙江	87461.9	6608.9	17036.7	551.8
上 海	167725.3	7433.1	57206.0	
江 苏	465334.7	25068.8	191650.3	467.3
浙 江	394537.7	14144.3	120592.7	2307.1
安 徽	183619.2	22601.4	54381.6	42.2
福 建	125550.9	5388.5	37443.3	32.7
江 西	147661.2	31175.1	44901.9	142.3
山 东	376390.5	20322.4	166105.5	6.5
河 南	192465.7	33887.0	31886.4	170.4
湖 北	214501.5	20356.6	65732.0	134.5
湖 南	237938.7	39433.5	55099.0	448.1
广 东	408948.2	49043.6	138986.8	4199.3
广 西	173703.1	22595.0	70692.3	3218.7
海 南	44953.9	2453.9	24077.3	
重 庆	153573.8	11381.3	32767.4	3639.1
四 川	373325.7	30867.9	104040.7	1763.3
贵 州	143976.5	19836.1	46308.8	54.0
云 南	131427.7	31955.2	34621.1	2.7
西 藏	21439.0	9991.7	1563.0	
陕 西	227329.9	13906.7	104878.7	1980.6
甘 肃	98806.2	15457.2	26941.6	173.7
青 海	60401.2	13624.7	34777.0	348.4
宁 夏	23133.8	4721.0	10780.3	
新 疆	176153.7	19604.2	72607.6	1230.0

单位：万元

假肢厂(站)专项拨款	其他经费	殡葬	补贴火化场经费	补贴殡葬类单位经费
10129.7	**14582.4**	**674587.0**	**289648.8**	**384938.2**
	905.2	20928.5	6436.6	14491.9
	1637.4	15693.7	1890.4	13803.3
358.0		35173.3	15179.5	19993.8
95.1	733.6	19342.0	17832.6	1509.4
		16766.4	3529.1	13237.3
	2.2	36643.5	18930.3	17713.2
	67.9	5646.7	1521.0	4125.7
410.1	141.7	5960.3	1589.8	4370.5
	467.3	68490.6	37091.2	31399.4
	2307.1	70779.5	33128.4	37651.1
	42.2	29692.2	16565.5	13126.7
	32.7	22008.0	13158.0	8850.0
142.3		5337.0	2551.6	2785.4
	6.5	21208.6	12642.7	8565.9
170.0	0.4	19305.1	12242.4	7062.7
10.0	124.5	26746.9	2932.7	23814.2
413.3	34.8	17663.6	3393.4	14270.2
3977.0	222.3	64798.5	20061.8	44736.7
	3218.7	21731.1	5916.1	15815.0
		5166.5	44.0	5122.5
	3639.1	24200.0	13445.3	10754.7
1762.3	1.0	38191.8	10127.4	28064.4
50.0	4.0	8652.4	4188.7	4463.7
2.3	0.4	19087.5	9684.2	9403.3
		1063.0	1063.0	
1965.6	15.0	21734.8	16315.0	5419.8
173.7		8180.3	1200.4	6979.9
	348.4	232.7	186.4	46.3
		176.8	15.7	161.1
600.0	630.0	23985.7	6785.6	17200.1

C-1-17续表5

地区	社会福利事业单位	社会福利院经费	在院人员生活费	儿童福利院经费	在院人员生活费	精神病人福利院经费
全 国	**1377526.4**	**559525.5**	**86840.9**	**157492.6**	**48408.7**	**180566.7**
中央级	21450.1					
北 京	18973.5	8393.3	712.2	2655.1	425.5	3885.6
天 津	13439.4	1882.1	378.7	2237.3		3764.1
河 北	32044.9	10074.1	1459.7	513.5	283.7	
山 西	19906.5	12851.0	1732.8	1348.7	848.5	
内蒙古	37904.6	13718.1	4156.0	3962.7	1360.0	7225.6
辽 宁	38813.6	20514.5	2934.0	2229.5	467.9	
吉 林	29529.1	11875.0	1595.7	1897.5	1669.7	9149.8
黑龙江	48798.1	8989.9	3508.2	4938.2	2022.2	19910.8
上 海	56739.2	36439.3	2054.8	5951.2	1871.7	10314.5
江 苏	110070.2	54472.6	6781.1	9753.3	997.3	23448.3
浙 江	138111.9	59784.1	2641.5	7360.8	838.0	2631.0
安 徽	43180.4	10418.1	2452.6	9019.9	3289.1	63.4
福 建	35470.1	13182.4	2975.3	2679.9	908.7	13416.7
江 西	22594.0	14221.5	2397.2	885.8	495.8	4345.0
山 东	59083.6	22849.0	4683.2	12160.2	5028.5	5263.8
河 南	62479.3	15297.7	3058.4	6738.7	2318.0	3158.9
湖 北	63130.7	41757.6	5142.2	9825.6	2449.7	593.6
湖 南	55167.9	22597.6	2029.3	4964.7	2905.4	5869.0
广 东	86678.4	61938.3	18731.4	9901.1	3141.5	5868.9
广 西	36622.1	15363.0	1267.4	4455.7	894.9	7139.8
海 南	2667.9	67.0	49.0	83.0	58.0	
重 庆	52563.0	17365.3	1956.2	10791.6	1785.7	13668.7
四 川	137630.7	33162.3	4339.7	10907.3	2991.4	9613.2
贵 州	33617.3	7717.2	1360.6	3474.5	1918.6	7601.6
云 南	17901.1	6751.3	576.8	975.1	217.0	2830.6
西 藏	8452.2	5814.1	715.8	2638.1	1817.0	
陕 西	31197.0	12137.7	3432.0	9055.9	1449.1	1330.9
甘 肃	15488.4	5129.2	1000.8	4442.6	820.2	3014.1
青 海	6096.0	1197.4	74.0	762.8	714.6	4112.4
宁 夏	7063.7	3389.0	365.2	2192.1	451.5	637.6
新 疆	34661.5	10175.8	2279.1	8690.2	3969.5	11708.8

单位：万元

在院人员生活费	补贴安置农场经费	其他社会福利单位	其他社会福利支出	社会救助	最低生活保障	城市最低生活保障	城市最低生活保障金
15472.4	**26008.0**	**453933.6**	**1074946.0**	**23473778.5**	**16508145.4**	**7192858.8**	**6797956.1**
		21450.1					
273.1		4039.5	46322.2	189310.7	107008.8	72044.6	69101.8
245.2		5555.9	18898.1	240289.3	162518.7	113512.3	102380.9
	105.8	21351.5	29088.0	729992.8	510635.1	208240.9	200451.2
		5706.8	24868.2	641175.8	487580.6	228096.4	223838.7
865.6		12998.2	30106.7	843269.6	644213.2	332371.7	324987.3
		16069.6	13633.2	747086.5	572908.7	394289.3	362788.7
585.6		6606.8	9376.0	651948.7	525980.4	366029.3	344077.4
1646.0	2999.3	11959.9	8506.1	1134486.3	868542.7	601098.2	508281.1
133.2		4034.2	46347.0	337321.5	156184.5	138790.2	133736.1
1530.7		22396.0	69587.5	861363.4	496858.1	135762.7	126296.4
35.6	1.0	68335.0	48602.2	512651.1	264382.6	44915.3	38542.3
20.3	112.0	23567.0	33721.4	987511.6	669277.7	281671.7	273088.3
1356.0	268.8	5922.3	25208.3	348290.4	206426.6	53547.5	50492.8
75.0		3141.7	43510.9	1010696.5	698154.9	355204.0	341434.1
1082.0		18810.6	109663.9	998124.5	678936.2	163875.6	151955.2
20.0	15537.4	21746.6	44737.5	1238963.2	901907.3	329212.6	323575.7
59.2		10953.9	38400.8	1179690.4	779099.1	391909.8	359843.0
317.0	81.0	21655.6	70126.6	1262120.1	872829.9	431434.5	422492.6
2315.2	87.3	8882.8	65241.6	968438.8	553022.4	159529.9	147947.6
618.3	295.0	9368.6	18843.9	843360.0	584525.3	144349.6	143968.0
		2517.9	10588.3	125418.3	76885.5	34118.6	33688.6
664.8		10737.4	29023.0	518833.2	245334.2	147530.6	140482.5
1666.4		83947.9	60831.3	1594515.8	1080056.8	490012.3	487363.8
871.3	5187.0	9637.0	35507.9	942113.8	786192.8	168125.7	160443.7
	1191.4	6152.7	27860.1	1361550.6	1147559.5	386222.6	383896.4
			369.1	87390.9	65987.5	25869.8	24773.9
198.2		8672.5	53632.1	925296.0	631097.5	245305.7	221588.8
54.7	142.0	2760.5	32565.0	981764.8	801649.2	251384.2	249420.1
		23.4	5322.4	252857.6	174348.2	96319.0	82437.8
116.0		845.0	392.0	202582.2	157439.5	62475.5	55198.3
723.0		4086.7	24064.7	755364.1	600601.9	339608.7	309383.0

C-1-17续表6

地　区	城市最低生活保障对象临时补助	农村最低生活保障	农村最低生活保障金	农村最低生活保障对象临时补助	临时救助合计	临时救助	流浪乞讨人员救助
全　国	**394902.7**	**9315286.6**	**8934745.1**	**380541.5**	**1061717.5**	**656943.5**	**404774.0**
中央级							
北　京	2942.8	34964.2	34332.2	632.0	31545.2	9507.0	22038.2
天　津	11131.4	49006.4	45147.0	3859.4	16614.2	13076.2	3538.0
河　北	7789.7	302394.2	293874.7	8519.5	28444.6	16182.4	12262.2
山　西	4257.7	259484.2	252338.3	7145.9	22497.2	13564.5	8932.7
内蒙古	7384.4	311841.5	302808.1	9033.4	29233.6	22921.1	6312.5
辽　宁	31500.6	178619.4	167172.3	11447.1	34729.8	16148.7	18581.1
吉　林	21951.9	159951.1	146614.7	13336.4	13671.5	6596.6	7074.9
黑龙江	92817.1	267444.5	232907.3	34537.2	40041.3	32774.1	7267.2
上　海	5054.1	17394.3	16793.6	600.7	32667.1	16024.6	16642.5
江　苏	9466.3	361095.4	342018.1	19077.3	51316.4	30037.4	21279.0
浙　江	6373.0	219467.3	206308.9	13158.4	53263.0	33927.1	19335.9
安　徽	8583.4	387606.0	377027.9	10578.1	40092.2	23239.6	16852.6
福　建	3054.7	152879.1	144911.3	7967.8	20373.3	10586.6	9786.7
江　西	13769.9	342950.9	338766.7	4184.2	21368.9	11290.4	10078.5
山　东	11920.4	515060.6	489090.7	25969.9	56677.3	38829.0	17848.3
河　南	5636.9	572694.7	561687.6	11007.1	35299.9	17512.3	17787.6
湖　北	32066.8	387189.3	337064.5	50124.8	57940.9	34087.3	23853.6
湖　南	8941.9	441395.4	429482.1	11913.3	49857.0	27316.8	22540.2
广　东	11582.3	393492.5	375945.1	17547.4	57594.7	18718.9	38875.8
广　西	381.6	440175.7	438600.7	1575.0	22245.6	9983.1	12262.5
海　南	430.0	42766.9	41826.2	940.7	8218.2	3724.5	4493.7
重　庆	7048.1	97803.6	91471.6	6332.0	62663.0	49711.8	12951.2
四　川	2648.5	590044.5	583843.7	6200.8	57442.2	27448.0	29994.2
贵　州	7682.0	618067.1	589037.0	29030.1	23366.6	13980.1	9386.5
云　南	2326.2	761336.9	756154.6	5182.3	33055.9	27622.5	5433.4
西　藏	1095.9	40117.7	39337.7	780.0	1530.5	906.8	623.7
陕　西	23716.9	385791.8	355229.5	30562.3	64579.8	52220.9	12358.9
甘　肃	1964.1	550265.0	549871.9	393.1	35161.1	28911.3	6249.8
青　海	13881.2	78029.2	63578.0	14451.2	22068.0	20331.5	1736.5
宁　夏	7277.2	94964.0	86365.8	8598.2	9360.8	8006.6	1354.2
新　疆	30225.7	260993.2	245137.3	15855.9	28797.7	21755.8	7041.9

单位：万元

流浪乞讨人员救助单位经费	流浪乞讨人员救助经费	特困人员供养	城市“三无”救助	农村特困供养	农村特困集中供养	农村特困集中供养保障金
166574.9	**238199.1**	**2149238.6**	**49961.9**	**2099276.7**	**828664.3**	**803321.3**
4050.4	17987.8	6134.6	1062.2	5072.4	2013.0	1901.9
873.4	2664.6	12250.7	184.8	12065.9	1397.3	1357.8
3625.1	8637.1	87009.4	218.3	86791.1	27733.9	26487.7
3198.6	5734.1	50977.1	338.3	50638.8	12555.4	12217.7
3171.3	3141.2	50369.5	10534.9	39834.6	12358.1	12278.8
12472.8	6108.3	60068.0	1262.5	58805.5	19733.7	18835.0
1861.4	5213.5	29446.5	849.3	28597.2	10028.2	9109.5
3175.5	4091.7	69513.2	99.1	69414.1	28930.3	27701.5
13324.2	3318.3	2057.6		2057.6	951.3	884.5
8131.9	13147.1	129206.2	2572.2	126634.0	65278.6	63526.0
8692.5	10643.4	29388.2	789.7	28598.5	28136.4	27157.2
3817.2	13035.4	137323.1	1327.9	135995.2	62555.6	62118.7
3839.9	5946.8	53218.7	492.9	52725.8	6990.5	6771.2
3544.9	6533.6	84109.7	2057.0	82052.7	48333.6	47789.5
9339.9	8508.4	106006.9	1996.8	104010.1	79896.8	77133.0
6056.3	11731.3	157595.3	1984.1	155611.2	66802.0	66285.8
11237.1	12616.5	115837.4	3183.9	112653.5	35594.2	31862.9
6308.3	16231.9	165051.6	1449.7	163601.9	53178.0	52198.4
18715.5	20160.3	176903.7	4323.6	172580.1	25103.9	23579.0
4713.0	7549.5	83182.3	114.2	83068.1	12765.2	12367.1
1579.8	2913.9	14277.7	62.4	14215.3	2494.9	2411.9
4913.9	8037.3	95902.6	8075.3	87827.3	35607.0	34430.6
9060.3	20933.9	187547.9	1577.6	185970.3	109936.3	109047.5
4641.9	4744.6	26721.5	1201.0	25520.5	12719.1	11837.5
1716.8	3716.6	38264.6	758.3	37506.3	11249.5	10946.8
192.2	431.5	5236.6	273.5	4963.1	3001.5	2876.6
5959.9	6399.0	83936.5	2166.7	81769.8	34720.0	32166.0
3158.7	3091.1	51402.8	244.1	51158.7	6840.5	6834.0
57.0	1679.5	9885.5	64.5	9821.0	1785.9	1494.8
926.1	428.1	5897.1	8.5	5888.6	2946.4	2851.4
4219.1	2822.8	24516.1	688.6	23827.5	7027.2	6861.0

C-1-17续表7

地 区	农村特困集中供养临时补助	农村特困分散供养	农村特困分散供养保障金	农村特困分散供养临时补助	其他社会救助	其他城市生活救助(含传统救济)	其他农村生活救助(含传统救济)
全 国	**25343.0**	**1270612.4**	**1234844.7**	**35767.7**	**717987.3**	**328056.0**	**389931.3**
中央级							
北 京	111.1	3059.4	2859.6	199.8	22329.8	16330.6	5999.2
天 津	39.5	10668.6	10295.6	373.0	6485.8	4445.7	2040.1
河 北	1246.2	59057.2	57692.5	1364.7	4654.4	1411.3	3243.1
山 西	337.7	38083.4	37859.2	224.2	3802.1	1294.6	2507.5
内蒙古	79.3	27476.5	27288.4	188.1	40005.0	9983.4	30021.6
辽 宁	898.7	39071.8	37949.7	1122.1	14229.1	8718.6	5510.5
吉 林	918.7	18569.0	18237.7	331.3	4059.5	2933.9	1125.6
黑龙江	1228.8	40483.8	38386.3	2097.5	14904.2	9029.7	5874.5
上 海	66.8	1106.3	966.1	140.2	117566.8	112032.8	5534.0
江 苏	1752.6	61355.4	59549.2	1806.2	58097.0	29021.1	29075.9
浙 江	979.2	462.1	450.7	11.4	61149.5	15049.1	46100.4
安 徽	436.9	73439.6	72964.9	474.7	12634.4	5743.9	6890.5
福 建	219.3	45735.3	44468.2	1267.1	10926.3	2200.9	8725.4
江 西	544.1	33719.1	33168.6	550.5	25318.2	10264.5	15053.7
山 东	2763.8	24113.3	22965.3	1148.0	8679.8	6563.3	2116.5
河 南	516.2	88809.2	87991.1	818.1	18048.0	5360.3	12687.7
湖 北	3731.3	77059.3	67374.1	9685.2	71441.0	28813.7	42627.3
湖 南	979.6	110423.9	108768.2	1655.7	18409.7	6196.7	12213.0
广 东	1524.9	147476.2	144613.9	2862.3	14024.9	7058.9	6966.0
广 西	398.1	70302.9	69376.6	926.3	62384.8	2124.3	60260.5
海 南	83.0	11720.4	11277.2	443.2	561.2	268.9	292.3
重 庆	1176.4	52220.3	49923.1	2297.2	23380.1	8611.5	14768.6
四 川	888.8	76034.0	75538.7	495.3	31260.1	5135.1	26125.0
贵 州	881.6	12801.4	12008.7	792.7	11928.0	2821.2	9106.8
云 南	302.7	26256.8	25661.4	595.4	15249.5	2709.3	12540.2
西 藏	124.9	1961.6	1918.6	43.0	480.2	233.6	246.6
陕 西	2554.0	47049.8	44335.4	2714.4	18618.4	9585.7	9032.7
甘 肃	6.5	44318.2	44112.3	205.9	3413.7	1174.1	2239.6
青 海	291.1	8035.1	7363.2	671.9	10006.1	7186.5	2819.6
宁 夏	95.0	2942.2	2800.6	141.6	3395.4	1478.9	1916.5
新 疆	166.2	16800.3	16679.6	120.7	10544.3	4273.9	6270.4

单位：万元

医疗救助	资助参加合作医疗	资助参加医疗保险	直接医疗救助	门诊救助	住院救助	优抚对象医疗补助
3036689.7	**367577.4**	**177257.7**	**2145715.3**	**237572.4**	**1908142.9**	**346139.3**
22292.3	660.1	3676.4	13357.5	6128.0	7229.5	4598.3
42419.9		6623.3	26701.1	403.2	26297.9	9095.5
99249.3	19655.5	2380.2	53341.2	5524.3	47816.9	23872.4
76318.8	9080.6	4815.7	54588.6	3222.9	51365.7	7833.9
79448.3	5789.4	4941.5	62436.7	3326.6	59110.1	6280.7
65150.9	9463.7	7383.4	39154.6	2473.4	36681.2	9149.2
78790.8	7673.9	4294.5	60547.7	13027.2	47520.5	6274.7
141484.9	12782.8	12141.5	110099.1	13809.7	96289.4	6461.5
28845.5	14.0	3703.1	23050.9	3275.4	19775.5	2077.5
125885.7	12155.6	4896.0	91372.1	14664.8	76707.3	17462.0
104467.8	2958.8	1813.1	84965.1	16438.2	68526.9	14730.8
128184.2	15504.7	6388.5	92365.9	9315.1	83050.8	13925.1
57345.5	6870.0	1608.4	42620.2	6644.1	35976.1	6246.9
181744.8	23697.9	9454.7	134920.6	20232.2	114688.4	13671.6
147824.3	19999.0	11067.6	77003.6	4059.8	72943.8	39754.1
126112.7	22634.6	6581.3	79036.0	2859.6	76176.4	17860.8
155372.0	18449.4	4392.0	119964.8	7044.7	112920.1	12565.8
155971.9	21338.4	9941.7	103414.6	24475.7	78938.9	21277.2
166893.1	13428.2	20026.8	112863.2	10451.0	102412.2	20574.9
91022.0	12614.1	1621.5	69934.8	1801.4	68133.4	6851.6
25475.7	1532.1	1795.4	20066.4	606.2	19460.2	2081.8
91553.3	5660.6	3968.1	65991.7	12173.3	53818.4	15932.9
238208.8	39291.9	18287.5	155724.5	17833.8	137890.7	24904.9
93904.9	12658.4	872.0	71028.8	1093.8	69935.0	9345.7
127421.1	36183.6	7584.3	73284.4	12200.0	61084.4	10368.8
14156.1	746.0	259.8	12650.6	2749.7	9900.9	499.7
127063.8	5933.4	890.8	109091.9	8938.6	100153.3	11147.7
90138.0	13754.6	4320.8	68129.6	3017.5	65112.1	3933.0
36549.8	3423.4	2665.0	28805.9	1468.5	27337.4	1655.5
26489.4	1882.4	1268.8	22295.7	3046.6	19249.1	1042.5
90904.1	11740.3	7594.0	66907.5	5267.1	61640.4	4662.3

C-1-17续表8

地 区	医疗救助	资助参加合作医疗	资助参加医疗保险	医疗救助	门诊救助	住院救助
全 国	**3036689.7**	**367577.4**	**177257.7**	**2145715.3**	**237572.4**	**1908142.9**
中央级						
北 京	22292.3	660.1	3676.4	13357.5	6128.0	7229.5
天 津	42419.9		6623.3	26701.1	403.2	26297.9
河 北	99249.3	19655.5	2380.2	53341.2	5524.3	47816.9
山 西	76318.8	9080.6	4815.7	54588.6	3222.9	51365.7
内蒙古	79448.3	5789.4	4941.5	62436.7	3326.6	59110.1
辽 宁	65150.9	9463.7	7383.4	39154.6	2473.4	36681.2
吉 林	78790.8	7673.9	4294.5	60547.7	13027.2	47520.5
黑龙江	141484.9	12782.8	12141.5	110099.1	13809.7	96289.4
上 海	28845.5	14.0	3703.1	23050.9	3275.4	19775.5
江 苏	125885.7	12155.6	4896.0	91372.1	14664.8	76707.3
浙 江	104467.8	2958.8	1813.1	84965.1	16438.2	68526.9
安 徽	128184.2	15504.7	6388.5	92365.9	9315.1	83050.8
福 建	57345.5	6870.0	1608.4	42620.2	6644.1	35976.1
江 西	181744.8	23697.9	9454.7	134920.6	20232.2	114688.4
山 东	147824.3	19999.0	11067.6	77003.6	4059.8	72943.8
河 南	126112.7	22634.6	6581.3	79036.0	2859.6	76176.4
湖 北	155372.0	18449.4	4392.0	119964.8	7044.7	112920.1
湖 南	155971.9	21338.4	9941.7	103414.6	24475.7	78938.9
广 东	166893.1	13428.2	20026.8	112863.2	10451.0	102412.2
广 西	91022.0	12614.1	1621.5	69934.8	1801.4	68133.4
海 南	25475.7	1532.1	1795.4	20066.4	606.2	19460.2
重 庆	91553.3	5660.6	3968.1	65991.7	12173.3	53818.4
四 川	238208.8	39291.9	18287.5	155724.5	17833.8	137890.7
贵 州	93904.9	12658.4	872.0	71028.8	1093.8	69935.0
云 南	127421.1	36183.6	7584.3	73284.4	12200.0	61084.4
西 藏	14156.1	746.0	259.8	12650.6	2749.7	9900.9
陕 西	127063.8	5933.4	890.8	109091.9	8938.6	100153.3
甘 肃	90138.0	13754.6	4320.8	68129.6	3017.5	65112.1
青 海	36549.8	3423.4	2665.0	28805.9	1468.5	27337.4
宁 夏	26489.4	1882.4	1268.8	22295.7	3046.6	19249.1
新 疆	90904.1	11740.3	7594.0	66907.5	5267.1	61640.4

单位：万元

优抚对象医疗补助	自然灾害生活救助	生活救济费	紧急抢救、安置、转移灾民支出	救灾储备	自然灾害灾后重建补助	其他救助
346139.3	**1485214.2**	**920698.3**	**84615.0**	**67017.2**	**303652.5**	**109231.2**
	19058.0		19058.0			
4598.3	4340.6	1227.0		1985.5	500.0	628.1
9095.5	1468.8	24.3		1444.5		
23872.4	37977.2	35998.7	618.9	455.0	425.0	479.6
7833.9	41607.6	36566.2	324.6	2608.4	569.8	1538.6
6280.7	45546.5	37171.0	124.7	593.1	4669.0	2988.7
9149.2	45235.2	16546.5		2456.3	23935.7	2296.7
6274.7	23891.1	16011.2	2807.9	248.0	4188.6	635.4
6461.5	30622.2	27726.7	101.0	1336.5	139.0	1319.0
2077.5	832.0					832.0
17462.0	24695.6	15064.3	140.1	679.9	1498.7	7312.6
14730.8	37955.5	26153.0	1583.8	4907.9	601.5	4709.3
13925.1	38823.3	29211.6	1092.8	1861.4	4580.5	2077.0
6246.9	35496.1	13667.6	1101.4	1062.6	8741.8	10922.7
13671.6	60781.4	39196.0	8880.0	3011.8	4742.3	4951.3
39754.1	24697.1	21786.3	27.3	458.2	446.5	1978.8
17860.8	31893.0	26295.2	601.5	1648.5	1468.2	1879.6
12565.8	98076.3	73275.0	4118.7	3472.5	10415.8	6794.3
21277.2	56585.6	42577.3	3318.0	716.9	5007.2	4966.2
20574.9	51051.2	23829.3	2774.6	4751.0	13213.3	6483.0
6851.6	54284.8	30222.0	2133.2	2831.5	15444.1	3654.0
2081.8	17857.7	12868.9	36.1	1175.8	2252.5	1524.4
15932.9	37817.3	28177.8	1712.1	2051.0	4110.0	1766.4
24904.9	104505.1	80044.0	3555.4	3186.2	12540.5	5179.0
9345.7	80434.3	54894.2	3824.3	2318.9	7875.8	11521.1
10368.8	196844.1	65769.1	2579.5	1134.6	114757.4	12603.5
499.7	19555.0	4381.9	12992.0	1670.6	41.2	469.3
11147.7	65003.2	44209.1	3794.2	3990.4	7309.4	5700.1
3933.0	58828.5	54102.0	443.6	978.7	1785.7	1518.5
1655.5	18329.5	5564.3	20.0	11941.8	41.0	762.4
1042.5	22038.7	19310.8	816.6	596.1	461.3	853.9
4662.3	99081.7	38827.0	6034.7	1443.6	51890.7	885.7

C-1-17续表9

地 区	民政管理事务	行政运行	一般行政管理事务	机关服务	拥军优属
全 国	**3996486.2**	**947561.5**	**191378.1**	**23025.5**	**226240.2**
中央级	72069.8	8316.5	18885.9	380.8	302.9
北 京	185927.9	33839.7	4552.0	1820.5	7531.9
天 津	186918.0	19158.7	28834.9	250.1	8424.6
河 北	100835.0	48070.6	3577.4	218.8	4899.8
山 西	75285.6	18334.3	3015.5	187.1	2994.5
内蒙古	94107.4	30745.7	2520.1	784.3	3693.8
辽 宁	241886.4	62287.6	6120.3	657.0	6958.2
吉 林	79903.8	11337.0	1785.2	109.8	2121.3
黑龙江	58034.4	12090.7	2351.9	323.1	1381.7
上 海	143389.5	20780.2			18087.5
江 苏	239760.2	57869.8	9220.2	1018.8	19683.1
浙 江	236926.2	58279.5	10133.5	926.8	14718.4
安 徽	79831.2	24621.5	3407.0	680.6	6128.1
福 建	85759.9	19445.5	4379.1	173.5	7782.8
江 西	57822.0	15413.7	5152.6	647.9	1432.7
山 东	188195.5	48073.9	6719.6	1713.0	15253.0
河 南	117263.5	35483.0	5125.1	2584.7	10623.1
湖 北	174746.7	34481.5	14305.6	857.6	5606.9
湖 南	137167.1	37009.1	8732.6	2060.8	4894.1
广 东	301490.5	63746.5	9069.7	1682.2	28236.7
广 西	125808.1	28303.9	5997.6	429.8	8552.7
海 南	37205.9	5829.2	1927.3	69.9	3913.7
重 庆	123741.6	19874.4	3931.7	813.3	4663.9
四 川	226877.8	65440.0	7295.1	1154.3	10350.4
贵 州	107073.6	41838.3	2815.5	57.7	5750.7
云 南	157863.8	41628.3	7285.2	1765.8	7555.7
西 藏	12753.6	4457.8	957.0	10.0	889.5
陕 西	150896.4	22705.2	2697.6	820.8	3162.7
甘 肃	40942.7	17089.6	1077.1	356.5	1322.5
青 海	31345.5	5004.5	849.5	46.3	702.8
宁 夏	34448.1	8291.3	2070.6		1074.0
新 疆	90208.5	27714.0	6585.7	423.7	7546.5

单位：万元

老龄事务	民间组织管理	行政区划和地名管理	基层政权和社区建设	部队供应	其他民政管理事务支出
335401.1	**78349.3**	**120698.0**	**1059137.2**	**50107.3**	**964588.0**
1598.2	21035.2	4755.0	442.5		16352.8
8179.3	3026.5	1017.3	66601.8	831.9	58527.0
2283.9	1395.2	338.7	106329.6	166.1	19736.2
4330.2	885.3	5637.9	12857.6	2522.0	17835.4
2548.9	172.5	4937.6	21344.2	1013.4	20737.6
1312.5	100.2	3265.3	5392.3	1089.2	45204.0
5112.6	881.0	4595.8	130906.3	1904.9	22462.7
2151.5	157.2	2166.7	24411.0	1226.8	34437.3
2843.9	369.3	3129.5	18567.6	687.8	16288.9
26508.0	8462.6	193.7	5924.7	1399.4	62033.4
28932.9	6424.2	3504.8	60332.6	1503.1	51270.7
34678.8	7795.8	6410.3	45907.0	2781.3	55294.8
6918.4	1341.8	2176.9	15518.3	1395.5	17643.1
6300.6	757.9	3185.5	14322.7	1124.4	28287.9
11423.5	240.2	2283.3	7950.7	1050.2	12227.2
4165.1	2266.8	6380.8	60949.2	4883.1	37791.0
6428.3	833.3	6480.1	19549.1	2787.2	27369.6
7043.5	687.5	4041.4	54283.6	2779.9	50659.2
6823.9	2397.1	7725.1	34490.3	1451.6	31582.5
18242.1	11445.0	5837.1	86509.5	3313.6	73408.1
10902.7	410.0	4730.1	38125.7	2494.3	25861.3
3143.8	264.1	901.0	4721.8	1086.2	15348.9
4547.5	434.3	2739.7	39626.3	1048.0	46062.5
25139.5	4284.8	7956.0	57887.4	1587.7	45782.6
8067.6	168.9	2086.6	13195.6	1755.9	31336.8
41439.6	756.2	6866.6	13588.1	1975.7	35002.6
226.0	8.3	2471.7	261.2	132.2	3339.9
28117.0	596.3	2764.0	70110.3	1200.2	18722.3
2129.8	177.5	3112.0	965.6	322.2	14389.9
4209.8	122.1	2755.8	10443.6	2629.9	4581.2
1241.0	208.2	1601.5	7163.8	60.0	12737.7
18410.7	244.0	4650.2	10457.2	1903.6	12272.9

C-1-17续表10

地 区	行政事业单位离退休	地方离退休人员经费	离休人员离休金	退休人员退休金	退职人员退职金	离退休人员其他费用
全 国	**501099.2**	**134711.0**	**8909.3**	**109940.4**	**2981.8**	**12879.5**
中央级	6302.9					
北 京	60898.0	35922.2	259.5	31664.9	457.3	3540.5
天 津	3781.8	2585.5	72.6	1960.9	22.2	529.8
河 北	27572.6	7945.1	1253.5	6172.9	108.2	410.5
山 西	10972.8	2128.6	197.5	1624.7	35.5	270.9
内蒙古	18345.6	1472.7	67.7	1240.6	49.0	115.4
辽 宁	26200.8	4972.3	454.4	3439.8	838.0	240.1
吉 林	9658.9	2387.4	337.4	1999.9	11.6	38.5
黑龙江	11056.0	182.6	8.3	174.3		
上 海	6080.9	1332.6	92.8	956.8		283.0
江 苏	27394.5	14267.0	1725.6	10235.0	209.4	2097.0
浙 江	24347.0	7362.2	354.3	6164.5	159.1	684.3
安 徽	16394.4	3561.6	583.3	2178.8	195.6	603.9
福 建	22707.3	10607.9	254.7	9742.6	123.2	487.4
江 西	11702.8	4966.4	301.3	4160.9	141.1	363.1
山 东	15396.2	4188.3	530.2	3172.5	37.1	448.5
河 南	22003.4	5346.9	697.7	4047.4	22.5	579.3
湖 北	19768.3	5196.9	449.3	4140.0	107.8	499.8
湖 南	8227.1	3329.5	189.0	2944.7	71.9	123.9
广 东	41977.2	2834.2	267.6	2076.0	185.9	304.7
广 西	17240.5	590.5	8.0	534.1		48.4
海 南	5243.0	453.8	18.4	422.4		13.0
重 庆	12364.6	492.9	1.9	428.2		62.8
四 川	29264.9	4926.6	175.5	4024.6	158.6	567.9
贵 州	1430.7	1290.9	57.8	1233.1		
云 南	16204.8	2606.2	168.7	2018.0		419.5
西 藏	1141.9	177.0		177.0		
陕 西	10016.7	1074.1	174.2	796.1	13.2	90.6
甘 肃	5608.3	1237.6	127.2	1079.6	13.0	17.8
青 海	2175.9	218.1	45.1	135.5	0.6	36.9
宁 夏	3401.6	21.0			21.0	
新 疆	6217.8	1032.4	35.8	994.6		2.0

单位：万元

一次性抚恤金	行政单位离退休	事业单位离退休	离退休人员管理机构	其他行政事业单位离退休支出	其他
7252.2	**201014.1**	**135130.5**	**3523.5**	**26720.1**	**1485487.2**
	4386.2	1410.9	505.8		25649.2
2401.7	13190.2	3418.9	1405.9	6960.8	176369.4
150.5	452.0	456.4	99.6	188.3	84370.9
249.4	8609.2	10488.3	30.0	500.0	8033.7
256.9	4127.9	4603.5	83.2	29.6	11772.7
91.8	11079.0	5710.0		83.9	53093.2
98.6	8660.3	8287.7		4280.5	63692.8
23.7	2577.7	4039.4		654.4	19748.8
	2820.8	7964.9		87.7	2846.8
163.1	4150.5	566.9		30.9	6984.9
1085.9	7812.1	4638.4	32.4	644.6	131620.1
78.8	10502.2	5467.5	110.1	905.0	56947.0
333.1	7349.0	2716.3	67.6	2699.9	44852.1
371.4	8187.4	2722.5	3.0	1186.5	38764.8
156.0	4086.3	2106.0	33.5	510.6	8072.5
298.7	3369.1	7836.1		2.7	42017.8
334.1	8326.2	7927.9	39.1	363.3	56357.3
319.3	8084.7	5169.2	456.9	860.6	25770.6
69.8	3525.8	1082.1		289.7	27686.8
74.8	19973.8	18238.1	115.8	815.3	165357.3
32.5	7796.9	8566.7		286.4	41973.5
13.0	4238.6	127.3	423.3		12515.0
58.5	7546.1	1865.8	53.3	2406.5	17509.3
115.7	15681.9	6705.7	13.0	1937.7	40920.3
	139.8				11345.4
413.0	9399.4	3434.2	0.2	764.8	113148.4
	291.5	673.4			8819.5
17.8	3563.5	5265.4	10.8	102.9	16813.1
17.8	2897.4	1408.6	40.0	24.7	31217.2
26.3	1426.2	531.6			49996.6
	2634.5	648.4		97.7	87749.8
	4127.9	1052.4		5.1	3470.4

C-1-18 支出水

地 区	优抚对象整体抚恤水平	定期抚恤水平	伤残抚恤	定期补助水平	在乡复退军人定期定量补助水平
全 国	**6953.95**	**13159.56**	**17645.81**	**2983.39**	**2745.15**
中央级					
北 京	27268.41	25853.05	15725.84	3726.46	3198.31
天 津	13240.10	22734.94	19944.46	6497.20	6219.19
河 北	5539.03	13712.92	16258.84	2272.17	2050.44
山 西	10007.28	11114.15	15876.32	3055.89	3231.72
内蒙古	18405.86	14465.80	14689.84	5075.14	5278.85
辽 宁	7596.53	12943.26	15614.03	2465.15	2861.14
吉 林	9578.44	15429.81	18829.60	2801.51	2697.16
黑龙江	7397.18	14773.05	14732.49	3611.49	3689.97
上 海	23464.74	11543.63	25101.99	4544.41	3777.18
江 苏	8794.55	16927.02	20335.61	2898.74	3057.13
浙 江	8111.62	22693.15	19429.70	2852.11	2548.80
安 徽	6010.20	12516.17	17291.47	2963.50	2848.33
福 建	6998.38	14663.07	17130.43	2876.66	2135.10
江 西	6875.12	13136.73	17127.52	3571.12	3974.21
山 东	7777.56	13964.92	23037.44	2496.29	2375.09
河 南	5631.56	11524.62	15557.08	2399.76	2034.67
湖 北	6783.01	11466.53	16091.05	3250.44	3072.72
湖 南	4885.01	11084.23	17329.41	2644.59	2249.39
广 东	7614.25	15994.15	17702.10	3894.05	2637.86
广 西	5250.65	13918.39	16024.54	2906.56	2838.62
海 南	8237.18	12347.10	16127.77	3148.49	3288.93
重 庆	6592.48	12961.87	16961.92	3803.85	3687.02
四 川	5821.72	11934.68	15616.00	3501.17	3246.57
贵 州	6208.28	12340.78	14763.22	3485.24	2970.98
云 南	5469.87	12728.61	17023.55	2302.02	2140.05
西 藏	13050.57	14071.01	8920.90	6559.04	10012.35
陕 西	8754.24	12969.20	15842.79	3897.88	3771.99
甘 肃	4891.74	13169.10	15540.02	2075.18	1355.27
青 海	11271.20	15929.79	10537.40	3282.68	2900.54
宁 夏	10113.36	13473.17	14451.39	3169.66	3435.84
新 疆	14481.63	10182.83	18226.17	6649.24	7182.70

平情况

单位：元/人·年、元/个·年

在乡红军老战士定期定量补助费水平	红军失散人员定期定量补助水平	“参战”退伍军人生活补贴水平	“涉核”退伍军人生活补助水平	烈士纪念建筑物管理单位补助水平
40049.79	**18453.34**	**4597.54**	**5494.54**	**631161.20**
56000.00		8696.62	10605.46	922200.00
		9431.72	10196.72	3050888.89
		4619.18	5324.05	439510.20
41666.67	17000.00	5073.80	4780.47	791310.34
40750.00	19000.00	5644.87	7052.24	3748111.11
50000.00		4236.23	5401.59	395260.87
	19000.00	6489.60	5508.21	508800.00
42166.67	19636.36	4709.45	4241.94	247500.00
		11190.00	10122.30	5734727.27
	19000.00	5434.26	7985.51	1077575.00
	19291.67	6187.66	6293.71	776852.94
	16709.36	4765.89	5049.87	541386.36
	18516.48	6827.15	8212.60	517857.14
40571.43	17750.88	6001.82	7516.23	277088.24
		4641.67	4911.48	679513.04
42333.33	19182.65	4363.91	4393.45	499838.38
41000.00	19055.72	4722.57	5173.50	500196.43
42000.00	18901.85	3790.51	9390.60	454000.00
	19970.59	6070.99	5939.76	375342.34
	18940.00	5123.44	5876.06	457916.67
	18222.22	3318.07	7393.94	480875.00
		4073.01	6852.75	327850.00
42046.51	18983.92	4875.55	5312.65	176687.50
42000.00	19166.67	4263.48	5099.53	380400.00
	19333.33	2520.84	7491.23	802047.62
36300.00	16500.00			14681.82
42211.54	18556.39	4561.15	4667.41	550425.00
42500.00	19500.00	4502.36	5914.10	212126.58
		6039.47	4083.45	368571.43
43000.00	18000.00	4353.30	4702.78	194777.78
43600.00	19000.00	7221.33	6416.06	2534666.67

C-1-18续表1

地　区	荣誉军人康复医院补助水平	荣誉军人康复医院在院人员补助水平	复员军人疗养院补助水平	复员军人疗养院在院人员补助水平	复退军人精神病院补助水平
全　国	**17401108.70**	**15896.32**	**10112361.11**	**12831.06**	**12058593.02**
中央级					
北　京					
天　津			5031000.00	1375.00	22302000.00
河　北	5224000.00		6607375.00	1468.19	14194500.00
山　西	4745666.67	18739.88	37435000.00	40043.71	8503714.29
内蒙古	20660000.00		150000.00		7203000.00
辽　宁	15171000.00				7915000.00
吉　林	24031500.00				1156666.67
黑龙江	26207000.00	17300.41			17556000.00
上　海	11412000.00	21066.67			
江　苏	38680000.00		5056250.00	11128.96	81745000.00
浙　江	63881000.00				63557000.00
安　徽	5186000.00				100000.00
福　建	1906000.00	16875.32			18068750.00
江　西	33898000.00	18798.51	479000.00	5175.84	55000.00
山　东	72314500.00	5134.02	22194285.71	14842.91	12292916.67
河　南	12968500.00	18166.26	6529500.00	20074.47	30793000.00
湖　北	34258000.00	29200.00	300000.00		14108500.00
湖　南	4951000.00		500000.00		5363625.00
广　东	15086500.00	8931.02	20158000.00	19644.59	10658625.00
广　西	20226000.00		8334000.00		20104000.00
海　南					
重　庆	7331666.67	18081.53			
四　川	18172200.00	14535.41	884500.00	4769.45	13231200.00
贵　州	5618333.33	11371.48			
云　南	21582000.00				839500.00
西　藏					
陕　西	44340000.00	206360.54	9249666.67	49038.22	16216666.67
甘　肃	3445000.00				1357000.00
青　海					
宁　夏	5021000.00				
新　疆	6528000.00	63515.08			90000.00

单位：元/个·年、元/人·年

复退军人精神病院在院人员补助水平	光荣院补助水平	光荣院在院人员补助水平	军队离休干部支出水平	军队退休干部支出水平	军队无军籍职工支出水平	孤儿补助水平
4429.16	**775235.08**	**6631.49**	**210481.22**	**102455.79**	**48624.16**	**10921.26**
	3483200.00	39531.51	126183.17	107194.66	54335.08	102582.71
6267.38	5130500.00	9494.17	120930.61	103739.16	47214.90	23814.39
	954038.76	5978.45	226001.89	118139.42	48064.99	9300.19
3363.20	850397.73	15110.77	154242.56	146819.41	47907.93	8605.17
2171.03	1138607.14	8960.95	154555.56	117463.83	43620.39	13849.26
1306.45	1471800.00	11153.26	763630.43	59723.43	48758.14	18365.34
67805.82	563920.00	3241.46	279134.39	86461.83	40594.41	7581.60
5572.56	227552.63	4779.52	522426.83	79558.04	47601.72	8853.18
			108909.59	106116.92	55782.08	37846.74
	1475125.00	12610.65	130140.03	119577.84	67586.73	14170.37
	651750.00	21217.16	128201.23	88861.18	59259.32	29302.47
	1293680.00	10098.17	135750.00	114105.23	43091.62	8373.06
9729.73	580076.92	8037.16	165084.86	114945.02	35952.74	8962.91
25550.00	269163.84	2530.17	171835.58	90999.07	32696.16	13476.46
8509.76	1233904.76	10484.78	150970.75	106322.68	55680.90	11590.28
9222.63	475318.18	5899.33	137177.83	107233.46	39051.32	7833.15
4062.90	850467.74	5991.30	159878.46	111835.80	49080.73	8587.83
2126.58	1031323.81	7907.26	92662.06	87064.21	34432.80	9041.06
5900.86	536688.89	13009.13	275061.39	125003.79	48608.23	12625.46
1262.42	274306.45	3689.68	146707.79	108722.40	53849.78	9568.48
	390777.78	15635.83	136097.56	176000.00	17524.98	14999.39
	3354714.29	17891.89	222122.58	104655.93	51211.87	10267.30
1377.26	623764.71	6368.75	207293.43	105538.18	41167.66	10398.83
	234045.45	5564.68	131857.92	104996.56	48163.04	9424.67
	40000.00	1367.04	103475.94	79653.64	24361.07	13425.43
			17625.97	201836.13	90221.35	17233.01
33915.91	1461687.50	11836.24	189608.08	111466.92	45200.07	11112.03
	35000.00	687.02	113043.96	83527.76	41663.12	7500.58
			935600.00	41465.39	67493.31	8375.15
	40666.67	5955.26	292560.98	17166.15	51320.12	6851.96
	1355913.04	3564.41	232589.04	134283.34	55283.90	8506.92

C-1-18续表2

地 区	康复辅具机构(站)专项拨款支出水平	补贴火化场人员水平	补贴殡葬类单位补助水平	社会福利院补助水平	社会福利院在院人员生活费补助水平
全 国	**4220708.33**	**630.35**	**849753.20**	**3256842.26**	**5671.16**
中央级					
北 京		703.59	2683685.19	9325888.89	4189.21
天 津		278.85	4929750.00	9410500.00	12137.82
河 北	3580000.00	801.27	1123247.19	2878314.29	4890.18
山 西	951000.00	8284.21	228696.97	6763684.21	6285.09
内蒙古		520.30	1018253.85	2689823.53	10572.50
辽 宁		683.90	503215.91	3798981.48	4789.65
吉 林		153.79	282582.19	1979166.67	3254.25
黑龙江	4101000.00	90.73	309964.54	1549982.76	4761.03
上 海				16563318.18	4843.18
江 苏		737.91	1231349.02	8511343.75	7419.67
浙 江		1037.55	1673382.22	6498271.74	2395.83
安 徽		620.59	805319.02	1965679.25	6946.85
福 建		670.56	560126.58	1997333.33	9105.59
江 西	1423000.00	381.62	219322.83	1354428.57	4835.27
山 东		215.47	498017.44	8788076.92	14532.66
河 南	850000.00	767.91	275886.72	2832907.41	6904.97
湖 北	50000.00	133.39	1360811.43	3451041.32	4071.67
湖 南	4133000.00	415.68	692728.16	2789827.16	2252.78
广 东	19885000.00	445.21	1424735.67	4185020.27	10956.21
广 西		754.14	1464351.85	1688241.76	2916.71
海 南		146.81	3201562.50	167500.00	1441.23
重 庆		1715.84	911415.25	5788433.33	3413.44
四 川	17623000.00	490.31	885312.30	2493406.02	4232.22
贵 州	500000.00	516.57	301601.35	1456075.47	6332.26
云 南	23000.00	1424.63	563071.86	1687825.00	2647.36
西 藏		13986.84		785689.19	1964.31
陕 西	19656000.00	3001.67	467224.14	3793031.25	7894.30
甘 肃	1737000.00	644.89	883531.65	1005725.49	6237.03
青 海		277.26	12861.11	1330444.44	1515.46
宁 夏		43.43	41307.69	4236250.00	2705.79
新 疆	6000000.00	2379.24	1048786.59	1413305.56	5795.76

单位：元/个·年、元/人·年、元/人次

儿童福利院补助水平	儿童福利院在院人员生活费补助水平	精神病人福利院补助水平	精神病人福利院在院人员生活费补助水平	城市最低生活保障补助水平（不含春节补助）	农村最低生活保障补助水平（不含春节补助）	农村特困集中供养救助水平
3294824.27	**11552.96**	**11958059.60**	**4847.29**	**3996.22**	**1822.10**	**5104.85**
2655100.00	3660.11	38856000.00	95061.51	8143.04	7028.09	10958.08
11186500.00		37641000.00	4207.63	7832.98	4353.57	11983.70
733571.43	17311.79			3641.45	1428.24	5752.13
1685875.00	13563.93			3735.01	2060.41	5617.63
4953375.00	16194.44	14451200.00	9316.86	5392.12	2600.94	9599.27
2229500.00	1823.15			5051.84	2103.78	6209.86
1897500.00	46509.04	13071142.86	3648.85	4744.13	1783.05	4182.25
3292133.33	15219.40	28444000.00	18003.95	4235.70	1971.14	6772.39
19837333.33	16833.08	34381666.67	794.15	7613.78	5440.63	8767.74
7502538.46	5505.60	21316636.36	3847.90	4513.65	2979.39	7731.96
6134000.00	5905.52	13155000.00	811.69	5263.90	3634.58	8427.86
2909645.16	11839.73	211333.33	1621.76	4222.98	1920.39	4171.79
2436272.73	10974.09	10320538.46	6490.20	3899.75	2021.61	7644.07
1771600.00	44936.18	14483333.33	4009.29	3694.84	2001.19	3920.19
9354000.00	20456.34	26319000.00	36246.41	4081.30	2060.05	5600.82
3546684.21	8969.20	5264833.33	163.32	2998.61	1429.57	4041.53
4094000.00	13684.36	2968000.00	789.33	4251.69	2112.77	5976.49
2364142.86	16989.80	6521111.11	2856.32	3321.56	1351.13	5220.75
2675972.97	14349.83	19563000.00	16843.83	4982.58	2447.49	9655.35
3182642.86	14097.54	17849500.00	5001.86	3736.44	1501.33	4709.19
415000.00	17402.38			4012.98	2226.03	10292.49
17986000.00	20774.48	15187444.44	3490.84	3744.01	1819.85	5644.74
2057981.13	13684.78	5059578.95	2632.12	3117.04	1439.90	4108.72
1737250.00	13348.12	3455272.73	4183.76	3991.04	1770.46	2545.60
375038.46	1918.95	7076500.00		3913.01	1660.84	2700.31
2638100.00	7944.59			5331.85	1228.40	2580.16
8232636.36	7801.89	13309000.00	4424.11	4356.22	2197.50	7294.58
2338210.53	6438.35	10047000.00	2172.29	3273.01	1632.04	7347.48
1089714.29	9527.34	41124000.00		4676.47	2000.59	3594.08
4384200.00	11235.55	6376000.00	3618.80	3577.99	2069.22	7403.02
1889173.91	13325.79	14636000.00	6356.36	3576.19	1860.50	5650.24

C-1-18续表3

地 区	农村特困分散供养救助水平	流浪乞讨人员救助单位补助水平	救助流浪乞讨人员每次补助水平	临时救助户次补助水平	资助参加合作医疗补助水平	资助参加医疗保险补助水平
全 国	**3584.79**	**816143.56**	**634.84**	**1002.35**	**80.84**	**106.39**
中央级						
北 京	11703.90	1841090.91	337.12	4320.38	243.12	1224.20
天 津	9793.10	623857.14	570.27	1563.54		210.95
河 北	3285.12	575412.70	1063.98	899.49	69.41	121.89
山 西	2901.35	336694.74	593.83	680.04	83.74	97.62
内蒙古	3675.25	813153.85	642.85	909.73	66.31	79.96
辽 宁	3657.11	1889818.18	978.38	524.15	135.73	189.82
吉 林	2044.80	364980.39	1453.69	629.20	94.11	60.74
黑龙江	4490.77	407115.38	1239.87	1628.49	100.45	104.55
上 海	7307.13	6662100.00	1198.72	396.26	4000.00	425.66
江 苏	5410.72	913696.63	1136.99	713.11	107.23	226.20
浙 江	4046.41	1704411.76	1687.74	1375.59	145.56	217.18
安 徽	2694.56	779020.41	892.44	1393.90	83.54	95.96
福 建	6444.22	914261.90	643.89	1292.59	99.32	137.37
江 西	3484.96	337609.52	673.94	903.79	120.27	131.39
山 东	3465.95	1583033.90	757.94	1618.77	116.87	158.01
河 南	2767.46	680483.15	680.80	922.51	74.00	92.69
湖 北	3983.73	796957.45	339.15	939.88	85.04	50.34
湖 南	2890.75	432075.34	282.56	582.00	79.63	72.83
广 东	6886.68	2495400.00	923.95	965.64	129.50	144.77
广 西	2774.61	506774.19	574.47	1568.54	67.80	108.98
海 南	4445.10	1579800.00	569.48	1149.86	64.46	150.47
重 庆	5021.09	1293131.58	1413.35	2101.62	62.72	63.61
四 川	3347.24	406291.48	817.35	589.23	94.00	115.29
贵 州	2094.23	595115.38	586.91	805.83	47.05	32.52
云 南	1586.27	238444.44	682.62	875.52	68.91	79.21
西 藏	7143.48	274571.43	355.67	546.66	477.41	47.11
陕 西	5655.70	662211.11	753.68	2015.40	95.18	73.35
甘 肃	3979.97	526450.00	846.88	1369.45	39.89	66.61
青 海	4334.86	51818.18	784.12	3182.27	71.61	138.03
宁 夏	3306.59	661500.00	304.83	719.62	75.03	68.93
新 疆	2862.01	827274.51	1223.05	617.85	82.81	81.96

单位：元/个·年、元/人·年、元/人次

直接医疗救助补助水平	门诊救助人次补助水平	住院救助人次补助水平	优抚对象医疗补助支出水平	救灾物资储备中心补助水平	老龄机构补助水平	军供站补助水平
852.87	**181.14**	**1584.42**	**792.99**	**863623.71**	**1471057.46**	**847839.26**
1367.22	822.22	3120.47	3520.09	1167941.18	5842357.14	319961.54
1352.08	33.33	3436.60	3803.58	7222500.00	1631357.14	830500.00
1831.23	632.81	2344.10	1076.78	413636.36	902125.00	840666.67
2439.54	718.69	2870.84	816.13	457614.04	268305.26	1013400.00
2239.65	676.54	2574.39	1727.89	1977000.00	625000.00	1815333.33
559.06	74.33	997.81	1512.21	982520.00	751852.94	828217.39
749.17	300.88	1266.46	1042.76	354285.71	488977.27	278818.18
1595.99	441.46	2553.90	1178.31	1670625.00	305795.70	529076.92
867.27	170.07	2701.57	1467.26		13254000.00	636090.91
357.03	70.88	1564.47	678.94	1133166.67	4822150.00	791105.26
364.48	92.86	1221.57	1502.24	926018.87	4281333.33	1264227.27
1054.90	676.02	1125.67	566.14	2326750.00	1257890.91	317159.09
334.00	70.16	1093.10	840.08	506000.00	1016225.81	624666.67
804.69	168.71	2402.22	1229.06	2151285.71	993347.83	700133.33
2201.23	409.34	2910.29	822.04	654571.43	281425.68	2034625.00
993.04	290.27	1092.32	515.03	1648500.00	783939.02	929066.67
1125.25	420.09	1256.88	396.53	771666.67	951824.32	1853266.67
920.80	618.77	1085.01	440.31	512071.43	563958.68	537629.63
1084.08	148.35	3042.37	1051.46	709104.48	1824210.00	1744000.00
750.69	789.60	749.72	578.50	1665588.24	1847915.25	1467235.29
1647.45	96.96	3282.59	952.90	2939500.00	3929750.00	5431000.00
241.28	57.03	896.41	655.03	586000.00	1684259.26	238181.82
1035.77	412.32	1287.55	730.18	318620.00	1174742.99	529233.33
3217.26	942.28	3343.52	782.04	1656357.14	831711.34	1755900.00
865.98	588.60	955.96	639.80	1620857.14	6278727.27	705607.14
2634.94	9159.56	2199.76	2994.01	355446.81	452000.00	440666.67
2290.02	626.13	3002.01	1146.78	2100210.53	2811700.00	750125.00
1692.47	196.35	2616.31	954.96	212760.87	210871.29	322200.00
1784.61	466.84	2103.57	4042.74	1531000.00	1002333.33	5259800.00
723.94	170.65	1487.06	1698.44	541909.09	496400.00	600000.00
885.59	105.70	2396.58	3147.86	656181.82	833063.35	1189750.00

C-1-19 中央专项基本

地 区	建设规模(平方米)	地方配套资金合计	中央对地方投资合计	社区 发改投资[2015] 1318号				养 发改	
				建设规模	小计	中央投资	地方投资	建设规模	小计
全 国	**3428896**	**405315**	**320000**	**235078**	**45963**	**20000**	**25963**	**2977027**	**635104**
北 京									
天 津	13000	7770	1200					13000	8970
河 北	188156	18994	17984	12561	2706	1225	1481	165995	32352
山 西	112614	22170	10300	3038	608	300	308	109576	31862
内蒙古	87152	9800	11800	12710	3270	800	2470	68042	17010
辽 宁	109541	14184	10912	8850	1994	800	1194	99258	22962
吉 林	93729	12047	11316	8589	1696	800	896	80840	20807
黑龙江	126441	18260	12490	11615	3215	810	2405	100496	25041
上 海	7800	3864	1288					7800	5152
江 苏	118734	23653	4500					118734	28153
浙 江	89085	27127	5100					89085	32227
安 徽	190498	13557	15303	16034	2542	1200	1342	164285	24158
福 建	80504	12958	4855					80504	17813
江 西	242588	22218	14300	13564	2443	1200	1243	216524	31575
山 东	124609	23708	5300					124609	29008
河 南	170173	15413	17525	13061	2065	1200	865	145823	29113
湖 北	206448	14602	17300	18437	2310	1200	1110	175111	27042
湖 南	237696	29600	17300	26328	4667	1200	3467	197168	39358
广 东	81500	17081	4546					81500	21627
广 西	122017	10577	16200	11354	2100	800	1300	108163	24177
海 南	34870	5024	5100					34870	10124
重 庆	107618	13983	11526	12480	2258	800	1458	88598	22343
四 川	184220	21674	17600	10622	2519	1200	1319	161608	33809
贵 州	144985	12474	12740	8935	1666	800	866	123170	21221
云 南	86698	5006	12200	6740	1280	800	480	69758	13978
西 藏	31340		6050	5200	1300	1300		26140	4750
陕 西	147170	11670	11800	7860	1482	800	682	128760	19888
甘 肃	91080	4516	12200	8000	1440	800	640	71080	12876
青 海	38250	3235	7400	2400	800	400	400	29850	8275
宁 夏	40530	3784	5859	3450	800	220	580	30680	7553
新 疆	87250	3076	13206	13250	2802	1345	1457	66000	11880
兵 团	32600	3290	4800						

建设投资对账单

单位：平方米、万元

老 投资[2015]1327号		儿童 发改投资[2015] 1329号				养老 发改投资[2015]726号			
中央投资	地方投资	建设规模	小计	中央投资	地方投资	建设规模	小计	中央投资	地方投资
274170	**360934**	**175141**	**34798**	**20000**	**14798**	**41650**	**9650**	**5830**	**3620**
1200	7770								
15659	16693	9600	1920	1100	820				
10000	21862								
10000	7010	6400	1320	1000	320				
10000	12962	1433	140	112	28				
10000	10807	4300	860	516	344				
9850	15191	5280	1134	800	334	9050	1360	1030	330
1288	3864								
4500	23653								
5100	27127								
13303	10855	10179	2160	800	1360				
4855	12958								
12000	19575	12500	2500	1100	1400				
5300	23708								
15225	13888	11289	1760	1100	660				
15000	12042	12900	2550	1100	1450				
15000	24358	14200	2875	1100	1775				
4546	17081								
15000	9177	2500	500	400	100				
5100	5024								
10000	12343	6540	908	726	182				
15000	18809	11990	2946	1400	1546				
10540	10681	12880	2327	1400	927				
10000	3978	10200	1948	1400	548				
4750									
10000	9888	10550	2100	1000	1100				
10000	2876	12000	2400	1400	1000				
6000	2275	6000	1560	1000	560				
4639	2914	6400	1290	1000	290				
10315	1565	8000	1600	1546	54				
						32600	8290	4800	3290

C-1-20 社会服务事业基本

地 区	在建规模	使用彩票公益金项目规模	在建项目总投资	开工累计完成投资	本年计划投资	本年实际完成投资
全 国	**40873388**	**10267014**	**8829431.5**	**4502462.2**	**2171593.4**	**2399011.9**
中央级	279057	141888	157928.2	73562.7	43573.0	22738.9
北 京	275488	12798	252369.9	136247.0	34758.1	35496.4
天 津	243631	201216	131421.5	40301.4	27264.0	34430.8
河 北	898050	613653	152890.7	98026.6	52869.0	59191.3
山 西	172466	3801	71414.4	21491.5	12566.4	12738.5
内蒙古	380987	163013	178491.0	71796.2	27108.6	44228.0
辽 宁	316419	170573	109988.1	77925.5	24034.9	30567.4
吉 林	39768	17000	12327.1	6184.1	3129.0	6184.1
黑龙江	650804	7910	133360.7	33414.0	48170.0	33242.0
上 海	81690	4986	56279.8	36199.0	2510.5	9279.3
江 苏	4083545	622304	1491455.9	790121.2	330110.1	295501.1
浙 江	753935	415685	391512.7	179134.6	73595.9	79059.7
安 徽	1255966	227684	148059.9	97640.9	107230.4	85378.3
福 建	425220	110826	175446.8	91231.8	25484.8	30209.7
江 西	1691518	974429	314217.0	212506.2	132826.2	155626.2
山 东	2241194	907795	902900.4	417361.1	171332.3	180588.3
河 南	601122	233506	197709.3	112685.7	42541.6	60207.3
湖 北	2417947	565226	524041.5	306147.2	114091.3	156024.5
湖 南	987220	495276	268822.8	145769.2	65877.7	72364.5
广 东	881554	591222	622282.8	254617.6	102436.0	97289.5
广 西	1669386	719912	405120.6	112900.1	86740.9	71530.2
海 南	258579	127578	45226.3	22627.2	19308.5	21241.5
重 庆	1592497	880539	304934.4	203135.9	101603.2	123756.5
四 川	646994	201879	177261.7	87341.1	57183.7	50405.8
贵 州	2334372	524923	318130.1	176239.8	124440.6	142348.7
云 南	2323874	139606	360017.1	161816.0	65987.1	135935.4
西 藏	20454	9330	17499.0	40533.0	4238.0	40533.0
陕 西	2267664	316709	219631.4	140384.0	43761.2	51076.2
甘 肃	414864	223119	277146.3	86747.3	44880.5	54204.5
青 海	240298	73338	82929.0	79592.0	62655.0	79079.5
宁 夏	9695234	239044	121791.7	36239.9	42089.7	34808.4
新 疆	731591	330246	206823.4	152542.4	77195.2	93746.4

建设投资情况总表

单位：万元、平方米、张

国家预算内投资	国内贷款	利用外资	福利彩票公益金	其他	本年完工项目规模	未投入使用项目建设床位数
927978.1	**47195.1**	**7909.0**	**616595.1**	**799334.6**	**10483623**	**416904**
16208.1			6530.8		25466	
18281.6			292.0	16922.8	82299	4253
6284.0	2450.0		25696.8		76553	1348
18570.8			13137.9	27482.6	237029	11941
7577.2			2825.3	2336.0	45307	3266
17001.2	1500.0		12598.9	13127.9	52016	7519
8766.8			18006.8	3793.8	99328	4608
4251.1			933.0	1000.0	32898	1010
32413.0			442.0	387.0	365690	7578
9211.6			67.7		24020	1927
134210.4	14100.0		44719.0	102471.7	1249173	32908
36381.1			33663.4	9015.2	131186	12227
46611.3			5182.2	33584.8	563663	21510
14312.4	279.8		9693.0	5924.5	111316	7140
32645.1		4840.0	47486.3	70654.8	988725	28329
48997.2			39370.2	92220.9	788705	43057
14982.6			16147.6	29077.1	290824	10085
44919.0	2350.0	1000.0	20860.4	86895.1	945130	17592
17437.5			30303.3	24623.7	377182	10617
56687.8			32340.8	8260.9	126518	26659
23363.3		369.0	37982.4	9815.5	336505	23453
6606.4	695.3		4192.1	9747.7	57356	1411
59452.0			34319.8	29984.7	886549	24944
30137.9	700.0		13589.0	5978.9	130982	10411
23330.7		1700.0	38379.0	78939.0	434327	39993
27001.3	22400.0		33647.1	52887.0	599081	21716
32475.0			3808.0	4250.0	25220	3175
17341.3			13557.3	20177.6	659328	9058
34168.4	2720.0		7930.1	9386.0	105004	6163
39615.5			5154.0	34310.0	223641	2897
8717.9			22855.3	3235.2	87013	6815
40018.6			40883.6	12844.2	325589	13294

C-1-21 提供住宿的机构

地 区	在建规模	使用彩票公益金项目规模	在建项目总投资	开工累计完成投资	本年计划投资	本年实际完成投资
全 国	**15931935**	**6014360**	**5638280.6**	**2726670.7**	**1288846.6**	**1473571.3**
中央级						
北 京	196887	12798	120882.4	67848.2	15299.3	16037.6
天 津	48532	6117	30391.6	20499.6	13774.0	20499.6
河 北	354654	222780	86443.3	60530.8	30879.0	31676.7
山 西	147699		58475.0	16865.5	10671.0	10285.6
内蒙古	229919	103745	94807.4	54318.2	18553.8	34222.2
辽 宁	179842	145048	72340.0	41222.3	18339.7	19222.5
吉 林	39768	17000	11301.1	6184.1	2350.0	6184.1
黑龙江	558054	5480	112964.0	24826.0	36955.0	24654.0
上 海	76604		50871.0	32154.3	2442.8	9211.6
江 苏	1738376	334847	1076134.2	497550.7	209080.8	180480.8
浙 江	455742	255981	276649.4	112800.0	49446.7	49449.2
安 徽	358142	87984	75501.3	61432.0	55512.3	59208.4
福 建	336655	110826	152107.5	78037.9	20245.2	24084.9
江 西	1255856	785476	253950.6	164019.3	102488.3	121526.3
山 东	1547261	578539	676548.4	259695.9	100390.2	113392.9
河 南	486878	177070	149680.9	86923.9	35915.4	50177.1
湖 北	1246483	311241	354967.5	207721.6	75061.7	105222.9
湖 南	439784	193356	188090.1	102354.0	41330.1	44087.2
广 东	670649	499836	364722.4	139539.6	66183.9	63855.4
广 西	1023392	433614	276162.4	52906.8	48151.6	32887.0
海 南	28477	3517	11038.0	6305.8	5352.0	6084.8
重 庆	646877	382776	127410.2	98912.0	41057.7	54401.2
四 川	305870	120250	123486.5	53879.6	39621.2	31776.6
贵 州	635346	374535	150905.2	92146.9	52290.4	66828.7
云 南	423989	93964	204944.1	84640.8	26802.6	73173.1
西 藏	19874	8750	15495.0	38739.0	2830.0	38739.0
陕 西	1419357	95720	101930.0	62846.6	24664.8	30001.8
甘 肃	254870	139820	147473.3	37104.6	20207.5	27148.0
青 海	114848	69488	42970.0	41170.0	38607.5	40657.5
宁 夏	289851	205483	89022.5	26926.4	34867.8	26826.4
新 疆	401399	238319	140615.3	96568.3	49474.3	61568.2

基本建设投资情况

单位：万元、平方米、张

国家预算内投资	国内贷款	利用外资	福利彩票公益金	其他	本年完工项目规模	未投入使用项目建设床位数
585038.2	**12880.0**	**5709.0**	**433278.8**	**436665.3**	**5570235**	**395365**
15745.6			292.0		50914	4253
5942.0	2450.0		12107.6		26553	1348
11636.1			6319.8	13720.8	100214	10779
7283.3			2098.3	904.0	36888	3240
16236.0	1500.0		6477.3	10008.9	49400	6491
8096.8			10347.1	778.6	35160	4452
4251.1			933.0	1000.0	32898	1010
24213.0			350.0	91.0	362940	6240
9211.6					23743	1927
94986.6	5160.0		32393.2	47941.0	828959	31216
20637.2			24649.5	4162.5	47962	12207
27127.7			3449.9	28630.8	368214	20769
11787.8			8372.6	3924.5	89644	7130
25985.0		4840.0	41928.3	48773.0	653066	27093
28959.5			29276.4	55157.0	499440	39975
8625.0			13840.1	27712.0	231900	9594
37646.0	350.0	500.0	10224.8	56502.1	267203	16373
8703.5			19280.3	16103.4	192715	10325
32201.6			28164.1	3489.7	75778	26647
8193.9		369.0	19183.0	5141.1	142449	21962
3506.4			1362.9	1215.5	8605	1154
19516.7			24458.3	10426.2	360197	24516
18112.0	700.0		9740.3	3224.3	75237	10220
15829.5			28406.9	22592.3	347261	39046
17431.4			24375.3	31366.4	153062	19830
30929.0			3560.0	4250.0	24320	3174
12605.3			8455.9	8940.6	77607	6995
10581.9	2720.0		4480.1	9366.0	71672	6163
21797.5			4050.0	14810.0	113251	2143
5898.0			18891.9	2036.5	55760	6671
21361.2			35809.9	4397.1	167223	12422

C-1-22 不提供住宿的机构

地　区	在建规模	使用彩票公益金项目规模	在建项目总投资	开工累计完成投资	本年计划投资	本年实际完成投资
全　国	**3404165**	**1257294**	**905128.4**	**561050.6**	**325293.3**	**369370.4**
中央级						
北　京	31385		89687.0	38343.0	9057.0	9057.0
天　津						
河　北	224872	112759	28868.6	16975.4	14179.4	16280.0
山　西	19765	3134	9476.4	3043.9	1305.4	1879.8
内蒙古	24481	22581	16147.2	3856.5	1451.2	1975.4
辽　宁	90155	8043	17733.1	16315.5	4931.2	5411.2
吉　林						
黑龙江	92150	1830	20346.7	8538.0	11165.0	8538.0
上　海						
江　苏	307111	121558	106044.7	61163.1	41359.8	37332.4
浙　江	115435	107718	9299.1	5724.9	4390.0	4497.2
安　徽	184048	107200	25568.6	14588.6	14408.6	13728.6
福　建	3930		2000.5	1588.1	20.0	88.0
江　西	169893	96535	21975.8	20028.8	11944.8	14771.8
山　东	367339	116181	123252.0	87119.4	30156.4	33980.4
河　南	26360	9060	30211.4	11306.5	2438.7	2253.6
湖　北	245558	22126	50796.0	36175.0	23283.0	31795.0
湖　南	173498	44611	38173.0	24270.1	14402.1	13688.1
广　东	35565	14563	9955.1	4996.8	2813.6	3051.0
广　西	321858	111971	33200.7	21650.8	17080.8	17280.3
海　南	88159	33967	14603.3	8045.5	7499.5	7195.5
重　庆	143228	83587	27970.9	19999.6	15543.4	19999.6
四　川	66457	19417	15530.7	12044.1	8313.1	9456.1
贵　州	110028	60811	44630.6	20463.0	11812.2	16706.1
云　南	67521	16707	25140.0	12959.5	9041.3	11393.8
西　藏			296.0	296.0	50.0	296.0
陕　西	57627	36915	17388.3	9143.5	6208.3	8443.5
甘　肃	60543	760	39089.0	33559.7	19997.0	19987.5
青　海	124650	3150	39205.0	37668.0	23447.5	37668.0
宁　夏	52741	28301	18298.2	5921.8	5395.2	5890.3
新　疆	199808	73809	30240.5	25265.5	13598.8	16726.2

基本建设投资情况

单位：万元、平方米、张

国家预算内投资	国内贷款	利用外资	福利彩票公益金	其他	本年完工项目规模	未投入使用项目建设床位数
152189.6			**70559.8**	**146621.0**	**1675124**	**21539**
2536.0				6521.0	31385	
3329.8			1155.4	11794.8	111025	1162
135.8			402.0	1342.0	8419	26
365.2			1328.2	282.0	2616	1028
670.0			1807.0	2934.2	17746	156
8200.0			80.0	258.0	2150	1338
17336.8			3061.2	16934.4	234141	1692
395.7			2293.0	1808.5	5192	20
9856.6			947.0	2925.0	37992	741
17.0			51.0	20.0	500	10
3977.0			2454.0	8340.8	104180	1236
8596.7			4849.8	20533.9	179050	3082
1288.9			444.6	520.1	18566	491
6332.0			6215.0	19248.0	159833	1219
6089.0			5976.3	1622.8	55607	292
1925.1			1053.4	72.5	22538	12
6115.7			8790.6	2374.0	76915	1491
2021.9			2725.7	2447.9	12816	257
10796.1			4552.9	4650.6	121608	428
6767.4			888.7	1800.0	44447	191
1451.2			6919.7	8335.2	28737	947
2440.5			4823.0	4130.3	53838	1886
296.0					900	1
1965.0			3714.5	2764.0	86453	2063
19767.5			200.0	20.0	19200	
17818.0			350.0	19500.0	109790	754
2554.9			2402.4	933.0	23593	144
9143.8			3074.4	4508.0	105887	872

C-1-23 其他社会服务机构

地 区	在建规模	使用彩票公益金项目规模	在建项目总投资	开工累计完成投资	本年计划投资
全 国	**19031863**	**1812951**	**1589766.0**	**891914.7**	**362585.2**
中央级					
北 京	47216		41800.5	30055.8	10401.8
天 津	195099	195099	101029.9	19801.8	13490.0
河 北	64891	24481	15670.1	7446.7	2124.7
山 西					
内蒙古	93700	3800	55536.4	6783.4	2730.2
辽 宁	40732	17132	19753.0	20143.0	602.0
吉 林					
黑龙江	600	600	50.0	50.0	50.0
上 海					
江 苏	1780980	114923	270923.0	209736.1	67615.1
浙 江	139027	18255	64949.0	45385.7	14360.8
安 徽	126813	31000	16410.0	13382.0	7260.0
福 建	66930		17838.8	7821.4	4477.6
江 西	193270	64452	15675.6	14482.1	14085.1
山 东	215162	138865	74831.0	48709.8	33136.0
河 南	63606	43876	11197.3	9811.5	1473.8
湖 北	834240	200500	96599.0	42487.0	10765.0
湖 南	369938	255309	39216.7	17725.6	7199.0
广 东	116521	30483	196853.9	82936.5	24572.1
广 西	108404	26919	19478.7	13373.0	3631.7
海 南	135255	89244	18469.1	7399.3	5898.1
重 庆	703666	333851	134047.9	74469.3	35269.2
四 川	214155	6700	10684.5	4251.0	1244.0
贵 州	1506130	28767	106091.0	55324.0	50894.0
云 南	1811114	16435	121970.0	60396.4	28456.2
西 藏					
陕 西	741540	153434	92460.0	66963.0	10540.0
甘 肃	108	108	3882.0	3851.0	500.0
青 海	800	700	600.0	600.0	600.0
宁 夏	9347382		12910.0	1565.7	265.7
新 疆	114584	18018	30838.6	26963.6	10943.1

基本建设投资情况

单位：万元、平方米

本年实际完成投资	国家预算内投资	国内贷款	利用外资	福利彩票公益金	其他	本年完工项目规模
403345.5	**123450.7**	**34315.1**	**2200.0**	**53492.3**	**189887.4**	**2622850**
10401.8					10401.8	
13931.2	342.0			13589.2		50000
5330.7	905.0			2458.7	1967.0	3150
3680.2	400.0			443.2	2837.0	
5689.0				5689.0		40732
50.0				12.0	38.0	600
63474.1	18799.1	8940.0		5941.0	29794.0	100304
18963.6	13428.0			2845.6	2690.0	76032
4203.0	2010.0			400.0	1793.0	112698
4167.4	2507.6	279.8			1380.0	9700
14352.1	809.1			1122.0	12421.0	187630
25391.3	10041.0			3997.0	11353.3	33200
4132.8	3794.7			338.1		20960
14145.0	941.0	2000.0	500.0	1750.0	8954.0	470756
13169.7	2020.0			4265.7	6884.0	126860
22516.7	20172.5			342.5	2001.7	11611
4484.8	560.0			2223.4	1701.4	17565
7084.6	400.0	695.3		18.5	5970.8	33335
39600.7	22756.6			1988.1	14856.0	385410
1808.7	854.1				954.6	6298
53008.0	5060.0		1700.0	259.0	45989.0	27621
48636.4	6429.4	22400.0		2889.0	16918.0	388341
11220.0	2641.0			321.0	8258.0	478068
891.0	891.0					1200
600.0				600.0		600
265.7					265.7	
12147.0	7688.6			1999.3	2459.1	40179

C-1-24 其他基本

地 区	在建规模	使用彩票公益金项目规模	在建项目总投资	开工累计完成投资	本年计划投资
全 国	**2505425**	**1182409**	**696256.5**	**322826.2**	**194868.3**
中央级	279057	141888	157928.2	73562.7	43573.0
北 京					
天 津					
河 北	253633	253633	21908.7	13073.7	5685.9
山 西	5002	667	3463.0	1582.1	590.0
内蒙古	32887	32887	12000.0	6838.1	4373.4
辽 宁	5690	350	162.0	244.7	162.0
吉 林			1026.0		779.0
黑龙江					
上 海	5086	4986	5408.8	4044.7	67.7
江 苏	257078	50976	38354.0	21671.3	12054.4
浙 江	43731	33731	40615.2	15224.0	5398.4
安 徽	586963	1500	30580.0	8238.3	30049.5
福 建	17705		3500.0	3784.4	742.0
江 西	72499	27966	22615.0	13976.0	4308.0
山 东	111432	74210	28269.0	21836.0	7649.7
河 南	24278	3500	6619.7	4643.8	2713.7
湖 北	91666	31359	21679.0	19763.6	4981.6
湖 南	4000	2000	3343.0	1419.5	2946.5
广 东	58819	46340	50751.4	27144.7	8866.4
广 西	215732	147408	76278.8	24969.5	17876.8
海 南	6688	850	1115.9	876.6	558.9
重 庆	98726	80325	15505.4	9755.0	9732.9
四 川	60512	55512	27560.0	17166.4	8005.4
贵 州	82868	60810	16503.3	8305.9	9444.0
云 南	21250	12500	7963.0	3819.3	1687.0
西 藏	580	580	1708.0	1498.0	1358.0
陕 西	49140	30640	7853.1	1430.9	2348.1
甘 肃	99343	82431	86702.0	12232.0	4176.0
青 海			154.0	154.0	
宁 夏	5260	5260	1561.0	1826.0	1561.0
新 疆	15800	100	5129.0	3745.0	3179.0

建设投资情况

单位：万元、平方米

本年实际完成投资	国家预算内投资	国内贷款	利用外资	福利彩票公益金	其他	本年完工项目规模
152724.7	**67299.6**			**59264.2**	**26160.9**	**615414**
22738.9	16208.1			6530.8		25466
5903.9	2699.9			3204.0		22640
573.1	158.1			325.0	90.0	
4350.2				4350.2		
244.7				163.7	81.0	5690
67.7				67.7		277
14213.8	3087.9			3323.6	7802.3	85769
6149.7	1920.2			3875.3	354.2	2000
8238.3	7617.0			385.3	236.0	44759
1869.4				1269.4	600.0	11472
4976.0	1874.0			1982.0	1120.0	43849
7823.7	1400.0			1247.0	5176.7	77015
3643.8	1274.0			1524.8	845.0	19398
4861.6				2670.6	2191.0	47338
1419.5	625.0			781.0	13.5	2000
7866.4	2388.6			2780.8	2697.0	16591
16878.1	8493.7			7785.4	599.0	99576
876.6	678.1			85.0	113.5	2600
9755.0	6382.6			3320.5	51.9	19334
7364.4	4404.4			2960.0		5000
5805.9	990.0			2793.4	2022.5	30708
2732.1	700.0			1559.8	472.3	3840
1498.0	1250.0			248.0		
1410.9	130.0			1065.9	215.0	17200
6178.0	2928.0			3250.0		12932
154.0				154.0		
1826.0	265.0			1561.0		7660
3305.0	1825.0				1480.0	12300

C-2-1 社会

地 区	机构和设施数	工商登记	编制登记	民政登记	设施
全 国	**413372**	**14965**	**24814**	**47267**	**326326**
中央级	2		2		
北 京	12792	539	679	976	10598
天 津	2621	222	94	285	2020
河 北	38912	530	700	820	36862
山 西	4713	330	678	737	2968
内蒙古	4691	135	510	331	3715
辽 宁	10102	1621	559	1556	6366
吉 林	3052	297	1053	220	1482
黑龙江	4469	266	493	1264	2446
上 海	7381	778	220	3295	3088
江 苏	44123	2538	1467	21983	18135
浙 江	33706	1743	922	2778	28263
安 徽	9699	342	505	1159	7693
福 建	6470	263	429	215	5563
江 西	5603	280	1808	741	2774
山 东	31146	1168	988	2457	26533
河 南	7552	678	1035	1374	4465
湖 北	14829	502	1810	723	11794
湖 南	14219	399	1999	319	11502
广 东	59183	172	1605	1017	56389
广 西	14057	110	560	234	13153
海 南	2107	17	46	156	1888
重 庆	8856	634	587	377	7258
四 川	22908	701	2620	1553	18034
贵 州	22812	29	989	229	21565
云 南	3872	225	450	273	2924
西 藏	545	7	96	407	35
陕 西	7794	173	652	689	6280
甘 肃	8951	60	354	170	8367
青 海	1341	20	52	16	1253
宁 夏	1249	55	110	280	804
新 疆	3615	131	742	633	2109

工作总表

单位：个、人

年末职工人数	女性	工商登记	编制登记	民政登记	设施
2820819	**1070074**	**1122369**	**274881**	**351713**	**1077376**
320	185		320		
81547	38680	24286	11666	10753	34886
34908	16124	16423	2326	5564	10621
124731	44724	29025	11914	10178	73711
50476	16786	27977	7368	5223	10018
34942	14900	11277	5696	3949	14123
143823	61096	81737	9554	12040	40729
36388	14935	15086	11262	2422	7886
41229	17545	10433	8859	9801	12319
126559	56348	60595	7379	44523	14105
453379	163387	229511	19065	114140	90877
265489	100218	172247	10638	14943	67816
68889	28439	17614	6415	10473	34932
42513	16712	14957	4238	2802	20629
48022	16717	24350	10475	4132	9365
233536	86747	88542	14892	24641	105724
102793	35814	54507	12415	11098	25390
98222	41069	31850	18615	5912	42072
85192	32510	26097	16781	3368	39214
201317	72773	14823	19500	12915	154336
39224	16525	7844	7403	4077	20156
12649	3938	1748	764	1217	8960
90525	34788	57710	5521	3913	23445
134457	49529	51299	18350	11152	53871
102983	26293	1835	8711	1615	90927
41878	13644	23393	4376	2554	11878
3441	1701	220	442	2730	67
45744	18075	10981	7779	5222	21889
28442	10016	3149	3886	1233	20304
7169	2446	1718	901	147	4444
11181	5059	3968	1627	1959	3638
28851	12351	7167	5743	7017	9044

C-2-1续表1

地 区	受教育程度		职业资格水平	
	大学专科人数	大学本科及以上人数	助理社会工作师人数	社会工作师人数
全 国	**426108**	**220567**	**20902**	**13699**
中央级	80	240		2
北 京	14842	12734	2130	975
天 津	5605	3727	923	228
河 北	10140	4542	274	283
山 西	5751	3299	146	145
内蒙古	7613	4367	593	259
辽 宁	21869	13902	587	424
吉 林	6475	3524	375	276
黑龙江	7904	4146	380	302
上 海	12420	6008	893	2059
江 苏	58983	30209	2234	1168
浙 江	25253	12167	1205	912
安 徽	13048	4347	747	344
福 建	3699	2126	555	415
江 西	4075	1258	160	126
山 东	50542	26590	774	582
河 南	14181	7469	585	381
湖 北	15417	7629	650	308
湖 南	15157	7158	752	508
广 东	37410	23962	4051	1962
广 西	5558	3524	355	289
海 南	1412	587	72	36
重 庆	12441	6265	685	424
四 川	25605	8918	846	588
贵 州	21442	7201	101	87
云 南	4464	2640	153	132
西 藏	207	130	3	1
陕 西	8992	3273	191	132
甘 肃	5229	3427	188	123
青 海	1107	567	46	60
宁 夏	1547	714	37	34
新 疆	7640	3917	211	134

单位：人、人次、时

年龄结构				志愿服务	
35岁及以下人数	36岁至45岁人数	46岁至55岁人数	56岁及以上人数	志愿者服务人次数	志愿服务时间
874620	**1100177**	**654115**	**191542**	**6508537**	**17275909.4**
215	50	38	17		
22796	30464	22579	5708	3592051	10486654.0
12147	12045	8212	2504	58394	98277.0
39887	45553	29946	9352	17623	64937.0
14723	19695	11822	4236	6481	17011.4
10005	13757	8547	2592	12249	26643.0
40772	60468	32113	10454	12680	28935.0
9526	16943	7215	2688	23347	46638.0
10918	17340	9396	3575	29144	86634.0
35554	42599	36007	12399	44042	123409.5
127368	179262	113384	33365	468707	981462.5
75791	96866	71359	21473	433253	733744.0
18785	29304	17006	3794	93246	213136.0
13173	17201	8862	3276	128605	360580.0
15608	20478	9443	2493	5771	17849.7
88389	87795	45548	11804	801569	1808037.7
38927	40740	16565	6561	5551	29668.0
27471	42246	21330	7175	70885	193362.0
22588	38205	20070	4264	35062	119906.0
71758	74126	41781	13652	69992	391484.9
11163	13659	11168	3234	2113	8591.0
3704	4742	3393	811	12258	21937.0
26489	35072	23042	5922	275146	602093.1
44563	54084	28560	7253	101057	290427.5
36080	39864	21667	5372	149024	297874.9
13405	18156	8662	1655	7918	42055.0
1864	1219	332	26	137	232.0
14401	17622	11291	2430	20208	59056.2
10514	10578	5862	1467	10981	54646.0
2467	3016	703	782	558	1605.0
3534	4709	2626	297	2591	6393.0
10035	12319	5586	911	17894	62629.0

C-2-1续表2

地 区	执行企业会计制度单位财务指标				执行行政	
	固定资产原价	营业收入	费用合计	营业利润	固定资产原价	上年结转和结余
全 国	**18045518.1**	**43959557.0**	**5392800.6**	**1211099.0**	**8376074.4**	**937524.3**
中央级					30229.4	3469.8
北 京	465598.0	550272.8	95658.9	1723.6	363608.0	222182.2
天 津	227463.5	595330.0	83006.5	5265.8	122407.2	9164.0
河 北	476389.3	978277.8	98524.8	3381.7	360870.2	34627.7
山 西	235413.5	224584.0	34068.9	-4661.1	190812.9	26214.4
内蒙古	64082.2	87967.6	13577.7	4822.6	183736.4	24176.0
辽 宁	1388079.0	1616440.9	191792.6	34791.7	303510.5	19861.8
吉 林	127199.3	246887.7	27375.4	-342.8	191540.1	7491.2
黑龙江	691825.6	154834.3	35649.9	1476.5	242285.6	10139.7
上 海	1258088.6	2709253.7	186309.2	149297.4	235613.1	18120.5
江 苏	3378122.0	11044167.6	1184045.6	216661.1	850801.2	59585.6
浙 江	5029893.2	14284917.2	2139761.4	532257.9	405292.4	33937.3
安 徽	161071.1	910030.0	67178.9	19951.1	223249.4	11422.5
福 建	136501.6	252029.4	45502.8	-77.1	94539.0	20717.1
江 西	101320.7	2006446.5	19069.6	4332.1	229667.3	47248.6
山 东	1092056.3	1749719.7	337511.6	133878.3	536531.1	10066.4
河 南	333735.2	501195.3	86526.3	21163.9	243698.9	12403.0
湖 北	308018.8	458044.7	89678.8	3506.9	468679.1	6999.7
湖 南	277378.6	630891.2	55680.0	5801.6	479710.0	8842.0
广 东	233248.9	277305.1	34910.7	5599.7	578699.4	69259.9
广 西	59960.3	272962.7	12091.2	-1955.4	154795.3	37355.2
海 南	17639.6	33002.8	6925.7	-1829.3	31184.0	13629.1
重 庆	664105.5	1840064.8	215492.2	34796.2	139262.6	35464.6
四 川	505094.7	1275967.9	113626.4	6182.7	571083.1	52884.4
贵 州	5782.0	15161.9	2439.7	904.9	164090.0	25358.1
云 南	378967.9	738883.1	135106.1	10345.7	178618.3	21590.9
西 藏	3598.0	498.0	359.0	139.0	65150.4	22522.0
陕 西	142359.5	314194.7	42910.1	19982.4	348447.7	18088.9
甘 肃	29771.3	10482.7	2469.8	85.8	111386.0	7080.3
青 海	8121.6	15681.5	3636.0	195.6	31246.6	8731.7
宁 夏	92238.8	68230.5	7173.0	-1925.3	75504.0	10224.9
新 疆	152393.5	95830.9	24741.8	5345.8	169825.2	28664.8

单位：万元

事业单位会计制度财务指标			执行民间非营利组织单位会计制度财务指标			
本年收入合计	本年支出合计	收支结余	固定资产原价	上年结余	本年收入合计	本年费用合计
8051375.2	**7452602.4**	**588258.0**	**2500456.1**	**87222.8**	**1130226.3**	**965823.9**
119533.4	98606.4	2496.7				
1099865.6	736603.3	38363.1	141076.7	11980.7	57429.0	67371.4
132402.0	130706.0	13024.6	21688.5	705.9	29015.2	19109.1
381515.1	361157.5	23442.5	249056.1	1043.1	19088.5	25818.3
161762.7	152644.5	22371.5	36386.1	295.5	2081.5	3607.5
121610.8	131311.9	26557.2	45337.0	1202.8	8499.5	6881.8
356681.9	437379.1	13906.5	72728.7	244.7	12156.9	14133.3
125214.4	117546.3	2862.2	10.0		78.1	40.0
106784.0	97073.2	2133.6	64748.5	4735.0	88447.9	7591.5
316404.8	298713.4	15205.9	183092.5	35986.2	348160.9	320539.3
603507.5	576518.0	63145.9	487744.1	-420.6	183561.2	192281.7
297588.9	270873.0	27880.9	120798.4	10090.1	68840.2	54066.7
144996.2	145095.0	3546.9	133406.9	319.2	22189.8	20844.0
158892.8	142925.3	14409.3	62267.2	2831.6	3508.3	4173.5
103592.3	70405.3	44498.9	20920.2		4389.4	5361.7
634778.9	639053.6	121.5	407338.1	119.0	121564.0	121565.1
232937.5	221745.9	8490.5	70449.2	2053.1	12053.1	12032.6
381369.2	364669.6	11268.3	35975.1	126.0	11474.1	11266.3
311735.9	311118.2	15992.6	12714.1	771.9	65790.5	4815.1
516911.4	509872.9	36024.5	61462.6	9622.2	18250.7	16572.1
182361.4	170544.1	13283.8	16586.7	1726.4	5220.6	5515.1
44518.5	41356.2	9176.1	2286.6	1402.5	1388.9	1107.7
200590.1	166580.3	70423.2	75208.6	351.1	19517.5	18413.5
368381.7	354619.8	18560.7	62803.0	1818.5	13758.6	17902.2
96453.1	109827.9	10101.8	38939.1	226.2	1801.9	2657.3
164264.9	162970.2	11861.9	11271.0	128.4	297.3	651.7
11791.3	26595.6	8038.4	468.0		6.1	3.2
338721.0	320139.9	16313.8	36658.0	-143.7	5378.8	5605.0
104897.9	87590.7	14312.8	18505.5		1390.6	904.4
27585.5	22937.2	2050.2	840.0		54.4	49.1
40365.4	42801.0	11796.3	3451.6		896.8	1063.8
163359.1	132621.1	16595.9	6238.0	7.0	3936.0	3879.9

C-2-2 提供住宿的社会

地 区	单位数	按登记类型分				按床位	
		工商登记	编制登记	民政登记	一个机构多块牌子	0～99张	100～299张
全 国	**31187**	**247**	**18022**	**11578**	**1340**	**17287**	**11447**
中央级	1		1				1
北 京	631	11	381	236	3	215	282
天 津	294	2	55	234	3	113	140
河 北	1160	3	496	536	125	573	440
山 西	841	1	358	420	62	582	230
内蒙古	735	1	402	310	22	424	251
辽 宁	1617	4	392	1165	56	1037	466
吉 林	767		742	7	18	479	235
黑龙江	926	7	281	621	17	572	267
上 海	660	2	56	599	3	216	345
江 苏	2464	12	1232	1186	34	983	1192
浙 江	1348	18	743	576	11	564	616
安 徽	1205	8	270	910	17	545	577
福 建	440	3	302	123	12	271	116
江 西	1667		1536	63	68	1146	476
山 东	2047	11	613	1417	6	753	1055
河 南	1232		719	503	10	745	429
湖 北	1884	23	1465	303	93	891	888
湖 南	1962	1	1701	172	88	1596	318
广 东	1588	48	1282	220	38	1107	368
广 西	611		351	179	81	457	124
海 南	98	3	32	54	9	63	27
重 庆	672	21	402	247	2	327	291
四 川	2928	58	2203	453	214	1562	1199
贵 州	936	1	708	143	84	646	273
云 南	534	6	311	204	13	303	195
西 藏	101		27	74		72	19
陕 西	691		435	209	47	343	254
甘 肃	447	1	168	118	160	296	128
青 海	60		35	16	9	37	16
宁 夏	120	1	55	55	9	61	43
新 疆	520	1	268	225	26	308	186

服务机构总表

单位:个、人

数分		按服务类型分				年末职工人数			
300～499张	500张以上	养老	精神病	儿童	其他		女性	工商登记	编制登记
1603	**850**	**27752**	**242**	**753**	**2440**	**385951**	**216236**	**6691**	**210469**
					1	185	130		185
71	63	597	1	12	21	15534	9773	396	7886
16	25	275	2	2	15	7072	4793	160	1944
96	51	1051	2	8	99	19014	10905	96	9461
23	6	712	8	13	108	8948	4016	7	4704
41	19	674	7	8	46	8065	4163	2	4288
80	34	1487	3	12	115	18633	10713	26	7931
36	17	681	14	10	62	8758	3485		7715
50	37	779	8	16	123	11822	5883	31	6379
68	31	630	3	4	23	24467	18166	158	3494
192	97	2329	12	32	91	34076	19653	353	16982
101	67	1269	3	12	64	17513	10812	468	9251
62	21	1076	4	36	89	12864	6363	140	4281
39	14	355	17	11	57	5916	2974	75	3449
34	11	1537	4	17	109	9943	3701		8982
176	63	1944	14	17	72	29477	16191	92	10632
30	28	1075	7	23	127	15670	8526		9753
62	43	1658	12	79	135	20451	11468	557	15887
34	14	1751	17	54	140	16999	8744	135	13740
66	47	1424	11	39	114	26435	16440	2408	16608
20	10	476	8	41	86	9608	6496		5767
2	6	83		2	13	1317	745	322	671
31	23	615	9	6	42	7961	4214	514	4174
114	53	2547	25	120	236	21003	10068	494	15098
11	6	804	22	26	84	5666	2615	15	4115
23	13	398	6	32	98	5610	3118	184	3559
7	3	81		10	10	1007	686		293
72	22	575	4	12	100	8832	4596		5632
15	8	348	6	29	64	4159	1989	9	2553
2	5	35	1	12	12	860	489		706
10	6	98	1	10	11	1572	1056	23	1106
19	7	388	11	48	73	6514	3265	26	3243

C-2-2续表1

地 区	年末职工人数		受教育程度		职业资格水平	
	民政登记	一个机构多块牌子	大学专科人数	大学本科及以上人数	助理社会工作师人数	社会工作师人数
全 国	**159028**	**9763**	**75792**	**50585**	**4624**	**4461**
中央级			71	114		2
北 京	7231	21	2652	2705	181	121
天 津	4960	8	1352	989	278	90
河 北	8309	1148	2952	2014	95	116
山 西	3690	547	1840	1286	32	88
内蒙古	3714	61	2017	1120	58	105
辽 宁	10008	668	4106	3165	114	159
吉 林	169	874	1194	923	52	107
黑龙江	5369	43	2209	1398	199	165
上 海	20738	77	1914	1220	265	443
江 苏	16449	292	6055	4498	437	444
浙 江	7765	29	2315	1773	165	184
安 徽	8296	147	1946	943	143	117
福 建	2322	70	991	942	120	136
江 西	512	449	1365	597	75	70
山 东	18693	60	7300	5559	307	293
河 南	5844	73	3468	1955	144	164
湖 北	3471	536	4463	2777	155	107
湖 南	2407	717	3948	2249	192	199
广 东	6864	555	4490	3392	664	424
广 西	3525	316	2959	1710	173	201
海 南	287	37	285	178	14	21
重 庆	3235	38	1553	1026	107	121
四 川	4343	1068	5489	2644	239	236
贵 州	1057	479	1739	977	50	39
云 南	1722	145	1445	1171	58	82
西 藏	714		65	55	1	1
陕 西	2913	287	2263	1127	86	88
甘 肃	840	757	1009	876	107	63
青 海	110	44	292	167	16	5
宁 夏	375	68	345	252	27	21
新 疆	3096	149	1700	783	70	49

单位：个、人、人次、时

年龄结构				按人员性质		志愿服务	
35岁及以下人数	36岁至45岁人数	46岁至55岁人数	56岁及以上人数	管理人员	专业技术技能人员	志愿者服务人次数	志愿服务时间
105962	**146062**	**106323**	**27604**	**148284**	**237667**	**511665**	**1472649.8**
138	29	13	5	28	157		
3942	5441	4806	1345	5209	10325	14300	28885.0
1699	2463	2383	527	2228	4844	8475	16280.0
6342	7360	4372	940	5206	13808	4476	15584.0
2586	3609	2257	496	3589	5359	5389	14515.2
1937	3154	2428	546	3234	4831	798	1794.0
3939	7520	5770	1404	8822	9811	5210	17514.0
2633	3777	2008	340	4423	4335	38	60.0
2970	5001	3296	555	5612	6210	283	1796.0
4945	8343	8142	3037	9276	15191	10962	25937.5
8107	11462	10871	3636	8783	25293	86286	215311.0
3940	5615	5961	1997	5490	12023	64383	120948.0
2974	4560	4194	1136	6349	6515	15073	48765.0
1717	2263	1477	459	2388	3528	20679	31529.0
1827	4519	3066	531	5504	4439	3589	12111.0
10252	11165	6585	1475	8597	20880	117759	282796.8
4895	5692	4047	1036	6590	9080	766	1914.0
5423	8180	5531	1317	7751	12700	20503	31771.0
4763	7335	3973	928	6579	10420	18728	72207.0
6519	10996	7545	1375	10020	16415	61708	367941.0
3434	3383	2183	608	2872	6736	1735	5785.0
567	427	246	77	436	881	3698	6318.0
1727	2505	2781	948	4057	3904	10674	30313.3
6253	7817	5308	1625	10905	10098	8678	18468.0
1783	2440	1246	197	3689	1977	7214	19658.0
1904	2249	1176	281	2400	3210	7344	40490.0
636	295	71	5	511	496	119	192.0
3225	3135	2074	398	3363	5469	6220	16818.0
1611	1558	836	154	1998	2161	285	870.0
381	346	107	26	348	512	542	1577.0
609	586	318	59	375	1197	2589	6385.0
2284	2837	1252	141	1652	4862	3162	18116.0

C-2-2续表2

地区	年末床位数	工商登记	编制登记	民政登记	一个机构多块牌子	年末收养人数	工商登记
全国	**3931555**	**66198**	**2230695**	**1539316**	**95346**	**2316072**	**27050**
中央级	150		150			149	
北京	140469	2591	82534	55142	202	79011	664
天津	54703	2180	12325	40114	84	28819	192
河北	168934	888	77419	78141	12486	77643	254
山西	69379	400	26211	37749	5019	36689	26
内蒙古	91342	300	45259	44058	1725	46324	300
辽宁	178188	266	72117	99942	5863	108577	150
吉林	76829		71890	1932	3007	44307	
黑龙江	125513	433	61940	62962	178	84740	422
上海	119254	478	14754	103035	987	79655	299
江苏	404939	2964	222521	176259	3195	219242	1146
浙江	229182	6194	123593	98919	476	102044	3453
安徽	155597	840	34138	118756	1863	85874	398
福建	56676	704	33036	22175	761	24447	319
江西	156083		146192	5330	4561	104015	
山东	331076	2874	113000	214159	1043	196508	246
河南	132433		75878	56079	476	88348	
湖北	243263	9748	195466	32540	5509	158469	1581
湖南	143636	800	118905	20665	3266	101949	308
广东	184339	16748	124377	40204	3010	87874	8481
广西	48722		23097	22105	3520	27474	
海南	12386	4592	3563	3421	810	6391	3817
重庆	90500	4168	52057	33937	338	55743	2077
四川	340990	7701	265115	55787	12387	246167	2307
贵州	73602	120	56671	11769	5042	41943	28
云南	62199	814	40347	19606	1432	35697	355
西藏	28129		15656	12473		24538	
陕西	92664		57710	31026	3928	60348	
甘肃	44866	90	20690	11514	12572	18874	90
青海	7727		5192	2306	229	3483	
宁夏	16207	245	8997	6525	440	9242	85
新疆	51578	60	29895	20686	937	31488	52

单位：张、人天、人、人次

编制登记	民政登记	一个机构多块牌子	老年人	青壮年	少年儿童	年末在院(站)人天数	家庭寄养儿童数量
1466206	**828245**	**41188**	**2152187**	**112941**	**97561**	**638646342**	**22361**
149			57	28	64	47998	
59560	21173	76	77488	2518	1467	27587563	445
9881	20118	44	27960	1965	310	7327071	363
43558	35579	5255	80525	2291	1830	26586725	256
17208	18903	2666	33015	2431	3357	10633294	1800
23602	22881	702	42998	3014	1473	13069887	34
49902	55299	3596	100715	5231	3001	29184549	323
42558	1078	671	36967	5147	2193	9428354	108
42565	41946	101	78560	4910	1564	20277454	104
11085	67808	463	73456	3972	2227	23754515	1135
142126	77806	1035	209559	8161	4393	63243530	554
56067	42547	111	96368	3297	2513	26467249	832
16780	68770	748	81104	2203	3389	25019311	2407
15080	10466	224	20906	3271	1912	8240747	970
98821	2639	2590	96424	2904	4722	21604316	1471
79413	122742	251	196129	3208	3315	63052152	381
51449	38443	156	79676	4319	6053	21882960	566
137467	19677	2468	145610	10468	5115	44186454	634
90974	10367	1474	90184	6305	6634	28921655	2415
61360	20525	1677	77007	5564	9472	28324004	667
14276	12790	877	21886	3158	2899	7382488	663
1847	999	125	6360	79	349	780521	7
34056	19384	226	51487	2922	1334	17050870	93
208620	31184	4844	229573	12828	4554	61565539	484
35095	5059	2262	37005	2305	3134	10884025	357
24411	10817	557	31429	2347	2364	8222721	1292
14826	9712		19257		5281	2475580	
44657	17974	2715	59040	3637	2669	17476864	536
11907	4508	4593	16513	756	3829	4386760	174
2711	875	24	1795	458	1357	891268	
5657	3367	154	8036	680	547	2181337	113
18538	12809	503	25098	2564	4240	6508581	3177

C-2-2续表3

地区	执行企业会计制度单位财务指标				执行行政	
	固定资产原价	营业收入	费用合计	营业利润	固定资产原价	上年结转和结余
全　国	**271230.0**	**25519.5**	**14689.6**	**-4732.0**	**6337256.1**	**494657.0**
中央级					12600.6	3469.8
北　京	82814.7	7749.6	1741.6	-1506.9	193313.3	47832.0
天　津	736.7	296.7	66.0		60488.1	7694.6
河　北	1916.0	334.2	333.2		283142.4	31877.4
山　西	1830.0	30.0	16.0		145237.1	19243.9
内蒙古	18.0				142655.5	17100.9
辽　宁	7272.1	130.0		32.2	215809.0	17649.4
吉　林	2.0				152087.2	4825.9
黑龙江	27.0	7.0	4.9		220134.6	5369.2
上　海	145.0	242.0	2025.0		130957.4	11203.5
江　苏	42943.3	1597.9	2780.9	-1353.6	663368.2	30930.8
浙　江	10579.2	2738.5	600.4	15.0	298665.9	23838.8
安　徽	1892.0	403.0	61.0		156775.5	7889.2
福　建	1564.2	449.4	85.9	-11.0	79896.7	16100.3
江　西	874.8	37.4	62.9	0.9	199763.6	9591.8
山　东	8520.0	549.0	421.2	9.9	378941.5	7026.8
河　南	60.0				156334.5	7878.1
湖　北	13066.0	760.0	202.0		385258.2	5316.5
湖　南	13731.0	660.0	660.0		415186.8	3697.4
广　东	27592.2	6153.8	2403.7	-56.3	476962.7	53271.7
广　西					111720.8	25511.5
海　南	2312.2	1219.5	1668.0	-1860.7	24274.0	11031.2
重　庆	19422.0	1716.8	866.3	-13.5	107159.4	3709.3
四　川	23260.6	286.8	546.4	7.0	460885.3	44575.9
贵　州	145.0	32.0	11.0	3.0	132376.0	12665.5
云　南	3181.0	74.0	41.4		146171.7	16342.8
西　藏					40162.8	2132.0
陕　西					274172.7	13404.2
甘　肃	450.0	1.0	5.0	1.0	86464.6	6133.3
青　海	500.0				13262.5	3550.5
宁　夏	6200.0		4.0		49892.5	8315.4
新　疆	175.0	50.9	82.8	1.0	123135.0	15477.4

单位：万元

事业单位会计制度财务指标			执行民间非营利组织单位会计制度财务指标			
本年收入合计	本年支出合计	收支结余	固定资产原价	上年结余	本年收入合计	本年费用合计
4984562.4	**4952283.0**	**348915.3**	**2074012.6**	**58074.5**	**666716.6**	**537332.5**
1497.3	9283.3	2496.7				
331362.4	343631.5	29961.1	137522.1	8478.4	51872.0	62719.7
100055.7	99806.4	11634.0	21090.4	533.8	28162.4	17736.0
264556.5	254134.3	19345.9	242463.4	1027.8	18366.3	24071.4
117033.1	117432.0	14074.4	35265.4	295.5	1823.5	3283.1
85057.5	97328.1	14772.7	45118.0	1202.8	8458.8	6836.8
295225.6	376398.9	12513.3	71068.2	210.7	11371.6	12255.2
48048.0	47753.2	2244.7			40.1	
91381.9	81915.5	2104.6	63164.9	4688.0	87885.4	7110.8
96345.8	94444.5	7945.9	119810.3	13870.7	179278.9	130041.4
452840.0	431763.4	27253.8	251875.7	-1048.8	40843.9	40728.4
202345.0	192692.0	6263.0	111997.7	9493.6	35929.1	27385.5
91254.7	92848.9	1509.3	121813.6	301.4	19674.9	18942.2
129606.6	117755.4	10334.8	61532.3	2811.0	3060.9	3782.7
57778.3	47676.3	13906.4	15840.8		398.4	958.5
472472.3	476957.1	121.5	377676.4		99306.0	99306.0
165514.5	160247.8	4802.4	66277.9	1607.0	10170.0	10247.4
316689.5	308093.4	9320.5	29293.0	126.0	8195.5	8203.1
230528.4	240441.2	6285.2	11485.3	507.1	4369.6	3415.4
364897.6	364100.2	23693.1	50655.2	9507.5	9755.6	10759.8
118010.4	113234.9	9527.1	15906.4	1615.2	5054.1	5283.2
28136.5	25807.4	6598.6	2072.8	1402.5	1178.4	1014.2
99875.5	71818.5	31659.2	72449.1	341.1	19037.6	17860.0
237225.9	224555.5	17766.9	38695.1	1042.3	9433.2	11799.3
45035.8	64974.1	5637.4	38031.6	147.0	1258.5	2055.2
88467.5	84148.3	6998.7	8759.0	55.3	295.2	632.1
3857.1	6435.7		450.0		6.1	3.2
231551.1	215043.9	11743.5	35210.3	-147.4	5278.8	5252.5
81766.2	72770.3	13541.0	18428.1		1337.4	704.1
13927.6	14060.9	1013.6	840.0		54.4	49.1
27773.5	31828.4	11497.2	3028.6		884.0	1041.8
94444.6	72901.7	12348.8	6191.0	6.0	3936.0	3854.4

C–2–3 养老服务

地 区	单位数	工商登记	编制登记	民政登记	一个机构多块牌子	0～99张	100～299张
全 国	**27752**	**247**	**15478**	**11265**	**762**	**14899**	**10698**
中央级							
北 京	597	11	350	235	1	198	272
天 津	275	2	37	234	2	101	137
河 北	1051	3	437	515	96	495	412
山 西	712	1	258	408	45	478	208
内蒙古	674	1	345	308	20	385	235
辽 宁	1487	4	302	1128	53	942	438
吉 林	681		664	7	10	423	217
黑龙江	779	7	177	587	8	466	235
上 海	630	2	28	597	3	198	339
江 苏	2329	12	1133	1182	2	895	1162
浙 江	1269	18	670	574	7	513	595
安 徽	1076	8	161	902	5	463	540
福 建	355	3	225	120	7	218	93
江 西	1537		1444	61	32	1041	457
山 东	1944	11	514	1417	2	696	1030
河 南	1075		582	488	5	638	393
湖 北	1658	23	1341	264	30	719	854
湖 南	1751	1	1554	159	37	1437	280
广 东	1424	48	1146	198	32	1012	319
广 西	476		260	174	42	352	103
海 南	83	3	21	54	5	53	22
重 庆	615	21	346	246	2	282	286
四 川	2547	58	2014	398	77	1293	1124
贵 州	804	1	607	143	53	552	244
云 南	398	6	194	195	3	212	157
西 藏	81		7	74		60	15
陕 西	575		325	209	41	250	239
甘 肃	348	1	105	114	128	226	105
青 海	35		23	12		21	10
宁 夏	98	1	41	55	1	45	40
新 疆	388	1	167	207	13	235	137

机构总表

单位：个、人

300～499张	500张以上	年末职工人数	女性	工商登记	编制登记	民政登记	一个机构多块牌子
1417	**738**	**318240**	**180915**	**6691**	**150667**	**154987**	**5895**
68	59	14180	8962	396	6580	7195	9
13	24	6360	4466	160	1233	4960	7
95	49	17368	10166	96	8217	8053	1002
21	5	6903	3053	7	2893	3593	410
37	17	6657	3563	2	2895	3709	51
78	29	16432	9750	26	6040	9780	586
33	8	6053	2250		5653	169	231
46	32	9065	4743	31	3843	5178	13
67	26	22725	17054	158	1806	20684	77
179	93	30717	17706	353	13802	16420	142
96	65	16118	10041	468	7898	7736	16
54	19	10435	5078	140	2074	8195	26
31	13	4165	1994	75	1751	2301	38
28	11	8710	3211		7931	497	282
158	60	26563	14563	92	7742	18693	36
23	21	11919	6497		6137	5753	29
50	35	15627	8782	557	11720	3184	166
24	10	13179	6738	135	10439	2263	342
52	41	21445	13961	2408	12378	6152	507
14	7	6364	4517		2771	3471	122
2	6	1137	674	322	509	287	19
29	18	6791	3609	514	3020	3219	38
89	41	14608	6650	494	10668	3043	403
7	1	4000	1779	15	2614	1057	314
18	11	3892	2228	184	2046	1615	47
6		796	560		82	714	
68	18	7180	3903		3998	2913	269
11	6	2677	1262	9	1266	818	584
1	3	381	190		319	62	
8	5	1124	758	23	713	375	13
11	5	4669	2207	26	1629	2898	116

C-2-3续表1

地　区	受教育程度		职业资格水平		
	大学专科人数	大学本科及以上人数	助理社会工作师人数	社会工作师人数	35岁及以下人数
全　国	**53956**	**31660**	**3363**	**3009**	**81374**
中央级					
北　京	2302	2082	138	104	3388
天　津	1203	738	262	69	1447
河　北	2658	1588	82	96	5866
山　西	1304	814	18	59	1943
内蒙古	1460	645	36	64	1422
辽　宁	3282	2462	81	129	3340
吉　林	676	441	46	101	1933
黑龙江	1449	672	181	128	2130
上　海	1383	724	192	353	4242
江　苏	5133	3110	346	297	6874
浙　江	1971	1288	129	144	3494
安　徽	1212	505	83	82	2240
福　建	468	466	77	77	987
江　西	990	393	39	50	1500
山　东	6377	4144	242	195	9102
河　南	1973	1086	97	77	3506
湖　北	3014	1089	104	65	3494
湖　南	2631	1538	146	160	3540
广　东	2863	2159	426	256	4675
广　西	1861	817	109	118	2004
海　南	234	137	11	18	511
重　庆	1158	513	74	62	1235
四　川	3038	1194	157	126	3659
贵　州	1001	586	23	26	1199
云　南	892	646	33	28	1327
西　藏	22	14			531
陕　西	1680	757	70	57	2620
甘　肃	590	477	86	44	1053
青　海	58	59	10	5	171
宁　夏	182	154	14	3	415
新　疆	891	362	51	16	1526

单位：人、人次、时

年龄结构			按人员性质分		志愿服务	
36岁至45岁人数	46岁至55岁人数	56岁及以上人数	管理人员	专业技术技能人员	志愿者服务人次数	志愿服务时间
122448	**90703**	**23715**	**122672**	**195568**	**459254**	**1317064.3**
5008	4513	1271	4539	9641	14291	28873.0
2290	2182	441	1965	4395	8275	15880.0
6710	3959	833	4741	12627	4193	14431.0
2871	1709	380	2967	3936	5238	14001.2
2792	1986	457	2711	3946	738	1434.0
6721	5095	1276	7801	8631	5111	17355.0
2538	1374	208	3290	2763	38	60.0
3991	2490	454	4314	4751	153	1216.0
7829	7791	2863	8695	14030	9768	23204.0
10397	10014	3432	8024	22693	78827	194390.0
5105	5611	1908	4874	11244	53398	95651.0
3718	3537	940	5001	5434	12915	41538.0
1735	1081	362	1746	2419	20659	31369.0
4035	2714	461	4757	3953	3061	9999.0
10331	5808	1322	7756	18807	101656	242443.8
4258	3262	893	5361	6558	743	1844.0
6569	4586	978	6508	9119	20101	31053.0
5654	3210	775	5193	7986	16601	62714.0
9214	6374	1182	7691	13754	61346	366341.0
2394	1545	421	1944	4420	1485	5205.0
364	194	68	371	766	3570	5960.0
2152	2529	875	3530	3261	9542	27464.3
5832	4057	1060	8333	6275	8394	17869.0
1860	839	102	2749	1251	5310	15722.0
1574	812	179	1717	2175	2902	14793.0
208	52	5	426	370	101	138.0
2568	1672	320	2591	4589	5494	14616.0
1017	508	99	1444	1233	275	790.0
149	54	7	205	176	22	130.0
418	245	46	274	850	2187	3169.0
2146	900	97	1154	3515	2860	17411.0

C-2-3续表2

地区	年末床位数	工商登记	编制登记	民政登记	一个机构多块牌子
全国	**3581382**	**66198**	**1935319**	**1512396**	**67469**
中央级					
北京	132574	2591	74921	54942	120
天津	51589	2180	9211	40114	84
河北	160625	888	72561	75862	11314
山西	62572	400	20820	37102	4250
内蒙古	85107	300	39243	43896	1668
辽宁	165461	266	61368	98504	5323
吉林	64551		61509	1932	1110
黑龙江	112453	433	50646	61313	61
上海	112249	478	7969	102815	987
江苏	388561	2964	208189	176098	1310
浙江	220440	6194	115379	98763	104
安徽	142422	840	23129	118036	417
福建	47592	704	24438	22020	430
江西	148315		140322	5050	2943
山东	316651	2874	99209	214159	409
河南	115993		60849	54948	196
湖北	224556	9748	180721	30930	3157
湖南	126776	800	104783	19250	1943
广东	161816	16748	104358	37888	2822
广西	37983		14756	21792	1435
海南	11371	4592	2768	3421	590
重庆	83473	4168	45070	33897	338
四川	302140	7701	239298	46849	8292
贵州	62428	120	47889	11769	2650
云南	50684	814	30669	18817	384
西藏	14735		2262	12473	
陕西	83976		49176	31026	3774
甘肃	36627	90	14615	11419	10503
青海	5022		3746	1276	
宁夏	14435	245	7545	6525	120
新疆	38205	60	17900	19510	735

单位：张、人天、人

年在院总人天数	年末在院人数	女性	工商登记	编制登记	民政登记	一个机构多块牌子
523147256	**2147272**	**526669**	**27050**	**1273670**	**814035**	**32517**
10642393	75538	15513	664	53735	21082	57
5049745	27273	11950	192	6919	20118	44
21303540	73862	13218	254	34464	34484	4660
8009025	33437	2311	26	12663	18479	2269
11276362	43488	6838	300	19799	22728	661
20587709	103524	19009	150	45490	54561	3323
8527483	40597	6390		38970	1078	549
17838027	79277	15219	422	38048	40734	73
22003007	73946	46535	299	5596	67588	463
55464693	210185	58277	1146	130794	77738	507
24804265	98966	33847	3453	52984	42494	35
21923871	80517	17426	398	11479	68401	239
5243310	19279	4609	319	8507	10323	130
20501356	102172	27328		97465	2635	2072
54123033	189661	49882	246	66617	122742	56
17383144	81246	17383		43275	37830	141
38043396	148403	37999	1581	126225	18671	1926
24516387	93109	23029	308	82112	9683	1006
22652367	78905	34552	8481	49525	19288	1611
5368919	22459	7295		9410	12559	490
442249	6062	2827	3817	1121	999	125
15877314	52397	12754	2077	30749	19345	226
53844495	227203	29967	2307	193911	26921	4064
9017959	36444	5401	28	30483	5059	874
5169727	31675	5341	355	20537	10602	181
1561178	11633	1239		1921	9712	
13146656	56372	10303		35683	17974	2715
2488165	15438	3091	90	7317	4454	3577
352678	1809	434		1577	232	
1629676	8342	1214	85	4884	3367	6
4355127	24053	5488	52	11410	12154	437

C-2-3续表3

地　区	在院人员按性质分				收养性机构年末在院人员
	优抚对象	“三无”和农村特困对象	自费人员	其他社会救济对象	老人
全　国	**75855**	**1123687**	**732116**	**9327**	**1900841**
中央级					
北　京	342	3174	30903	293	32563
天　津	506	945	21730	125	22195
河　北	4082	30749	28850	451	66203
山　西	2165	20379	7111	144	27574
内蒙古	1554	15546	23614	232	40409
辽　宁	3790	30482	47468	76	80052
吉　林	4557	29034	4269	61	36020
黑龙江	3649	36707	30431	101	73243
上　海	144	2232	70394	550	71816
江　苏	6567	107162	83086	1129	193479
浙　江	796	23257	70578	70	93588
安　徽	1544	54176	20198	114	76151
福　建	640	3903	12791	21	15846
江　西	7877	80341	9705	1092	93589
山　东	6861	103824	62194		174249
河　南	6075	49690	19192	312	71074
湖　北	7661	100982	29860	62	132477
湖　南	5605	65241	13734	206	81194
广　东	1405	26950	43240	658	66278
广　西	797	4639	13643	765	19144
海　南	68	771	4470	1	5314
重　庆	666	24192	27268	71	50317
四　川	4786	191022	21231	728	214834
贵　州	299	29237	3706	1579	33287
云　南	336	19731	3420	107	25650
西　藏	11	4042	54		11633
陕　西	1753	38816	11668	55	49035
甘　肃	458	10487	2977	184	12742
青　海	33	1221	253	10	1353
宁　夏	217	4972	1616		7061
新　疆	611	9783	12462	130	22471

单位：张、人、人次、平方米

在院人数按年龄分		在院人员按类型分			康复和医疗门诊人次数	机构建筑面积
青壮年	少年儿童	自理（完全自理）	介助（半自理）	介护（不能自理）		
69004	**41908**	**1374763**	**401378**	**235612**	**8084319**	**71808320**
2463	296	11556	10636	13130	332368	2224343
1334	87	11225	4211	8180	168605	981418
1687	1638	45038	14790	9700	224625	3867732
1353	2582	24194	4144	3171	44209	1636467
1571	650	30452	8542	3636	7679	1592205
4215	690	60493	15623	8841	90059	2181611
3681	738	28891	7386	4162	61181	1291949
3316	235	60189	10530	6075	83425	1443494
2060	70	20266	24209	29471	129789	2993716
4442	2577	124665	46398	29435	880451	7683736
2837	1175	63150	21779	12671	785373	3506186
1338	964	56433	16651	5369	74889	2485522
440	1069	8630	5017	3708	69841	1051914
2671	4109	80599	17102	2668	15390	3178884
1999	635	139867	26723	10293	425139	8484214
2857	2844	57722	13158	5895	163898	2284308
7841	2559	98587	29711	14579	540338	4665990
3986	4007	62515	18941	7731	227010	3386726
2689	6522	31786	18153	25550	1436994	3101305
840	1655	9031	5955	6653	115443	1000230
79	273	4794	291	581	7664	208071
1736	344	40766	6972	4659	214055	1659996
6717	1809	180009	35086	8265	492829	4767051
888	1669	27409	7521	914	1278206	953831
912	530	18510	6620	1962	20730	870974
		11400	217	16		317580
3153	635	34785	13484	4554	84072	1693221
512	1179	10472	2756	1205	69979	539834
170	65	1181	351	56	3605	123903
520	74	4425	2530	700	8793	486630
697	228	15723	5891	1782	27680	1145277

C-2-3续表4

地　区	执行企业会计制度单位财务指标				执行行政	
	固定资产原价	营业收入	费用合计	营业利润	固定资产原价	上年结转和结余
全　国	**269522.9**	**25305.0**	**14331.7**	**-4576.6**	**4942530.4**	**339179.4**
中央级						
北　京	82814.7	7749.6	1741.6	-1506.9	162020.0	43868.9
天　津	736.7	296.7	66.0		50040.0	6412.9
河　北	1916.0	334.2	333.2		238512.3	28175.5
山　西	1830.0	30.0	16.0		112607.6	16106.9
内蒙古	18.0				117224.0	11586.6
辽　宁	7272.1	130.0		32.2	179617.0	14274.7
吉　林	2.0				126295.5	2744.5
黑龙江	27.0	7.0	4.9		165019.0	2525.4
上　海	145.0	242.0	2025.0		68066.3	2889.8
江　苏	41236.2	1383.4	2423.0	-1198.2	558714.9	20921.2
浙　江	10579.2	2738.5	600.4	15.0	253345.1	20662.4
安　徽	1892.0	403.0	61.0		116035.0	3086.1
福　建	1564.2	449.4	85.9	-11.0	49125.0	10010.6
江　西	874.8	37.4	62.9	0.9	183853.1	8923.6
山　东	8520.0	549.0	421.2	9.9	303410.2	7026.8
河　南	60.0				102860.0	4405.3
湖　北	13066.0	760.0	202.0		316861.6	2426.5
湖　南	13731.0	660.0	660.0		355068.4	3229.1
广　东	27592.2	6153.8	2403.7	-56.3	348779.1	44389.2
广　西					61238.8	16946.5
海　南	2312.2	1219.5	1668.0	-1860.7	21098.6	9508.4
重　庆	19422.0	1716.8	866.3	-13.5	82468.6	1831.7
四　川	23260.6	286.8	546.4	7.0	345039.0	16328.2
贵　州	145.0	32.0	11.0	3.0	104812.4	4928.5
云　南	3181.0	74.0	41.4		93270.0	10360.6
西　藏					33810.6	2132.0
陕　西					226249.6	7465.0
甘　肃	450.0	1.0	5.0	1.0	51341.8	1411.5
青　海	500.0				7686.7	760.6
宁　夏	6200.0		4.0		35618.6	5339.5
新　疆	175.0	50.9	82.8	1.0	72441.6	8500.9

单位：万元

事业单位会计制度财务指标			执行民间非营利组织单位会计制度财务指标			
本年收入合计	本年支出合计	收支结余	固定资产原价	上年结余	本年收入合计	本年费用合计
3606158.0	**3642155.4**	**199761.2**	**2048109.3**	**57019.4**	**658400.8**	**524493.6**
279707.3	281965.1	18311.6	137522.1	8478.4	51872.0	62719.7
74964.1	77996.3	6926.0	21090.4	533.8	28162.4	17736.0
233119.9	225830.4	12827.9	236679.4	1027.8	17515.4	23098.3
92159.9	89173.2	12117.6	34520.4	295.5	1749.5	3107.2
54846.2	68867.8	6943.8	45118.0	1202.8	8458.8	6836.8
263018.5	344764.3	11160.4	70286.2	207.7	11163.4	12005.3
26740.8	27059.7	34.0			40.1	
59095.4	55644.9	1362.2	61429.7	4567.2	87808.6	4508.8
40963.2	38685.7	1681.7	119710.3	13870.7	179278.9	130040.4
342726.5	338132.3	11479.2	251865.7	-1048.8	40837.9	40724.4
147039.9	141485.5	5070.6	111895.7	9493.6	35789.1	27245.5
63267.3	65864.5	1499.1	120883.6	301.4	19674.9	18812.2
79500.8	77433.5	3840.2	61532.3	2811.0	3060.9	3782.7
47440.4	38661.0	13032.9	15751.8	0.0	398.4	958.5
392423.2	396908.0	121.5	377676.4	0.0	99306.0	99306.0
113495.4	109144.8	2433.3	65865.9	1487.0	9528.8	9600.6
227430.0	222661.1	3243.3	27018.0	120.0	7071.8	7261.9
158372.1	172972.8	2556.7	11421.3	504.1	4353.6	3380.4
255516.6	256745.4	19604.4	50256.8	9331.7	8493.7	9524.6
54086.3	52395.9	6067.9	15612.4	1591.6	5020.8	5157.1
23798.1	21457.8	6536.9	2072.8	1402.5	1178.4	1014.2
44167.9	35229.4	10675.0	72449.1	341.1	19037.6	17860.0
133424.1	126846.9	8324.4	26691.4	439.4	5549.4	6227.0
21885.1	23841.5	2688.7	38031.6	147.0	1258.5	2055.2
63211.7	55954.4	4578.1	8734.0	55.3	295.2	625.9
1577.1	1250.5		450.0		6.1	3.2
181603.8	166715.3	6563.9	35210.3	-147.4	5278.8	5252.5
64155.8	58603.8	5920.6	18428.1		1337.4	704.1
8122.0	7866.0	1013.6	710.0		54.4	48.9
21229.6	25804.0	8516.2	3028.6		884.0	1041.8
37069.0	36193.6	4629.5	6167.0	6.0	3936.0	3854.4

C-2-4 城市养老

地区	单位数	0~99张	100~299张	300~499张	500张以上
全　国	**7656**	**3618**	**3124**	**591**	**323**
中央级					
北　京	167	65	70	15	17
天　津	213	75	111	9	18
河　北	331	126	154	32	19
山　西	116	58	50	7	1
内蒙古	272	121	120	22	9
辽　宁	844	571	217	49	7
吉　林					
黑龙江	473	316	128	22	7
上　海	415	156	210	37	12
江　苏	837	308	401	75	53
浙　江	369	124	176	35	34
安　徽	300	147	121	19	13
福　建	118	36	54	19	9
江　西	178	107	65	2	4
山　东	740	298	320	89	33
河　南	314	179	110	18	7
湖　北	240	136	85	10	9
湖　南	142	75	58	5	4
广　东	251	95	111	28	17
广　西	166	87	62	12	5
海　南	18	4	8	1	5
重　庆	270	107	133	21	9
四　川	285	150	102	22	11
贵　州	116	78	37	1	
云　南	115	52	50	9	4
西　藏	7	5	1	1	
陕　西	117	32	56	21	8
甘　肃	52	19	26	4	3
青　海	7	3	2		2
宁　夏	21	8	8	4	1
新　疆	162	80	78	2	2

服务机构

单位:个、人

年末职工人数	女性	受教育程度 大学专科人数	受教育程度 大学本科及以上人数	职业资格水平 助理社会工作师人数	职业资格水平 社会工作师人数
132296	**83927**	**21608**	**10026**	**1345**	**905**
5580	3793	667	379	18	16
5427	3974	898	503	239	35
6545	4163	968	245	22	12
1712	911	256	115	6	10
3483	2117	625	161	8	13
8667	5607	1833	1190	19	61
4498	2422	716	283	146	93
14707	11217	658	289	125	258
14384	8834	2844	1432	137	72
6717	4457	777	456	32	28
4158	2522	650	166	29	20
2339	1084	152	71	17	13
1723	609	149	35	4	3
12608	7604	3394	1835	109	47
4842	3004	714	296	54	26
3417	2233	605	182	4	2
2755	1637	524	343	15	16
9205	6305	1177	436	143	50
3461	2536	1111	395	42	42
657	378	123	82	6	11
3961	2442	685	245	30	18
2359	1271	451	161	31	9
966	488	199	92	5	10
1583	916	367	249	7	9
82	63		1		
2642	1603	512	201	33	26
769	417	146	65	57	4
42	20	15	12		
190	133	23	2	1	
2817	1167	369	104	6	1

C-2-4续表1

地区	按人员性质分		年龄结构			
	管理人员	专业技术技能人员	35岁及以下人数	36岁至45岁人数	46岁至55岁人数	56岁及以上人数
全国	**44245**	**88051**	**33359**	**49386**	**38635**	**10916**
中央级						
北京	1155	4425	1158	1818	1969	635
天津	1581	3846	1230	1944	1860	393
河北	1796	4749	2177	2372	1647	349
山西	655	1057	621	736	272	83
内蒙古	1344	2139	686	1521	1030	246
辽宁	3941	4726	1489	3695	2798	685
吉林						
黑龙江	1919	2579	1052	1937	1200	309
上海	7018	7689	2911	5000	5156	1640
江苏	3579	10805	3360	4935	4457	1632
浙江	1769	4948	1517	1984	2424	792
安徽	1507	2651	1089	1371	1343	355
福建	820	1519	553	991	550	245
江西	802	921	258	972	433	60
山东	3508	9100	4580	4753	2678	597
河南	2043	2799	1183	1663	1474	522
湖北	1278	2139	589	1228	1290	310
湖南	701	2054	752	1186	618	199
广东	2308	6897	2015	3754	2892	544
广西	777	2684	1117	1252	823	269
海南	154	503	390	178	64	25
重庆	1798	2163	759	1258	1381	563
四川	1086	1273	706	910	561	182
贵州	560	406	260	419	247	40
云南	437	1146	615	669	234	65
西藏	2	80	39	29	12	2
陕西	804	1838	1020	985	554	83
甘肃	317	452	285	319	137	28
青海	25	17	18	19	5	
宁夏	46	144	43	98	40	9
新疆	515	2302	887	1390	486	54

单位：人、人次、时

志愿服务		年末床位数		年在院总人天数	年末在院人数	
志愿者服务人次数	志愿服务时间		光荣间床位			女性
169238	**395772.3**	**1163900**	**9188**	**147104519**	**596180**	**221676**
10037	19997.0	33829		4417760	14529	7357
7555	14460.0	38705	70	4424456	20674	10815
2007	7133.0	57841	621	8054558	26941	7445
3819	11353.0	13905	355	1096088	7149	794
455	860.0	40452	56	5460041	21759	4581
1887	7687.0	83667	621	11275396	46956	11545
30	30.0					
		51316	340	6331474	32723	7927
807	2076.0	66673		13995823	46835	30618
35912	71422.0	150598	849	17020003	68141	24415
27022	50359.0	82431	192	8788066	35283	14389
8666	27221.0	42500	89	5261899	18887	7158
1545	2080.0	24252	32	3171591	10793	2529
610	2220.0	18208	300	1678244	8316	3470
55146	129146.3	124760	1378	16539421	58650	21886
123	155.0	38698	338	4651434	22850	7105
		35146	1999	4361160	16381	6601
964	2830.0	18945	160	2421139	10225	4670
2000	8420.0	52176	43	8841977	29373	16432
380	770.0	21290	596	2684176	11933	4134
		8057	11	196408	4731	2442
3735	11308.0	39491	232	6480088	22393	7600
684	1502.0	36405	147	3583696	18430	5732
2524	6253.0	10480	160	995919	4040	1257
162	506.0	16665	34	833538	7681	1175
2		2262		231105	1921	439
692	2108.0	23643	285	1538673	12172	4855
150	430.0	9153	112	428535	3445	912
15	80.0	1507		34532	202	93
		3544	96	230402	1523	293
2309	15366.0	17301	72	2076917	11244	3007

C-2-4续表2

地区	在院人员按性质分				在院人员按	
	优抚对象	"三无"和农村特困对象	自费人员	其他社会救济对象	老人	青壮年
全 国	**7351**	**78593**	**477762**	**1564**	**582690**	**10339**
中央级						
北 京	200	277	13446	219	13919	596
天 津	130	571	19626	125	19640	947
河 北	323	5506	18610	90	26475	293
山 西	149	1301	5008	1	7033	16
内蒙古	98	873	19943	6	21535	198
辽 宁	1027	6417	37094	22	46519	423
吉 林						
黑龙江	1110	5739	21028	47	31300	1317
上 海	63	484	45935	140	46112	722
江 苏	1239	10016	54919	140	67004	783
浙 江	264	3021	30209	58	34772	490
安 徽	153	1645	16502	32	18700	62
福 建	37	199	10557		10670	109
江 西	200	6029	1980		8069	15
山 东	749	6007	50341		58015	600
河 南	485	4250	17078	75	22240	535
湖 北	136	1729	13041	20	15935	401
湖 南	180	2279	7163	79	9376	737
广 东	26	2552	25836	7	27863	876
广 西	129	698	9631	56	11662	179
海 南	14	79	4460	1	4731	
重 庆	65	1379	20857	27	22175	216
四 川	80	7466	7920	284	17676	239
贵 州	75	1272	2545	33	3718	128
云 南	90	2474	1975	74	7534	112
西 藏		915	54		1921	
陕 西	232	2132	9577	22	11994	152
甘 肃	22	1197	2162		3326	27
青 海		39	163		202	
宁 夏	66	413	583		1459	64
新 疆	9	1634	9519	6	11115	102

单位：张、人天、人、人次、平方米

年龄分	在院人员按类型分			康复和医疗门诊人次数	机构建筑面积
少年儿童	自理（完全自理）	介助（半自理）	介护（不能自理）		
3151	**336998**	**137473**	**121709**	**1733792**	**25765826**
14	3714	4283	6532	140046	853681
87	9255	3448	7971	106726	816688
173	14421	7034	5486	11620	1895619
100	5513	914	722	2287	339194
26	14976	4465	2318		702039
14	34024	8523	4409	24689	1046763
106	25653	3321	3749	25289	696479
1	12268	13074	21493	16685	1728975
354	33193	17623	17325	167486	3575320
21	20078	9914	5291	95638	1515430
125	9475	6296	3116	15709	653146
14	4913	3594	2286	7097	484220
232	6298	1364	654	3998	432466
35	41364	11332	5954	167462	3798459
75	13019	6683	3148	36307	877425
45	9308	3964	3109	10002	942079
112	5625	2618	1982	30505	492702
634	9055	7065	13253	734279	930840
92	4615	3303	4015	11858	397632
	4316	107	308		149859
2	16294	3900	2199	59434	894335
515	12776	4191	1463	13362	686544
194	2694	1017	329	8877	134369
35	6269	963	449	1650	252940
	1688	217	16		20280
26	5248	4148	2776	17223	489102
92	2434	546	465	12947	213960
	167	30	5	80	43071
	805	562	156	764	79527
27	7540	2974	730	11772	622684

C-2-4续表3

地区	执行企业会计制度单位财务指标				执行行政	
	固定资产原价	营业收入	费用合计	营业利润	固定资产原价	上年结转和结余
全　国	**229024.1**	**21922.2**	**13576.7**	**-4641.8**	**915217.4**	**25566.9**
中央级						
北　京	70267.4	4705.8	1548.4	-1556.8	31078.7	6592.8
天　津	736.7	296.7	66.0		25459.6	2191.8
河　北	1916.0	334.2	333.2		33396.8	75.0
山　西	1830.0	30.0	16.0		21723.5	1949.9
内蒙古	18.0				17209.5	448.3
辽　宁	270.0	130.0		32.2	35242.2	3294.2
吉　林						
黑龙江	22.0	2.0	1.4		56655.4	26.9
上　海	135.0	242.0	2025.0		14440.1	333.3
江　苏	40906.2	1333.4	2373.0	-1198.2	166821.0	3512.4
浙　江	10175.3	2662.9	532.8	15.0	63511.1	2602.8
安　徽	1892.0	368.0	26.0		7206.8	-199.5
福　建	1564.2	449.4	85.9	-11.0	9115.4	59.9
江　西	640.0				21074.5	20.0
山　东	7820.0	519.0	396.8	6.9	52931.8	
河　南					23789.9	26.0
湖　北	12916.0	655.0	202.0		14409.1	
湖　南	13730.0	660.0	660.0		131451.5	379.0
广　东	26591.4	6153.8	2159.3	-62.7	55624.4	1819.4
广　西					5255.4	505.0
海　南	2312.2	1219.5	1668.0	-1860.7	9997.3	
重　庆	19422.0	1716.8	866.3	-13.5	19976.6	40.8
四　川	5929.7	286.8	479.4	3.0	15907.9	1488.9
贵　州	45.0	32.0	11.0	3.0	2630.9	15.8
云　南	3180.0	74.0	41.4		13313.8	228.5
西　藏					762.4	
陕　西					18897.2	5.8
甘　肃	450.0	1.0	5.0	1.0	15285.6	74.1
青　海					1493.1	54.7
宁　夏	6200.0				12458.0	8.0
新　疆	55.0	49.9	79.8		18097.9	13.1

单位：万元

事业单位会计制度财务指标			执行民间非营利组织单位会计制度财务指标			
本年收入合计	本年支出合计	收支结余	固定资产原价	上年结余	本年收入合计	本年费用合计
208075.5	**202720.1**	**8098.5**	**1461914.5**	**40270.8**	**506644.5**	**375390.3**
12194.8	12435.7	-172.9	68008.0	1924.8	32440.6	42239.4
18264.1	16584.2	1013.0	16886.4	533.8	24803.8	14409.7
7090.9	6764.7	841.5	174677.2	1188.4	13793.0	18686.2
4844.9	5515.7	1258.2	12898.6	152.0	546.5	939.3
2938.2	3118.3	276.4	39426.9	1202.8	7609.4	5951.3
12096.6	14447.7	826.2	57372.7	186.2	8241.1	9436.6
2648.9	2567.0	3.0	59189.5	4534.1	87537.4	4133.3
3781.2	3578.0	214.4	48990.2	5627.9	134267.8	87234.9
33655.8	30789.9	932.2	196130.9	-1078.3	30827.7	32391.6
18832.3	17436.0	1105.9	84172.4	8684.6	26219.3	19195.0
1811.4	1680.8	3.0	63438.6	283.8	12059.0	10163.0
1341.3	1030.8	87.0	55735.7	2472.8	2303.2	2745.0
2198.8	1928.3		15670.0		253.4	839.4
10369.8	10369.8		250968.9		61779.1	61779.1
4650.2	4458.9	275.5	56650.4	1480.2	8551.6	8628.6
2505.5	2468.5		26459.0	116.0	6661.0	6949.1
8422.5	9643.3		10593.7	495.1	3516.0	2570.7
39853.2	37808.6	938.0	41696.4	9045.7	7092.8	8190.3
3624.7	2929.3	577.6	14258.4	1319.6	4909.5	4777.9
654.1	757.7	-17.7	1900.0	1402.5	1178.4	1004.5
3969.5	4133.3	-123.8	71751.1	341.1	18998.1	17820.5
909.9	1464.5		10481.4	230.3	2753.3	4146.8
446.5	462.4		24946.8	147.0	1124.9	1860.6
1210.4	988.3	21.5	4902.0	22.3	232.2	400.5
65.5	65.5					
3144.5	3122.1	-34.7	30369.3	-41.9	4259.8	4117.6
880.1	906.7		16681.0		576.4	609.0
680.1	664.0	70.7	75.0		6.0	0.4
597.5	492.0	3.5	1735.0		282.2	436.6
4392.3	4108.1		5849.0		3821.0	3733.4

C-2-5 农村养老

地区	单位数	0～99张	100～299张	300～499张	500张以上
全国	**15587**	**8511**	**6390**	**508**	**178**
中央级					
北京	273	93	139	25	16
天津	37	14	18	2	3
河北	431	153	202	50	26
山西	412	261	140	9	2
内蒙古	301	213	75	9	4
辽宁	502	315	177	7	3
吉林	594	390	183	20	1
黑龙江	161	58	76	13	14
上海	192	40	117	25	10
江苏	1285	466	707	90	22
浙江	753	327	377	34	15
安徽	661	253	374	32	2
福建	94	88	5	1	
江西	1058	735	310	10	3
山东	996	264	663	55	14
河南	548	300	242	3	3
湖北	1131	440	668	16	7
湖南	1322	1147	170	5	
广东	899	760	133	5	1
广西	120	113	6	1	
海南	44	33	11		
重庆	305	165	139	1	
四川	1955	960	934	43	18
贵州	574	398	173	3	
云南	195	109	78	5	3
西藏					
陕西	338	123	172	35	8
甘肃	215	165	43	5	2
青海	17	12	5		
宁夏	58	25	30	2	1
新疆	116	91	23	2	

服务机构

单位:个、人

年末职工人数		受教育程度		职业资格水平	
	女性	大学专科人数	大学本科及以上人数	助理社会工作师人数	社会工作师人数
109350	**54078**	**12353**	**3271**	**401**	**396**
5373	3223	540	251	11	9
394	229	150	27	4	4
5983	3402	544	143	8	9
3011	1139	394	111		4
1627	719	265	66	1	3
4112	2322	389	141	5	3
3385	1472	398	166	24	85
2283	1168	305	48	20	18
6392	4642	436	161	25	15
11855	6235	1168	258	35	25
5957	3288	552	98	48	54
4569	1610	144	35	13	4
421	172	13	4	1	1
4273	1373	350	3	3	4
9935	4974	1810	516	36	8
3991	1882	358	88	1	17
7369	3683	855	88	9	7
5609	2384	533	89	23	33
4744	2465	298	92	28	27
362	220	40	22		5
82	60				
1548	453	89	31	3	
8647	3307	1385	287	51	34
1818	724	392	250	9	3
1202	722	182	71	9	1
2445	1257	408	147	11	4
869	343	195	39	4	7
126	52	18	7	4	4
417	295	32	3	3	
551	263	110	29	12	8

C-2-5续表1

地区	按人员性质分		年龄结构			
	管理人员	专业技术技能人员	35岁及以下人数	36岁至45岁人数	46岁至55岁人数	56岁及以上人数
全　国	**47236**	**62114**	**23857**	**44330**	**32419**	**8744**
中央级						
北　京	1579	3794	1206	2010	1671	486
天　津	184	210	45	208	124	17
河　北	1503	4480	1887	2605	1256	235
山　西	1393	1618	730	1268	830	183
内蒙古	599	1028	304	724	476	123
辽　宁	2103	2009	794	1725	1262	331
吉　林	2037	1348	1074	1413	824	74
黑龙江	1173	1110	496	1113	605	69
上　海	1259	5133	1005	2206	2184	997
江　苏	3180	8675	1996	4082	4319	1458
浙　江	2235	3722	987	2007	2172	791
安　徽	2571	1998	662	1693	1717	497
福　建	232	189	39	201	164	17
江　西	2561	1712	581	1911	1504	277
山　东	2978	6957	3272	4214	1985	464
河　南	2105	1886	1096	1456	1178	261
湖　北	3418	3951	1558	3320	2086	405
湖　南	2922	2687	986	2798	1424	401
广　东	2132	2612	768	1910	1627	439
广　西	215	147	50	192	103	17
海　南	63	19	15	34	20	13
重　庆	1136	412	88	521	699	240
四　川	5460	3187	1627	3666	2636	718
贵　州	1488	330	556	952	279	31
云　南	727	475	403	471	278	50
西　藏						
陕　西	1000	1445	888	875	581	101
甘　肃	518	351	316	333	193	27
青　海	75	51	67	50	9	
宁　夏	138	279	126	146	125	20
新　疆	252	299	235	226	88	2

单位：人、人次、时、人天、张

志愿服务		年末床位数		年在院总人天数	年末在院人数	
志愿者服务人次数	志愿服务时间		光荣间床位			女性
168575	**636735.3**	**1771284**	**45713**	**306115051**	**1151825**	**223619**
66	492.0	53065	43	5509261	17773	6695
220	420.0	7214		306940	2068	944
1897	6230.0	73780	3369	10241467	33337	4169
738	1115.0	35600	776	5331738	19372	1079
83	374.0	29734	354	4046271	15546	1176
2140	8449.0	47165	585	6616269	28008	4186
		46348	1883	6295141	30574	4324
		41253	1221	8483885	30927	4448
8634	19598.0	38611	5	6453136	22445	12834
25944	68787.0	197877	4722	34853529	120866	29179
12948	23325.0	105213	456	11748606	47201	12541
2129	6157.0	86281	756	14970703	54635	8622
780	875.0	5534	138	641663	2263	648
1150	3440.0	98516	7571	14358215	69681	18878
28259	67416.0	158632	7133	35760353	112321	26363
150	340.0	56809	2700	10631834	46040	8412
11080	15224.0	141065	3630	27918748	102487	23382
12199	48331.0	80640	2584	17581055	63911	12790
45782	333184.0	58285	1520	7131662	23875	7400
		3907	528	775958	2631	578
250		1403		87898	419	171
2866	7591.3	30944	79	7182821	22941	1969
5017	10056.0	227958	2618	45832913	186929	19403
1435	4683.0	43223	123	6999172	27977	3106
117	457.0	21561	888	3522067	14799	3131
2277	6711.0	48356	1291	9689663	35075	4077
80	230.0	16911	565	1447652	7867	1432
		1345		139441	711	164
2040	2040.0	6463	121	893105	4033	593
294	1210.0	7591	54	663885	5113	925

C-2-5续表2

地　区	在院人员按性质分				在院人员按	
	优抚对象	“三无”和农村特困对象	自费人员	其他社会救济对象	老人	青壮年
全　国	**35492**	**929846**	**158926**	**4840**	**1110367**	**33168**
中央级						
北　京	18	2024	15410	74	16651	1075
天　津	62	77	1928		2057	11
河　北	299	21735	8736	191	32623	603
山　西	384	16374	1615	134	17961	937
内蒙古	510	11936	2097	208	14467	841
辽　宁	1660	19671	6325	8	26243	1660
吉　林	3587	25616	1121	18	27823	2392
黑龙江	1739	26156	2116	53	29608	1281
上　海	48	1565	20021	409	21174	1202
江　苏	4779	92141	22959	624	118682	1721
浙　江	331	18024	27984	7	46021	1130
安　徽	399	50037	2342	10	53760	705
福　建	36	928	1299		2235	5
江　西	2542	61175	4378	1080	66919	1628
山　东	4183	95357	10501		111496	634
河　南	3593	40253	1557		44264	1272
湖　北	4337	88376	8026	13	95580	5568
湖　南	2235	56271	1615	77	61607	1503
广　东	548	17077	5204	29	23333	337
广　西	5	1580	1021	2	2550	66
海　南		291			418	
重　庆	277	20625	1884	38	22091	780
四　川	2861	175030	7003	308	181296	4992
贵　州	53	25188	600	1464	27243	269
云　南	157	13609	654	19	13959	629
西　藏						
陕　西	227	32947	1754		33651	1331
甘　肃	304	6928	493	60	7241	248
青　海		666			691	17
宁　夏	100	3445	149		3763	263
新　疆	218	4744	134	14	4960	68

单位：张、人、人次、平方米

年龄分	在院人员按类型分			康复和医疗门诊人次数	机构建筑面积
少年儿童	自理（完全自理）	介助（半自理）	介护（不能自理）		
8290	**885545**	**206754**	**59526**	**1810007**	**31114870**
47	7080	5244	5449	38020	1152254
	1472	489	107	16484	113936
111	25187	5699	2451	9007	1326020
474	16415	2328	629	4808	894406
238	12255	2724	567	500	474443
105	21125	5057	1826	16324	594606
359	21601	5720	3253	32910	811428
38	23930	5764	1233	11723	437377
69	7405	9967	5073	90954	1033449
463	87250	26431	7185	361156	3093505
50	35396	8603	3202	420053	1236389
170	44198	9235	1202	21059	1396121
23	1667	440	156	224	117930
1134	55674	12619	1388	4060	1802890
191	94613	14104	3604	115412	4182230
504	40487	4371	1182	47464	881632
1339	75331	19473	7683	241006	2513784
801	48631	12865	2415	54594	1806511
205	15572	5543	2760	94322	1072628
15	1842	625	164	194	102729
1	285	95	39		23295
70	20922	1600	419	13397	421250
641	155621	26458	4850	134439	3213193
465	22085	5784	108	12056	602295
211	10090	4056	653	9421	381738
93	26612	7331	1132	17811	853164
378	6352	1280	235	41363	161887
3	467	215	29	292	51320
7	2278	1520	235	773	189197
85	3702	1114	297	181	173262

C-2-5续表3

地区	执行企业会计制度单位财务指标				执行行政	
	固定资产原价	营业收入	费用合计	营业利润	固定资产原价	上年结转和结余
全　国	**40498.8**	**3382.8**	**755.0**	**65.2**	**1835851.7**	**14599.1**
中央级						
北　京	12547.3	3043.8	193.2	49.9	44970.9	1377.5
天　津					5.0	
河　北					75251.4	715.3
山　西					25716.6	160.0
内蒙古					34450.3	315.2
辽　宁	7002.1				35798.6	314.7
吉　林	2.0				70570.9	413.6
黑龙江	5.0	5.0	3.5		53452.6	168.5
上　海	10.0				1580.2	16.4
江　苏	330.0	50.0	50.0		236430.7	194.7
浙　江	403.9	75.6	67.6		83620.4	3615.9
安　徽		35.0	35.0		67209.5	384.5
福　建					3642.7	
江　西	234.8	37.4	62.9	0.9	115611.7	36.5
山　东	700.0	30.0	24.4	3.0	68029.0	
河　南	60.0				39905.3	
湖　北	150.0	105.0			152254.3	549.0
湖　南	1.0				92761.0	693.3
广　东	1000.8		244.4	6.4	133480.9	2938.1
广　西					3446.6	5.0
海　南					1665.3	2.5
重　庆					23817.1	0.3
四　川	17330.9		67.0	4.0	202636.8	1688.6
贵　州	100.0				77280.7	242.2
云　南	1.0				36295.1	647.4
西　藏						
陕　西					111916.7	59.7
甘　肃					12358.6	22.2
青　海	500.0				1408.1	
宁　夏			4.0		15372.2	
新　疆	120.0	1.0	3.0	1.0	14912.5	38.0

单位：万元

事业单位会计制度财务指标			执行民间非营利组织单位会计制度财务指标			
本年收入合计	本年支出合计	收支结余	固定资产原价	上年结余	本年收入合计	本年费用合计
303317.6	**378233.1**	**2278.2**	**562500.5**	**16420.6**	**150046.6**	**147415.6**
10217.7	8767.2	499.5	69514.1	6553.6	19431.4	20480.3
55.2	48.2	0.5	4204.0		3358.6	3326.3
16991.4	17039.2	174.0	62002.2	-160.6	3722.4	4412.1
4060.7	3808.4		18621.8	43.5	1203.0	1651.5
6930.3	6794.2	130.6	5691.1		849.4	885.5
8947.3	88133.7	2.8	12888.5	6.5	2922.3	2558.7
10561.3	10635.6					
5097.7	4973.9	212.5	1747.2	22.1	271.2	312.6
1374.6	1147.8	20.4	70720.1	8242.8	45011.1	42805.5
50102.9	55363.6	21.0	55315.8	29.5	9690.0	8264.6
21888.0	21350.9	597.0	27435.6	797.0	9224.2	7716.1
10299.8	9563.4	16.1	57445.0	17.6	7615.9	8649.2
663.4	666.9		5796.6	338.2	757.7	1037.7
9893.7	8699.9		39.0		2.0	3.0
14581.1	14581.1		126707.5		37526.9	37526.9
6659.6	6086.4	4.0	9211.5	6.8	940.0	963.0
29526.2	27584.5	59.7	549.0		375.8	312.8
19220.1	18320.2	36.0	827.6	9.0	837.6	809.7
16100.6	16242.7	312.5	1520.4	101.0	910.4	1049.3
173.8	204.9		1354.0	272.0	111.3	379.2
398.6	398.6		172.8			9.7
7282.4	7130.1		48.0		16.0	16.0
24128.5	22800.9	167.7	14609.0	208.1	2788.1	2030.2
4059.3	3951.9	2.6	4093.0		23.1	92.6
2902.5	2813.0	21.9	3452.0	33.0	13.0	221.4
8843.5	8613.5	-3.7	4841.0	-105.5	1019.0	1134.9
10583.8	10568.4	3.1	1747.1		761.0	95.1
196.0	196.0		635.0		48.4	48.5
867.7	873.2		1293.6		601.8	605.2
709.9	874.8		18.0	6.0	15.0	18.0

C-2-6 社会

地区	单位数	0～99张	100～299张	300～499张	500张以上
全国	**1717**	**620**	**705**	**225**	**167**
中央级					
北京	9	1	4	1	3
天津	2		2		
河北	35	12	16	6	1
山西	19	7	7	3	2
内蒙古	51	13	29	5	4
辽宁	54	11	27	11	5
吉林	60	16	27	11	6
黑龙江	58	23	17	8	10
上海	22	1	12	5	4
江苏	64	13	21	13	17
浙江	92	15	36	27	14
安徽	53	25	23	1	4
福建	66	28	24	11	3
江西	105	54	41	7	3
山东	26	6	7	8	5
河南	54	26	18	2	8
湖北	121	19	69	16	17
湖南	81	37	28	12	4
广东	148	52	56	18	22
广西	91	55	33	1	2
海南	4	1	2		1
重庆	30	2	13	6	9
四川	133	37	65	21	10
贵州	53	23	26	3	1
云南	40	15	20	3	2
西藏	74	55	14	5	
陕西	32	13	7	10	2
甘肃	51	16	32	2	1
青海	9	5	2	1	1
宁夏	8	3	1	1	3
新疆	72	36	26	7	3

福利院

单位:个、人

年末职工人数	女性	受教育程度		职业资格水平	
		大学专科人数	大学本科及以上人数	助理社会工作师人数	社会工作师人数
43411	**26903**	**9963**	**7726**	**1108**	**1020**
1090	782	357	368	21	19
96	46	36	32	5	2
992	637	286	186	23	29
442	258	114	59	1	7
931	479	342	210	20	36
1995	1076	470	488	38	47
1732	461	194	228	19	7
1571	884	258	184	9	10
1583	1173	270	256	42	76
2968	1824	624	833	149	127
2653	1811	425	345	44	56
1082	677	233	122	27	39
791	453	167	169	41	44
1351	683	255	153	14	6
753	440	226	246	44	28
1170	652	322	198	31	25
2877	1827	817	313	61	36
2706	1788	874	546	83	75
6037	4423	947	1135	216	124
1997	1492	521	269	55	61
215	156	51	29	4	1
1077	617	278	198	32	43
2220	1307	612	352	39	60
807	388	256	152	8	8
584	359	157	172	9	13
714	497	22	13	0	0
892	449	280	124	17	16
569	289	150	97	11	17
173	102	20	14	6	1
421	279	107	96	9	2
922	594	292	139	30	5

C-2-6续表1

地区	按人员性质分		年龄结构			
	管理人员	专业技术技能人员	35岁及以下人数	36岁至45岁人数	46岁至55岁人数	56岁及以上人数
全 国	**16001**	**27410**	**13604**	**16696**	**11016**	**2095**
中央级						
北 京	184	906	395	371	290	34
天 津	16	80	47	25	19	5
河 北	312	680	401	327	214	50
山 西	181	261	117	188	126	11
内蒙古	455	476	282	345	264	40
辽 宁	989	1006	524	762	612	97
吉 林	834	898	517	824	349	42
黑龙江	839	732	376	699	455	41
上 海	410	1173	304	609	445	225
江 苏	548	2420	1055	902	800	211
浙 江	649	2004	542	930	882	299
安 徽	502	580	345	425	269	43
福 建	325	466	209	309	216	57
江 西	674	677	353	584	370	44
山 东	230	523	253	248	189	63
河 南	439	731	554	377	202	37
湖 北	909	1968	867	1183	676	151
湖 南	713	1993	1041	870	712	83
广 东	2368	3669	1498	2921	1483	135
广 西	651	1346	696	742	462	97
海 南	37	178	48	86	68	13
重 庆	508	569	287	333	392	65
四 川	1117	1103	799	777	546	98
贵 州	455	352	278	323	191	15
云 南	266	318	183	251	129	21
西 藏	424	290	492	179	40	3
陕 西	309	583	304	302	232	54
甘 肃	244	325	225	222	100	22
青 海	74	99	74	68	24	7
宁 夏	56	365	222	129	59	11
新 疆	283	639	316	385	200	21

单位：人、人次、时、张、人天

志愿服务		年末床位数		年在院总人天数	年末在院人数	
志愿者服务人次数	志愿服务时间		光荣间床位			女性
90857	**210193.5**	**377201**	**14100**	**55843393**	**210868**	**71741**
4160	8320.0	3078		620530	2882	1428
		440		113880	312	68
22	88.0	6274	1212	1089511	3739	874
65	130.0	4473		1006305	2787	331
200	200.0	10940	172	1434798	4361	1018
284	419.0	12874	363	2235882	8359	2946
		14654	189	1789752	8011	1596
145	1160.0	13734	502	2689532	10601	2707
327	1530.0	6915	5	1548573	4651	3083
16154	51652.0	27405	402	3335866	10780	4592
6352	9807.0	30069	648	4024277	14429	6657
1830	7609.0	7607	408	1288640	3795	1525
18282	28260.0	11736	702	1192657	3670	1300
514	1739.0	14275	911	1809575	9300	2067
5597	13543.5	7910	185	1176225	3910	1438
319	856.0	9797	998	1616684	5674	1611
8018	13739.0	32159	2613	4609664	18927	6805
933	2570.0	15274	626	3287915	10932	4661
13180	24347.0	41751	1395	6240261	20873	10333
1015	3835.0	9045	675	1586039	5965	2331
3280	5840.0	680		124095	391	184
2017	5977.0	12135	311	2091767	6687	3120
2583	5894.0	27733	278	3742693	15732	4448
1209	4420.0	6236	250	784268	2970	830
2515	13206.0	7013	80	795253	4558	1035
99	138.0	12473		1330073	9712	800
1341	2890.0	6908	571	1586815	4654	1279
45	130.0	6898	48	585683	3018	747
7	50.0	1824	75	178230	675	177
147	1129.0	3969	100	492640	2053	326
217	715.0	10922	381	1435310	6460	1424

C-2-6续表2

地区	在院人员按性质分				在院人员按	
	优抚对象	“三无”和农村特困对象	自费人员	其他社会救济对象	老人	青壮年
全国	**5965**	**101074**	**85462**	**2649**	**159679**	**21802**
中央级						
北京	13	844	2023		1857	790
天津		292	20		78	234
河北	16	2645	526	12	2153	437
山西	1	2386	270	9	536	283
内蒙古	108	2705	1480	18	3457	520
辽宁	211	4136	3630	42	6002	1816
吉林	409	2923	2752	43	6592	1040
黑龙江	346	4684	5324		9820	690
上海	18	183	4438	1	4516	135
江苏	80	4831	5142	365	7116	1917
浙江	89	2207	11864	5	12375	979
安徽	99	2259	1337	72	2693	439
福建	236	2636	777	21	2312	326
江西	255	5928	2616		6626	407
山东	176	2460	1224		2957	544
河南	614	4626	293	235	2531	914
湖北	1076	9125	7625	29	16187	1599
湖南	501	5872	4236	39	6282	1654
广东	316	7159	11716	604	13874	1341
广西	59	2328	2721	703	3824	593
海南		391			49	79
重庆	28	2185	4451	6	5682	733
四川	254	8185	5963	135	13814	1271
贵州	36	2352	257	82	1724	275
云南	36	3648	791	14	4103	171
西藏	11	3127			9712	
陕西	578	3668	235		2593	1551
甘肃	72	2349	322	94	2126	206
青海	33	516	90	10	460	153
宁夏	40	1114	884		1793	193
新疆	254	3310	2455	110	5835	512

单位：人、人次、平方米

年龄分	在院人员按类型分			康复和医疗门诊人次数	家庭寄养儿童数量	机构建筑面积
少年儿童	自理（完全自理）	介助（半自理）	介护（不能自理）			
29387	**111677**	**48435**	**50756**	**2895086**	**7131**	**11194931**
235	692	1074	1116	140163	11	184472
	113	126	73	1533	118	10675
1149	1521	1036	1182	11635	256	220935
1968	575	523	1689	2107	1752	138338
384	2501	1142	718	6800	20	335563
541	4272	1755	2332	21061	101	375707
379	5799	1382	830	25311	89	330668
91	8177	1388	1036	26413	1	265776
	593	1168	2890	22150		227736
1747	3758	2272	4750	138223	251	937744
1075	7441	2827	4161	96251	388	715807
663	1991	771	1033	9178	352	326264
1032	1652	831	1187	59588	296	344213
2267	6663	2152	485	1495	486	569965
409	2240	995	675	39236		270610
2229	2582	1747	1345	27150	99	296687
1141	9984	5461	3482	115812	177	925351
2996	5390	2560	2982	63280	1100	755573
5658	6434	5334	9105	483072	486	930039
1548	1972	1630	2363	87351	520	394741
263	101	79	211	7314	7	20300
272	3285	1432	1970	103963	93	299002
647	10145	3793	1794	93746	43	737347
971	1977	568	425	1252403	65	139432
284	2141	1565	852	9659	29	213229
	9712					297300
510	2295	1784	575	9105	98	232843
686	1662	900	456	15637	49	156027
62	547	106	22	3233		29512
67	1336	411	306	7256		210086
113	4126	1623	711	14961	244	302990

C-2-6续表3

地区	执行行政事业单位会计制度财务指标				
	固定资产原价	上年结转和结余	本年收入合计	本年支出合计	收支结余
全国	**1289267.2**	**90764.9**	**731361.4**	**676324.2**	**63984.6**
中央级					
北京	62629.6	1399.8	34813.1	33656.9	5364.4
天津	3293.4	217.6	2741.9	2638.8	360.8
河北	25849.4	2847.2	12388.2	13199.3	1463.0
山西	19660.6	2455.9	11645.7	11668.6	582.6
内蒙古	42635.8	1856.4	18783.8	18010.1	2574.0
辽宁	54777.7	3373.8	38891.4	40595.1	2847.2
吉林	49454.2	2249.9	14794.8	15024.4	34.0
黑龙江	35267.5	995.1	14237.8	13795.0	996.3
上海	51042.9	2487.0	34479.3	32618.8	1409.7
江苏	112131.9	10492.0	80298.0	76486.3	3651.3
浙江	88695.7	3157.9	58551.6	55452.0	1856.9
安徽	21730.1	400.9	10834.8	10579.0	490.8
福建	25114.6	4125.8	17234.5	16646.2	734.3
江西	26150.1	1175.6	8595.0	7350.8	-1.1
山东	22265.7		26447.3	26447.3	
河南	12492.1	2967.4	14239.0	12550.1	448.9
湖北	92349.3	419.9	41809.0	40730.0	529.9
湖南	86299.8	419.1	43358.0	37596.7	1407.7
广东	117059.7	19890.9	80490.5	75625.9	7215.5
广西	36192.6	8291.4	23146.3	22581.2	2940.4
海南	4306.7	1680.9	7169.9	3879.6	4484.5
重庆	34280.1	698.6	26467.1	19389.1	7631.8
四川	85676.5	8047.1	36056.5	32109.6	4687.3
贵州	19469.5	2230.2	6930.0	8282.9	626.1
云南	20664.2	1650.8	7236.8	5752.7	1336.9
西藏	33048.2	2132.0	1511.6	1185.0	
陕西	51912.9	2516.5	30103.3	17614.2	2588.8
甘肃	15918.0	555.0	8369.8	6699.2	1758.4
青海	4270.8	5.7	1123.6	1046.3	80.0
宁夏	7141.2	923.3	9853.5	8159.2	5114.4
新疆	27486.4	1101.2	8759.3	8953.9	769.8

单位：万元

执行民间非营利组织单位会计制度财务指标			
固定资产原价	上年结余	本年收入合计	本年费用合计
23694.3	**328.0**	**1709.7**	**1687.7**
3000.0	100.0		516.4
25.0	15.0		10.0
		40.1	
493.0	11.0		62.9
419.0		320.2	68.2
287.7	12.0	345.6	334.4
42.8		143.0	116.1
4.0		37.2	9.0
10.0	4.0	35.0	
7040.0	185.0	490.5	285.0
650.0		23.5	23.5
1601.0	1.0	8.0	50.0
8991.8		110.5	102.0
380.0		50.0	4.0
450.0		6.1	3.2
300.0		100.0	103.0

C-2-7 光荣

地区	单位数	0~99张	100~299张	300~499张	500张以上
全国	**1106**	**883**	**191**	**27**	**5**
中央级					
北京	10	8	2		
天津	6	3	3		
河北	129	101	22	5	1
山西	88	81	6	1	
内蒙古	28	24	4		
辽宁	35	21	13	1	
吉林	25	17	6	1	1
黑龙江	38	31	6	1	
上海					
江苏	8	8			
浙江	12	11	1		
安徽	25	8	15	2	
福建	26	22	3		1
江西	177	132	38	7	
山东	21	11	10		
河南	44	35	8		1
湖北	62	35	21	6	
湖南	105	91	13	1	
广东	45	42	3		
广西	62	61	1		
海南	9	9			
重庆	7	6	1		
四川	51	44	5	1	1
贵州	44	41	3		
云南	2	2			
西藏					
陕西	16	14	2		
甘肃	5	4	1		
青海					
宁夏	3	2		1	
新疆	23	19	4		

院

单位:个、人

年末职工人数	女性	受教育程度		职业资格水平	
		大学专科人数	大学本科及以上人数	助理社会工作师人数	社会工作师人数
9407	**4478**	**2340**	**977**	**118**	**135**
185	82	44	67	3	
135	79	58	31	3	15
1585	835	276	71	8	3
758	314	262	91	3	19
295	125	105	62	1	
468	217	162	144	8	6
511	110	84	47	3	9
225	118	21	9	3	1
77	54	15	12	3	
50	29	24	8	3	1
210	117	43	26	5	2
173	96	27	30	3	5
918	307	100	13	15	26
158	87	57	27	6	3
428	230	122	22	3	
815	472	299	85	16	6
824	364	200	70	11	12
387	226	69	32	9	12
253	144	66	28	8	3
59	27	14	2		
44	18	20	22	1	
295	149	106	36	2	6
188	86	85	18		3
12	7	3	1		1
125	75	37	4	1	
42	5	7	4		2
17	11	2			
170	94	32	15		

C-2-7续表1

地区	按人员性质分		年龄结构		
	管理人员	专业技术技能人员	35岁及以下人数	36岁至45岁人数	46岁至55岁人数
全国	**4105**	**5302**	**2659**	**4089**	**2279**
中央级					
北京	97	88	41	58	68
天津	75	60	37	50	45
河北	391	1194	552	700	293
山西	309	449	216	338	170
内蒙古	104	191	61	118	109
辽宁	212	256	150	203	99
吉林	293	218	167	211	121
黑龙江	92	133	62	74	77
上海					
江苏	20	57	13	31	16
浙江	20	30	8	30	12
安徽	76	134	45	98	54
福建	72	101	42	78	47
江西	556	362	171	447	241
山东	41	117	58	58	36
河南	181	247	159	188	73
湖北	349	466	206	380	200
湖南	351	473	215	354	227
广东	191	196	117	152	107
广西	135	118	65	110	65
海南	36	23	12	22	18
重庆	31	13	16	15	13
四川	178	117	92	128	54
贵州	134	54	42	102	41
云南	7	5	2	2	2
西藏					
陕西	80	45	45	54	21
甘肃	34	8	15	12	11
青海					
宁夏	2	15	5	5	6
新疆	38	132	45	71	53

单位：人、人次、人天、张、时

56岁及以上人数	志愿服务：志愿者服务人次数	志愿服务：志愿服务时间	年末床位数	光荣间床位	年在院总人天数
380	**16886**	**40195.0**	**76363**	**29268**	**11177945**
18	12	32.0	662	596	49702
3	300	600.0	668	460	119140
40	251	955.0	10704	3422	1372830
34	571	1240.0	3787	1954	454065
7			1711	635	317997
16	800	800.0	2732	985	380700
12	8	30.0	2791	241	442082
12			2818	548	317765
17	95	130.0	380	265	76730
	4200	6350.0	542	349	37107
13	200	351.0	2973	1575	325921
6	52	154.0	1737	570	193691
59	260	810.0	14658	5738	2625369
6	5665	15540.0	1672		279787
8	50	230.0	3108	1387	364299
29	921	1969.0	7316	3058	1066130
28	1655	5883.0	6061	2944	1184007
11	384	390.0	1946	629	201507
13	90	600.0	2190	895	243651
7	40	120.0	365	129	32658
	924	2588.0	400	103	67933
21	81	245.0	3783	1617	481241
3	58	116.0	1125	179	184839
6	54	312.0	130	50	13350
5	175	630.0	709	415	154280
4			250	134	13282
1			145	135	3800
1	40	120.0	1000	255	174082

C-2-7续表2

地区	年末在院人数	在院人员		
		女性	优抚对象	"三无"和农村特困对象
全国	**43411**	**7452**	**22637**	**13469**
中央级				
北京	138	33	111	29
天津	346	110	156	5
河北	4186	404	2916	856
山西	1722	62	1344	258
内蒙古	929	63	803	32
辽宁	1486	297	820	258
吉林	1554	470	561	495
黑龙江	2489	137	400	128
上海				
江苏	278	78	251	2
浙江	131		82	
安徽	945	69	833	104
福建	529	97	313	140
江西	12301	2741	4422	7124
山东	899	106	866	
河南	1806	129	1144	531
湖北	4592	999	2067	1752
湖南	3729	768	2642	754
广东	862	172	363	162
广西	864	147	529	33
海南	125	30	54	10
重庆	227	39	179	2
四川	1492	191	1063	245
贵州	641	162	114	405
云南	8		7	
西藏				
陕西	463	14	425	36
甘肃	82		39	13
青海				
宁夏	16	2	11	
新疆	571	132	122	95

单位：人

按性质分		在院人员按年龄分		
自费人员	其他社会救济对象	老人	青壮年	少年儿童
6386	**89**	**41435**	**1166**	**810**
24		136	2	
98		344	2	
372	18	4071	86	29
86		1673	9	40
94		924	3	2
343	4	1200	256	30
396		1305	249	
1963	1	2461	28	
23		274	2	2
		102		29
17		938	1	6
76		529		
515		11587	255	459
		899		
128	2	1748	27	31
723		4480	88	24
442	11	3670	5	54
160	18	819	19	24
209	4	862	2	
10		116		9
45		226	1	
177	1	1455	31	6
131		545	57	39
		8		
		459	4	
	30	29	30	23
		16		
354		559	9	3

C-2-7续表3

地区	在院人员按类型分			康复和医疗门诊人次数	机构建筑面积
	自理(完全自理)	介助(半自理)	介护(不能自理)		
全国	**35218**	**6073**	**2120**	**155860**	**2429127**
中央级					
北京	70	35	33	14139	33936
天津	195	122	29	2104	25120
河北	3215	731	240	15032	345214
山西	1322	313	87	5157	187277
内蒙古	719	188	22		62342
辽宁	1072	242	172	15015	95211
吉林	1291	184	79	2960	89853
黑龙江	2375	57	57	20000	41262
上海					
江苏	220	53	5	1006	11090
浙江	65	49	17	16	13206
安徽	769	158	18	4154	97541
福建	381	134	14	551	37871
江西	11330	836	135	362	329420
山东	752	118	29	1975	59443
河南	1377	279	150	13071	137089
湖北	3574	745	273	30518	198734
湖南	2758	700	271	6960	285666
广东	555	167	140	372	106792
广西	542	211	111	824	69900
海南	92	10	23	350	14617
重庆	180	33	14	10531	14163
四川	1093	348	51	7357	62109
贵州	551	75	15	2917	9420
云南	5	2	1		1114
西藏					
陕西	332	92	39	422	51831
甘肃	22	11	49	32	2100
青海					
宁夏	6	7	3		7520
新疆	355	173	43	35	39286

单位：万元、人、人次、平方米

执行行政事业单位会计制度财务指标				
固定资产原价	上年结转和结余	本年收入合计	本年支出合计	收支结余
182555.2	**11982.2**	**72889.5**	**72849.3**	**6424.6**
7678.0	581.6	3692.1	3940.0	612.8
3488.2	20.0	2870.6	2887.7	
29138.8	132.5	10376.7	10762.9	37.1
11175.0	2056.8	9177.7	9411.5	855.2
8675.1	2954.7	3533.4	4756.7	2388.8
9015.3	1922.0	4788.2	4669.7	2016.4
3729.5	81.0	1384.7	1399.7	
5360.6	30.7	1018.2	967.6	29.2
2599.9		709.7	747.6	
505.8	228.0	803.1	733.9	
9322.6	323.3	2242.4	2187.7	139.2
2243.3	137.3	1654.9	1575.6	64.6
15567.0	4.9	3109.0	3107.3	
4885.8		1618.9	1618.9	
4734.1	25.7	1449.0	1502.7	1.2
19898.2	38.1	6369.3	6252.1	
18106.1	3.0	5701.1	5550.2	
5219.7	67.5	2545.3	2995.6	-170.3
4206.7	365.4	937.9	978.7	11.4
1283.6		278.8	268.8	
1544.0		1085.1	842.1	246.0
5189.0	66.7	3077.8	2632.9	193.0
1411.0		32.4	53.4	
100.0				
2679.1		2056.5	2060.8	
107.2		91.0	91.0	
50.0		5.0	5.0	
4641.6	2943.0	2280.7	849.2	

C-2-8 荣誉军人

地区	单位数	编制登记	一个机构多块牌子	0~99张	100~299张	300~499张	500张以上
全国	**46**	**41**	**5**	**14**	**17**	**8**	**7**
中央级							
北京							
天津							
河北	1	1			1		
山西	6	6		4	2		
内蒙古	1	1			1		
辽宁	1	1				1	
吉林	2	2			1	1	
黑龙江	1	1				1	
上海	1	1		1			
江苏	1	1			1		
浙江	1	1					1
安徽	1	1			1		
福建	1	1			1		
江西	1	1					1
山东	2	2				2	
河南	4	4		2	1		1
湖北	1	1					1
湖南	2	1	1		1		1
广东	2	2			1		1
广西	1	1			1		
海南							
重庆	3	3		2		1	
四川	5	3	2	1	2	1	1
贵州	3	2	1	2	1		
云南	1	1			1		
西藏							
陕西	1	1				1	
甘肃	1	1		1			
青海							
宁夏	1		1	1			
新疆	1	1			1		

康复疗养院

单位:个、人

年末职工人数	女性	受教育程度 大学专科人数	大学本科及以上人数	职业资格水平 助理社会工作师人数	社会工作师人数
5566	**3045**	**1445**	**2177**	**40**	**65**
212	110	36	133	4	1
218	99	41	60	2	5
73	39	18	46	1	2
162	82	33	30		4
425	207				
126	28				
43	22	19	18		4
252	183	65	96		3
517	367	123	304		1
140	52	48	36		
56	27	18	19	2	1
287	180	71	159	3	8
553	280	69	361	5	15
462	272	107	195		2
338	181	83	151	4	3
355	182	139	173		1
219	122	94	88	5	11
57	22	22	20	3	2
161	79	86	17	8	1
435	288	183	152	2	1
107	48	30	33		
101	48	35	24	1	
183	87	95	28		
46	18	9	21		
6	3	5	1		
32	19	16	12		

C-2-8续表1

地 区	按人员性质分		年龄结构		
	管理人员	专业技术技能人员	35岁及以下人数	36岁至45岁人数	46岁至55岁人数
全 国	**1143**	**4423**	**2194**	**1624**	**1409**
中央级					
北 京					
天 津					
河 北	61	151	83	57	48
山 西	61	157	45	84	72
内蒙古	38	35	16	25	20
辽 宁		162	45	55	50
吉 林	126	299	175	90	80
黑龙江	28	98	43	47	36
上 海	8	35	22	14	6
江 苏	53	199	140	36	51
浙 江	63	454	395	77	37
安 徽	140		27	38	68
福 建	2	54	22	14	15
江 西	56	231	96	53	127
山 东	138	415	200	169	151
河 南	40	422	116	219	118
湖 北	28	310	92	135	88
湖 南	28	327	194	102	52
广 东	94	125	60	87	56
广 西	7	50	7	20	26
海 南					
重 庆	57	104	85	25	44
四 川	37	398	215	105	102
贵 州	33	74	24	33	47
云 南	18	83	34	32	33
西 藏					
陕 西	17	166	34	78	57
甘 肃	2	44	17	12	15
青 海					
宁 夏	2	4	2	4	
新 疆	6	26	5	13	10

单位：人、人次、张、人天、时

56岁及以上人数	志愿服务		年末床位数		年在院总人天数
	志愿者服务人次数	志愿服务时间		光荣间床位	
339	**754**	**2830.0**	**10052**	**1714**	**1451291**
24			200		60450
17			535	79	54614
12			100	25	8900
12			322	72	60155
80			600		350
			380		12300
1			50	50	5475
25			220	40	65236
8	586	2306.0	634	60	204575
7			200		73000
5			250	100	38500
11	150	420.0	750		21028
33			800		127970
9			736	195	76712
23			528	200	75000
7			618		24798
16			465	35	123015
4			230	20	69337
7			503	190	54705
13			1110	298	169299
3			229		52159
2	18	104.0	100	58	50
14			300	200	53655
2			62	62	7560
			30		9000
4			100	30	3448

C-2-8续表2

地 区	年末在院人数	女性	在院人员	
			优抚对象	“三无”和农村特困对象
全 国	**5768**	**1579**	**2154**	**538**
中央级				
北 京				
天 津				
河 北	200	67	71	
山 西	316	45	192	60
内蒙古	20		20	
辽 宁	148	35	72	
吉 林	300			
黑龙江	54		54	
上 海	15		15	
江 苏	177		26	151
浙 江	556	260	30	5
安 徽	191	52	60	131
福 建	100	35	18	
江 西	636	87	408	
山 东	193	31	96	
河 南	311	93	145	30
湖 北	455	208	35	
湖 南	310	110	47	25
广 东	293	137	30	
广 西	190	101	19	
海 南				
重 庆	149	26	117	1
四 川	686	193	502	96
贵 州	216	46	21	20
云 南	46		46	
西 藏				
陕 西	147	53	101	19
甘 肃	21		21	
青 海				
宁 夏	30			
新 疆	8		8	

单位：人

按性质分		在院人员按年龄分		
自费人员	其他社会救济对象	老人	青壮年	少年儿童
2614	**12**	**4033**	**1678**	**57**
136		195	5	
64		223	93	
		11	9	
76		88	60	
		300		
		54		
		14	1	
		167	10	
521		318	238	
		60	131	
82		100		
216	12	263	366	7
97		163	30	
136		217	89	5
420		265	180	10
238		209	67	34
233		264	28	1
61		190		
31		143	6	
103		504	182	
173		57	159	
		46		
27		130	17	
		20	1	
		30		
		2	6	

C-2-8续表3

地　区	在院人员按类型分			康复和医疗门诊人次数	机构建筑面积
	自理（完全自理）	介助（半自理）	介护（不能自理）		
全　国	**2821**	**1887**	**1060**	**1111430**	**941535**
中央级					
北　京					
天　津					
河　北	28	93	79	53257	5000
山　西	285	8	23	17334	47217
内蒙古		9	11	379	12949
辽　宁		46	102	12970	69325
吉　林	200	100			60000
黑龙江	54				2600
上　海			15		3556
江　苏		10	167	93512	47676
浙　江	170	386		173415	25355
安　徽		191		24789	12450
福　建	17	18	65	2381	67680
江　西	574	56	6	5475	40043
山　东	164	19	10	39367	81100
河　南	217	58	36	39906	61724
湖　北	355	68	32	143000	72042
湖　南	71	160	79	69088	38275
广　东	48	38	207	124949	31500
广　西	4	186		15160	30306
海　南					
重　庆	85	7	57	26730	31245
四　川	355	225	106	234877	66010
贵　州	102	77	37	1953	68315
云　南	5	34	7		21953
西　藏					
陕　西	85	42	20	32157	32000
甘　肃	2	19			5860
青　海					
宁　夏		30			300
新　疆		7	1	731	7055

单位：万元、人次、平方米、人

执行行政事业单位会计制度财务指标				
固定资产原价	上年结转和结余	本年收入合计	本年支出合计	收支结余
231923.6	**36748.7**	**164049.2**	**150431.1**	**25084.5**
5417.0		4653.0	4632.0	
3857.5	4174.0	4149.9	3672.5	3792.9
5166.0	2268.8	2083.7	3083.6	
6542.0	511.2	2863.0	2890.0	
2540.9				
560.0		575.0	575.0	
1003.1	53.1	1328.1	1341.1	37.2
9968.8	2291.9	6790.4	6117.0	2965.3
11861.0	7533.0	23346.0	22975.0	
2925.9				
2382.0		1583.0	1583.0	
3196.4	7468.2	13690.9	8125.1	13034.0
87816.4	1530.1	16165.1	16635.8	
10042.8	-23.2	9860.3	9266.6	
22835.0		12048.2	11085.3	962.9
5974.8		9454.9	9495.6	-40.7
9404.5		12099.7	11416.3	
4693.2	5317.9	4372.3	4682.5	99.7
2850.8	1092.0	5363.8	3734.8	2921.0
19132.6	415.6	19975.1	19663.3	57.7
1199.4	1086.2	1741.1	1522.8	1254.5
1868.4	2696.6	4565.8	1717.5	
7622.3	270.2	4643.3	4653.9	
1504.1	63.1	1068.2	517.7	
1558.7		1628.4	1044.7	

C-2-9 复员军人

地区	单位数	0~99张	100~299张	300~499张	500张以上
全国	**36**	**13**	**14**	**6**	**3**
中央级					
北京					
天津	1			1	
河北	8	2	4	1	1
山西	1			1	
内蒙古	1		1		
辽宁					
吉林					
黑龙江					
上海					
江苏	4	3	1		
浙江					
安徽					
福建					
江西	2	1	1		
山东	7	2	3	1	1
河南	2		1		1
湖北	1		1		
湖南	1	1			
广东	2		2		
广西	1	1			
海南					
重庆					
四川	2	1		1	
贵州					
云南					
西藏					
陕西	3	2		1	
甘肃					
青海					
宁夏					
新疆					

疗养院

单位:个、人

年末职工人数	女性	受教育程度		职业资格水平	
		大学专科人数	大学本科及以上人数	助理社会工作师人数	社会工作师人数
2639	**1481**	**734**	**1272**	**30**	**69**
109	59	18	52		1
836	495	198	433	3	13
245	108	51	170	2	1
5	2				
83	42	37	18		7
11	4	1	1		
790	486	166	435	19	36
71	38	20	10		
7	4	4			
102	20	60	30		
144	75	58	63	4	9
16	9	4	6		
42	28	29	6		
178	111	88	48	2	2

C-2-9续表1

地区	按人员性质分		年龄结构		
	管理人员	专业技术技能人员	35岁及以下人数	36岁至45岁人数	46岁至55岁人数
全　国	**443**	**2196**	**937**	**790**	**724**
中央级					
北　京					
天　津	17	92	51	6	44
河　北	76	760	236	288	238
山　西	54	191	63	90	76
内蒙古	3	2			5
辽　宁					
吉　林					
黑龙江					
上　海					
江　苏	14	69	17	32	22
浙　江					
安　徽					
福　建					
江　西	5	6	1	5	5
山　东	152	638	320	195	224
河　南	37	34	39	15	12
湖　北	7		4	3	
湖　南	10	92	62	32	8
广　东	34	110	31	68	43
广　西	7	9	7	1	6
海　南					
重　庆					
四　川	6	36	18	15	9
贵　州					
云　南					
西　藏					
陕　西	21	157	88	40	32
甘　肃					
青　海					
宁　夏					
新　疆					

单位：人、人次、人天、张、时

56岁及以上人数	志愿服务：志愿者服务人次数	志愿服务：志愿服务时间	年末床位数	光荣间床位	年在院总人天数
188	**1467**	**4292.0**	**6663**	**1085**	**1226304**
8			300		78840
74			1620	310	466384
16			400		60059
			120	21	5175
12	370	1110.0	340	193	97900
	132	528.0	150		7052
51	901	2254.0	1595		214211
5			710	116	34310
			150	45	1720
			98		11203
2			341	100	102191
2			56		8000
	23	152.0	330	50	29234
	36	208.0			
18	5	40.0	453	250	110025

C-2-9续表2

地区	年末在院人数	女性	在院人员	
			优抚对象	“三无”和农村特困对象
全国	**3701**	**602**	**2256**	**167**
中央级				
北京				
天津	216	13	158	
河北	1125	259	457	7
山西	163		95	
内蒙古	15		15	
辽宁				
吉林				
黑龙江				
上海				
江苏	256	13	192	21
浙江				
安徽				
福建				
江西	135	85	50	85
山东	910	58	791	
河南	94	33	94	
湖北	35	4	10	
湖南	80	30		40
广东	213	78	122	
广西	56	4	56	
海南				
重庆				
四川	91		26	
贵州				
云南				
西藏				
陕西	312	25	190	14
甘肃				
青海				
宁夏				
新疆				

单位：人

按性质分		在院人员按年龄分		
自费人员	其他社会救济对象	老人	青壮年	少年儿童
966	**173**	**2637**	**851**	**213**
58		76	140	
470	140	686	263	176
68		148	15	
		15		
43		236	9	11
		125		10
31		719	191	
		74	20	
25		30	5	
40		50	20	10
91		125	88	
		56		
65		89	2	
75	33	208	98	6

C-2-9续表3

地区	在院人员按类型分			康复和医疗门诊人次数	机构建筑面积
	自理（完全自理）	介助（半自理）	介护（不能自理）		
全国	**2504**	**756**	**441**	**378144**	**362032**
中央级					
北京					
天津	190	26		41758	15000
河北	666	197	262	124074	74944
山西	84	58	21	12516	30035
内蒙古	1	14			4869
辽宁					
吉林					
黑龙江					
上海					
江苏	244	9	3	119068	18401
浙江					
安徽					
福建					
江西	60	75			4100
山东	734	155	21	61687	92372
河南	40	20	34		29751
湖北	35				14000
湖南	40	38	2	2583	8000
广东	122	6	85		29507
广西	56			56	4922
海南					
重庆					
四川	19	71	1	9048	1850
贵州					
云南					
西藏					
陕西	213	87	12	7354	34281
甘肃					
青海					
宁夏					
新疆					

单位：人、人次、平方米、万元

执行行政事业单位会计制度财务指标				
固定资产原价	上年结转和结余	本年收入合计	本年支出合计	收支结余
119410.5	**7695.6**	**69524.4**	**73035.5**	**1548.0**
5611.1	465.6	2653.0	2997.1	121.5
32078.5	751.4	20953.4	21273.7	597.5
16539.5	30.0	5143.7	4885.3	288.4
529.8		40.0	40.0	
3768.2		2114.9	2114.9	
341.0	66.0	254.6	142.0	
33072.8	5496.7	23759.3	27773.4	
1400.0	167.7	1102.9	1133.5	137.1
283.5		78.5	78.2	0.3
880.0		720.0	720.0	
8529.6		7799.4	8101.1	241.9
683.2	159.7	821.1	903.4	161.3
126.0		56.0	31.0	
15567.3	558.5	4027.6	2841.9	

C-2-10 军休

地区	单位数	0~99张	100~299张	300~499张
全国	**1604**	**1240**	**257**	**52**
中央级				
北京	138	31	57	27
天津	16	9	3	1
河北	116	101	13	1
山西	70	67	3	
内蒙古	20	14	5	1
辽宁	51	24	4	9
吉林				
黑龙江	48	38	8	1
上海				
江苏	130	97	31	1
浙江	42	36	5	
安徽	36	30	6	
福建	50	44	6	
江西	16	12	2	2
山东	152	115	27	3
河南	109	96	13	
湖北	102	89	10	2
湖南	98	86	10	1
广东	77	63	13	1
广西	35	35		
海南	8	6	1	1
重庆				
四川	116	100	16	
贵州	14	10	4	
云南	45	34	8	1
西藏				
陕西	68	66	2	
甘肃	24	21	3	
青海	2	1	1	
宁夏	7	6	1	
新疆	14	9	5	

所

单位：个、人

500张以上	年末职工人数	女性	受教育程度 大学专科人数	大学本科及以上人数
55	**15571**	**7003**	**5513**	**6211**
23	1952	1082	694	1017
3	199	79	43	93
1	1215	524	350	377
	517	224	186	208
	243	82	105	100
14	1028	446	395	469
1	362	123	149	148
1	1098	534	380	461
1	224	89	70	77
	276	100	94	120
	385	162	91	173
	147	55	64	29
7	1766	692	655	724
	955	419	330	277
1	804	382	351	270
1	828	363	301	287
	709	345	220	313
	218	94	97	77
	124	53	46	24
	610	300	272	200
	114	45	39	41
2	410	176	148	129
	715	321	260	205
	382	190	83	251
	40	16	5	26
	73	37	13	52
	177	70	72	63

C-2-10续表1

地 区	职业资格水平		按人员性质分	
	助理社会工作师人数	社会工作师人数	管理人员	专业技术技能人员
全 国	**321**	**419**	**9499**	**6072**
中央级				
北 京	85	60	1524	428
天 津	11	12	92	107
河 北	14	29	602	613
山 西	4	13	314	203
内蒙古	5	10	168	75
辽 宁	11	8	556	472
吉 林				
黑龙江	3	6	263	99
上 海				
江 苏	22	63	630	468
浙 江	2	4	138	86
安 徽	9	17	205	71
福 建	13	13	295	90
江 西		3	103	44
山 东	23	58	709	1057
河 南	8	7	516	439
湖 北	10	11	519	285
湖 南	14	23	468	360
广 东	21	23	564	145
广 西	1	5	152	66
海 南	1	6	81	43
重 庆				
四 川	32	16	449	161
贵 州	1	2	79	35
云 南	7	4	262	148
西 藏				
陕 西	6	9	360	355
甘 肃	14	14	329	53
青 海			31	9
宁 夏	1	1	30	43
新 疆	3	2	60	117

单位：人、人次、时

年龄结构				志愿服务	
35岁及以下人数	36岁至45岁人数	46岁至55岁人数	56岁及以上人数	志愿者服务人次数	志愿服务时间
4764	**5533**	**4221**	**1053**	**11477**	**27046.2**
588	751	515	98	16	32.0
37	57	90	15	200	400.0
530	361	263	61	16	25.0
151	167	163	36	45	163.2
73	59	82	29		
338	281	274	135		
101	121	117	23	8	56.0
293	379	349	77	352	1289.0
45	77	84	18	2290	3504.0
72	93	86	25	90	200.0
122	142	89	32		
40	63	34	10	245	842.0
419	694	545	108	6088	14544.0
359	340	205	51	101	263.0
178	320	246	60	82	121.0
290	312	169	57	850	3100.0
186	322	166	35		
62	77	60	19		
46	44	24	10		
202	231	149	28	6	20.0
39	31	34	10	84	250.0
90	149	136	35		
241	234	195	45	1004	2237.0
195	119	52	16		
12	12	16			
17	36	15	5		
38	61	63	15		

C–2–10续表2

地区	执行行政事业单位会计制度财务指标				
	固定资产原价	上年结转和结余	本年收入合计	本年支出合计	收支结余
全　国	**368304.8**	**151822.0**	**2056940.4**	**2088562.1**	**92342.8**
中央级					
北　京	15662.8	33917.2	218789.6	223165.3	12007.8
天　津	12182.7	3517.9	48379.3	52840.3	5430.2
河　北	37380.4	23654.1	160666.3	152158.6	9714.8
山　西	13934.9	5280.3	53137.3	50211.2	5340.3
内蒙古	8557.5	3743.2	20536.8	33064.9	1574.0
辽　宁	38241.2	4858.8	195432.0	194028.1	5467.8
吉　林					
黑龙江	13722.9	1304.2	35517.8	32766.4	121.2
上　海					
江　苏	26994.4	4430.2	169054.8	166513.0	3909.4
浙　江	5151.1	3524.8	23618.9	23537.7	1510.8
安　徽	7640.1	2176.9	38078.9	41853.6	850.0
福　建	6627.0	5687.6	57023.7	55931.0	2954.3
江　西	1912.4	152.4	9698.4	9307.6	
山　东	34408.7		299481.7	299481.7	121.5
河　南	10495.8	1241.7	75534.4	74146.6	1566.6
湖　北	14832.2	1419.5	135093.3	134462.5	1690.5
湖　南	19595.2	1734.7	71495.5	91646.8	1153.7
广　东	19460.3	19673.3	96627.9	104555.2	11066.8
广　西	6761.1	2302.1	21010.2	20115.9	2277.5
海　南	3845.7	7825.0	15296.7	16153.1	2070.1
重　庆					
四　川	16370.2	4621.3	49220.3	48144.7	3218.7
贵　州	2820.9	1354.1	8675.8	9568.1	805.5
云　南	21028.5	5137.3	47296.2	44682.9	3197.8
西　藏					
陕　西	17654.1	4054.3	128785.1	127808.9	4013.5
甘　肃	6168.3	697.1	43162.9	39820.8	4159.1
青　海	514.7	700.2	6122.3	5959.7	862.9
宁　夏	597.2	4408.2	9905.9	16274.6	3398.3
新　疆	5744.5	4405.6	19298.4	20362.9	3859.7

单位：万元、户、人

机构内的户数	分散安置户数	年末机构管理军休干部人数	分散安置人数	本年发放离退休金
175919	**45096**	**182136**	**46617**	**2644989.9**
41940	2583	42678	2462	228230.8
4262	1450	5073	1416	35524.1
10206	6185	11337	7003	1111265.0
3872	2168	4042	2114	36821.4
2050	1132	2019	1161	23465.5
18701	401	18937	370	121836.3
158		158		
2952	60	2777	294	15307.3
11741	2681	12558	2871	136493.5
1551	161	1500	134	14818.6
2861	615	2886	822	31045.7
4083	1467	3566	1642	43619.2
1758	54	1838	35	7259.1
21282	6150	18922	6144	182543.8
6135	1682	6171	1700	55165.7
8192	3058	8250	2724	93594.9
5140	548	5096	1174	52464.4
6852	3454	7585	4169	74836.9
1265	471	1289	469	13801.6
866	410	793	397	8289.2
4821	776	4631	788	40708.2
1135	460	1101	501	12242.3
5215	1415	5026	443	152000.3
3607	4964	8547	4998	93407.6
3353	2221	3229	2224	34846.8
346	127	348	127	4931.7
284	19	708	21	8014.2
1291	384	1071	414	12455.8

C-2-11 智障与精神疾病

地　区	单位数	单位数按登记类型分			单位数按床位数量分	
		编制登记	民政登记	一个机构多块牌子	0～99张	100～299张
全　国	**242**	**226**	**4**	**12**	**44**	**87**
中央级						
北　京	1	1				1
天　津	2	2				
河　北	2	2				
山　西	8	8				7
内蒙古	7	7				4
辽　宁	3	3			1	1
吉　林	14	10		4	2	4
黑龙江	8	8				1
上　海	3	3				
江　苏	12	11		1		5
浙　江	3	3				1
安　徽	4	4			2	1
福　建	17	17			1	9
江　西	4	3		1	3	1
山　东	14	14			1	5
河　南	7	7			3	1
湖　北	12	12			1	1
湖　南	17	16		1	4	5
广　东	11	11			2	5
广　西	8	8				2
海　南						
重　庆	9	9			5	1
四　川	25	22		3	6	6
贵　州	22	21		1	11	8
云　南	6	6				4
西　藏						
陕　西	4	4				2
甘　肃	6	5	1		1	4
青　海	1	1				1
宁　夏	1			1		
新　疆	11	8	3		1	7

服务机构总表

单位:个、人

300～499张	500张以上	年末职工人数	女性	年末职工人数按登记类型分：编制登记	民政登记	受教育程度：大学专科人数	大学本科及以上人数
56	**55**	**25736**	**15278**	**25012**	**150**	**8561**	**8462**
		171	138	171		56	66
2		349	169	349		62	89
	2	512	272	512		76	267
	1	1073	609	1073		200	273
2	1	538	280	538		206	199
1		353	175	353		177	83
1	7	1296	737	761		182	190
3	4	1244	460	1244		260	359
1	2	544	346	544		185	149
4	3	1765	1099	1765		472	834
1	1	154	102	154		19	69
	1	538	303	538		237	121
6	1	1113	695	1113		377	235
		162	94	162		52	55
8		1738	1083	1738		527	901
2	1	1046	623	1046		412	396
5	5	2662	1654	2662		725	1266
4	4	1724	1146	1724		568	382
2	2	1217	686	1217		415	427
3	3	1573	1162	1573		671	457
	3	484	250	484		162	157
5	8	2595	1447	2556		1303	708
	3	665	378	665		375	84
1	1	418	246	418		161	170
1	1	345	166	345		122	110
1		412	251	399	13	97	188
		204	146	204		108	55
1		110	63	110		43	20
2	1	731	498	594	137	311	152

C-2-11续表1

地　区	职业资格水平		按人员性质分		年龄	
	助理社会工作师人数	社会工作师人数	管理人员	专业技术技能人员	35岁及以下人数	36岁至45岁人数
全　国	**238**	**246**	**5085**	**20651**	**10486**	**8308**
中央级						
北　京			4	167	101	47
天　津	5		120	229	111	77
河　北	4	5	71	441	130	202
山　西	3	6	137	936	357	414
内蒙古	1	8	100	438	200	127
辽　宁	4	1	95	258	78	145
吉　林			386	910	312	619
黑龙江	9	4	361	883	373	441
上　海	19	11	134	410	261	109
江　苏	18	28	178	1587	695	514
浙　江	2	5	27	127	55	62
安　徽		1	319	219	223	179
福　建	20	17	176	937	519	322
江　西	5	7	127	35	44	69
山　东	16	16	367	1371	720	460
河　南	7	22	110	936	412	346
湖　北	14	13	414	2248	1234	778
湖　南		2	343	1381	507	789
广　东	56	34	219	998	497	453
广　西	10	12	166	1407	819	400
海　南						
重　庆	6	12	92	392	183	153
四　川	20	16	521	2074	1489	601
贵　州	3	3	252	413	196	242
云　南	3	3	113	305	190	123
西　藏						
陕　西	5	10	40	305	117	106
甘　肃	1	3	62	350	192	142
青　海			48	156	90	89
宁　夏	5	2	9	101	50	52
新　疆	2	5	94	637	331	247

单位：人、人次、时、张

结构		志愿服务		年末床位数	光荣间床位	床位按登记类型分	
46岁至55岁人数	56岁及以上人数	志愿者服务人次数	志愿服务时间			编制登记	民政登记
5635	**1307**	**12605**	**31328.0**	**77561**	**2617**	**77308**	**253**
19	4			150		150	
114	47			957		957	
136	44			1129		1129	
250	52	2	2.0	1892	445	1892	
175	36			2063	27	2063	
121	9			800	25	800	
325	40			4457	110	4457	
408	22			4163	425	4163	
100	74	550	980.0	1800		1800	
458	98	1441	3003.0	5660	10	5660	
33	4	7000	18500.0	1110		1110	
78	58	110	500.0	765		765	
217	55			4285	67	4285	
46	3	132	528.0	421		421	
466	92	2969	6558.0	3597		3597	
246	42			1876	2	1876	
461	189			5576	340	5576	
360	68			5217	261	5217	
235	32	12	60.0	4104	11	4104	
281	73			3405	152	3405	
114	34			2381		2381	
399	106			10792	7	10792	
175	52			3235	177	3235	
85	20	54	312.0	1960		1960	
103	19	50	200.0	1260	360	1260	
70	8			1091	110	1051	40
13	12			260	28	260	
8				350		350	
139	14	285	685.0	2805	60	2592	213

C-2-11续表2

地区	年在院总人天数	年末在院人数	女性	在院人数按登记类型分	
				编制登记	民政登记
全国	**18819378**	**63154**	**18217**	**62935**	**219**
中央级					
北京	10486	27	15	27	
天津	280959	844	231	844	
河北	305565	979	175	979	
山西	517061	1587	195	1587	
内蒙古	565403	1636	414	1636	
辽宁	267090	732	145	732	
吉林	600050	2114	584	2114	
黑龙江	487099	2244	745	2244	
上海	612198	1680	475	1680	
江苏	1781671	5173	1704	5173	
浙江	233085	639	246	639	
安徽	225094	623	111	623	
福建	1051303	3849	1279	3849	
江西	68779	357	35	357	
山东	715320	2886	486	2886	
河南	619143	1764	444	1764	
湖北	1318737	4560	1751	4560	
湖南	1040142	4119	1308	4119	
广东	1074477	3731	1017	3731	
广西	918709	3255	912	3255	
海南					
重庆	695111	2109	611	2109	
四川	3246867	9788	3001	9788	
贵州	760141	2412	539	2412	
云南	293750	1468	405	1468	
西藏					
陕西	344460	1021	269	1021	
甘肃	140742	393	136	367	26
青海	88330	242	98	242	
宁夏	117000	350	195	350	
新疆	440606	2572	691	2379	193

单位:人天、人

在院人员按性质分				在院人员按年龄分		
优抚对象	“三无”和农村特困对象	自费人员	其他社会救济对象	老人	青壮年	少年儿童
9720	**16932**	**26801**	**5635**	**21193**	**40314**	**1647**
		27		14		13
157	255	340	92	213	631	
566	90	323		442	534	3
564	252	771		479	1077	31
116	453	942	125	238	1398	
337	114	281		138	594	
426	1025	293	193	707	1366	41
170	1800	274		663	1578	3
50	113	901	616	534	1146	
910	2264	1792	21	1724	3425	24
97	47	417		218	416	5
325	60	237	1	194	424	5
366	1076	2318	89	1018	2800	31
	257	100		124	233	
1627	323	469		1677	1209	
250	150	712	276	224	1436	104
489	681	2459	343	1652	2584	324
779	911	1415	272	1577	2242	300
559	642	981	1339	933	2666	132
357	543	1970	183	966	2116	173
62	685	1348		919	1186	4
769	1899	4982	1330	3653	5932	203
43	759	1082	546	961	1341	110
111	750	145	178	283	1182	3
437	345	254		517	484	20
100	197	59	31	152	233	8
17	9	216		82	137	23
9	218	123		150	160	40
27	1014	1570		741	1784	47

C-2-11续表3

地 区	在院人员按类型分			康复和医疗门诊人次数	机构建筑面积
	自理（完全自理）	介助（半自理）	介护（不能自理）		
全 国	**32735**	**22979**	**7440**	**3000518**	**2928362**
中央级					
北 京	2	2	23	140013	7993
天 津	797	47		73106	20571
河 北	488	461	30	63396	87308
山 西	1000	537	50	59399	89537
内蒙古	944	629	63	69915	73670
辽 宁	622	63	47		23419
吉 林	1203	807	104	90207	88000
黑龙江	1271	945	28	16733	22200
上 海	715	965		6151	81648
江 苏	2719	1563	891	178016	250660
浙 江	369	204	66		56500
安 徽	38	540	45	52329	24704
福 建	2457	820	572	315065	155654
江 西	258	73	26		8462
山 东	2195	529	162	71103	191524
河 南	378	883	503	269890	79692
湖 北	1717	2259	584	493273	291374
湖 南	2065	1146	908	259541	158938
广 东	2225	1191	315	95758	94426
广 西	1430	1261	564	238418	381041
海 南					
重 庆	1082	740	287	50966	94440
四 川	4304	3788	1696	216807	243711
贵 州	1301	968	143	61050	52568
云 南	461	888	119	20324	106819
西 藏					
陕 西	814	159	48	25642	74237
甘 肃	154	207	32	85454	37484
青 海	215	19	8		20000
宁 夏	15	295	40	7200	1200
新 疆	1496	990	86	40762	110581

单位：人、人次、平方米、万元

执行行政事业单位会计制度财务指标				
固定资产原价	上年结转和结余	本年收入合计	本年支出合计	收支结余
491220.6	**55121.7**	**638823.2**	**576549.9**	**74878.1**
6482.1	1807.4	12678.2	11772.6	7387.6
6366.5	346.2	12172.5	10046.2	2472.4
20396.3	855.0	12019.8	11137.9	1270.0
19423.5	1282.5	15465.3	19251.2	374.5
4153.6	2949.2	14254.7	13631.1	3643.4
6739.1	1077.7	7591.8	7106.2	
9826.4	1224.3	10415.0	9700.8	1974.4
19308.0	1303.0	8868.0	9121.0	
18378.1	469.1	16742.0	16362.1	380.0
58596.3	3712.4	67864.3	54957.2	9352.0
9027.7	631.7	16596.2	15012.8	722.0
3212.7	-7.5	2913.4	3104.4	-47.5
18537.7	766.7	34097.3	26918.9	2580.5
674.2		1975.0	1516.9	
35077.1		45773.1	45773.1	
15031.3	159.0	25582.5	24984.5	-81.0
34010.6	1671.7	56725.6	53644.3	4483.3
22469.2	282.0	44661.3	38297.6	3381.0
29681.6	4798.2	30430.8	30280.4	2444.1
24957.7	4061.9	36716.2	33618.1	1894.2
8818.3		27032.3	18089.0	8943.3
54750.1	10581.6	69069.7	62293.0	5663.7
8510.7	1182.8	10778.4	11308.5	1190.4
18444.0	2832.9	8962.6	8587.8	1078.4
9659.3	3311.8	9060.9	10291.0	1903.1
6251.0	2396.9	7810.2	5562.4	5743.2
1651.6	2748.1	4112.4	4110.5	
675.8	1990.9	2010.0	1775.5	2225.4
20110.1	2686.2	26443.7	18294.9	5899.7

C-2-12 福利类

地区	单位数	编制登记	一个机构多块牌子	0～99张	100～299张	300～499张	500张以上
全国	**151**	**144**	**7**	**36**	**51**	**29**	**35**
中央级							
北京	1	1			1		
天津	1	1				1	
河北							
山西	1	1			1		
内蒙古	5	5			3	2	
辽宁							
吉林	7	7		1	1		5
黑龙江	7	7			1	2	4
上海	3	3				1	2
江苏	11	10	1		5	4	2
浙江	2	2				1	1
安徽	3	3		2	1		
福建	13	13		1	6	5	1
江西	3	2	1	2	1		
山东	2	2			1	1	
河南	6	6		3	1	2	
湖北	2	2		1			1
湖南	9	8	1	2	5	1	1
广东	3	3		2			1
广西	4	4			1	1	2
海南							
重庆	9	9		5	1		3
四川	19	17	2	5	4	4	6
贵州	22	21	1	11	8		3
云南	4	4			2	1	1
西藏							
陕西	1	1					1
甘肃	3	3			3		
青海	1	1			1		
宁夏	1		1			1	
新疆	8	8		1	4	2	1

精神病院和医院

单位:个、人

年末职工人数		受教育程度		职业资格水平		按人员性质分	
	女性	大学专科人数	大学本科及以上人数	助理社会工作师人数	社会工作师人数	管理人员	专业技术技能人员
14393	**8357**	**5236**	**4318**	**123**	**139**	**2689**	**11704**
171	138	56	66			4	167
232	112	62	89	5		30	202
89	45	34	29	1	1	25	64
342	165	142	100	1	6	82	260
691	404	156	166			130	561
1198	439	246	334	9	4	345	853
544	346	185	149	19	11	134	410
1485	927	424	665	18	25	162	1323
78	49	8	36			19	59
242	168	111	53		1	23	219
920	573	324	225	17	17	146	774
159	93	52	55	5	7	126	33
234	115	57	89	4	4	39	195
752	450	340	245	4	10	92	660
365	184	127	72			56	309
889	579	259	222		2	185	704
648	419	205	325	1	2	35	613
848	590	319	277	4	3	87	761
484	250	162	157	6	12	92	392
1831	963	978	474	11	12	368	1463
665	378	375	84	3	3	252	413
301	181	118	131	2	2	93	208
127	49	31	63	5	9	8	119
190	129	56	25	1	1	24	166
204	146	108	55			48	156
110	63	43	20	5	2	9	101
594	402	258	112	2	5	75	519

C-2-12续表1

地区	年龄结构				志愿服务		年末床位数	光荣间床位
	35岁及以下人数	36岁至45岁人数	46岁至55岁人数	56岁及以上人数	志愿者服务人次数	志愿服务时间		
全　国	**5898**	**4628**	**3111**	**756**	**2545**	**5845.0**	**49430**	**1200**
中央级								
北　京	101	47	19	4			150	
天　津	72	70	60	30			657	
河　北								
山　西	16	30	39	4			150	
内蒙古	116	77	123	26			1358	7
辽　宁								
吉　林	166	310	191	24			4035	60
黑龙江	357	427	392	22			3683	425
上　海	261	109	100	74	550	980.0	1800	
江　苏	620	414	368	83	1441	3003.0	4633	10
浙　江	35	19	21	3			910	
安　徽	127	53	20	42	110	500.0	265	
福　建	419	264	192	45			3441	67
江　西	44	69	43	3	132	528.0	371	
山　东	82	57	70	25	244	530.0	430	
河　南	359	222	138	33			1276	2
湖　北	49	130	115	71			893	
湖　南	256	457	145	31			2036	215
广　东	267	261	110	10			1914	6
广　西	467	202	149	30			1999	
海　南								
重　庆	183	153	114	34			2381	
四　川	1059	460	251	61			7950	3
贵　州	196	242	175	52			3235	177
云　南	130	87	66	18	18	104.0	1560	
西　藏								
陕　西	74	30	21	2	50	200.0	650	200
甘　肃	36	105	44	5			451	
青　海	90	89	13	12			260	28
宁　夏	50	52	8				350	
新　疆	266	192	124	12			2592	

单位：张、人天、人、人次、时

年在院总人天数	年末在院人数	在院人员按性质分				
		女性	优抚对象	“三无”和农村特困对象	自费人员	其他社会救济对象
11650679	**39543**	**11940**	**2391**	**13522**	**17925**	**3743**
10486	27	15			27	
212704	657	221		255	310	92
12190	149	55	2	66	81	
339110	1014	233	80	427	507	
585785	2009	544	324	1022	293	193
333699	2135	739	81	1780	274	
612198	1680	475	50	113	901	616
1451974	4160	1239	630	2202	1107	21
160085	439	221	60	47	254	
45688	123	64		35	87	1
762596	3035	823	257	755	1934	89
68279	347	30		247	100	
108957	304	101	74	191	34	
446985	1181	444		150	712	276
273750	763	39		13	670	
405084	1560	545	230	404	784	
501696	1710	543	40	253	210	1119
451191	1886	580	136	382	1166	
695111	2109	611	62	685	1348	
2310818	7089	2330	182	1416	4102	581
760141	2412	539	43	759	1082	546
226225	1094	321	31	652	57	178
163520	455	155	51	311	93	
91910	234	104	32	116	49	31
88330	242	98	17	9	216	
117000	350	195	9	218	123	
415167	2379	676		1014	1404	

C-2-12续表2

地区	在院人员按年龄分			在院人员按类型分			康复和医疗门诊人次数	机构建筑面积
	老人	青壮年	少年儿童	自理（完全自理）	介助（半自理）	介护（不能自理）		
全　国	**12549**	**25952**	**1042**	**20298**	**14113**	**5132**	**1512244**	**1676791**
中央级								
北　京	14		13	2	2	23	140013	7993
天　津	157	500		657			39722	10894
河　北								
山　西	39	92	18	125	19	5	451	8262
内蒙古	204	810		354	599	61	25466	62206
辽　宁								
吉　林	603	1365	41	1140	767	102	90207	83000
黑龙江	554	1578	3	1162	945	28	16733	19800
上　海	534	1146		715	965		6151	81648
江　苏	1313	2826	21	2043	1291	826	73443	208368
浙　江	158	276	5	209	171	59		35000
安　徽	116	6	1	38	40	45	14360	8161
福　建	593	2412	30	2002	761	272	299576	130830
江　西	114	233		250	71	26		7262
山　东	189	115		267	27	10	3002	13381
河　南	108	974	99	262	421	498	217438	52956
湖　北	742	21			702	61	18360	34035
湖　南	566	828	166	902	222	436	65654	30010
广　东	373	1302	35	1461	152	97	62607	42563
广　西	568	1160	158	992	479	415	94348	302627
海　南								
重　庆	919	1186	4	1082	740	287	50966	94440
四　川	2483	4409	197	2686	2908	1495	162300	166487
贵　州	961	1341	110	1301	968	143	61050	52568
云　南	195	896	3	441	540	113	14254	50389
西　藏								
陕　西	137	298	20	435	14	6		28154
甘　肃	40	186	8	115	106	13	8181	19575
青　海	82	137	23	215	19	8		20000
宁　夏	150	160	40	15	295	40	7200	1200
新　疆	637	1695	47	1427	889	63	40762	104981

单位：人、人次、平方米、万元

执行行政事业单位会计制度财务指标				
固定资产原价	上年结转和结余	本年收入合计	本年支出合计	收支结余
268832.1	**30724.4**	**380044.1**	**332149.6**	**58175.2**
6482.1	1807.4	12678.2	11772.6	7387.6
2127.0		9432.6	7475.8	1956.8
600.1		2384.4	2384.4	
1873.6	2949.2	7739.7	8078.1	2681.4
9055.8	1224.3	10037.2	9305.0	1974.4
18421.0	1303.0	8371.0	8624.0	
18378.1	469.1	16742.0	16362.1	380.0
38676.5	2070.5	53646.7	45352.3	9348.6
6990.7	39.7	6866.2	5630.8	
1034.2	-7.5	2913.4	3104.4	-47.5
16555.7	693.3	27982.3	22215.8	2221.8
654.2		1975.0	1516.9	
2854.0		5369.0	5369.0	
8923.0	159.0	16198.8	16360.8	-81.0
400.0	70.0	1120.0	1059.0	131.0
9315.6	282.0	22126.1	18646.7	3381.0
16505.2	2526.2	20463.2	18322.8	
12736.7	2075.5	21447.3	18872.5	846.9
8818.3		27032.3	18089.0	8943.3
35296.8	4014.2	51527.8	45207.2	5663.7
8510.7	1182.8	10778.4	11308.5	1190.4
15724.6	346.2	6579.6	6733.2	
3835.3	2020.4	2106.8	4217.8	1184.1
2675.4	73.9	2242.0	2242.0	2887.6
1651.6	2748.1	4112.4	4110.5	
675.8	1990.9	2010.0	1775.5	2225.4
20060.1	2686.2	26161.7	18012.9	5899.7

C-2-13 复退军人

地区	单位数	0~99张	100~299张	300~499张	500张以上	年末职工人数	女性
全国	**91**	**8**	**36**	**27**	**20**	**11343**	**6921**
中央级							
北京							
天津	1			1		117	57
河北	2				2	512	272
山西	7		6		1	984	564
内蒙古	2		1		1	196	115
辽宁	3	1	1	1		353	175
吉林	7	1	3	1	2	605	333
黑龙江	1			1		46	21
上海							
江苏	1				1	280	172
浙江	1		1			76	53
安徽	1				1	296	135
福建	4		3	1		193	122
江西	1	1				3	1
山东	12	1	4	7		1504	968
河南	1				1	294	173
湖北	10		1	5	4	2297	1470
湖南	8	2		3	3	835	567
广东	8		5	2	1	569	267
广西	4		1	2	1	725	572
海南							
重庆							
四川	6	1	2	1	2	764	484
贵州							
云南	2		2			117	65
西藏							
陕西	3		2	1		218	117
甘肃	3	1	1	1		222	122
青海							
宁夏							
新疆	3		3			137	96

精神病院

单位：个、人

受教育程度		职业资格水平		按人员性质分	
大学专科人数	大学本科及以上人数	助理社会工作师人数	社会工作师人数	管理人员	专业技术技能人员
3325	**4144**	**115**	**107**	**2396**	**8947**
				90	27
76	267	4	5	71	441
166	244	2	5	112	872
64	99		2	18	178
177	83	4	1	95	258
26	24			256	349
14	25			16	30
48	169		3	16	264
11	33	2	5	8	68
126	68			296	
53	10	3		30	163
				1	2
470	812	12	12	328	1176
72	151	3	12	18	276
598	1194	14	13	358	1939
309	160			158	677
210	102	55	32	184	385
352	180	6	9	79	646
325	234	9	4	153	611
43	39	1	1	20	97
91	47		1	32	186
41	163		2	38	184
53	40			19	118

C-2-13续表1

地区	年龄结构				志愿服务		年末床位数	
	35岁及以下人数	36岁至45岁人数	46岁至55岁人数	56岁及以上人数	志愿者服务人次数	志愿服务时间		光荣间床位
全国	**4588**	**3680**	**2524**	**551**	**10060**	**25483.0**	**29673**	**1418**
中央级								
北京								
天津	39	7	54	17			300	
河北	130	202	136	44			1129	
山西	341	384	211	48	2	2.0	1742	445
内蒙古	84	50	52	10			705	20
辽宁	78	145	121	9			800	25
吉林	146	309	134	16			1872	50
黑龙江	16	14	16				480	
上海								
江苏	75	100	90	15			1027	
浙江	20	43	12	1	7000	18500.0	200	
安徽	96	126	58	16			500	
福建	100	58	25	10			844	
江西			3				50	
山东	638	403	396	67	2725	6028.0	3167	
河南	53	124	108	9			600	
湖北	1185	648	346	118			4683	340
湖南	251	332	215	37			3181	46
广东	230	192	125	22	12	60.0	2190	5
广西	352	198	132	43			1406	152
海南								
重庆								
四川	430	141	148	45			2934	5
贵州								
云南	60	36	19	2	36	208.0	400	
西藏								
陕西	43	76	82	17			610	160
甘肃	156	37	26	3			640	110
青海								
宁夏								
新疆	65	55	15	2	285	685.0	213	60

单位：人、人次、时、张、人天

年在院总人天数	年末在院人数	在院人员按性质分				
		女性	优抚对象	“三无”和农村特困对象	自费人员	其他社会救济对象
7202279	**23701**	**6301**	**7332**	**3451**	**8922**	**1892**
68255	187	10	157		30	
305565	979	175	566	90	323	
504871	1438	140	562	186	690	
226293	622	181	36	26	435	125
267090	732	145	337	114	281	
14265	105	40	102	3		
153400	109	6	89	20		
329697	1013	465	280	62	685	
73000	200	25	37		163	
179406	500	47	325	25	150	
288707	814	456	109	321	384	
500	10	5		10		
606363	2582	385	1553	132	435	
172158	583		250			
1044987	3797	1712	489	668	1789	343
635058	2559	763	549	507	631	272
572781	2021	474	519	389	771	220
467518	1369	332	221	161	804	183
969629	2789	695	590	524	926	749
67525	374	84	80	98	88	
180940	566	114	386	34	161	
48832	159	32	68	81	10	
25439	193	15	27		166	

C-2-13续表2

地区	在院人员按年龄分			在院人员按类型分			康复和医疗门诊人次数	机构建筑面积
	老人	青壮年	少年儿童	自理（完全自理）	介助（半自理）	介护（不能自理）		
全 国	**8665**	**14431**	**605**	**12464**	**8929**	**2308**	**1488274**	**1320376**
中央级								
北 京								
天 津	56	131		140	47		33384	9677
河 北	442	534	3	488	461	30	63396	87308
山 西	440	985	13	875	518	45	58948	81275
内蒙古	34	588		590	30	2	44449	11464
辽 宁	138	594		622	63	47		23419
吉 林	104	1		63	40	2		73154
黑龙江	109			109				2400
上 海								
江 苏	411	599	3	676	272	65	104573	42292
浙 江	60	140		160	33	7		21500
安 徽	78	418	4		500		37969	16543
福 建	425	388	1	455	59	300	15489	24824
江 西	10			8	2			1200
山 东	1488	1094		1928	502	152	68101	178143
河 南	116	462	5	116	462	5	52452	26736
湖 北	910	2563	324	1717	1557	523	474913	257339
湖 南	1011	1414	134	1163	924	472	193887	128928
广 东	560	1364	97	764	1039	218	33151	51863
广 西	398	956	15	438	782	149	144070	78414
海 南								
重 庆								
四 川	1191	1592	6	1645	943	201	54507	77873
贵 州								
云 南	88	286		20	348	6	6070	56430
西 藏								
陕 西	380	186		379	145	42	25642	46083
甘 肃	112	47		39	101	19	77273	17909
青 海								
宁 夏								
新 疆	104	89		69	101	23		5600

单位：人、人次、平方米、万元

执行行政事业单位会计制度财务指标				
固定资产原价	上年结转和结余	本年收入合计	本年支出合计	收支结余
222388.5	**24397.3**	**258779.1**	**244400.3**	**16702.9**
4239.5	346.2	2739.9	2570.4	515.6
20396.3	855.0	12019.8	11137.9	1270.0
18823.4	1282.5	13080.9	16866.8	374.5
2280.0		6515.0	5553.0	962.0
6739.1	1077.7	7591.8	7106.2	
770.6		377.8	395.8	
887.0		497.0	497.0	
19919.8	1641.9	14217.6	9604.9	3.4
2037.0	592.0	9730.0	9382.0	722.0
2178.5				
1982.0	73.4	6115.0	4703.1	358.7
20.0				
32223.1		40404.1	40404.1	
6108.3		9383.7	8623.7	
33610.6	1601.7	55605.6	52585.3	4352.3
13153.6		22535.2	19650.9	
13176.4	2272.0	9967.6	11957.6	2444.1
12221.0	1986.4	15268.9	14745.6	1047.3
19453.3	6567.4	17541.9	17085.8	
2719.4	2486.7	2383.0	1854.6	1078.4
5824.0	1291.4	6954.1	6073.2	719.0
3575.6	2323.0	5568.2	3320.4	2855.6
50.0		282.0	282.0	

C-2-14 儿童服务

地区	单位数	单位数按登记类型分			单位数按床位数量分	
		编制登记	民政登记	一个机构多块牌子	0~99张	100~299张
全　国	**753**	**394**	**33**	**326**	**415**	**236**
中央级						
北　京	12	10	1	1	4	5
天　津	2	2				1
河　北	8	5	1	2	6	2
山　西	13	4	3	6	10	3
内蒙古	8	7	1		1	5
辽　宁	12	9	1	2	7	2
吉　林	10	8		2	3	3
黑龙江	16	16			2	13
上　海	4	3	1		2	1
江　苏	32	10		22	18	9
浙　江	12	10		2	1	8
安　徽	36	27	1	8	13	17
福　建	11	6	3	2	5	4
江　西	17	7		10	12	3
山　东	17	14		3	3	4
河　南	23	19	2	2	11	8
湖　北	79	23		56	64	9
湖　南	54	20	3	31	38	11
广　东	39	26	9	4	20	14
广　西	41	8		33	29	11
海　南	2	2			1	1
重　庆	6	5	1		2	2
四　川	120	30	1	89	92	19
贵　州	26	17		9	11	12
云　南	32	20	2	10	15	14
西　藏	10	10			4	2
陕　西	12	11		1	3	6
甘　肃	29	13		16	11	14
青　海	12	4	2	6	7	2
宁　夏	10	4		6	7	1
新　疆	48	44	1	3	13	30

机构总表

单位:个、人

300～499张	500张以上	年末职工人数	女性	年末职工人数按登记类型分		
				编制登记	民政登记	一个机构多块牌子
71	**31**	**13789**	**8903**	**10982**	**575**	**2232**
2	1	536	394	498	36	2
1		126	84	126		
		61	32	41	6	14
		177	74	62	21	94
1	1	345	185	343	2	
1	2	445	263	355	9	81
2	2	423	175	321		102
1		445	282	445		
	1	422	346	375	47	
4	1	600	433	486		114
2	1	478	356	470		8
5	1	820	538	708	20	92
2		155	109	116	21	18
2		192	104	129		63
7	3	454	312	433		21
2	2	906	750	869	18	19
5	1	765	480	434		331
5		695	357	346	61	288
5		1156	725	863	249	44
1		754	479	567		187
		20	15	20		
	2	292	227	276	16	
7	2	921	548	562	4	355
2	1	266	159	202		64
2	1	340	230	226	16	98
1	3	162	113	162		
1	2	249	135	248		1
3	1	522	288	397		125
1	2	192	133	111	46	35
1	1	258	213	203		55
5		612	364	588	3	21

C-2-14续表1

地区	受教育程度		职业资格水平		按人员性质分	
	大学专科人数	大学本科及以上人数	助理社会工作师人数	社会工作师人数	管理人员	专业技术技能人员
全国	**4254**	**3815**	**398**	**543**	**5023**	**8766**
中央级						
北京	166	259	16	13	144	392
天津	36	71	8	13	48	78
河北	12	3		1	18	43
山西	40	34	2	8	66	111
内蒙古	140	93	12	18	111	234
辽宁	144	228	8	6	127	318
吉林	72	65	1	2	123	300
黑龙江	151	148	3	24	264	181
上海	113	165	20	40	72	350
江苏	163	220	30	56	129	471
浙江	110	190	15	20	133	345
安徽	212	152	34	17	462	358
福建	31	64	5	14	84	71
江西	55	18	6	1	83	109
山东	131	222	22	36	167	287
河南	488	130	13	30	178	728
湖北	269	209	22	19	247	518
湖南	219	106	17	14	259	436
广东	206	175	52	46	459	697
广西	190	195	18	17	293	461
海南	3				12	8
重庆	79	176	17	31	88	204
四川	331	253	16	31	556	365
贵州	111	88	10	4	167	99
云南	63	134	6	22	156	184
西藏	26	26	1		57	105
陕西	73	83	5	10	101	148
甘肃	141	91	13	8	166	356
青海	85	33	4		57	135
宁夏	93	42	8	16	49	209
新疆	301	142	14	26	147	465

单位：人、人次、时

年龄结构				志愿服务	
35岁及以下人数	36岁至45岁人数	46岁至55岁人数	56岁及以上人数	志愿者服务人次数	志愿服务时间
5575	**4938**	**2853**	**423**	**21815**	**72456.5**
200	172	138	26	9	12.0
61	37	21	7		
17	35	9			
38	71	59	9		
187	82	64	12		
148	151	134	12		
149	144	79	51		
203	156	80	6		
214	86	97	25		
238	166	171	25	3733	7955.0
178	149	133	18		
284	285	224	27	1267	4840.0
61	60	33	1		
63	68	58	3	132	528.0
222	134	79	19	9100	23754.0
315	444	142	5		
302	286	150	27	165	372.0
248	301	128	18	545	2324.0
439	445	254	18		
339	268	129	18		
3	10	7			
187	56	41	8	5	5.0
345	341	193	42	53	157.0
127	86	46	7	1672	3075.0
131	154	50	5	4146	24661.0
92	59	11		18	54.0
98	84	62	5	45	62.5
196	211	101	14		
93	77	20	2	518	1431.0
127	83	42	6	402	3216.0
270	237	98	7	5	10.0

C-2-14续表2

地　区	执行行政事业单位会计制度财务指标					为儿童提供服务机构床位数
	固定资产原价	上年结转和结余	本年收入合计	本年支出合计	收支结余	
全　国	**376718.6**	**41542.9**	**287361.0**	**245969.6**	**36935.0**	**100112**
中央级						
北　京	18201.9	717.4	17734.7	16869.4	1498.0	1910
天　津	1602.4	806.2	6498.9	5230.6	2136.1	668
河　北	629.2	104.0	1256.9	1467.9	104.0	584
山　西	1930.7	186.5	694.2	681.6	2.6	1180
内蒙古	13302.8	1536.0	6949.8	6265.7	2551.1	1633
辽　宁	7960.8	1607.1	8925.0	9018.6	561.4	3371
吉　林	7626.1	785.3	3297.8	3402.6	94.7	3110
黑龙江	21856.5	661.3	14156.9	7541.8	715.4	2847
上　海	18311.3	381.4	14948.8	14661.5	608.1	2091
江　苏	11541.1	3895.8	16749.1	13971.4	4811.3	4064
浙　江	13707.3	1616.0	14512.5	12191.7	642.0	2654
安　徽	17085.3	2596.7	12625.6	11056.9	-25.8	5967
福　建	3360.0	1239.4	5402.6	3407.7	1418.3	1504
江　西	3373.7		485.8	409.8		1658
山　东	18920.0		15258.9	15258.9		5390
河　南	16570.9	795.0	7778.1	7369.4	1100.2	4217
湖　北	10599.0	259.1	10898.2	10251.6	463.0	4753
湖　南	21786.9	39.4	8177.8	9205.5		4429
广　东	31293.3	1034.7	18844.2	18435.8	606.3	4911
广　西	6899.1	438.4	7111.0	7471.4	506.5	3082
海　南	660.0	18.4	96.0	91.0		163
重　庆	7321.3	1809.3	16246.4	7069.7	10986.0	2489
四　川	23990.5	14851.9	12045.0	12700.0	1769.7	7978
贵　州	5119.7	1441.4	3258.8	3658.9	138.0	3430
云　南	16575.0	977.4	5614.3	5178.6	530.4	3780
西　藏	6101.8		1910.0	4454.8		5769
陕　西	22280.4	1486.8	26184.2	23898.4	2876.5	2915
甘　肃	16242.9	873.0	4518.2	3531.3	891.0	4321
青　海	3170.0		371.4	371.4		1920
宁　夏	11584.6	330.0	2553.0	2351.0	509.0	840
新　疆	17114.1	1055.0	22256.9	8494.7	1441.2	6484

单位：万元

按登记类型分			为儿童提供服务机构年末收养人数			按登记类型分		
编制登记	民政登记	一个机构多块牌子		女性	儿童	编制登记	民政登记	一个机构多块牌子
77813	**3555**	**18744**	**56084**	**19043**	**53021**	**48283**	**2230**	**5571**
1660	200	50	1214	443	1158	1105	91	18
668			223	82	223	223		
334	50	200	177	44	177	107	6	64
450	173	557	744	181	744	312	124	308
1601	32		840	321	823	817	23	
2861	50	460	2690	987	2299	2398	19	273
2810		300	1514	39	1414	1392		122
2847			1487	557	1326	1487		
2021	70		1987	804	1987	1917	70	
2415		1649	2154	982	1792	1696		458
2372		282	1365	584	1333	1313		52
4647	130	1190	3275	1298	2420	2756	14	505
1130	155	219	838	345	807	633	143	62
1085		573	614	39	613	612		2
4766		624	2680	979	2680	2485		195
3897	210	110	3111	1172	3078	2901	210	
2562		2191	2209	773	2200	1723		486
2965	571	893	2596	1222	2302	2022	312	262
3927	814	170	2494	874	2403	1871	561	62
1120		1962	1119	418	938	774		345
163			76	27	76	76		
2449	40		986	405	986	947	39	
5118	20	2840	2646	1018	2475	2228	7	411
2353		1077	1483	573	1346	1059		424
2572	160	1048	1842	336	1831	1349	117	376
5769			5281	1419	5281	5281		
2903		12	2014	781	2014	2014		
2671		1650	2664	846	2641	1739		925
850	850	220	1269	243	1269	765	480	24
520		320	432	151	432	294		138
6307	30	147	4060	1100	3953	3987	14	59

C-2-15 儿童

地区	单位数	0～99张	100～299张	300～499张	500张以上	年末职工人数	女性
全国	**478**	**177**	**203**	**67**	**31**	**12038**	**8235**
中央级							
北京	10	4	4	1	1	485	373
天津	2		1	1		126	84
河北	7	5	2			48	31
山西	8	5	3			122	63
内蒙古	8	1	5	1	1	345	185
辽宁	10	5	2	1	2	424	257
吉林	10	3	3	2	2	423	175
黑龙江	15	2	12	1		437	276
上海	3	2			1	360	289
江苏	13	2	6	4	1	546	406
浙江	12	1	8	2	1	478	356
安徽	31	11	14	5	1	798	535
福建	11	5	4	2		155	109
江西	5	2	1	2		101	79
山东	13		3	7	3	423	299
河南	19	8	7	2	2	848	723
湖北	24	16	3	4	1	476	354
湖南	21	9	7	5		371	236
广东	37	19	14	4		1050	719
广西	14	6	7	1		610	420
海南	2	1	1			20	15
重庆	6	2	2		2	292	227
四川	53	28	16	7	2	681	459
贵州	20	6	11	2	1	226	144
云南	26	9	14	2	1	324	219
西藏	10	4	2	1	3	162	113
陕西	11	2	6	1	2	248	135
甘肃	19	3	13	2	1	438	259
青海	7	2	2	1	2	177	127
宁夏	5	2	1	1	1	238	205
新疆	46	12	29	5		606	363

收养机构

单位:个、人

受教育程度		职业资格水平		按人员性质分		年龄结构	
大学专科人数	大学本科及以上人数	助理社会工作师人数	社会工作师人数	管理人员	专业技术技能人员	35岁及以下人数	36岁至45岁人数
3561	**3406**	**344**	**492**	**4056**	**7982**	**4947**	**4216**
156	221	11	11	93	392	180	157
36	71	8	13	48	78	61	37
12			1	8	40	15	25
26	27	2	8	45	77	27	55
140	93	12	18	111	234	187	82
131	220	8	6	109	315	142	146
72	65	1	2	123	300	149	144
151	140	3	24	261	176	200	151
87	154	17	35	61	299	187	68
139	214	29	54	108	438	212	143
110	190	15	20	133	345	178	149
202	147	34	16	450	348	280	273
31	64	5	14	84	71	61	60
12	12	1	1	23	78	32	25
124	217	20	35	150	273	209	120
455	114	10	27	160	688	290	418
146	163	17	13	113	363	201	168
87	43	11	8	110	261	146	142
179	149	40	34	406	644	381	415
134	148	16	12	203	407	286	212
3				12	8	3	10
79	176	17	31	88	204	187	56
232	185	12	24	385	296	256	233
87	79	9	4	132	94	114	75
59	129	6	22	143	181	125	149
26	26	1		57	105	92	59
73	82	5	10	101	147	97	84
110	75	8	7	114	324	172	182
79	31	4		46	131	86	71
87	30	8	16	34	204	123	71
296	141	14	26	145	461	268	236

C-2-15续表1

地区	年龄结构		志愿服务		年末床位数		年在院总人天数
	46岁至55岁人数	56岁及以上人数	志愿者服务人次数	志愿服务时间		光荣间床位	
全　国	**2521**	**354**	**21119**	**69821.5**	**89430**	**576**	**15294074**
中央级							
北　京	127	21	9	12.0	1460		424325
天　津	21	7			668		85410
河　北	8				554		59815
山　西	33	7			976		228328
内蒙古	64	12			1633		306525
辽　宁	124	12			3291		936750
吉　林	79	51			3110		131037
黑龙江	80	6			2747		484975
上　海	81	24			1991		405850
江　苏	167	24	3671	7711.0	3265	6	661171
浙　江	133	18			2654		517939
安　徽	218	27	1267	4840.0	5413	20	1013977
福　建	33	1			1504		302235
江　西	44		132	528.0	965		40272
山　东	75	19	8939	23346.0	5106		897229
河　南	136	4			3832	28	943306
湖　北	97	10	35	132.0	3151		653403
湖　南	79	4	217	696.0	3321	376	624181
广　东	237	17			4571		799067
广　西	104	8			1943		231699
海　南	7				163		12165
重　庆	41	8	5	5.0	2489		313741
四　川	156	36	53	157.0	6503	29	797865
贵　州	32	5	1672	3075.0	3252	16	524635
云　南	45	5	4146	24661.0	3541	80	412752
西　藏	11		18	54.0	5769		834788
陕　西	62	5	45	62.5	2903		677940
甘　肃	76	8			3693	19	464984
青　海	18	2	503	1316.0	1800		273769
宁　夏	38	6	402	3216.0	693		146675
新　疆	95	7	5	10.0	6469	2	1087266

单位：人、人次、时、张、人天

年末在院人数	女性	在院人员按性质分				在院人员按年龄分		
		优抚对象	“三无”和农村特困对象	自费人员	其他社会救济对象	老人	青壮年	少年儿童
54816	**18669**	**1911**	**42104**	**1512**	**1247**	**1231**	**1832**	**51753**
1174	442		1070	104		1	55	1118
223	82		223					223
177	44		164					177
732	181		476		223			732
840	321		840				17	823
2690	987	1541	863	129	64		391	2299
1514	39		390		22		100	1414
1467	552	150	1182	135		161		1306
1933	782		1836	97				1933
2113	982	4	1991	41		68	294	1751
1365	584		1189	167	9		32	1333
3265	1295	27	2636	352	240	414	441	2410
838	345		838				31	807
610	39		610			1		609
2674	977		2488					2674
3096	1157	68	2731	75		23	10	3063
1995	669		1907	32	10	1	8	1986
2366	1170	5	1818	30		281	13	2072
2358	874		1720	135	16	7	84	2267
1072	413		905				181	891
76	27		76					76
986	405		980	6				986
2583	1011		2093	42	34	136	35	2412
1477	572	4	1172	23	81	78	59	1340
1841	336		1631		24	11		1830
5281	1419	8	1646					5281
2014	781		2014					2014
2295	689	2	1738	127	360	12	11	2272
1269	243		789					1269
432	151		384					432
4060	1100	102	3704	17	164	37	70	3953

C-2-15续表2

地区	在院人员按类型分			康复和医疗门诊人次数	家庭寄养儿童数量	机构建筑面积
	自理(完全自理)	介助(半自理)	介护(不能自理)			
全国	**25086**	**10739**	**18991**	**873042**	**15230**	**2624631**
中央级						
北京	295	61	818	1170	434	105238
天津	33	12	178	301	245	12712
河北	147		30			6620
山西	498	86	148	730	48	19428
内蒙古	345	206	289	166772	14	162975
辽宁	1881	677	132	23818	222	76686
吉林	1234	244	36	11359	19	229017
黑龙江	1003	271	193	179	103	97435
上海	250	243	1440	3758	1135	35074
江苏	438	213	1462	19401	303	91259
浙江	97	159	1109	37626	444	54390
安徽	633	1037	1595	24570	2055	187023
福建	463	174	201	110	674	27148
江西	360	12	238		985	17980
山东	911	563	1200	52901	381	167108
河南	1373	519	1204	6788	467	126115
湖北	527	437	1031	74707	457	57932
湖南	784	485	1097	2155	1315	67678
广东	588	576	1194	232595	181	97524
广西	93	441	538	17187	143	40532
海南	30	19	27			4300
重庆	297	225	464	39241		71614
四川	838	1162	583	28514	441	124956
贵州	726	337	414	1896	292	47009
云南	693	291	857	3497	1263	114294
西藏	5257	22	2			114617
陕西	606	408	1000		438	86587
甘肃	967	527	801	41930	125	109529
青海	564	705		41		31194
宁夏	132	64	236	190	113	24120
新疆	3023	563	474	81606	2933	216538

单位：人、人次、平方米、万元

执行行政事业单位会计制度财务指标				
固定资产原价	上年结转和结余	本年收入合计	本年支出合计	收支结余
355255.3	**40987.6**	**275316.9**	**234254.0**	**36253.7**
17604.7	658.4	15520.5	14978.1	1206.7
1602.4	806.2	6498.9	5230.6	2136.1
268.2		452.9	452.9	
1930.7	186.5	691.2	678.6	2.6
13302.8	1536.0	6949.8	6265.7	2551.1
7957.8	1607.1	8908.4	9002.0	561.4
7626.1	785.3	3297.8	3402.6	94.7
20641.5	661.3	13902.5	7233.7	690.4
17839.3	89.4	13836.8	13518.5	347.1
11541.1	3895.8	16749.1	13971.4	4811.3
13707.3	1616.0	14512.5	12191.7	642.0
16914.8	2596.7	12625.6	11056.9	-25.8
3360.0	1239.4	5402.6	3407.7	1418.3
1823.7		376.8	300.8	
18398.9		14626.6	14626.6	
16497.9	795.0	7748.1	7339.4	1100.2
10488.0	259.1	10808.2	10143.6	463.0
14378.9	34.2	5562.0	6593.8	
24519.6	1034.7	15326.9	15126.3	606.3
6864.1	438.4	7111.0	7470.9	506.5
660.0	18.4	96.0	91.0	
7321.3	1809.3	16246.4	7069.7	10986.0
23840.5	14851.9	11998.0	12647.0	1769.7
5041.7	1441.4	3197.9	3617.0	138.0
16562.8	977.4	5515.4	5115.2	530.4
6101.8		1910.0	4454.8	
22280.4	1486.8	26184.2	23898.4	2876.5
15360.6	777.9	4167.5	3237.7	891.0
3170.0		371.4	371.4	
10551.6	330.0	2547.0	2345.0	509.0
17096.8	1055.0	22174.9	8415.0	1441.2

C-2-16 未成年人

地区	单位数					年末职工人数	
		0~99张	100~299张	300~499张	500张以上		女性
全国	**275**	**238**	**33**	**4**		**1751**	**668**
中央级							
北京	2		1	1		51	21
天津							
河北	1	1				13	1
山西	5	5				55	11
内蒙古							
辽宁	2	2				21	6
吉林							
黑龙江	1		1			8	6
上海	1		1			62	57
江苏	19	16	3			54	27
浙江							
安徽	5	2	3			22	3
福建							
江西	12	10	2			91	25
山东	4	3	1			31	13
河南	4	3	1			58	27
湖北	55	48	6	1		289	126
湖南	33	29	4			324	121
广东	2	1		1		106	6
广西	27	23	4			144	59
海南							
重庆							
四川	67	64	3			240	89
贵州	6	5	1			40	15
云南	6	6				16	11
西藏							
陕西	1	1				1	
甘肃	10	8	1	1		84	29
青海	5	5				15	6
宁夏	5	5				20	8
新疆	2	1	1			6	1

救助保护中心

单位:个、人

受教育程度		职业资格水平		按人员性质分		年龄结构	
大学专科人数	大学本科及以上人数	助理社会工作师人数	社会工作师人数	管理人员	专业技术技能人员	35岁及以下人数	36岁至45岁人数
693	**409**	**54**	**51**	**967**	**784**	**628**	**722**
10	38	5	2	51		20	15
	3			10	3	2	10
14	7			21	34	11	16
13	8			18	3	6	5
	8			3	5	3	5
26	11	3	5	11	51	27	18
24	6	1	2	21	33	26	23
10	5		1	12	10	4	12
43	6	5		60	31	31	43
7	5	2	1	17	14	13	14
33	16	3	3	18	40	25	26
123	46	5	6	134	155	101	118
132	63	6	6	149	175	102	159
27	26	12	12	53	53	58	30
56	47	2	5	90	54	53	56
99	68	4	7	171	69	89	108
24	9	1		35	5	13	11
4	5			13	3	6	5
	1				1	1	
31	16	5	1	52	32	24	29
6	2			11	4	7	6
6	12			15	5	4	12
5	1			2	4	2	1

C-2-16续表1

地　区	年龄结构		志愿服务		本年在站救助人次数		
	46岁至55岁人数	56岁及以上人数	志愿者服务人次数	志愿服务时间		从其他站转入的	女性
全　国	**332**	**69**	**696**	**2635.0**	**47087**	**3988**	**5809**
中央级							
北　京	11	5			586		58
天　津							
河　北	1				43		
山　西	26	2			1579		
内蒙古							
辽　宁	10				97	5	20
吉　林							
黑龙江					20		
上　海	16	1			54		
江　苏	4	1	62	244.0	1612	212	110
浙　江							
安　徽	6				506	222	125
福　建							
江　西	14	3			1561	85	451
山　东	4		161	408.0	309		12
河　南	6	1			772		25
湖　北	53	17	130	240.0	16766	489	369
湖　南	49	14	328	1628.0	7612	850	3173
广　东	17	1			763	533	156
广　西	25	10			3438	148	373
海　南							
重　庆							
四　川	37	6			6677	880	657
贵　州	14	2			694	303	162
云　南	5				42	20	5
西　藏							
陕　西					7		3
甘　肃	25	6			1092	49	108
青　海	2		15	115.0	154		
宁　夏	4				2488	192	2
新　疆	3				215		

单位：人、人次、时

未成年人	肢体残疾人	智障及精神病人	救治的危重病人	自主返乡	跨省接送
47087	**1437**	**2095**	**65**	**1881**	**2432**
586					43
43					
1579					1
97	16	34		32	
20					
54					
1612	7	6		190	353
506	2	51	2	68	68
1561	15	7			400
309				60	4
772	12				
16766	107	114		478	428
7612	1047	1428		434	354
763	60	43			316
3438	59	284	28	150	48
6677	14	75	9	113	34
694	72	34		16	285
42				10	10
7		1			
1092	24	13	22	244	73
154			4		
2488	2	5		86	15
215					

C-2-16续表2

地区	床位数	成年人床位数	未成年人床位数	年末在站人数	女性	未成年人	本年在站人天数	在站滞留三个月以上人数
全国	**10682**		**10682**	**1268**	**374**	**1268**	**295827**	**356**
中央级								
北京	450		450	40	1	40	19582	3
天津								
河北	30		30					
山西	204		204	12		12	362	
内蒙古								
辽宁	80		80				868	
吉林								
黑龙江	100		100	20	5	20	400	
上海	100		100	54	22	54	18410	
江苏	799		799	41		41	18954	35
浙江								
安徽	554		554	10	3	10	5618	9
福建								
江西	693		693	4		4	8089	
山东	284		284	6	2	6	2358	3
河南	385		385	15	15	15	10946	
湖北	1602		1602	214	104	214	49351	10
湖南	1108		1108	230	52	230	20370	58
广东	340		340	136		136	60891	117
广西	1139		1139	47	5	47	30236	64
海南								
重庆								
四川	1475		1475	63	7	63	38410	25
贵州	178		178	6	1	6	1797	8
云南	239		239	1		1	95	
西藏								
陕西	12		12				447	1
甘肃	628		628	369	157	369	4129	13
青海	120		120				4	
宁夏	147		147				4510	10
新疆	15		15					

单位:张、人、人天、万元

残疾人人数	未成年人人数	执行行政事业单位会计制度财务指标				
		固定资产原价	上年结转和结余	本年收入合计	本年支出合计	收支结余
193	**340**	**21463.3**	**555.3**	**12044.1**	**11715.6**	**681.3**
	3	597.2	59.0	2214.2	1891.3	291.3
		361.0	104.0	804.0	1015.0	104.0
				3.0	3.0	
		3.0		16.6	16.6	
		1215.0		254.4	308.1	25.0
		472.0	292.0	1112.0	1143.0	261.0
8	35					
2	9	170.5				
		1550.0		109.0	109.0	
	3	521.1		632.3	632.3	
		73.0		30.0	30.0	
4	9	111.0		90.0	108.0	
16	57	7408.0	5.2	2615.8	2611.7	
91	117	6773.7		3517.3	3309.5	
61	64	35.0			0.5	
	24	150.0		47.0	53.0	
	8	78.0		60.9	41.9	
		12.2		98.9	63.4	
1	1					
5	5	882.3	95.1	350.7	293.6	
5	5	1033.0		6.0	6.0	
		17.3		82.0	79.7	

C-2-17 其他提供住宿的

地区	单位数	单位数按登记类型分			单位数按	
		编制登记	民政登记	一个机构多块牌子	0～99张	100～299张
全国	**2440**	**1929**	**276**	**235**	**1735**	**648**
中央级	1	1				1
北京	21	20		1	13	5
天津	15	14		1	12	2
河北	99	52	20	27	65	33
山西	108	88	9	11	90	16
内蒙古	46	43	1	2	35	10
辽宁	115	78	36	1	79	34
吉林	62	60		2	44	18
黑龙江	123	80	34	9	100	23
上海	23	22	1		16	5
江苏	91	78	4	9	60	26
浙江	64	60	2	2	45	18
安徽	89	78	7	4	39	48
福建	57	54		3	39	18
江西	109	82	2	25	81	26
山东	72	71		1	43	27
河南	127	111	13	3	80	42
湖北	135	89	39	7	103	30
湖南	140	112	10	18	108	32
广东	114	99	13	2	68	37
广西	86	75	5	6	68	18
海南	13	9		4	7	6
重庆	42	42			35	6
四川	236	139	54	43	164	62
贵州	84	64		20	69	14
云南	98	91	7		66	31
西藏	10	10			5	5
陕西	100	95		5	82	15
甘肃	64	45	3	16	52	12
青海	12	7	2	3	6	6
宁夏	11	11			8	3
新疆	73	49	14	10	53	19

社会服务机构总表

单位:个、人

床位数量分		年末职工人数		年末职工人数按登记类型分		
300~499张	500张以上		女性	编制登记	民政登记	一个机构多块牌子
39	**18**	**28186**	**11140**	**23808**	**3316**	**1062**
		185	130	185		
	3	647	279	637		10
	1	237	74	236		1
1		1073	435	691	250	132
2		795	280	676	76	43
1		525	135	512	3	10
	2	1403	525	1183	219	1
		986	323	980		6
		1068	398	847	191	30
	2	776	420	769	7	
4	1	994	415	929	29	36
1		763	313	729	29	5
2		1071	444	961	81	29
		483	176	469		14
2		879	292	760	15	104
2		722	233	719		3
3	2	1799	656	1701	73	25
1	1	1397	552	1071	287	39
		1401	503	1231	83	87
6	3	2617	1068	2150	463	4
		917	338	856	54	7
		160	56	142		18
1		394	128	394		
9	1	2879	1423	1312	1296	271
	1	735	299	634		101
1		960	414	869	91	
		49	13	49		
2	1	1058	392	1041		17
		548	188	491	9	48
		83	20	72	2	9
		80	22	80		
1		502	196	432	58	12

C-2-17续表1

地区	受教育程度		职业资格水平		按人员性质分		年龄	
	大学专科人数	大学本科及以上人数	助理社会工作师人数	社会工作师人数	管理人员	专业技术技能人员	35岁及以下人数	36岁至45岁人数
全　国	**9021**	**6648**	**625**	**663**	**15504**	**12682**	**8527**	**10368**
中央级	71	114		2	28	157	138	29
北　京	128	298	27	4	522	125	253	214
天　津	51	91	3	8	95	142	80	59
河　北	206	156	9	14	376	697	329	413
山　西	296	165	9	15	419	376	248	253
内蒙古	211	183	9	15	312	213	128	153
辽　宁	503	392	21	23	799	604	373	503
吉　林	264	227	5	4	624	362	239	476
黑龙江	349	219	6	9	673	395	264	413
上　海	233	182	34	39	375	401	228	319
江　苏	287	334	43	63	452	542	300	385
浙　江	215	226	19	15	456	307	213	299
安　徽	285	165	26	17	567	504	227	378
福　建	115	177	18	28	382	101	150	146
江　西	268	131	25	12	537	342	220	347
山　东	265	292	27	46	307	415	208	240
河　南	595	343	27	35	941	858	662	644
湖　北	455	213	15	10	582	815	393	547
湖　南	530	223	29	23	784	617	468	591
广　东	1006	631	130	88	1651	966	908	884
广　西	237	241	36	54	469	448	272	321
海　南	48	41	3	3	53	107	53	53
重　庆	154	180	10	16	347	47	122	144
四　川	817	489	46	63	1495	1384	760	1043
贵　州	252	219	14	6	521	214	261	252
云　南	329	221	16	29	414	546	256	398
西　藏	17	15		1	28	21	13	28
陕　西	388	177	6	11	631	427	390	377
甘　肃	181	120	7	8	326	222	170	188
青　海	41	20	2		38	45	27	31
宁　夏	27	36			43	37	17	33
新　疆	197	127	3	2	257	245	157	207

单位：人、人次、时、张、人天

结构		志愿服务		年末床位数				年在院（站）总人天数
46岁至55岁人数	56岁及以上人数	志愿者服务人次数	志愿服务时间		编制登记	民政登记	一个机构多块牌子	
7132	**2159**	**17991**	**51801.0**	**170958**	**140255**	**23112**	**7591**	**14805340**
13	5			150	150			47998
136	44			5835	5803		32	958447
66	32	200	400.0	1489	1489			65801
268	63	283	1153.0	6596	3395	2229	972	798140
239	55	149	512.0	3735	3049	474	212	409344
203	41	60	360.0	2539	2352	130	57	187842
420	107	99	159.0	8556	7088	1388	80	499434
230	41			3261	3114		147	112272
318	73	130	580.0	6050	4284	1649	117	456419
154	75	644	1753.5	3114	2964	150		715050
228	81	2285	9963.0	6654	6257	161	236	748800
184	67	3985	6797.0	4978	4732	156	90	366094
355	111	781	1887.0	6443	5597	590	256	801069
146	41	20	160.0	3295	3183		112	347517
248	64	264	1056.0	5689	4364	280	1045	316823
232	42	4034	10041.0	5438	5428		10	432748
397	96	23	70.0	10347	9256	921	170	681877
334	123	237	346.0	8378	6607	1610	161	1121291
275	67	1582	7169.0	7214	5940	844	430	866805
682	143	350	1540.0	13508	11988	1502	18	980431
228	96	250	580.0	4252	3816	313	123	364198
45	9	128	358.0	852	632		220	37852
97	31	1127	2844.0	2157	2157			164704
659	417	231	442.0	19988	9907	8918	1163	1919426
186	36	232	861.0	4509	3194		1315	179230
229	77	242	724.0	5775	5146	629		517376
8				7625	7625			79614
237	54	631	1939.5	4513	4371		142	201251
157	33	10	80.0	2827	2353	55	419	115608
20	5	2	16.0	525	336	180	9	49942
23	7			582	582			25785
115	23	12	10.0	4084	3096	933	55	236152

C-2-17续表2

地区	执行企业会计制度单位财务指标				执行行政	
	固定资产原价	营业收入	费用合计	营业利润	固定资产原价	上年结转和结余
全国	**1707.1**	**214.5**	**357.9**	**-155.4**	**526786.5**	**58813.0**
中央级					12600.6	3469.8
北京					6609.3	1438.3
天津					2479.2	129.3
河北					23604.6	2742.9
山西					11275.3	1668.0
内蒙古					7975.1	1029.1
辽宁					21492.1	689.9
吉林					8339.2	71.8
黑龙江					13951.1	879.5
上海					26201.7	7463.2
江苏	1707.1	214.5	357.9	-155.4	34515.9	2401.4
浙江					22585.8	928.7
安徽					20442.5	2213.9
福建					8874.0	4083.6
江西					11862.6	668.2
山东					21534.2	
河南					21872.3	2518.8
湖北					23787.0	959.2
湖南					15862.3	146.9
广东					67208.7	3049.6
广西					18625.2	4064.7
海南					2515.4	1504.4
重庆					8551.2	68.3
四川					37105.7	2814.2
贵州					13933.2	5112.8
云南					17882.7	2171.9
西藏					250.4	
陕西					15983.4	1140.6
甘肃					12628.9	1451.9
青海					754.2	41.8
宁夏					2013.5	655.0
新疆					13469.2	3235.3

单位：万元

事业单位会计制度财务指标			执行民间非营利组织单位会计制度财务指标			
本年收入合计	本年支出合计	收支结余	固定资产原价	上年结余	本年收入合计	本年费用合计
452220.2	**487608.1**	**37341.0**	**25903.3**	**1055.1**	**8315.8**	**12838.9**
1497.3	9283.3	2496.7				
21242.2	33024.4	2763.9				
6420.2	6533.3	99.5				
18159.9	15698.1	5144.0	5784.0		850.9	973.1
8713.7	8326.0	1579.7	745.0		74.0	175.9
9006.8	8563.5	1634.4				
15690.3	15509.8	791.5	782.0	3.0	208.2	249.9
7594.4	7590.1	141.6				
9261.6	9607.8	27.0	1735.2	120.8	76.8	2602.0
23691.8	24735.2	5276.1	100.0			1.0
25500.1	24702.5	1611.3	10.0		6.0	4.0
24196.4	24002.0	-171.6	102.0		140.0	140.0
12448.4	12823.1	83.5	930.0			130.0
10605.9	9995.3	2495.8				
7877.1	7088.6	873.5	89.0			
19017.1	19017.1					
18658.5	18749.1	1349.9	412.0	120.0	641.2	646.8
21635.7	21536.4	1130.9	2275.0	6.0	1123.7	941.2
19317.2	19965.3	347.5	64.0	3.0	16.0	35.0
60106.0	58638.6	1038.3	398.4	175.8	1261.9	1235.2
20096.9	19749.5	1058.5	294.0	23.6	33.3	126.1
4242.4	4258.6	61.7				
12428.9	11430.4	1054.9				
22687.1	22715.6	2009.1	12003.7	602.9	3883.8	5572.3
9113.5	26165.2	1620.3				
10678.9	14427.5	811.8	25.0			6.2
370.0	730.4					
14702.2	14139.2	400.0				
5282.0	5072.8	986.2				
1321.8	1713.0		130.0			0.2
1980.9	1897.9	246.6				
8675.0	9918.5	378.4	24.0			

C-2-18 生活无着人员

地区	单位数	0~99张	100~299张	300~499张	500张以上	年末职工人数	女性
全国	**1766**	**1494**	**232**	**27**	**13**	**17419**	**5939**
中央级							
北京	20	13	4		3	604	265
天津	14	12	1		1	212	71
河北	62	54	8			465	134
山西	90	81	7	2		600	216
内蒙古	39	34	4	1		411	106
辽宁	64	48	15		1	839	256
吉林	51	44	7			729	245
黑龙江	77	70	7			690	200
上海	19	16	2		1	334	109
江苏	70	56	11	3		753	300
浙江	51	44	7			515	167
安徽	44	31	11	2		427	137
福建	42	35	7			333	110
江西	93	80	11	2		578	180
山东	55	43	10	2		476	146
河南	85	66	15	3	1	1059	365
湖北	86	71	13	1	1	863	311
湖南	113	98	15			1010	340
广东	73	45	19	6	3	1763	558
广西	66	62	4			439	145
海南	10	7	3			112	38
重庆	38	35	2	1		334	109
四川	156	137	18	1		1165	434
贵州	72	65	6		1	454	181
云南	66	60	6			453	158
西藏	7	5	2			34	10
陕西	89	81	5	2	1	912	335
甘肃	50	48	2			410	157
青海	6	5	1			44	10
宁夏	9	7	2			67	20
新疆	49	41	7	1		334	126

救助管理站

单位：个、人

受教育程度		职业资格水平		按人员性质分	
大学专科人数	大学本科及以上人数	助理社会工作师人数	社会工作师人数	管理人员	专业技术技能人员
6195	**4952**	**490**	**535**	**10765**	**6654**
123	271	27	4	499	105
50	79	3	8	79	133
120	109	9	13	199	266
239	142	8	14	338	262
166	157	6	11	236	175
369	263	14	20	506	333
177	182	2	2	463	266
266	171	4	5	474	216
144	149	20	37	294	40
248	281	41	56	370	383
174	192	17	13	341	174
139	127	15	14	282	145
82	152	15	28	265	68
187	102	21	11	350	228
169	209	22	40	195	281
362	207	14	27	515	544
316	158	15	10	386	477
432	175	25	22	580	430
645	472	112	71	1274	489
132	147	13	18	283	156
40	29	3	3	43	69
131	151	8	16	293	41
452	324	40	55	860	305
179	150	11	5	317	137
158	150	10	10	237	216
8	9		1	13	21
334	148	6	11	545	367
151	96	5	8	270	140
29	9	2		16	28
18	32			38	29
155	109	2	2	204	130

C-2-18续表1

地区	年龄结构				志愿服务	
	35岁及以下人数	36岁至45岁人数	46岁至55岁人数	56岁及以上人数	志愿者服务人次数	志愿服务时间
全国	**5742**	**6368**	**4193**	**1116**	**16626**	**48158.5**
中央级						
北京	246	192	130	36		
天津	71	57	63	21	200	400.0
河北	157	167	106	35	124	491.0
山西	215	188	155	42	149	512.0
内蒙古	99	112	169	31	60	360.0
辽宁	258	265	246	70	21	41.0
吉林	195	342	166	26		
黑龙江	202	256	206	26	130	580.0
上海	121	79	84	50	276	1064.0
江苏	261	279	158	55	2236	9854.0
浙江	149	214	102	50	3919	6709.0
安徽	130	140	126	31	509	1275.0
福建	137	105	63	28	20	160.0
江西	159	251	127	41	132	528.0
山东	162	160	128	26	4034	10041.0
河南	435	366	205	53	23	70.0
湖北	289	334	173	67	217	295.0
湖南	379	439	154	38	1582	7169.0
广东	490	633	528	112	350	1540.0
广西	121	152	112	54	250	580.0
海南	40	36	29	7	128	358.0
重庆	98	125	85	26	1082	2754.0
四川	395	450	266	54	231	442.0
贵州	175	164	93	22	177	724.0
云南	130	191	106	26	146	186.0
西藏	7	19	8			
陕西	353	322	191	46	616	1919.5
甘肃	144	135	106	25	10	80.0
青海	13	15	13	3	2	16.0
宁夏	13	29	18	7		
新疆	98	151	77	8	2	10.0

单位：人、人次、时

本年在站救助人次数	从其他站转入的	女性	未成年人	老年人	肢体残疾人
3186825	**161103**	**602977**	**101669**	**306567**	**130249**
530364	2180	195678	8716	16533	1594
46497	63	918	363	671	305
46630	904	7765	1587	6149	1997
81667	2232	13980	5425	10121	4846
33214	5978	5721	875	3529	2318
57000	2012	9427	2677	9124	4342
33028	2585	5276	1222	5916	1382
31649	2346	4328	2256	7600	2483
25996	897	5307	1989	2598	660
110083	9562	14494	6862	8112	2424
59603	942	10548	2049	6936	1710
91074	10874	16208	5242	13145	5902
61090	1418	4499	1904	3582	2204
91394	29665	9787	3533	12981	3152
80985	2957	12682	4173	7038	3475
125542	9371	26755	6538	21357	9290
328848	10527	41467	4016	31183	6753
518655	11871	108831	7024	51430	22531
173082	11479	15186	4837	9710	8317
103392	3215	11635	4395	7033	1891
38735	294	9560	1282	2323	985
49255	3285	8738	1400	6627	2320
219447	20721	29981	9128	24995	14360
65480	3773	7636	3948	9624	3873
37041	3189	4111	4076	3158	3826
11312	311	685	154	394	890
65996	3871	7417	2823	9093	3880
30090	3482	5493	1483	7692	2980
9973	114	1438	11	305	3391
9233	710	1547	218	647	249
20470	275	5879	1463	6961	5919

C-2-18续表2

地区	智障及精神病人	救治的危重病人	自主返乡	跨省接送	床位数
全国	**442162**	**27312**	**892526**	**85080**	**102720**
中央级					
北京	6344	697	15593	1937	5486
天津	640	59	7172	322	1289
河北	4458	1141	28361	1880	2988
山西	8068	266	32712	1561	2645
内蒙古	5635	408	14762	929	1839
辽宁	5352	659	17741	3843	5207
吉林	1683	317	9924	787	2251
黑龙江	2898	58	7420	2399	2687
上海	1618	141	10271	597	1765
江苏	13547	1045	46166	6328	4471
浙江	9377	1224	31170	2664	2973
安徽	16679	689	27510	3981	3607
福建	1883	369	40557	803	1933
江西	7031	81	23504	4457	4060
山东	7377	221	32973	4595	3695
河南	16604	9707	36354	4831	5856
湖北	49787	748	61322	8279	4948
湖南	204860	976	94415	8125	5088
广东	6964	2892	92045	2889	7864
广西	9921	238	22383	2614	2260
海南	19505	1575	29293	78	513
重庆	3992	337	35101	1326	1717
四川	18124	1256	69121	10911	6734
贵州	3939	156	31013	1536	3057
云南	1752	878	11516	486	1892
西藏	8		118	48	7624
陕西	3767	549	33250	2698	4018
甘肃	2799	100	14851	1616	1548
青海	5237		1294		189
宁夏	1014	195	2541	891	542
新疆	1299	330	12073	1669	1974

单位：人、张、人天、人次

成年人床位数	儿童床位数	年末在站人数	女性	儿童	本年在站人天数
83616	**19104**	**33714**	**6412**	**2875**	**8403061**
4677	809	2232	117	549	958447
1081	208	479	171	103	65801
2371	617	1010	280	61	271341
1933	712	532	168	23	235372
1422	417	202	48	23	72514
3841	1366	757	89	143	173668
1558	693	82	26		57887
2193	494	506	37	58	152709
1531	234	873	345	62	349845
3629	842	1537	593	128	549569
2410	563	810	273	42	250312
2696	911	1008	448	64	345740
1243	690	309	89	16	174812
3392	668	868	35	70	182023
2655	1040	1281	406	135	416170
4560	1296	1614	518	188	431380
3908	1040	2218	608	90	838995
4527	561	1620	376	117	530273
6072	1792	1993	340	267	696670
1806	454	366	108	26	183675
377	136	253	153	28	37072
1250	467	251	79	32	140163
5771	963	1782	351	251	621275
2578	479	1514	95	25	96974
1686	206	310	22	28	111030
7624		7624	447	114	79614
3428	590	931	82	70	178131
1260	288	282	16	105	102783
189					8811
434	108	115	31	19	25485
1514	460	355	61	38	64520

C-2-18续表3

地　区	本年不在站救助人次数	未成年人	在站滞留三个月以上人数	残疾人人数	未成年人人数
全　国	**518194**	**17967**	**14597**	**6843**	**849**
中央级					
北　京	2621	110	38	2	3
天　津	228	12	492	29	46
河　北	34504	285	530	182	53
山　西	13316	1192	679	426	31
内蒙古	15650	79	166	108	18
辽　宁	5336	145	196	120	25
吉　林	2836	43	108	18	4
黑龙江	1332	38	23	12	4
上　海	1632	27	787	331	56
江　苏	3936	338	1355	840	18
浙　江	3460	1	698	272	27
安　徽	54485	2389	630	435	20
福　建	31268	702	331	223	13
江　西	3992	191	130	113	8
山　东	30963	686	464	329	15
河　南	46002	2795	462	204	25
湖　北	26386	2060	1210	730	32
湖　南	48190	1662	1833	987	64
广　东	44353	261	1248	169	208
广　西	24586	1065	943	383	28
海　南	12433	587	110	93	17
重　庆	7612	65	245	69	18
四　川	29996	455	883	278	46
贵　州	14666	170	281	77	13
云　南	17363	858	18	12	5
西　藏	820	49			
陕　西	18900	542	438	270	32
甘　肃	5318	911	106	20	7
青　海	11292	161	65	10	
宁　夏	2323	25	66	53	8
新　疆	2395	63	62	48	5

单位：万元

执行行政事业单位会计制度财务指标				
固定资产原价	上年结转和结余	本年收入合计	本年支出合计	收支结余
316093.1	**46807.1**	**344421.0**	**368222.8**	**29611.1**
4695.3	1438.3	19527.2	31196.4	2763.9
1781.2	129.3	5650.2	5789.2	73.6
16593.6	2262.8	12985.6	10626.2	4959.9
9682.3	1654.8	7204.4	7134.2	1273.6
5299.9	951.2	7131.3	6726.2	1527.6
12569.7	599.5	12162.1	12187.5	673.3
5194.8	71.8	6128.1	6117.6	132.4
5646.4	747.3	7063.1	7582.8	33.1
16913.2	6959.0	15307.5	15989.1	5077.6
24280.6	2273.6	22291.1	21543.0	1097.6
9310.2	1563.7	17511.4	17594.7	359.4
8236.9	191.3	10157.9	10171.2	20.8
4189.1	2794.5	7811.9	7257.8	1432.1
5661.7	226.7	6089.2	5447.5	556.8
12291.3		12226.2	12226.2	
9507.0	2033.5	12435.2	12378.3	880.9
20994.2	943.7	17142.8	17076.0	1072.9
10664.1	78.4	15956.4	16494.5	88.5
47658.9	2729.0	49702.8	48692.9	1035.1
8302.4	2781.8	10908.8	10530.4	1074.1
1712.1	1390.5	3727.7	3752.8	58.4
7240.5	55.5	10673.7	9832.7	884.6
18484.2	2274.2	17784.7	18327.7	1489.3
10055.9	5198.5	4684.8	19886.8	704.7
8084.5	1270.5	6324.9	6938.8	647.7
250.4		16.0	376.4	
12197.4	1087.8	12613.6	12182.1	218.1
9791.1	1399.2	4192.8	4017.2	949.9
228.1	41.8	940.1	970.9	
1240.7	542.7	1581.4	1612.7	146.8
7335.4	3116.2	6488.1	7563.0	378.4

C-2-19 军

地区	单位数	0～99张	100～299张	300～499张	500张以上
全　国	**320**	**194**	**97**	**20**	**9**
中央级					
北　京	1			1	
天　津	1		1		
河　北	9	7	2		
山　西	6	4	2		
内蒙古	5	3	2		
辽　宁	12	8	3		1
吉　林	11	7	4		
黑龙江	11	4	6		1
上　海	1		1		
江　苏	16	10	5	1	
浙　江	10	5	4	1	
安　徽	35	28	6	1	
福　建	11	8	3		
江　西	14	9	3	2	
山　东	17	10	6	1	
河　南	25	13	10		2
湖　北	9	4	3	1	1
湖　南	13	9	3	1	
广　东	13	5	6	1	1
广　西	13	8	3	2	
海　南	2	2			
重　庆	4	3		1	
四　川	14	7	2	4	1
贵　州	8	3	3	2	
云　南	22	10	11	1	
西　藏	3	3			
陕　西	10	8	2		
甘　肃	9	6	2		1
青　海	4	3	1		
宁　夏	1	1			
新　疆	10	6	3		1

供站

单位：个、人

年末职工人数	女性	受教育程度		职业资格水平	
		大学专科人数	大学本科及以上人数	助理社会工作师人数	社会工作师人数
5201	**2023**	**1645**	**1123**	**54**	**51**
43	14	5	27		
25	3	1	12		
88	29	19	39		1
104	39	48	23	1	1
98	27	45	26		1
225	72	80	56	3	2
257	78	87	45	3	2
172	70	75	47	2	4
42	10	11	7	2	
199	89	36	51	1	7
145	65	40	34	2	2
510	265	116	20	9	2
102	51	26	17	2	
286	106	80	27		1
246	87	96	83	5	6
592	214	203	133	6	8
218	75	80	44		
255	116	64	45	1	1
244	110	93	86	4	9
243	97	74	76	4	2
38	14	4	6		
60	19	23	29	2	
201	61	79	49	3	1
97	37	26	28		1
301	154	86	40	2	
15	3	9	6		
117	49	50	20		
121	26	30	16	2	
37	10	12	11		
10	2	8	2		
110	31	39	18		

C-2-19续表1

地区	按人员性质分		年龄
	管理人员	专业技术技能人员	35岁及以下人数
全国	**2833**	**2368**	**1091**
中央级			
北京	23	20	7
天津	16	9	9
河北	43	45	24
山西	62	42	17
内蒙古	72	26	20
辽宁	144	81	39
吉林	161	96	44
黑龙江	109	63	31
上海	37	5	9
江苏	71	128	21
浙江	96	49	17
安徽	178	332	62
福建	69	33	9
江西	185	101	60
山东	112	134	46
河南	365	227	188
湖北	82	136	50
湖南	164	91	59
广东	152	92	53
广西	150	93	52
海南	6	32	8
重庆	54	6	24
四川	110	91	44
贵州	79	18	44
云南	123	178	37
西藏	15		6
陕西	57	60	37
甘肃	48	73	24
青海	20	17	14
宁夏	4	6	2
新疆	26	84	34

单位:人、人次、时

结构			志愿服务	
36岁至45岁人数	46岁至55岁人数	56岁及以上人数	志愿者服务人次数	志愿服务时间
1992	**1678**	**440**	**632**	**1554.0**
22	6	8		
2	3	11		
22	30	12		
48	30	9		
39	32	7		
89	71	26		
134	64	15		
83	50	8		
5	19	9		
93	62	23	49	109.0
50	62	16	66	88.0
203	197	48	272	612.0
30	53	10		
93	110	23	132	528.0
80	104	16		
215	153	36		
87	58	23	12	42.0
98	78	20		
90	83	18		
87	78	26		
15	14	1		
19	12	5	45	90.0
71	68	18		
23	25	5	25	47.0
151	92	21	6	18.0
9				
44	33	3	15	20.0
44	47	6		
14	7	2		
3	5			
29	32	15	10	

C-2-19续表2

地区	执行企业会计制度单位财务指标				执行行政事业单位	
	固定资产原价	营业收入	费用合计	营业利润	固定资产原价	上年结转和结余
全国	**1707.1**	**214.5**	**357.9**	**-155.4**	**155962.4**	**6351.6**
中央级						
北京					1914.0	
天津					698.0	
河北					3492.4	427.5
山西					802.0	13.2
内蒙古					2571.9	40.3
辽宁					3382.1	4.6
吉林					3144.4	
黑龙江					7499.7	132.2
上海					2504.5	132.9
江苏	1707.1	214.5	357.9	-155.4	9935.3	127.8
浙江					13275.6	-635.0
安徽					11308.1	2022.6
福建					3091.2	110.7
江西					6200.9	441.5
山东					9242.9	
河南					12079.8	485.3
湖北					2392.8	15.5
湖南					4508.4	0.3
广东					15841.8	320.6
广西					6050.8	1172.9
海南					803.3	113.9
重庆					1310.7	12.8
四川					11530.5	318.4
贵州					938.0	-107.7
云南					9292.2	864.4
西藏						
陕西					2907.2	52.8
甘肃					2257.2	52.7
青海					526.1	
宁夏					722.8	112.3
新疆					5737.8	119.1

单位：万元、张、人次、人天

会计制度财务指标			床位数	接待人次数		本年在站人天数
本年收入合计	本年支出合计	收支结余			接待军队人次数	
82721.2	**83491.2**	**3715.8**	**37899**	**4666095**	**3549129**	**2490314**
1715.0	1828.0		349	167000	167000	
770.0	744.1	25.9	200	12800	12800	
1860.4	1960.7	154.1	494	49621	44621	3900
1508.3	1183.8	306.1	433	58369	46390	87475
1655.2	1600.3	106.8	490	64003	64003	57889
1792.5	1684.7	112.4	1361	45412	35967	141880
1466.3	1472.5	9.2	1010	90763	54900	54385
2198.5	2025.0	-6.1	1700	35065	24780	97942
1303.2	1420.3	14.5	179	94822	49767	
3169.0	3119.5	513.7	1672	196096	86007	115441
6475.0	6198.3	-531.0	1364	337632	230235	89766
2245.5	2606.9	62.7	2140	202916	134458	297997
1565.9	1343.4	74.7	1177	114635	109281	127810
1787.9	1641.1	316.7	1349	172424	108739	133800
6790.9	6790.9		1743	260753	244093	16578
5831.2	5978.7	469.0	3217	414433	217594	30328
4472.9	4430.4	58.0	1740	130723	121945	54301
2985.5	3280.1	259.0	1134	310297	255725	247659
8421.9	8037.4	3.2	3278	234845	219468	105990
5589.6	5172.8	294.0	1609	109967	109729	82283
514.7	505.8	3.3	139	45475	45475	780
1755.2	1597.7	170.3	440	153202	150762	24541
3863.6	3630.1	519.8	3689	343112	342906	135405
2626.7	2384.9	297.4	1249	131377	108530	52935
4354.0	6588.7	164.1	2920	452370	195968	393575
354.0	354.0		1	78000	78000	
1713.2	1581.7	181.9	445	73500	73500	23090
1009.0	995.6	36.3	1044	95614	95614	1967
381.7	742.1		156	84100	84000	
399.5	285.2	99.8				
2144.9	2306.5		1177	106769	36872	112597

C-2-20 安置

地区	单位数	0～99张	100～299张	300～499张	500张以上	年末职工人数
全国	**15**	**14**		**1**		**590**
中央级						
北京						
天津						
河北						
山西						
内蒙古						
辽宁						
吉林						
黑龙江						
上海						
江苏						
浙江						
安徽	2	2				50
福建	4	4				48
江西						
山东						
河南						
湖北						
湖南	3	3				51
广东						
广西	2	2				181
海南						
重庆						
四川	1	1				45
贵州	1	1				104
云南	1			1		82
西藏						
陕西	1	1				29
甘肃						
青海						
宁夏						
新疆						

农场

单位:个、人

女性	受教育程度		职业资格水平		按人员性质分	
	大学专科人数	大学本科及以上人数	助理社会工作师人数	社会工作师人数	管理人员	专业技术技能人员
181	**109**	**73**	**27**	**39**	**282**	**308**
12	3	4	1		50	
15	7	8	1		48	
12	13	1	1		10	41
54	19	12	17	34	22	159
10	6	2	1		6	39
43	31	11	2		87	17
27	26	26	4	5	30	52
8	4	9			29	

C-2-20续表1

地区	年龄结构				志愿服务		年末床位数
	35岁及以下人数	36岁至45岁人数	46岁至55岁人数	56岁及以上人数	志愿者服务人次数	志愿服务时间	
全国	**153**	**206**	**153**	**78**	**36**	**208.0**	**793**
中央级							
北京							
天津							
河北							
山西							
内蒙古							
辽宁							
吉林							
黑龙江							
上海							
江苏							
浙江							
安徽	4	7	7	32			40
福建	4	11	30	3			185
江西							
山东							
河南							
湖北							
湖南	11	28	9	3			38
广东							
广西	77	64	24	16			70
海南							
重庆							
四川	2	20	15	8			30
贵州	20	38	45	1			80
云南	35	27	10	10	36	208.0	300
西藏							
陕西		11	13	5			50
甘肃							
青海							
宁夏							
新疆							

单位：人、人次、时

年在院总人天数	年末在院人数	女性	在院人员按性质分：“三无”和农村特困对象	在院人员按性质分：其他社会救济对象	在院人员按年龄分：老人	在院人员按年龄分：青壮年	在院人员按年龄分：少年儿童
100330	**600**	**164**	**541**	**47**	**330**	**265**	**5**
14600	40		40		40		
44895	172	47	167	5	167		5
9715	30	11	30		30		
19410	44	24		42	32	12	
10950	30		30		30		
365	1		1		1		
365	273	82	273		20	253	
30	10				10		

C-2-20续表2

地区	在院人员按类型分			康复和医疗门诊人次数	机构建筑面积
	自理（完全自理）	介助（半自理）	介护（不能自理）		
全国	**237**	**153**	**210**	**378**	**221076**
中央级					
北京					
天津					
河北					
山西					
内蒙古					
辽宁					
吉林					
黑龙江					
上海					
江苏					
浙江					
安徽		34	6		12948
福建	154	17	1	62	26414
江西					
山东					
河南					
湖北					
湖南	18	12		36	99800
广东					
广西	22	20	2		57500
海南					
重庆					
四川	3	10	17	280	2000
贵州	1				1800
云南	29	60	184		19614
西藏					
陕西	10				1000
甘肃					
青海					
宁夏					
新疆					

单位：万元

执行行政事业单位会计制度财务指标				
固定资产原价	上年结转和结余	本年收入合计	本年支出合计	收支结余
7458.8	**1328.6**	**6928.9**	**7827.8**	**679.4**
370.5				
1593.7	1178.4	1228.1	1394.1	989.0
54.8	28.2	105.3	64.7	
4272.0	110.0	3598.5	4046.3	-309.6
47.7		31.4	357.1	
241.3		1590.2	1590.2	
	12.0			
878.8		375.4	375.4	

C-2-21 其他提供住宿的

地区	单位数	0～99张	100～299张	300～499张	500张以上	年末职工人数	女性
全国	**339**	**227**	**97**	**11**	**4**	**4976**	**2997**
中央级	1		1			185	130
北京							
天津							
河北	28	11	16	1		520	272
山西	12	9	3			91	25
内蒙古	2	1	1			16	2
辽宁	39	31	7		1	339	197
吉林							
黑龙江	35	30	5			206	128
上海	3		2		1	400	301
江苏	5	4		1		42	26
浙江	3	1	1	1		103	81
安徽	8	6	2			84	30
福建							
江西	2	1	1			15	6
山东							
河南	17	14	2		1	148	77
湖北	40	32	8			316	166
湖南	11	7	4			85	35
广东	28	23	5			610	400
广西	5	4	1			54	42
海南	1		1			10	4
重庆							
四川	65	26	30	8	1	1468	918
贵州	3	3				80	38
云南	9	6	3			124	75
西藏							
陕西							
甘肃	5	4	1			17	5
青海	2	1	1			2	
宁夏	1	1				3	
新疆	14	12	2			58	39

社会服务机构

单位：个、人

受教育程度		职业资格水平		按人员性质分	
大学专科人数	大学本科及以上人数	助理社会工作师人数	社会工作师人数	管理人员	专业技术技能人员
1072	**500**	**54**	**38**	**1624**	**3352**
71	114		2	28	157
67	8			134	386
9				19	72
		3	3	4	12
54	73	4	1	149	190
8	1			90	116
78	26	12	2	44	356
3	2	1		11	31
1				19	84
27	14	1	1	57	27
1	2	4		2	13
30	3	7		61	87
59	11			114	202
21	2	2		30	55
268	73	14	8	225	385
12	6	2		14	40
4	6			4	6
280	114	2	7	519	949
16	30	1		38	42
59	5		14	24	100
	8			8	9
				2	
1	2			1	2
3		1		27	31

C-2-21续表1

地区	年龄结构				志愿服务
	35岁及以下人数	36岁至45岁人数	46岁至55岁人数	56岁及以上人数	志愿者服务人次数
全国	**1541**	**1802**	**1108**	**525**	**697**
中央级	138	29	13	5	
北京					
天津					
河北	148	224	132	16	159
山西	16	17	54	4	
内蒙古	9	2	2	3	
辽宁	76	149	103	11	78
吉林					
黑龙江	31	74	62	39	
上海	98	235	51	16	368
江苏	18	13	8	3	
浙江	47	35	20	1	
安徽	31	28	25		
福建					
江西	1	3	11		
山东					
河南	39	63	39	7	
湖北	54	126	103	33	8
湖南	19	26	34	6	
广东	365	161	71	13	
广西	22	18	14		
海南	5	2	2	1	
重庆					
四川	319	502	310	337	
贵州	22	27	23	8	30
云南	54	29	21	20	54
西藏					
陕西					
甘肃	2	9	4	2	
青海		2			
宁夏	2	1			
新疆	25	27	6		

单位：人、人次、时、张、人天

志愿服务时间	年末床位数	光荣间床位	年在院总人天数	年末在院人数	女性
1880.5	**29546**	**260**	**3811635**	**15158**	**4506**
	150		47998	149	78
662.0	3114	85	522899	1615	277
	657	40	86497	389	16
	210		57439	158	
118.0	1988		183886	874	406
	1663	14	205768	1226	70
689.5	1170		365205	1169	440
	511		83790	193	97
	641		26016	264	37
	656		142732	411	27
	280		1000	4	1
	1274	23	220169	613	129
9.0	1690	80	227995	1079	362
	954	3	79158	475	150
	2366	5	177771	751	308
	313		78830	231	47
	200				
	9535	2	1151796	4628	1863
90.0	123		28956	89	51
312.0	663		12406	129	38
	235		10858	97	
	180		41131	163	85
	40		300	3	
	933	8	59035	448	24

C-2-21续表2

地区	在院人员按性质分				在院人员按年龄分	
	优抚对象	“三无”和农村特困对象	自费人员	其他社会救济对象	老人	青壮年
全国	**246**	**2805**	**9938**	**496**	**12721**	**1457**
中央级			149		57	28
北京						
天津						
河北		272	1274	57	1533	70
山西		57	288	38	388	1
内蒙古		19	140		130	28
辽宁	27	167	658	2	831	31
吉林						
黑龙江		43	657	25	1210	16
上海		649	370		233	766
江苏		80	85		193	
浙江	8		256		252	12
安徽	4	82	222		411	
福建						
江西		4			4	
山东						
河南	22	157	249		570	16
湖北		270	809		1012	35
湖南	59	236	131	2	386	64
广东		79	413	233	211	125
广西		55	44	132	89	9
海南						
重庆						
四川	70	541	3628	7	4486	75
贵州	48	5	52		63	17
云南			95		129	
西藏						
陕西						
甘肃	1	41	55		96	
青海					12	151
宁夏					2	
新疆	7	48	363		423	13

单位：人、人次、平方米

少年儿童	在院人员按类型分			康复和医疗门诊人次数	机构建筑面积
	自理（完全自理）	介助（半自理）	介护（不能自理）		
980	**7803**	**3863**	**3492**	**105401**	**690402**
64	32	106	11	4135	30000
12	995	447	173	5018	95065
	271	111	7		10938
	130	28			2600
12	469	171	234	1925	44707
	907	170	149		35577
170	86	301	782	799	31613
	115	78		3374	4100
	255	4	5	435	2999
	260	138	13		12800
	4				7000
27	343	105	165	250	58853
32	647	266	166	10798	47640
25	318	108	49	166	11050
415	174	198	379	71376	70156
133	197	33	1	23	14270
67	2093	1364	1171	6075	131932
9	75	10	4	990	13949
	36	65	28		23159
1	64	15	18	26	10294
	163				23500
1	2	1			400
12	167	144	137	11	7800

C-2-21续表3

地区	执行行政事业单位会计制度财务指标				
	固定资产原价	上年结转和结余	本年收入合计	本年支出合计	收支结余
全国	**47272.2**	**4325.7**	**18149.1**	**28066.3**	**3334.7**
中央级	12600.6	3469.8	1497.3	9283.3	2496.7
北京					
天津					
河北	3518.6	52.6	3313.9	3111.2	30.0
山西	791.0		1.0	8.0	
内蒙古	103.3	37.6	220.3	237.0	
辽宁	5540.3	85.8	1735.7	1637.6	5.8
吉林					
黑龙江	805.0				
上海	6784.0	371.3	7081.1	7325.8	184.0
江苏	300.0		40.0	40.0	
浙江			210.0	209.0	
安徽	527.0		45.0	45.0	
福建					
江西					
山东					
河南	285.5		392.1	392.1	
湖北	400.0		20.0	30.0	
湖南	635.0	40.0	270.0	126.0	
广东	3708.0		1981.3	1908.3	
广西					
海南					
重庆					
四川	7043.3	221.6	1007.4	400.7	
贵州	2698.0	22.0	211.8	2303.3	618.2
云南	506.0	25.0		900.0	
西藏					
陕西					
甘肃	580.6		80.2	60.0	
青海					
宁夏	50.0				
新疆	396.0		42.0	49.0	

单位：万元

执行民间非营利组织单位会计制度财务指标			
固定资产原价	上年结余	本年收入合计	本年费用合计
25903.3	**1055.1**	**8315.8**	**12838.9**
5784.0		850.9	973.1
745.0		74.0	175.9
782.0	3.0	208.2	249.9
1735.2	120.8	76.8	2602.0
100.0			1.0
10.0		6.0	4.0
102.0		140.0	140.0
930.0			130.0
89.0			
412.0	120.0	641.2	646.8
2275.0	6.0	1123.7	941.2
64.0	3.0	16.0	35.0
398.4	175.8	1261.9	1235.2
294.0	23.6	33.3	126.1
12003.7	602.9	3883.8	5572.3
25.0			6.2
130.0			0.2
24.0			

C-2-22 不提供住宿的

地 区	机构和设施数	工商登记	编制登记	民政登记	设施
全 国	**382185**	**14718**	**6792**	**35689**	**324986**
中央级	1		1		
北 京	12161	528	298	740	10595
天 津	2327	220	39	51	2017
河 北	37752	527	204	284	36737
山 西	3872	329	320	317	2906
内蒙古	3956	134	108	21	3693
辽 宁	8485	1617	167	391	6310
吉 林	2285	297	311	213	1464
黑龙江	3543	259	212	643	2429
上 海	6721	776	164	2696	3085
江 苏	41659	2526	235	20797	18101
浙 江	32358	1725	179	2202	28252
安 徽	8494	334	235	249	7676
福 建	6030	260	127	92	5551
江 西	3936	280	272	678	2706
山 东	29099	1157	375	1040	26527
河 南	6320	678	316	871	4455
湖 北	12945	479	345	420	11701
湖 南	12257	398	298	147	11414
广 东	57595	124	323	797	56351
广 西	13446	110	209	55	13072
海 南	2009	14	14	102	1879
重 庆	8184	613	185	130	7256
四 川	19980	643	417	1100	17820
贵 州	21876	28	281	86	21481
云 南	3338	219	139	69	2911
西 藏	444	7	69	333	35
陕 西	7103	173	217	480	6233
甘 肃	8504	59	186	52	8207
青 海	1281	20	17		1244
宁 夏	1129	54	55	225	795
新 疆	3095	130	474	408	2083

社会服务机构和设施总表

单位:个、人

年末职工人数	女性	工商登记	编制登记	民政登记	设施
2434868	**854158**	**1110477**	**69294**	**187484**	**1063991**
135	55		135		
66013	28907	23847	3822	3479	34793
27836	11331	16238	406	579	10598
105717	33819	28841	2532	1781	72408
41528	12770	27866	2762	1429	9449
26877	10737	11177	1501	137	14055
125190	50383	81486	1836	1807	39918
27630	11747	14829	3793	1996	6996
29407	11662	10230	2641	4260	12229
102092	38182	60395	3926	23743	14028
419303	143734	228959	2267	97492	90397
247976	89406	171634	1522	7033	66846
56025	22076	16964	2609	1667	34641
36597	13738	14780	880	378	20492
38079	13016	24064	1765	3334	8794
204059	70556	88204	4489	5702	104770
87123	27288	53915	3229	4662	25276
77771	29601	31075	2937	2223	41462
68193	23766	25707	3283	706	38318
174882	56333	12171	3123	5807	153750
29616	10029	7601	1866	309	19834
11332	3193	1388	129	892	8921
82564	30574	57136	1403	618	23398
113454	39484	50604	3439	6608	52676
97317	23678	1723	4685	461	90379
36268	10526	22908	1096	531	11688
2434	1015	205	161	2001	67
36912	13479	10864	2254	2192	21442
24283	8027	3019	1445	272	19506
6309	1957	1681	228		4400
9609	4003	3935	530	1574	3570
22337	9086	7031	2600	3811	8890

C-2-22续表1

地　区	受教育程度		职业资格水平	
	大学专科人数	大学本科及以上人数	助理社会工作师人数	社会工作师人数
全　国	**350316**	**169982**	**16278**	**9238**
中央级	9	126		
北　京	12190	10029	1949	854
天　津	4253	2738	645	138
河　北	7188	2528	179	167
山　西	3911	2013	114	57
内蒙古	5596	3247	535	154
辽　宁	17763	10737	473	265
吉　林	5281	2601	323	169
黑龙江	5695	2748	181	137
上　海	10506	4788	628	1616
江　苏	52928	25711	1797	724
浙　江	22938	10394	1040	728
安　徽	11102	3404	604	227
福　建	2708	1184	435	279
江　西	2710	661	85	56
山　东	43242	21031	467	289
河　南	10713	5514	441	217
湖　北	10954	4852	495	201
湖　南	11209	4909	560	309
广　东	32920	20570	3387	1538
广　西	2599	1814	182	88
海　南	1127	409	58	15
重　庆	10888	5239	578	303
四　川	20116	6274	607	352
贵　州	19703	6224	51	48
云　南	3019	1469	95	50
西　藏	142	75	2	
陕　西	6729	2146	105	44
甘　肃	4220	2551	81	60
青　海	815	400	30	55
宁　夏	1202	462	10	13
新　疆	5940	3134	141	85

单位：人、人次、时

年龄结构				志愿服务	
35岁及以下人数	36岁至45岁人数	46岁至55岁人数	56岁及以上人数	志愿者服务人次数	志愿服务时间
768658	**954115**	**547792**	**163943**	**5996872**	**15803259.6**
77	21	25	12		
18854	25023	17773	4363	3577751	10457769.0
10448	9582	5829	1977	49919	81997.0
33545	38193	25574	8405	13147	49353.0
12137	16086	9565	3740	1092	2496.2
8068	10603	6119	2046	11451	24849.0
36833	52948	26343	9050	7470	11421.0
6893	13166	5207	2364	23309	46578.0
7948	12339	6100	3020	28861	84838.0
30609	34256	27865	9362	33080	97472.0
119261	167800	102513	29729	382421	766151.5
71851	91251	65398	19476	368870	612796.0
15811	24744	12812	2658	78173	164371.0
11456	14938	7385	2817	107926	329051.0
13781	15959	6377	1962	2182	5738.7
78137	76630	38963	10329	683810	1525240.9
34032	35048	12518	5525	4785	27754.0
22048	34066	15799	5858	50382	161591.0
17825	30870	16097	3336	16334	47699.0
65239	63130	34236	12277	8284	23543.9
7729	10276	8985	2626	378	2806.0
3137	4315	3147	733	8560	15619.0
24762	32567	20261	4974	264472	571779.8
38310	46267	23252	5625	92379	271959.5
34297	37424	20421	5175	141810	278216.9
11501	15907	7486	1374	574	1565.0
1228	924	261	21	18	40.0
11176	14487	9217	2032	13988	42238.2
8903	9020	5026	1313	10696	53776.0
2086	2670	596	756	16	28.0
2925	4123	2308	238	2	8.0
7751	9482	4334	770	14732	44513.0

C-2-22续表2

地区	执行企业会计制度单位财务指标				执行行政	
	固定资产原价	营业收入	费用合计	营业利润	固定资产原价	上年结转和结余
全国	**17774288.1**	**43934037.5**	**5378111.0**	**1215831.0**	**2038818.3**	**442867.3**
中央级					17628.8	
北京	382783.3	542523.2	93917.3	3230.5	170294.7	174350.2
天津	226726.8	595033.3	82940.5	5265.8	61919.1	1469.4
河北	474473.3	977943.6	98191.6	3381.7	77727.8	2750.3
山西	233583.5	224554.0	34052.9	-4661.1	45575.8	6970.5
内蒙古	64064.2	87967.6	13577.7	4822.6	41080.9	7075.1
辽宁	1380806.9	1616310.9	191792.6	34759.5	87701.5	2212.4
吉林	127197.3	246887.7	27375.4	-342.8	39452.9	2665.3
黑龙江	691798.6	154827.3	35645.0	1476.5	22151.0	4770.5
上海	1257943.6	2709011.7	184284.2	149297.4	104655.7	6917.0
江苏	3335178.7	11042569.7	1181264.7	218014.7	187433.0	28654.8
浙江	5019314.0	14282178.7	2139161.0	532242.9	106626.5	10098.5
安徽	159179.1	909627.0	67117.9	19951.1	66473.9	3533.3
福建	134937.4	251580.0	45416.9	-66.1	14642.3	4616.8
江西	100445.9	2006409.1	19006.7	4331.2	29903.7	37656.8
山东	1083536.3	1749170.7	337090.4	133868.4	157589.6	3039.6
河南	333675.2	501195.3	86526.3	21163.9	87364.4	4524.9
湖北	294952.8	457284.7	89476.8	3506.9	83420.9	1683.2
湖南	263647.6	630231.2	55020.0	5801.6	64523.2	5144.6
广东	205656.7	271151.3	32507.0	5656.0	101736.7	15988.2
广西	59960.3	272962.7	12091.2	-1955.4	43074.5	11843.7
海南	15327.4	31783.3	5257.7	31.4	6910.0	2597.9
重庆	644683.5	1838348.0	214625.9	34809.7	32103.2	31755.3
四川	481834.1	1275681.1	113080.0	6175.7	110197.8	8308.5
贵州	5637.0	15129.9	2428.7	901.9	31714.0	12692.6
云南	375786.9	738809.1	135064.7	10345.7	32446.6	5248.1
西藏	3598.0	498.0	359.0	139.0	24987.6	20390.0
陕西	142359.5	314194.7	42910.1	19982.4	74275.0	4684.7
甘肃	29321.3	10481.7	2464.8	84.8	24921.4	947.0
青海	7621.6	15681.5	3636.0	195.6	17984.1	5181.2
宁夏	86038.8	68230.5	7169.0	-1925.3	25611.5	1909.5
新疆	152218.5	95780.0	24659.0	5344.8	46690.2	13187.4

单位：万元

事业单位会计制度财务指标			执行民间非营利组织单位会计制度财务指标			
本年收入合计	本年支出合计	收支结余	固定资产原价	上年结余	本年收入合计	本年费用合计
3066812.8	**2500319.4**	**239342.7**	**426443.5**	**29148.3**	**463509.7**	**428491.4**
118036.1	89323.1					
768503.2	392971.8	8402.0	3554.6	3502.3	5557.0	4651.7
32346.3	30899.6	1390.6	598.1	172.1	852.8	1373.1
116958.6	107023.2	4096.6	6592.7	15.3	722.2	1746.9
44729.6	35212.5	8297.1	1120.7		258.0	324.4
36553.3	33983.8	11784.5	219.0		40.7	45.0
61456.3	60980.2	1393.2	1660.5	34.0	785.3	1878.1
77166.4	69793.1	617.5	10.0		38.0	40.0
15402.1	15157.7	29.0	1583.6	47.0	562.5	480.7
220059.0	204268.9	7260.0	63282.2	22115.5	168882.0	190497.9
150667.5	144754.6	35892.1	235868.4	628.2	142717.3	151553.3
95243.9	78181.0	21617.9	8800.7	596.5	32911.1	26681.2
53741.5	52246.1	2037.6	11593.3	17.8	2514.9	1901.8
29286.2	25169.9	4074.5	734.9	20.6	447.4	390.8
45814.0	22729.0	30592.5	5079.4		3991.0	4403.2
162306.6	162096.5		29661.7	119.0	22258.0	22259.1
67423.0	61498.1	3688.1	4171.3	446.1	1883.1	1785.2
64679.7	56576.2	1947.8	6682.1		3278.6	3063.2
81207.5	70677.0	9707.4	1228.8	264.8	61420.9	1399.7
152013.8	145772.7	12331.4	10807.4	114.7	8495.1	5812.3
64351.0	57309.2	3756.7	680.3	111.2	166.5	231.9
16382.0	15548.8	2577.5	213.8		210.5	93.5
100714.6	94761.8	38764.0	2759.5	10.0	479.9	553.5
131155.8	130064.3	793.8	24107.9	776.2	4325.4	6102.9
51417.3	44853.8	4464.4	907.5	79.2	543.4	602.1
75797.4	78821.9	4863.2	2512.0	73.1	2.1	19.6
7934.2	20159.9	8038.4	18.0			
107169.9	105096.0	4570.3	1447.7	3.7	100.0	352.5
23131.7	14820.4	771.8	77.4		53.2	200.3
13657.9	8876.3	1036.6				
12591.9	10972.6	299.1	423.0		12.8	22.0
68914.5	59719.4	4247.1	47.0	1.0		25.5

C–2–23 社区服务

地区	单位数	农村	年末职工人数	女性
全国	**360956**	**184542**	**1276128**	**467755**
中央级				
北京	11528	5116	40782	19965
天津	2069	485	11222	6676
河北	37106	30550	75426	24414
山西	3222	1476	11435	4524
内蒙古	3754	1041	14989	7052
辽宁	6684	1244	42018	24972
吉林	1757	577	10172	6581
黑龙江	3103	415	18163	7882
上海	5865	377	40615	16039
江苏	38986	16126	188447	58037
浙江	30370	19065	74931	29565
安徽	7969	3280	37495	15112
福建	5619	2256	20988	8240
江西	3339	413	12421	5196
山东	27637	14760	112831	44016
河南	5345	1932	30362	10119
湖北	12165	4313	44384	18521
湖南	11488	6222	39529	15239
广东	57108	18524	160546	51776
广西	13094	11757	20144	6606
海南	1968	1509	9809	2754
重庆	7412	3830	24415	10687
四川	18762	8664	59482	20229
贵州	21622	18170	93772	22489
云南	2990	1210	12453	4542
西藏	329	200	2001	861
陕西	6696	3975	23938	9321
甘肃	8177	5927	19877	6484
青海	1130	577	4314	1250
宁夏	1006	356	5154	2789
新疆	2656	195	14013	5817

机构和设施总表

单位：个、人

受教育程度		职业资格水平		年龄结构
大学专科人数	大学本科及以上人数	助理社会工作师人数	社会工作师人数	35岁及以下人数
260007	**123740**	**14295**	**7712**	**390955**
9987	8560	1901	792	11811
3207	2194	587	116	3793
5560	1495	120	110	22016
1993	776	72	24	2934
4001	2554	498	119	5374
12893	8075	384	199	14023
3949	1654	231	124	2267
4685	2077	169	121	5018
8408	3779	530	1509	10788
33620	16476	1546	570	52520
13630	6410	939	426	21048
9351	2641	434	194	9949
2258	832	424	260	6049
1543	236	63	37	3483
33039	15663	380	190	42749
5448	2479	369	131	6974
8580	3528	310	187	12527
8794	4046	497	264	10502
31735	19388	3228	1449	59059
1701	988	152	76	4756
985	319	38	4	2149
6119	2568	500	254	6904
13073	4163	531	285	16186
18768	5508	42	44	32646
2104	971	63	37	3439
71	25	2		1088
4767	1225	59	25	5740
3758	2164	72	50	7580
737	309	20	50	1298
786	237	6	9	1239
4457	2400	128	56	5046

C-2-23续表1

地　区	年龄结构			志愿
	36岁至45岁人数	46岁至55岁人数	56岁及以上人数	志愿者服务人次数
全　国	**492777**	**291927**	**100109**	**5551376**
中央级				
北　京	13999	11861	3111	3551007
天　津	3645	2670	1114	48969
河　北	26388	19674	7348	10442
山　西	4580	2504	1417	875
内蒙古	6326	2473	775	11329
辽　宁	16069	7785	4125	2824
吉　林	5914	1766	225	20
黑龙江	7566	3170	2409	19756
上　海	14457	12146	3224	30370
江　苏	73963	47124	14840	365550
浙　江	28757	17896	7230	311017
安　徽	16558	8870	2118	40912
福　建	7805	4755	2378	54
江　西	4957	2523	1458	788
山　东	42362	21099	6621	659679
河　南	14087	5433	3868	4757
湖　北	18439	8613	4805	48909
湖　南	15438	11065	2459	10324
广　东	57595	32008	11884	6618
广　西	6501	6546	2341	
海　南	3956	2999	705	8560
重　庆	9415	5954	2142	248091
四　川	24993	14486	3817	4953
贵　州	36286	19813	5027	138097
云　南	5859	2473	682	500
西　藏	724	189		
陕　西	9666	6915	1617	8260
甘　肃	6863	4329	1084	10515
青　海	1734	380	701	2
宁　夏	2362	1462	76	
新　疆	5513	2946	508	8198

单位：人、人次、时、张

服务					
志愿服务时间	床位数合计	日间照料床位数	农村	留宿照料床位数	农村
14714623.7	**2981379**	**1212564**	**743263**	**1768815**	**1199748**
10405345.0	10260	5691	2365	4569	505
79297.0	12642	6377	3480	6265	5163
37706.0	340892	198774	166449	142118	107905
2477.2	25909	14241	9250	11668	9163
24605.0	129346	14624	1416	114722	110265
5339.0	40648	20117	5283	20531	9441
	4823	3962	223	861	1
66523.0	68886	23529	3709	45357	14382
90342.0	16214	2397	3	13817	994
727080.5	223400	140787	58453	82613	28400
534093.0	257671	135760	99995	121911	61603
110708.0	206691	19385	7388	187306	152597
179.0	81781	20157	9964	61624	33977
2467.0	26893	12830	8965	14063	10812
1461798.4	329480	137014	89176	192466	108274
27631.0	242184	67165	43273	175019	127663
159505.0	75190	43405	15869	31785	11042
25051.0	91518	33932	24982	57586	44573
19135.9	61385	31645	13343	29740	12872
	122462	21885	20095	100577	95306
15619.0	8188	2270	1275	5918	4344
533582.8	95713	28192	12770	67521	58659
16954.0	188206	52200	23581	136006	87981
266843.9	88859	41465	30674	47394	39702
1250.0	56048	17332	6394	38716	20659
28518.0	57093	30818	23980	26275	21339
53200.0	85368	70028	52203	15340	12865
	14087	4684	1759	9403	4799
	3527	2061	853	1466	1391
19373.0	16015	9837	6093	6178	3071

C-2-23续表2

地区	年末收养人数合计	日间照料人数	农村	留宿照料人数	农村
全国	**944514**	**236765**	**160547**	**707749**	**527064**
中央级					
北京	3705	1966	1090	1739	211
天津	1392	442	240	950	887
河北	45690	18945	17787	26745	17180
山西	8610	3182	1648	5428	4838
内蒙古	76032	4934	644	71098	69132
辽宁	6277	1402	446	4875	3279
吉林	475	454	57	21	1
黑龙江	29432	6682	2429	22750	7831
上海	1104	1104			
江苏	36884	18540	10686	18344	8429
浙江	49951	10299	7490	39652	11928
安徽	65397	1282	3	64115	54545
福建	14278	3697	406	10581	5601
江西	16393	7784	7385	8609	8280
山东	119983	39888	26599	80095	45857
河南	139975	34067	27688	105908	79228
湖北	18462	7931	3414	10531	4683
湖南	46996	18113	13885	28883	30423
广东	7055	3060	818	3995	2137
广西	49528	7117	6521	42411	40904
海南	2279	426	362	1853	1695
重庆	63207	15870	8032	47337	41601
四川	68413	6830	4926	61583	47878
贵州	13266	2001	1748	11265	10010
云南	17889	2151	762	15738	11381
西藏					
陕西	23289	8953	7760	14336	12733
甘肃	5761	3414	2895	2347	2233
青海	2395	91	10	2304	1205
宁夏	806	246	186	560	551
新疆	9590	5894	4630	3696	2403

单位：人、人次、人天、个、平方米

本年收养照料人天数	老年人活动人次数	社区服务志愿者组织数	注册社区志愿者人数	城镇便民、利民服务网点数	机构建筑面积
73598363	**17818781**	**95693**	**2271509**	**248643**	**96859126**
508878	2064118	11801	994529	5247	2101855
		84		4491	864539
3547804	814632	570	60	3136	6299075
439264	185323	416	10920	5023	740970
17732856	1152019	956	8923	6721	2816122
260	643	817	39466	7841	1949540
1987	78827	464	1308	57	421780
51674	63288	1150	49785	8210	1319513
220186	5731	2794	114386	15061	1335192
2242463	3607505	12458	170221	31832	9001051
103056	1162845	1920	37250	34445	7961543
5343547	75088	907	8002	6567	3347240
892464	11486	485	92	1209	1440895
78804	41887	697	2005	1650	622161
19922904	4039647	6387	27279	30127	14726477
2280675	145629	147	881	1565	4907011
58365	236527	609	1946	4519	2940847
5170685	65562	1164	603	3978	3547697
231654	448258	8108	375082	7250	8583673
3146037	1317556	5		1302	2310812
18980	12045	2	40	19	396677
7297943	1685000	33891	274782	12517	2723713
1601594	348271	1009	107483	26246	5707533
171185	1003	6684	10664	15309	3792004
1056329	31000	1	30	42	1533668
	120			3	19900
1339121	35220	1501	34876	2624	1996623
32570	131449			6938	1458336
			40		361490
3010				1090	287721
104068	58102	666	856	3624	1343468

C-2-23续表3

地区	执行企业会计制度单位财务指标				执行行政	
	固定资产原价	营业收入	费用合计	营业利润	固定资产原价	上年结转和结余
全　国	**6993.3**	**2366.2**	**1349.4**	**119.9**	**272605.2**	**13333.5**
中央级						
北　京	8.0	557.9	151.0	3.5	42212.1	3000.1
天　津					406.2	2.5
河　北	2066.0		0.2		9860.3	4.0
山　西	0.2	7.0	3.0		11385.3	97.9
内蒙古					727.0	
辽　宁	123.0	682.9	709.6	23.2	768.6	22.0
吉　林	500.0	7.0			934.0	
黑龙江	21.0	112.6	8.0	2.0	1577.0	41.0
上　海					11396.5	1653.4
江　苏	837.7	380.7	146.7	46.7	48572.4	322.1
浙　江	221.2				11681.9	1283.1
安　徽	343.0	220.0	62.0		7539.0	84.3
福　建	82.0	24.0	2.5	12.0	74.7	5.0
江　西	221.0	190.0	55.0		871.0	3.0
山　东	186.0	70.0	22.0	21.0	8021.8	
河　南					7407.1	2.1
湖　北	597.1	20.0	7.5	9.7	8574.3	
湖　南	120.0				3667.2	
广　东	510.0				10925.6	1764.1
广　西					270.1	
海　南					700.0	
重　庆					1871.2	
四　川	112.6	58.3	46.1	0.8	18291.1	670.4
贵　州					5328.4	4114.3
云　南	145.5	9.6	123.0	1.0	3133.3	
西　藏					8810.7	170.0
陕　西					15288.4	
甘　肃	5.0				1937.0	
青　海						
宁　夏					13053.9	3.2
新　疆	894.0	26.2	12.8		17319.1	91.0

单位：万元

事业单位会计制度财务指标			执行民间非营利组织单位会计制度财务指标			
本年收入合计	本年支出合计	收支结余	固定资产原价	上年结余	本年收入合计	本年费用合计
221765.6	**213990.7**	**7669.5**	**424984.1**	**28617.3**	**457778.2**	**426179.7**
40816.1	43895.4	2708.7	3554.6	3502.3	5557.0	4651.7
620.0	606.0	4.5	598.1	172.1	852.8	1373.1
7816.5	7777.3		6592.7	15.3	722.2	1746.9
1200.6	1197.7		1120.7		258.0	324.4
620.0	625.0		219.0		40.7	45.0
539.6	451.6	17.0	1660.5	34.0	785.3	1878.1
2034.1	2029.1	4.0	10.0		38.0	40.0
3028.3	2894.8	19.3	1583.6	47.0	562.5	480.7
54919.4	48022.1	789.3	62798.0	22022.6	165257.2	188412.7
43050.9	42306.7	2787.6	235868.4	628.2	142717.3	151553.3
5469.8	5124.4	223.4	8622.1	467.6	32499.1	26681.2
3067.9	2829.5		11223.4	2.0	1571.2	1684.0
301.6	278.8	2.0	734.9	20.6	447.4	390.8
347.0	342.0		5079.4		3991.0	4403.2
6940.3	6983.9		29661.7	119.0	22258.0	22259.1
3307.8	2637.1	100.0	3744.6	152.7	1132.1	1776.5
3176.1	3199.4	97.3	6682.1		3278.6	3063.2
788.0	658.0		1228.8	264.8	61420.9	1399.7
8820.9	8849.5	188.9	10807.4	114.7	8495.1	5812.3
15.0	15.0		680.3	111.2	166.5	231.9
			213.8		210.5	93.5
1140.4	1185.6		2759.5	10.0	479.9	553.5
1076.4	946.2	1.0	24107.9	776.2	4325.4	6102.9
19404.2	15019.2	645.4	907.5	79.2	543.4	602.1
381.7	1184.2		2512.0	73.1	2.1	19.6
220.0	200.6		18.0			
6111.1	6369.1		1447.7	3.7	100.0	352.5
32.2	26.2		77.4		53.2	200.3
5.4	72.7	2.1	423.0		12.8	22.0
6514.3	8263.6	79.0	47.0	1.0		25.5

C-2-24 社区服务

地区	单位数	农村	为居民提供便民办事服务的机构	为居民提供活动场所的机构	为居民提供养老等服务的机构
全国	**863**	**26**	**576**	**167**	**87**
中央级					
北京	17		11	4	4
天津	13		11	2	
河北	28	1	17	7	2
山西	26	2	14	4	1
内蒙古	3		2	2	1
辽宁	27		11	8	1
吉林	13	2	5		
黑龙江	39		22	8	2
上海	8		6		
江苏	66	1	47	8	3
浙江	26	1	14	3	1
安徽	49	1	35	3	3
福建	25		18	4	
江西	45	2	29	6	3
山东	121		104	52	24
河南	43	3	24	7	7
湖北	33		28	2	3
湖南	54	4	46	9	8
广东	29	2	17	3	4
广西	5		2	2	
海南	2				2
重庆	11		6	4	
四川	70	1	39	10	6
贵州	17	1	14	1	2
云南	8		4	3	
西藏					
陕西	51		33	7	2
甘肃	20	5	9	4	7
青海					
宁夏	3		3		
新疆	11		5	4	1

指导中心

单位：个、人

农村	为居民提供便民信息服务的机构	年末职工人数	女性	受教育程度 大学专科人数	大学本科及以上人数
4	**251**	**8299**	**3643**	**2328**	**1838**
	5	471	276	93	169
	1	75	32	19	29
	2	300	175	69	9
	10	93	40	12	14
	1	15	10	8	5
	8	223	123	95	84
	8	49	19	16	11
	9	307	185	107	121
	2	103	58	28	61
	17	485	247	140	114
1	10	1105	156	90	80
	6	451	157	66	50
	3	129	68	17	26
1	7	264	150	66	27
	68	1958	920	810	598
1	6	370	203	101	43
	4	285	128	71	57
	42	340	153	113	45
1	7	178	87	47	81
	1	18	9	9	3
		4	1	3	
	1	30	12	6	15
	20	375	139	123	75
		88	34	25	7
	1	55	27	15	31
	11	330	140	131	44
		69	28	15	2
		42	18		
	1	87	48	33	37

C-2-24续表1

地区	职业资格水平		年龄结构			
	助理社会工作师人数	社会工作师人数	35岁及以下人数	36岁至45岁人数	46岁至55岁人数	56岁及以上人数
全　国	**245**	**158**	**2925**	**3754**	**1354**	**266**
中央级						
北　京	8	17	119	199	136	17
天　津	1		23	23	24	5
河　北			119	116	56	9
山　西	2	2	41	30	19	3
内蒙古			3	8	4	
辽　宁	2	3	71	103	46	3
吉　林		2	15	22	10	2
黑龙江	6	7	126	136	43	2
上　海	8	28	48	31	18	6
江　苏	24	9	160	184	105	36
浙　江	11	5	177	862	58	8
安　徽	100	11	181	202	57	11
福　建	4	9	41	67	17	4
江　西	5	1	65	157	31	11
山　东	21	24	996	708	202	52
河　南	3	2	145	151	60	14
湖　北	3	5	83	135	58	9
湖　南	14	4	115	144	69	12
广　东	11	15	67	69	28	14
广　西			5	9	4	
海　南		1		3	1	
重　庆	1	1	6	15	9	
四　川	10	2	93	128	138	16
贵　州	1	2	41	31	15	1
云　南			10	26	16	3
西　藏						
陕　西	8	4	106	121	81	22
甘　肃	2	1	30	23	14	2
青　海						
宁　夏			9	11	21	1
新　疆		3	30	40	14	3

单位：人、人次、时、张

志愿服务		床位数合计	日间照料床位数		留宿照料床位数	
志愿者服务人次数	志愿服务时间			农村		农村
70930	**148770.0**	**23541**	**15413**	**6075**	**8128**	**860**
5298	8186.0	2203	420		1783	
		118	110		8	
838	3636.0	1812	792	700	1020	700
6	6.0	64	58		6	6
25	51.0	60	60			
30	120.0	368	358		10	
		599	589	130	10	
		2502	1364		1138	
8692	17440.0					
604	1229.0	465	463		2	
		4295	4294	4199	1	
2759	3594.0	497	382		115	20
		114	45		69	
		629	512	140	117	62
50511	107409.0	1580	1405		175	
		3287	572	7	2715	
		323	238		85	
87	532.0	417	332		85	
		183	132	45	51	
		20	20			
		320	100		220	
16	67.0	1985	1829	770	156	
325	644.0	296	90	61	206	50
		130	70		60	
1729	5806.0	785	730		55	
		477	436	23	41	22
		2	2			
10	50.0	10	10			

C-2-24续表2

地区	年末收养人数合计	日间照料人数	农村	留宿照料人数	农村
全国	**4454**	**1766**	**584**	**2688**	**502**
中央级					
北京	981	160		821	
天津					
河北	1131	458	438	673	438
山西	14	14			
内蒙古	12	12			
辽宁	10	10			
吉林					
黑龙江	803	59		744	
上海					
江苏	101	101			
浙江					
安徽	17	5		12	2
福建	14			14	
江西	209	147	140	62	62
山东	392	371		21	
河南	361	96	6	265	
湖北	2	2			
湖南	233	185		48	
广东	10	10			
广西					
海南					
重庆	24	15		9	
四川	75	69		6	
贵州					
云南	30	30			
西藏					
陕西	35	22		13	
甘肃					
青海					
宁夏					
新疆					

单位：人、人次、人天、个、平方米

本年收养照料人天数	老年人活动人次数	社区服务志愿者组织数	注册社区志愿者人数	城镇便民、利民服务网点数	机构建筑面积
266665	**179203**	**6105**	**469730**	**12207**	**960325**
213890	86000	4040	358711	6	100707
		20			11574
					20130
1420	211	3		21	11231
4380	1625				4450
					97185
					2890
					19552
		996	70626	1	6847
10143	2442	187	50	2114	91042
				1815	23350
	5402	3	412	50	26972
		41		312	13972
625		5		25	19025
27315	15491	470	900	3938	185205
	1255			178	84862
	2860	1		1308	49522
7808	8600	6		190	49490
	40987	257	38000	1320	17277
					800
					400
156	5279	31	591	49	13950
286	5408	2	17	802	27110
				1	6300
					9594
642	3404	42	423	59	48044
	239			18	8030
					1244
		1			9570

C-2-24续表3

地　区	执行企业会计制度单位财务指标				执行行政	
	固定资产原价	营业收入	费用合计	营业利润	固定资产原价	上年结转和结余
全　国	**611.0**	**366.2**	**165.2**	**32.5**	**77725.2**	**5360.0**
中央级						
北　京					29979.5	1567.8
天　津					241.4	2.5
河　北	20.0				103.0	
山　西	0.2	7.0	3.0		46.5	11.9
内蒙古					25.0	
辽　宁					54.0	22.0
吉　林						
黑龙江	2.0				273.0	
上　海					4915.0	542.8
江　苏	35.7	50.7	43.7	31.7	1151.5	299.1
浙　江	0.1				8541.5	1265.9
安　徽	343.0	220.0	62.0		1072.4	
福　建						
江　西			0.1		175.0	
山　东	180.0	39.0	16.0		7156.4	
河　南					4291.5	0.1
湖　北					7018.8	
湖　南					2877.2	
广　东					5438.9	1602.7
广　西					22.6	
海　南						
重　庆					262.0	
四　川		49.5	40.4	0.8	525.6	42.0
贵　州					5.0	
云　南						
西　藏						
陕　西					1417.4	
甘　肃					1610.0	
青　海						
宁　夏					183.9	3.2
新　疆	30.0				338.1	

单位：万元

事业单位会计制度财务指标			执行民间非营利组织单位会计制度财务指标			
本年收入合计	本年支出合计	收支结余	固定资产原价	上年结余	本年收入合计	本年费用合计
50663.2	**51562.2**	**3457.9**	**6654.5**	**24.0**	**2049.3**	**3155.9**
24492.0	26227.5	2092.7				
447.8	445.7	0.5	61.6		34.7	651.8
687.7	572.7		33.5		19.8	8.1
153.9	141.9		1.0			1.0
154.0	154.0					
279.3	284.3	17.0	108.0		10.4	10.6
126.1	125.1					
359.0	359.0		6.0		2.0	5.7
2881.7	2517.2	789.8	11.4		279.5	98.8
3491.1	3539.5	128.6	1071.4		386.5	570.1
1542.2	1685.8	219.4	178.0	12.5	135.2	554.5
532.3	449.0		18.0		32.0	9.0
203.8	191.0		32.0	10.5	37.0	54.3
157.0	152.0		329.0		171.0	189.8
3607.4	3607.4		4643.5		894.9	894.9
1512.8	889.7	99.8	30.1	1.0	31.3	40.2
1744.9	1812.9	97.3				
473.0	393.0					
1937.3	1926.5	10.7	48.5			41.0
5.0	5.0					
215.0	215.0					
192.8	257.3		73.5		15.0	25.9
5.0	5.0					
	67.0		5.0			0.1
5367.5	5368.8					
4.0	4.0					
5.4	68.7	2.1	4.0			0.1
85.2	97.2					

C-2-25 社区服务

地　区	单位数	农村	为居民提供便民办事服务的机构	为居民提供活动场所的机构	为居民提供养老等服务的机构
全　国	**24138**	**8392**	**16900**	**5195**	**2926**
中央级					
北　京	199	18	162	74	19
天　津	345	144	203	138	4
河　北	697	93	167	181	335
山　西	536	210	228	245	48
内蒙古	834	61	717	277	7
辽　宁	812	111	520	108	143
吉　林	645	390	617	28	38
黑龙江	637	129	449	195	53
上　海	265	12	224	21	2
江　苏	2667	1039	1562	548	709
浙　江	2744	1935	1606	616	509
安　徽	1224	615	810	135	196
福　建	227	50	127	55	50
江　西	356	53	238	77	11
山　东	1241	368	1049	540	283
河　南	737	163	520	83	120
湖　北	565	80	445	98	27
湖　南	507	136	473	100	33
广　东	2893	950	1827	805	44
广　西	83	12	37	32	1
海　南	68		55	2	12
重　庆	323	49	265	130	8
四　川	1633	162	1442	175	79
贵　州	1525	722	1382	101	59
云　南	131	38	79	23	31
西　藏	239	200	239		
陕　西	391	127	271	114	1
甘　肃	791	486	546	107	99
青　海	30	14	15	14	
宁　夏	70	7	68	2	2
新　疆	723	18	557	171	3

中心

单位:个、人

				受教育程度	
农村	为居民提供便民信息服务的机构	年末职工人数	女性	大学专科人数	大学本科及以上人数
1101	**3025**	**147284**	**57517**	**39227**	**21389**
	88	2078	1192	505	819
	21	2040	1116	589	314
69	51	2324	1064	509	194
4	17	1965	836	420	144
	199	5198	2713	1731	1122
22	79	6580	3508	2120	1835
	18	2158	1287	508	425
10	70	6428	2163	1864	746
	18	5120	2590	1748	1304
259	181	25543	5368	6997	1052
424	61	10982	4455	2908	1483
99	174	6859	2829	1857	866
5	8	1264	530	220	118
	33	1488	724	300	57
38	650	8837	3554	3008	2168
53	43	4661	1752	1008	448
1	71	3447	1320	558	240
2	411	2922	1250	749	380
25	288	12826	5854	3228	3504
	13	324	117	63	28
		673	180	65	28
	80	1807	801	545	262
9	260	7035	2383	1685	555
6	101	10923	3600	2709	1664
14	13	897	374	225	143
		1659	801	25	10
	5	2095	698	483	129
60	46	2955	1733	874	624
	4	171	66	43	19
	10	806	468	46	44
1	12	5219	2191	1637	664

C-2-25续表1

地区	职业资格水平		年龄结构			
	助理社会工作师人数	社会工作师人数	35岁及以下人数	36岁至45岁人数	46岁至55岁人数	56岁及以上人数
全国	**2974**	**1445**	**53255**	**56495**	**27640**	**9894**
中央级						
北京	32	26	488	782	657	151
天津	124	16	607	863	489	81
河北	11	13	913	926	400	85
山西	4	4	699	930	279	57
内蒙古	186	59	2123	2188	702	185
辽宁	12	14	2317	2451	1426	386
吉林	27	12	514	1419	216	9
黑龙江	40	20	1486	1884	1384	1674
上海	209	165	2256	1452	970	442
江苏	205	89	9867	10014	3876	1786
浙江	393	97	2926	4134	3009	913
安徽	79	33	2108	3001	1486	264
福建	34	12	332	615	279	38
江西	36	14	463	635	344	46
山东	52	6	4064	3167	1294	312
河南	27	29	1734	1808	604	515
湖北	21	21	1168	1309	787	183
湖南	73	25	912	1391	504	115
广东	1287	691	6176	3967	2102	581
广西	1		108	133	69	14
海南	3	3	204	302	122	45
重庆	5	12	483	831	446	47
四川	44	48	2155	3072	978	830
贵州	2	4	3992	3949	2246	736
云南	7	7	287	355	217	38
西藏	2		929	660	70	
陕西	2	1	687	684	520	204
甘肃	9	7	1333	1085	491	46
青海			62	73	33	3
宁夏		1	78	209	502	17
新疆	47	16	1784	2206	1138	91

单位：人、人次、时、张

志愿服务		床位数合计	日间照料床位数		留宿照料床位数	
志愿者服务人次数	志愿服务时间			农村		农村
1660318	**4314398.0**	**128083**	**87054**	**26393**	**41029**	**13033**
1387003	3771668.5	658	607	48	51	2
46769	74897.0	2417	2147	766	270	
1738	2592.0	7192	5845	1957	1347	185
300	750.0	2817	1764	201	1053	70
2392	4770.0	1026	984	48	42	
765	1780.0	3901	2017	264	1884	834
20		1069	956		113	
		6432	3814	399	2618	99
6571	10450.0	2003	2003			
6313	15039.0	14811	10425	2636	4386	2613
96584	161641.0	23702	20647	11873	3055	1155
3600	8992.0	20229	8255	2677	11974	5516
		589	303	80	286	46
30	96.0	879	861	11	18	
41040	99418.5	4921	3862	510	1059	205
16	24.0	10172	5309	321	4863	807
		1561	1004	188	557	156
3512	7370.0	1319	865	242	454	216
2870	6780.0	2471	1791	770	680	290
		48	40		8	1
		696	183		513	
36171	82717.0	1637	1129	58	508	50
1980	2249.0	6765	3873	133	2892	48
15379	44986.0	3785	2822	1718	963	549
60	60.0	1692	979	160	713	40
934	2437.0	806	493	148	313	53
199	1150.0	3338	3019	1012	319	88
		501	501	112		
		85	78		7	
6072	14531.0	561	478	61	83	10

C-2-25续表2

地区	年末收养人数合计	日间照料人数	农村	留宿照料人数	农村
全国	**20865**	**11955**	**1475**	**8910**	**2605**
中央级					
北京	194	189	21	5	
天津					
河北	153	153	153		
山西	593	593	100		
内蒙古	254	239		15	
辽宁	380	1		379	368
吉林	175	175			
黑龙江	5149	2835	378	2314	80
上海	919	919			
江苏	1732	453	199	1279	1156
浙江	1008	845	281	163	66
安徽	1432	1048		384	44
福建					
江西	88	88			
山东	1562	1162	111	400	131
河南	4297	1685	20	2612	316
湖北	223	95	42	128	128
湖南	248	194	5	54	
广东	247	206	28	41	33
广西	18	18			
海南	76			76	
重庆	873	541	53	332	30
四川	358	127	13	231	2
贵州	369	32	31	337	243
云南	101			101	
西藏					
陕西	79	55	30	24	
甘肃	104	103	10	1	
青海					
宁夏					
新疆	233	199		34	8

单位：人、人次、人天、个、平方米

本年收养照料人天数	老年人活动人次数	社区服务志愿者组织数	注册社区志愿者人数	城镇便民、利民服务网点数	机构建筑面积
692345	**1783561**	**43686**	**671212**	**127545**	**8627703**
10347	702812	3934	422246	4302	196900
		43		1577	172752
	506	198	30	2403	233006
556	194	393	10920	3798	86655
9413	435370	735	6882	5003	462086
		244	340	3272	291232
1987	188	426			99020
		11		6279	244057
219716	5411	1725	40081	14408	101136
30052	90275	521	13561	3837	1041972
	99515	1305	36197	28715	1039469
12000	11360	99	1300	2264	322923
		129	75	176	94174
12728	5600	272	1940	1031	81895
278118	173174	1747	10455	9057	737275
	9735	45	210	992	388275
	29856	142		406	146509
20157	3670	136		1009	187154
	32472	197		945	712015
				20	22319
					14200
94979	103077	29419	86700	2764	198002
520	22143	186	35830	13908	418847
	670	1164	3421	13457	331101
					72661
	120			3	11950
1740	2016	79	300	416	150153
	1990			4820	204186
					7944
				539	38571
32	53407	536	724	2144	519264

C-2-25续表3

地 区	执行企业会计制度单位财务指标				执行行政	
	固定资产原价	营业收入	费用合计	营业利润	固定资产原价	上年结转和结余
全 国	**1600.5**	**620.1**	**298.8**	**35.2**	**56099.8**	**6973.8**
中央级						
北 京	8.0	557.9	151.0	3.5	11911.9	1432.3
天 津					164.8	
河 北	15.0				93.0	
山 西					1448.5	
内蒙古					633.0	
辽 宁					59.0	
吉 林	500.0	1.0			3.0	
黑龙江	2.0				427.0	5.0
上 海					6045.4	1110.6
江 苏					1783.2	14.0
浙 江					427.2	1.2
安 徽					1188.0	
福 建					46.0	5.0
江 西	21.0		4.9		646.0	3.0
山 东	6.0	31.0	6.0	21.0	855.4	
河 南					476.1	
湖 北	597.0	20.0	7.5	9.7	1128.3	
湖 南						
广 东	35.0				1288.3	160.4
广 西						
海 南					50.0	
重 庆					558.5	
四 川					307.6	
贵 州					5260.0	4114.3
云 南	110.5	9.6	123.0	1.0	140.0	
西 藏					2297.3	85.0
陕 西					4157.0	
甘 肃	5.0				98.0	
青 海						
宁 夏					243.0	
新 疆	301.0	0.6	6.4		14364.3	43.0

单位：万元

事业单位会计制度财务指标			执行民间非营利组织单位会计制度财务指标			
本年收入合计	本年支出合计	收支结余	固定资产原价	上年结余	本年收入合计	本年费用合计
113374.6	**105239.0**	**1552.3**	**19098.6**	**565.2**	**40141.1**	**13191.9**
15644.6	16988.4	616.0				
172.2	160.3	4.0	269.5	30.1	107.8	137.9
770.0	770.0		9.0	9.3	9.5	18.9
534.5	540.8		147.0		252.0	237.0
465.0	465.0		13.0		15.7	15.7
119.0	32.0		156.5		180.5	215.7
224.0	220.0	4.0	10.0			2.0
1590.6	1326.3	19.3	51.1	5.0	94.0	105.9
50507.6	44635.1	-0.6	494.5	220.1	986.2	1118.6
5642.3	5114.5	5.0	12108.2	226.0	3677.9	4892.1
2009.3	2038.5		703.7	5.0	898.9	588.2
225.1	213.1		73.0	2.0	37.0	13.0
45.0	43.0	2.0	6.0	4.0	9.0	12.9
119.3	119.3		1416.1		67.0	460.1
3309.9	3353.5		1854.3		1851.1	1851.1
302.1	296.1		125.5	1.1	17.0	577.4
740.2	728.2		80.1		257.0	257.0
31.0			72.2		30095.0	97.0
5974.6	6029.6	178.2	1256.9	62.0	1517.0	2422.9
			90.0			20.0
170.4	170.4					
207.0	182.0		73.0	0.6	40.0	91.6
19358.2	15011.2	645.4	12.0		26.5	22.9
179.7	118.5		5.0		2.0	1.0
110.0	100.3		18.0			
270.6	585.6					
2.0	2.0					
	2.0		54.0			7.8
4650.4	5993.3	79.0				25.2

C-2-26 社区

地 区	单位数	农村	为居民提供便民办事服务的机构	为居民提供活动场所的机构	为居民提供养老等服务的机构
全 国	**128083**	**62892**	**91369**	**28996**	**15062**
中央级					
北 京	6409	3672	5282	3091	522
天 津	1307	182	1049	179	23
河 北	1876	204	1166	224	666
山 西	1669	677	994	464	93
内蒙古	880	18	560	279	1
辽 宁	3952	696	2910	238	552
吉 林	1070	185	1056		9
黑龙江	1356	71	754	351	50
上 海	2881	329	1391	1072	20
江 苏	16123	8751	7977	2021	6750
浙 江	11803	9053	9025	1540	816
安 徽	3048	966	2502	348	31
福 建	2897	892	2048	379	504
江 西	1022	71	631	253	32
山 东	10561	5941	8136	5268	2553
河 南	882	150	707	86	10
湖 北	4555	1018	3247	906	225
湖 南	3578	891	2905	935	389
广 东	13284	6400	8494	4077	195
广 西	616	101	425	52	36
海 南	1639	1280	1256	273	20
重 庆	2342	399	1741	742	144
四 川	8790	4068	6640	825	543
贵 州	17076	15027	14665	3922	528
云 南	1433	363	1194	105	39
西 藏	90		90		
陕 西	2486	627	1785	488	52
甘 肃	1891	631	1028	516	193
青 海	455	33	341	53	
宁 夏	669	192	456	139	64
新 疆	1443	4	914	170	2

服务站

单位：个、人

农村	为居民提供便民信息服务的机构	年末职工人数	女性	受教育程度	
				大学专科人数	大学本科及以上人数
7974	**23345**	**522047**	**205400**	**122317**	**49947**
57	2865	28003	14050	7046	5759
	234	7119	4933	2347	1695
118	39	8424	4299	2349	509
78	151	5463	2168	889	469
1	156	4502	2225	1236	896
147	472	25463	15796	9023	5330
	5	7831	5173	3397	1157
28	209	5778	2850	1853	648
	400	12098	6503	1464	600
4514	1799	70911	24707	13669	5742
655	920	29751	10808	5117	1998
5	300	14179	6161	4186	1024
81	252	11904	5164	1531	499
	106	3644	1580	480	64
1088	4851	45024	18454	14304	5690
4	80	3909	1608	1089	331
92	472	17653	6847	4036	1253
97	2528	15334	7096	4107	1755
39	854	43738	13055	7283	3195
	155	5866	2780	1044	566
9	191	7904	2268	896	290
32	258	11355	5815	4131	1538
381	2918	27076	9364	6911	1699
448	2175	73375	16277	14358	3321
16	108	7364	2614	1369	469
		342	60	46	15
1	220	10927	4937	3128	785
79	170	4651	1911	1522	749
	61	1906	789	537	229
4	27	3335	1974	540	184
	369	7218	3134	2429	1488

C-2-26续表1

地　区	职业资格水平		年龄结构			
	助理社会工作师人数	社会工作师人数	35岁及以下人数	36岁至45岁人数	46岁至55岁人数	56岁及以上人数
全　国	**6616**	**2769**	**168496**	**205067**	**117141**	**31343**
中央级						
北　京	1803	714	7651	9835	8220	2297
天　津	441	84	2992	2188	1681	258
河　北	25	55	3956	2902	1227	339
山　西	17	4	1482	2265	1346	370
内蒙古	143	37	1809	1791	707	195
辽　宁	209	142	8779	9412	4230	3042
吉　林	204	110	1656	4439	1523	213
黑龙江	63	39	2182	2885	516	195
上　海	194	83	1271	5213	4319	1295
江　苏	902	294	18044	28067	19775	5025
浙　江	311	192	9943	10276	6825	2707
安　徽	67	30	4192	6894	2802	291
福　建	315	177	4327	4554	2396	627
江　西	6	15	1266	1675	594	109
山　东	75	96	16775	17256	8072	2921
河　南	8	1	1531	1390	670	318
湖　北	88	43	5262	7874	3368	1149
湖　南	259	115	4773	5154	4515	892
广　东	654	154	16434	15956	9323	2025
广　西	76	17	2911	1906	914	135
海　南	30		1846	3376	2060	622
重　庆	361	181	4266	4392	2297	400
四　川	252	119	7882	11552	6571	1071
贵　州	13	9	25257	29053	15569	3496
云　南	14	2	2445	3316	1277	326
西　藏			159	64	119	
陕　西	41	12	3113	4420	2883	511
甘　肃	12	10	1946	1662	857	186
青　海	8	9	826	878	177	25
宁　夏	6	5	843	1717	740	35
新　疆	19	20	2677	2705	1568	268

单位：人次、张、人 、时

志愿服务		床位数合计	日间照料床位数		留宿照料床位数	
志愿者服务人次数	志愿服务时间			农村		农村
3433753	**9320787.3**	**295575**	**248231**	**113304**	**47344**	**20345**
2151205	6587939.5	2466	2414	823	52	
1200	2400.0	2444	2099	1047	345	
1509	1555.0	12730	7576	1620	5154	2154
565	1712.0	4243	4178	2911	65	49
5402	11740.0	45			45	45
2014	3409.0	8640	7072	487	1568	353
		3131	2393	93	738	1
19756	66523.0	5949	3325	408	2624	471
8452	51795.0	291	291			
163955	341096.5	76831	72957	32727	3874	1852
208382	359299.0	44948	39993	32145	4955	3272
24433	50836.0	5291	3217	696	2074	650
		8442	7881	3703	561	140
545	715.0	897	847	41	50	
467342	1008602.5	32170	28826	10084	3344	1300
13	16.0	1617	1147	77	470	22
29936	112540.0	10129	8184	1496	1945	431
4941	12165.0	3781	2981	771	800	218
3548	10751.9	7454	4239	1808	3215	489
		676	500	8	176	35
8560	15619.0	1725	731	305	994	652
201490	429612.0	5261	4261	302	1000	72
2767	14227.0	14701	10224	3229	4477	2629
120139	210402.9	23941	18867	15258	5074	4256
		3365	2564	419	801	176
4097	15184.0	3466	2081	530	1385	241
1435	7910.0	7360	6689	2048	671	376
2		1733	1281		452	418
		872	824	261	48	36
2065	4737.0	976	589	7	387	7

C-2-26续表2

地区	年末收养人数合计	日间照料人数	农村	留宿照料人数	农村
全　国	**35548**	**32086**	**14006**	**3462**	**4273**
中央级					
北　京	419	419	158		
天　津	52	52	52		
河　北	145	89		56	
山　西	1129	1129	685		
内蒙古					
辽　宁	40	39	4	1	
吉　林	300	279	57	21	1
黑龙江	346	120	8	226	160
上　海	181	181			
江　苏	13648	13369	7975	279	2828
浙　江	1484	1464	509	20	
安　徽	237	57		180	
福　建	591	543	144	48	18
江　西	102	102			
山　东	8348	7789	2611	559	475
河　南	153	53	23	100	
湖　北	873	804	337	69	35
湖　南	1032	876	368	156	30
广　东	117	112	84	5	5
广　西	108	108	4		
海　南	158	88	64	70	70
重　庆	2930	2436	214	494	12
四　川	1263	873	237	390	142
贵　州	861	405	290	456	391
云　南	142	72	20	70	50
西　藏					
陕　西	615	411	50	204	8
甘　肃	252	198	112	54	48
青　海					
宁　夏					
新　疆	22	18		4	

单位：人、人次、人天、个、平方米

本年收养照料人天数	老年人活动人次数	社区服务志愿者组织数	注册社区志愿者人数	城镇便民、利民服务网点数	机构建筑面积
2757732	**5088549**	**34731**	**956827**	**80980**	**30149902**
48208	575061	3827	213572	939	1119063
		21		2914	487398
20568	865	160	30	130	213992
13000	132000			1158	318445
	367452	150	1616	1583	207812
	643	573	39126	4111	752349
	78639	38	1308	57	307599
		1139	49785	1709	559211
470	320	43	2093	548	576646
998872	2676711	10782	148355	17015	4053789
44060	87594	555	853	3903	2765116
3600	49090	776	6040	3698	855341
179554	2910	239	17	423	519776
10121	36251	316	60	523	159856
1004620	424519	3560	9469	14096	4649189
2500	4500	19		99	496270
16482	51107	433	1758	2605	1116662
107113	27105	956	30	2705	736285
		402	188495	1867	1967987
22200	41434	5		1249	108763
18615		2	40	19	267554
226492	417563	3785	181664	8826	873197
32760	92940	788	71208	4061	2109768
	321	5501	7090	1827	2828188
				30	464573
					7950
8497	4789	532	34086	1872	719515
	12040			982	336560
					117160
				551	188212
	4695	129	132	1480	265676

C-2-26续表3

地区	执行企业会计制度单位财务指标				执行行政	
	固定资产原价	营业收入	费用合计	营业利润	固定资产原价	上年结转和结余
全国	**558.0**	**31.6**	**6.4**		**58837.1**	**227.3**
中央级						
北京						
天津						
河北					706.9	
山西					9566.8	86.0
内蒙古					65.0	
辽宁					20.0	
吉林		6.0			931.0	
黑龙江						
上海					132.1	
江苏	2.0				13093.8	3.0
浙江						
安徽					95.0	
福建					1.1	
江西						
山东					10.0	
河南						
湖北					375.2	
湖南					704.0	
广东	5.0				3750.1	
广西						
海南					650.0	
重庆					50.7	
四川					1756.8	5.3
贵州						
云南					704.0	
西藏					6513.4	85.0
陕西					4866.0	
甘肃						
青海						
宁夏					12572.0	
新疆	551.0	25.6	6.4		2273.2	48.0

单位：万元

事业单位会计制度财务指标			执行民间非营利组织单位会计制度财务指标			
本年收入合计	本年支出合计	收支结余	固定资产原价	上年结余	本年收入合计	本年费用合计
30159.9	**28743.6**	**4.1**	**165350.6**	**2157.7**	**81140.2**	**81075.5**
4778.4	4778.4		3965.0		138.4	154.0
486.2	489.0		1.0			0.2
	5.0					0.6
6.0			106.4		75.6	93.1
1684.0	1684.0				38.0	38.0
366.6	244.2		3.6		35.9	3.6
1509.3	862.2	0.1	11887.9	1928.2	8802.4	7361.5
17724.0	16334.7		132116.5	165.4	53231.1	56849.5
122.6		4.0	566.6	15.7	12011.7	8707.8
96.5	76.5		110.0		24.0	24.0
5.0			3.1		5.1	5.1
70.7	70.7		827.3		828.0	826.3
23.0	23.0		11167.4		5431.0	5431.0
606.5	579.5		138.0			42.0
238.0	226.0		256.6		209.9	212.7
			2273.6	24.4	197.5	707.8
			298.3			31.4
			123.8		73.5	73.5
115.0	115.0					
107.4	78.5		760.5	24.0	34.1	404.9
	603.8					
110.0	100.3					
429.0	396.7		510.0			5.1
			6.0			100.6
			188.0		4.0	2.8
1681.7	2076.1		41.0			

C-2-27 社区养老

地 区	单位数	农村	年末职工人数	女性
全 国	**26067**	**16493**	**122218**	**42953**
中央级				
北 京	23	14	673	108
天 津	126	119	498	152
河 北	860	467	3954	1950
山 西	240	153	1783	745
内蒙古	886	145	2619	1060
辽 宁	189	63	1988	940
吉 林				
黑龙江	503	107	3054	1374
上 海	70	5	342	234
江 苏	3615	2375	20241	6723
浙 江	3496	2344	12254	4467
安 徽	1301	1088	7192	2293
福 建	1055	664	4152	1337
江 西	249	186	1316	497
山 东	1094	536	8921	4302
河 南	1753	1233	13380	3681
湖 北	894	362	3845	1903
湖 南	1237	913	4817	1301
广 东	621	410	3608	704
广 西	1071	934	2233	748
海 南	44	38	73	23
重 庆	856	618	3309	1491
四 川	2272	1120	8532	3260
贵 州	1199	995	3404	981
云 南	1018	578	3032	1113
西 藏				
陕 西	477	367	1677	730
甘 肃	506	411	3266	416
青 海	175	105	1212	150
宁 夏	46	32	130	47
新 疆	191	111	713	223

单位：万元

受教育程度		职业资格水平		年龄结构
大学专科人数	大学本科及以上人数	助理社会工作师人数	社会工作师人数	35岁及以下人数
15195	**8574**	**1568**	**644**	**26105**
46	34	7	11	25
101	62	6	3	21
423	223	45	21	758
176	60	20	1	243
431	102	21		654
185	179	144	27	302
213	220	49	39	653
12	6	9	16	205
3027	1529	178	68	5730
1519	710	132	66	2185
600	191	79	32	1010
255	78	43	46	722
187	22	11	6	304
1778	1148	82	14	2301
1352	1195	280	62	1829
595	336	22	12	680
844	734	77	20	922
266	215	88	26	402
96	19	7	30	218
		5		23
272	117	11	14	542
1226	601	148	70	2299
546	259	17	26	1232
393	216	22	20	538
181	50	4	1	360
169	108	16	8	1470
69	35	7	4	199
13				16
220	125	38	1	262

C-2-27续表1

地区	年龄结构			志愿
	36岁至45岁人数	46岁至55岁人数	56岁及以上人数	志愿者服务人次数
全　国	**45565**	**33183**	**17365**	**109831**
中央级				
北　京	34	563	51	748
天　津	286	139	52	500
河　北	1501	1283	412	1573
山　西	458	266	816	4
内蒙古	1233	517	215	2820
辽　宁	751	519	416	
吉　林				
黑龙江	1253	833	315	
上　海	42	38	57	292
江　苏	6999	5847	1665	63789
浙　江	4384	3541	2144	3658
安　徽	2662	2542	978	3272
福　建	1282	1342	806	30
江　西	513	387	112	213
山　东	3689	2482	449	24764
河　南	6391	2981	2179	4728
湖　北	1614	1115	436	
湖　南	2008	1445	442	446
广　东	551	484	2171	
广　西	763	812	440	
海　南	20	21	9	
重　庆	1026	1304	437	1322
四　川	3135	2111	987	98
贵　州	1223	582	367	1210
云　南	1554	691	249	230
西　藏				
陕　西	531	611	175	134
甘　肃	999	504	293	
青　海	243	98	672	
宁　夏	81	21	12	
新　疆	339	104	8	

单位：人次、张、人、时

服务					
志愿服务时间	床位数合计	日间照料床位数	农村	留宿照料床位数	农村
266933.5	**1342302**	**257938**	**144051**	**1084364**	**715469**
1680.0	1697	2		1695	443
1000.0	7150	1517	1317	5633	5163
6645.0	50327	9183	4500	41144	21535
9.2	11203	2419	1363	8784	7844
5758.0	24611	12491	900	12120	9265
	16230	6382	2915	9848	3694
	42578	13442	2605	29136	7293
665.0	13817			13817	994
133252.0	66542	24957	14338	41585	13800
6483.0	108210	27980	14612	80230	46306
9000.0	151456	4019	1998	147437	127814
90.0	50182	3919	3243	46263	26979
1656.0	22749	10387	8713	12362	10750
61156.3	141082	5325	2806	135757	65406
27591.0	207875	51644	37384	156231	120181
	27826	9764	2494	18062	5642
2235.0	49825	5680	3502	44145	34643
	15721	8476	5199	7245	3704
	27637	1994	1618	25643	21887
	2026	432	432	1594	1594
2804.0	43131	3965	2165	39166	35984
243.0	123787	16672	8259	107115	73428
5075.0	42214	7008	5438	35206	29688
980.0	40510	10503	4556	30007	16259
609.0	19663	2393	1377	17270	14577
	14117	9865	7001	4252	3886
	9275	625	338	8650	4090
	509	387	100	122	100
2.0	10352	6507	4878	3845	2520

C-2-27续表2

地　区	年末收养人数合计	日间照料人数	农村	留宿照料人数	农村
全　国	**557184**	**76158**	**53254**	**481026**	**338902**
中央级					
北　京	407			407	200
天　津	1336	388	188	948	887
河　北	17344	276	154	17068	8746
山　西	5399	512	159	4887	4395
内蒙古	10537	4357	562	6180	4324
辽　宁	2528	801	84	1727	693
吉　林					
黑龙江	17590	3225	1854	14365	3529
上　海					
江　苏	14840	2788	1611	12052	2911
浙　江	22155	1475	810	20680	11155
安　徽	57342	35		57307	49322
福　建	9462	243	243	9219	4596
江　西	15994	7447	7245	8547	8218
山　东	66034	1875	1083	64159	33987
河　南	127053	28484	24342	98569	75528
湖　北	11180	2569	857	8611	3177
湖　南	25748	2660	726	23088	17041
广　东	4659	2209	465	2450	1144
广　西	12763	643	527	12120	10938
海　南	904	100	100	804	804
重　庆	31524	2864	1653	28660	26221
四　川	52272	3327	2797	48945	38653
贵　州	10510	1315	1178	9195	8193
云　南	14733	1795	620	12938	9204
西　藏					
陕　西	13413	1432	1125	11981	10632
甘　肃	1377	610	568	767	767
青　海	2385	81		2304	1205
宁　夏	77	40		37	37
新　疆	7618	4607	4303	3011	2395

单位：人、人天、个、平方米

本年收养照料人天数	老年人活动人次数	社区服务志愿者组织数	注册社区志愿者人数	城镇便民、利民服务网点数	机构建筑面积
37342818	**4877163**	**7923**	**6623**	**5347**	**18488811**
47265					19402
					119243
1110533	285691				875508
376983	23360				191025
2312122	325300	71	425	77	332706
260					489958
51674	63288				240341
		1	50		310611
873383	557775	432	699	3187	870651
51776	949135	34	80	2	1250983
5111171	6	3			1392598
712910	8196	26		277	545753
55330	36	100	5	60	135420
12083553	1678689	137	4373	1128	2658527
2278175	109637	18		19	2383918
5000	9666			24	462671
2970445	23000	28		20	968047
228134	374311	6124	595	16	238876
976135	170560			8	463648
365	12045				49989
4504740	192759	119	1	350	646652
1249702	62641	22	334		1714700
171185		8	21	8	332137
1006620	31000			5	775044
1104707	68	800		57	231928
				109	136955
			40		177077
					13474
60650					460969

C-2-27续表3

地　区	执行企业会计制度单位财务指标				执行行政	
	固定资产原价	营业收入	费用合计	营业利润	固定资产原价	上年结转和结余
全　国	**1319.7**	**804.3**	**723.3**	**25.2**	**45219.7**	**55.0**
中央级						
北　京						
天　津						
河　北	1030.0				4066.4	4.0
山　西						
内蒙古						
辽　宁	123.0	682.9	709.6	23.2	635.5	
吉　林						
黑龙江	17.0	112.6	8.0	2.0	813.0	36.0
上　海						
江　苏					16390.0	
浙　江	21.0				532.0	15.0
安　徽					4421.0	
福　建	1.0				15.0	
江　西					50.0	
山　东						
河　南					1638.5	
湖　北	0.1					
湖　南					50.0	
广　东	70.0				0.3	
广　西						
海　南						
重　庆						
四　川	22.6	8.8	5.7		14971.0	
贵　州						
云　南	35.0				1380.0	
西　藏						
陕　西					50.0	
甘　肃					30.0	
青　海						
宁　夏					55.0	
新　疆					122.0	

单位：万元

事业单位会计制度财务指标			执行民间非营利组织单位会计制度财务指标			
本年收入合计	本年支出合计	收支结余	固定资产原价	上年结余	本年收入合计	本年费用合计
7962.9	**7199.7**		**54289.0**	**647.6**	**55190.5**	**25486.6**
			1239.1	-34.7	258.2	258.1
602.2	595.0		1794.5	6.0	434.5	1311.1
			707.0		5.0	48.5
135.3	135.3		73.7		45.0	122.5
706.1	776.6		1302.3	22.0	342.0	226.4
2058.4	2173.7		13528.9	89.8	9510.8	8669.4
1102.0	238.0		1100.2	53.0	6949.7	6351.0
1595.4	1595.4		9866.3		638.3	1079.1
			332.0		96.0	31.5
			50.0		30.0	30.0
			4301.9		1458.3	1458.3
1174.8	1174.8		3045.5	150.6	559.0	496.9
			4755.0		2209.0	2266.0
12.0	12.0		304.0	6.0	30275.4	300.2
0.3	0.3		16.0			4.1
			3.0		26.5	26.5
					137.0	
			52.0		38.7	99.1
317.5	179.7		7571.7	308.7	2017.1	2494.4
			735.9	44.2	55.0	17.5
166.9	225.9		2412.0			1.1
5.0	5.0		930.0	2.0	100.0	186.9
4.0	3.0		5.0			0.2
	2.0		162.0		5.0	7.8
83.0	83.0		1.0			

C-2-28 社区互助型

地区	单位数	农村	年末职工人数	女性
全国	**62027**	**55517**	**123658**	**38445**
中央级				
北京	226	170	680	292
天津				
河北	24468	22537	44396	13793
山西	173	130	558	134
内蒙古	822	816	1084	164
辽宁	112	111	279	97
吉林				
黑龙江	59	57	267	80
上海				
江苏	435	193	2269	949
浙江	458	235	898	465
安徽	134	76	581	274
福建	1218	595	2122	561
江西				
山东	5228	4528	19936	6619
河南	34		69	30
湖北	2570	2036	6929	3061
湖南	4497	4008	11064	3462
广东				
广西	10893	10669	9688	1920
海南	3	3	5	1
重庆	1683	1376	2585	810
四川	1917	1511	3911	938
贵州	1430	1292	4020	1043
云南	87	69	119	41
西藏				
陕西	2885	2625	7494	2383
甘肃	2115	1944	3391	972
青海	468	425	1021	243
宁夏	84	83	237	88
新疆	28	28	55	25

养老设施

单位：个、人

受教育程度		职业资格水平		年龄结构
大学专科人数	大学本科及以上人数	助理社会工作师人数	社会工作师人数	35岁及以下人数
12102	**4685**	**231**	**247**	**32874**
206	76			163
1298	228	2	6	12344
131	8			171
99	17	3		170
75	13	8	3	49
15	101		1	26
189	38	3	5	268
20	5	5	1	291
104	27	16	2	160
118	42	3	3	451
3636	1986	88	15	8019
24	2			24
874	238	36	61	2066
1960	896	30	85	2294
163	136	4	6	790
1				1
545	156	2	1	620
569	225	5	4	860
708	149	2		1134
1				4
766	211	1	1	1255
416	88	20	16	1316
88	26	3	37	207
75				156
21	17			35

C-2-28续表1

地　区	年龄结构			志愿
	36岁至45岁人数	46岁至55岁人数	56岁及以上人数	志愿者服务人次数
全　国	**45128**	**34048**	**11248**	**69885**
中央级				
北　京	280	198	39	
天　津				
河　北	14403	13004	4645	4657
山　西	159	190	38	
内蒙古	498	221	154	
辽　宁	106	89	19	
吉　林				
黑龙江	150	90	1	
上　海				
江　苏	989	861	151	413
浙　江	338	196	73	
安　徽	233	161	27	218
福　建	892	310	468	
江　西				
山　东	6419	4203	1295	34326
河　南	39	6		
湖　北	3043	1533	287	18640
湖　南	4844	3055	806	540
广　东				
广　西	2930	4268	1700	
海　南	2	2		
重　庆	1040	749	176	322
四　川	1617	1023	411	
贵　州	1577	1051	258	701
云　南	76	32	7	
西　藏				
陕　西	3437	2250	552	1227
甘　肃	1432	482	140	8841
青　海	540	72	1	
宁　夏	66			
新　疆	18	2		

单位：人次、张、人 、时

服务 志愿服务时间	床位数合计	日间照料床位数	农村	留宿照料床位数	农村
211647.1	**707013**	**362149**	**313107**	**344864**	**318970**
	1821	1821	1349		
23000.0	194093	128626	118940	65467	61907
	2665	2560	2232	105	105
	102909	521	468	102388	100828
	614	473	473	141	111
	3898	185	155	3713	3513
1688.0	6033	4254	1146	1779	984
	4969	3978	3316	991	138
719.0	3075	1141	351	1934	1574
	15502	3543	1871	11959	6051
84967.1	124846	78824	70913	46022	40755
	1459	804		655	
46080.0	18197	14876	10272	3321	2666
1060.0	30508	22138	19653	8370	7267
	93433	18859	18461	74574	73369
	18	9	9	9	9
1377.0	12025	6071	3982	5954	5740
	14321	11136	8661	3185	1500
4680.0	15305	11638	7453	3667	3178
	851	782	485	69	24
3966.0	27978	22856	20278	5122	4901
44110.0	28283	24016	20589	4267	3188
	2578	2277	1309	301	291
	1096	301	281	795	795
	536	460	460	76	76

C-2-28续表2

地区	年末收养人数合计	日间照料人数	农村	留宿照料人数	农村
全国	**211111**	**77656**	**69583**	**133455**	**136667**
中央级					
北京	1178	1178	900		
天津					
河北	18912	13542	13482	5370	5365
山西	587	587	587		
内蒙古	64995	135	82	64860	64765
辽宁	289	289	289		
吉林					
黑龙江	1784	52	52	1732	1732
上海					
江苏	1056	186	27	870	400
浙江	457	240		217	
安徽	1129	82	3	1047	922
福建	1037	50	19	987	987
江西					
山东	36553	23262	21899	13291	11251
河南	929	274		655	
湖北	4249	4105	2178	144	54
湖南	17551	13473	12409	4078	12690
广东					
广西	36445	6179	5988	30266	29962
海南					
重庆	7905	3751	2405	4154	4101
四川	4074	1963	1616	2111	864
贵州	580	249	249	331	286
云南	154	130	103	24	13
西藏					
陕西	8858	6853	6375	2005	1984
甘肃	1845	1046	910	799	777
青海	10	10	10		
宁夏	534	20		514	514
新疆					

单位：人、人次、人天、个、平方米

本年收养照料人天数	老年人活动人次数	社区服务志愿者组织数	注册社区志愿者人数	城镇便民、利民服务网点数	机构建筑面积
29335651	**3698754**	**556**	**692**	**2437**	**14267039**
177973	700245				70498
2374098	526094	180		251	3433393
					26925
15391461	4592			34	1711406
					12620
					27766
68411	6530			690	99695
					100614
216776	230				56958
				4	197900
5211818	739826	113	362	348	3007738
					8538
23528	42829	32	160		546338
1921586	890			4	1185906
2118600	1022155				1651077
					300
1435258	419877	195	31	114	390793
159907	158861			7	342713
	12	11	132		224495
13000				6	29421
223235	22233	25	7	205	727629
	54380			774	327531
					59109
					17312
					10364

C-2-29 其他社区服务

地区	单位数	农村	年末职工人数	女性
全国	**119778**	**41222**	**352622**	**119797**
中央级				
北京	4654	1242	8877	4047
天津	278	40	1490	443
河北	9177	7248	16028	3133
山西	578	304	1573	601
内蒙古	329	1	1571	880
辽宁	1592	263	7485	4508
吉林	29		134	102
黑龙江	509	51	2329	1230
上海	2641	31	22952	6654
江苏	16080	3767	68998	20043
浙江	11843	5497	19941	9214
安徽	2213	534	8233	3398
福建	197	55	1417	580
江西	1667	101	5709	2245
山东	9392	3387	28155	10167
河南	1896	383	7973	2845
湖北	3548	817	12225	5262
湖南	1615	270	5052	1977
广东	40281	10762	100196	32076
广西	426	41	2015	1032
海南	212	188	1150	281
重庆	2197	1388	5329	1758
四川	4080	1802	12553	4145
贵州	375	133	1962	554
云南	313	162	986	373
西藏				
陕西	406	229	1415	433
甘肃	2854	2450	5545	1424
青海	2		4	2
宁夏	134	42	604	194
新疆	260	34	721	196

单位：人、个

受教育程度		职业资格水平		年龄结构
大学专科人数	大学本科及以上人数	助理社会工作师人数	社会工作师人数	35岁及以下人数
68838	**37307**	**2661**	**2449**	**107300**
2091	1703	51	24	3365
151	94	15	13	150
912	332	37	15	3926
365	81	29	13	298
496	412	145	23	615
1395	634	9	10	2505
28	61			82
633	241	11	15	545
5156	1808	110	1217	7008
9598	8001	234	105	18451
3976	2134	87	65	5526
2538	483	93	86	2298
117	69	25	13	176
510	66	5	1	1385
9503	4073	62	35	10594
1874	460	51	37	1711
2446	1404	140	45	3268
1021	236	44	15	1486
20911	12393	1188	563	35980
326	236	64	23	724
20	1			75
620	480	120	45	987
2559	1008	72	42	2897
422	108	7	3	990
101	112	20	8	155
78	6	3	6	219
762	593	13	8	1485
		2		4
112	9		3	137
117	69	24	16	258

C-2-29续表1

地区	年龄结构			志愿
	36岁至45岁人数	46岁至55岁人数	56岁及以上人数	志愿者服务人次数
全　国	**136768**	**78561**	**29993**	**206659**
中央级				
北　京	2869	2087	556	6753
天　津	285	337	718	500
河　北	6540	3704	1858	127
山　西	738	404	133	
内蒙古	608	322	26	690
辽　宁	3246	1475	259	15
吉　林	34	17	1	
黑龙江	1258	304	222	
上　海	7719	6801	1424	6363
江　苏	27710	16660	6177	130476
浙　江	8763	4267	1385	2393
安　徽	3566	1822	547	6630
福　建	395	411	435	24
江　西	1977	1167	1180	
山　东	11123	4846	1592	41696
河　南	4308	1112	842	
湖　北	4464	1752	2741	333
湖　南	1897	1477	192	798
广　东	37052	20071	7093	200
广　西	760	479	52	
海　南	253	793	29	
重　庆	2111	1149	1082	8786
四　川	5489	3665	502	92
贵　州	453	350	169	343
云　南	532	240	59	210
西　藏				
陕　西	473	570	153	139
甘　肃	1662	1981	417	40
青　海				
宁　夏	278	178	11	
新　疆	205	120	138	51

单位：人次、张、人 、时

服务					
志愿服务时间	床位数合计	日间照料床位数		留宿照料床位数	
			农村		农村
452087.8	**484865**	**241779**	**140333**	**243086**	**131071**
35871.0	1415	427	145	988	60
1000.0	513	504	350	9	
278.0	74738	46752	38732	27986	21424
	4917	3262	2543	1655	1089
2286.0	695	568		127	127
30.0	10895	3815	1144	7080	4449
	24	24			
	7527	1399	142	6128	3006
9992.0	103	103	3		
234776.0	58718	27731	7606	30987	9151
6670.0	71547	38868	33850	32679	10732
37567.0	26143	2371	1666	23772	17023
89.0	6952	4466	1067	2486	761
	1739	223	60	1516	
100245.0	24881	18772	4863	6109	608
	17774	7689	5484	10085	6653
885.0	17154	9339	1419	7815	2147
1689.0	5668	1936	814	3732	2229
1604.0	35556	17007	5521	18549	8389
	668	492	8	176	14
	3703	895	529	2808	2089
17072.8	33339	12666	6263	20673	16813
168.0	26647	8466	2529	18181	10376
1056.0	3318	1040	746	2278	1981
210.0	9500	2434	774	7066	4160
516.0	4395	2265	1647	2130	1567
30.0	31793	26003	21530	5790	5305
	963	469	211	494	460
53.0	3580	1793	687	1787	458

C-2-29续表2

地　区	年末收养人数合计	日间照料人数	农村	留宿照料人数	农村
全　国	**115352**	**37144**	**21645**	**78208**	**44115**
中央级					
北　京	526	20	11	506	11
天　津	4	2		2	
河　北	8005	4427	3560	3578	2631
山　西	888	347	117	541	443
内蒙古	234	191		43	43
辽　宁	3030	262	69	2768	2218
吉　林					
黑龙江	3760	391	137	3369	2330
上　海	4	4			
江　苏	5507	1643	874	3864	1134
浙　江	24847	6275	5890	18572	707
安　徽	5240	55		5185	4255
福　建	3174	2861		313	
江　西					
山　东	7094	5429	895	1665	13
河　南	7182	3475	3297	3707	3384
湖　北	1935	356		1579	1289
湖　南	2184	725	377	1459	662
广　东	2022	523	241	1499	955
广　西	194	169	2	25	4
海　南	1141	238	198	903	821
重　庆	19951	6263	3707	13688	11237
四　川	10371	471	263	9900	8217
贵　州	946			946	897
云　南	2729	124	19	2605	2114
西　藏					
陕　西	289	180	180	109	109
甘　肃	2183	1457	1295	726	641
青　海					
宁　夏	195	186	186	9	
新　疆	1717	1070	327	647	

单位：人、人次、人天、个、平方米

本年收养照料人天数	老年人活动人次数	社区服务志愿者组织数	注册社区志愿者人数	城镇便民、利民服务网点数	机构建筑面积
3203152	**2191551**	**2692**	**166425**	**20127**	**24365346**
11195					595285
					73572
42605	1476	32		352	1523046
47305	29558	20		46	106689
15480	17680			24	97662
				458	306196
					12271
				222	228586
		29	1536	104	339952
261602	273772	536	7556	4989	2843902
7220	26601	26	120	10	2782011
	9000	26	250	555	692448
	380	50		17	69320
		4		11	225965
1317480	1007948	360	1720	1560	3488543
	20502	65	671	277	1545148
13355	100209	1	28	176	619145
143576	2297	38	573	50	420815
3520	488	1128	147992	3102	5647518
29102	83407			25	64205
					64234
1036318	546445	342	5795	414	601119
158419	6278	11	94	7468	1094395
				16	69783
36709		1	30	1	182375
300	2710	23	60	15	119354
32570	62800			235	445074
					200
3010					28908
43386					77625

C-2-29续表3

地区	执行企业会计制度单位财务指标					执行行政
	固定资产原价	营业收入	费用合计	营业利润	固定资产原价	上年结转和结余
全国	**2904.1**	**544.0**	**155.7**	**27.0**	**34723.4**	**717.4**
中央级						
北京					320.7	
天津						
河北	1001.0		0.2		4891.0	
山西					323.5	
内蒙古					4.0	
辽宁					0.1	
吉林						
黑龙江					64.0	
上海					304.0	
江苏	800.0	330.0	103.0	15.0	16153.9	6.0
浙江	200.1				2181.2	1.0
安徽					762.6	84.3
福建	81.0	24.0	2.5	12.0	12.6	
江西	200.0	190.0	50.0			
山东						
河南					1001.0	2.0
湖北					52.0	
湖南	120.0				36.0	
广东	400.0				448.0	1.0
广西					247.5	
海南						
重庆					1000.0	
四川	90.0				730.1	623.1
贵州					63.4	
云南					909.3	
西藏						
陕西					4798.0	
甘肃					199.0	
青海						
宁夏						
新疆	12.0				221.5	

单位：万元

事业单位会计制度财务指标			执行民间非营利组织单位会计制度财务指标			
本年收入合计	本年支出合计	收支结余	固定资产原价	上年结余	本年收入合计	本年费用合计
19605.0	**21246.2**	**2655.2**	**179591.4**	**25222.8**	**279257.1**	**303269.8**
679.5	679.5		2315.5	3537.0	5298.8	4393.6
			267.0	142.0	710.3	583.4
978.2	1061.2		790.7		120.0	254.8
26.0	26.0		264.7		1.0	37.7
1.0	1.0		206.0		25.0	28.7
			1215.9	34.0	473.8	1436.2
6.0	188.7		220.6	20.0	88.6	139.1
20.8	7.6		50404.2	19874.3	155189.1	179833.8
14135.1	15144.3	2654.0	77043.4	147.0	75911.0	80572.2
693.7	1162.1		6073.6	381.4	12503.6	10479.7
618.6	495.5		1156.1		839.9	558.9
47.8	44.8		361.8	6.1	300.3	287.0
			2457.0		2895.0	2897.0
			7694.6	119.0	12622.7	12623.8
318.1	276.5	0.2	543.5		524.8	662.0
84.5	78.8		1709.0		812.6	498.2
34.0	27.0		596.0	258.8	840.6	789.8
908.7	893.1		7212.4	28.3	6780.6	2636.5
10.0	10.0		379.0	111.2	140.0	174.0
640.0	685.2		2707.5	10.0	441.2	454.4
251.7	248.7	1.0	15629.2	442.9	2219.2	3086.1
41.0	3.0		159.6	35.0	461.9	561.7
35.1	169.0		90.0	73.1	0.1	17.4
39.0	13.0		7.7	1.7		160.5
22.2	17.2		66.4		53.2	99.5
			15.0		3.8	3.5
14.0	14.0		5.0	1.0		0.3

C−2−30 老龄事业

地区	单位数	编制登记	民政登记	一个机构多块牌子
全　国	**2280**	**1787**	**62**	**431**
中央级				
北　京	14	11		3
天　津	14	11		3
河　北	48	26	7	15
山　西	95	87	1	7
内蒙古	21	21		
辽　宁	68	45	7	16
吉　林	44	41		3
黑龙江	93	72	7	14
上　海	20	18	2	
江　苏	60	49	2	9
浙　江	81	53	2	26
安　徽	55	51		4
福　建	62	51		11
江　西	115	100	2	13
山　东	148	139		9
河　南	82	74	4	4
湖　北	74	56		18
湖　南	121	56	1	64
广　东	100	66		34
广　西	59	42	1	16
海　南	8	5		3
重　庆	27	20		7
四　川	214	180		34
贵　州	97	79	3	15
云　南	66	61	1	4
西　藏	5	2	3	
陕　西	100	97		3
甘　肃	101	86		15
青　海	42	5		37
宁　夏	25	23	2	
新　疆	221	160	17	44

机构情况

单位：个、人

年末职工人数	女性	受教育程度		职业资格水平	
		大学专科人数	大学本科及以上人数	助理社会工作师人数	社会工作师人数
9316	**4082**	**3383**	**3375**	**102**	**141**
140	63	28	109	1	6
57	31	16	37		2
200	74	57	69	15	2
444	184	219	84	6	8
83	42	30	48	1	5
261	130	90	117	6	1
173	83	53	37	3	1
314	157	111	103	4	3
159	93	40	97	5	22
244	119	70	101	4	8
302	145	91	129	6	4
160	53	48	80		2
175	69	65	68	1	1
368	141	156	64		6
1043	327	366	495	2	11
319	138	103	80	10	5
288	122	124	95		1
366	159	145	78	3	5
315	139	112	149	9	10
190	92	82	68	2	1
21	13	9	11		1
111	58	45	45	2	4
718	337	283	290	4	8
363	173	162	149		
368	159	138	140	7	4
8	1	1	4		
724	322	257	200	1	1
501	209	118	100	2	
77	42	18	7		
106	43	48	42	1	1
718	364	298	279	7	18

C-2-30续表

地 区	年龄结构 35岁及以下人数	36岁至45岁人数	46岁至55岁人数	56岁及以上人数	志愿服务 志愿者服务人次数	志愿服务时间
全 国	**2382**	**3534**	**2823**	**577**	**362319**	**904610.2**
中央级						
北 京	33	52	44	11	25539	51084.0
天 津	19	14	24		300	600.0
河 北	71	80	43	6	75	270.0
山 西	134	180	104	26	210	
内蒙古	16	37	26	4	122	244.0
辽 宁	90	76	76	19	4264	5361.0
吉 林	50	70	46	7	23289	46578.0
黑龙江	64	120	108	22	9105	18315.0
上 海	45	57	50	7	1380	3120.0
江 苏	70	74	81	19	1308	6203.0
浙 江	81	112	86	23	37916	47223.0
安 徽	37	57	47	19	35191	49660.0
福 建	33	57	75	10	107860	328830.0
江 西	96	155	101	16	1100	2100.0
山 东	242	386	343	72	3089	8984.0
河 南	130	127	57	5	14	87.0
湖 北	56	111	91	30	1149	1480.0
湖 南	81	144	126	15	3885	16804.0
广 东	93	106	96	20	1606	4208.0
广 西	35	68	74	13	278	2106.0
海 南	4	11	3	3		
重 庆	22	31	48	10	4153	12685.0
四 川	164	265	231	58	87025	253922.0
贵 州	72	130	140	21	1700	7131.0
云 南	82	132	118	36	45	225.0
西 藏	3	3	2		18	40.0
陕 西	250	264	173	37	5092	11962.2
甘 肃	109	207	163	22	71	236.0
青 海	9	50	18		2	12.0
宁 夏	19	36	37	14	2	8.0
新 疆	172	322	192	32	6531	25132.0

单位：万元、人、人次、时

执行行政事业单位会计制度财务指标				
固定资产原价	上年结转和结余	本年收入合计	本年支出合计	收支结余
82909.0	**7887.5**	**217196.3**	**219093.2**	**4815.7**
720.8	39.7	24082.4	24316.2	
141.9	1115.7	3784.3	3190.5	1407.8
239.5	23.3	1138.7	1158.5	1.3
732.4	161.4	4105.2	3938.1	7.4
285.2	211.3	2137.9	2133.1	176.8
724.7	7.5	3460.0	4089.7	87.2
5661.4	20.0	1510.6	1496.5	1.3
2978.1	51.8	2898.7	3740.4	9.7
9499.0	1310.5	16720.6	16518.4	617.5
7385.3	14.6	5760.2	5677.5	23.6
3137.6	359.5	11313.6	11416.5	36.7
310.5	2.9	2097.3	2105.2	
617.2	419.1	7416.2	7221.3	475.0
942.1	10.8	2199.6	2295.0	
4954.4		15835.9	15835.9	
358.7	8.9	2449.9	2353.0	1.5
1687.5	51.6	7315.2	7324.0	49.8
1052.6	2.9	2254.0	2355.9	
8153.8	347.9	20480.6	21005.7	150.8
922.9	320.4	5921.5	6155.2	156.0
21.5	342.0	50.1	829.4	312.2
2240.5	16.8	3836.9	3647.9	200.8
7537.7	68.5	15284.6	13466.3	42.7
1352.6	727.9	7060.4	7035.0	123.8
10496.7	1381.5	7611.1	8852.1	727.0
3022.5		50.9	42.0	
2634.0	547.8	30842.4	31032.7	170.1
1836.9	180.0	2418.1	2352.9	
136.0	0.1	154.8	50.6	
793.3	40.3	1441.8	1338.5	10.4
2331.7	102.8	5562.8	6119.2	26.3

C-2-31 居家养老

地 区	老龄人口情况							老年维权
	60岁及以上老年人口数	65岁及以上老年人口数	80岁及以上老年人口数	100岁及以上老年人口数	纯老年人家庭人口数	老龄系统接待来信来访次数	老年法律援助中心	涉老案件数
全 国	**217387412**	**143311066**	**29936281**	**72306**	**31245431**	**494182**	**21439**	**77394**
中央级								
北 京	3064353	2078059	545815	2342	482903	51321	242	748
天 津	2303700	1469301	334098	309	231339	4163	44	4091
河 北	11017783	7334254	1353766	2460	857088	12109	576	16603
山 西	4612233	3052439	593917	990	676155	7022	776	707
内蒙古	3677221	2381353	419702	362	673875	3048	101	347
辽 宁	7967525	5059359	1044970	1574	2107223	15242	1286	2651
吉 林	5010000	3130000	600000	771	812651	731	47	90
黑龙江	4915204	2997531	593715	867	900269	3661	553	948
上 海	4333812	2768466	773701	2501	844661	41228	348	7721
江 苏	15749170	10874955	2334377	5626	3126371	114581	1265	3895
浙 江	9840267	6528657	1562791	2228	2342570	34871	836	3163
安 徽	11097380	7445664	1605078	3658	1312502	9209	578	1541
福 建	5575455	3590038	891589	2112	1023703	6801	1306	2489
江 西	6584715	3848779	842382	2971	278091	6057	367	478
山 东	17061372	11154095	2392410	5837	4235527	7223	2080	2410
河 南	12160370	8282955	1857199	5116	1074915	6153	1023	939
湖 北	9692651	6329740	1255054	2389	818180	12263	899	2172
湖 南	11520192	7970845	1798295	2565	2126135	29550	935	2686
广 东	11743040	7936012	1951124	6691	791379	13382	935	535
广 西	8102433	5578017	1166693	6416	425465	12274	280	682
海 南	1209542	867427	209505	1747	54997	1855	19	220
重 庆	6774076	4543910	932207	1459	1518868	5961	486	7968
四 川	17476721	11438519	2058277	4833	1882073	33933	1708	4571
贵 州	5787382	3791999	607569	1256	392945	6691	1076	572
云 南	5910403	3684112	772999	1419	697557	9971	1987	5093
西 藏	185035	134721	23276	73	1282	560		
陕 西	5890085	3729008	673652	801	628526	16842	480	1765
甘 肃	3780329	2553075	354343	393	287271	8239	536	281
青 海	697662	471397	75666	145	118187		2	20
宁 夏	845738	454135	51117	77	74295	7960	125	431
新 疆	2801563	1832244	260994	2318	448428	11281	543	1577

服务情况

单位：个、人

老龄事业发展情况									
	老年活动设施			老年福利			老年医疗护理机构		
维权协调组织数	老年活动站/中心/室数	老年人参与人数	年末活动人次数	享受高龄补贴的老年人数	享受护理补贴的老年人数	享受养老服务补贴的老年人数	老年医院数	床位数	
71399	**370581**	**46565600**	**224214678**	**21551154**	**264906**	**2578631**	**2576**	**137633**	
3144	6756	813260	5863121	322463	1880	128046	19	2711	
1258	1869	396975	543122	17943	971	7639	32	1746	
1851	9188	884528	37579626	857534	14748	14715	112	2467	
1927	19585	1230120	3561074	296186	150		82	2682	
259	1317	275004	3406406	360258	13	4277	4	111	
1904	7021	988802	2136174	125483	869	2148	39	1378	
715	1580	84220	138228	9464	1429	2508	16	237	
695	3395	468871	2772953	108586	10728	4210	296	6571	
2777	6424	464173	11118522	163662	48390	186243	32	4262	
6338	20990	4811633	68875351	2313815	27201	158701	302	27844	
3711	31497	7771491	18506224	1267764	27005	146477	37	4940	
2187	7459	1321468	3262460	1370186	18723	78868	43	6900	
2011	18332	1852304	3455360	518541	17358	57203	42	3065	
1829	10609	1116600	2008078	404474	1230	598	78	1591	
5513	55280	2722484	4395030	1340505	20213	173316	81	10511	
2706	33176	1334628	1932454	375734	1395	14333	200	4822	
2821	9847	1963413	13551936	973731	7178	14435	127	5942	
3365	17423	2382334	3293030	321131	11166	142118	160	8449	
1696	16743	2364250	6409269	3202633	958	12118	77	6778	
1681	5860	1034176	2205523	951034	928	7637	37	4767	
126	830	293890	406285	160392	41	1780	2	50	
2549	6152	2125810	3422291	262920	7582	23118	13	802	
9103	24979	3985177	12081415	1379830	26903	658302	281	16377	
2331	16449	871775	1990796	441779	3948	679856	168	2993	
3010	15126	2801980	7821348	900392	455	8365	71	4603	
	10	3414	3583	21560	5				
2841	6687	950620	1411336	2375264	10019	6317	150	3301	
1946	3888	547142	884616	139135	3083	45203	60	450	
	609	90800	126001	300675					
674	864	156713	323762	31033		75	2	26	
431	10636	457545	729304	237047	337	25	13	1257	

C-2-31续表

地区	老年医疗护理机构							老龄事业
	老年临终关怀医院数	床位数	年底在院人数	老年人协会个数	参加人数	村、居老年人协会	参加人数	乡、街道老年人协会
全国	**706**	**33819**	**15111**	**450795**	**48693123**	**368893**	**38374350**	**38835**
中央级								
北京	3	152	42	5664	409084	5402	353136	129
天津	1	30	25	3197	333239	2967	284940	210
河北	37	390	150	23955	653778	18247	637669	3143
山西	69	4679	295	19150	933992	16776	751764	876
内蒙古				1695	194151	1217	95770	287
辽宁	8	850	138	10654	945545	8834	732831	1152
吉林				1327	71039	801	47452	71
黑龙江	44	1171	501	7368	925879	4986	545736	1711
上海	10	259	183	2257	234739	2034	181801	206
江苏	73	8664	5696	19210	4122832	17156	3405615	1189
浙江	3	466	457	30583	7821917	29325	8504173	789
安徽	8	194	116	12750	1438138	11209	1172331	1164
福建	33	1798	954	16072	2275301	14189	1923772	842
江西	6	287	204	20767	1420500	9423	930538	1014
山东	19	1780	906	67361	2156777	54672	1415060	7935
河南	19	441	330	18103	1123318	14285	813550	1147
湖北	70	411	217	15378	1978482	12359	1257163	1153
湖南	87	2633	1000	29011	3045824	24965	2299666	2229
广东	22	2330	710	16066	2397846	12865	1854559	1474
广西	3	200	140	9531	1786028	8237	1354932	831
海南				783	127582	585	81257	172
重庆	2	75	30	10075	2729676	8503	1508010	1304
四川	114	4081	1522	41330	5864967	35645	3995645	3969
贵州	18	130	65	17898	1264044	14887	972566	2098
云南	39	1212	807	16292	2329431	9560	1601563	1390
西藏				9	1655			
陕西	16	1346	441	15596	1180687	13310	959690	816
甘肃	1	200	180	10091	508343	8963	458223	651
青海				773	29039	723	13214	35
宁夏				1427	83922	1209	59163	177
新疆	1	40	2	6422	305368	5559	162561	671

单位：人、人次、时、万元

发展情况							老年学校	
参加人数	县、市老年人协会	参加人数	老年基金会	事业投入经费	其他老年社团组织	参加人数	老年学校个数	在校人数
7899197	**6830**	**2878167**	**2146**	**27034**	**38776**	**3984394**	**52624**	**7328143**
56151	4	6059	1	2	6088	213748	2410	237009
46296	5	2098			1070	110979	463	110062
162149	713	117646	503	27	447	138880	251	41921
132535	700	61290	2	28	174	49755	1241	98171
42437	153	45418			44	4586	54	9109
227854	166	17676			2959	99107	1191	143083
17120	7	9300	1	6	117	20921	328	28505
372356	223	30724	2		164	12746	276	30338
50248	7	3719	14	4941	297	20589	1227	496533
569361	226	97489	8	6446	9310	551873	3711	1299348
516168	43	384828	265	1566	1323	170210	9682	936064
212276	193	59590	1	8	795	82165	2884	253474
233599	77	45091	261	7588	512	247984	12032	1041805
437547	318	157271	13	102	1442	96644	1138	222223
333838	453	238815	6	270	2891	105136	1261	258349
131603	324	34122	15	59	319	36575	2266	159913
467250	520	185269	3	136	565	212953	881	205708
534375	370	193742	25	370	911	264339	1029	166916
253692	239	76148	593	1453	2547	166925	493	100582
279965	101	78808	3	81	827	84877	609	80775
22161	21	19728	192		57	7194	8	2458
589467	262	251555	6	439	976	530745	1945	239961
1390514	462	379404	7	213	1478	422498	2153	528924
276153	534	70571	14	383	1396	87533	1757	186851
229487	432	217431	75	666	1007	127683	1977	321444
	5	725						
140226	95	29568	29	419	496	74954	257	51510
71122	43	14507	3	3	148	33128	41	14542
14871	6	2237	94	1824	87	1558	102	1016
20815	34	6406			100	3398	19	2699
67561	94	40932	10	7	229	4711	938	58850

C-2-32 为残疾人提供

地区	单位数	年末职工人数	#女性	#残疾职工	#女残疾职工	残疾职工工资总额	残疾职工养老保险总额
全国	**14585**	**1113183**	**367219**	**429000**	**134628**	**18221518.6**	**271262.5**
中央级							
北京	528	23936	8373	9649	2985	22765.6	5585.3
天津	220	16238	4483	6263	1939	664832.3	3768.4
河北	449	28601	8723	11713	2965	21456.5	5157.2
山西	332	28062	7355	13014	3480	24092.3	3375.5
内蒙古	134	11177	3359	4463	1327	6591.7	1180.2
辽宁	1617	81486	24734	36491	9758	77116.7	20038.1
吉林	295	14817	4418	6787	1746	16388564.0	475.6
黑龙江	258	10222	3314	5249	1564	6371.6	1312.4
上海	776	60395	21608	19466	6752	97654.7	29279.4
江苏	2435	228994	84914	78486	29799	182920.2	54058.6
浙江	1724	171630	59186	60363	21561	172321.6	54364.8
安徽	335	17119	6342	6736	2071	13293.2	2602.7
福建	259	14818	5165	7355	1446	57297.2	10397.1
江西	285	24326	7281	9620	2570	100919.8	546.8
山东	1154	88288	25470	32943	9417	74205.1	24156.5
河南	680	54020	15986	23161	6636	34222.2	1343.9
湖北	478	31148	10076	12469	4296	26708.4	11800.8
湖南	407	26356	7554	13021	3542	20846.5	3401.8
广东	134	12508	3788	5310	1513	10735.8	903.4
广西	112	7619	2533	2893	785	48409.6	3317.6
海南	14	1388	383	1025	330	3894.5	9.5
重庆	613	57136	19449	21002	6322	59094.3	18814.8
四川	646	51148	17898	20360	5761	71292.7	10814.2
贵州	32	1882	495	798	312	1951.3	218.1
云南	223	23038	5659	9405	2198	13920.2	1496.3
西藏	7	205	70	99	31	150.6	23.0
陕西	176	10903	3308	3898	1322	6274.8	1704.6
甘肃	59	3055	1033	1169	341	2335.9	349.1
青海	20	1681	577	867	278	1836.9	12.4
宁夏	54	3935	985	1533	372	4515.1	6.7
新疆	129	7052	2700	3392	1209	4927.3	747.7

服务的机构总表

单位:个、人、万元

残疾职工补贴	纳税总额	增值税总额	营业税总额	所得税总额	应减免税金总额	实际减免税金总额	盈利总额
30939.1	**1397915.6**	**1130969.2**	**56935.7**	**178880.0**	**706746.2**	**660159.8**	**814055.7**
2525.7	20910.0	14058.3	1382.4	1503.6	25270.3	21074.9	1643.8
32.8	5571.8	4142.7	172.7	1231.3	3856.8	3257.7	2814.2
435.6	14957.1	11776.1	565.0	565.3	10849.9	7570.8	1067.7
494.9	21799.0	16842.4	476.6	478.1	15719.8	11010.2	5258.5
124.4	6361.9	5994.2	178.1	163.8	3669.2	2880.3	1425.3
185.6	44867.6	51013.9	899.5	4232.4	36688.8	39019.6	13280.5
28.6	1039.5	1182.4		5.5	1039.5	703.5	26.0
187.1	482.9	354.0	77.8	61.1	287.9	287.9	-155.9
8449.3	126839.9	76147.6	20195.6	49184.7	78045.5	73631.0	134450.5
3961.3	362396.9	298573.1	7966.9	36812.1	194588.6	170612.6	127827.4
982.5	456306.7	458918.1	6080.6	47526.9	144641.4	165699.2	356179.8
389.1	12672.9	11099.9	125.2	861.8	8106.9	7414.5	12194.2
125.0	2131.3	1382.3	60.6	48.7	842.4	1059.0	522.2
168.2	54583.8	2966.1	491.5	695.7	17267.3	18272.8	6385.2
6727.1	120719.1	66983.9	8509.0	19690.4	69651.2	62757.5	76528.0
92.2	10249.3	7057.3	192.1	794.5	7582.3	6579.7	2897.9
406.8	7042.3	9530.1	273.8	2372.6	7876.3	6792.1	3969.0
1101.3	5367.8	3014.2	679.4	165.9	6301.1	4639.1	1193.2
234.3	8160.9	2791.2	117.6	349.9	4309.3	3669.9	3206.5
15.8	1177.4	859.4	103.9	3.8	382.1	358.7	-40.7
	250.0	223.0		10.0	250.0	223.0	70.0
1216.5	103162.2	64385.5	6458.8	11615.1	57994.0	39084.6	61726.8
2693.6	3935.3	3828.2	747.6	232.6	5546.1	6453.9	1809.4
51.6	86.2	85.0	1.2		32.9	32.9	43.5
131.7	2644.2	4508.2	227.9	6.4	1879.7	3706.8	-9547.0
101.3	1500.7	11200.2	301.7	252.5	825.9	566.3	8036.9
14.3							
21.0	38.0				234.7	234.7	
6.7	605.0		605.0		1526.0	1526.0	355.0
34.8	2055.9	2051.9	45.2	15.3	1480.3	1040.6	887.8

C-2-32续表

地区	执行企业会计制度单位财务指标			
	固定资产原价	营业收入	费用合计	营业利润
全国	**17767294.8**	**43931671.3**	**5375459.6**	**1215711.1**
中央级				
北京	382775.3	541965.3	93766.3	3227.0
天津	226726.8	595033.3	82940.5	5265.8
河北	472407.3	977943.6	98191.4	3381.7
山西	233583.3	224547.0	34049.9	-4661.1
内蒙古	64064.2	87967.6	13577.7	4822.6
辽宁	1380683.9	1615628.0	191083.0	34736.3
吉林	126697.3	246880.7	27375.4	-342.8
黑龙江	691777.6	154714.7	35637.0	1474.5
上海	1257943.6	2709011.7	184284.2	149297.4
江苏	3334341.0	11042189.0	1181118.0	217968.0
浙江	5019092.8	14282178.7	2139161.0	532242.9
安徽	158836.1	909407.0	66896.3	19951.1
福建	134855.4	251556.0	45391.1	-78.1
江西	100224.9	2006219.1	18927.7	4331.2
山东	1083350.3	1749100.7	337068.4	133847.4
河南	333675.2	501195.3	86526.3	21163.9
湖北	294355.7	457264.7	89469.3	3497.2
湖南	263527.6	630231.2	54681.6	5801.6
广东	205146.7	271151.3	31973.2	5656.0
广西	59960.3	272962.7	12084.2	-1955.4
海南	15327.4	31783.3	5257.7	31.4
重庆	644683.5	1838348.0	214625.9	34809.7
四川	481721.5	1275622.8	112930.6	6174.9
贵州	5637.0	15129.9	2367.9	901.9
云南	375641.4	738799.5	134892.4	10344.7
西藏	3598.0	498.0	359.0	139.0
陕西	142359.5	314194.7	42907.6	19982.4
甘肃	29316.3	10481.7	2464.8	84.8
青海	7621.6	15681.5	3636.0	195.6
宁夏	86038.8	68230.5	7169.0	-1925.3
新疆	151324.5	95753.8	24646.2	5344.8

单位：万元

执行行政事业单位会计制度财务指标				
固定资产原价	上年结转和结余	本年收入合计	本年支出合计	收支结余
20726.8	**316.4**	**33477.5**	**29280.9**	**6417.3**
84.0		245.0	237.0	
5807.6		6167.1	7122.2	1.6
561.0	-42.4	2048.9	545.9	1460.6
14.9		42.6	42.6	
3656.4	100.0	4490.5	3612.1	978.5
154.0		10370.5	7478.4	2892.1
		15.0	16.7	
5596.7	-236.0	1650.6	1904.5	-236.0
2041.5	476.7	3309.8	3169.9	727.8
1413.4	18.1	2148.3	2780.5	
45.0		53.0	53.0	
465.3		640.5	615.1	
887.0		2295.7	1703.0	592.7

C-2-33 为残疾人提供

地 区	单位数	年末职工人数	#女 性	#残疾职工	#女残疾职工	残疾职工工资总额	残疾职工养老保险总额
全 国	**11435**	**883187**	**295865**	**335109**	**108040**	**18034756.9**	**216928.9**
中央级							
北 京	498	22357	7603	9186	2804	21702.9	5178.2
天 津	219	16233	4483	6261	1939	664829.1	3767.3
河 北	309	21185	6007	8651	2079	15514.0	3837.3
山 西	171	18067	5372	8501	2656	15850.7	2440.6
内蒙古	54	4042	1601	1312	555	2836.5	312.3
辽 宁	1294	62349	18849	28813	7427	66211.2	17062.7
吉 林	285	14167	4223	6564	1671	16388484.0	475.6
黑龙江	224	9179	3021	4729	1450	5918.2	1295.5
上 海	762	59917	21469	19324	6736	97230.2	29117.9
江 苏	2351	224195	82969	76525	29148	178761.0	44653.7
浙 江	1526	155551	54705	54528	19639	154983.6	48997.0
安 徽	215	12101	4467	4667	1494	9990.1	1617.4
福 建	133	7190	2629	3374	426	54258.5	10279.1
江 西	242	19265	5882	7797	2496	96942.8	371.7
山 东	1011	79318	23025	29710	8426	67597.6	22407.6
河 南	515	39601	11827	17196	4551	25259.7	1248.8
湖 北	244	15326	4759	6435	2250	13507.0	887.6
湖 南	266	17763	5543	8439	2534	14218.5	2285.2
广 东	98	9498	3105	4215	1173	9106.7	771.5
广 西	40	2426	738	884	249	43588.2	1164.6
海 南	7	419	124	381	111	674.5	9.5
重 庆	334	26137	7864	9418	2542	22793.0	7828.5
四 川	268	20718	7980	8100	2564	48361.2	7895.4
贵 州	8	275	96	134	46	379.5	36.1
云 南	75	8529	1621	3309	750	5461.6	779.2
西 藏							
陕 西	147	8814	2582	2997	921	4403.0	1166.2
甘 肃	43	2225	859	891	304	1853.1	325.4
青 海	4	102	60	18	2	32.0	
宁 夏	12	599	167	216	82	129.8	
新 疆	80	5639	2235	2534	1015	3878.7	717.0

工作岗位的福利企业

单位：人、万元

残疾职工补贴	纳税总额	增值税总额	营业税总额	所得税总额	应减免税金总额	实际减免税金总额	盈利总额
27455.4	**1268069.1**	**1027521.5**	**47194.0**	**165435.8**	**628857.6**	**591639.3**	**752759.5**
2503.2	19246.3	13844.3	548.9	1146.0	24053.5	19921.4	615.0
32.8	5571.8	4142.7	172.7	1231.3	3856.8	3257.7	2814.2
258.8	10707.1	9665.5	544.8	385.6	8010.2	5995.5	2080.3
448.1	11976.0	10169.7	443.2	477.4	7145.3	5533.7	3136.3
51.6	1927.6	1683.9	29.0	77.0	1230.4	931.5	386.0
183.6	36765.6	43641.4	753.0	3216.9	30344.3	33924.4	7863.2
28.6	1039.5	1182.4		5.5	1039.5	703.5	26.0
181.0	482.9	354.0	77.8	61.1	287.9	287.9	-155.9
8449.3	126839.9	76147.6	20195.6	49184.7	78045.5	73631.0	134203.3
3932.0	360083.9	294150.1	7803.2	36736.2	192240.3	169371.7	126258.8
982.5	436918.7	431881.1	6080.6	46671.9	135381.4	152290.2	349599.8
242.7	11496.3	10217.0	108.8	767.8	7480.9	6823.0	11518.1
99.7	1558.3	862.3	45.6	36.7	511.9	828.5	522.2
68.0	54583.8	2962.1	491.5	695.7	17263.3	18272.8	6385.2
6458.8	110596.2	61281.4	8191.4	18428.7	62047.7	58006.5	72266.0
87.0	9038.9	6019.4	185.9	707.5	7080.4	6340.8	2467.4
122.7	6819.3	4480.9	54.9	1703.0	3607.5	3163.0	596.0
495.6	4752.0	2925.2	679.4	165.9	6034.7	4331.0	1114.8
196.2	7646.2	2542.4	103.8	334.9	3838.4	3268.0	3264.7
2.8	478.8	217.0	65.3	3.8	36.5	32.0	31.0
	250.0	223.0		10.0	250.0	223.0	70.0
279.6	42894.6	34306.7	128.0	3110.1	34731.6	21583.3	18669.9
2181.9	1230.0	864.1	150.0	20.0	1109.3	566.6	2608.8
21.3	86.2	85.0	1.2		20.9	20.9	43.5
23.5	2167.4	1218.6		6.4	1291.7	1025.2	-1913.5
82.3	892.0	10431.5	301.4	238.7	445.8	284.9	7439.6
12.5							
29.3	2019.8	2022.2	38.0	13.0	1471.9	1021.3	848.8

C-2-33续表1

地区	单位数	年末职工人数	受教育程度		职业资
			大学专科人数	大学本科及以上人数	助理社会工作师人数
全　国	**11435**	**883187**	**59341**	**24454**	**766**
中央级					
北　京	498	22357	1745	706	22
天　津	219	16233	959	322	54
河　北	309	21185	880	474	5
山　西	171	18067	1006	588	5
内蒙古	54	4042	231	64	6
辽　宁	1294	62349	3343	1263	66
吉　林	285	14167	515	293	34
黑龙江	224	9179	605	283	4
上　海	762	59917	1748	519	61
江　苏	2351	224195	18413	8476	179
浙　江	1526	155551	8239	3254	74
安　徽	215	12101	916	227	22
福　建	133	7190	155	54	3
江　西	242	19265	719	192	5
山　东	1011	79318	8751	3900	48
河　南	515	39601	1899	547	12
湖　北	244	15326	475	272	3
湖　南	266	17763	1055	227	7
广　东	98	9498	549	469	68
广　西	40	2426	87	27	1
海　南	7	419	4		
重　庆	334	26137	2091	1102	27
四　川	268	20718	2732	505	23
贵　州	8	275	31	12	
云　南	75	8529	307	36	4
西　藏					
陕　西	147	8814	1006	386	25
甘　肃	43	2225	82	30	1
青　海	4	102	4		5
宁　夏	12	599	12	8	1
新　疆	80	5639	782	218	1

单位:个、人、人次、时

格水平	年龄结构				志愿服务	
社会工作师人数	35岁及以下人数	36岁至45岁人数	46岁至55岁人数	56岁及以上人数	志愿者服务人次数	志愿服务时间
626	**283212**	**348260**	**199060**	**52655**	**36266**	**66345.0**
10	5907	10071	5244	1135	800	800.0
16	6510	5819	3063	841	450	1700.0
14	8575	7964	4023	623	880	4610.0
	5402	6763	4309	1593		
6	800	1428	862	952		
42	17163	27851	14205	3130	262	578.0
24	3354	5891	2912	2010		
2	2434	3782	2438	525		
45	19248	19330	15374	5965	870	2760.0
74	64771	90968	53881	14575	11317	19665.0
274	46177	54741	43271	11362	18637	28064.0
5	3605	5722	2522	252	641	1285.0
4	2317	3666	970	237	12	42.0
2	7991	8298	2585	391	18	
12	31779	29504	14804	3231	1530	4625.0
20	19437	13607	5317	1240	8	20.0
1	4627	7132	3024	543	10	80.0
2	3784	10334	3005	640	456	1189.0
34	4074	3919	1219	286		
	855	842	656	73		
3	239	118	48	14		
11	7627	10567	6650	1293	105	220.0
13	7842	8499	3548	829		
	75	120	67	13	21	168.0
1	2231	3618	2415	265		
5	3820	3314	1466	214	189	399.0
1	481	1287	281	176	60	140.0
	10	50	19	23		
	268	218	86	27		
5	1809	2837	796	197		

C-2-33续表2

地区	执行企业会计制度单位财务指标			
	固定资产原价	营业收入	费用合计	营业利润
全国	**15231258.3**	**37954044.1**	**4625273.8**	**1116346.6**
中央级				
北京	346746.7	512159.2	81621.3	3165.0
天津	226640.8	594986.3	82921.3	5273.8
河北	356402.8	804451.1	64669.3	8859.7
山西	142827.9	137208.7	27077.2	-4534.9
内蒙古	31137.9	57809.5	6705.8	632.0
辽宁	1237182.3	1197110.1	146658.9	28594.7
吉林	109824.3	225034.7	22604.4	1213.2
黑龙江	683595.6	143752.7	33633.0	1495.0
上海	1253830.2	2697425.2	180952.1	148960.4
江苏	3282206.3	10922399.8	1170554.2	217264.0
浙江	4707055.2	13124354.8	2063483.7	524851.4
安徽	111976.5	670945.5	42868.4	8534.1
福建	81311.3	153279.8	15632.7	-281.8
江西	91945.9	2000399.1	18951.7	4331.2
山东	976984.4	1582302.9	307976.9	124659.4
河南	281341.3	366846.4	66157.4	9641.0
湖北	112884.2	164370.6	36079.5	6420.8
湖南	96329.3	469622.0	26399.8	963.8
广东	190751.9	214670.9	23884.9	5271.1
广西	22804.4	87619.5	7736.9	-1891.0
海南	1329.1	2610.0	13.0	
重庆	289035.9	621883.7	80855.8	7643.9
四川	231176.9	702326.0	51076.6	445.5
贵州	1338.0	5925.1	621.7	362.3
云南	115070.6	224170.4	10072.7	-7798.3
西藏				
陕西	83057.4	177497.9	28932.6	16712.9
甘肃	8406.6	5601.2	463.7	-34.2
青海	570.0			
宁夏	11928.0	2128.0	2693.1	67.0
新疆	145566.6	85153.0	23975.2	5524.6

单位：万元

执行行政事业单位会计制度财务指标				
固定资产原价	上年结转和结余	本年收入合计	本年支出合计	收支结余
1050.8	**0.5**	**1565.9**	**2291.7**	**111.8**
14.9		42.6	42.6	
154.0		56.5	56.5	
		15.0	16.7	
558.5	0.5	1104.2	1104.2	111.8
278.4		294.6	1018.7	
45.0		53.0	53.0	

C-2-34 民政部门直属

地 区	单位数	年末职工人数	#女 性	#残疾职工	#女残疾职工	残疾职工工资总额	残疾职工养老保险总额
全 国	**24**	**1602**	**507**	**121**	**21**	**538.7**	**37.5**
中央级							
北 京	1	97	25	7		85.3	
天 津	1	5		2		3.2	1.1
河 北	1	17	4	2	1	3.9	
山 西	1	83	30	2		7.5	
内蒙古	1	41		25		68.0	13.0
辽 宁							
吉 林							
黑龙江	1	23	6	8	2	17.0	6.8
上 海	1	77	30	2		21.8	
江 苏	1	155	43	2		20.0	
浙 江							
安 徽	1	10	10	2	1	4.0	
福 建							
江 西	1	68	8	14		16.8	0.3
山 东	1	116	30	4		13.9	5.0
河 南	2	128	34	12	2	6.9	1.5
湖 北	2	152	43	3	2	9.6	
湖 南	1	100	36	3	1	15.8	
广 东	2	78	17	9	2	35.2	
广 西							
海 南							
重 庆							
四 川	1	155	74	3	2	108.4	
贵 州	1	58	22	2	1	10.0	
云 南	1	74	33	5	1	45.0	
西 藏							
陕 西	1	88	24	12	4	39.0	9.0
甘 肃	1	44	20	1	1	1.8	0.8
青 海							
宁 夏							
新 疆	1	33	18	1	1	5.6	

康复辅具机构

单位：个、人、万元

残疾职工补贴	纳税总额	增值税总额	营业税总额	所得税总额	应减免税金总额	实际减免税金总额	盈利总额
10.5	**75.5**	**259.1**	**11.6**	**2.9**	**373.4**	**571.4**	**-23.4**
3.8	15.0	10.0	2.6	1.8	14.0	14.0	-25.0
4.5							
	52.8	39.9	4.5	1.1			1.6
0.2		4.0			4.0		
2.0							
	7.7	3.2	4.5		355.4	355.4	
		202.0				202.0	

C-2-34续表1

地区	单位数	年末职工人数	受教育程度		职业资
			大学专科人数	大学本科及以上人数	助理社会工作师人数
全国	**24**	**1602**	**444**	**345**	**36**
中央级					
北京	1	97	27	29	
天津	1	5			
河北	1	17	3	5	
山西	1	83	18	27	
内蒙古	1	41			
辽宁					
吉林					
黑龙江	1	23	5		
上海	1	77	13	7	
江苏	1	155	80	15	2
浙江					
安徽	1	10	2		
福建					
江西	1	68	8	4	1
山东	1	116	27	22	
河南	2	128	30	30	6
湖北	2	152	40	24	
湖南	1	100	25	32	1
广东	2	78	21	36	12
广西					
海南					
重庆					
四川	1	155	55	50	10
贵州	1	58	12	25	
云南	1	74	33	9	1
西藏					
陕西	1	88	27	17	2
甘肃	1	44	11	9	1
青海					
宁夏					
新疆	1	33	7	4	

单位：个、人、人次、时

格水平	年龄结构			
社会工作师人数	35岁及以下人数	36岁至45岁人数	46岁至55岁人数	56岁及以上人数
32	**480**	**421**	**499**	**202**
1	46	21	21	9
			5	
	5	4	4	4
2	15	26	39	3
		2	12	27
	13	5	4	1
	5	35	27	10
1	87	40	20	8
1	2	4	4	
	2	12	17	37
	10	31	65	10
7	53	30	28	17
1	39	34	56	23
1	33	30	23	14
7	26	29	18	5
8	76	24	46	9
	18	24	14	2
1	29	9	34	2
	8	38	29	13
2	7	5	28	4
	6	18	5	4

C-2-34续表2

地区	执行企业会计制度单位财务指标			
	固定资产原价	营业收入	费用合计	营业利润
全　国	**26239.0**	**17176.4**	**7846.4**	**-706.0**
中央级				
北　京	2239.6	3584.0	956.1	-376.9
天　津	86.0	47.0	19.2	-8.0
河　北				
山　西	8534.0	522.0	193.0	-102.0
内蒙古	205.0	130.0	153.0	
辽　宁				
吉　林				
黑龙江	185.3	164.3	39.5	9.5
上　海	2583.1	2069.7	983.8	-18.7
江　苏				
浙　江				
安　徽	474.0	979.0	394.0	-166.0
福　建				
江　西				
山　东	3261.0	2596.0	1383.0	-10.0
河　南	4502.0	1983.0	775.0	-179.0
湖　北	25.7	36.6	21.8	-0.2
湖　南				
广　东	1527.3	3479.8	2426.0	271.3
广　西				
海　南				
重　庆				
四　川				
贵　州				
云　南				
西　藏				
陕　西	2616.0	1585.0	502.0	-126.0
甘　肃				
青　海				
宁　夏				
新　疆				

单位:万元

执行行政事业单位会计制度财务指标				
固定资产原价	上年结转和结余	本年收入合计	本年支出合计	收支结余
19676.0	**315.9**	**31911.6**	**26989.2**	**6305.5**
84.0		245.0	237.0	
5807.6		6167.1	7122.2	1.6
561.0	-42.4	2048.9	545.9	1460.6
3656.4	100.0	4490.5	3612.1	978.5
		10314.0	7421.9	2892.1
5596.7	-236.0	1650.6	1904.5	-236.0
1483.0	476.2	2205.6	2065.7	616.0
1135.0	18.1	1853.7	1761.8	
465.3		640.5	615.1	
887.0		2295.7	1703.0	592.7

C-2-35 其他为残疾人

地 区	单位数	年末职工人数	#女 性	#残疾职工	#女残疾职工
全 国	**3126**	**228394**	**70847**	**93770**	**26567**
中央级					
北 京	29	1482	745	456	181
天 津					
河 北	139	7399	2712	3060	885
山 西	160	9912	1953	4511	824
内蒙古	79	7094	1758	3126	772
辽 宁	323	19137	5885	7678	2331
吉 林	10	650	195	223	75
黑龙江	33	1020	287	512	112
上 海	13	401	109	140	16
江 苏	83	4644	1902	1959	651
浙 江	198	16079	4481	5835	1922
安 徽	119	5008	1865	2067	576
福 建	126	7628	2536	3981	1020
江 西	42	4993	1391	1809	74
山 东	142	8854	2415	3229	991
河 南	163	14291	4125	5953	2083
湖 北	232	15670	5274	6031	2044
湖 南	140	8493	1975	4579	1007
广 东	34	2932	666	1086	338
广 西	72	5193	1795	2009	536
海 南	7	969	259	644	219
重 庆	279	30999	11585	11584	3780
四 川	377	30275	9844	12257	3195
贵 州	23	1549	377	662	265
云 南	147	14435	4005	6091	1447
西 藏	7	205	70	99	31
陕 西	28	2001	702	889	397
甘 肃	15	786	154	277	36
青 海	16	1579	517	849	276
宁 夏	42	3336	818	1317	290
新 疆	48	1380	447	857	193

服务的机构

单位:个、人、万元

残疾职工工资总额	残疾职工养老保险总额	残疾职工补贴	纳税总额	增值税总额
186223.0	**54296.1**	**3473.2**	**129771.0**	**103188.6**
977.4	407.1	22.5	1663.7	214.0
5938.6	1319.9	176.8	4250.0	2110.6
8234.1	934.9	46.8	9823.0	6672.7
3687.2	854.9	69.0	4419.3	4300.3
10905.5	2975.4	2.0	8102.0	7372.5
80.0				
436.4	10.1	1.6		
402.7	161.5			
4139.2	9404.9	29.3	2260.2	4383.1
17338.0	5367.8		19388.0	27037.0
3299.1	985.3	146.4	1176.6	882.9
3038.7	118.0	25.3	573.0	520.0
3960.2	174.8	100.0		
6593.6	1743.9	266.3	10122.9	5702.5
8955.6	93.6	5.2	1210.4	1037.9
13191.8	10913.2	284.1	223.0	5049.2
6612.2	1116.6	605.7	615.8	89.0
1593.9	131.9	38.1	514.7	248.8
4821.4	2153.0	13.0	698.6	642.4
3220.0				
36301.3	10986.3	936.9	60267.6	30078.8
22823.1	2918.8	511.7	2697.6	2960.9
1561.8	182.0	30.3		
8413.6	717.1	108.2	476.8	3289.6
150.6	23.0			
1832.8	529.4	19.0	608.7	566.7
481.0	22.9	1.8		
1804.9	12.4	21.0	38.0	
4385.3	6.7	6.7	605.0	
1043.0	30.7	5.5	36.1	29.7

C-2-35续表1

地区	营业税总额	所得税总额	应减免税金总额	实际减免税金总额	盈利总额
全国	**9730.1**	**13441.3**	**77515.2**	**67949.1**	**61319.6**
中央级					
北京	833.5	357.6	1216.8	1153.5	1028.8
天津					
河北	20.2	179.7	2839.7	1575.3	-1012.6
山西	33.4	0.7	8574.5	5476.5	2122.2
内蒙古	146.5	85.0	2424.8	1934.8	1064.3
辽宁	146.5	1015.5	6344.5	5095.2	5417.3
吉林					
黑龙江					
上海					247.2
江苏	159.2	74.8	2348.3	1240.9	1567.0
浙江		855.0	9260.0	13409.0	6580.0
安徽	16.4	94.0	626.0	591.5	676.1
福建	15.0	12.0	330.5	230.5	
江西					
山东	317.6	1261.7	7603.5	4751.0	4262.0
河南	6.2	87.0	501.9	238.9	430.5
湖北	218.9	669.6	4268.8	3629.1	3373.0
湖南			266.4	308.1	78.4
广东	13.8	15.0	470.9	401.9	-58.2
广西	38.6		345.6	326.7	-71.7
海南					
重庆	6330.8	8505.0	23262.4	17501.3	43056.9
四川	593.1	212.6	4081.4	5531.9	-799.4
贵州			12.0	12.0	
云南	227.9		588.0	2681.6	-7633.5
西藏					
陕西	0.3	13.8	380.1	79.4	597.3
甘肃					
青海			234.7	234.7	
宁夏	605.0		1526.0	1526.0	355.0
新疆	7.2	2.3	8.4	19.3	39.0

单位：个、人、万元

单位数	年末职工人数	受教育程度		职业资格水平	
		大学专科人数	大学本科及以上人数	助理社会工作师人数	社会工作师人数
3126	**228394**	**15179**	**6228**	**512**	**110**
29	1482	91	59	2	5
139	7399	285	103	25	6
160	9912	100	29	7	2
79	7094	1108	291	2	1
323	19137	1000	571	13	9
10	650	91	50	15	8
33	1020	37	7		
13	401	3	7		8
83	4644	285	68	8	8
198	16079	678	205	6	1
119	5008	330	114	121	1
126	7628	60	45		
42	4993	6	10		
142	8854	388	172	4	9
163	14291	2439	1844		
232	15670	929	407	175	1
140	8493	522	49	39	4
34	2932	99	18		
72	5193	115	114	3	
7	969	82	37	18	2
279	30999	2330	998	31	29
377	30275	3051	719	16	10
23	1549	192			
147	14435	295	151	11	3
7	205	1			
28	2001	259	32	11	
15	786	45	10		
16	1579	18	4	5	3
42	3336	177	59		
48	1380	163	55		

C-2-35续表2

地区	年龄结构				志愿服务	
	35岁及以下人数	36岁至45岁人数	46岁至55岁人数	56岁及以上人数	志愿者服务人次数	志愿服务时间
全　国	**76230**	**96032**	**47114**	**9018**	**12207**	**24648.0**
中央级						
北　京	665	476	308	33	146	236.0
天　津						
河　北	2274	3227	1545	353	50	182.0
山　西	2996	3974	2297	645		
内蒙古	1593	2593	2641	267		
辽　宁	4986	8541	3950	1660		
吉　林	183	209	202	56		
黑龙江	186	553	238	43		
上　海	184	136	39	42		
江　苏	1193	2200	1033	218	47	94.0
浙　江	4060	7251	3946	822		
安　徽	1658	1967	1141	242	305	706.0
福　建	2847	3169	1451	161		
江　西	1903	2101	958	31		
山　东	2549	3686	2297	322	20	38.0
河　南	6341	6346	1269	335		
湖　北	4132	7496	3688	354	52	81.0
湖　南	2569	4158	1605	161	341	905.0
广　东	1364	958	576	34		
广　西	1314	2229	1481	169		
海　南	712	189	59	9		
重　庆	9861	12213	7429	1496	11050	22200.0
四　川	12920	11838	4681	836		
贵　州	688	486	275	100	186	206.0
云　南	5548	6126	2378	383		
西　藏	45	94	50	16		
陕　西	747	740	439	75		
甘　肃	345	364	70	7		
青　海	666	746	144	23	10	
宁　夏	1186	1365	672	113		
新　疆	515	601	252	12		

单位：万元、人、人次、时

执行企业会计制度单位财务指标			
固定资产原价	营业收入	费用合计	营业利润
2509797.5	**5960450.8**	**743641.4**	**100070.5**
33789.0	26222.1	11188.9	438.9
116004.5	173492.5	33522.1	-5478.0
82221.4	86816.3	6779.7	-24.2
32721.3	30028.1	6718.9	4190.6
143501.6	418517.9	44424.1	6141.6
16873.0	21846.0	4771.0	-1556.0
7996.7	10797.7	1964.5	-30.0
1530.3	9516.8	2348.3	355.7
52134.7	119789.2	10563.8	704.0
312037.6	1157823.9	75677.3	7391.5
46385.6	237482.5	23793.5	11583.0
53544.1	98276.2	29781.7	203.7
8279.0	5820.0		
103104.9	164201.8	27708.5	9198.0
47831.9	132365.9	19593.9	11701.9
181445.8	292857.5	53368.0	-2923.4
167198.3	160609.2	28620.2	4837.8
12867.5	53000.6	6196.1	113.6
37155.9	185343.2	4354.3	-64.4
13998.3	29173.3	5244.7	31.4
355647.6	1216464.3	133770.1	27165.8
250544.6	573296.8	61957.3	5729.4
4299.0	9204.8	1807.0	539.6
260570.8	514629.1	124869.0	18143.0
3598.0	498.0	359.0	139.0
56686.1	135111.8	13475.5	3395.5
20909.7	4880.5	2001.1	119.0
7051.6	15681.5	3636.0	195.6
74110.8	66102.5	4475.9	-1992.3
5757.9	10600.8	671.0	-179.8

C-2-36 残疾人教育

地　区	职业培训基地数（个）	本年度城镇职业培训人数（人次）	残疾人就业服务机构（个）	残疾人就业人数（万人）
全　国	**6942**	**393242**	**2820**	**2108.2**
北　京	61	11003	17	14.6
天　津	30	2929	20	10.9
河　北	203	25242	188	103.4
山　西	501	8476	122	47.7
内蒙古	72	10495	80	37.6
辽　宁	165	14561	117	71.6
吉　林	208	12141	68	46.5
黑龙江	132	14308	126	34.9
上　海	28	16472	18	9.2
江　苏	252	19576	112	96.3
浙　江	352	15773	103	43.1
安　徽	86	12326	95	87.3
福　建	352	11114	92	39.6
江　西	231	9360	87	72.1
山　东	1031	19698	135	147.9
河　南	269	38179	162	223.8
湖　北	321	10367	105	115.4
湖　南	265	7387	133	123.1
广　东	186	13835	135	77.8
广　西	47	10915	119	73.1
海　南	11	2480	21	8.2
重　庆	39	6050	38	60.5
四　川	474	36657	137	191.4
贵　州	85	5146	80	81.4
云　南	136	8773	138	101.6
西　藏	5	116	2	1.5
陕　西	509	12856	120	72.6
甘　肃	63	19723	97	63.6
青　海	38	1309	31	5.9
宁　夏	40	2028	19	12.8
新　疆	747	12821	92	29.0
兵团	3	1126	10	1.9
黑龙江农垦			1	1.6

指标解释：

1.职业培训基地数：指承担着残疾人就业前培训，在职培训、下岗失业人员转岗转业培训、农村务工人员培训等项职能的实体的个数。

2.本年度城镇职业培训人数：指本年度城镇残疾人中在各类职业培训机构（基地）接受培训（含统计时正在接受培训）的实际人次数。

3.残疾人就业服务机构：指截止到本年度12月31日，省（自治区、直辖市）、地（州、盟）、市（地市级市、县级市）、县（旗）、市辖区各级残联所建的残疾人就业服务机构数。

4.残疾人就业人数：包括城镇就业残疾人和农村在业残疾人，其中城镇就业残疾人指截止到本年度12月31日城镇（非农业户口）残疾人集中就业、分散按比例就业（包括实施按比例就业前已在社会各单位就业的残疾人）、辅助性就业、公益性岗位就业、个体及其他形式就业的人数，农村在业残疾人指截止到本年度12月31日农村残疾人（农业户口）从事各种生产劳动，包括种植业、养殖业、家庭手工业及在各种类型企事业、服务业、商业及个体从业的实际人数。

就业情况

省市县乡残联实有人员（人）	高等院校录取残疾考生（人）	接收托养服务残疾人（人）	农村贫困残疾人危房改造（户）
111471	**10186**	**1005127**	**68517**
1255	251	120372	551
964	131	30837	206
5566	339	20663	1327
4515	253	14823	
3095	315	18555	7292
4120	320	32288	2497
3004	444	15413	42
3335	202	17457	195
1040	86	30072	282
5009	663	65180	588
5736	562	111089	3122
3364	460	17113	6534
2488	271	25628	3809
3812	271	19578	2837
5903	520	55432	1186
8074	819	22654	938
3277	351	22731	290
5276	357	22831	7948
7388	371	33723	6118
3267	275	35602	2749
643	74	15754	
1932	265	28445	4096
8517	470	48022	1162
2739	327	14991	442
3570	594	25784	1670
277	12	5150	
4495	329	22921	2209
3966	296	20620	4859
1051	138	22863	1694
709	102	15317	
2760	267	42578	3726
101	46	9095	134
223	5	1546	14

5.高等院校录取残疾考生：指本年度高等特殊教育院校和普通高等院校录取的残疾考生数。
6.接收托养服务残疾人：指本年度接受机构托养和居家托养的智力、精神、无生活自理能力、长期需要专人照料或护理的残疾人数。
7.农村贫困残疾人危房改造：指本年度完成危房改造的农村贫困残疾人户数。

C-2-37 孤儿和

地 区	孤儿数	集中供养孤儿	社会散居孤儿	收养登记合计	中国公民收养登记
全 国	**502105**	**91712**	**410393**	**22348**	**19406**
中央级					
北 京	2152	1740	412	174	122
天 津	862	599	263	87	61
河 北	16060	2137	13923	377	348
山 西	13545	2783	10762	258	85
内蒙古	5526	1175	4351	183	84
辽 宁	7727	3242	4485	221	166
吉 林	5196	1510	3686	32	17
黑龙江	7465	1459	6006	44	34
上 海	1964	1864	100	199	145
江 苏	17691	3420	14271	2329	2128
浙 江	4827	2483	2344	3390	3308
安 徽	26993	3525	23468	878	763
福 建	6012	1982	4030	1264	1187
江 西	23133	5400	17733	414	291
山 东	17534	3232	14302	2414	2280
河 南	43261	5321	37940	729	373
湖 北	23704	3919	19785	748	644
湖 南	43616	5428	38188	1086	1007
广 东	38845	9924	28921	1458	1012
广 西	23614	2405	21209	1586	1435
海 南	1636	333	1303	112	112
重 庆	11085	1264	9821	214	173
四 川	29684	4086	25598	1012	950
贵 州	21047	2802	18245	284	207
云 南	23802	2111	21691	1565	1450
西 藏	5798	5581	217	475	475
陕 西	12515	2631	9884	377	188
甘 肃	20608	2963	17645	96	53
青 海	16268	1412	14856	42	31
宁 夏	6890	438	6452	47	37
新 疆	23045	4543	18502	253	240

家庭收养

单位：人、件

香港居民	澳门居民	台湾居民	华侨	外国人收养登记	协议解除收养关系登记	#中国公民
105	**3**	**42**	**29**	**2942**	**388**	**385**
				52	1	1
				26	7	7
				29	9	9
				173		
1				99		
12	1	4	1	55	5	5
				15		
1		1		10	3	3
		6		54	4	4
		1	1	201	21	21
1		1	9	82	14	14
1				115	10	10
11	1	9	2	77	69	69
				123	64	64
1		3	4	134	49	49
		1	4	356	8	8
1		1	1	104	7	7
2		4		79	12	12
53	1	3		446	10	9
4		3		151	3	3
12		2	1			
3		2	1	41	12	11
2			1	62	49	49
				77	11	11
		1	4	115		
				189	18	17
				43	2	2
				11		
				10		
				13		

C-2-38 被收养的

地 区	被收养人合计	女性	残疾儿童	社会福利机构抚养的孤儿	#被外国人收养
全 国	**22363**	**14751**	**3290**	**10704**	**2804**
中央级					
北 京	174	94	51	51	51
天 津	87	48	23	56	26
河 北	380	226	52	166	29
山 西	258	61	16	223	173
内蒙古	183	82	18	117	99
辽 宁	221	124	30	102	52
吉 林	32	11		24	15
黑龙江	44	23	8	9	
上 海	199	152	57	100	54
江 苏	2329	1457	867	1074	201
浙 江	3397	2669	69	2014	81
安 徽	878	567	23	384	115
福 建	1264	973	87	459	75
江 西	416	325	115	268	123
山 东	2414	1465	210	866	134
河 南	729	374	392	544	350
湖 北	748	495	118	320	104
湖 南	1087	718	81	406	79
广 东	1460	1001	422	1174	446
广 西	1587	1271	162	621	151
海 南	112	84		66	
重 庆	214	123	36	68	39
四 川	1009	580	15	374	62
贵 州	285	207	71	159	77
云 南	1565	1124	102	214	2
西 藏	475	24		473	
陕 西	377	212	176	223	189
甘 肃	96	54	39	63	43
青 海	42	18	10	26	11
宁 夏	47	32	10	18	10
新 疆	254	157	30	42	13

儿童情况

单位：人

社会孤儿数	#被外国人收养	近亲属抚养人数	生父母有特殊困难无力抚养人数	#被外国人收养	其他
5645	**113**	**1143**	**539**	**9**	**4332**
97		3	2		21
		21	4		6
103		26	7		78
1		7	5		22
11		5	25		25
79		21	3		16
2			1		5
9		13	6	3	7
65		8			26
253		137	16		849
985		113	7		278
336		57	14		87
489		43	5		268
72		7	3		66
974		68	10		496
37		45	35	6	68
114		70	46		198
204		164	67		246
117		81	11		77
502		33	46		385
12		9	9		16
64		21	13		48
333		74	98		130
33		2	6		85
553	113	35	32		731
1		1			
69		12	36		37
14		7	3		9
6		4	1		5
21			4		4
89		56	24		43

C-2-39 救助、低保

地区	单位数	年末职工人数	女性	受教育 大学专科人数
全国	**965**	**7651**	**3428**	**2638**
中央级				
北京	16	122	66	30
天津	1	8	5	
河北	5	33	20	18
山西	92	750	354	278
内蒙古	19	233	130	64
辽宁	13	91	31	17
吉林	67	880	251	186
黑龙江	34	293	148	85
上海	7	92	54	16
江苏	7	19	6	2
浙江	14	68	42	15
安徽	26	104	36	36
福建	21	65	38	20
江西	68	430	207	162
山东	13	66	31	21
河南	47	368	174	114
湖北	68	626	294	274
湖南	77	737	294	289
广东	4	34	19	2
广西	106	543	292	195
海南	3	17	11	6
重庆	36	279	153	76
四川	52	265	130	114
贵州	56	879	361	377
云南	13	54	27	16
西藏	10	26	10	10
陕西	27	263	134	104
甘肃	21	141	51	34
青海				
宁夏	14	93	44	42
新疆	28	72	15	35

服务机构

单位：个、人

程度	职业资格水平		年龄结构	
大学本科及以上人数	助理社会工作师人数	社会工作师人数	35岁及以下人数	36岁至45岁人数
3104	**140**	**155**	**3760**	**2989**
84	6	7	51	44
8		2	8	
13		3	16	10
309	15	12	379	261
144	22	16	96	108
40		5	41	24
231	11	9	459	368
156	1	4	95	147
64	13	9	52	32
13	1	1	12	4
41	2	8	31	25
59	5	5	42	45
32	2	7	32	29
96	11	10	152	228
39	1	7	39	22
104	1	3	215	107
219	5	7	231	303
201	7	14	321	311
32	3		21	5
284	2	2	246	236
10		1	3	8
194	13	3	147	97
86	6	12	130	109
391	5	2	585	235
36	1		25	28
15			19	7
85	4	3	159	79
73		1	92	34
32	2	2	24	55
13	1		37	28

C-2-39续表

地区	年龄结构		志愿服务	
	46岁至55岁人数	56岁及以上人数	志愿者服务人次数	志愿服务时间
全国	**791**	**111**	**1737**	**5180.0**
中央级				
北京	24	3	30	60.0
天津				
河北	7			
山西	101	9	6	19.0
内蒙古	28	1		
辽宁	10	16		
吉林	50	3		
黑龙江	46	5		
上海	7	1		
江苏	3		15	40.0
浙江	10	2		
安徽	15	2	96	
福建	4			
江西	42	8	33	221.0
山东	5		3	10.0
河南	40	6		
湖北	79	13	12	36.0
湖南	87	18	812	2338.0
广东	7	1		
广西	58	3	100	700.0
海南	6			
重庆	31	4	382	1103.0
四川	21	5		
贵州	56	3	174	352.0
云南	1			
西藏				
陕西	22	3	54	241.0
甘肃	13	2	20	60.0
青海				
宁夏	12	2		
新疆	6	1		

单位：万元、人、人次、时

执行行政事业单位会计制度财务指标				
固定资产原价	上年结转和结余	本年收入合计	本年支出合计	收支结余
16314.6	**3305.9**	**87072.1**	**87074.4**	**5826.3**
262.6	291.7	13066.5	13147.2	244.7
126.1		696.8	378.3	
28.9		70.0	68.8	
1572.9	141.1	5764.7	5869.3	5.2
350.9	7.3	1726.4	1733.7	
40.7	6.5	509.1	484.1	
796.9	159.0	6311.2	5804.2	559.2
602.2		1139.8	1152.0	
612.5	530.9	11066.8	12233.4	34.6
10.0		107.4	107.4	
108.9	18.0	953.7	915.8	18.8
161.0	1.2	783.3	850.8	5.4
77.7	3.3	429.6	391.9	34.1
549.0	6.0	1561.3	1598.8	
77.2		398.6	398.6	
1128.3	175.0	1244.0	1204.1	31.3
1737.5	125.0	5929.1	6017.7	-33.5
1707.1	136.1	8734.8	7165.2	748.7
925.2	355.5	1213.0	1344.3	
1329.5	197.7	2968.3	2928.2	191.9
36.9	82.6	2871.2	2907.3	29.8
966.1	3.9	3743.5	3683.5	40.5
287.2	832.1	2312.2	2374.4	2.4
1389.3	170.5	3666.4	3719.3	35.2
19.7	59.5	7848.2	8442.2	3829.0
306.7		352.8	352.8	
461.7		1285.2	1224.1	49.0
399.2		121.5	285.6	
113.0	3.0	156.7	276.4	
129.7		40.0	15.0	

C-2-40 城市最低

地 区	城市最低生活保障人数	按人员性质分类			老年人	成	
		#女 性	#残疾人	#三无人员		在职人员	灵活就业
全 国	**17010975**	**7271290**	**1656916**	**438288**	**2934761**	**310890**	**3773190**
中央级							
北 京	84860	37268	18388	1763	13027	4674	10486
天 津	130705	65646	20190	1358	14977	3788	10712
河 北	550471	249798	43925	7603	95513	8589	111155
山 西	599298	265020	44353	8856	73083	15716	163952
内蒙古	602708	295716	57560	8	83060	1535	205381
辽 宁	718132	304990	114927	10268	97901	7337	99891
吉 林	725269	357165	81840	8340	120083	13	530332
黑龙江	1199994	503993	129914	23080	117904	7069	211458
上 海	175650	65114	29249	592	5296	12690	2056
江 苏	279810	123314	36376	4240	80462	4646	26872
浙 江	73220	27996	22483	3054	18300	2765	8386
安 徽	646672	276116	75502	32108	208403	5978	113392
福 建	129477	50814	20875	4442	33308	1852	24085
江 西	924083	382196	145366	50882	183943	25206	210786
山 东	372321	155929	30079	6921	64490	14364	80236
河 南	1079085	438891	73733	28484	214046	10758	199751
湖 北	846352	401423	45707	16149	154466	68049	281114
湖 南	1271969	523145	74507	44141	304037	14779	124590
广 东	296930	117965	36655	14033	66997	8432	64393
广 西	385308	146547	26179	19681	91873	6942	128834
海 南	83949	38118	9436	1552	11525	840	9069
重 庆	375219	171522	63035		67862	737	73746
四 川	1563548	604943	213500	49166	311675	16519	320091
贵 州	402010	163483	26926	14009	68818	4555	86027
云 南	981076	374836	53969	36186	153159	22539	222646
西 藏	46464	19937	3385	8205	9707	4532	8783
陕 西	508672	242728	25070	2822	37338	4714	114167
甘 肃	762050	297909	37242	8653	67577	7509	142273
青 海	176282	87968	7876	3039	25212	4714	31063
宁 夏	154272	66117	12729	3911	18672	1911	37127
新 疆	865119	414683	75940	24742	122047	17138	120336

生活保障

单位：人、户

年人		未成年人		城市最低生活保障户数
登记失业	未登记失业	在校生	其 他	
2641439	**3940229**	**2359345**	**1051121**	**9574057**
21677	13868	12231	8897	50130
38105	30337	19760	13026	77439
79952	141241	87085	26936	312482
61524	114893	130660	39470	310165
84942	167255	37811	22724	364139
179611	169550	126676	37166	414854
4842	3950	65937	112	470491
247414	438455	137596	40098	702577
55969	61417	36017	2205	121888
34079	85745	35061	12945	155244
10978	19548	8734	4509	50107
58708	161974	72328	25889	398448
20478	32151	12640	4963	75518
159440	141747	114638	88323	442816
91894	59869	42935	18533	201190
198492	235673	127979	92386	637747
110243	143147	60377	28956	489832
245434	337604	153460	92065	742333
31491	61935	49275	14407	151870
46323	42796	37003	31537	198698
5847	41732	9716	5220	38852
51141	98851	63180	19702	226019
230711	396109	187241	101202	925095
41937	115138	61370	24165	224566
168135	199452	152614	62531	613245
4570	8406	7355	3111	27776
82695	59022	132128	78608	254191
140915	219365	145141	39270	316776
18873	42118	34950	19352	86858
19106	36965	31662	8829	80941
95913	259916	165785	83984	411770

C-2-41 农村最低生活

地 区	农村最低生活保障人数	女 性	老年人	未成年人	残疾人
全 国	**49035544**	**17950423**	**20061001**	**5247896**	**4575465**
中央级					
北 京	48850	19815	20540	5757	17100
天 津	103701	42989	29180	17761	17991
河 北	2057594	735872	1251466	105819	167509
山 西	1224701	468746	719597	60758	137527
内蒙古	1164224	557924	683755	30650	89949
辽 宁	794627	290542	364467	56231	109617
吉 林	822267	394808	465806	29850	50220
黑龙江	1181589	469519	600101	63141	79935
上 海	30867	15398	10463	1664	10466
江 苏	1147947	445189	475823	124997	118628
浙 江	567628	206831	227564	73070	128604
安 徽	1963293	828458	936633	148302	273377
福 建	716811	260786	227503	78654	103180
江 西	1692827	618912	502636	275248	329861
山 东	2374164	876119	1426507	146644	194661
河 南	3929062	1180719	2035595	298469	359960
湖 北	1595368	718031	651135	110477	207065
湖 南	3178693	1054323	1391280	274646	197131
广 东	1536045	486243	483472	302823	147439
广 西	2921414	972810	1009402	488912	169659
海 南	187896	82953	41452	33186	15442
重 庆	502634	226274	125236	96745	83058
四 川	4054741	1257840	1832063	410835	667113
贵 州	3327023	1190548	1174822	493701	216463
云 南	4552840	1726937	1344596	507810	254796
西 藏	320234	120481	134280	61360	15206
陕 西	1616515	677567	554884	151884	139000
甘 肃	3369222	1227874	740718	487332	123394
青 海	317797	84608	55825	61995	17617
宁 夏	417384	144574	143529	31285	42188
新 疆	1317586	566733	400671	217890	91309

保障和临时救助

单位：人、户、户次

农村居民最低生活保障户数	临时救助户次	按户籍性质分类		按属地分类	
		城市家庭户次	农村家庭户次	当地常住人口户次	非当地常住人口户次
28462464	**6554018**	**2500662**	**4053356**	**6335043**	**218975**
29828	22005	8175	13830	21995	10
49052	83632	73549	10083	83607	25
1532916	179907	36311	143596	175106	4801
955622	199467	46803	152664	196358	3109
907009	251955	104503	147452	232877	19078
524218	308091	167464	140627	284651	23440
631540	104841	67159	37682	104466	375
741810	201255	90210	111045	198760	2495
24813	404396	358631	45765	399464	4932
625250	421217	141413	279804	418005	3212
362357	246636	43460	203176	244610	2026
1164222	166723	97808	68915	163757	2966
375987	81902	26877	55025	81282	620
819612	124923	57819	67104	123762	1161
1730832	239868	64780	175088	237704	2164
3090233	189833	53731	136102	178627	11206
1055225	362677	123496	239181	357733	4944
1865947	469362	163860	305502	443075	26287
712017	193850	65801	128049	168254	25596
1179258	63646	7402	56244	62664	982
80126	32391	5108	27283	32298	93
273904	236540	108237	128303	230933	5607
2482609	465827	165212	300615	452094	13733
1672757	173488	29671	143817	165225	8263
2518503	315499	50668	264831	312456	3043
119783	16588	9466	7122	15750	838
748796	259109	68599	190510	245568	13541
1123384	211116	35522	175594	208050	3066
111744	63890	11674	52216	59019	4871
321548	111261	13540	97721	111170	91
631562	352123	203713	148410	325723	26400

C-2-42 特困人员

地区	农村特困人员供养总数	集中供养人数	女性	老年人	未成年人	残疾人
全国	**5167743**	**1623288**	**277503**	**1432006**	**46731**	**271015**
中央级						
北京	4451	1837	181	1421	16	1015
天津	12060	1166	135	1034	8	280
河北	227987	48215	4085	43519	339	8408
山西	153611	22350	1357	18176	277	5328
内蒙古	87635	12874	1112	10133	87	3966
辽宁	138616	31778	3236	27493	528	6638
吉林	114789	23978	2487	16379	143	7835
黑龙江	132867	42718	7633	32878	822	11826
上海	2599	1085	219	987	4	205
江苏	197823	84427	14338	79462	1054	12340
浙江	34527	33385	4687	31146	346	4932
安徽	422497	149949	19895	139251	2312	17825
福建	80116	9145	1174	7774	170	1996
江西	220050	123294	39021	105563	10259	18076
山东	212224	142652	26862	137682	1191	12215
河南	486194	165289	32045	151329	5120	22010
湖北	252992	59557	11617	52333	296	13001
湖南	483850	101859	21448	90002	3795	16495
广东	240147	26000	5138	24527	375	2683
广西	280486	27107	4528	25079	680	4020
海南	28791	2424	642	2379	13	109
重庆	167082	63080	6421	54675	566	12175
四川	494722	267568	28983	231240	7125	47119
贵州	111092	49965	9535	39989	5323	7774
云南	207185	41660	10367	33698	2182	10611
西藏	14379	11633	4312	9544	1215	1488
陕西	130787	47597	7379	39092	702	13444
甘肃	120663	9310	1433	7816	312	2038
青海	23505	4969	1858	4275	435	707
宁夏	12878	3980	790	3349	47	1221
新疆	71138	12437	4585	9781	989	3235

救助供养

单位：人

分散供养人数	女 性	老年人	未成年人	残疾人	城市“三无”救助人数	传统救济
3544455	**594319**	**2988960**	**132120**	**663280**	**68003**	**637520**
2614	186	2133	13	1414	571	
10894	1014	9415	55	2500		3
179772	15121	158379	2443	32074	144	5998
131261	11744	94759	4713	39412	130	11141
74761	4838	60172	435	17487	12422	20852
106838	12059	91491	2408	21360	1669	7007
90811	16555	57595	1884	33641	1144	1290
90149	16711	63832	2183	31152	1148	1609
1514	210	1232	9	436		16
113396	14828	107596	1517	11346	2741	49130
1142	174	1025	16	204	1286	4862
272548	42474	245508	5113	36903	1289	44723
70971	10248	55200	2504	19457	816	4732
96756	32343	81610	8719	14881	8165	30542
69572	12931	66065	667	6613	2036	590
320905	56995	290612	9901	40035	249	23694
193435	31033	169005	1213	36484	7678	20089
381991	73231	322343	18963	64741	2421	101538
214147	30694	195724	7341	24024	3987	1495
253379	41868	229222	10761	34563	1880	118118
26367	7378	24734	387	2289	1	65
104002	8946	88726	1813	17472	10749	13563
227154	30558	194280	7276	41663		60555
61127	12422	43420	10447	10771	1375	23804
165525	40802	112066	16249	50176	89	38134
2746	1622	2740	424	403	255	68
83190	12909	62232	3330	25077	2831	26820
111353	21636	92058	2949	25427	1483	26278
18536	5867	14228	2694	3311	59	128
8898	2321	6506	207	2646	20	14
58701	24601	45052	5486	15318	1365	662

C-2-43 医疗

地区	资助参加基本医疗保险人数	医疗救助人次数	民政部门认定并实施医疗救助		
			资助参加基本医疗保险人数	民政部门直接救助人次数	
					住院救助人次
全　国	**66346834**	**28891179**	**62130148**	**25158725**	**12043159**
中央级					
北　京	57182	97759	57182	97698	23168
天　津	313973	197481	313973	197481	76523
河　北	3093201	301164	3027209	291286	203988
山　西	1577711	223766	1577711	223766	178922
内蒙古	1518680	282452	1491111	278779	229608
辽　宁	1160407	712729	1086239	700367	367618
吉　林	1640494	857110	1522479	808200	375224
黑龙江	2495744	700051	2433901	689848	377029
上　海	87031	265787	87031	265787	73200
江　苏	1694702	4636898	1350009	2559202	490308
浙　江	1154634	3230586	286753	2331129	560976
安　徽	2769797	936605	2521783	875586	737793
福　建	896363	1303018	808767	1276065	329121
江　西	2773912	1701922	2690000	1676686	477427
山　东	2606982	362239	2411578	349820	250641
河　南	3828037	815900	3768647	795897	697383
湖　北	3353518	1140489	3042004	1066113	898417
湖　南	4283043	1185320	4044635	1123093	727538
广　东	2453505	1045745	2420208	1041093	336620
广　西	2124356	954422	2009388	931603	908789
海　南	376561	123565	356983	121803	59283
重　庆	1572984	2877024	1526352	2735080	600378
四　川	6215073	1589777	5766087	1503473	1070952
贵　州	3061106	226689	2958803	220774	209166
云　南	6273660	868169	6208261	846257	638985
西　藏	70769	48011	70769	48011	45009
陕　西	785012	517608	744865	476380	333621
甘　肃	4540357	427905	4097133	402546	248870
青　海	671120	161413	671120	161413	129957
宁　夏	484488	316047	434957	307977	129444
新　疆	2412432	783528	2344210	755512	257201

救助

单位：人、人次

	民政部门认定、有关方面实施医疗救助			
门诊救助人次	资助参加基本医疗保险人数	直接救助人次数	住院救助人次数	门诊救助人次数
13115566	**4216686**	**3732454**	**1035740**	**2696714**
74530		61	55	6
120958				
87298	65992	9878	8553	1325
44844				
49171	27569	3673	2789	884
332749	74168	12362	12352	10
432976	118015	48910	33708	15202
312819	61843	10203	8289	1914
192587				
2068894	344693	2077696	333918	1743778
1770153	867881	899457	205942	693515
137793	248014	61019	48962	12057
946944	87596	26953	4286	22667
1199259	83912	25236	11590	13646
99179	195404	12419	9284	3135
98514	59390	20003	18238	1765
167696	311514	74376	60652	13724
395555	238408	62227	44168	18059
704473	33297	4652	2269	2383
22814	114968	22819	18587	4232
62520	19578	1762	1761	1
2134702	46632	141944	36324	105620
432521	448986	86304	70567	15737
11608	102303	5915	5574	341
207272	65399	21912	21886	26
3002				
142759	40147	41228	28393	12835
153676	443224	25359	23823	1536
31456				
178533	49531	8070	8070	
498311	68222	28016	15700	12316

C-2-44 救灾储

地区	单位数	年末职工人数		受教育程度		职业资
			女性	大学专科人数	大学本科及以上人数	助理社会工作师人数
全国	**776**	**2288**	**724**	**745**	**737**	**40**
中央级						
北京	17	75	21	18	35	
天津	2	27	10	7	17	3
河北	11	51	11	16	13	
山西	57	166	48	71	30	5
内蒙古	3	21	6	6	8	
辽宁	25	144	51	73	55	
吉林	7	37	12	7	3	
黑龙江	8	36	11	12	16	
上海	1	1				
江苏	6	13	5	3	8	
浙江	53	113	38	26	20	3
安徽	8	28	9	14	5	1
福建	21	40	16	5	16	3
江西	14	39	15	7	6	
山东	7	38	10	11	19	2
河南	10	74	16	17	39	1
湖北	45	134	59	53	46	
湖南	14	39	9	20	10	
广东	67	208	86	65	65	6
广西	17	59	27	21	27	2
海南	4	13	5	3	9	
重庆	35	60	16	18	23	1
四川	100	290	89	111	96	5
贵州	14	38	8	15	19	3
云南	7	54	22	9	34	4
西藏	47	93	36	17	21	
陕西	19	95	25	28	22	1
甘肃	46	86	25	32	26	
青海	78	105	18	13	23	
宁夏	11	50	10	24	5	
新疆	22	61	10	23	21	

备机构

单位：个、人、人次、时

格水平	年龄结构				志愿服务	
社会工作师人数	35岁及以下人数	36岁至45岁人数	46岁至55岁人数	56岁及以上人数	志愿者服务人次数	志愿服务时间
40	**827**	**912**	**454**	**95**	**981**	**2507.5**
	19	38	14	4		
	12	10	4	1		
3	15	16	16	4		
1	41	75	39	11		
	7	6	8			
1	45	46	39	14		
	13	16	8			
	14	11	10	1		
				1		
2	7	1	5		70	201.0
1	36	40	32	5		
2	8	9	8	3		
4	14	16	8	2		
	17	11	10	1		
3	7	17	11	3		
1	27	24	19	4		
1	42	68	18	6	50	55.0
	20	14	5		32	83.0
2	86	88	31	3	60	200.0
	14	25	18	2		
	8	3	2			
1	17	25	13	5	614	1675.0
9	117	124	46	3	66	98.5
1	25	10	2	1	75	115.0
3	33	14	7		2	
	56	29	5	3		
1	27	37	21	10	9	72.0
	32	39	15			
	29	57	15	4		
	21	21	8			
4	18	22	17	4	3	8.0

C-2-44续表

地区	执行行政事业单位会计制度财务指标				
	固定资产原价	上年结转和结余	本年收入合计	本年支出合计	收支结余
全　国	**117914.9**	**46245.6**	**52991.3**	**63434.2**	**72684.3**
中央级					
北　京	2434.8		2961.1	6384.2	13696.0
天　津	2252.8		6464.0	6973.4	
河　北	799.6	53.1	2369.4	2400.3	
山　西	979.4	1676.3	5539.5	3124.0	10795.0
内蒙古	1537.4	235.5	1089.1	366.7	
辽　宁	3804.9	138.7	2859.0	2453.0	420.0
吉　林	1026.8		321.3	288.5	30.0
黑龙江	933.8	59.4	765.1	497.1	
上　海					
江　苏	41.0	2384.3	2251.3	1841.5	
浙　江	1811.8		292.0	292.3	500.0
安　徽	2089.7	128.7	163.0	265.6	
福　建	274.2	309.0	568.9	346.1	800.0
江　西	798.0		96.0	101.8	
山　东	3143.2		887.9	910.3	
河　南	2419.4	1150.0	1288.0	1052.4	
湖　北	2973.8	2.0	1103.4	1032.7	4530.0
湖　南	206.3		12.6	12.1	11000.0
广　东	7713.5	3438.6	4077.8	6181.1	13191.0
广　西	3108.6	98.5	1724.1	1724.6	700.0
海　南	1005.2	1.0	297.7	297.2	1823.3
重　庆	2395.5	5801.0	4177.5	2448.8	3225.0
四　川	30154.9	501.4	1835.0	1988.5	4590.0
贵　州					
云　南	2747.3	2158.3	490.1	2229.6	3960.0
西　藏	10970.6	20220.0	693.4	13032.8	400.0
陕　西	4621.1	223.4	2390.0	1618.4	200.0
甘　肃	2861.7	505.7	613.1	332.2	1294.0
青　海	13548.2	4814.8	5137.2	771.1	650.0
宁　夏	7111.9	2345.8	1560.7	674.8	500.0
新　疆	4149.5	0.1	963.1	3793.1	380.0

单位：万元、平方米、顶

库房建筑面积	仓储面积	#租用仓储面积	#空余仓储面积	仓储物资种类			
				单帐篷	#中央储备	棉帐篷	#中央储备
1194024.3	**1007399.4**	**72684**	**91180**	**547858**	**132621**	**173655**	**51409**
29892.0	26876.0	13696	1860	6515		1757	
10466.0	9420.0		60	12962	9858	10026	4516
28310.5	23610.7		4240	1164		2756	
25056.5	30071.0	10795	1304	18049		9093	
134836.9	101246.1		17233	3915	216	10431	310
46850.0	41095.0	420	1237	16732	9739	12813	12302
	30.0	30					
4644.7	4024.7		85	305			
2000.0	2000.0			120			
8897.0	7487.0			2321		500	
12972.0	10822.0	500	1300	248	150	50	
11858.0	11068.0		3858	11899	6599	422	
21611.0	20156.6	800	260	29293	900	1510	
9999.0	8161.0		160	2850	50	690	200
18395.0	17300.0		5000	9710	3680	2050	
19870.0	15638.0		550	37030	14589	2030	1900
56395.0	41350.0	4530	2340	8099	4286	1235	485
17008.0	25453.0	11000	815	12418	10415	2636	1036
58988.2	52540.0	13191	3515	29035		623	
19132.0	15864.0	700	1250	5375	53	1093	
4155.0	4113.3	1823	300	9537	63		
18454.0	16806.0	3225	561	14606	450		
210445.9	153391.3	4590	24665	168196	34694	26881	5066
18498.0	15318.0		390	1048	190	5903	
38404.2	34508.5	3960	3000	17158	4739		
33426.7	30371.0	400	1220	18266	150	16810	4390
55091.7	54308.0	200	100	37848	9009	7192	5064
78734.7	64587.3	1294	13766	41500	9148	13731	4000
71464.3	63412.9	650	211	3829	2252	17535	1510
104903.0	88250.0	500	200	15159		12384	
23265.0	18120.0	380	1700	12671	11391	13504	10630

C-2-45 民政部门

地 区	直接接收捐赠情况			间接接收
	捐赠款数额	捐赠衣被合计	捐赠其他物资价值	捐赠款数额
全 国	**442029.5**	**4537.0**	**52408.2**	**42562.3**
中央级				
北 京	88479.8	118.2	16290.0	
天 津	7496.4			33.5
河 北	380.4	0.2		
山 西	1357.5	24.6	80.4	18.2
内蒙古	61.2	1.4	0.8	
辽 宁	2800.0	364.0	66.8	5.7
吉 林	2229.8			
黑龙江	650.1	0.1	10.0	
上 海	6806.0	466.8		
江 苏	99061.7	398.0	946.8	22485.0
浙 江	6683.5	9.0	91.2	617.9
安 徽	610.0	827.0	10.0	71.0
福 建	616.8		5.7	
江 西	7822.3	148.1	28420.1	654.0
山 东	8538.9			
河 南	3885.7	416.0	43.2	172.9
湖 北	2203.6	1.0	133.2	53.6
湖 南	21919.6	118.9	115.9	2602.5
广 东	79246.9	670.2	819.5	5959.4
广 西	263.2	280.0	0.5	100.0
海 南	327.6	0.3		
重 庆	45075.7	2.3	3533.3	2243.2
四 川	22347.7	296.1	685.3	6110.5
贵 州	9541.5	6.0	444.1	91.5
云 南	4018.0	373.1	332.1	1209.5
西 藏	15397.9	1.0	153.6	30.5
陕 西	392.5	4.0	11.2	101.4
甘 肃	1129.3	2.8	207.1	
青 海	367.9			
宁 夏	147.2			2.0
新 疆	2170.8	7.9	7.4	

接收的社会捐赠

单位：万元、万件、人次、个

捐赠情况		受益人次数	社会捐赠接收工作站、点数		
捐赠衣被合计	捐赠其他物资价值			社会捐赠接收工作站数	慈善超市数
172.5	**6164.4**	**18384078**	**30362**	**12810**	**9654**
		2312086	1648	31	166
		18503	812	448	48
		7487	674	557	49
		21783	1068	575	254
		1191	461	11	164
0.8		90839	881	664	163
		34649	301	219	115
		6623	913	367	539
		2895	3422	200	154
		3007353	3543	1019	2295
1.3		91813	453	206	154
		16344	350	243	104
9.0		15514	799	318	463
0.6		208963	542	211	59
		91737	2340	1137	757
8.0	0.5	70175	770	483	68
	0.2	214447	690	481	254
1.5	340.1	288591	1529	584	762
	4.9	1882462	963	564	152
		180974	1165	614	294
		1700	39	13	8
26.4	372.6	9217557	1769	951	601
40.0	13.7	407184	2517	1193	1428
		72810	1096	674	207
	5431.1	48459	149	131	16
1.9	1.3	327	39	35	1
3.0		11471	402	180	42
		34901	306	226	85
		200	37	23	6
		1026	235	92	152
80.0		24014	449	360	94

C-2-46 福利彩票发

地 区	单位数	编制登记	民政登记	一个机构多块牌子	年末职工人数	女性	受教育 大学专科人数
全 国	**861**	**704**	**64**	**93**	**11972**	**5114**	**4059**
中央级	1	1			135	55	9
北 京	17	17			141	60	51
天 津	10	10			101	44	14
河 北	13	13			291	132	82
山 西	12	12			257	126	109
内蒙古	15	15			255	103	112
辽 宁	19	19			431	174	169
吉 林	52	46		6	581	107	75
黑龙江	20	19		1	164	66	59
上 海	18	3	14	1	222	110	51
江 苏	79	75	2	2	849	367	263
浙 江	70	41	11	18	620	278	195
安 徽	48	24	22	2	673	343	262
福 建	13	10	1	2	327	130	103
江 西	45	31	1	13	153	49	47
山 东	18	18			725	295	234
河 南	52	45	7		593	234	189
湖 北	53	42		11	439	210	207
湖 南	76	76			642	272	218
广 东	65	56		9	751	330	250
广 西	30	26		4	740	340	276
海 南	3	3			49	18	20
重 庆	1	1			162	44	37
四 川	12	11		1	894	509	429
贵 州	13	13			265	119	105
云 南	12	12			113	48	51
西 藏	2	1	1		32	13	14
陕 西	39	26		13	583	160	152
甘 肃	20	13	1	6	238	113	52
青 海	2	2			93	53	17
宁 夏	10	5	4	1	242	124	106
新 疆	21	18		3	211	88	101

行机构情况

单位:个、人、人次、时

程度	职业资格水平		年龄结构				志愿服务	
大学本科及以上人数	助理社会工作师人数	社会工作师人数	35岁及以下人数	36岁至45岁人数	46岁至55岁人数	56岁及以上人数	志愿者服务人次数	志愿服务时间
3896	**184**	**125**	**6274**	**3832**	**1550**	**316**	**2362**	**6210.7**
126			77	21	25	12		
76	3	4	59	45	29	8	3	6.0
68		1	45	38	14	4		
64	2	2	166	88	30	7		
103	1		135	78	38	6		
88	4	1	152	59	33	11		
202			240	108	68	15	16	32.0
92	5	1	273	246	49	13		
44	2	7	69	70	22	3		
63		1	98	60	34	30	80	190.0
333	35	22	420	288	121	20	1036	2989.0
158	7	5	313	232	65	10	650	1250.0
208	11	5	410	187	69	7		
86	1		123	118	76	10		
13	5	1	54	66	26	7	111	422.7
336	16	22	353	247	103	22		
187	25	2	305	203	80	5		
124	1		198	170	68	3	63	112.0
193	2	15	350	220	64	8	190	530.0
274	44	20	380	231	121	19		
201	9	4	397	266	69	8		
18	2	4	15	16	18			
109	1		93	44	23	2		
241	2		685	142	55	12		
95	1	1	163	80	19	3	60	180.0
28	1		45	50	14	4	3	18.0
7			15	12	5			
92	1	4	230	196	99	58	140	451.0
90	3	1	115	84	35	4	10	30.0
34		1	55	24	13	1		
75		1	160	63	17	2		
68			81	80	48	2		

C-2-46续表

地区	执行行政事业单位会计制度财务指标				
	固定资产原价	上年结转和结余	本年收入合计	本年支出合计	收支结余
全国	**758130.9**	**123212.4**	**1088326.8**	**937147.7**	**126638.5**
中央级	17628.8		118036.1	89323.1	
北京	15603.1	614.8	25082.0	23548.7	1629.0
天津	20362.0	349.8	15130.5	14064.2	372.7
河北	35191.7	1082.5	61510.9	54234.9	863.8
山西	13391.0	3526.7	17407.3	11935.7	2371.0
内蒙古	32556.4	3872.7	22074.0	18766.8	9468.6
辽宁	60884.3	705.0	20645.2	19072.7	737.1
吉林	14325.4	1298.5	29600.5	21974.2	53.0
黑龙江	10987.8	4197.3	4784.0	4681.5	
上海	117.2	-5.5	20117.3	16899.3	3136.3
江苏	87403.2	25341.6	77031.2	72008.6	28895.3
浙江	40508.9	5942.1	46342.9	30095.9	19286.8
安徽	29243.7	3249.4	35024.4	34501.0	2072.9
福建	7250.8	2836.7	16796.7	13235.1	2442.0
江西	16657.3	5570.8	18642.8	13250.4	
山东	78159.1	3039.6	85427.2	85151.1	
河南	49207.7	735.1	45226.6	42358.2	1474.0
湖北	28743.4	647.6	27941.0	27512.7	49.9
湖南	33689.7	4871.1	53110.1	46802.2	6039.5
广东	41974.4	9427.2	80090.8	74070.9	8776.4
广西	15223.5	10446.2	31971.6	24953.2	773.8
海南	2551.7	696.0	7959.4	7077.1	1593.2
重庆	12101.2	25814.3	30756.0	26055.8	30514.5
四川	2138.9	513.2	43010.7	44198.6	-838.1
贵州	15487.2	7173.1	16494.8	14329.8	2932.2
云南	8629.7	416.2	53308.7	49191.8	307.2
西藏	404.6		6616.1	6466.7	149.4
陕西	35163.9	383.3	23205.1	20234.4	2701.5
甘肃	14462.9	261.3	17556.4	9611.2	
青海	3612.2	7.0	5373.1	4803.2	576.8
宁夏	4036.6	-559.9	9304.5	8427.2	259.7
新疆	10432.6	758.7	22748.9	8311.5	

单位：万元

执行民间非营利组织单位会计制度财务指标			
固定资产原价	上年结余	本年收入合计	本年费用合计
1459.4	**531.0**	**5731.5**	**2311.7**
484.2	92.9	3624.8	2085.2
178.6	128.9	412.0	
369.9	15.8	943.7	217.8
426.7	293.4	751.0	8.7

C-2-47 优抚对象享受

地区	抚恤、补助优抚对象总人数	在院集中供养人数	定期抚恤人数合计	烈属	城市
全国	**8970288**	**76730**	**264975**	**160948**	**35110**
中央级					
北京	44391	127	1572	410	188
天津	46098	109	830	334	143
河北	567184	3091	10847	5037	843
山西	179764	2729	7814	5271	450
内蒙古	48914	833	1696	801	374
辽宁	222382	2945	6133	2382	580
吉林	122521	3076	4139	2319	1207
黑龙江	118751	1739	4556	2881	1282
上海	39870	194	5294	4359	3822
江苏	481575	4989	14428	6834	954
浙江	299097	610	4758	2425	526
安徽	460194	2343	8753	4294	1155
福建	188639	916	8337	6399	572
江西	295368	5308	18613	16288	2335
山东	898504	9820	25173	13886	2529
河南	749023	13247	15152	7250	1443
湖北	473408	5523	30412	22600	2385
湖南	868211	7118	26001	17036	3574
广东	428232	898	7520	4904	2098
广西	292105	555	4068	2597	364
海南	26659	51	2227	1950	312
重庆	264581	838	5166	2615	719
四川	841662	4597	25308	13741	3934
贵州	222427	173	3178	1636	399
云南	353159	272	6393	3673	770
西藏	4667	542	1690	1163	267
陕西	249604	2260	8311	4189	687
甘肃	121555	567	2188	669	184
青海	15011	128	584	273	82
宁夏	12324	621	410	176	61
新疆	34408	511	3424	2556	871

定期抚恤、补助情况

单位：人

农　村	因公牺牲军人遗属	城　市	农　村	病故军人遗属	城　市	农　村
125838	**43711**	**11452**	**32259**	**60316**	**18232**	**42084**
222	152	78	74	1010	694	316
191	137	55	82	359	243	116
4194	2394	543	1851	3416	849	2567
4821	993	207	786	1550	348	1202
427	417	183	234	478	250	228
1802	1228	381	847	2523	733	1790
1112	644	361	283	1176	677	499
1599	734	390	344	941	461	480
537	144	116	28	791	629	162
5880	1985	483	1502	5609	805	4804
1899	909	211	698	1424	476	948
3139	1943	513	1430	2516	741	1775
5827	956	172	784	982	283	699
13953	1102	292	810	1223	391	832
11357	4862	1094	3768	6425	1848	4577
5807	3770	806	2964	4132	1166	2966
20215	4608	627	3981	3204	736	2468
13462	3848	1240	2608	5117	1612	3505
2806	896	497	399	1720	886	834
2233	524	112	412	947	229	718
1638	122	79	43	155	65	90
1896	997	297	700	1554	475	1079
9807	5439	1341	4098	6128	1829	4299
1237	597	139	458	945	238	707
2903	998	216	782	1722	496	1226
896	235	61	174	292	28	264
3502	1771	445	1326	2351	523	1828
485	674	167	507	845	174	671
191	93	40	53	218	48	170
115	113	44	69	121	68	53
1685	426	262	164	442	231	211

C-2-47续表

地　区	定期补助人数合计	在乡退伍红军老战士	在乡西路红军老战士	红军失散人员	在乡复员军人
全　国	**7968445**	**177**	**64**	**3708**	**792440**
中央级					
北　京	31107	1			3075
天　津	38156				2008
河　北	513530				24329
山　西	149433	6		1	19514
内蒙古	35495	4		1	7097
辽　宁	187876	2			23119
吉　林	100330			1	17399
黑龙江	98607	5	1	11	24699
上　海	27507				2103
江　苏	419475			1	40724
浙　江	271970			48	18517
安　徽	419462			203	29533
福　建	168464			182	14489
江　西	256578	3	4	1132	22580
山　东	774963				73147
河　南	672521	3		219	47887
湖　北	411783	1	1	341	38187
湖　南	791171	2		866	107688
广　东	396244			34	19391
广　西	277481			200	25711
海　南	22264			9	3642
重　庆	239092				23831
四　川	756982	4	39	311	99188
贵　州	204919	1		6	23934
云　南	328546			3	30580
西　藏	1245	90		2	21
陕　西	219857	52		133	29838
甘　肃	108973	2	14	2	8748
青　海	10938				1600
宁　夏	9867		1	1	1738
新　疆	23609	1	4	1	8123

单位：人

抗　日	带病回乡退伍军人	60岁以上农村籍退伍军人	参战退役人员	参试退役人员	部分60周岁以上烈士子女(含错杀被平反人员子女)	其　他
26545	**1183750**	**3924604**	**1409601**	**184840**	**241257**	**228004**
197	1573	20373	3138	806	1942	199
124	11524	14813	7528	61	1229	993
3398	47913	336249	49669	18747	29912	6711
1990	26485	71108	8835	6924	12557	4003
165	9674	15587	1453	134	894	651
303	13430	108418	6426	3897	2608	29976
345	11224	65344	3221	1218	1674	249
477	10177	54824	4901	372	1538	2079
22	562	21767	2421	556		98
4116	50263	236268	33261	4348	15011	39599
139	17948	202341	24353	2448	1563	4752
1047	133424	196215	33070	11690	8336	6991
32	9974	102612	30443	254	7019	3491
253	42856	91708	41857	2681	51257	2500
7016	91224	479837	71302	14969	44484	
2056	87160	398345	94095	25871	15305	3636
1591	107421	171652	66335	8461	11991	7393
611	159891	321240	177837	8231	12055	3361
313	28008	165063	152653	9279	3100	18716
72	3436	91573	85601	3655	3529	63776
555	1161	8335	7907	66	435	709
32	65372	85320	55790	5657	1263	1859
224	179813	314509	125765	19306	7037	11010
50	13356	82079	84043	211	313	976
73	22774	95037	173690	114	2000	4348
	163	302				667
838	25656	90301	43329	22442	3103	5003
162	4590	69883	16942	6147	784	1861
2	1458	5307	988	1390	138	57
21	589	4827	1135	360	73	1143
321	4651	3367	1613	4545	107	1197

C-2-48 伤残人员和

地区	伤残人员合计	按伤残				
		一级	因战	因公	因病	二级
全国	**736868**	**3545**	**941**	**2366**	**238**	**2296**
中央级						
北京	11712	44	1	39	4	40
天津	7112	31		30	1	21
河北	42807	231	21	189	21	103
山西	22517	76	18	56	2	34
内蒙古	11723	51	6	43	2	20
辽宁	28373	133	21	109	3	85
吉林	18052	139	24	105	10	75
黑龙江	15588	66	15	37	14	45
上海	7069	23	3	19	1	18
江苏	47672	182	52	116	14	137
浙江	22369	66	10	52	4	101
安徽	31979	152	33	103	16	55
福建	11838	46	3	41	2	27
江西	20177	106	31	60	15	183
山东	98368	300	79	212	9	295
河南	61350	286	56	198	32	213
湖北	31213	165	54	96	15	78
湖南	51039	436	220	204	12	260
广东	24468	98	17	69	12	43
广西	10556	40	17	21	2	26
海南	2168	9	1	7	1	6
重庆	20323	118	48	58	12	39
四川	59372	213	70	132	11	167
贵州	14330	104	33	70	1	41
云南	18220	144	45	88	11	72
西藏	1732	7		7		13
陕西	21436	130	47	79	4	41
甘肃	10394	62	9	49	4	17
青海	3489	23	6	16	1	6
宁夏	2047	25		25		4
新疆	7375	39	1	36	2	31

优待情况

单位：人

等级分类						
			三 级			
因 战	因 公	因 病		因 战	因 公	因 病
304	**1579**	**413**	**16824**	**4199**	**10235**	**2390**
2	29	9	193	30	125	38
1	17	3	112	25	68	19
11	68	24	759	140	462	157
5	23	6	432	133	234	65
2	13	5	168	29	115	24
16	54	15	592	164	376	52
24	37	14	632	180	334	118
2	32	11	343	51	173	119
1	16	1	115	19	73	23
33	86	18	1330	524	693	113
	60	41	467	41	281	145
8	33	14	677	186	416	75
2	20	5	168	17	130	21
5	152	26	367	65	183	119
12	248	35	3261	827	2175	259
26	149	38	1165	330	579	256
8	53	17	645	106	415	124
65	172	23	1412	391	856	165
4	23	16	433	107	263	63
7	13	6	210	71	113	26
3	1	2	46	15	27	4
4	24	11	432	90	294	48
22	123	22	1256	251	857	148
15	20	6	273	92	160	21
10	28	34	432	148	176	108
	9	4	64	1	62	1
13	26	2	381	95	251	35
	16	1	198	25	138	35
1	3	2	63	22	38	3
	3	1	42	6	32	4
2	28	1	156	18	136	2

C-2-48续表1

地区	按伤残							
	四级	因战	因公	因病	五级	因战	因公	因病
全国	**12607**	**1551**	**7154**	**3902**	**51342**	**14245**	**24726**	**12371**
中央级								
北京	142	24	84	34	498	95	333	70
天津	81	15	50	16	520	70	232	218
河北	634	82	271	281	3084	560	1277	1247
山西	260	38	123	99	1509	561	683	265
内蒙古	116	14	53	49	610	105	424	81
辽宁	237	63	110	64	1925	651	1042	232
吉林	603	153	267	183	2192	582	1414	196
黑龙江	321	7	72	242	1053	408	477	168
上海	109	10	53	46	372	89	191	92
江苏	957	130	570	257	3459	1082	1331	1046
浙江	403	18	169	216	1245	207	497	541
安徽	335	47	224	64	1940	549	947	444
福建	141	11	72	58	1160	126	376	658
江西	638	29	218	391	1427	239	646	542
山东	2319	159	1947	213	6973	2699	3474	800
河南	1785	201	696	888	4863	1106	1909	1848
湖北	490	38	282	170	1860	347	1000	513
湖南	875	214	532	129	4115	1334	2052	729
广东	247	49	126	72	1452	359	585	508
广西	72	18	40	14	715	256	373	86
海南	22	6	9	7	145	45	72	28
重庆	303	38	193	72	1191	349	648	194
四川	828	105	579	144	3863	1045	1903	915
贵州	106	14	77	15	790	309	386	95
云南	198	28	59	111	1103	447	479	177
西藏	43	2	38	3	92	2	87	3
陕西	94	10	60	24	1569	364	711	494
甘肃	108	9	72	27	690	109	480	101
青海	15	4	10	1	222	39	176	7
宁夏	31	5	24	2	106	20	66	20
新疆	94	10	74	10	599	91	455	53

单位：人

等级分类									
六级	因战	因公	因病	七级	因战	因公	八级	因战	因公
166243	**37122**	**90076**	**39045**	**217094**	**50471**	**166623**	**211659**	**55498**	**156161**
1914	329	1333	252	3630	617	3013	4008	680	3328
1454	230	910	314	2023	280	1743	2198	330	1868
10284	1536	5199	3549	12295	2236	10059	12256	2212	10044
4688	1459	2319	910	7066	2200	4866	6526	1915	4611
3103	356	2295	452	3611	563	3048	3216	555	2661
6251	1896	3584	771	8539	2802	5737	9055	3288	5767
5430	1274	3625	531	3812	717	3095	3170	653	2517
3304	1221	1472	611	5034	2396	2638	4978	2697	2281
1179	231	657	291	2017	363	1654	2614	499	2115
12136	3226	6199	2711	13027	3534	9493	13330	3958	9372
4358	480	2049	1829	5702	742	4960	8646	994	7652
7552	1539	3856	2157	9343	1960	7383	9157	2224	6933
3412	313	1309	1790	2765	450	2315	3171	589	2582
4075	767	2018	1290	5551	941	4610	6245	1348	4897
26046	6984	14932	4130	30126	8216	21910	23022	7219	15803
14965	3405	7751	3809	17023	3876	13147	15185	3595	11590
6422	955	3450	2017	9594	1507	8087	9330	1738	7592
11005	2808	5788	2409	14685	3694	10991	14745	4214	10531
4741	1076	2442	1223	6612	1518	5094	8470	2477	5993
1921	595	907	419	3137	992	2145	3472	1293	2179
458	136	214	108	567	173	394	630	200	430
3788	798	2171	819	6959	1293	5666	6096	1576	4520
12421	2436	6777	3208	18634	3885	14749	17493	4352	13141
2392	629	1288	475	4626	1128	3498	4883	1632	3251
3096	904	1557	635	5774	1808	3966	6322	2407	3915
226	3	220	3	533	6	527	428	4	424
4972	905	2539	1528	6884	1409	5475	6433	1516	4917
1994	227	1222	545	3482	384	3098	3154	469	2685
568	120	404	44	1326	241	1085	982	249	733
493	70	365	58	592	126	466	607	133	474
1595	214	1224	157	2125	414	1711	1837	482	1355

C-2-48续表2

地区	按伤残等级分类						按人员	
	九级			十级			残疾军人	伤残国家机关工作人员
		因战	因公		因战	因公		
全国	**33891**	**1436**	**32455**	**21367**	**1098**	**20269**	**681204**	**31191**
中央级								
北京	878	14	864	365	7	358	10577	420
天津	399	11	388	273	6	267	6370	135
河北	2049	28	2021	1112	28	1084	40527	1382
山西	741	16	725	1185	55	1130	21274	921
内蒙古	565	10	555	263	8	255	8840	1892
辽宁	992	30	962	564	11	553	25467	1130
吉林	1062	13	1049	937	16	921	13370	2384
黑龙江	324	11	313	120	9	111	14714	431
上海	400	16	384	222	12	210	6530	130
江苏	1873	140	1733	1241	74	1167	45995	882
浙江	976	22	954	405	13	392	21685	354
安徽	1760	55	1705	1008	42	966	29352	1849
福建	681	12	669	267	3	264	11191	309
江西	1024	109	915	561	95	466	18537	888
山东	3851	86	3765	2175	55	2120	95177	1687
河南	3195	180	3015	2670	137	2533	58201	1863
湖北	1707	50	1657	922	37	885	29322	1114
湖南	2311	183	2128	1195	118	1077	45848	3340
广东	1396	69	1327	976	66	910	23738	272
广西	650	34	616	313	34	279	9486	391
海南	204	24	180	81	8	73	2056	45
重庆	894	32	862	503	28	475	19102	679
四川	2419	125	2294	2078	109	1969	54993	2535
贵州	647	29	618	468	57	411	12888	867
云南	717	52	665	362	37	325	16277	804
西藏	174	1	173	152	2	150	710	730
陕西	616	36	580	316	20	296	20219	887
甘肃	464	18	446	225	5	220	9521	558
青海	201	4	197	83		83	2541	607
宁夏	92	4	88	55		55	1680	199
新疆	629	22	607	270	6	264	5016	1506

单位：人

种类分类		优抚对象享受医疗保障人数	优待				烈士褒扬	
伤残人民警察	伤残民兵民工		优待优抚对象户数	优待军属户数	优待总金额	固定优待军属总额	本年新增享受烈士待遇的人数	零散烈士纪念设施
19948	**4525**	**4364991**	**3170333**	**858330**	**1929547.5**	**766241.3**	**341**	**11838**
675	40	13063	27509	6436	319526.6	17572.9		130
576	31	23913	9136	4801	12334.6	6581.4	101	4
679	219	221702	183574	52420	100379.6	55894.4	31	1095
215	107	95988	58160	19027	60193.8	27957.9	13	864
855	136	36349	25733	16278	36568.0	12424.0	6	100
1471	305	60502	69627	14851	27740.4	7653.4	1	84
2148	150	60174	14224	1697	9173.0	3013.1	2	428
378	65	54837	38474	10960	12455.4	3725.9		60
398	11	14159	23706	7282	35189.9	15917.3	3	5
654	141	257194	241330	45557	143162.6	55049.9	3	587
180	150	98059	116209	39187	96237.1	50936.2	21	285
601	177	245965	145199	41013	146478.9	29858.1	7	317
202	136	74361	103525	12092	37282.3	11024.6	1	252
563	189	111236	70536	26323	33572.2	11734.1	6	531
1141	363	483604	538501	91332	211245.1	130913.2	21	500
1115	171	346791	247015	94760	116660.0	79627.7	43	434
691	86	316898	197790	32664	98780.6	30501.0	8	618
1773	78	483237	218398	61204	56057.3	26260.0	9	384
421	37	195679	88594	35650	74047.9	28686.9		1468
180	499	118438	152409	34199	43943.9	14680.6	10	628
30	37	21847	9908	4852	5083.3	2501.0	1	737
470	72	243240	192077	26105	38966.8	16002.1	1	356
1479	365	341081	206518	75110	99201.2	46887.6	13	759
528	47	119504	45618	27623	24768.9	18508.7	4	373
658	481	162063	54219	24665	15375.0	6688.5	9	193
188	104	1669	1522	748	1167.1	771.6	1	1
228	102	97209	30531	28097	51524.0	46037.9	9	287
277	38	41185	23908	11699	7254.5	2943.2	1	286
260	81	4095	1506	980	1545.2	991.2		29
132	36	6138	3080	865	1575.8	578.3		7
782	71	14811	31797	9853	12056.5	4318.6	16	36

C-2-49 离退休、

地 区	本年接收人员合计	军队离退休干部	离 休	地方离退休干部	离 休	军队退休士官	军队无军籍职工
全 国	**19429**	**9102**	**600**	**409**	**81**	**410**	**9508**
中央级							
北 京	4216	2536	3	4		5	1671
天 津	355	189				4	162
河 北	1296	473	28	52	1	43	728
山 西	111	25	5	3		7	76
内蒙古	275	75	1			17	183
辽 宁	1389	642	72	4	1	35	708
吉 林	543	145		27		16	355
黑龙江	226	93	5			2	131
上 海	744	451		9			284
江 苏	1299	498	7	45		17	739
浙 江	366	201	13	2		2	161
安 徽	495	224	36	75	22	34	162
福 建	517	122		3	1	3	389
江 西	122	40				5	77
山 东	772	419		56	55	68	229
河 南	535	218	1	4		39	274
湖 北	585	292				12	281
湖 南	340	86		1		14	239
广 东	521	215	37			4	302
广 西	165	87		2		4	72
海 南	128	44	1			2	82
重 庆	253	107				9	137
四 川	805	377		40		26	362
贵 州	90	32		3		1	54
云 南	285	169				15	101
西 藏	1048	623	385	41			384
陕 西	834	380	1	4		9	441
甘 肃	577	93	3	20	1	11	453
青 海	123	52	1	8			63
宁 夏	63	33				2	28
新 疆	351	161	1	6		4	180

退职人员

单位：人

本年实有人数合计	军队离退休干部	离休	地方离退休干部	离休	军队退休士官	军队无军籍职工	军队离退休干部服务站
376047	**220880**	**19725**	**26360**	**1131**	**7669**	**121138**	**201**
76294	46001	1818	6029	28	571	23693	
7894	5225	490	840	2	84	1745	
19566	11456	1059	1433	99	1122	5555	22
5601	2553	437	285	33	254	2509	7
4090	2554	252	281	10	117	1138	7
32003	22400	1702	1055	121	378	8170	25
7861	4354	253	42		314	3151	
5550	3473	328	19	1	77	1981	20
11972	7604	542	149	5	11	4208	7
21569	12932	1264	2128	169	254	6255	3
8175	4392	651	1375	42	48	2360	9
5409	3232	620	549	102	220	1408	12
7984	3660	436	3050	13	68	1206	3
4280	1257	371	1373	57	192	1458	1
25721	17694	2598	718	89	1242	6067	11
12324	7184	911	937	119	559	3644	12
15264	7865	938	1404	84	223	5772	1
12118	5480	796	1892	34	222	4524	9
14115	7830	505	290	27	68	5927	3
3403	1993	154	27		45	1338	13
2349	779	41	20	1	9	1541	1
5899	3702	155	129	1	147	1921	10
16610	9521	685	979	23	581	5529	11
2330	1334	183	248	9	12	736	1
11871	6784	748	330	7	82	4675	4
1048	623	385	41			384	
16252	9976	842	245	33	238	5793	5
8015	3914	364	288	16	340	3473	1
2298	816	10	31	2	32	1419	
1019	634	41			57	328	
7163	3658	146	173	4	102	3230	3

C-2-50 军队离退休

地区	单位数	年末职工人数		受教育程度		职业资
			女性	大学专科人数	大学本科及以上人数	助理社会工作师人数
全　国	**271**	**3696**	**1650**	**1232**	**1865**	**84**
中央级						
北　京	25	368	183	92	239	10
天　津	1	41	26	10	31	1
河　北	21	271	140	92	82	3
山　西	4	38	19	11	20	
内蒙古	1	18	8	7	11	
辽　宁	11	422	155	71	298	2
吉　林	33	595	202	290	185	20
黑龙江	2	8	3	7		
上　海	21	332	162	120	160	17
江　苏	3	18	9	4	7	
浙　江	12	142	76	29	102	
安　徽	9	60	22	24	20	2
福　建	7	46	22	8	20	1
江　西	1	3	1	2		
山　东	7	155	58	39	90	3
河　南	5	83	43	45	24	4
湖　北	6	70	20	13	47	
湖　南	14	83	43	25	34	
广　东	6	92	43	22	66	9
广　西	4	53	26	10	38	2
海　南						
重　庆	40	331	141	148	167	3
四　川	16	155	100	63	51	3
贵　州	2	5	3	2	3	
云　南	6	91	47	30	52	1
西　藏						
陕　西	6	64	27	14	47	
甘　肃	1	2	1		2	
青　海	1	19	11	1	18	
宁　夏						
新　疆	6	131	59	53	51	3

人员管理中心

单位:个、人、人次、时

格水平	年龄结构				志愿服务	
社会工作师人数	35岁及以下人数	36岁至45岁人数	46岁至55岁人数	56岁及以上人数	志愿者服务人次数	志愿服务时间
110	**1326**	**1276**	**875**	**219**	**1114**	**3997.0**
22	109	118	130	11		
1	25	10	4	2		
6	142	87	40	2	796	3330.0
3	13	12	8	5	1	
3	9	4	5			
4	145	113	122	42	86	86.0
2	186	286	79	44		
	2	6				
18	126	79	101	26	20	40.0
3	7	8	3			
3	59	33	41	9		
1	19	18	18	5		
	16	17	11	2		
	1	2				
12	65	49	36	5	102	230.0
7	15	41	20	7		
	11	35	21	3		
4	25	46	10	2	9	34.0
14	39	39	13	1		
2	27	18	7	1		
1	74	136	101	20	32	105.0
	51	43	40	21		
	3	2				
1	45	30	15	1	24	72.0
1	50	8	5	1	44	100.0
	1	1				
1	15	2		2		
1	46	33	45	7		

C-2-50续表

地区	执行行政事业单位会计		
	固定资产原价	上年结余	收入合计
全国	**171980.6**	**198920.3**	**1162499.4**
中央级			
北京	67946.2	168412.9	653125.0
天津	500.0		426.0
河北	4152.9	206.0	25066.2
山西	737.6	741.8	3362.3
内蒙古	136.4	2209.1	6912.5
辽宁	8344.9	550.7	27824.9
吉林	9000.6	1187.5	35116.5
黑龙江	9.0		181.7
上海	9241.0	1836.3	105109.1
江苏	500.0		15.0
浙江	3685.2	1075.9	26423.4
安徽	882.8	12.1	8354.0
福建	1939.5	264.0	1340.7
江西	3.0		
山东	6267.8		24425.4
河南	4623.5	1926.9	5999.0
湖北	13933.0	797.2	9231.2
湖南	1531.0	63.0	3097.8
广东	10931.3	438.3	19557.2
广西	4488.3	780.5	16105.9
海南			
重庆	7354.9	119.3	55540.1
四川	3040.6	3597.0	60896.7
贵州	1.8	6.2	29.8
云南	2288.7	1067.5	3637.4
西藏			
陕西	457.9	3289.9	39727.2
甘肃			
青海	146.4	359.3	2655.3
宁夏			
新疆	9836.3	9978.9	28339.1

单位：人、万元

制度财务指标		年末机构管理军休干部人数		本年发放离退休金
支出合计	收支结余		分散安置人数	
766557.0	**14935.4**	**13673**	**11650**	**190416**
271950.5	3111.4			
426.0				
22504.7	2463.0	785	265	7818
2992.3	536.4	132	10	1882
8143.1	978.5	563	563	6868
28344.9	30.7	549	338	9394
35871.1		99	7	2089
181.7				
99124.6	1440.9	6824	6814	87760
15.0				
25969.0	1274.6	524	524	5140
7414.4	55.8			
1255.4	198.5			52
3.0				
24425.4				139
4096.2	610.0			
1422.6	797.2			127
3157.0	17.5	9	9	306
19333.7	9.9	654	654	9152
15314.7	791.9			4210
56470.0	192.0	3327	2297	41405
61582.9	1494.2			
29.8				
4309.7		38		11363
40877.3	871.1			
2935.9	78.7	169	169	2712
28406.1	-16.9			

C-2-51 军队离退休

地区	单位数	年末职工人数	女性	受教育 大学专科人数
全　国	**27**	**584**	**238**	**193**
中央级				
北　京	11	402	160	104
天　津	1	11	3	
河　北	1	3		3
山　西				
内蒙古				
辽　宁	2	14	5	5
吉　林				
黑龙江	1	4		3
上　海	2	50	26	15
江　苏	3	41	16	19
浙　江				
安　徽				
福　建				
江　西	1	22	14	18
山　东				
河　南				
湖　北				
湖　南	1	4	2	1
广　东				
广　西				
海　南	1	18	7	14
重　庆				
四　川	2	13	5	11
贵　州				
云　南				
西　藏				
陕　西				
甘　肃	1	2		
青　海				
宁　夏				
新　疆				

人员活动中心

单位：个、人、人次、时

程度	职业资格水平		年龄结构	
大学本科及以上人数	助理社会工作师人数	社会工作师人数	35岁及以下人数	36岁至45岁人数
179	**4**	**4**	**182**	**200**
112	1	3	139	146
11			4	1
			2	
8			3	7
1			2	2
28	2	1	21	11
11	1		3	13
3				2
1			1	2
2			6	8
2			1	6
				2

C-2-51续表

地区	年龄结构		志愿服务	
	46岁至55岁人数	56岁及以上人数	志愿者服务人次数	志愿服务时间
全　国	**151**	**51**	**155**	**305.0**
中央级				
北　京	88	29		
天　津	4	2		
河　北	1			
山　西				
内蒙古				
辽　宁	4		5	5.0
吉　林				
黑龙江				
上　海	15	3	150	300.0
江　苏	20	5		
浙　江				
安　徽				
福　建				
江　西	13	7		
山　东				
河　南				
湖　北				
湖　南	1			
广　东				
广　西				
海　南	2	2		
重　庆				
四　川	3	3		
贵　州				
云　南				
西　藏				
陕　西				
甘　肃				
青　海				
宁　夏				
新　疆				

单位：万元

执行行政事业单位会计制度财务指标				
固定资产原价	上年结转和结余	本年收入合计	本年支出合计	收支结余
71785.6	**35295.0**	**41374.1**	**23312.0**	**31168.3**
29125.1	1694.5	7385.6	8038.7	515.6
25824.3		2158.0	2034.0	99.3
654.0		201.0	199.0	
6741.4		1565.5	1565.5	
		854.0	854.0	
5426.1	322.5	4278.0	3185.9	327.4
2676.6	-10.7	1997.8	1218.0	804.1
263.0	32001.1	18204.5	2151.3	28780.9
706.7	11.6	136.0	136.0	
180.0	1276.0	4505.0	3864.0	641.0
188.4		66.7	65.6	
		22.0		

C-2-52 烈士纪念

地区	单位数	年末职工人数		受教育程度		职业资
			女性	大学专科人数	大学本科及以上人数	助理社会工作师人数
全国	**1464**	**10050**	**3948**	**3095**	**2059**	**115**
中央级						
北京	5	47	16	17	20	3
天津	9	131	53	40	50	
河北	98	841	305	192	210	9
山西	58	376	160	106	47	3
内蒙古	9	101	37	37	39	2
辽宁	46	323	131	102	108	2
吉林	30	375	93	115	56	4
黑龙江	24	203	81	86	61	1
上海	11	226	90	92	64	
江苏	80	678	261	169	203	21
浙江	34	170	76	35	75	3
安徽	44	386	159	119	50	8
福建	28	138	58	34	31	
江西	68	317	112	42	37	
山东	115	913	349	366	295	11
河南	99	1304	578	429	180	13
湖北	56	682	299	259	90	1
湖南	59	437	194	115	38	4
广东	111	428	152	65	73	8
广西	24	268	113	112	67	9
海南	8	17	2	4	3	
重庆	20	70	26	24	33	
四川	176	489	187	194	71	7
贵州	40	113	30	39	22	
云南	21	97	22	36	12	2
西藏	44	69	24	28	3	
陕西	40	342	182	115	40	1
甘肃	79	383	111	88	47	2
青海	7	18	6	7	5	
宁夏	9	29	8	7	4	
新疆	12	79	33	21	25	1

建筑物管理机构

单位：个、人、人次、时

格水平	年龄结构				志愿服务	
社会工作师人数	35岁及以下人数	36岁至45岁人数	46岁至55岁人数	56岁及以上人数	志愿者服务人次数	志愿服务时间
183	3030	3882	2548	590	28355	74832.5
4	15	13	10	9	226	238.0
	32	45	41	13	200	400.0
21	263	329	191	58	904	3255.0
5	88	137	126	25		
3	21	40	31	9		
4	97	113	84	29	13	20.0
	108	166	95	6		
	51	77	64	11		
3	42	59	72	53	210	720.0
35	171	241	222	44	3078	9879.0
6	46	60	51	13	650	2166.0
11	81	177	118	10	1028	2012.0
3	25	61	35	17		
	82	127	102	6	132	528.0
23	344	326	200	43	19387	49555.5
41	535	476	255	38	6	16.0
2	185	278	141	78	137	242.0
	139	173	106	19	285	765.0
2	97	160	147	24		
3	85	91	76	16		
	1	6	10			
	17	39	12	2	45	209.0
7	138	224	95	32	335	985.0
	22	51	35	5	1497	3221.0
	24	41	31	1		
	2	55	10	2		
4	145	145	48	4	200	495.0
5	141	136	92	14	20	110.0
	4	5	7	2	2	16.0
	8	3	14	4		
1	21	28	27	3		

C-2-52续表

地　区	执行行政事业单位会计制度财务指标				
	固定资产原价	上年结转和结余	本年收入合计	本年支出合计	收支结余
全　国	**526450.7**	**14350.7**	**162109.7**	**160429.3**	**11903.6**
中央级					
北　京	11990.0	296.5	1984.5	1690.9	192.6
天　津	12305.8	1.4	3066.7	3227.2	18.4
河　北	26716.9	1381.4	18540.9	18442.7	702.4
山　西	16777.2	625.3	7350.0	6155.4	2158.7
内蒙古	5487.6	539.2	1993.4	2215.4	317.2
辽　宁	6392.0	782.0	4053.0	4518.7	254.2
吉　林	7707.8	0.3	2272.2	2329.5	
黑龙江	5063.1	421.0	1750.5	1156.2	
上　海	68363.4	1268.9	7847.8	8285.2	914.0
江　苏	35036.9	602.9	14286.6	14457.7	545.6
浙　江	45692.2	1419.9	4448.5	4367.1	777.6
安　徽	26247.2	54.7	4251.6	4279.6	-14.0
福　建	4408.2	779.7	2432.5	2441.3	388.4
江　西	9259.3	107.5	2713.9	2440.8	351.0
山　东	56966.1		28391.3	28391.3	
河　南	22204.8	526.9	7865.1	7754.5	91.7
湖　北	22115.0	-40.2	5493.2	6455.0	-193.3
湖　南	21808.6	59.9	2703.7	2912.2	9.6
广　东	21112.9	216.6	17758.5	14970.8	2989.9
广　西	17731.6	0.4	5644.6	6218.3	1766.7
海　南	2414.7	200.3	698.6	573.8	
重　庆	5173.8		1520.2	1270.2	250.0
四　川	42962.3	2361.9	5022.9	3537.3	327.0
贵　州	6113.2	23.9	1451.9	1550.8	
云　南	3717.8	147.0	371.9	1831.8	
西　藏	1472.5		1.0	65.0	
陕　西	15603.0	240.3	3555.9	3687.0	34.2
甘　肃	2958.4		1749.9	1597.2	4.7
青　海	541.3		315.5	315.5	
宁　夏	502.8	77.1	122.8	183.0	17.0
新　疆	1604.3	2255.9	2450.6	3107.9	

单位：万元、平方米、个、人次

管理单位占地面积	烈士纪念建筑物面积	烈士纪念建筑物数	纪念馆(陈列馆)个数	藏品数	参观人次数	本机构管理的其他烈士纪念园地数
44416867.2	**5658892.5**	**34625**	**1360**	**233896**	**70992932**	**592**
71116.0	26225.0	42	7	1044	405400	6
339913.3	43191.3	35	13	1563	1218060	
3405216.8	257576.4	530	80	38049	4189233	78
1336898.0	345731.5	148	51	3809	1654909	1
476623.0	44110.0	29	15	255	414802	1
1799738.4	263255.0	404	26	16184	1077107	6
623270.0	26469.0	400	27	5806	976726	5
414838.1	79567.8	535	17	7137	2685782	1
385450.0	43204.7	65	16	2627	1800531	5
2867589.5	499545.0	402	110	19915	7589794	5
1165820.1	97237.3	133	35	6125	1730808	16
4775797.8	271404.0	831	197	6959	4627273	5
741089.6	64913.7	154	23	1465	3395170	25
776503.0	178018.0	790	42	5545	688986	147
5227172.0	505106.1	704	159	31319	8572128	10
2523300.5	237762.2	910	99	10011	3944464	86
2875346.7	538083.5	528	104	21060	3956158	61
1330931.1	371684.9	227	20	3462	1767447	1
1472726.0	116783.7	245	12	1905	5238755	7
2267419.4	173777.1	64	10	2219	1759564	6
503024.0	138215.0	482	23	856	431702	25
220442.0	63282.8	124	18	2759	2631047	36
5590903.8	608540.2	3979	96	9987	3703022	14
806519.0	256744.0	225	12	424	1139831	11
515187.9	103109.7	79	12	2150	530539	6
92520.0	40226.0	82	43	5702	76020	1
490923.0	91364.0	83	37	4589	1686818	2
644048.0	88905.0	264	37	8723	2585877	20
103805.2	33640.0	22025	6	10800	85000	4
237244.0	40879.6	72	5	859	129250	1
335491.0	10340.0	34	8	588	300729	

C-2-53 自然灾害损失

地区	人口受灾情况			
	受灾人口	死亡人口	失踪人口	紧急转移安置人口
合计	**18620.3**	**819**	**148**	**644.4**
北京	5.5			
天津				
河北	1699.5	12		0.2
山西	863.3	10		0.5
内蒙古	584.4	26		1.5
辽宁	715.6	10		0.7
吉林	450.5			0.5
黑龙江	249.7	3		0.7
上海	16.9	1		14.2
江苏	534.8	10		17.2
浙江	704.6	67	12	185.2
安徽	1069.7	27		45.1
福建	370.9	46	4	99.9
江西	628.3	50		48.8
山东	1173.2	11		0.4
河南	516.5	19		1.2
湖北	1100.2	48	6	15.9
湖南	1221.4	30	2	38.8
广东	848.7	31	5	38.3
广西	768.3	59	1	27.7
海南	144.9	5	1	8
重庆	189.2	29	3	3.9
四川	997.5	69	19	26.6
贵州	588	64	4	18.5
云南	1279.2	87	17	10.9
西藏	55.4	36	2	14.1
陕西	583	36	68	6.2
甘肃	658	3		0.7
青海	189.5	12	3	0.1
宁夏	131			0.03
新疆	219.9	18	1	17.6
兵团	62.7			1

情况总表

单位：万人次、人、千公顷、万间、亿元

农作物受灾情况		房屋倒损情况			直接经济损失
受灾面积	绝收面积	倒塌房屋	严重损坏房屋	一般损坏房屋	
21769.8	**2232.7**	**24.8**	**49.2**	**201.3**	**2704.1**
6.2	0.9			0.1	1.3
1798.8	169.5	0.1	0.2	1.2	107.5
1142.6	140.4	0.1	0.4	1.1	103.3
2700.8	315	0.1	0.1	2.2	113.5
1482.8	240.5			0.1	65.1
846.2	74	0.005	0.1	0.6	81.9
1175.3	68.8	0.1	1	1.4	39.5
12.3	1.1				3.5
615.5	41	0.3	0.6	15.5	84.9
393.2	58	0.3	0.6	2.6	228.2
966.7	149	0.9	2.3	8.2	118.9
203.3	26.5	1.8	2.2	12	189.1
455.3	39.5	1.4	1.4	3.9	69.7
1379	98.9	0.2	0.2	1	80.7
225.1	12.2	0.7	0.8	4.1	44
1115.6	90.5	1.7	2	4.5	82.2
765.1	88.5	1.6	3.3	7.9	126.7
846.3	92.9	1	2.1	12.9	315.3
545.7	32.3	1.2	1.2	4.8	48.5
41.2	3.7			0.03	14.2
70.8	9.1	0.9	1	2.9	22
562.7	57	2.3	5	24.6	132
224.4	29.5	0.7	3.4	11.1	72.6
1028.3	111.6	0.8	5	36	141.9
11.8	1.8	2.4	3.9	8.8	107.2
744.3	73.7	0.4	0.7	2.3	72.7
1011.2	76.2	0.1	0.4	4.2	61.6
220.5	21.6	0.1	0.1	0.4	12
218.8	27.2	0.1	0.02	0.1	8.3
551.4	60.7	5	10	24.1	109
408.6	21.1	0.5	1.2	2.7	46.8

C-2-54 旱灾

地 区	人口受灾情况		
	受灾人口	因旱需生活救助人口	因旱饮水困难需救助人口
合 计	**5436.5**	**854.9**	**454.2**
北 京	0.6		
天 津			
河 北	894.8	44	16.8
山 西	624	164.9	24.2
内蒙古	404.7	123	62.2
辽 宁	678.6	36.2	29.6
吉 林	402.3	18.4	0.4
黑龙江	79.9	0.9	
上 海			
江 苏			
浙 江			
安 徽			
福 建			
江 西			
山 东	664.7	95.3	75.6
河 南			
湖 北	43.5	5.5	4.5
湖 南			
广 东	47.8	7.3	7.3
广 西	99.3	13.7	8.6
海 南	11.2		
重 庆			
四 川	165.4	39.3	21.6
贵 州	61.9	23.1	11.9
云 南	522.6	165	125.1
西 藏	9.7	2.9	0.3
陕 西	272.3	13.3	10.4
甘 肃	228.6	31.2	18.8
青 海	112.7	0.3	
宁 夏	99.6	69.1	36.5
新 疆	0.1	0.1	
兵 团	12.2	1.4	0.4

损失情况

单位:万人次、千公顷、万头、亿元

农作物受灾情况		损失情况	
受灾面积	绝收面积	饮水困难大牲畜	直接经济损失
10609.7	**1046.1**	**498.8**	**486.4**
0.2	0.2		0.1
1112.7	81.7	9.2	47.5
1023.4	126	5.4	71
2171.7	254	252.4	81.5
1429.5	233	4.4	60
700	60		73.6
484.1	10.1		8.9
883.2	65.4	15.6	32
117.7	12.1	1.1	4.1
147.7	19		6.2
160	3.1	2.8	1.6
4.2			1.5
222.9	10.7	12.7	6.1
18.9	2.2	3	1
514.9	47.9	100	23.7
1.3	0.3	4.8	0.6
561.6	38.1		22.4
533.1	47.5	8.9	21.6
126.5	5.4	3.2	5.6
172.1	22.6	75.3	4.7
128.9	2.1		0.1
95.1	4.7		12.6

C-2-55 风雹灾害

地区	人口受灾情况			
	受灾人口（万人次）	死亡人口（人）	失踪人口（人）	紧急转移安置人口
合计	**3202.3**	**116**		**5.7**
北京	4.6			
天津				
河北	592	11		0.07
山西	182.7	2		0.1
内蒙古	75.6	9		0.1
辽宁	25.6	3		0.02
吉林	35.1			0.01
黑龙江	38.3	2		
上海	0.0002	1		
江苏	115.8	8		0.7
浙江	1			0.01
安徽	133.8	8		0.3
福建	0.5			
江西	27.5	11		0.3
山东	262.3	6		0.1
河南	452.1	13		0.2
湖北	99.5			0.5
湖南	24.4	1		0.1
广东	21.3	4		
广西	9.2	4		0.1
海南				
重庆	21.1	2		0.1
四川	147.1	10		1.3
贵州	114.1	2		1.2
云南	145.3	8		0.2
西藏	3.8	1		0.001
陕西	210.3	3		0.1
甘肃	241.7	2		0.01
青海	39.5	3		0.01
宁夏	21.2			0.01
新疆	122.8	2		0.1
兵团	34.1			0.02

损失情况

单位：万人次、人、千公顷、万间、亿元

农作物受灾情况		房屋倒损情况			直接经济损失
受灾面积	绝收面积	倒塌房屋	严重损坏房屋	一般损坏房屋	
2918	**309.1**	**1.3**	**5.1**	**61.2**	**322.7**
5.3	0.7			0.1	1.1
346.8	54.7	0.04	0.1	1.1	48.6
55.8	5.1	0.03	0.1	0.6	21.2
301.5	37.9	0.01	0.03	0.2	16.1
46.5	6.6	0.004	0.01	0.1	4.7
121.8	10.1	0.001	0.01	0.4	5.7
146.5	15.1		0.1	0.5	5.6
97	6	0.1	0.2	7.6	15.8
0.8	0.002	0.0001	0.001	0.01	0.1
118.7	6.5	0.1	0.3	0.9	6
0.2	0.1			0.01	0.1
16	0.9	0.1	0.1	0.3	1.7
207.6	23.4	0.1	0.1	0.6	17.8
152.6	8.9	0.3	0.5	3.9	30.5
50.5	2.7	0.1	0.2	1.1	4.3
11.8	0.3			0.3	0.8
4.4				5.7	2.2
3.2	0.3			0.5	0.3
10.2	1.5			1.3	1.9
71.7	12.8	0.1	1.3	11.8	13.4
40.8	6.5	0.1	0.5	4.5	6.9
112	13.8	0.02	1.4	17.6	16.8
1.4	0.3	0.01	0.01	0.02	0.6
75.5	10.7	0.1		0.7	28.9
263	20.2	0.02	0.1	1.1	29
49.8	11.9	0.01	0.02	0.04	2.9
38.1	2.8	0.04	0.001	0.01	2.3
309.4	36.5			0.2	20.3
259.1	12.8	0.0002	0.01	0.01	17.1

C-2-56 台风灾害

地区	人口受灾情况			
	受灾人口	死亡人口	失踪人口	紧急转移安置人口
合计	**2375.6**	**48**	**9**	**359.5**
北京				
天津				
河北				
山西				
内蒙古				
辽宁				
吉林				
黑龙江				
上海	15.2			14.2
江苏	224.8			7.2
浙江	667.6	15	3	182.8
安徽	128.8	4		22.6
福建	268.5	8	2	70.1
江西	58.6	1		11.1
山东	4.1			
河南				
湖北				
湖南				
广东	613.5	18	4	30.3
广西	275.9	1		13.4
海南	112.6	1		7.8
重庆				
四川				
贵州				
云南	6			0.01
西藏				
陕西				
甘肃				
青海				
宁夏				
新疆				
兵团				

注：台风灾害损失包含台风风暴潮。

损失情况

单位：万人次、人、千公顷、万间、亿元

农作物受灾情况		房屋倒损情况			直接经济损失
受灾面积	绝收面积	倒塌房屋	严重损坏房屋	一般损坏房屋	
1721.1	**181.5**	**2.3**	**5.4**	**21.7**	**684.2**
7.9					2.3
259.3	22	0.1	0.2	1.2	17.4
368.4	56.1	0.3	0.6	2.5	219.5
99	8.1	0.3	0.7	2.3	31.8
126.3	13.1	0.5	1.4	7	88.6
40.1	2.5	0.1	0.1	0.1	6.2
6				0.02	0.1
616.5	69	0.7	2	7	288
160.6	6.9	0.3	0.4	1.5	17.7
36.2	3.7			0.03	12.4
0.8	0.1	0.004	0.001	0.01	0.2

C-2-57 地震灾害

地　区	人口受灾情况			
	受灾人口（万人次）	死亡人口（人）	失踪人口（人）	紧急转移安置人口
合　计	**98.6**	**34**	**2**	**36.9**
北　京				
天　津				
河　北				
山　西	2.3			0.8
内蒙古				
	0.1			0.04
辽　宁				
吉　林				
黑龙江				
上　海	4.2	2		0.2
江　苏				
浙　江				
安　徽				
福　建				
江　西				
山　东				
河　南				
湖　北				
湖　南				
广　东	4.6			0.1
广　西	4.7			0.3
海　南	18.6			8.4
	30.4	28	2	13.8
重　庆				
四　川	3.6	1		0.6
贵　州				
云　南				
西　藏	26.1	3		12
	4			0.7
陕　西				
甘　肃				
青　海				
宁　夏				
新　疆				
兵　团				

损失情况

单位：万人次、人、千公顷、万间、亿元

农作物受灾情况		房屋倒损情况			直接经济损失
受灾面积	绝收面积	倒塌房屋	严重损坏房屋	一般损坏房屋	
0.5		**6.5**	**13.2**	**43.1**	**201.4**
			0.002	1.5	3.4
			0.04	0.1	0.1
			0.6	0.9	0.8
0.3			0.1	3.8	11
0.1			0.1	0.7	6.1
0.1		0.03	2.1	12	12.3
		2.3	3.8	8.5	103.2
		0.02	0.2	3	1
		3.7	5.2	10.2	54.5
		0.4	1.1	2.4	9

C-2-58 低温冷冻和

地 区	人口受灾情况			
	受灾人口（万人次）	死亡人口（人）	失踪人口（人）	紧急转移安置人口
合 计	**729.6**	**8**		**0.5**
北 京	0.1			
天 津				
河 北	31.4			
山 西	26.1			
内蒙古	52.1			
辽 宁				
吉 林	0.3			
黑龙江	24.5			0.0004
上 海				
江 苏	64.8			
浙 江				
安 徽	28.7			0.1
福 建				
江 西				
山 东	51.1	4		0.1
河 南	4.8			
湖 北	43.9			0.1
湖 南	0.9			
广 东				
广 西				
海 南				
重 庆				
四 川	3.4			
贵 州	6			
云 南	204			0.01
西 藏	6.3	4		0.005
陕 西	13.5			
甘 肃	114.2			
青 海	25.7			
宁 夏	8.1			
新 疆	9.3			0.2
兵 团	10.4			

雪灾损失情况

单位:万人次、人、千公顷、万间、亿元

农作物受灾情况		房屋倒损情况			直接经济损失
受灾面积	绝收面积	倒塌房屋	严重损坏房屋	一般损坏房屋	
900.3	**36.5**	**0.1**	**0.1**	**0.7**	**89**
					0.1
57.1	2	0.0002			2.2
32	2.6			0.0002	5.3
42.4	1.9				2.5
0.2					0.04
63	3.4	0.002	0.003	0.02	2.4
58.8	1.6	0.002	0.004	0.01	4.6
58.1	1.5	0.01	0.01	0.004	6.8
43.1	1.7			0.1	22.3
19.9	0.5				1.2
73.7	1.3				3.8
0.7	0.2				0.1
9.7	0.2				0.3
4	0.1				0.1
169.7	7.9	0.01	0.1	0.1	20.1
1.5	0.0001	0.02	0.01	0.02	0.8
16.3	5.2				2
134.5	1.5				2.6
34.4	0.5	0.004	0.01		1.9
4					0.6
29.7	1.8			0.4	3.6
47.5	2.6	0.0002	0.01	0.003	5.7

C-2-59 洪涝、滑坡和

地 区	人口受灾情况			
	受灾人口（万人次）	死亡人口（人）	失踪人口（人）	紧急转移安置人口
合 计	**6777.5**	**575**	**126**	**241.8**
北 京	0.2			
天 津				
河 北	181.3	1		0.1
山 西	30.5	8		0.4
内蒙古	49.6	17		0.6
辽 宁	11.4	1		0.7
吉 林	12.7			0.4
黑龙江	107	1		0.7
上 海	1.7			
江 苏	129.4	1		9.3
浙 江	36	39		2.4
安 徽	774.2	13		21.9
福 建	101.9	35	1	29.8
江 西	542.2	38		37.4
山 东	191	1		0.2
河 南	59.6	6		1
湖 北	913.3	47	6	15.3
湖 南	1196.1	28	2	38.7
广 东	166.1	6	1	8
广 西	383.9	49	1	14.2
海 南	21.1	2		0.2
重 庆	168.1	27	3	3.8
四 川	677	57	19	25.2
贵 州	401.3	62	4	17
云 南	382.7	79	17	2.3
西 藏	5.2	3		0.3
陕 西	86.9	32	68	6.1
甘 肃	69.9			0.04
青 海	11.5	9	3	0.1
宁 夏	2.1			0.02
新 疆	61.6	13	1	5.3
兵 团	2			0.3

泥石流灾害损失情况

单位:万人次、人、千公顷、万间、亿元

农作物受灾情况		房屋倒损情况			直接经济损失
受灾面积	绝收面积	倒塌房屋	严重损坏房屋	一般损坏房屋	
5620.2	**659.5**	**14.6**	**25.4**	**74.6**	**919.9**
0.7				0.002	0.03
282.2	31.1	0.03	0.05	0.1	9.2
31.4	6.7	0.1	0.3	0.5	5.8
185.2	21.2	0.1	0.1	0.5	9.7
6.8	0.9	0.01	0.002	0.02	0.4
24.2	3.9	0.004	0.02	0.1	2.5
481.7	40.2	0.1	0.9	0.9	22.6
4.4	1.1				1.2
200.4	11.4	0.1	0.2	6.7	47.1
24	1.9			0.1	8.5
690.9	132.9	0.5	0.7	4.1	73.5
76.8	13.3	1.3	0.8	5	100.4
399.2	36.1	1.2	1.2	3.5	61.8
239.1	8.4	0.1	0.1	0.2	8.5
52.6	2.8	0.4	0.3	0.2	12.3
873.7	74.4	1.6	1.8	3.4	70
752.6	88	1.6	3.3	7.6	125.8
77.7	4.9	0.3	0.1	0.2	18.9
221.9	22	0.9	0.8	2.8	28.9
0.8					0.3
60.6	7.6	0.9	1	1.6	20.1
258.1	33.3	2.2	3.6	9	101.2
160.6	20.7	0.6	2.8	5.9	58.5
230.8	41.9	0.7	1.4	6.3	68.8
7.6	1.2	0.03	0.1	0.2	2
90.9	19.7	0.3	0.7	1.6	19.4
80.6	7	0.02	0.1	0.1	7.4
9.8	3.8	0.1	0.1	0.3	1.5
4.6	1.8	0.01	0.02	0.1	0.7
83.4	20.3	1.3	4.8	13.3	30.5
6.9	1	0.1	0.1	0.3	2.4

C-3-1 成员组

地区	单位数	年末职工人数	女性	受教育程度 大学专科人数	大学本科及以上人数	职业资 助理社会工作师人数
全国	**1342960**	**10157149**	**3019335**	**1754174**	**1086825**	**37006**
中央级	2316	34064	14993	368	24632	437
北京	16632	158793	69881	38739	59728	3872
天津	10488	63097	27723	16907	22338	1026
河北	72237	557141	189757	56149	32866	2058
山西	42928	259143	75395	49711	20419	204
内蒙古	26681	147517	47327	35262	12820	258
辽宁	36394	273967	85712	57960	46523	1098
吉林	21802	108618	25127	14167	4147	728
黑龙江	26503	205893	73563	34284	12273	287
上海	19102	202440	50103	68934	23471	1466
江苏	101880	685786	195259	154544	96097	5620
浙江	76078	510926	154631	113411	62452	1966
安徽	42617	333223	89544	68800	40344	2982
福建	40723	344828	78513	32457	26565	792
江西	35789	277787	79570	32855	10608	668
山东	123855	683201	179874	161332	96386	1034
河南	80974	460396	128718	77621	36240	337
湖北	57008	442546	140112	85423	29681	1708
湖南	73320	420581	134762	82490	47247	583
广东	80199	744003	297991	174745	111403	3557
广西	38393	434708	91908	46729	28598	493
海南	8429	67934	21296	8261	6333	25
重庆	26443	218603	88770	47921	44512	2422
四川	93200	758935	231385	107141	68538	1350
贵州	29231	270822	67653	39720	41103	102
云南	35387	518786	175626	47291	29368	571
西藏	6037	37457	10334	1294	886	
陕西	44956	375121	88135	35453	17598	194
甘肃	36096	260894	42531	23499	11185	939
青海	8252	44048	10563	4175	1116	47
宁夏	7611	65793	12316	7662	4933	34
新疆	21399	190098	40263	28869	16415	148

织总表

单位：个、人、人次、时

格水平	年龄结构				志愿服务	
社会工作师人数	35岁及以下人数	36岁至45岁人数	46岁至55岁人数	56岁及以上人数	志愿者服务人次数	志愿服务时间
30385	**3074793**	**3946241**	**2206906**	**929209**	**2802525**	**9620706.4**
6571	8993	13151	7507	4413		
2556	50459	54520	40407	13407	735126	4146993.0
311	16167	18568	18017	10345	19526	54825.0
2268	130379	274450	117388	34924	52391	238676.0
140	75851	92607	63319	27366	5811	11581.0
208	46351	54820	33133	13213	18136	43944.0
466	77350	99073	57821	39723	30688	37727.0
1758	20484	74672	9272	4190	21	30.0
358	73476	78653	42582	11182	633	1790.0
2449	64443	66379	48166	23452	30040	88921.0
1578	190601	253998	170931	70256	261585	648907.0
1220	153414	196068	106321	55123	169530	363270.0
862	95924	130963	79810	26526	105075	248668.0
439	83164	116149	89635	55880	3621	3925.0
161	90438	123252	49057	15040	1549	4065.0
403	193934	290242	153483	45542	257621	648903.4
212	158514	173880	91297	36705	4504	4518.0
918	147762	152745	111641	30398	21169	72803.0
274	141987	171074	82041	25479	179611	566010.0
2606	330996	231599	132015	49393	38239	99327.0
602	103106	156786	111398	63418	8582	28464.0
32	20818	30979	12404	3733		
2110	80994	76218	44013	17378	322839	888877.8
503	257733	283470	136685	81047	86628	286846.0
56	70836	113091	61159	25736	425624	1072010.2
125	152041	181483	106648	78614	1468	2402.0
	8564	13098	10563	5232	9	
140	96241	129945	116423	32512	4315	17856.0
965	61924	125866	58481	14623	1518	2036.0
10	10320	22422	9227	2079	8413	12187.0
8	9913	45273	7632	2975	4	
76	51616	100747	28430	9305	8249	25144.0

C-3-1续表

地区	执行企业会计制度单位财务指标					执行行政
	固定资产原价	营业收入	费用合计	营业利润	固定资产原价	上年结转和结余
全国	**2727337.9**	**1580476.7**	**29720.1**	**62691.9**	**21466812.6**	**1388906.6**
中央级						
北京	2458738.3	1525429.8	29346.8	61648.9	427581.1	121295.9
天津					147810.4	19920.4
河北	5444.5				2420273.6	22100.8
山西					589354.8	7572.2
内蒙古					101070.1	4.4
辽宁	1397.8				158668.9	14088.3
吉林	216.0	2.0	2.0		77286.4	678.9
黑龙江	6701.2	26.0	0.6		373328.3	34764.7
上海	187570.3	52399.4	122.0	1034.4	1034562.3	110973.1
江苏		140.0	105.0		5731671.0	730387.6
浙江	409.0				3485469.9	96279.3
安徽					489488.0	23610.2
福建	203.0	385.0			121002.7	1560.6
江西	11538.1	1432.0	65.0	6.0	142705.0	-389.8
山东					1426036.5	
河南	7012.0	36.0			259920.4	1591.6
湖北	155.4				884220.0	666.2
湖南	1212.0				267196.3	2419.3
广东	24671.5	38.5	27.7	2.6	1750474.8	67692.2
广西	347.0				172669.6	1620.4
海南					23193.6	625.1
重庆					182354.5	2554.6
四川	2996.4				263376.7	28075.2
贵州	7.5				39071.3	2767.0
云南	2022.0				416207.3	93488.2
西藏	9714.0		40.0		20491.4	10.0
陕西	6.0				165038.0	959.5
甘肃	29.5				158475.1	505.9
青海	4.6				6902.4	5.0
宁夏	975.5				36467.6	45.0
新疆	5966.3	588.0	11.0		94444.6	3034.8

单位：万元

事业单位会计制度财务指标			执行民间非营利组织单位会计制度财务指标			
本年收入合计	本年支出合计	收支结余	固定资产原价	上年结余	本年收入合计	本年费用合计
8332765.3	**7226575.1**	**83096.8**	**25309976.9**	**11167688.4**	**29665645.8**	**24413337.8**
			953052.1		5569041.1	4424685.2
261107.1	334373.0	5818.0	1201051.3	1724446.8	1790230.3	1188879.0
113960.4	116918.2		429764.9	18394.3	193439.6	275263.6
336315.8	331275.7	4850.0	1567216.7	642838.2	5555114.9	1898736.2
152181.1	169209.3	575.2	341266.1	12508.9	190658.8	171520.7
65428.8	65047.7	337.0	85720.4	1051.1	78971.5	80078.1
361695.1	100905.8	1357.4	1188167.6	881840.8	409881.2	424516.2
33818.2	32960.0	16.0	10751.9	342.2	97415.5	22852.3
321118.3	64337.0	45.7	151151.6	2280.8	33601.6	195235.6
490604.0	425853.7	21800.0	306221.8	2510002.8	2655448.1	2291482.2
984412.6	859000.0	3405.5	2367764.6	2069236.8	2914549.1	2641884.3
1221201.6	1025931.6	16809.0	2526305.3	1025169.3	1686143.4	1476087.1
176471.8	166073.9	61.5	1152652.3	300366.8	592402.9	576388.7
139291.9	140175.1		373482.5	150297.8	254943.9	269846.8
85967.3	85967.0	117.0	332173.3	7875.1	271353.5	943075.2
1217124.9	1217100.6		676685.9	6512.5	1037668.0	1026906.6
145344.1	141123.1	248.8	723848.0	53378.1	707252.0	448680.3
203247.9	200222.1	184.1	578818.2	4869.9	570452.7	533812.1
258274.6	252163.8	954.3	545989.8	71910.9	327112.7	342067.4
847359.8	614044.8	22541.2	6267734.4	318039.4	1970916.9	2193775.8
91277.9	55641.2	149.0	183420.4	72636.0	102615.2	91582.7
19581.3	19593.8	230.0	72979.5	204.4	335332.1	99572.1
72770.3	71997.5	569.1	676138.2	195072.6	620052.8	524578.2
179179.1	201796.9	2659.3	845196.8	666671.2	942780.6	1339099.5
317809.6	316116.8	68.1	298856.7	45866.2	155892.7	141828.0
86036.2	77820.0	258.6	575161.3	257002.2	288360.5	328531.1
730.1	754.1		4976.7	13863.7	3398.7	2953.5
65403.5	58592.7		543786.3	5275.2	117289.2	204679.8
34292.3	25560.9	10.0	115385.1	3861.9	53400.2	54788.7
1131.4	1087.0		54556.2	969.2	29943.7	34931.9
6585.4	6689.7		59241.3	27110.5	38765.0	91500.6
43042.9	48242.1	32.0	100459.7	77792.8	71217.4	73518.3

C-3-2 社会组

地　区	单位数	年末职工人数	女性	受教育程度 大学专科人数	大学本科及以上人数	职业资格水平 助理社会工作师人数	社会工作师人数
全　国	**662425**	**7347892**	**2241648**	**1398843**	**966440**	**20173**	**24206**
中央级	2316	34064	14993	368	24632	437	6571
北　京	9721	124162	51499	27808	51227	899	1429
天　津	5137	40676	16878	11161	19097	135	79
河　北	19328	369688	155341	44755	30529	1920	2153
山　西	12511	148418	49002	38567	15539	80	39
内蒙古	13248	93553	29066	28051	10434	139	183
辽　宁	20669	203846	56629	38251	40187	263	102
吉　林	10606	73716	13044	13372	3583	684	1728
黑龙江	13567	148331	53926	21676	9422	97	324
上　海	13355	175287	34224	61750	19683	470	2120
江　苏	80385	574738	160966	129541	86338	2236	636
浙　江	43784	385560	119093	93926	55836	413	504
安　徽	24630	255607	66579	57936	37851	1999	497
福　建	23956	276227	60877	28847	25878	488	278
江　西	15358	201551	58807	28154	9357	517	137
山　东	43411	357529	85427	104060	71811	714	322
河　南	29472	246082	79400	47250	28238	271	111
湖　北	27605	324578	102283	73451	27039	1260	757
湖　南	27766	257929	87850	65842	43718	355	200
广　东	53958	616820	262511	158502	105425	2137	2062
广　西	22196	354569	72178	40542	27371	381	556
海　南	5357	52898	17717	6388	6156	2	32
重　庆	15360	163302	70342	37121	41265	1635	1737
四　川	40011	547520	178712	84637	62239	858	362
贵　州	10533	182063	47691	34195	40295	82	42
云　南	21128	447877	161007	42283	28229	510	105
西　藏	572	11970	4476	748	666		
陕　西	19699	277783	63573	32295	16712	168	129
甘　肃	18730	192871	29876	19363	9534	908	957
青　海	3633	25717	6585	3380	874	34	8
宁　夏	4857	53289	8022	6267	4577	6	3
新　疆	9566	129671	23074	18356	12698	75	43

织总表

单位:个、人、人次、时

年龄结构				志愿服务	
35岁及以下人数	36岁至45岁人数	46岁至55岁人数	56岁及以上人数	志愿者服务人次数	志愿服务时间
2498325	**2729883**	**1404928**	**714756**	**478768**	**1221227.4**
8993	13151	7507	4413		
42609	43303	28465	9785		
9742	12013	11368	7553	850	1700.0
99718	197727	54421	17822	7598	30888.0
52787	50065	29730	15836	2197	4221.0
34043	31928	18593	8989	1444	4102.0
60109	72040	37666	34031	558	1125.0
19549	41334	8716	4117	20	30.0
62147	46736	29978	9470		
58714	58095	39039	19439	356	792.0
164094	209686	138054	62904	60745	132906.0
127288	142235	69734	46303	58069	108493.0
81890	94188	57938	21591	37888	86526.0
70784	81869	70793	52781	6	
76041	80786	32957	11767	10	
124170	146182	65638	21539	103291	275726.4
115393	80441	30716	19532	13	34.0
124581	103499	73263	23235	2783	5589.0
107929	93065	40590	16345	131420	392813.0
307362	186505	87685	35268	38177	99207.0
90724	128779	81078	53988		
18077	24191	8193	2437		
67516	52925	28691	14170	28063	56278.0
212327	194080	78530	62583	70	286.0
50368	77066	35834	18795	2524	12174.0
133103	150722	89158	74894	507	1231.0
4568	4547	2187	668		
81049	91211	82223	23300	1508	4131.0
47216	91690	42989	10976	46	5.0
6471	14300	3844	1102	32	
7044	39996	3721	2528		
31919	75528	15629	6595	593	2970.0

C-3-2续表1

地　区	行政执法	行政处罚数	并处没收违法经营额/违法所得	并处罚款
全　国	**2951**	**2928**	**7**	**8**
中央级				
北　京	123	122	7	7
天　津				
河　北	155	155		
山　西	13	13		
内蒙古	25	25		
辽　宁				
吉　林	4	4		
黑龙江				
上　海	16	16		
江　苏	71	68		
浙　江	13	13		
安　徽	13	13		
福　建				
江　西				
山　东	1662	1656		1
河　南	14	1		
湖　北	92	92		
湖　南				
广　东	90	90		
广　西	24	24		
海　南				
重　庆	171	171		
四　川	227	227		
贵　州	72	72		
云　南				
西　藏				
陕　西	41	41		
甘　肃				
青　海				
宁　夏	1	1		
新　疆	124	124		

单位：起

(1) 警告	(2) 限期（责令）停止活动	(3) 撤销登记	取缔非法社会组织	#并处没收非法财产
901	**60**	**1967**	**23**	**1**
54		68	1	
		155		
		13		
		25		
		4		
		16		
42	18	8	3	
9		4		
		13		
706	16	934	6	1
		1	13	
12	1	79		
51	3	36		
		24		
17	14	140		
4	1	222		
		72		
3	2	36		
		1		
3	5	116		

C-3-2续表2

地　区	执行行政事业单位会计制度财务指标				
	固定资产原价	上年结转和结余	本年收入合计	本年支出合计	收支结余
全　国	**276899.1**	**23062.1**	**515717.5**	**228967.1**	**1985.3**
中央级					
北　京					
天　津					
河　北	1134.9	15.0	439.9	276.5	
山　西	3045.0		2060.6	1763.1	2.0
内蒙古	6898.4	4.4	5238.9	5217.5	337.0
辽　宁	1240.1	270.7	4894.2	4790.2	
吉　林	505.0	24.0	1445.6	1068.6	
黑龙江	20448.4	4.0	262388.2	407.5	
上　海					
江　苏	142069.5	18364.8	199501.0	186465.5	496.9
浙　江	10.1		23.0	8.0	
安　徽	8.0		4.5	4.5	
福　建	7920.9	4.0	1978.0	1819.0	
江　西	8500.2		2567.5	2416.0	117.0
山　东					
河　南	2499.2	206.0	1613.7	529.4	
湖　北	3350.0		3410.3	2559.3	
湖　南	7971.8	1495.4	6845.9	7303.2	954.3
广　东	7622.7	256.4	1950.7	1282.8	
广　西	3489.8	1217.0	1212.4	1098.4	
海　南	1937.0	18.0	993.2	996.2	
重　庆	1577.2	18.6	712.5	712.5	
四　川	1762.1		1708.2	1020.0	
贵　州	2770.4	131.3	1931.1	1190.8	68.1
云　南	8570.6	356.5	2041.9	1550.0	
西　藏	4152.1		0.2	0.2	
陕　西	4115.1	6.5	750.1	563.7	
甘　肃	25794.7	256.3	6082.0	779.3	10.0
青　海	95.0		2.0	3.0	
宁　夏	5206.8		4213.0	4213.0	
新　疆	4204.1	413.2	1708.9	928.9	

单位：万元

执行民间非营利组织单位会计制度财务指标			
固定资产原价	上年结余	本年收入合计	本年费用合计
22833898.0	**11070290.0**	**28774009.2**	**23608642.7**
953052.1		5569041.1	4424685.2
1201051.3	1724446.8	1790167.6	1188879.0
429742.0	18394.3	193439.6	275227.6
1535069.3	642747.8	5549526.9	1887335.5
243503.9	11847.5	163945.7	156318.1
81158.8	1051.1	75763.1	76555.5
1129742.3	880373.7	389089.0	403853.6
10751.9	342.2	97380.8	22852.3
141974.6	2247.8	26386.5	189555.7
306221.8	2510002.8	2655447.1	2290984.0
1776745.3	2062993.7	2702128.0	2476990.4
1741529.3	1021176.4	1425125.9	1282573.6
1133580.8	300366.8	585769.6	569334.7
255553.0	127472.0	192257.6	218205.5
314833.0	6802.1	260197.0	928014.3
676685.9	6512.5	1037668.0	1026906.6
624918.3	53369.1	664559.6	401455.7
525448.4	4869.9	497937.6	477134.5
521806.1	71910.9	322343.7	337831.9
6123029.7	307762.3	1945732.1	2140283.5
181040.6	72602.0	101673.8	90216.0
71686.5	204.4	335047.1	99287.1
607155.3	194798.6	585775.3	492477.1
783016.1	659915.3	925634.8	1304085.9
163184.5	16343.7	105462.5	89390.7
473109.0	243013.0	270572.1	307323.6
4630.7	13863.7	3398.7	2953.5
543786.3	5275.2	117289.2	204679.8
102629.7	3861.9	52361.8	53414.9
28817.7	939.2	25092.1	28866.8
56356.6	26990.5	38310.2	90546.9
92087.2	77792.8	69485.1	70423.2

C-3-3 社会

地区	单位数	年末职工人数		受教育程度		职业资
			女性	大学专科人数	大学本科及以上人数	助理社会工作师人数
全　国	**328500**	**3901849**	**912812**	**544786**	**375358**	**8298**
中央级	1974	30166	13330		24406	437
北　京	3961	39591	12616	8860	20830	157
天　津	2408	12053	4113	1583	7603	14
河　北	9871	235453	95778	13180	10389	1598
山　西	6562	77358	20856	19234	6813	26
内蒙古	7538	55714	13767	17859	5700	8
辽　宁	8655	99931	14792	13921	12202	39
吉　林	5540	36699	4804	4712	1550	466
黑龙江	5871	99829	37968	9578	5061	53
上　海	4003	32736	6215	14504	4565	199
江　苏	35137	236898	58794	61446	26144	773
浙　江	20745	142144	33693	37650	19004	174
安　徽	12637	113618	14757	17204	9150	1552
福　建	15251	196445	29182	17084	8251	132
江　西	8303	109358	19859	16763	4759	25
山　东	17378	132789	25456	34079	27080	203
河　南	11758	79336	18071	10871	5587	107
湖　北	12118	178265	46498	27163	8071	43
湖　南	13208	119458	29231	23491	16392	110
广　东	24904	187131	41466	39276	26392	192
广　西	12949	245467	32435	20266	15811	261
海　南	2445	25644	5769	3675	4068	
重　庆	7221	46554	9274	7784	7518	321
四　川	20645	338463	91304	31148	32947	408
贵　州	6236	134592	28616	21885	31724	11
云　南	14115	378745	129627	29413	13303	95
西　藏	536	11778	4397	710	611	
陕　西	10627	182101	30155	13799	5151	37
甘　肃	14306	163954	21409	11629	5633	789
青　海	2320	17320	4498	1702	466	17
宁　夏	3285	43433	3093	3602	1871	2
新　疆	5993	98826	10989	10715	6306	49

团体

单位:个、人、人次、时

格水平	年龄结构				志愿服务	
社会工作师人数	35岁及以下人数	36岁至45岁人数	46岁至55岁人数	56岁及以上人数	志愿者服务人次数	志愿服务时间
12050	**981945**	**1550535**	**883240**	**486129**	**209196**	**499677.8**
6571	7607	11982	6814	3763		
146	7744	19771	9254	2822		
7	2834	3378	3185	2656	300	600.0
1417	41650	151141	31856	10806	1455	5534.0
15	16592	28730	20296	11740	1915	3069.0
2	17363	19377	12438	6536	746	2606.0
21	16636	34334	20296	28665	270	579.0
205	11789	17684	5839	1387		
142	46470	28419	19037	5903		
352	8064	9862	8019	6791	116	312.0
152	48086	84809	65375	38628	25240	59121.0
290	31380	57585	38689	14490	48888	91004.0
333	25319	47469	27931	12899	9489	20014.0
30	33849	57626	56845	48125		
42	37180	40375	23517	8286	10	
120	39785	51793	28996	12215	43504	119454.8
26	34562	27418	11573	5783		
73	66261	52684	49466	9854	312	836.0
62	36351	46011	25592	11504	61088	162899.0
212	43538	74927	45627	23039	352	1107.0
510	48339	94497	67395	35236		
32	9126	11445	3695	1378		
317	10298	15806	12107	8343	13612	27559.0
96	109830	119339	55106	54188	69	286.0
18	26915	62107	29055	16515	641	1988.0
55	96586	126790	82486	72883	398	936.0
	4505	4480	2137	656		
10	39964	56351	68568	17218	721	1673.0
767	36994	82478	35073	9409	45	
3	3978	9280	3253	809		
	3505	36011	2396	1521		
24	18845	66576	11324	2081	25	100.0

C-3-3续表1

地区	社会组织负责人	女性	中央级社团	省级社团
			按活动	
全国	**663189**	**122143**	**1974**	**29233**
中央级	24439	8222	1974	
北京	15556	3575		1687
天津	5961	483		976
河北	17016	2015		970
山西	8584	875		705
内蒙古	14524	2627		787
辽宁	11440	1824		840
吉林	7918	702		763
黑龙江	9563	1308		1053
上海	20406	4391		1248
江苏	54383	8320		1035
浙江	45666	8383		1118
安徽	17726	2153		1016
福建	17706	3030		1088
江西	13808	2077		811
山东	53018	10545		900
河南	17845	3515		1162
湖北	29220	4904		981
湖南	28257	4981		921
广东	54204	18783		1733
广西	19167	2434		873
海南	7281	837		855
重庆	23545	3867		1028
四川	37795	6284		1214
贵州	34570	2528		763
云南	18883	2836		956
西藏	771	61		218
陕西	19001	3126		908
甘肃	18334	5419		559
青海	2729	332		561
宁夏	3141	88		699
新疆	10732	1618		805

单位：人、个

区域分		当年新增单位数	当年年检单位数	行业性社团
地级社团	县级社团			
80220	**217073**	**30400**	**241113**	**41253**
		33	1853	401
	2274	325	3508	152
	1432	106	2163	299
2835	6066	824	8313	1649
2207	3650	428	4131	764
2604	4147	1028	5547	1742
3784	4031	333	5156	2275
1899	2878	253	4125	296
2359	2459	372	4206	531
	2755	145	3709	121
6024	28078	4182	29219	3423
4808	14819	1526	17973	1746
3757	7864	1451	8244	1620
3426	10737	1118	10524	2462
2421	5071	312	6337	517
5764	10714	1620	13223	5973
3869	6727	995	9817	1008
3415	7722	938	9861	1336
4020	8267	1130	10072	2043
8801	14370	2916	17487	1838
2552	9524	1485	7626	925
501	1089	187	1333	327
	6193	497	5649	1175
4317	15114	1492	14330	2499
1405	4068	600	2977	984
2833	10326	1313	11577	1159
117	201	12	406	167
2015	7704	1321	6001	924
1712	12035	2774	7767	983
511	1248	162	1731	243
582	2004	208	1722	289
1682	3506	314	4526	1382

C-3-3续表2

地区	社会组织					
	科技与研究	生态环境	教育	卫生	社会服务	文化
全　国	**16624**	**6812**	**10429**	**9950**	**47898**	**32998**
中央级	60	6	36	24	23	55
北　京	360	69	149	167	501	364
天　津	40	21	55	50	294	116
河　北	475	152	274	478	1348	1064
山　西	697	102	267	141	964	870
内蒙古	483	118	285	160	841	860
辽　宁	350	139	294	445	1061	723
吉　林	181	64	207	169	1466	520
黑龙江	291	104	203	252	1059	777
上　海	656	52	154	192	540	332
江　苏	1430	507	912	930	8890	3969
浙　江	1315	505	845	617	2167	2035
安　徽	671	237	316	359	2189	1347
福　建	496	396	727	420	2349	1891
江　西	244	209	375	427	1311	809
山　东	1080	287	455	508	2296	2099
河　南	792	288	448	360	1313	1266
湖　北	777	206	281	403	1552	1235
湖　南	774	418	580	447	1787	1298
广　东	1256	322	820	580	3827	2709
广　西	556	106	273	172	2243	756
海　南	280	22	57	48	205	328
重　庆	422	110	244	179	580	591
四　川	679	630	744	779	3114	1933
贵　州	237	105	173	155	761	641
云　南	380	234	312	465	1465	1374
西　藏	20	23	13	23	107	50
陕　西	549	132	203	210	1136	1291
甘　肃	252	910	190	285	1334	945
青　海	147	126	95	188	241	156
宁　夏	197	79	261	106	222	194
新　疆	477	133	181	211	712	400

单位：个

按行业分类

体育	法律	工商业服务	宗教	农业及农村发展	职业及从业组织	其他
23300	**3269**	**36654**	**4991**	**62151**	**20652**	**52772**
18	5	1536	4	9	3	195
258	60	602	43	581	160	647
72	21	93	17	175	86	1368
694	95	1159	182	1628	657	1665
618	76	640	91	658	386	1052
587	61	829	66	1517	404	1327
547	117	774	145	1048	679	2333
331	106	233	68	639	210	1346
479	86	509	89	832	523	667
372	42	788	69	65	253	488
4301	309	3205	375	3326	1659	5324
1771	226	3635	360	1708	2105	3456
963	138	1238	208	2493	942	1536
1005	150	1433	365	2176	1138	2705
674	107	808	162	1245	659	1273
1211	169	2239	227	4021	1409	1377
800	146	1483	282	2151	716	1713
857	137	1592	187	1929	638	2324
770	160	1436	238	2159	1221	1920
1996	130	4039	277	1628	1167	6153
445	49	743	95	4454	592	2465
186	20	370	12	450	148	319
419	37	914	96	2401	428	800
1384	211	1532	355	4715	1537	3032
406	56	789	113	1184	583	1033
751	238	1215	309	4208	768	2396
10	9	35	9	113	7	117
433	55	988	180	4161	438	851
308	63	494	203	7145	719	1458
252	57	113	35	461	25	424
92	47	179	31	1308	115	454
290	86	1011	98	1563	277	554

C-3-3续表3

地　区	行政执法	行政处罚数	并处没收违法经营额/违法所得	并处罚款
全　国	**1681**	**1679**	**7**	**7**
中央级				
北　京	71	70	7	7
天　津				
河　北	105	105		
山　西	7	7		
内蒙古	22	22		
辽　宁				
吉　林	4	4		
黑龙江				
上　海				
江　苏	33	33		
浙　江	4	4		
安　徽	11	11		
福　建				
江　西				
山　东	914	913		
河　南	1	1		
湖　北	55	55		
湖　南				
广　东	59	59		
广　西	20	20		
海　南				
重　庆	100	100		
四　川	118	118		
贵　州	12	12		
云　南				
西　藏				
陕　西	23	23		
甘　肃				
青　海				
宁　夏	1	1		
新　疆	121	121		

单位：起

⑴ 警告	⑵ 限期（责令）停止活动	⑶ 撤销登记	取缔非法社会组织	并处没收非法财产
533	**31**	**1115**	**2**	
54		16	1	
		105		
		7		
		22		
		4		
26	5	2		
3		1		
		11		
400	7	506	1	
		1		
11	1	43		
27	3	29		
		20		
9	10	81		
		118		
		12		
3		20		
		1		
	5	116		

C-3-3续表4

地　区	执行行政事业单位会计制度财务指标				
	固定资产原价	上年结转和结余	本年收入合计	本年支出合计	收支结余
全　国	**276899.1**	**515717.5**	**23062.1**	**228967.1**	**1985.3**
中央级					
北　京					
天　津					
河　北	1134.9	439.9	15.0	276.5	
山　西	3045.0	2060.6		1763.1	2.0
内蒙古	6898.4	5238.9	4.4	5217.5	337.0
辽　宁	1240.1	4894.2	270.7	4790.2	
吉　林	505.0	1445.6	24.0	1068.6	
黑龙江	20448.4	262388.2	4.0	407.5	
上　海					
江　苏	142069.5	199501.0	18364.8	186465.5	496.9
浙　江	10.1	23.0		8.0	
安　徽	8.0	4.5		4.5	
福　建	7920.9	1978.0	4.0	1819.0	
江　西	8500.2	2567.5		2416.0	117.0
山　东					
河　南	2499.2	1613.7	206.0	529.4	
湖　北	3350.0	3410.3		2559.3	
湖　南	7971.8	6845.9	1495.4	7303.2	954.3
广　东	7622.7	1950.7	256.4	1282.8	
广　西	3489.8	1212.4	1217.0	1098.4	
海　南	1937.0	993.2	18.0	996.2	
重　庆	1577.2	712.5	18.6	712.5	
四　川	1762.1	1708.2		1020.0	
贵　州	2770.4	1931.1	131.3	1190.8	68.1
云　南	8570.6	2041.9	356.5	1550.0	
西　藏	4152.1	0.2		0.2	
陕　西	4115.1	750.1	6.5	563.7	
甘　肃	25794.7	6082.0	256.3	779.3	10.0
青　海	95.0	2.0		3.0	
宁　夏	5206.8	4213.0		4213.0	
新　疆	4204.1	1708.9	413.2	928.9	

单位：万元

执行民间非营利组织单位会计制度财务指标			
固定资产原价	上年结余	本年收入合计	本年费用合计
3519025.5	**3052677.8**	**5898014.5**	**6477432.5**
840163.3		2207320.9	1294387.2
246802.4	542558.1	419650.8	218937.8
25186.5	693.4	54833.8	82729.6
68228.4	384811.5	72342.2	992194.3
65568.4	4736.7	50253.7	48289.7
17065.2	649.0	22770.2	22435.8
285458.2	5616.1	43716.2	72583.3
4983.2	18.0	5760.9	10095.4
19733.3	812.7	6838.8	39608.9
24366.0	601543.0	459714.7	356126.8
496248.6	18458.5	450768.4	393765.2
127401.3	395451.3	363121.5	308332.7
118916.8	10304.8	90671.7	95430.7
27384.2	106707.0	80064.3	80300.2
73084.1	2099.1	31669.9	675761.1
119926.2	3960.5	323838.0	312605.1
36404.6	8021.0	36184.3	31414.2
65046.9	374.7	142096.4	132285.0
148037.2	394.0	72565.3	67007.5
287254.8	118989.3	497702.2	677916.2
29581.6	71619.9	18209.2	20566.4
2702.8	84.3	14984.7	15514.5
55126.2	14650.4	123044.8	125202.1
108207.8	634746.8	100905.7	126296.4
49226.1	12838.1	52372.5	35198.2
58165.2	34134.8	40990.1	59898.1
3288.4	287.3	405.0	510.7
47433.4	2072.1	44763.3	114597.1
33637.0	57.0	28819.0	25456.9
9944.9	9.0	22274.3	22193.9
9801.7		8532.4	7779.8
14650.8	75979.4	10829.3	12011.7

C-3-4 基金

地区	单位数	年末职工人数		受教育程度		职业资
			女性	大学专科人数	大学本科及以上人数	助理社会工作师人数
全国	**4784**	**25028**	**7251**	**5455**	**6373**	**207**
中央级	240	2303	820			
北京	382	2852	1877	381	1315	
天津	70	111	25	15	90	
河北	61	274	105	85	164	3
山西	67	169	66	112	49	1
内蒙古	102	414	137	319	79	
辽宁	72	437	107	205	66	24
吉林	81	103	23			
黑龙江	86	140	5	3	5	4
上海	270	1317	203	942	271	
江苏	543	2115	538	151	152	8
浙江	436	1202	415	468	530	2
安徽	100	376	34	27	57	
福建	221	1323	212	114	90	12
江西	52	243	53	140	78	
山东	118	471	108	223	168	12
河南	120	428	51	222	164	
湖北	106	880	164	305	377	
湖南	223	1270	153	292	718	
广东	677	4088	1170	280	749	2
广西	57	616	207	136	39	1
海南	62	385	62	68	109	
重庆	64	405	136	138	233	12
四川	143	944	130	260	130	
贵州	46	209	5	94	34	17
云南	93	262	91	74	155	14
西藏	13	29	12		18	
陕西	95	536	42	40	61	5
甘肃	54	558	157	145	157	90
青海	30	30				
宁夏	59	295	134	97	197	
新疆	41	243	9	119	118	

会

单位：个、人、人次、时

格水平	年龄结构				志愿服务	
社会工作师人数	35岁及以下人数	36岁至45岁人数	46岁至55岁人数	56岁及以上人数	志愿者服务人次数	志愿服务时间
233	**9126**	**6776**	**5549**	**3577**	**280**	**1145.0**
	853	686	467	297		
	2509	1		342		
	20	30	35	26		
4	96	79	52	47		
2	33	23	38	75	260	1045.0
	146	112	65	91		
6	81	90	215	51		
	89	14				
7	2	4	134			
36	464	392	206	255		
4	726	514	627	248	10	50.0
2	486	462	195	59		
	18	193	77	88		
	212	296	446	369		
	50	177	16			
2	202	214	31	24	10	50.0
1	37	73	144	174		
	204	323	245	108		
	272	330	402	266		
2	1482	1136	967	503		
1	118	271	175	52		
	76	76	178	55		
32	98	191	43	73		
	260	312	242	130		
	61	66	74	8		
3	60	86	67	49		
	4	9	14	2		
3	119	151	137	129		
128	213	191	130	24		
	8	15	7			
	75	150	47	23		
	52	109	73	9		

C-3-4续表1

地 区	社会组织负责人数	女性	公募基金会	按性 非公募基金会
全 国	**12487**	**2852**	**1548**	**3198**
中央级	1571	347	98	104
北 京	2686	752	43	339
天 津	64	25	20	50
河 北	71	26	10	51
山 西	73	6	24	43
内蒙古	295	3	94	8
辽 宁	72	25	49	23
吉 林	61	12	24	57
黑龙江	47	17	39	47
上 海	700	200	56	214
江 苏	612	35	202	341
浙 江	521	82	143	293
安 徽	102	2	22	78
福 建	240	34	37	184
江 西	134	24	20	32
山 东	130	21	42	76
河 南	401	58	40	80
湖 北	759	149	23	83
湖 南	1065	140	121	102
广 东	1470	655	116	561
广 西	96	30	23	34
海 南	223	47	18	44
重 庆	246	41	27	37
四 川	143	19	58	85
贵 州	79	18	31	15
云 南	91	1	46	47
西 藏	23	8	8	5
陕 西	365	57	30	65
甘 肃	8	4	20	34
青 海	30		18	12
宁 夏	59	13	25	34
新 疆	50	1	21	20

单位:人、个

质分		当年登记单位数	当年年检单位数
涉外基金会	境外基金代表机构		
9	**29**	**622**	**3881**
9	29	12	180
		66	299
		7	55
		5	49
		8	59
		7	80
		5	72
		2	54
		10	65
		71	196
		59	483
		52	380
		21	82
		36	138
		2	43
		13	96
		12	102
		13	95
		29	185
		114	513
		6	51
		4	46
		12	53
		15	126
		6	38
		17	80
			13
		6	69
		4	53
		1	29
		4	59
		3	38

C-3-4续表2

地区	社会组织					
	科技与研究	生态环境	教育	卫生	社会服务	文化
全国	**96**	**64**	**1346**	**186**	**1624**	**259**
中央级	3		2	1	13	1
北京	24	9	65	24	175	47
天津	3		25	3	25	9
河北	1		7	1	2	
山西			26		32	9
内蒙古		2	27	46	4	5
辽宁			27		24	
吉林		2	22	1	46	1
黑龙江	2	5	21	5	43	2
上海	12	6	64	17	126	22
江苏	3	3	153	8	183	16
浙江	8		174	6	131	17
安徽	3	3	26	2	39	5
福建		3	104	8	64	5
江西	2	1	21	1	20	1
山东	4	2	33	4	24	10
河南		1	17	1	2	6
湖北		3	47	1	33	6
湖南	2		130		15	11
广东	17	7	153	21	392	45
广西	1		14	5	29	1
海南	1	3	21	2	11	8
重庆	2		24	2	26	3
四川	4		54	2	24	4
贵州			8		30	
云南		7	23	21	26	2
西藏		1	4	1	1	4
陕西	1		22	2	5	13
甘肃	2	3	15	1	27	3
青海		3	5		7	3
宁夏	1		10		42	
新疆			2		3	

单位：个

按行业分类							
体育	法律	工商业服务	宗教	农业及农村发展	职业及从业组织	国际及涉外组织	其他
35	**56**	**201**	**31**	**54**	**19**	**29**	**784**
		179				29	12
4	3			3			28
2							3
			3				47
				2			16
1	20						
	8	1					
2	1	1	1	1	1		1
3		8	2		2		8
3	3	2	5	23	5		136
4	1	1	3	13			78
1	1	1			7		12
		4	1				32
1	2		2	1			
2	1	2		1			35
1							92
2	4		1	2			7
2	1		4	1	2		55
5	1		1	1			34
				1			6
	4	1	4	2			5
	1	1	2				3
1	2			1	1		50
1							7
							14
	2						
	1		1	1			49
				1	1		1
			1				11
							6
							36

C-3-4续表3

地区	行政执法	行政处罚数	(1) 警告	(2) 限期（责令）停止活动	(3) 撤销登记
全国	**16**	**16**	**11**	**1**	**4**
中央级					
北京					
天津					
河北					
山西					
内蒙古					
辽宁					
吉林					
黑龙江					
上海					
江苏					
浙江	9	9	6		3
安徽					
福建					
江西					
山东					
河南					
湖北	1	1			1
湖南					
广东	1	1	1		
广西					
海南					
重庆					
四川	5	5	4	1	
贵州					
云南					
西藏					
陕西					
甘肃					
青海					
宁夏					
新疆					

单位：起、万元

执行民间非营利组织单位会计制度财务指标			
固定资产原价	上年结余	本年收入合计	本年费用合计
357515.6	**3515647.7**	**5310811.5**	**4186391.7**
83814.7		3254534.8	3020480.1
10027.0	387288.9	251492.2	6616.7
3000.0	10000.0	1750.0	803.0
1404.7	14393.6	14628.8	707.2
1346.0		9395.0	11029.3
428.0	10.0	10614.0	8064.5
3956.3		32741.6	29694.0
328.7		500.0	1007.9
215.0		210.0	473.0
	1113248.0	347672.0	224468.2
4051.2	1883781.2	678567.7	424481.8
9873.3	75893.7	131703.1	98755.3
1137.3		1845.5	459.2
30273.0		28609.0	28169.3
745.0		11524.0	9336.4
1371.7		5231.4	4915.6
126.0	35.0	1116.0	144.6
1515.1		55278.2	30899.6
921.0		1539.8	343.3
96679.6	421.8	374941.4	197088.2
584.2	4.9	54.1	75.1
1018.0		2800.0	560.0
69283.0	300.8	54511.8	48958.7
1260.0		3765.0	3765.0
361.2			365.9
313.7	29.8	18383.4	15266.6
801.3	13017.5	2339.1	1989.5
2666.0		12.0	148.8
27.0	1.5	5.0	10.4
4250.0		1152.0	865.0
14297.6	17221.0	13654.6	14259.5
11440.0		240.0	2190.0

C–3–5 民办

地 区	单位数	年末职工人数		受教育程度		职业资
			女性	大学专科人数	大学本科及以上人数	助理社会工作师人数
全 国	**329141**	**3421015**	**1321585**	**848602**	**584709**	**11668**
中央级	102	1595	843	368	226	
北 京	5378	81719	37006	18567	29082	742
天 津	2659	28512	12740	9563	11404	121
河 北	9396	133961	59458	31490	19976	319
山 西	5882	70891	28080	19221	8677	53
内蒙古	5608	37425	15162	9873	4655	131
辽 宁	11942	103478	41730	24125	27919	200
吉 林	4985	36914	8217	8660	2033	218
黑龙江	7610	48362	15953	12095	4356	40
上 海	9082	141234	27806	46304	14847	271
江 苏	44705	335725	101634	67944	60042	1455
浙 江	22603	242214	84985	55808	36302	237
安 徽	11893	141613	51788	40705	28644	447
福 建	8484	78459	31483	11649	17537	344
江 西	7003	91950	38895	11251	4520	492
山 东	25915	224269	59863	69758	44563	499
河 南	17594	166318	61278	36157	22487	164
湖 北	15381	145433	55621	45983	18591	1217
湖 南	14335	137201	58466	42059	26608	245
广 东	28377	425601	219875	118946	78284	1943
广 西	9190	108486	39536	20140	11521	119
海 南	2850	26869	11886	2645	1979	2
重 庆	8075	116343	60932	29199	33514	1302
四 川	19223	208113	87278	53229	29162	450
贵 州	4251	47262	19070	12216	8537	54
云 南	6920	68870	31289	12796	14771	401
西 藏	23	163	67	38	37	
陕 西	8977	95146	33376	18456	11500	126
甘 肃	4370	28359	8310	7589	3744	29
青 海	1283	8367	2087	1678	408	17
宁 夏	1513	9561	4795	2568	2509	4
新 疆	3532	30602	12076	7522	6274	26

非企业

单位:个、人、人次、时

格水平	年龄结构				志愿服务	
社会工作师人数	35岁及以下人数	36岁至45岁人数	46岁至55岁人数	56岁及以上人数	志愿者服务人次数	志愿服务时间
11923	**1507254**	**1172572**	**516139**	**225050**	**269292**	**720404.6**
	533	483	226	353		
1283	32356	23531	19211	6621		
72	6888	8605	8148	4871	550	1100.0
732	57972	46507	22513	6969	6143	25354.0
22	36162	21312	9396	4021	22	107.0
181	16534	12439	6090	2362	698	1496.0
75	43392	37616	17155	5315	288	546.0
1523	7671	23636	2877	2730	20	30.0
175	15675	18313	10807	3567		
1732	50186	47841	30814	12393	240	480.0
480	115282	124363	72052	24028	35495	73735.0
212	95422	84188	30850	31754	9181	17489.0
164	56553	46526	29930	8604	28399	66512.0
248	36723	23947	13502	4287	6	
95	38811	40234	9424	3481		
200	84183	94175	36611	9300	59777	156221.6
84	80794	52950	18999	13575	13	34.0
684	58116	50492	23552	13273	2471	4753.0
138	71306	46724	14596	4575	70332	229914.0
1848	262342	110442	41091	11726	37825	98100.0
45	42267	34011	13508	18700		
	8875	12670	4320	1004		
1388	57120	36928	16541	5754	14451	28719.0
266	102237	74429	23182	8265	1	
24	23392	14893	6705	2272	1883	10186.0
47	36457	23846	6605	1962	109	295.0
	59	58	36	10		
116	40966	34709	13518	5953	787	2458.0
62	10009	9021	7786	1543	1	5.0
5	2485	5005	584	293	32	
3	3464	3835	1278	984		
19	13022	8843	4232	4505	568	2870.0

C-3-5续表1

地区	社会组织负责人	女性	按性 法人
全国	**484475**	**160016**	**260479**
中央级	102	64	100
北京	16731	7663	5054
天津	3574	1488	2581
河北	12201	3732	6112
山西	7306	1844	5396
内蒙古	8205	2281	3771
辽宁	13122	4823	9396
吉林	18152	1618	2934
黑龙江	8368	3005	4399
上海	23411	10210	7990
江苏	50247	13851	39081
浙江	28403	10211	18829
安徽	14984	4540	8906
福建	8482	3113	7091
江西	11078	3593	4550
山东	57673	17143	19817
河南	28378	9915	12699
湖北	23628	6330	12820
湖南	21640	7071	9493
广东	31651	12108	25929
广西	10784	4263	6091
海南	4621	1503	2641
重庆	18171	7820	7182
四川	26314	9768	15163
贵州	5449	1529	2385
云南	7755	2560	4906
西藏	14	7	14
陕西	11301	3734	6278
甘肃	4854	1329	3148
青海	1789	542	1194
宁夏	1797	362	1171
新疆	4290	1996	3358

单位：人、个

质分			
合伙	个体	当年登记单位数	当年年检单位数
8791	**59871**	**39505**	**241099**
1	1	18	80
10	314	555	4495
9	69	299	2006
333	2951	1538	6863
100	386	664	3882
285	1552	873	4154
221	2325	956	6678
26	2025	241	3448
208	3003	663	4787
35	1057	1041	7344
819	4805	6308	36015
474	3300	3185	18989
457	2530	1436	8917
379	1014	745	5686
273	2180	375	5520
1028	5070	4178	17718
1168	3727	1757	13490
418	2143	1415	12399
498	4344	1591	10381
136	2312	3348	20028
209	2890	1665	6250
53	156	457	1801
104	789	939	6159
603	3457	2035	13175
242	1624	485	2156
217	1797	853	5141
2	7		17
250	2449	826	6386
152	1070	567	3010
17	72	127	897
25	317	144	675
39	135	221	2552

C-3-5续表2

地区	社会组织					
	科技与研究	生态环境	教育	卫生	社会服务	文化
全国	**16447**	**433**	**182547**	**24021**	**49426**	**16620**
中央级	21		7	7	23	19
北京	377	7	2967	344	958	260
天津	48	3	1359	210	466	98
河北	563		5249	1794	852	286
山西	618	2	3668	288	543	297
内蒙古	407	4	3453	261	697	218
辽宁	352	15	7124	1555	1573	264
吉林	174		3135	235	1020	151
黑龙江	634	8	4853	212	1160	164
上海	406	21	3148	167	2977	564
江苏	915	54	9256	2596	20444	2741
浙江	1393	29	12932	871	2610	1351
安徽	563	9	6459	1941	1498	431
福建	482	11	5983	408	348	490
江西	261	2	5258	537	323	220
山东	3433	16	10583	2709	2879	2445
河南	909	48	11247	2143	1124	749
湖北	672	113	7206	1110	1538	1170
湖南	336	16	11384	808	504	561
广东	1220	31	18956	677	3016	1503
广西	213	4	7711	228	355	215
海南	174		1789	417	141	163
重庆	144		5755	103	853	105
四川	508	11	13255	1488	1302	608
贵州	197	2	2930	426	291	92
云南	226	6	5061	427	413	216
西藏	2		14			2
陕西	573	7	5635	1107	597	519
甘肃	365	4	2319	503	260	370
青海	54		780	78	85	109
宁夏	63	10	851	48	164	95
新疆	144		2220	323	412	144

单位：个

按行业分类							
体育	法律	工商业服务	宗教	农业及农村发展	职业及从业组织	国际及涉外组织	其他
14342	**449**	**3355**	**114**	**1417**	**601**	**7**	**19362**
	1	12				3	9
334	21	15	1	17	8		69
242	1	20		1	146		65
372	5	34	4	17	12		208
247	3	37	2	10	7		160
238	6	41	3	15	10		255
453	9	52	18	9	17		501
185	3	10	1	6	1		64
407	3	15	3	2	5		144
583	27	217		48	11	4	909
2329	39	758	20	206	61		5286
1118	17	203	1	47	43		1988
403	1	101	11	80	8		388
423	2	83	4	7	12		231
213	4	22		14	4		145
1781	135	418	5	51	49		1411
910	9	73	7	4	6		365
353	61	273	7	712	78		2088
267	2	100	6	34	2		315
1004	7	239	5	7	30		1682
341	1	20		1	1		100
82		16		1	18		49
359	2	61	1	24	12		656
444	34	344	3	44	9		1173
153	3	22	2	8	7		118
340	4	42	4	5	4		172
	1	2					2
221	38	50		11	4		215
170	5	38	4	33	25		274
56	4	2			1		114
114		27		2	9		130
200	1	8	2	1	1		76

C-3-5续表3

地区	行政执法	行政处罚数	并处罚款	(1) 警告	(2) 限期(责令)停止活动	(3) 撤销登记
全国	**1254**	**1233**	**1**	**357**	**28**	**848**
中央级						
北京	52	52				52
天津						
河北	50	50				50
山西	6	6				6
内蒙古	3	3				3
辽宁						
吉林						
黑龙江						
上海	16	16				16
江苏	38	35		16	13	6
浙江						
安徽	2	2				2
福建						
江西						
山东	748	743	1	306	9	428
河南	13					
湖北	36	36		1		35
湖南						
广东	30	30		23		7
广西	4	4				4
海南						
重庆	71	71		8	4	59
四川	104	104				104
贵州	60	60				60
云南						
西藏						
陕西	18	18			2	16
甘肃						
青海						
宁夏						
新疆	3	3		3		

单位：起、万元

取缔非法社会组织		执行民间非营利组织单位会计制度财务指标			
	并处没收非法财产	固定资产原价	上年结余	本年收入合计	本年费用合计
21	**1**	**18957356.9**	**4501964.5**	**17565183.2**	**12944818.5**
		29074.1		107185.4	109817.9
		944221.9	794599.8	1119024.6	963324.5
		401555.5	7700.9	136855.8	191695.0
		1465436.2	243542.7	5462555.9	894434.0
		176589.5	7110.8	104297.0	96999.1
		63665.6	392.1	42378.9	46055.2
		840327.8	874757.6	312631.2	301576.3
		5440.0	324.2	91119.9	11749.0
		122026.3	1435.1	19337.7	149473.8
		281855.8	795211.8	1848060.4	1710389.0
3		1276445.5	160754.0	1572791.9	1658743.4
		1604254.7	549831.4	930301.3	875485.6
		1013526.7	290062.0	493252.4	473444.8
		197895.8	20765.0	83584.3	109736.0
		241003.9	4703.0	217003.1	242916.8
5	1	555388.0	2552.0	708598.6	709385.9
13		588387.7	45313.1	627259.3	369896.9
		458886.4	4495.2	300563.0	313949.9
		372847.9	71516.9	248238.6	270481.1
		5739095.3	188351.2	1073088.5	1265279.1
		150874.8	977.2	83410.5	69574.5
		67965.7	120.1	317262.4	83212.6
		482746.1	179847.4	408218.7	318316.3
		673548.3	25168.5	820964.1	1174024.5
		113597.2	3505.6	53090.0	53826.6
		414630.1	208848.4	211198.6	232158.9
		541.0	558.9	654.6	453.3
		493686.9	3203.1	72513.9	89933.9
		68965.7	3803.4	23537.8	27947.6
		14622.8	930.2	1665.8	5807.9
		32257.3	9769.5	16123.2	68507.6
		65996.4	1813.4	58415.8	56221.5

C-3-6 自治组

地区	单位数	居民1000户以下	居民1000户－3000户	居民3000户以上	社区居委会（村委会）成员	#中共党员
全国	**680535**	**483032**	**159392**	**38111**	**2809257**	**1603313**
中央级						
北京	6911	4235	2183	493	34631	20060
天津	5351	3646	1416	289	22421	8970
河北	52909	42548	8868	1493	187453	91332
山西	30417	24875	4512	1030	110725	48509
内蒙古	13433	9087	3774	572	53964	27482
辽宁	15725	7774	5777	2174	70121	35760
吉林	11196	6662	3419	1115	34902	1799
黑龙江	12936	6575	5100	1261	57562	25837
上海	5747	2140	3294	313	27153	13870
江苏	21495	8834	9755	2906	111048	72202
浙江	32294	24202	7098	994	125366	56751
安徽	17987	7488	7885	2614	77616	50644
福建	16767	12599	3683	485	68601	25383
江西	20431	12411	7172	848	76236	29091
山东	80444	65959	11888	2597	325672	267725
河南	51502	34185	14665	2652	214314	114843
湖北	29403	20461	6804	2138	117968	81990
湖南	45554	34546	8727	2281	162652	106779
广东	26241	16030	7488	2723	127183	87883
广西	16197	10832	4560	805	80139	53994
海南	3072	2614	322	136	15036	11323
重庆	11083	6072	3910	1101	55301	32779
四川	53189	39632	10435	3122	211415	113835
贵州	18698	15659	2464	575	88759	41213
云南	14259	9289	4300	670	70909	48400
西藏	5465	5336	125	4	25487	18309
陕西	25257	20867	3429	961	97338	47054
甘肃	17366	13726	3049	591	68023	28574
青海	4619	3701	375	543	18331	7031
宁夏	2754	1995	579	180	12504	7795
新疆	11833	9052	2336	445	60427	26096

织总表

单位：个、人

#女性	社区居委会（村委会）主任	#主任、书记"一肩挑"	#女性	受教育程度 大学专科人数
777687	**678538**	**239042**	**107379**	**355331**
18382	6869	4064	2033	10931
10845	5296	1860	1145	5746
34416	52817	10105	5471	11394
26393	30297	12066	3004	11144
18261	13433	2123	2678	7211
29083	15690	6980	4321	19709
12083	11126	3438	2382	795
19637	12885	2591	3636	12608
15879	5644	1290	3216	7184
34293	21417	5807	4872	25003
35538	32076	2764	3703	19485
22965	17900	3632	2684	10864
17636	16698	1353	2000	3610
20763	20378	1957	3874	4701
94447	80444	59623	12888	57272
49318	51334	21177	12131	30371
37829	29353	24184	2573	11972
46912	45501	21294	4163	16648
35480	26156	18464	3569	16243
19730	16165	4127	1775	6187
3579	3070	2158	259	1873
18428	11061	779	1841	10800
52673	52994	4680	10133	22504
19962	18595	1727	2604	5525
14619	14199	6185	1568	5008
5858	5465	2692	1138	546
24562	25216	1942	1712	3158
12655	17314	1653	2468	4136
3978	4618	1245	604	795
4294	2746	1474	539	1395
17189	11781	5608	2395	10513

C-3-6续表1

地区	受教育程度	职业资格水平		年龄结构			
	大学本科及以上人数	助理社会工作师人数	社会工作师人数	35岁及以下人数	36岁至45岁人数	46岁至55岁人数	56岁及以上人数
全国	**120385**	**16833**	**6179**	**576468**	**1216358**	**801978**	**214453**
中央级							
北京	8501	2973	1127	7850	11217	11942	3622
天津	3241	891	232	6425	6555	6649	2792
河北	2337	138	115	30661	76723	62967	17102
山西	4880	124	101	23064	42542	33589	11530
内蒙古	2386	119	25	12308	22892	14540	4224
辽宁	6336	835	364	17241	27033	20155	5692
吉林	564	44	30	935	33338	556	73
黑龙江	2851	190	34	11329	31917	12604	1712
上海	3788	996	329	5729	8284	9127	4013
江苏	9759	3384	942	26507	44312	32877	7352
浙江	6616	1553	716	26126	53833	36587	8820
安徽	2493	983	365	14034	36775	21872	4935
福建	687	304	161	12380	34280	18842	3099
江西	1251	151	24	14397	42466	16100	3273
山东	24575	320	81	69764	144060	87845	24003
河南	8002	66	101	43121	93439	60581	17173
湖北	2642	448	161	23181	49246	38378	7163
湖南	3529	228	74	34058	78009	41451	9134
广东	5978	1420	544	23634	45094	44330	14125
广西	1227	112	46	12382	28007	30320	9430
海南	177	23		2741	6788	4211	1296
重庆	3247	787	373	13478	23293	15322	3208
四川	6299	492	141	45406	89390	58155	18464
贵州	808	20	14	20468	36025	25325	6941
云南	1139	61	20	18938	30761	17490	3720
西藏	220			3996	8551	8376	4564
陕西	886	26	11	15192	38734	34200	9212
甘肃	1651	31	8	14708	34176	15492	3647
青海	242	13	2	3849	8122	5383	977
宁夏	356	28	5	2869	5277	3911	447
新疆	3717	73	33	19697	25219	12801	2710

单位：个、人、人次、时

志愿服务		居民(村民)小组	当年完成选举的居(村)委会数	当年完成选举的居(村)选民登记总数			
志愿者服务人次数	志愿服务时间				本届登记选民数	参加投票人数	委托投票人数
2323757	**8399479.0**	**6038906**	**164645**	**212091025**	**186896907**	**159437341**	**9161414**
735126	4146993.0	84898	2503	4781147	4008275	2710503	82551
18676	53125.0	94358	3453	4060978	3604952	3464539	105988
44793	207788.0	295662	41189	32164546	30315268	26501792	1420174
3614	7360.0	121238	5503	3852698	3081279	2689215	127571
16692	39842.0	75823	11328	11021222	9746680	7801741	404735
30130	36602.0	182743	2189	4893391	3435297	2786284	84023
1		80202	2214	2696515	2200429	1799495	37300
633	1790.0	134720	1917	6256630	3338869	2872046	20703
29684	88129.0	206110	5064	11440280	10560425	9919117	658088
200840	516001.0	357056	2517	6619791	6409801	4982917	459133
111461	254777.0	326115	3591	5979514	5224997	5507159	263692
67187	162142.0	286653	3280	9819262	8535112	7488235	446467
3615	3925.0	175448	15623	24428104	20197982	16483155	655210
1539	4065.0	181603	1194	2641962	2255130	1961015	15088
154330	373177.0	542957	18880	16831602	15823420	12548562	1962902
4491	4484.0	400910	2851	5017435	4615756	3611289	86988
18386	67214.0	238606	3849	9274183	8151886	5772830	509937
48191	173197.0	480281					
62	120.0	264685					
8582	28464.0	280406	251	1110302	804507	632605	72166
		28744	903	1399861	1272675	764532	43857
294776	832599.8	94391	3	4128	4128	3179	
86558	286560.0	420141	6078	8270880	7614305	6734428	199440
423100	1059836.2	184198	3635	6664181	6182214	5423620	146101
961	1171.0	171592	3154	7928378	7144672	6455496	182003
9		16672	3097	982092	955560	885403	18609
2807	13725.0	137728	15103	16509882	15118688	14096187	904109
1472	2031.0	92845	3978	6027569	5175676	4889682	234452
8381	12187.0	14708	27	35731	35661	19430	14714
4		14921	499	665128	523240	333684	2237
7656	22174.0	52492	772	713633	560023	299201	3176

C-3-6续表2

地　区	执行企业会计制度单位财务指标				执行行政	
	固定资产原价	营业收入	费用合计	营业利润	固定资产原价	上年结转和结余
全　国	**2727337.9**	**1580476.7**	**281523.3**	**62691.9**	**21189913.5**	**1365844.5**
中央级						
北　京	2458738.3	1525429.8	257191.8	61648.9	427581.1	121295.9
天　津					147810.4	19920.4
河　北	5444.5		68.0		2419138.7	22085.8
山　西					586309.8	7572.2
内蒙古					94171.7	
辽　宁	1397.8		7.8		157428.8	13817.6
吉　林	216.0	2.0	2.0		76781.4	654.9
黑龙江	6701.2	26.0	261.3		352879.9	34760.7
上　海	187570.3	52399.4	22583.0	1034.4	1034562.3	110973.1
江　苏		140.0	140.0		5589601.5	712022.8
浙　江	409.0				3485459.8	96279.3
安　徽					489480.0	23610.2
福　建	203.0	385.0	385.0		113081.8	1556.6
江　西	11538.1	1432.0	708.4	6.0	134204.8	-389.8
山　东					1426036.5	
河　南	7012.0	36.0	36.0		257421.2	1385.6
湖　北	155.4				880870.0	666.2
湖　南	1212.0				259224.5	923.9
广　东	24671.5	38.5	62.9	2.6	1742852.1	67435.8
广　西	347.0		1.0		169179.8	403.4
海　南					21256.6	607.1
重　庆					180777.3	2536.0
四　川	2996.4		9.1		261614.6	28075.2
贵　州	7.5				36300.9	2635.7
云　南	2022.0				407636.7	93131.7
西　藏	9714.0		40.0		16339.3	10.0
陕　西	6.0				160922.9	953.0
甘　肃	29.5				132680.4	249.6
青　海	4.6				6807.4	5.0
宁　夏	975.5				31260.8	45.0
新　疆	5966.3	588.0	27.0		90240.5	2621.6

单位：万元

事业单位会计制度财务指标			执行民间非营利组织单位会计制度财务指标			
本年收入合计	本年支出合计	收支结余	固定资产原价	上年结余	本年收入合计	本年费用合计
7817047.8	**6997608.0**	**81111.5**	**2476078.9**	**97398.4**	**891636.6**	**804695.1**
261107.1	334373.0	5818.0			62.7	
113960.4	116918.2		22.9			36.0
335875.9	330999.2	4850.0	32147.4	90.4	5588.0	11400.7
150120.5	167446.2	573.2	97762.2	661.4	26713.1	15202.6
60189.9	59830.2		4561.6		3208.4	3522.6
356800.9	96115.6	1357.4	58425.3	1467.1	20792.2	20662.6
32372.6	31891.4	16.0			34.7	
58730.1	63929.5	45.7	9177.0	33.0	7215.1	5679.9
490604.0	425853.7	21800.0			1.0	498.2
784911.6	672534.5	2908.6	591019.3	6243.1	212421.1	164893.9
1221178.6	1025923.6	16809.0	784776.0	3992.9	261017.5	193513.5
176467.3	166069.4	61.5	19071.5		6633.3	7054.0
137313.9	138356.1		117929.5	22825.8	62686.3	51641.3
83399.8	83551.0		17340.3	1073.0	11156.5	15060.9
1217124.9	1217100.6					
143730.4	140593.7	248.8	98929.7	9.0	42692.4	47224.6
199837.6	197662.8	184.1	53369.8		72515.1	56677.6
251428.7	244860.6		24183.7		4769.0	4235.5
845409.1	612762.0	22541.2	144704.7	10277.1	25184.8	53492.3
90065.5	54542.8	149.0	2379.8	34.0	941.4	1366.7
18588.1	18597.6	230.0	1293.0		285.0	285.0
72057.8	71285.0	569.1	68982.9	274.0	34277.5	32101.1
177470.9	200776.9	2659.3	62180.7	6755.9	17145.8	35013.6
315878.5	314926.0		135672.2	29522.5	50430.2	52437.3
83994.3	76270.0	258.6	102052.3	13989.2	17788.4	21207.5
729.9	753.9		346.0			
64653.4	58029.0					
28210.3	24781.6		12755.4		1038.4	1373.8
1129.4	1084.0		25738.5	30.0	4851.6	6065.1
2372.4	2476.7		2884.7	120.0	454.8	953.7
41334.0	47313.2	32.0	8372.5		1732.3	3095.1

C-3-7 村民

地区	单位数	居民1000户以下	居民1000户—3000户	居民3000户以上	社区居委会（村委会）成员
全国	**580856**	**443920**	**115494**	**21442**	**2297061**
中央级					
北京	3936	3598	320	18	14207
天津	3686	3230	418	38	12000
河北	48974	40908	7066	1000	168253
山西	28087	24159	3301	627	99935
内蒙古	11110	8393	2516	201	42347
辽宁	11569	7023	3776	770	44882
吉林	9327	6119	2423	785	28193
黑龙江	9077	5305	3277	495	40025
上海	1593	988	552	53	6098
江苏	14486	6749	6167	1570	72577
浙江	27901	22172	5300	429	105396
安徽	14688	6581	6215	1892	60409
福建	14429	11430	2735	264	56711
江西	16947	10608	5735	604	62736
山东	73811	62080	9871	1860	293510
河南	46925	32112	12903	1910	191393
湖北	25109	18866	5079	1164	96345
湖南	40448	31971	6814	1663	140053
广东	19632	13907	4578	1147	89481
广西	14273	10153	3705	415	68262
海南	2561	2343	175	43	12227
重庆	8220	5221	2702	297	38102
四川	46240	36192	8172	1876	180436
贵州	16612	14439	1774	399	76727
云南	12024	8451	3314	259	57874
西藏	5257	5174	80	3	24076
陕西	22743	19640	2550	553	84886
甘肃	16032	13181	2421	430	61472
青海	4143	3452	190	501	16154
宁夏	2272	1867	362	43	9630
新疆	8744	7608	1003	133	42664

委员会

单位:个、人

#中共党员	#女性	社区居委会（村委会）主任	#主任、书记“一肩挑”	#女性
1327149	**525741**	**579383**	**198337**	**66672**
10282	4121	3927	2296	297
4716	2737	3641	712	107
82658	24422	48912	8810	3775
44129	20889	27979	11004	2087
21725	10741	11110	1101	1309
23476	10988	11546	3931	1457
649	9306	9263	2497	1467
19423	8348	9029	1388	1346
4524	2101	1573	431	485
48571	17051	14463	3448	2260
45282	25632	27717	1656	2102
40358	15113	14609	2744	1614
20537	12443	14368	997	1077
24132	14646	16914	1300	2735
243691	83851	73811	55111	10497
104733	39513	46768	19480	10284
67371	26152	25072	20979	866
92133	37679	40403	18750	2626
63191	18735	19590	13661	1398
47288	14188	14244	3568	1108
9384	2657	2560	1757	178
22482	9808	8208	271	780
96425	41547	46098	3562	8045
35693	14584	16523	1376	1732
39913	10537	11978	5346	1086
17193	5413	5257	2610	1097
40780	18869	22714	1411	923
25936	9861	15986	1288	1938
6049	2796	4142	1032	388
6152	2148	2264	1130	217
18273	8865	8714	4690	1391

C-3-7续表1

地　区	受教育程度		职业资格水平	
	大学专科人数	大学本科及以上人数	助理社会工作师人数	社会工作师人数
全　国	**214575**	**56481**	**1700**	**557**
中央级				
北　京	3335	1137	93	18
天　津	1954	423	1	3
河　北	6785	738	21	21
山　西	8274	3846	2	6
内蒙古	3241	717	1	3
辽　宁	8690	1405	39	24
吉　林	43	17		
黑龙江	6992	1014	98	15
上　海	2180	881	78	26
江　苏	13687	4414	679	148
浙　江	13154	2944	91	38
安　徽	6183	1137	130	36
福　建	1855	185	47	9
江　西	2599	843	2	7
山　东	47168	18198	51	7
河　南	25042	6602	17	46
湖　北	5626	904	5	4
湖　南	11254	2065	42	27
广　东	5161	870	152	56
广　西	3505	262	9	12
海　南	1130	27		
重　庆	4887	757	38	9
四　川	15869	4484	69	20
贵　州	3481	456	2	7
云　南	2594	390	6	6
西　藏	379	129		
陕　西	978	139	3	3
甘　肃	2857	871	1	4
青　海	256	56	5	1
宁　夏	329	113	1	
新　疆	5087	457	17	1

单位：人、人次、时

年龄结构				志愿服务	
35岁及以下人数	36岁至45岁人数	46岁至55岁人数	56岁及以上人数	志愿者服务人次数	志愿服务时间
429430	**1002011**	**680743**	**184877**	**882621**	**2443060.2**
1262	4586	6401	1958	1280	2750.0
2165	3800	4219	1816	11746	31899.0
24275	68839	58874	16265	37708	175569.0
19798	37795	31349	10993	200	277.0
8289	17879	12324	3855	969	1212.0
7524	17424	15007	4927	1035	1492.0
156	27781	225	31	1	
6635	22769	9239	1382	633	1790.0
1476	2196	2038	388	16045	48982.0
16082	28804	22561	5130	77572	193790.0
19847	45831	31854	7864	33992	91400.0
9166	29350	17696	4197	34362	86412.0
9597	28892	15636	2586	2782	2950.0
11080	35127	13635	2894	5	6.0
61509	129967	79992	22042	122768	301895.0
36618	82984	55822	15969	4484	4484.0
17640	39924	32452	6329	964	1448.0
27768	67526	36624	8135	33131	128572.0
13597	30168	34196	11520	62	120.0
9080	23566	27137	8479	252	324.0
2015	5538	3589	1085		
7406	16553	11681	2462	98196	279678.0
37040	76272	50647	16477	57413	218032.0
17333	31390	22098	5906	337193	846322.2
15799	25191	14150	2734	716	911.0
3557	8161	8030	4328	9	
12345	33708	30548	8285	1574	8527.0
12725	30927	14378	3442	1472	2031.0
3120	6982	5154	898	6049	12187.0
1927	3888	3401	414	1	
12599	18193	9786	2086	7	

C-3-7续表2

地区	当年完成选举的村委会数	当年完成选举的村选民登记数	本届登记选民数	参加投票人数	委托投票人数
全　国	**134675**	**149455947**	**134197410**	**118633157**	**7410406**
中央级					
北　京	260	160304	146485	120418	21386
天　津	2782	3291789	2949057	2953020	87577
河　北	39748	30844480	29035059	25305813	1365852
山　西	5290	3749419	2993822	2627319	126162
内蒙古	9617	7920530	7292418	5955243	322125
辽　宁	900	1882078	1707298	1496923	71207
吉　林	1645	1928852	1763118	1527012	34330
黑龙江	1444	5484105	2737463	2395869	16017
上　海	1278	3103232	3025709	2973772	319746
江　苏	1234	3190136	3117903	2577410	301205
浙　江	3191	4776366	4041005	4462994	225988
安　徽	1659	3990733	3607064	3335314	225928
福　建	13542	20119677	16914761	14659177	630201
江　西	865	2175602	1816780	1580436	1495
山　东	17280	14102341	13812195	10990383	1847684
河　南					
湖　北	234	845147	801911	651816	151901
湖　南					
广　东					
广　西	214	928552	623469	478420	71381
海　南	778	1143600	1143227	658109	38063
重　庆					
四　川	5446	7002623	6532324	5790146	166887
贵　州	3109	5831876	5410111	4746187	133194
云　南	2570	5653371	5469861	5180025	165478
西　藏	3023	933598	909125	841266	17904
陕　西	14231	15290371	13963738	13109062	852148
甘　肃	3471	4637699	3928697	3812725	214195
青　海					
宁　夏	381	177389	176848	155191	50
新　疆	483	292077	277962	249107	2302

单位：个、人、次

经推举产生的村民代表数	女性	当年召开村民会议次数	当年召开村民代表会议的次数	自然村	村委会小组数
7346594	**1591133**	**361509**	**676302**	**1863300**	**4691632**
16653	5838	528	2106	3884	27913
45417	9455	1153	2696	3137	39937
1277942	218658	35415	67979	65317	255296
124735	24605	8099	14894	45007	105553
358135	85544	15801	27353	39949	54466
134912	6187	634	1293	31133	76433
25177	4047	293	477	11239	54226
417194	4204	924	1503	15892	73223
202758	65144	2364	4461	1324	25899
72366	17686	4932	25956	67538	217863
144253	49812	24322	13125	91746	256874
522069	212798	1367	3436	132427	243246
423566	104372	5708	24339	64417	145035
23892	1105	1000	1142	103277	166668
1862433	459139	182716	358967	91756	460400
78990	13603	956	1934	154803	361161
68841	11447	5917	14718	95610	193542
				109791	423503
95605	21627	3413	7585	139573	214181
16930	4653	4110	3704	156858	245843
24822	2695	577	851	16548	25243
				6048	68240
127709	25839	6789	9412	76131	363233
230301	67450	26607	49147	81848	159532
253181	77736	1507	929	118756	148128
44654	5456	400	322	14144	15552
536994	74900	24074	36418	56885	121519
185730	14426	1578	990	46053	86515
				5635	13628
8449	960	253	466	6747	12734
22886	1747	72	99	9827	36046

C-3-7续表3

地 区	执行企业会计制度单位财务指标				执行行政	
	固定资产原价	营业收入	费用合计	营业利润	固定资产原价	上年结转和结余
全 国	**2704509.9**	**1579491.0**	**280586.6**	**62685.9**	**16798589.7**	**518776.8**
中央级						
北 京	2458738.2	1525429.8	257191.8	61648.9	337528.4	106511.1
天 津					129090.7	19658.9
河 北	4973.3		68.0		2269697.2	13807.5
山 西					560199.2	1611.0
内蒙古					72953.7	
辽 宁	708.9		7.8		126615.7	10906.7
吉 林	56.0	2.0	2.0		69168.5	556.3
黑龙江	17.3	14.0	15.5		125316.1	34190.8
上 海	187570.3	52399.4	22583.0	1034.4	871311.4	68679.3
江 苏		140.0	140.0		4726410.2	27130.5
浙 江	409.0				2693115.3	62479.2
安 徽					372039.5	4432.7
福 建	75.0				80976.9	1814.8
江 西	10082.0	1083.0	499.0		113720.1	-445.3
山 东					1135141.5	
河 南	6174.0	30.0	30.0		222407.6	1208.9
湖 北	127.4				316348.8	581.5
湖 南	12.0				192330.9	898.9
广 东	21796.6	11.8	34.4	2.6	1338621.3	60752.1
广 西	33.0		1.0		141184.1	299.6
海 南					17442.9	322.7
重 庆					108538.9	2518.5
四 川	2848.4		9.1		197738.3	20144.5
贵 州	7.5				32400.9	2194.7
云 南	1751.0				271346.2	77296.0
西 藏	7404.0				5085.3	10.0
陕 西	6.0				140560.5	925.3
甘 肃	29.5				63702.2	229.0
青 海					5686.3	
宁 夏	751.0				16937.0	41.0
新 疆	939.5	381.0	5.0		44974.1	20.6

单位：万元

事业单位会计制度财务指标			执行民间非营利组织单位会计制度财务指标			
本年收入合计	本年支出合计	收支结余	固定资产原价	上年结余	本年收入合计	本年费用合计
5635632.6	**5113531.0**	**66720.6**	**2034784.1**	**63544.8**	**738113.6**	**644103.6**
138715.6	201304.1	342.5				
101979.7	104695.9					
316185.6	303326.4	4850.0	31255.0	64.0	4893.7	10722.7
87477.7	88058.6	4.0	92148.3	601.0	25070.1	14291.4
45448.8	45107.4		1636.5		2231.0	2548.5
52980.5	56156.1	1325.5	50868.9	1214.1	17393.9	15167.0
27272.5	27380.7	14.0				
43772.4	48101.1	45.7	7711.0	33.0	6232.2	4967.3
344464.2	286092.1	24861.7				
498338.7	402338.6	2085.0	417545.7	999.7	148123.3	114314.8
965823.8	810416.8	10320.8	751739.8	3992.9	240734.5	169596.6
136558.0	125236.8	57.0	17071.2		5844.1	6043.9
102346.3	103169.4		85887.9	11336.0	48935.2	39559.0
45149.6	45455.8		15333.3	993.0	10083.0	11067.7
1019861.2	1019861.2					
121427.4	119162.5	242.2	91404.8	4.0	40242.5	44371.7
152961.8	150971.2		45921.3		64061.5	51438.9
182088.9	178324.0		19943.6		3720.4	3484.7
539437.0	329616.2	20175.1	105386.7	9989.1	23516.4	38621.4
79283.7	43844.1	149.0	648.3	34.0	900.2	1227.8
12906.4	12871.8	230.0	802.0		184.0	184.0
40088.6	39370.3	562.8	49681.2	260.0	24374.1	22949.9
145499.1	151824.2	1407.3	48881.7	4340.9	13000.4	28920.6
287334.8	286761.7		117236.0	27649.2	43369.7	42810.2
50690.2	45801.4	36.0	39934.0	1943.9	8456.5	11992.1
725.9	725.9		116.0			
56656.5	50749.0					
24709.2	21457.9		12380.2		1024.9	1328.8
940.2	921.5		20225.2	30.0	3888.4	4808.5
1722.7	1629.2		2766.5	60.0	407.4	777.9
12785.6	12799.1	12.0	8259.0		1426.2	2908.2

C-3-8 社区

地 区	单位数	居民1000户以下	居民1000户–3000户	居民3000户以上	社区居委会（村委会）成员
全 国	**99679**	**39112**	**43898**	**16669**	**512196**
中央级					
北 京	2975	637	1863	475	20424
天 津	1665	416	998	251	10421
河 北	3935	1640	1802	493	19200
山 西	2330	716	1211	403	10790
内蒙古	2323	694	1258	371	11617
辽 宁	4156	751	2001	1404	25239
吉 林	1869	543	996	330	6709
黑龙江	3859	1270	1823	766	17537
上 海	4154	1152	2742	260	21055
江 苏	7009	2085	3588	1336	38471
浙 江	4393	2030	1798	565	19970
安 徽	3299	907	1670	722	17207
福 建	2338	1169	948	221	11890
江 西	3484	1803	1437	244	13500
山 东	6633	3879	2017	737	32162
河 南	4577	2073	1762	742	22921
湖 北	4294	1595	1725	974	21623
湖 南	5106	2575	1913	618	22599
广 东	6609	2123	2910	1576	37702
广 西	1924	679	855	390	11877
海 南	511	271	147	93	2809
重 庆	2863	851	1208	804	17199
四 川	6949	3440	2263	1246	30979
贵 州	2086	1220	690	176	12032
云 南	2235	838	986	411	13035
西 藏	208	162	45	1	1411
陕 西	2514	1227	879	408	12452
甘 肃	1334	545	628	161	6551
青 海	476	249	185	42	2177
宁 夏	482	128	217	137	2874
新 疆	3089	1444	1333	312	17763

居委会

单位:个、人

#中共党员	#女性	社区居委会（村委会）主任	#主任、书记“一肩挑”	#女性
276164	**251946**	**99155**	**40705**	**40707**
9778	14261	2942	1768	1736
4254	8108	1655	1148	1038
8674	9994	3905	1295	1696
4380	5504	2318	1062	917
5757	7520	2323	1022	1369
12284	18095	4144	3049	2864
1150	2777	1863	941	915
6414	11289	3856	1203	2290
9346	13778	4071	859	2731
23631	17242	6954	2359	2612
11469	9906	4359	1108	1601
10286	7852	3291	888	1070
4846	5193	2330	356	923
4959	6117	3464	657	1139
24034	10596	6633	4512	2391
10110	9805	4566	1697	1847
14619	11677	4281	3205	1707
14646	9233	5098	2544	1537
24692	16745	6566	4803	2171
6706	5542	1921	559	667
1939	922	510	401	81
10297	8620	2853	508	1061
17410	11126	6896	1118	2088
5520	5378	2072	351	872
8487	4082	2221	839	482
1116	445	208	82	41
6274	5693	2502	531	789
2638	2794	1328	365	530
982	1182	476	213	216
1643	2146	482	344	322
7823	8324	3067	918	1004

C-3-8续表1

地区	受教育程度		职业资格水平	
	大学专科人数	大学本科及以上人数	助理社会工作师人数	社会工作师人数
全国	**140756**	**63904**	**15133**	**5622**
中央级				
北京	7596	7364	2880	1109
天津	3792	2818	890	229
河北	4609	1599	117	94
山西	2870	1034	122	95
内蒙古	3970	1669	118	22
辽宁	11019	4931	796	340
吉林	752	547	44	30
黑龙江	5616	1837	92	19
上海	5004	2907	918	303
江苏	11316	5345	2705	794
浙江	6331	3672	1462	678
安徽	4681	1356	853	329
福建	1755	502	257	152
江西	2102	408	149	17
山东	10104	6377	269	74
河南	5329	1400	49	55
湖北	6346	1738	443	157
湖南	5394	1464	186	47
广东	11082	5108	1268	488
广西	2682	965	103	34
海南	743	150	23	
重庆	5913	2490	749	364
四川	6635	1815	423	121
贵州	2044	352	18	7
云南	2414	749	55	14
西藏	167	91		
陕西	2180	747	23	8
甘肃	1279	780	30	4
青海	539	186	8	1
宁夏	1066	243	27	5
新疆	5426	3260	56	32

单位：人、人次、时

年龄结构				志愿服务	
35岁及以下人数	36岁至45岁人数	46岁至55岁人数	56岁及以上人数	志愿者服务人次数	志愿服务时间
147038	**214347**	**121235**	**29576**	**1441136**	**5956418.8**
6588	6631	5541	1664	733846	4144243.0
4260	2755	2430	976	6930	21226.0
6386	7884	4093	837	7085	32219.0
3266	4747	2240	537	3414	7083.0
4019	5013	2216	369	15723	38630.0
9717	9609	5148	765	29095	35110.0
779	5557	331	42		
4694	9148	3365	330		
4253	6088	7089	3625	13639	39147.0
10425	15508	10316	2222	123268	322211.0
6279	8002	4733	956	77469	163377.0
4868	7425	4176	738	32825	75730.0
2783	5388	3206	513	833	975.0
3317	7339	2465	379	1534	4059.0
8255	14093	7853	1961	31562	71282.0
6503	10455	4759	1204	7	
5541	9322	5926	834	17422	65766.0
6290	10483	4827	999	15060	44625.0
10037	14926	10134	2605		
3302	4441	3183	951	8330	28140.0
726	1250	622	211		
6072	6740	3641	746	196580	552921.8
8366	13118	7508	1987	29145	68528.0
3135	4635	3227	1035	85907	213514.0
3139	5570	3340	986	245	260.0
439	390	346	236		
2847	5026	3652	927	1233	5198.0
1983	3249	1114	205		
729	1140	229	79	2332	
942	1389	510	33	3	
7098	7026	3015	624	7649	22174.0

C-3-8续表2

地 区	当年完成选举的居委会数	当年完成选举的居选民登记数	
			本届登记选民数
全 国	**29970**	**62635078**	**52699497**
中央级			
北 京	2243	4620843	3861790
天 津	671	769189	655895
河 北	1441	1320066	1280209
山 西	213	103279	87457
内蒙古	1711	3100692	2454262
辽 宁	1289	3011313	1727999
吉 林	569	767663	437311
黑龙江	473	772525	601406
上 海	3786	8337048	7534716
江 苏	1283	3429655	3291898
浙 江	400	1203148	1183992
安 徽	1621	5828529	4928048
福 建	2081	4308427	3283221
江 西	329	466360	438350
山 东	1600	2729261	2011225
河 南	2851	5017435	4615756
湖 北	3615	8429036	7349975
湖 南			
广 东			
广 西	37	181750	181038
海 南	125	256261	129448
重 庆	3	4128	4128
四 川	632	1268257	1081981
贵 州	526	832305	772103
云 南	584	2275007	1674811
西 藏	74	48494	46435
陕 西	872	1219511	1154950
甘 肃	507	1389870	1246979
青 海	27	35731	35661
宁 夏	118	487739	346392
新 疆	289	421556	282061

单位：个、人

参加投票人数	委托投票人数	居委会小组数
40804184	**1751008**	**1347274**
2590085	61165	56985
511519	18411	54421
1195979	54322	40366
61896	1409	15685
1846498	82610	21357
1289361	12816	106310
272483	2970	25976
476177	4686	61497
6945345	338342	180211
2405507	157928	139193
1044165	37704	69241
4152921	220539	43407
1823978	25009	30413
380579	13593	14935
1558179	115218	82557
3611289	86988	39749
5121014	358036	45064
		56778
		50504
154185	785	34563
106423	5794	3501
3179		26151
944282	32553	56908
677433	12907	24666
1275471	16525	23464
44137	705	1120
987125	51961	16209
1076957	20257	6330
19430	14714	1080
178493	2187	2187
50094	874	16446

C-3-8续表3

地　区	执行企业会计制度单位财务指标				执行行政	
	固定资产原价	营业收入	费用合计	营业利润	固定资产原价	上年结转和结余
全　国	**22828.0**	**985.7**	**936.7**	**6.0**	**4391323.8**	**847067.7**
中央级						
北　京	0.1				90052.7	14784.8
天　津					18719.7	261.5
河　北	471.2				149441.5	8278.3
山　西					26110.6	5961.2
内蒙古					21218.0	
辽　宁	688.9				30813.1	2910.9
吉　林	160.0				7612.9	98.6
黑龙江	6683.9	12.0	245.8		227563.8	569.9
上　海					163250.9	42293.8
江　苏					863191.3	684892.3
浙　江					792344.5	33800.1
安　徽					117440.5	19177.5
福　建	128.0	385.0	385.0		32104.9	-258.2
江　西	1456.1	349.0	209.4	6.0	20484.7	55.5
山　东					290895.0	
河　南	838.0	6.0	6.0		35013.6	176.7
湖　北	28.0				564521.2	84.7
湖　南	1200.0				66893.6	25.0
广　东	2874.9	26.7	28.5		404230.8	6683.7
广　西	314.0				27995.7	103.8
海　南					3813.7	284.4
重　庆					72238.4	17.5
四　川	148.0				63876.3	7930.7
贵　州					3900.0	441.0
云　南	271.0				136290.5	15835.7
西　藏	2310.0		40.0		11254.0	
陕　西					20362.4	27.7
甘　肃					68978.2	20.6
青　海	4.6				1121.1	5.0
宁　夏	224.5				14323.8	4.0
新　疆	5026.8	207.0	22.0		45266.4	2601.0

单位：万元

事业单位会计制度财务指标			执行民间非营利组织单位会计制度财务指标			
本年收入合计	本年支出合计	收支结余	固定资产原价	上年结余	本年收入合计	本年费用合计
2181415.2	**1884077.0**	**14390.9**	**441294.8**	**33853.6**	**153523.0**	**160591.5**
122391.5	133068.9	5475.5			62.7	
11980.7	12222.3		22.9			36.0
19690.3	27672.8		892.4	26.4	694.3	678.0
62642.8	79387.6	569.2	5613.9	60.4	1643.0	911.2
14741.1	14722.8		2925.1		977.4	974.1
303820.4	39959.5	31.9	7556.4	253.0	3398.3	5495.6
5100.1	4510.7	2.0			34.7	
14957.7	15828.4		1466.0		982.9	712.6
146139.8	139761.6	-3061.7			1.0	498.2
286572.9	270195.9	823.6	173473.6	5243.4	64297.8	50579.1
255354.8	215506.8	6488.2	33036.2		20283.0	23916.9
39909.3	40832.6	4.5	2000.3		789.2	1010.1
34967.6	35186.7		32041.6	11489.8	13751.1	12082.3
38250.2	38095.2		2007.0	80.0	1073.5	3993.2
197263.7	197239.4					
22303.0	21431.2	6.6	7524.9	5.0	2449.9	2852.9
46875.8	46691.6	184.1	7448.5		8453.6	5238.7
69339.8	66536.6		4240.1		1048.6	750.8
305972.1	283145.8	2366.1	39318.0	288.0	1668.4	14870.9
10781.8	10698.7		1731.5		41.2	138.9
5681.7	5725.8		491.0		101.0	101.0
31969.2	31914.7	6.3	19301.7	14.0	9903.4	9151.2
31971.8	48952.7	1252.0	13299.0	2415.0	4145.4	6093.0
28543.7	28164.3		18436.2	1873.3	7060.5	9627.1
33304.1	30468.6	222.6	62118.3	12045.3	9331.9	9215.4
4.0	28.0		230.0			
7996.9	7280.0					
3501.1	3323.7		375.2		13.5	45.0
189.2	162.5		5513.3		963.2	1256.6
649.7	847.5		118.2	60.0	47.4	175.8
28548.4	34514.1	20.0	113.5		306.1	186.9

C-3-9 其他社会服务

地区	单位数	工商登记	编制登记	民政登记	一个机构多块牌子	年末职工人数	女性	受教育 大学专科人数
全国	**6594**	**788**	**4109**	**568**	**1129**	**94224**	**30864**	**26269**
中央级								
北京	64	4	60			1945	651	381
天津	42	2	32	8		913	278	215
河北	221	5	198	8	10	3740	1060	743
山西	138	15	86	12	25	1392	536	440
内蒙古	161	27	127	4	3	2176	619	724
辽宁	459	31	247	170	11	6073	1906	1764
吉林	211	34	163	2	12	4908	1123	1642
黑龙江	175	18	145	9	3	3238	1045	1058
上海	92	56	36			3546	1450	709
江苏	341	56	230	44	11	4942	1600	1386
浙江	293	57	201	10	25	3824	1019	1035
安徽	209	25	145	27	12	3200	1058	824
福建	202	32	139	3	28	2986	856	482
江西	201	7	157	6	31	2030	641	354
山东	282	19	246	9	8	4404	1421	1550
河南	296	30	247	16	3	6327	2003	1780
湖北	270	17	207	11	35	4220	1645	1550
湖南	324	32	190	4	98	3732	1306	1402
广东	447	52	254	24	117	8356	2367	1813
广西	175	25	115		35	2360	916	806
海南	63	5	9	10	39	336	86	62
重庆	168	30	97	22	19	2471	1023	711
四川	444	46	262	27	109	5227	1933	1484
贵州	378	59	96	12	211	4106	1578	1143
云南	201	27	155	10	9	1482	417	483
西藏	24		4	20		74	39	37
陕西	168	32	121	8	7	2877	1035	703
甘肃	225	17	54	11	143	1327	511	333
青海	37	12	7	5	13	281	66	90
宁夏	88	6	20	34	28	413	179	101
新疆	195	10	59	42	84	1318	497	464

机构总表

单位：个、人、人次、时

程度	职业资格水平		年龄结构				志愿服务	
大学本科及以上人数	助理社会工作师人数	社会工作师人数	35岁及以下人数	36岁至45岁人数	46岁至55岁人数	56岁及以上人数	志愿者服务人次数	志愿服务时间
11848	**851**	**756**	**31533**	**35944**	**20675**	**6072**	**21783**	**67110.0**
485	58	38	648	541	575	181	398	2091.0
328	3	6	257	223	282	151	406	945.0
285	14	24	1303	1442	754	241	321	1331.0
318	3	10	532	499	270	91		
310	9	18	606	810	602	158		
1021	51	47	2073	2124	1432	444	157	286.0
439	6	13	1388	1730	1277	513		
486	16	15	793	1407	811	227	5	
407	12	27	1003	1099	998	446	1998	10158.0
777	87	58	1486	1899	1190	367	1382	4688.0
577	41	43	1105	1380	1017	322	4526	7975.0
257	97	46	1030	1295	723	152	1327	3989.0
248	38	48	894	1289	623	180	6	16.0
99	24	24	655	907	397	71	234	856.0
794	46	63	1577	1710	903	214	5041	13495.0
524	42	40	2949	2267	903	208		
416	42	33	1466	1680	847	227	175	195.0
447	26	21	1541	1378	675	138	1468	5964.0
852	113	52	2621	3376	1896	463	228	264.0
345	29	21	863	905	448	144		
35	2		95	135	92	14	215	
383	14	18	708	1028	551	184	2518	8890.0
549	41	41	1634	2200	1112	281	29	162.0
478	6	9	1508	1724	708	166	858	4198.0
215	19	17	512	590	201	179	9	32.0
14			53	14	7			
322	4	14	938	1074	689	176	347	1075.0
190	2	4	575	422	291	39		
41			80	139	53	9		
79	1	5	98	158	130	27		
127	5	1	542	499	218	59	135	500.0

C-3-9续表

地区	执行企业会计制度单位财务指标				执行行政	
	固定资产原价	营业收入	费用合计	营业利润	固定资产原价	上年结转和结余
全国	**970507.7**	**1074715.6**	**276506.6**	**218696.8**	**1884846.3**	**88285.3**
中央级						
北京	52972.6	118660.1	38300.9	58820.5	105403.3	-1449.6
天津	5998.2	3990.9	1707.1	798.4	42836.7	7486.2
河北	3898.0	4086.0	3745.4	-49.4	78538.6	4188.8
山西	12266.0	3046.3	1463.4	-605.8	32421.8	1069.8
内蒙古	15164.4	7168.6	3790.7	177.5	31817.2	973.7
辽宁	38649.7	27700.0	15387.3	293.7	99792.5	3106.0
吉林	19961.6	1983.2	766.1	247.1	74690.3	478.3
黑龙江	15133.8	8004.8	5550.1	1608.9	83154.0	10946.6
上海	252938.9	460305.5	69094.7	94335.8	6360.6	1899.3
江苏	38281.1	62800.9	11602.8	28707.4	185541.5	14140.7
浙江	34634.7	45233.6	14229.3	7060.2	100355.9	5753.1
安徽	16250.0	11121.4	4225.4	1200.7	51397.0	1598.2
福建	57699.1	25102.4	12404.4	1640.3	41150.6	9387.9
江西	7866.4	3952.2	1441.8	140.1	69694.8	218.2
山东	7273.2	4655.3	2072.5	316.8	97681.7	
河南	21572.8	8857.4	5785.4	649.7	53181.4	87.8
湖北	9255.1	10581.9	5425.9	1318.7	86872.0	3348.6
湖南	30820.1	12180.8	5316.2	516.4	70296.5	787.2
广东	48986.9	39796.4	12251.0	8431.9	248189.8	7993.4
广西	29006.2	77287.6	9113.7	1619.0	46365.3	5307.7
海南	3774.3	3782.5	2043.4	621.6	8702.4	2531.8
重庆	36300.0	24688.6	8709.8	1104.8	38930.4	1216.6
四川	44679.7	35981.7	12388.0	1968.7	84871.3	286.9
贵州	87262.7	45610.7	19420.7	5129.2	18511.6	303.6
云南	42618.5	5131.7	1854.5	677.1	34332.9	846.8
西藏	375.7				1701.2	140.0
陕西	22565.7	16627.9	7405.1	900.5	24027.1	1099.8
甘肃	3489.3	5334.4	757.0	1070.0	19020.6	89.0
青海	993.5	30.0	30.0		1595.7	2.6
宁夏	2088.5	232.0	150.7	-3.0	7679.7	604.4
新疆	7731.0	780.8	73.3		39731.9	3841.9

单位：万元

事业单位会计制度财务指标			执行民间非营利组织单位会计制度财务指标			
本年收入合计	本年支出合计	收支结余	固定资产原价	上年结余	本年收入合计	本年费用合计
1378451.0	**1322894.3**	**71053.9**	**64594.5**	**6341.5**	**16510.0**	**11523.0**
121855.4	123541.8	12229.1				
45810.9	39330.8	6972.7	83.8		163.5	147.3
41677.4	40257.8	5265.1	150.0		71.0	8.0
22031.5	22269.8	117.9				
21473.9	21665.6	649.6	125.0		11.0	14.0
85085.5	80128.7	3272.9	7140.4	692.4	2148.2	1210.7
13210.9	13553.7	-234.8				
40950.4	38361.2	460.0	49.0			54.2
11337.6	11319.4	1655.9				
124723.4	119109.2	4486.6	5319.0		2518.6	1891.2
106148.5	98058.5	3968.8	563.0	2047.8	1422.2	718.9
43953.9	42438.9	1839.3	3801.4	1777.0	1278.3	1181.6
33182.8	33415.5	2484.3	3.0		7.9	0.3
19253.3	16164.6	146.1	22.5		26.0	18.3
77474.4	77474.4		3282.2		1766.1	1766.1
29525.5	29001.4	375.6	383.0		162.0	5.4
85054.3	75637.7	4686.5	69.0		64.3	64.3
42738.8	43579.3	-86.8	1480.0		108.5	49.0
182981.6	178340.8	6777.4	1194.2	3.0	348.1	19.0
33296.6	30843.5	3622.4	1.0		63.0	
6773.9	5871.2	1927.6	30.1			
39387.6	36200.5	4405.8	13450.4		972.1	937.0
56794.0	52068.0	654.9	15287.6	1374.3	4500.0	2380.4
6714.5	7512.4	-811.3	3332.0		222.5	358.1
16131.6	15155.8	600.4	25.9		21.7	16.5
744.0	746.4					
24725.3	24199.5	1250.8	1116.5		67.5	73.0
11304.1	11615.7	100.0	75.2		5.5	5.6
861.2	795.6		3897.0		30.0	32.3
5588.3	5746.7	670.6	3171.3	447.0	430.0	421.8
27659.9	28489.9	3566.5	542.0		102.0	150.0

C-3-10 婚姻登记

地 区	单位数	编制登记	民政登记	一个机构多块牌子	年末职工人数	女性	受教育程度	
							大学专科人数	大学本科及以上人数
全 国	**2064**	**1211**	**173**	**680**	**10373**	**6734**	**4194**	**2931**
中央级								
北 京	10	10			114	87	21	83
天 津	14	6	8		184	103	54	117
河 北	43	31	4	8	381	281	119	37
山 西	72	44	7	21	317	213	144	83
内蒙古	31	31			152	100	78	56
辽 宁	107	89	11	7	715	491	258	298
吉 林	65	64	1		481	299	111	93
黑龙江	34	31	3		231	153	89	50
上 海	18	18			156	113	44	85
江 苏	86	61	19	6	584	383	246	170
浙 江	68	50	2	16	338	247	128	156
安 徽	46	31	9	6	302	180	154	63
福 建	44	33		11	151	102	57	52
江 西	74	54	3	17	307	206	90	26
山 东	110	102	1	7	893	588	382	329
河 南	40	33	4	3	331	219	116	44
湖 北	95	84	3	8	589	432	271	139
湖 南	118	79	2	37	672	415	319	127
广 东	133	71	4	58	671	422	288	182
广 西	67	51		16	285	203	149	81
海 南	47	1	8	38	62	26	12	12
重 庆	50	39	11		311	176	101	126
四 川	127	59	12	56	627	386	309	147
贵 州	230	34	3	193	446	256	217	150
云 南	34	22	9	3	133	82	46	36
西 藏	22	2	20		41	29	24	6
陕 西	52	48		4	317	201	118	63
甘 肃	146	20	2	124	364	220	155	67
青 海	1			1	2	2		
宁 夏	49	2	20	27	103	66	42	37
新 疆	31	11	7	13	113	53	52	16

服务机构总表

单位:个、人、人次、时、处

职业资格水平		年龄结构				志愿服务		办理婚姻登记事务的处数
助理社会工作师人数	社会工作师人数	35岁及以下人数	36岁至45岁人数	46岁至55岁人数	56岁及以上人数	志愿者服务人次数	志愿服务时间	
194	**205**	**4896**	**4009**	**1335**	**133**	**12945**	**34234.0**	**5714**
6	5	64	35	15		4	4.0	16
1		71	46	51	16	206	545.0	18
2	9	207	146	28		129	573.0	361
1	3	154	121	39	3			137
		43	75	32	2			121
16	9	344	260	98	13	50	96.0	223
6	5	209	174	90	8			69
2		113	100	16	2	5		204
3	14	71	62	15	8	20	40.0	22
20	18	302	200	65	17	279	783.0	112
14	12	167	128	41	2	3856	6725.0	111
15	14	131	122	47	2	520	1218.0	115
11	11	65	76	9	1			137
5	6	127	131	48	1			123
16	24	407	360	117	9	4953	13240.0	171
5	8	194	103	32	2			194
18	9	260	245	82	2	35	40.0	112
8	7	361	232	75	4	668	3094.0	151
15	12	318	256	91	6	208	220.0	290
4	1	90	143	48	4			134
		29	33			215		164
9	15	115	141	53	2	1589	6771.0	101
9	14	277	251	84	15	15	97.0	754
1		243	158	44	1	122	569.0	714
7	7	50	76	7		9	32.0	193
		36	4	1				102
	2	161	118	37	1	62	187.0	184
		209	100	45	10			177
			2					231
		36	54	12	1			105
		42	57	13	1			168

C-3-10续表

地区	执行企业会计制度单位财务指标 固定资产原价	营业收入	费用合计	营业利润	执行行政 固定资产原价	上年结转和结余
全国	**377.4**	**419.5**	**272.5**	**12.6**	**78720.9**	**950.1**
中央级						
北京					419.0	10.3
天津	38.0	125.2	95.2	5.5	1621.5	63.5
河北	13.0				244.1	12.1
山西	4.0				185.1	3.1
内蒙古					509.1	6.5
辽宁	0.8	7.5	1.5		2212.0	48.7
吉林	10.6	1.0	0.2		568.5	2.3
黑龙江					1224.9	0.6
上海					1523.9	101.0
江苏		5.0	5.0		1196.5	51.3
浙江					1387.7	40.8
安徽					723.8	48.3
福建					330.4	88.9
江西	11.0	12.5	2.4		50525.7	
山东					3989.3	
河南					156.7	
湖北	1.0				1506.3	78.4
湖南					1283.6	25.8
广东	11.0	20.4	57.6		2707.5	127.6
广西	63.0	108.7	92.8	-0.9	555.6	33.5
海南	1.5	4.4			27.4	0.1
重庆		79.8			1805.9	52.3
四川	3.0				2306.1	6.0
贵州					164.8	
云南	110.0	55.0	17.8	8.0	248.2	9.0
西藏	8.5				427.2	140.0
陕西					405.1	
甘肃					64.6	
青海						
宁夏	30.0				139.0	
新疆	72.0				261.4	

单位：万元

事业单位会计制度财务指标			执行民间非营利组织单位会计制度财务指标			
本年收入合计	本年支出合计	收支结余	固定资产原价	上年结余	本年收入合计	本年费用合计
49942.8	**51303.3**	**691.0**	**926.9**		**1158.0**	**964.2**
1930.5	1946.0	1.3				
3216.5	3231.6	76.9	83.8		163.5	147.3
942.1	953.6	1.1				
434.1	510.9					
814.2	862.8	2.9				
3353.9	3597.3	3.1	8.0		13.4	15.4
1335.3	1329.8	2.0				
1200.9	1263.1					
5208.9	5123.0	93.8				
4017.9	4020.4	53.9	89.3		284.1	275.4
2899.6	2997.9	12.5	168.0		259.0	164.0
1210.6	1224.4	-4.3	73.4		55.1	55.5
684.9	772.7	56.3	3.0		5.9	0.3
488.8	483.1	2.8	22.5		26.0	18.3
6071.7	6071.7					
502.1	515.1		3.0			3.2
2936.6	2868.1	-1.5	3.0		49.8	49.8
1906.1	1955.5	-4.1			6.5	
2973.9	3133.3	69.1	15.0		10.0	12.0
603.5	646.9	4.6	1.0		63.0	
138.0	147.4		0.1			
3408.5	3137.3	320.6	380.4		82.4	58.5
1144.3	1215.7		42.3		99.6	140.4
255.5	256.9		8.0		16.0	6.6
310.3	1128.5		25.9		21.7	16.5
117.0	51.4					
1510.2	1516.0					
74.4	75.4		0.2			1.0
10.0	25.0				2.0	
242.5	242.5					

C-3-11 结婚登

地 区	登记结婚件数	登记结婚人数	按居住		
			内地居民登记结婚件数	内地居民登记结婚人数	涉外及华侨、港澳台居民登记结婚件数
全 国	**12247056**	**24494112**	**12205888**	**24408074**	**41168**
中央级					
北 京	166018	332036	165000	330000	1018
天 津	101238	202476	100898	201796	340
河 北	609442	1218884	608863	1217726	579
山 西	346789	693578	346642	693284	147
内蒙古	217857	435714	217668	435336	189
辽 宁	316977	633954	315283	630566	1694
吉 林	234453	468906	233671	467342	782
黑龙江	318224	636448	316724	633448	1500
上 海	141827	283654	140049	280098	1778
江 苏	786037	1572074	784445	1568890	1592
浙 江	392478	784956	389399	778798	3079
安 徽	739101	1478202	737989	1475978	1112
福 建	349417	698834	344309	688618	5108
江 西	306158	612316	305234	610468	924
山 东	701034	1402068	699949	1399898	1085
河 南	1094357	2188714	1093463	2186926	894
湖 北	572954	1145908	571636	1143272	1318
湖 南	542664	1085328	540969	1081938	1695
广 东	840411	1680822	832694	1665442	7717
广 西	421289	842578	419676	839352	1613
海 南	83066	166132	82416	164832	650
重 庆	292570	585140	291841	583682	729
四 川	741526	1483052	740186	1480372	1340
贵 州	492606	985212	492213	984426	393
云 南	458235	916470	455202	910404	3033
西 藏	15442	30884	15433	29351	9
陕 西	355978	711956	355542	711084	436
甘 肃	220327	440654	220169	440338	158
青 海	51066	102132	51038	99835	28
宁 夏	60900	121800	60862	121724	38
新 疆	276615	553230	276425	552850	190

记服务

单位:对、人

地分类

内地居民	#女 性	香港居民	澳门居民	台湾居民	华 侨	外国人
39770	26089	4696	1331	8423	5744	22372
933	664	68	5	143	18	869
336	262	9	3	56	9	267
578	316	14	9	74	12	471
25	13	9	3	15	8	234
186	119	8	6	28	6	144
1684	1322	86	15	195	93	1315
780	552	27	9	115	38	595
1497	997	41	15	177	290	980
1642	1245	127	15	324	42	1406
1577	1261	61	18	495	22	1011
2275	1328	56	12	258	2443	1114
1108	546	41	10	241	16	808
5040	3207	703	93	1717	942	1721
923	487	51	14	263	19	578
1069	740	40	11	180	22	848
862	571	56	14	265	27	564
1313	1028	115	34	456	20	698
1694	1336	147	75	749	36	689
7676	5324	2436	827	840	1526	2129
1611	999	136	49	400	62	968
650	506	192	9	335	19	95
727	584	59	29	223	13	407
1334	1024	99	27	437	27	756
393	293	55	18	132	16	172
3008	382	19	2	111	5	2921
9	46					9
433	297	24	7	104	10	294
156	116	11	1	61	2	85
28	20			4		24
38	20	1		10		27
185	484	5	1	15	1	173

C-3-11续表

地区	按婚姻状况分类			
	初婚人数	再婚人数	#女性	#恢复结婚件数
全国	**21089700**	**3404412**	**1772263**	**398527**
中央级				
北京	229546	102490	49274	13441
天津	174859	27617	14039	12812
河北	987465	231419	124982	2107
山西	623132	70446	38628	8992
内蒙古	330999	104715	58154	14917
辽宁	575281	58673	29712	22623
吉林	424231	44675	22461	19901
黑龙江	553715	82733	42181	27390
上海	198938	84716	41908	15457
江苏	1322105	249969	128813	38291
浙江	648666	136290	69969	10619
安徽	1240023	238179	124099	29453
福建	608249	90585	41014	1407
江西	527676	84640	44285	10374
山东	1104987	297081	157628	1955
河南	2116748	71966	35836	33625
湖北	1079852	66056	33475	6966
湖南	892489	192839	103851	13368
广东	1501835	178987	85208	27356
广西	739950	102628	57659	7063
海南	151307	14825	7172	1327
重庆	412757	172383	90612	15473
四川	1138435	344617	186571	29669
贵州	953016	32196	16180	8277
云南	782890	133580	67082	2100
西藏	29293	1591	765	14
陕西	598491	113465	61578	6997
甘肃	426481	14173	7164	2726
青海	92146	9986	5307	255
宁夏	103105	18695	9589	1700
新疆	521033	32197	17067	11872

单位:对、人

按年龄分类				
20～24岁	25～29岁	30～34岁	35～39岁	40岁及以上
6438557	**9657075**	**2881476**	**1553068**	**3963936**
24366	154441	69130	31098	53001
34821	91323	36252	15396	24684
443969	464806	119288	58389	132432
198646	251196	67763	43191	132782
87422	175119	59112	31194	82867
99844	267114	96061	50533	120402
83558	173026	63844	39967	108511
100939	198508	82394	57556	197051
22624	118808	56668	26224	59330
374380	591326	132382	80218	393768
142272	344777	102939	49481	145487
468694	521197	122167	86760	279384
163304	310633	84333	34418	106146
189984	243160	64479	39069	75624
316624	713919	155808	70841	144876
673957	858958	213937	141047	300815
291852	469554	126685	65964	191853
272068	485915	140888	64016	122441
490868	718631	230655	90905	149763
217317	331866	139760	60809	92826
42098	59117	26268	12067	26582
167484	202990	65328	33481	115857
429148	532069	163378	98507	259950
272929	299198	126932	86786	199367
259975	287510	113849	77305	177831
10835	13141	3712	1744	1452
187231	334397	79644	33804	76880
134865	185939	43463	18442	57945
22236	32521	11678	7745	27952
37117	44512	12471	7388	20312
177130	181404	70208	38723	85765

C-3-12 离婚登

地区	总计	民政部门合计	内地居民登记离婚	涉外及华侨、港澳台居民登记离婚	#外国人
全国	**3841407**	**3148779**	**3142542**	**6237**	**2659**
北京	82194	73000	72746	254	178
天津	51931	46507	46431	76	54
河北	199048	157180	157121	59	44
山西	72207	54166	54153	13	8
内蒙古	91883	71400	71382	18	11
辽宁	152348	126826	126557	269	193
吉林	127410	113263	113144	119	77
黑龙江	189802	162094	161923	171	93
上海	66612	58302	57902	400	268
江苏	229281	188789	188546	243	140
浙江	139580	115062	114669	393	148
安徽	181207	149042	148912	130	72
福建	89286	72589	71632	957	283
江西	95163	79099	79006	93	48
山东	240933	185305	185153	152	113
河南	252274	213156	213058	98	37
湖北	166886	144684	144491	193	78
湖南	180924	150901	150711	190	44
广东	193360	167544	166142	1402	290
广西	104413	83521	83344	177	72
海南	15137	11827	11706	121	16
重庆	137326	120220	120079	141	54
四川	286183	241360	241133	227	107
贵州	108395	81293	81224	69	19
云南	109073	85231	85068	163	140
西藏	2374	1812	1812	0	0
陕西	97299	74097	74038	59	34
甘肃	46185	29155	29134	21	12
青海	12773	7592	7586	6	5
宁夏	18136	13315	13310	5	5
新疆	101784	70,447	70,429.00	1816	

说明：全国的含有军事。

记服务

单位：件(对)、人

法院部门合计	判决离婚	调解离婚	离婚案件收案	判决不离	调解不离
692628	**212258**	**480370**	**1408432**	**274475**	**60531**
9194	3081	6113	21863	4018	254
5424	1650	3774	13451	3289	563
41868	12644	29224	86810	18041	1226
18041	5445	12596	43167	6277	5328
20483	6707	13776	37450	2630	1671
25522	8575	16947	52546	9014	1471
14147	5431	8716	27491	3624	411
27708	6388	21320	42079	1890	1034
8310	2639	5671	17871	4195	276
40492	10575	29917	95262	24101	4081
24518	7487	17031	52713	12635	1405
32165	9012	23153	71024	17089	1650
16697	7683	9014	35324	8362	481
16064	5818	10246	36804	7951	2043
55628	19406	36222	121126	28600	7322
39118	13844	25274	83174	21090	2361
22202	6661	15541	47732	12046	1057
30023	10585	19438	61921	15997	2159
25816	10548	15268	52902	11247	1184
20892	8129	12763	37443	8250	1324
3310	1215	2095	5871	905	698
17106	5667	11439	34263	8121	1019
44823	11741	33082	84801	16278	2573
27102	6722	20380	46703	6289	1582
23842	6673	17169	44161	5009	3008
562	71	491	832	16	76
23202	5356	17846	50135	6216	6149
17030	4836	12194	37267	6266	2407
5181	1225	3956	10182	898	858
4821	1504	3317	11373	2146	823
31337	4940	26397	44691	1985	4037

C-3-13 殡葬服务

地 区	单位数	工商登记	编制登记	民政登记	年末职工人数	女性	受教育程度 大学专科人数	大学本科及以上人数
全 国	**4530**	**788**	**2898**	**395**	**83851**	**24130**	**22075**	**8917**
中央级								
北 京	54	4	50		1831	564	360	402
天 津	28	2	26		729	175	161	211
河 北	178	5	167	4	3359	779	624	248
山 西	66	15	42	5	1075	323	296	235
内蒙古	130	27	96	4	2024	519	646	254
辽 宁	352	31	158	159	5358	1415	1506	723
吉 林	146	34	99	1	4427	824	1531	346
黑龙江	141	18	114	6	3007	892	969	436
上 海	74	56	18		3390	1337	665	322
江 苏	255	56	169	25	4358	1217	1140	607
浙 江	225	57	151	8	3486	772	907	421
安 徽	163	25	114	18	2898	878	670	194
福 建	158	32	106	3	2835	754	425	196
江 西	127	7	103	3	1723	435	264	73
山 东	172	19	144	8	3511	833	1168	465
河 南	256	30	214	12	5996	1784	1664	480
湖 北	175	17	123	8	3631	1213	1279	277
湖 南	206	32	111	2	3060	891	1083	320
广 东	314	52	183	20	7685	1945	1525	670
广 西	108	25	64		2075	713	657	264
海 南	16	5	8	2	274	60	50	23
重 庆	118	30	58	11	2160	847	610	257
四 川	317	46	203	15	4600	1547	1175	402
贵 州	148	59	62	9	3660	1322	926	328
云 南	167	27	133	1	1349	335	437	179
西 藏	2		2		33	10	13	8
陕 西	116	32	73	8	2560	834	585	259
甘 肃	79	17	34	9	963	291	178	123
青 海	36	12	7	5	279	64	90	41
宁 夏	39	6	18	14	310	113	59	42
新 疆	164	10	48	35	1205	444	412	111

机构总表

单位:个、人、人次、时

职业资格水平		年龄结构				志愿服务	
助理社会工作师人数	社会工作师人数	35岁及以下人数	36岁至45岁人数	46岁至55岁人数	56岁及以上人数	志愿者服务人次数	志愿服务时间
657	**551**	**26637**	**31935**	**19340**	**5939**	**8838**	**32876.0**
52	33	584	506	560	181	394	2087.0
2	6	186	177	231	135	200	400.0
12	15	1096	1296	726	241	192	758.0
2	7	378	378	231	88		
9	18	563	735	570	156		
35	38	1729	1864	1334	431	107	190.0
	8	1179	1556	1187	505		
14	15	680	1307	795	225		
9	13	932	1037	983	438	1978	10118.0
67	40	1184	1699	1125	350	1103	3905.0
27	31	938	1252	976	320	670	1250.0
82	32	899	1173	676	150	807	2771.0
27	37	829	1213	614	179	6	16.0
19	18	528	776	349	70	234	856.0
30	39	1170	1350	786	205	88	255.0
37	32	2755	2164	871	206		
24	24	1206	1435	765	225	140	155.0
18	14	1180	1146	600	134	800	2870.0
98	40	2303	3120	1805	457	20	44.0
25	20	773	762	400	140		
2		66	102	92	14		
5	3	593	887	498	182	929	2119.0
32	27	1357	1949	1028	266	14	65.0
5	9	1265	1566	664	165	736	3629.0
12	10	462	514	194	179		
		17	10	6			
4	12	777	956	652	175	285	888.0
2	4	366	322	246	29		
		80	137	53	9		
1	5	62	104	118	26		
5	1	500	442	205	58	135	500.0

C-3-13续表1

地区	火化炉数	全年遗体火化数	国际运尸数	外国人	港澳台	侨民
全国	**6063**	**4595065**	**632**	**434**	**195**	**3**
中央级						
北京	86	91482	112	110	2	
天津	67	67792				
河北	376	189443				
山西	65	21526				
内蒙古	159	67828				
辽宁	368	276801				
吉林	169	98899				
黑龙江	255	175231				
上海	95	127798	46	45	1	
江苏	536	502655				
浙江	348	319294				
安徽	267	266931				
福建	224	196225				
江西	202	66863				
山东	504	586755				
河南	323	159425				
湖北	330	219860				
湖南	159	81635	2	2		
广东	419	450619	466	275	189	2
广西	99	78448				
海南	6	2997	4		3	1
重庆	126	78360	2	2		
四川	284	206549				
贵州	136	81087				
云南	186	67977				
西藏	6	760				
陕西	98	54353				
甘肃	54	18614				
青海	50	6723				
宁夏	10	3615				
新疆	56	28520				

单位:具、个、台

穴位数	#本年销售穴位数	安葬数	#本年安葬数	格位数	#格位存放数	#本年格位存放数
15811006	**657044**	**10379760**	**654835**	**1057245**	**443155**	**47322**
689399	15291	546703	20767	65100	47482	1661
284220	5160	307806	6623	47442	31928	1840
265020	7407	114931	7856	12078	7068	980
131052	3753	65870	4064	28352	8371	722
289634	15899	232373	22750	20905	7636	824
806917	97341	547208	51840	7042	3481	1275
25951	1851	17260	2771	25480	14446	2550
242985	24795	209947	27780			
1921132	71274	1349108	47858	94127	83863	5531
1507746	93218	1300186	54290	75165	45770	1785
1119407	31564	815713	46332	16374	10674	807
418384	16248	308215	39184	3754	1947	1768
290860	15497	227130	18047	26166	6423	313
174810	9354	69634	10787			
263441	7367	173054	18909			
275668	8979	163176	8051	22630	8649	1543
919013	23089	623588	50902	3855	1594	111
451717	21283	222838	23327	20273	2568	531
1275492	32627	770514	31519	334210	88717	12219
348434	14058	212613	13649	33907	8360	4476
36370	2598	22061	2812			
661209	18378	349831	17762	87624	27605	1524
1263526	42301	803803	40439	14994	10739	1997
449102	21797	219702	23700	17472	3980	372
533735	10138	144712	16634	50	15	10
426544	24368	391500	22690	98415	20009	2653
113982	6991	90591	7721			
5359	1169	2346	322			
30981	3235	20895	3736			
588916	10014	56452	11713	1830	1830	1830

C-3-13续表2

地 区	执行企业会计制度单位财务指标				执行行政	
	固定资产原价	营业收入	费用合计	营业利润	固定资产原价	上年结转和结余
全 国	**970130.3**	**1074296.1**	**276234.1**	**218684.2**	**1806125.4**	**87335.2**
中央级						
北 京	52972.6	118660.1	38300.9	58820.5	104984.3	-1459.9
天 津	5960.2	3865.7	1611.9	792.9	41215.2	7422.7
河 北	3885.0	4086.0	3745.4	-49.4	78294.5	4176.7
山 西	12262.0	3046.3	1463.4	-605.8	32236.7	1066.7
内蒙古	15164.4	7168.6	3790.7	177.5	31308.1	967.2
辽 宁	38648.9	27692.5	15385.8	293.7	97580.5	3057.3
吉 林	19951.0	1982.2	765.9	247.1	74121.8	476.0
黑龙江	15133.8	8004.8	5550.1	1608.9	81929.1	10946.0
上 海	252938.9	460305.5	69094.7	94335.8	4836.7	1798.3
江 苏	38281.1	62795.9	11597.8	28707.4	184345.0	14089.4
浙 江	34634.7	45233.6	14229.3	7060.2	98968.2	5712.3
安 徽	16250.0	11121.4	4225.4	1200.7	50673.2	1549.9
福 建	57699.1	25102.4	12404.4	1640.3	40820.2	9299.0
江 西	7855.4	3939.7	1439.4	140.1	19169.1	218.2
山 东	7273.2	4655.3	2072.5	316.8	93692.4	
河 南	21572.8	8857.4	5785.4	649.7	53024.7	87.8
湖 北	9254.1	10581.9	5425.9	1318.7	85365.7	3270.2
湖 南	30820.1	12180.8	5316.2	516.4	69012.9	761.4
广 东	48975.9	39776.0	12193.4	8431.9	245482.3	7865.8
广 西	28943.2	77178.9	9020.9	1619.9	45809.7	5274.2
海 南	3772.8	3778.1	2043.4	621.6	8675.0	2531.7
重 庆	36300.0	24608.8	8709.8	1104.8	37124.5	1164.3
四 川	44676.7	35981.7	12388.0	1968.7	82565.2	280.9
贵 州	87262.7	45610.7	19420.7	5129.2	18346.8	303.6
云 南	42508.5	5076.7	1836.7	669.1	34084.7	837.8
西 藏	367.2				1274.0	
陕 西	22565.7	16627.9	7405.1	900.5	23622.0	1099.8
甘 肃	3489.3	5334.4	757.0	1070.0	18956.0	89.0
青 海	993.5	30.0	30.0		1595.7	2.6
宁 夏	2058.5	232.0	150.7	-3.0	7540.7	604.4
新 疆	7659.0	780.8	73.3		39470.5	3841.9

单位：万元

事业单位会计制度财务指标			执行民间非营利组织单位会计制度财务指标			
本年收入合计	本年支出合计	收支结余	固定资产原价	上年结余	本年收入合计	本年费用合计
1328508.2	**1271591.0**	**70362.9**	**63667.6**	**6341.5**	**15352.0**	**10558.8**
119924.9	121595.8	12227.8				
42594.4	36099.2	6895.8				
40735.3	39304.2	5264.0	150.0		71.0	8.0
21597.4	21758.9	117.9				
20659.7	20802.8	646.7	125.0		11.0	14.0
81731.6	76531.4	3269.8	7132.4	692.4	2134.8	1195.3
11875.6	12223.9	-236.8				
39749.5	37098.1	460.0	49.0			54.2
6128.7	6196.4	1562.1				
120705.5	115088.8	4432.7	5229.7		2234.5	1615.8
103248.9	95060.6	3956.3	395.0	2047.8	1163.2	554.9
42743.3	41214.5	1843.6	3728.0	1777.0	1223.2	1126.1
32497.9	32642.8	2428.0			2.0	
18764.5	15681.5	143.3				
71402.7	71402.7		3282.2		1766.1	1766.1
29023.4	28486.3	375.6	380.0		162.0	2.2
82117.7	72769.6	4688.0	66.0		14.5	14.5
40832.7	41623.8	-82.7	1480.0		102.0	49.0
180007.7	175207.5	6708.3	1179.2	3.0	338.1	7.0
32693.1	30196.6	3617.8				
6635.9	5723.8	1927.6	30.0			
35979.1	33063.2	4085.2	13070.0		889.7	878.5
55649.7	50852.3	654.9	15245.3	1374.3	4400.4	2240.0
6459.0	7255.5	-811.3	3324.0		206.5	351.5
15821.3	14027.3	600.4				
627.0	695.0					
23215.1	22683.5	1250.8	1116.5		67.5	73.0
11229.7	11540.3	100.0	75.0		5.5	4.6
861.2	795.6		3897.0		30.0	32.3
5578.3	5721.7	670.6	3171.3	447.0	428.0	421.8
27417.4	28247.4	3566.5	542.0		102.0	150.0

C-3-14 殡仪

地区	单位数	年末职工人数		受教育程度		职业资
			女性	大学专科人数	大学本科及以上人数	助理社会工作师人数
全国	**1821**	**46725**	**12108**	**13206**	**4868**	**404**
中央级						
北京	12	602	151	154	126	23
天津	10	405	86	100	86	2
河北	153	2786	590	511	202	12
山西	27	389	101	88	82	2
内蒙古	66	1176	299	393	133	2
辽宁	81	2753	759	751	303	12
吉林	47	1948	267	1192	229	
黑龙江	96	2431	731	778	343	13
上海	15	1086	302	322	163	3
江苏	92	2801	677	730	379	52
浙江	77	2201	445	639	230	20
安徽	69	2077	600	477	128	66
福建	63	1810	437	184	87	17
江西	84	1264	317	159	37	8
山东	123	2811	564	972	389	23
河南	116	3606	1012	1049	243	22
湖北	84	2499	840	893	191	21
湖南	72	1536	443	525	176	6
广东	89	4323	986	921	402	73
广西	33	773	242	274	71	9
海南	2	70	20	13	11	
重庆	38	866	285	292	138	3
四川	87	1865	517	495	164	9
贵州	49	1721	591	353	130	1
云南	78	747	169	255	110	1
西藏	2	33	10	13	8	
陕西	44	1081	319	382	165	3
甘肃	27	442	146	80	85	1
青海	20	95	19	39	10	
宁夏	7	65	25	18	14	
新疆	58	463	158	154	33	

馆

单位:个、人、人次、时

格水平	年龄结构				志愿服务	
社会工作师人数	35岁及以下人数	36岁至45岁人数	46岁至55岁人数	56岁及以上人数	志愿者服务人次数	志愿服务时间
278	**15036**	**17957**	**10621**	**3111**	**5311**	**20602.0**
14	174	165	185	78	52	52.0
	104	71	145	85	100	200.0
13	893	1105	623	165	184	726.0
7	92	145	120	32		
6	308	430	339	99		
15	874	1027	635	217	48	89.0
3	374	654	535	385		
14	556	1028	668	179		
7	424	297	248	117	1628	9768.0
28	769	1022	797	213	588	1180.0
18	594	832	600	175	231	368.0
26	659	830	479	109	175	533.0
22	533	764	402	111		
2	354	574	285	51	234	856.0
29	910	1096	638	167	88	255.0
9	1745	1264	503	94		
8	825	981	525	168	105	115.0
4	603	547	326	60	755	2710.0
17	1290	1792	1003	238		
6	324	256	135	58		
	26	24	17	3		
3	270	371	183	42	656	1590.0
11	577	821	368	99		
4	573	806	285	57	227	1445.0
2	314	300	107	26		
	17	10	6			
6	394	384	254	49	230	640.0
3	233	110	83	16		
	33	46	16			
1	13	21	27	4		
	181	184	84	14	10	75.0

C-3-14续表1

地区	火化炉数	全年遗体火化数	国际运尸数	外国人
全国	**6063**	**4595065**	**632**	**434**
中央级				
北京	86	91482	112	110
天津	67	67792		
河北	376	189443		
山西	65	21526		
内蒙古	159	67828		
辽宁	368	276801		
吉林	169	98899		
黑龙江	255	175231		
上海	95	127798	46	45
江苏	536	502655		
浙江	348	319294		
安徽	267	266931		
福建	224	196225		
江西	202	66863		
山东	504	586755		
河南	323	159425		
湖北	330	219860		
湖南	159	81635	2	2
广东	419	450619	466	275
广西	99	78448		
海南	6	2997	4	
重庆	126	78360	2	2
四川	284	206549		
贵州	136	81087		
云南	186	67977		
西藏	6	760		
陕西	98	54353		
甘肃	54	18614		
青海	50	6723		
宁夏	10	3615		
新疆	56	28520		

单位:具、个、台

港澳台	侨民	穴位数	#本年销售穴位数	安葬数	#本年安葬数
195	**3**	**2737909**	**84577**	**1452907**	**195692**
2		10653	180	9322	186
		28628	488	22983	1415
		66142	3153	27075	3088
		131995	8120	111722	10068
		15125	681	50805	14493
		1795	108	1692	1057
		130690	7827	122788	15515
1		79	79	87	87
		114847	2749	100281	2898
		111718	3206	74220	17636
		110673	2235	60366	22647
		125047	6226	117592	8949
		154469	8295	55352	9465
		72762	822	58587	11720
		32672	1201	16582	779
		116466	6556	120342	32019
		149843	5961	101239	8323
189	2	143953	2633	76920	3602
		4612	1351	1273	179
3	1				
		115559	3257	67155	3234
		29768	1593	18577	1975
		43730	3365	8801	4670
		313022	4952	53957	11920
		149400	1865	139993	1717
		21948	1677	17726	1808
		5645	588	1683	582
		536668	5409	15787	5660

C-3-14续表2

地 区	执行企业会计制度单位财务指标				执行行政	
	固定资产原价	营业收入	费用合计	营业利润	固定资产原价	上年结转和结余
全 国	**309605.8**	**152954.3**	**55169.7**	**16563.9**	**1411543.2**	**49074.6**
中央级						
北 京					52318.2	-2136.0
天 津					24310.0	
河 北	348.0	471.0	370.0	-60.0	67564.9	2573.5
山 西	671.0	54.0	41.0	18.0	24181.4	840.1
内蒙古	5097.7	1462.5	1598.1	-86.7	28812.6	883.9
辽 宁	10800.4	4246.9	3995.5	-1490.2	81390.8	3016.6
吉 林	17546.0	520.8	149.9	120.5	62849.2	
黑龙江	7508.9	1875.1	2078.1	154.9	74015.1	10000.9
上 海	92139.6	78774.4	16004.7	14031.2	4107.2	
江 苏	6780.7	2711.3	503.5	621.2	161924.3	11194.5
浙 江	4873.5	4072.2	1395.7	556.5	89118.6	3793.8
安 徽	3774.3	2217.8	1091.7	121.0	35678.4	265.5
福 建	48580.1	15634.9	8521.3	41.7	31808.7	5568.0
江 西	6298.1	1759.0	683.2	22.1	14497.1	203.2
山 东	645.0	54.4	148.0		83657.6	
河 南	4176.1	923.2	310.2	103.1	48316.0	-10.8
湖 北	1664.5	110.0	110.0		61544.1	2301.0
湖 南	8198.7	3623.4	1882.2	23.0	48603.5	596.1
广 东	6115.8	2408.7	1682.3	85.3	201917.6	5520.6
广 西	10035.5	2775.6	2080.4	-319.8	26653.4	2139.0
海 南	48.0	1792.0	852.7	363.0	599.7	282.2
重 庆	10725.4	3086.9	1465.3	43.5	30075.5	922.6
四 川	11418.3	7546.5	2120.2	151.0	58582.3	-789.8
贵 州	38391.2	15840.8	7952.4	2059.6	15307.9	184.0
云 南	3821.0	50.0			31988.6	736.0
西 藏	367.2				1274.0	
陕 西	2840.0	157.2	54.0	5.0	17858.0	926.0
甘 肃	200.0	15.0	6.0		18317.6	42.0
青 海	711.0				1524.0	
宁 夏					6191.6	21.7
新 疆	5829.8	770.7	73.3		6555.3	

单位：万元

事业单位会计制度财务指标			执行民间非营利组织单位会计制度财务指标			
本年收入合计	本年支出合计	收支结余	固定资产原价	上年结余	本年收入合计	本年费用合计
888386.8	**851069.9**	**30181.6**	**26637.8**	**1996.0**	**3461.0**	**3299.3**
35439.3	33114.0	-1298.5				
18451.7	17581.2	200.6				
30117.7	30597.9	2160.3	150.0		71.0	8.0
14277.0	14655.1	117.5				
16951.4	17129.4	565.8	112.0		11.0	11.0
58363.9	55767.7	2395.1	53.0		2.0	3.3
6034.0	6176.3	-91.3				
31637.8	28969.3	460.0	3.0			0.8
1690.3	1648.5					
87224.7	82079.3	6007.0	2389.0		450.0	450.0
83606.6	77767.5	978.0				
30467.1	29810.5	1241.2	2720.0	1774.0	1016.0	973.0
19886.9	17991.2	1689.6				
14655.9	12604.7	143.3				
62293.2	62293.2		878.8		1258.0	1258.0
21063.1	21129.3	53.1	370.0		150.0	0.2
54516.8	49607.0	4479.4				
32903.7	33650.5	-96.9				
138161.7	134335.6	5353.6				
12249.4	11347.9	1317.1				
845.0	687.5	514.8				
28940.3	27728.7	2141.2	12735.0		372.0	370.0
34561.5	33466.6	531.5	200.0			40.0
4746.7	4772.7	-888.7	1180.0		20.0	2.0
14498.2	12716.5	573.5				
627.0	695.0					
20164.6	19635.0	1088.0	310.0		28.0	19.0
8588.6	8804.1	100.0				
723.5	660.5		3897.0		30.0	32.3
1655.8	1226.8	446.4	1252.0	222.0	53.0	83.7
3043.4	2420.4		388.0			48.0

C-3-15 公

地区	单位数	年末职工人数		受教育程度		职业资
			女性	大学专科人数	大学本科及以上人数	助理社会工作师人数
全国	**1567**	**27277**	**9412**	**5632**	**2306**	**166**
中央级						
北京	34	1146	374	193	224	29
天津	7	203	63	30	61	
河北	14	392	132	67	27	
山西	27	608	197	171	136	
内蒙古	24	554	156	161	73	3
辽宁	217	2195	539	592	289	16
吉林	52	2036	524	212	87	
黑龙江	32	448	121	127	46	1
上海	50	2260	1018	328	134	5
江苏	110	1163	407	287	107	8
浙江	74	820	212	101	54	2
安徽	63	681	233	159	43	13
福建	31	406	163	73	29	1
江西	6	137	46	41	21	8
山东	40	615	241	177	66	7
河南	48	1146	395	264	78	4
湖北	63	866	298	263	55	3
湖南	78	1020	360	328	80	8
广东	113	2166	694	299	116	15
广西	27	598	266	172	78	5
海南	7	150	29	26	4	2
重庆	52	1106	488	255	64	2
四川	147	2198	852	456	179	21
贵州	50	1535	648	390	110	
云南	42	392	110	91	19	8
西藏						
陕西	39	1214	433	116	41	1
甘肃	37	436	121	71	21	
青海	14	175	42	47	31	
宁夏	16	176	66	26	9	1
新疆	53	435	184	109	24	3

墓

单位：个、人、人次、时

格水平	年龄结构				志愿服务	
社会工作师人数	35岁及以下人数	36岁至45岁人数	46岁至55岁人数	56岁及以上人数	志愿者服务人次数	志愿服务时间
137	**8124**	**10012**	**6803**	**2338**	**2823**	**10466.0**
16	368	319	361	98	333	2026.0
	49	65	52	37		
2	127	139	69	57	8	32.0
	260	203	92	53		
	163	185	168	38		
10	739	671	594	191	48	80.0
2	713	664	575	84		
1	92	222	95	39		
	495	723	727	315	350	350.0
9	295	515	236	117	480	2648.0
1	172	239	286	123	415	746.0
5	217	276	153	35	510	1850.0
	108	170	88	40		
15	53	62	16	6		
10	238	218	127	32		
14	368	467	223	88		
14	280	357	183	46	35	40.0
8	366	389	209	56	40	150.0
3	628	818	544	176		
3	194	269	113	22		
	24	59	62	5		
	287	417	267	135	38	64.0
15	626	883	543	146	12	63.0
2	485	617	333	100	482	2116.0
5	82	118	54	138		
1	280	478	343	113	27	116.0
	97	184	147	8		
	42	87	37	9		
1	30	56	70	20		
	246	142	36	11	45	185.0

C-3-15续表1

地 区	执行企业会计制度单位财务指标			
	固定资产原价	营业收入	费用合计	营业利润
全 国	**643212.3**	**917582.3**	**217844.2**	**201912.8**
中央级				
北 京	52972.6	118660.1	38300.9	58820.5
天 津	5960.2	3865.7	1611.9	792.9
河 北	3537.0	3615.0	3375.4	10.6
山 西	11591.0	2992.3	1422.4	-623.8
内蒙古	9528.7	5656.1	2180.6	259.2
辽 宁	27848.5	23445.6	11390.3	1783.9
吉 林	1679.7	1181.0	234.4	198.2
黑龙江	7046.9	5379.7	2711.2	1264.0
上 海	160799.3	381531.1	53090.0	80304.6
江 苏	28735.0	59781.9	10681.0	28196.8
浙 江	29667.2	40810.3	12768.3	6495.4
安 徽	12475.7	8903.6	3133.7	1079.7
福 建	8052.0	8503.5	3480.1	1411.6
江 西	1542.3	2180.7	756.2	118.0
山 东	6628.2	4600.9	1924.5	316.8
河 南	17396.7	7934.2	5475.2	546.6
湖 北	7589.6	10471.9	5315.9	1318.7
湖 南	16017.4	8190.4	2918.0	493.4
广 东	42844.1	37366.1	10511.1	8346.6
广 西	18907.7	74403.3	6940.5	1939.7
海 南	3714.8	1986.1	1190.7	258.6
重 庆	22074.6	21345.9	7231.3	1060.3
四 川	32852.8	28254.1	10079.8	1832.3
贵 州	48724.6	29458.9	11058.3	3066.6
云 南	38687.5	5026.7	1836.7	669.1
西 藏				
陕 西	19361.7	16470.7	7351.1	895.5
甘 肃	2929.3	5319.4	708.0	1060.0
青 海	282.5	30.0	30.0	
宁 夏	2018.5	217.0	136.7	-3.0
新 疆	1746.2	0.1		

单位：万元

执行行政事业单位会计制度财务指标				
固定资产原价	上年结转和结余	本年收入合计	本年支出合计	收支结余
205638.0	**16102.7**	**282649.2**	**263115.6**	**24017.2**
33091.8	639.1	67453.1	76356.0	8581.8
10129.6	3735.0	19439.8	14909.8	1948.7
2901.8	1009.1	6441.0	4591.2	2171.2
7660.8	226.0	6303.5	6077.7	
646.8		1876.6	1774.2	
15082.2	15.6	18574.9	17065.9	850.0
1647.3		2454.1	2378.7	80.0
5473.3	945.1	7116.6	6683.5	
19161.9	1737.9	28564.6	24461.3	1959.2
6401.8	1714.2	10282.6	7516.3	2923.2
8337.6	1284.4	10996.3	9899.6	601.4
376.5	24.0	2834.4	1501.1	402.0
525.0		330.0	330.0	
9249.8		8508.9	8508.9	
3423.5	-2.3	4496.6	3962.7	304.6
16061.4	979.2	22626.8	18232.4	198.6
12175.2	125.9	5056.6	5098.1	
15180.2	1834.2	19035.7	18134.4	775.1
2370.4		5794.3	3809.1	1976.7
279.0	788.0	805.8	176.5	
3286.9		3538.5	2439.0	1099.5
17180.2	548.1	16523.3	13050.5	97.4
1129.0	0.5	30.1	850.1	
652.3	60.0	173.4	130.2	1.0
1729.1		1357.9	1373.8	-41.3
256.9	-2.0	2034.1	2126.2	
987.7	440.7	2828.7	3391.1	88.1
10240.0		7171.0	8287.3	

C-3-15续表2

地区	执行民间非营利组织单位会计制度财务指标				穴位数
	固定资产原价	上年结余	本年收入合计	本年费用合计	
全国	**25083.8**	**4097.5**	**9841.9**	**4673.9**	**13073097**
中央级					
北京					678746
天津					255592
河北					198878
山西					131052
内蒙古	13.0			3.0	157639
辽宁	7077.4	692.4	2129.2	1191.4	791792
吉林					24156
黑龙江	46.0			53.4	112295
上海					1921053
江苏	2636.1		592.4	365.8	1392899
浙江	315.0	2047.8	920.2	296.9	1007689
安徽	1008.0		207.2	146.7	307711
福建			2.0		165813
江西					20341
山东	2300.0		185.1	185.1	190679
河南			10.0		242996
湖北	37.0		12.0	12.0	802547
湖南	1480.0		102.0	49.0	301874
广东	1164.2		337.1	6.0	1131539
广西					343822
海南	30.0				36370
重庆	90.0		408.8	347.5	545650
四川	4545.3	1354.3	4292.4	1280.0	1233758
贵州	2144.0		186.5	349.5	405372
云南					220713
西藏					
陕西	706.5		9.5	24.0	277144
甘肃	70.0		5.5	4.5	92034
青海					5359
宁夏	1267.3	3.0	340.0	257.1	25336
新疆	154.0		102.0	102.0	52248

单位：万元、个、具

#本年销售穴位数	安葬数	#本年安葬数	格位数	格位存放数	本年格位存放数
572467	**8926853**	**459143**	**980107**	**395808**	**45529**
15111	537381	20581	65100	47482	1661
4672	284823	5208	47442	31928	1840
4254	87856	4768	12078	7068	980
3753	65870	4064	28352	8371	722
7779	120651	12682	20905	7636	824
96660	496403	37347	7042	3481	1275
1743	15568	1714	25480	14446	2550
16968	87159	12265			
71195	1349021	47771	94127	83863	5531
90469	1199905	51392	5505	958	150
28358	741493	28696	9896	8669	675
14013	247849	16537	3754	1947	1768
9271	109538	9098	26166	6423	313
1059	14282	1322			
6545	114467	7189			
7778	146594	7272	22630	8649	1543
16533	503246	18883	3855	1594	111
15322	121599	15004	20273	2568	531
29994	693594	27917	334210	88717	12219
12707	211340	13470	33907	8360	4476
2598	22061	2812			
15121	282676	14528	86624	27075	1498
40708	785226	38464	14994	10739	1997
18432	210901	19030	17472	3980	372
5186	90755	4714	50	15	10
22503	251507	20973	98415	20009	2653
5314	72865	5913			
1169	2346	322			
2647	19212	3154			
4605	40665	6053	1830	1830	1830

C-3-16 骨灰

地区	单位数	年末职工人数		受教育程度	
			女性	大学专科人数	大学本科及以上人数
全国	**15**	**90**	**18**	**13**	**7**
中央级					
北京					
天津					
河北					
山西					
内蒙古					
辽宁	1	5		3	2
吉林					
黑龙江					
上海					
江苏	3	17	7	4	3
浙江	1	3	1		
安徽					
福建					
江西					
山东					
河南					
湖北					
湖南					
广东	9	50		1	
广西					
海南					
重庆	1	15	10	5	2
四川					
贵州					
云南					
西藏					
陕西					
甘肃					
青海					
宁夏					
新疆					

堂

单位：个、人、人次、时

年龄结构			
35岁及以下人数	36岁至45岁人数	46岁至55岁人数	56岁及以上人数
14	**64**	**9**	**3**
1	2	2	
7	8	2	
	1	1	1
2	48		
4	5	4	2

C-3-16续表

地区	执行企业会计制度单位财务指标				执行行政事业单位会计制度财务指标		
	固定资产原价	营业收入	费用合计	营业利润	固定资产原价	本年收入合计	本年支出合计
全　国	**6302.6**	**614.0**	**461.5**	**-106.9**	**418.0**	**125.0**	**125.0**
中央级							
北　京							
天　津							
河　北							
山　西							
内蒙古							
辽　宁							
吉　林							
黑龙江							
上　海							
江　苏	2765.4	302.7	413.3	-110.6	418.0	45.0	45.0
浙　江	37.2	135.3	35.0	2.7			
安　徽							
福　建							
江　西							
山　东							
河　南							
湖　北							
湖　南							
广　东						80.0	80.0
广　西							
海　南							
重　庆	3500.0	176.0	13.2	1.0			
四　川							
贵　州							
云　南							
西　藏							
陕　西							
甘　肃							
青　海							
宁　夏							
新　疆							

单位：万元、个、具

执行民间非营利组织单位会计制度财务指标				格位数		
固定资产原价	上年结余	本年收入合计	本年费用合计		格位存放数	本年格位存放数
17.0	**3.0**	**237.6**	**1.6**	**77138**	**47347**	**1793**
2.0		0.6	0.6			
		236.0		69660	44812	1635
				6478	2005	132
15.0	3.0	1.0	1.0			
				1000	530	26

C-3-17 殡葬管

地区	单位数	年末职工人数		受教育程度		职业资
			女性	大学专科人数	大学本科及以上人数	助理社会工作师人数
全国	**1127**	**9759**	**2592**	**3224**	**1736**	**87**
中央级						
北京	8	83	39	13	52	
天津	11	121	26	31	64	
河北	11	181	57	46	19	
山西	12	78	25	37	17	
内蒙古	40	294	64	92	48	4
辽宁	53	405	117	160	129	7
吉林	47	443	33	127	30	
黑龙江	13	128	40	64	47	
上海	9	44	17	15	25	1
江苏	50	377	126	119	118	7
浙江	73	462	114	167	137	5
安徽	31	140	45	34	23	3
福建	64	619	154	168	80	9
江西	37	322	72	64	15	3
山东	9	85	28	19	10	
河南	92	1244	377	351	159	11
湖北	28	266	75	123	31	
湖南	56	504	88	230	64	4
广东	103	1146	265	304	152	10
广西	48	704	205	211	115	11
海南	7	54	11	11	8	
重庆	27	173	64	58	53	
四川	83	537	178	224	59	2
贵州	49	404	83	183	88	4
云南	47	210	56	91	50	3
西藏						
陕西	33	265	82	87	53	
甘肃	15	85	24	27	17	1
青海	2	9	3	4		
宁夏	16	69	22	15	19	
新疆	53	307	102	149	54	2

理机构

单位:个、人、人次、时

格水平	年龄结构				志愿服务	
社会工作师人数	35岁及以下人数	36岁至45岁人数	46岁至55岁人数	56岁及以上人数	志愿者服务人次数	志愿服务时间
136	**3463**	**3902**	**1907**	**487**	**704**	**1808.0**
3	42	22	14	5	9	9.0
6	33	41	34	13	100	200.0
	76	52	34	19		
	26	30	19	3		
12	92	120	63	19		
13	115	164	103	23	11	21.0
3	92	238	77	36		
	32	57	32	7		
6	13	17	8	6		
3	113	154	90	20	35	77.0
12	172	180	89	21	24	136.0
1	23	67	44	6	122	388.0
15	188	279	124	28	6	16.0
1	121	140	48	13		
	22	36	21	6		
9	642	433	145	24		
2	101	97	57	11		
2	211	210	65	18	5	10.0
20	383	462	258	43	20	44.0
11	255	237	152	60		
	16	19	13	6		
	32	94	44	3	235	465.0
1	154	245	117	21	2	2.0
3	207	143	46	8	27	68.0
3	66	96	33	15		
5	103	94	55	13	28	132.0
1	36	28	16	5		
	5	4				
3	19	27	21	2		
1	73	116	85	33	80	240.0

C-3-17续表

地区	执行企业会计制度单位财务指标				执行行政	
	固定资产原价	营业收入	费用合计	营业利润	固定资产原价	上年结转和结余
全国	**11009.6**	**3145.5**	**2758.7**	**314.4**	**188526.2**	**22157.9**
中央级						
北京					19574.3	37.0
天津					6775.6	3687.7
河北					7827.8	594.1
山西					394.5	0.6
内蒙古	538.0	50.0	12.0	5.0	1848.7	83.3
辽宁					1107.5	25.1
吉林	725.3	280.4	381.6	-71.6	9625.3	476.0
黑龙江	578.0	750.0	760.8	190.0	2440.7	
上海					729.5	1798.3
江苏					2840.8	1157.0
浙江	56.8	215.8	30.3	5.6	3447.8	204.3
安徽					6657.2	
福建	1067.0	964.0	403.0	187.0	8635.0	3707.0
江西	15.0				4147.0	15.0
山东					785.0	
河南					1285.2	100.9
湖北					7760.2	-10.0
湖南	6604.0	367.0	516.0		8234.2	39.4
广东	16.0	1.2			28384.5	511.0
广西					16785.9	3135.2
海南	10.0				7796.3	1461.5
重庆					3762.1	241.7
四川	405.6	181.1	188.0	-14.6	6802.7	522.6
贵州	146.9	311.0	410.0	3.0	1909.9	119.1
云南					1443.8	41.8
西藏						
陕西	364.0				4034.9	173.8
甘肃	360.0		43.0	10.0	381.5	49.0
青海					71.7	2.6
宁夏	40.0	15.0	14.0		361.4	142.0
新疆	83.0	10.0			22675.2	3841.9

单位：万元

事业单位会计制度财务指标			执行民间非营利组织单位会计制度财务指标				殡仪服务站
本年收入合计	本年支出合计	收支结余	固定资产原价	上年结余	本年收入合计	本年费用合计	
157347.2	**157280.5**	**16164.1**	**11929.0**	**245.0**	**1811.5**	**2584.0**	**28**
17032.5	12125.8	4944.5					
4702.9	3608.2	4746.5					
4176.6	4115.1	932.5					
1016.9	1026.1	0.4					
1831.7	1899.2	80.9					
4792.8	3697.8	24.7			3.0		
3387.5	3668.9	-225.5					2
995.1	1445.3						
4438.4	4547.9	1562.1					
4871.2	8503.2	-3533.5	204.6		956.1	800.0	
9359.7	9776.8	55.1	80.0		243.0	258.0	
1279.9	1504.4	1.0		3.0		6.4	
9776.6	13150.5	336.4					4
3778.6	2746.8						
600.6	600.6		103.4		323.0	323.0	
3463.7	3394.3	17.9	10.0		2.0	2.0	
4974.1	4930.2	10.0	29.0		2.5	2.5	
2872.4	2875.2	14.2					
22730.3	22657.5	579.6					
14649.4	15039.6	324.0					
4985.1	4859.8	1412.8					
3500.3	2895.5	844.5	245.0		108.9	161.0	4
4564.9	4335.2	26.0	10500.0	20.0	108.0	920.0	2
1682.2	1632.7	77.4					
1149.7	1180.6	25.9					
1692.6	1674.7	204.1	100.0		30.0	30.0	
607.0	610.0		5.0			0.1	
137.7	135.1						
1093.8	1103.8	136.1	652.0	222.0	35.0	81.0	
17203.0	17539.7	3566.5					16

C-4-1 其他

地区	单位数	编制登记	民政登记	年末职工人数	女性	受教育程度 大学专科人数	大学本科及以上人数
全国	**2078**	**2023**	**55**	**17056**	**7784**	**4266**	**6451**
中央级	28	28		1129	537	112	956
北京	70	70		788	364	138	463
天津	20	20		180	94	53	107
河北	36	35	1	561	357	94	101
山西	77	77		522	246	138	132
内蒙古	20	20		337	136	80	92
辽宁	112	106	6	862	312	191	258
吉林	24	24		183	74	37	37
黑龙江	32	32		507	281	98	136
上海	54	40	14	525	262	106	284
江苏	71	71		572	261	140	239
浙江	155	154	1	784	346	158	366
安徽	27	27		158	63	52	40
福建	62	62		273	140	70	151
江西	420	418	2	1549	550	317	245
山东	56	55	1	464	206	126	159
河南	118	117	1	1648	775	443	613
湖北	81	75	6	692	311	204	246
湖南	97	95	2	913	437	303	279
广东	40	38	2	454	237	128	228
广西	76	76		903	412	312	231
海南	13	13		96	32	41	35
重庆	21	21		124	42	47	49
四川	137	137		1012	506	315	454
贵州	90	74	16	616	257	200	184
云南	23	23		159	57	57	48
西藏							
陕西	41	41		505	244	133	128
甘肃	32	32		202	57	52	74
青海	5	5		25	8	8	3
宁夏	13	10	3	96	40	20	22
新疆	27	27		217	140	93	91

事业单位

单位：个、人、人次、时

职业资格水平		年龄结构				志愿服务	
助理社会工作师人数	社会工作师人数	35岁及以下人数	36岁至45岁人数	46岁至55岁人数	56岁及以上人数	志愿者服务人次数	志愿服务时间
284	**408**	**5985**	**6042**	**3930**	**1099**	**13123**	**42957.5**
6	12	483	320	243	83		
23	27	248	252	231	57		
7	9	40	70	53	17	300	600.0
1	3	307	178	64	12	680	2930.0
2	21	108	207	171	36		
	5	116	116	89	16		
	3	252	375	141	94	2	6.0
3	4	87	54	27	15		
6	2	155	146	180	26		
14	45	178	188	102	57	54	138.0
21	26	168	206	145	53	710	2095.0
17	64	289	240	212	43	7410	24834.0
8	3	24	69	59	6	132	276.0
8	22	102	103	61	7	12	80.0
29	15	475	790	258	26	701	2795.0
7	10	170	148	114	32	2204	5955.5
36	20	631	507	391	119	60	200.0
10	16	211	275	159	47	85	123.0
5	13	333	328	169	83	467	1765.0
7	13	180	151	90	33		
23	26	338	306	207	52	100	800.0
6	3	34	34	23	5		
1	1	29	57	31	7	100	200.0
31	28	452	289	217	54		
4	6	206	196	177	37		
1	1	64	57	28	10	6	18.0
1		175	193	110	27	70	102.0
2	1	60	66	60	16	30	40.0
3	3	5	7	12	1		
	1	11	17	50	18		
2	5	54	97	56	10		

C-4-1续表

地区	执行企业会计制度单位财务指标			
	固定资产原价	营业收入	费用合计	营业利润
全国	**23596.3**	**23795.9**	**11117.8**	**1270.4**
中央级	6287.7	15684.1	6677.7	962.0
北京	188.2	2067.1	346.8	620.2
天津				
河北				
山西				
内蒙古				
辽宁				
吉林				
黑龙江				
上海				
江苏	43.7	856.6	412.1	82.8
浙江	1257.4	79.7	565.8	-460.4
安徽	883.0	70.0	93.0	-1.0
福建				
江西	157.8	101.7	88.6	
山东				
河南				
湖北	110.0	2.4	2.4	
湖南				
广东				
广西	10266.6	3149.3	1876.5	-208.9
海南				
重庆				
四川	2006.7	1443.0	953.8	279.8
贵州	2374.2	342.0	101.1	-4.1
云南				
西藏				
陕西				
甘肃				
青海				
宁夏				
新疆	21.0			

单位：万元

执行行政事业单位会计制度财务指标				
固定资产原价	上年结转和结余	本年收入合计	本年支出合计	收支结余
461428.0	**96640.5**	**419863.5**	**434490.9**	**71357.0**
105490.4	28584.6	77481.3	60492.2	44966.2
52941.5	6576.9	33885.0	40432.3	7140.5
2748.7	-308.9	3808.3	4003.8	21.4
5252.3	132.9	3972.7	3979.0	8.1
2947.7	52.3	7735.9	5425.6	63.5
1413.7	725.3	4192.4	3968.4	409.6
9427.8	3248.5	10440.5	12858.9	307.4
84.9		565.8	590.3	
8495.3	144.8	4298.2	4298.8	
32001.1	-719.1	27298.4	25260.9	745.8
13818.1	2139.2	32332.3	31673.8	1217.9
18483.4	3673.0	38754.1	36812.6	3002.6
616.9	0.3	872.1	994.5	15.4
5382.7	963.6	6923.7	12516.1	1698.0
7527.0	2717.9	11943.5	13632.6	1345.0
1787.4	145.2	6582.3	6535.7	
22294.3	6929.4	18063.8	17532.0	-414.9
15058.4	539.9	14883.3	15097.6	-183.2
13104.1	-251.0	15895.5	16019.0	232.9
36410.8	19070.0	20716.9	19187.0	2222.2
27211.5	1011.0	9763.2	10025.1	-174.9
1451.5	439.6	6958.9	6374.0	985.8
2611.4	62.8	1887.1	1912.4	37.5
28649.3	7472.0	22750.2	26989.7	3267.5
7391.9	7279.8	19651.1	20795.2	841.2
724.6	132.8	1314.7	1947.1	
25187.5	3540.0	4582.9	5490.8	83.2
1399.9	23.2	3195.3	22708.5	-0.7
736.2	912.9	759.3	735.4	
456.0		450.8	450.8	
10321.7	1401.6	7904.0	5750.8	3519.0

06

附 录

《中国民政统计年鉴-2015》勘误

1.第13页，第4行，社会组织增加值为“638.6”亿元改为“650.3”亿元。

2.第93页，“农村资助参加合作医疗人数”修改为“民政部门资助参加合作医疗人数”。

3.第119页，单位为“万人”。

4.第122页，“被收养人合计”分类有误，见第492页C-2-30。

5.第127页，删除：“民政部门直接接收的捐赠”一行。

6.第152页，“十二五”时期 “374385.92”改为“526047.92”；“11189.38”改为“15603.48”；“2.99”改为“2.97”

7.第153页，最后一行：“其他”2014年“133.1”改为“463.6”。

8.第155页，B-1-17单位为“亿元”。

9.第158页，“十二五”时期“75.3”修改为“104.3”。

10.第166页，2012年“23169”改为“23189”；“4141”改为“4121”。

11.第164页，B-2-5表表头“城乡各类服务机构和设施合计”应为“城乡各类社区服务机构和设施合计”。

12.第569页，“当年新增单位数”，“当年年检单位数”指标与“社会组织职工中共党员人数”不存在包含 关系。